AF408755

# Jim's Blog
## Volume 2

Jim

West Martian Limited Company
1st Edition, March 2024

First printing 2024
The publisher can be contacted at westmartian.com
ISBN-13: 979-8-218-39884-2 Paperback

# Contents

# Jim's Blog
## Volume 2

## Puritanism, progressivism, and entertainment

2013-01-05 15:49:31

I have been watching the English dubbed Japanese anime "Speed Grapher", which is pretty good except for the horrendously heavy handed propaganda.

In the anime, money is revolting, immoral and disgusting, sex is revolting, immoral and disgusting, and male sexual pleasure obtained at the expense of females (there being no such thing as male sexual pleasure obtained with female pleasure) is the most utterly disgusting, revolting, and abhorrent of them all. There is no such thing as entrepreneurship or capital formation. Rich people get rich by stealing it, and/or prostituting women against their will. Rich people do not save, invest, or create. They somehow profit by creating financial crises. And, did I mention, all sex in the anime is disgusting, especially heterosex (with the exception of one chick that has a good time killing and raping)

Still, a surprisingly good anime. I could put up with the anti capitalist propaganda, and I could have put up with the anti sex propaganda if only the phallocentric male oppressers were having good dirty fun cruelly oppressing women, rather than putting the viewer off sex altogether. The one female that was having sex fun with her guns was not really enough. All sex scenes in the anime were fetish retardant, were disgusting.

When Ayn Rand depicts a rich sexist male raping a woman, she expects her readers to get off on it, as she quite obviously did. Which may be part of why Ayn Rand still outsells all these progressives. Money is fun, sex is fun, stories that celebrate people having fun are fun. Propaganda about the evils of money and sex is no fun. That progressives are puritans is evident from their dourness and total humorlessness.

## Guns, murder, and race

2013-01-07 10:30:39

Stolen from the comment section of Steve Sailer's excellent blog.

Someone who wishes to remain anonymous[1] has assembled data showing that American whites murder at about the same rate as whites in countries with strict gun control, American "Hispanics" murder at about the same rate as they do in their native countries, which generally have strict gun control, and that American blacks murder at about the same rate as blacks do world wide, mostly in countries with strict gun control.

The main factor by far in homicide rates is race.

Another significant factor is national IQ. East Asians in high IQ countries have markedly lower murder rates than East Asians in low IQ countries. Similarly, Central Americans. Possibly high IQ nations carry out policies discouraging murder more effectively than low IQ nations, and members of high IQ races are more easily influenced by such pressures. Blacks, however, seem unaffected by the national IQ.

Anonymous explains how he constructed the graph:

---

[1]https://isteve.blogspot.com.au/2012/12/two-part-interview-with-me-in.html?showComment=1356668949146#c823662547890589596

I took the step of plotting homicide rate vs IQ of country. There is a very
definite link between IQ and homicide rate, and it seems mainly to function
as an upper bound. That is, the higher the IQ of the country, the lower
the possible homicide rate. Higher IQ seems to be a civilizing factor. But
within the greater homicide rates seemingly afforded by lower IQ, there is
a great deal of variance. There are some relatively non-homicidal, low IQ
populations. So there is more at work here than IQ.

...

2

Looking at the country table and clicking to sort by sub-region, the exceptions stuck out.

3

It seemed evident to me that the exceptions were probably of an racial/ethnic nature. ...
1. The geographically logical groupings that wikipedia uses are roughly similar to racial groupings.
2. The genetic maps of the world made by Cavalli Sforza shows racial clines
that more closely matches the variation seen in the homicide rates, and would
explain the exceptions (note that this map does not include modern settlement).

4

The big sub-region exception in North Africa vs Sub-Saharan Africa is well
explained genetically, being more Arab than African.
3. Colonies consisting primarily of founding country ethnic stock (e.g. Southern Europe -> Argentina, Chile, Uruguay, Western/Northern Europe ->
USA, Australia, Canada) have homicide rates very similar to the founding
countries.

So I separated homicide rate vs. country IQ by racial grouping, to make this
relation clearer. (I cribbed this idea from La Griffe Du Lion[5]) I used marker
color to divide the broad racial categories – Europeans, Asians/North Africans,
Amerinds, and Africans. Within those I selected regions, especially when I
knew that there was relatedness, I grouped close ethnicities together as best
I could.

Because of the topical nature of USA homicide rates, I also broke out the
largest racial groupings within the USA – whites, blacks and Hispanics (mostly
Amerind). Once broken out like that, it is evident that within that country,

[2]https://en.wikipedia.org/wiki/List_of_countries_by_intentional_homicide_rate#By_subregion
[3]https://en.wikipedia.org/wiki/List_of_countries_by_intentional_homicide_rate#By_country
[4]https://en.wikipedia.org/wiki/File:The_history_and_geography_of_human_genes_Luigi_Luca_Cavalli-
Sforza_map_genetic.png
[5]https://www.lagriffedulion.f2s.com/sft.htm

the homicide rates appear to be largely of a racial origin. The USA's white homicide rate of around ~2/100k fits perfectly within the European range, including the areas from which most of its white people are drawn (Western, Northern-Germanic, Southern Europe). The USA's black homicide rate is very similar to that of the West/Central African areas from which the slaves were taken (e.g.Benin, Ghana, Guinea, Nigeria, Senegal and Cote I'voire, Siera Leone, Angola etc.). The Hispanic homicide rate appears to be very similar to that of Mexico, where most of the Hispanic population comes from. I used the FBI stats to tease this information out.

[6]

Because the data suits a log scale better, I graphed it that way here[7].

... race/ethnicity is a very good predictor of homicide rate. It is very hard to make an honest case that gun ownership is much of a factor at all in causing homicides. The evidence suggests that people(s) kill people, not guns. In heavily armed Switzerland, white USA, Serbia etc., the homicide rate is low. In mostly disarmed Netherlands, Poland and Italy, the homicide rate is also low. The common factor here is the European background.

In sub-Saharan African areas with more guns (Equatorial Guinea, Angola), homicide rates are high. In sub-Saharan African areas that have very few guns (Ghana, Ethiopia, Eritrea, in fact most of sub-Saharan Africa) homicide rates are also high. The common factor here is the sub-Saharan racial background.

Anonymous suggests that instead of gun control, we apply ....

That black homicide rates seem to be insensitive to national IQ is consistent with the eighteenth century belief that to maintain acceptable behavior among a black population requires forms of coercion more extreme and direct than are required for other races.

## Law of conservation of pussy

### 2013-01-13 08:31:25

Reading the manosphere blogs, I notice a lot of husbands complaining that their wife has sex with them once a month, and, of course, no end of nice guys getting no sex at all.

A fertile age woman generally has sex at least once a week. As Saint Paul observed, few people have the capacity for continence, whether male or female. So if husband is not getting any, chances are that someone else is getting a piece of his wife. It is not in a woman's nature to be content with sex once a month.

The law of conservation of pussy is that if some men are not getting some, other men must be getting a lot.

Allegedly, in the ancestral environment, half as many men reproduced as women, though the source for this conclusion is hard to track down. With the abolition of old

---

[6]https://i.imgur.com/dCa9U.jpg
[7]https://i.imgur.com/J5Iuv.jpg

style marriage, we seem to have reverted to the system where a minority of males have sex with the majority of females during the female fertile years.

If ten year old girls were not restrained, most of them would be banging thirty and forty year old men. While ten year old boys are completely uninterested in sex and regard it as disgusting, girls start taking an interest in males well before puberty. Preteen girls are primarily interested in older males, and, just as male homosexuals don't much like male homosexuals, preferring manly men or twelve year old boys, preteen girls don't much like adult males that like preteen girls. Preteen girls are especially interested in older males that have recently had an adult sexual relationship with an adult female, are especially interested in divorced men, separated men, and widowers.

We don't let preteen girls follow their desires because it is likely to be bad for them and bad for society. Seems to me that letting adult women follow their desires is worse for them and worse for society. All women are immature until menopause.

In the ancestral environment women seldom got to make their own sexual choices, and have not evolved to be very good at it.

## Aaron Swartz needed killing

### 2013-01-17 07:16:51

Moldbug is back![8]

Though for some reason he is not as wonderfully long winded as he usually is.

> "Civil disobedience" is no more than a way for the overdog to say to the underdog: I am so strong that you cannot enforce your "laws" upon me. I am strong and might makes right - I give you the law, not you me.

Thoreau was an even better example of this than Aaron Swartz.

> You'll note the tone of this manifesto, which is the typical vaunting, bullying tone of the powerful addressing the powerless. Your so-called laws are worthless, it says, because law means nothing without power. It is we who have the power, we who make the real laws.

>

> ...

>

> Then [Aaron Swartz] takes his beliefs seriously, and speaks actual truth to actual power. Well, ya know, power doesn't like that much.

Thoreau, of course, unlike Aaron Swartz, was never so careless as to speak the actual truth to actual power.

Thoreau seems to have pretty much agreed with the Moldbuggian analysis of the civil war, except, of course, that the armed faith that was to conquer America was supposedly individualist, and while he knew it was a religion, felt it was not a church, and therefore exempted from the first amendment, that his brand of individualism could only be imposed at gunpoint by the state, that his brand of anti statism required a vastly more powerful federal government. Thoreau pretty much agrees with Moldbug that the civil war was a theocratic war to impose the true religion on all by centralized state power, the difference

---

[8]https://unqualified-reservations.blogspot.com.au/2013/01/noam-chomsky-killed-aaron-swartz.html

being that Moldbug thinks the religion was statist, oppressive, and untrue, while Thoreau thinks the religion is true, individualist, and anti statist, despite requiring conscription, taxation, warfare, and a vast increase in state power.

Thoreau prefigures the innumerable protests we have recently seen where the Cathedral revolts against itself by demanding more power and money for itself.

Hurray Moldbug!

## Students against a democratic society

2013-01-20 12:41:55

Excerpts from Carlyle, predicting social decay, in the context of today's headlines showing social decay.[9]

But, as Carlyle observed, in 1848, most of the Kings ran away at the first whiff of gunpowder. He hoped that they might be replaced by a sterner breed of Kings. They are not showing up yet. But, if enough people reject democracy, equality, and all that, perhaps they will.

But I don't think so. I am with Froude, who longed for the return of pirates, rather than Kings, who recollected the good old days when Britain failed to notice that its colonialists were bandits, and continued to fail to notice their transition from mobile bandits to stationary bandits.

## Courage and Nerdliness

2013-01-24 13:55:28

The Audacious Epigone reminds us of the courage of John Derbyshire who told us:

> To the dissident, the only thing worth pondering about the proposition is, is it true? If it is, then no king's command can falsify it; and if it is not, then not even the assent of a hundred million will make it true.

Predictably, one year after he said this, he was persecuted for speaking truth to power.

The dissident, therefore, has disturbing characteristics in common with the nerd, in fearlessly pursuing obscure knowledge that is of little personal use to him, or likely to be actively harmful to him. Who could be nerdlier than Stephen McIntyre of Climate Audit[10]?

But, on the other hand, Steve McIntyre defeated the united forces of the state, academia, and the scientific establishment by exposing the hockey stick fraud. After seven years of struggle, in 2012 October, the scientific establishment quietly decided that no further hockey sticks shall be published or publishable, and quietly conceded that the medieval climatic optimum happened. He won, the entire marshaled and united forces of official science lost. He is now pursuing mopping up operations to get the worst offenders punished. They are unlikely to be punished, but that they are discredited (and thus all of

---

[9]https://radishmag.files.wordpress.com/2013/01/radish-1-1.pdf
[10]https://climateaudit.org/

official science discredited) is implicitly admitted by the retreat. There is something not very nerdly about such a victory.

The entire forces of official science, including those that had absolutely no relevant knowledge or expertise, thousands of scientists and every scientific organization, officially endorsed the Hockey stick as official science and official government truth.

Warmism was a massive overreach by the left. The plan was have a climate treaty organization centrally planning the world economy, to reduce the world population and living standards to sustainable level– to kill off about six billion with artificial famine, and reduce most of the few survivors to serfs working the fields with digging sticks under the whips of their carbon overlords, that being what it means to reduce carbon emissions without increasing nuclear power. Less power, less industrial civilization, therefore less people. We can only support the world population by using a lot of power, and at present the only practical sources for lots of power are carbon or uranium.

But the first step in this program, the food to fuel program, which is causing the deaths of a mere five million or so per year for[11] the most utterly miniscule reduction in carbon emissions, has turned out to be politically unsustainable. Raising that from millions of deaths to many hundreds of millions of deaths per year, which is what is needed to make a significant dent in carbon emissions and properly empower our new carbon overlords, was never going to fly.

Global warming was a proposal for a ridiculously extreme expansion of leftist power and the government run economy, which is to say, the leftist run economy, so defeating it was an important victory, for which Steve McIntyre deserves a major part of the credit, but it was merely a defensive victory, while on so many other fronts, the left marches on from victory to victory.

I have been watching "High School of the Dead", a Japanese anime with wonderful and beautifully done, though quite improbable, boob animations.

The secondary male character in "High School of the Dead" is a total nerd, a fanboy. What is he a fanboy of? American gun culture and American guns, which are of course totally unavailable in Japan. He knows the English language words for various gun parts, which I do not, and frequently speaks about guns in barely recognizable English, the way that American fans of Japanese anime speak about Japanese anime in broken Japanese. He can not only take a gun apart and put it together, which I can do, but does so while reciting the English language instructions and naming the gun parts, while I have no idea what they are named and am apt to wind up with mysterious strange looking bits left over.

In the story end of the world disaster ensues, he gets guns, quite a lot of guns, becomes very good at using them with quite improbable swiftness– and yet he, unlike the main character, remains a total nerd, even though his kill count is way higher than that of all the other characters put together, even though he saves every major character's life time after time, usually saving several major characters in every episode.

The obsessive pursuit of useless knowledge (dinosaurs, star trek episodes, and, in Japan, guns) is the distinctive characteristic of a nerd. Obviously someone in the US who pursues extensive knowledge of guns is not a nerd, but an expert. Someone in Japan

---

[11] https://www.theoildrum.com/node/3495

who pursues extensive knowledge of guns in the US is a nerd. People who pursue useless knowledge tend to wind up as low status, thus are assumed to be low status, and the anime rests on this assumption, even though in the story the nerd's knowledge has suddenly become tremendously useful.

However, genuinely speaking truth to power, though almost useless, is, I would argue, not nerdly, since when power is based on lies, truth is, in the long run, apt to win, thus he who speaks the truth, has at least some small prospect of being a hero on the winning side, particularly if he times it right.

Rule by priests rests on lies. When priests become discredited, rule by soldiers, or brigands, may ensue, which is apt to be an improvement. Indeed, I would argue that rule by brigands is the best, for when they rule, they cease to be brigands, as we see in Munshi Abdullah's account of early British colonialists.

Someone who speaks truth to power has a non negligible chance of winding up on the winning side and becoming an ideologue of the winning side, at least if he times it correctly. When soldiers or brigands come to power, they are apt to bring some new priests to power with them, thus defeating the massed forces of the establishment, as Steve McIntyre did, was not only an enormously impressive feat, and brought personal benefit to Steve McIntyre in that he, and you, did not wind up as serfs farming wheat with a digging stick, but there is a small but non zero possibility of a new establishment, in which case he will quite likely wind up as part of the new establishment priesthood, while all those who officially endorsed the Hockey Stick find themselves no longer part of the establishment priesthood.

Democracy is become unsustainable, due to hordes of bastards, the government importing a new people, ever increasing welfare, free medical care, the abolition of old style marriage, the total inability of government to budget, and so on and so forth. Democracy, equality, social justice, and all that stuff, is going to go, thus at this point in history, it may well be becoming less nerdly to be a dissident.

## Fed has no gold

### 2013-01-25 07:35:24

Supposedly, the Federal Reserve has mountain of gold, seven thousand tonnes stashed in various places in the US. By an astonishing coincidence, it owes banks in other nations seven thousand tonnes of gold.

The Fed owes the German government fifteen hundred tonnes of gold. Germany asked for its gold back. The Fed did not want to give it. So Germany asked for three hundred tonnes of gold back. The fed agreed, in principle, to return three hundred tonnes of Germany's gold– *over seven years.*

Why so long?

This only makes sense is the fed has considerably less than three hundred tonnes left and they hope to quietly purchase three hundred tonnes over the next seven years using freshly printed money. Stalling is going to create fear. If the fed is stalling, it can only be because it has absolutely no alternative but to stall.

Recall the bank run scene in "It's a wonderful life". Imagine if the bankers had said,

"No problem, we have your money, but, alas, due to postal delays and that our clerks a bit slow counting it is going to take seven years."

## Why MRAs are whiny mangina losers

### 2013-01-26 15:34:36

The Men's Rights Activist program is real equality for men and women, wherein women make their own decisions *and* take the consequences of their own decisions. It is a logically consistent and libertarian position, but can never be an emotionally consistent position because it is a cold, callous, nasty, hateful position that no one believes in, no one supports, a position that can never be popular.

The only logically and emotionally consistent position.that can ever be popular, is Pauline male supremacism, male supremacism in accordance with the doctrines of Saint Paul the Apostle, a position that condescends to women gently and affectionately..

Don't be a Men's Rights Activist. Be a Male Supremacist. It is more likely to be politically successful, and you are more likely to get laid.

MRAs pitifully whine about discrimination against men: Why, they ask, is it that whenever women don't like the consequences of their own decisions, they demand that someone else (men) make it all better?

To have women independent of male authority while men take the consequences of female decisions is a society that is grossly unnatural in one way, thus hard to achieve.

To have women independent of male authority and also have women take the consequences of their own decisions is a society that is grossly unnatural in two ways, thus twice as hard to achieve.

To answer the MRA question: Why should women not face the consequences of their own decisions?

It is because women, like children, need special protection, special privilege, are frequently incompetent at making life decisions, and usually need to have their decisions supervised and restrained by fathers or husbands. Women without male authority in their lives are in trouble. They are at best to be pitied (widows, spinsters, and orphans) and at worst to be despised (sluts and tramps). In most societies, in all healthy societies, it is normative for a woman to be subject to male authority. Any woman not so subject is viewed with pity or disapproval, usually both.

No one believes that women should take the consequences of their own decisions. Progressives certainly don't believe it, feminists believe it even less, and not even men's rights activists really believe it, for to believe in it at emotional level they have to demonize women as sluts, tramps, gold diggers etc, which destroys their relationships with women and results in them ending up alone.

Nor does anyone believe that women should make their own decisions, should be independent of male authority. Most women engage in doublethink and crimestop while treating the man in their lives with eighteenth century respect and picking up his socks. For feminists to believe in independence at emotional level, to stop themselves from picking up their husband's socks, they have to demonize men as rapists, which destroys their relationships with men and results in them ending up alone.

If a woman gets away with not treating the man in her life with respect and not picking up his socks, she feels as guilty about it as if she had been raised in the eighteenth century, and pretty soon she is rationalizing her behavior with one hundred and one reasons why he is evil and hateful, thus does not deserve respect or socks, and, pretty soon, why he does not deserve sex.

## Bad tactics

The MRA tactic of demanding equality and whining pitifully about the lack thereof is doomed to fail

It is entirely pointless to accuse progressives of hypocrisy or to demand that they live up to their own standards. A progressive will find the accusation incomprehensible. To a progressive, hypocrisy does not mean a non progressive acting contrary to the rules that the non progressive himself has agreed are morally right, it means a non progressive acting contrary to the rules that progressives have agreed are morally right. These rules apply to non progressives, and *only* to non progressives. If you accuse a progressive of hypocrisy, it is like accusing him of racism because affirmative action discriminates against whites. He absolutely will not understand you. The accusation can never make any sense to him.

Progressives own the word hypocrisy much as they own the word racism. A progressive cannot be hypocritical, and cannot be racist. By definition, only non progressives can be hypocritical, just as only non progressives can be racist.

Progressives cannot be hypocritical, because they are justified by faith, as Christians used to be before the Churches became another megaphone for progressives.

The proposition that women are not entitled to special protection, and especially not entitled to special protection from the consequences of their own decisions, is entirely unsaleable. No one believes it, not even MRAs. Every MRA believes in his heart that good women are entitled to such protection. To hold an MRA position consistently, he has to disbelieve in the existence of good women, which is apt to have bad effects on his sex life.

The MRA position is the genuinely equalist position, and the equalist position is unsaleable. The only unprogressive position that can possibly win widespread support is that good women, who are normally under the authority of husbands or fathers, deserve special protection, that the social authority of husbands and fathers needs legal and moral support, and that sluts and tramps, women who's behavior is abnormal and bad, in that they have chosen to be independent of male authority, do not deserve special protection, that sluts and tramps need to face the consequences of their own decisions, that some wicked women, just a few of them, not very many, need to face the consequences of their own decisions.

To rein back special legal protection for women without restoring male authority follows logically from what progressives theoretically believe, believe intellectually, but at an emotional level they do not believe it, no one believes it, no one can ever be persuaded of it.

The only way to rein back special legal protection for women is to give legal backing to male authority, and then rein back special legal protection to those bad women whose own non normative decisions have rendered them independent of male authority.

Women will never be expected to face the consequences of their own decisions, legally, socially, or morally. Independent women will never be legally expected to face the consequences of their own decisions until the Pauline rules once again get legal support as they did back in the eighteenth century.

Male supremacism on the Pauline model is necessary for civilization, since it gives men ability and motive to invest in posterity, necessary for society, because children need fathers, and is the only political tactic capable of achieving the rollback of the feminist imperative that Men's Rights Activists want.

## Radish defends slavery

### 2013-01-29 11:21:23

As usual, good reactionary stuff.[12]

You favor abolishing welfare: What do propose to do with all the able bodied people that are too lazy or too violent or have too short a time preferance to hold down a job?

Once upon a time, such people were put on the chain gang. Progressives did not like private individuals owning slaves, but they just love governments owning slaves. Look how they loved communist china, and look how bitterly outraged and indignant they became when the Chinese government realized that most people do better work as employees, rather than slaves.

## People of negative economic value

### 2013-02-01 05:56:24

The racial problem is that stupid people can vote, that incentives for good behavior are weak or nonexistent, and that some people are unresponsive to incentives. Stop voting, ensure that everyone has good incentives, and then the problem is reduced those people unresponsive to incentives, a markedly smaller problem.

Nations with slightly higher IQ are markedly wealthier than nations with lower IQ, but individuals with markedly higher IQ are not markedly wealthier than individuals with markedly lower IQ.

The difference between nations is well approximated if we suppose that people with an IQ above 105 all have roughly comparable productivity, and are responsible for producing almost everything, and people with IQ below 105 have negligible productivity, and are all parasites[13]. But individual wages do not fit this picture. Obviously a low IQ person who is working for a living in private enterprise must be producing value at least equal to his wages.

Moving from a nation with low average IQ to a nation with high average IQ substantially benefits the migrant. No one wants to move in the other direction.

This only makes sense if people with high average IQ produce large benefits to those around them, and people with low average IQ produce large costs to those around them, negative externalities.

---

[12]https://radishmag.wordpress.com/2013/01/25/volume-1-issue-3-slavery-in-america-was-it-really-so-bad/
[13]https://www.lagriffedulion.f2s.com/sft.htm

A family with an income of about sixty thousand is arguably better off not working. Thus an IQ of 105 is about the IQ where a man is likely to be earning enough money for it to be financially sensible for a woman to marry him and stay married to him and become a housewife for much of her life, rather than "marrying" Uncle Sam The Big Pimp. It is about the IQ where it becomes sensible to work, rather than be a parasite. Of course there are lots of people with an IQ well below 105 who work, but they tend to be looked down on as chumps, rednecks etc. Our ruling elite does not much like such people. Pop music is apt to denigrate them, television shows condescend to them. The show "Married with Children" implied that no one from the wrong side of the bell curve should get married or hold down a job.

That people with high average IQ benefit everyone is obvious, particularly in the extreme cases, for example Bill Gates and Steve Jobs.

But what about the reverse, costs?

Obviously working people with IQ below 105 must be producing something, or else no one would pay them, but to fit the observed distribution, that contribution must be cancelled out on average by the negative externalities produced by low IQ people, and especially the negative externalities produced by non working low IQ people.

That the problem is externalities fits the fact that low IQ people can still get jobs, and also the fact that it is a good idea to be surrounded by high IQ people and a bad idea to be surrounded by stupid people, explains "white privilege". Blacks prefer to hang out with blacks, but hanging out with low IQ people has bad consequences.

Repeating in slightly different words: The observed distribution of national GDPs makes sense if those stupid people with jobs are producing value similar to their wages, but have negative externalities, and those stupid people without jobs are producing nothing, and have larger negative externalities that cancel out the production of working people with IQ below 105.

Stupid people produce negative externalities.

Directly through bad work performance, as for example with government employees, who tend to be low performing members of low performing racial voting blocks, for example the American DMV and TSA. It is far more unpleasant to go through US airport security than Israeli airport security, because Israeli airport security is operated by humans, and US airport security by subhumans.

By being individually and personally unemployable in private enterprise. Many people, a great many people, due to stupidity, a propensity to punch out their boss or customers, steal stuff, or a time preference too short to allow them to contract to exchange labor for money, just cannot work for a living in private employment, and instead live on welfare, government employment, crime, and so on and so forth, producing a wide variety of negative externalities.

Directly through crime. Subhumans render places unsafe and unpleasant.

Directly through political redistribution, through the supposedly peaceful political process of voting, through rioting, and through the threat of rioting. Detroit was destroyed by individual crimes, by voting for criminals and more crime, through routine arson, through large scale rioting managed by community organizers with the collaboration and support of police, and through supposedly peaceful political and legal changes obtained by voting under the continual threat of more riots and more arson.

Through the bad apple effect, that people learn from each other. A black person who passes out drunk in a public place is apt to get violent when woken up by a guard, and a person who is culturally raised as a black is likely to take his example from the high status people in his environment (thugs), and thus pass out drunk in a public place, and become belligerent when woken up by a guard. Someone raised white is substantially less likely to pass out drunk in a public place, and if woken up by a guard, more likely to be apologetic about it. Stupid people tend to set an example that people around them are apt to follow, thus have a negative externality by their social influence. The man raised white, when a policeman stops him, imitates his dad or his employer. The man raised black, when a policeman stops him, imitates what he thinks a thug or a pimp would do.

Because stupid excludes smart: Academia these days values conformity more than performance. The dumber the average, the less smart people conform, and thus the more smart people are excluded from Academia, and thus from the elite.

Bad average effect: A high IQ person cannot communicate over too great a difference, thus high IQ people among a mass of stupids are rendered isolated and ineffectual (nerds).

Negative externalities need to be met by political control of those producing negative externalities, by measures against people causing negative externalities, a doctrine you have doubtless heard from every leftist complaining about pollution. It provides an intelligent rationale for intelligent people to justify meddling in other people's affairs, leading to leftists discovering ever more new forms of pollution whose effects are ever less significant, and whose clean up costs victimize ever increasing numbers of people, and render those people ever less free. At present, the regulated levels of most major pollutants are about one thousandth the levels that produce statistically noticeable effects, or they regulate things like dust that are probably not much influenced by human activity.

It also provides an intelligent rationale for dealing with problem groups, which produce much greater externalities than any pollutant that the left can dream up. If we don't need to do anything about problem groups, we don't need to do anything about pollution.

Conversely, if you claim that your ideal society will be able to deal with some externalities, for example anarcho capitalism can deal pretty effectively with major point sources of pollution, though not with diffuse sources of pollution, then your ideal society really should do something in at least some ways about at least some problem groups.

Anarchocapitalists tend to assume that everyone has positive economic value, or savings, or insurance, or a support network, and those that do not are sufficiently few, and sufficiently appealing (the deserving poor) to be taken care of by private charity.

But, what, however about the undeserving poor? For example people who are not only stupid, but whose stupidity inclines them to display unpleasant personal characteristics at inopportune times, such as during job interviews or conversations with police or guards. By and large, the people who are unemployable at any wage, any job, are for the most part not only stupid but also scary, unpleasant, menacing, nasty people.

People of negative economic value tend to be overwhelmingly of certain races and not others, for both genetic and cultural reasons, thus the difficult to see and measure problem of people of negative economic value tends to manifest as the highly visible problem of race. To suppose that all people of one race have positive economic value is clearly false, and to suppose that all people of another race have negative economic value is clearly ridiculous, but nonetheless any measure that efficiently addresses the problem of people of negative economic value is going to have radically disparate impact, and thus will look racist, and indeed, will be racist, racist in the old fashioned colonialist style, will occasionally result in terrible things happening where the victims of those terrible things are almost all of a particular race.

In the West Indies as depicted in the book "the west indies as they are", if I correctly understand his depiction of the workhouse, it took a firm hand with the idle. The workhouse functioned rather as a nokill dogpound does today. An occupant was likely to be sold into slavery, or if he could not be sold, given away into slavery, or if he could not be given away, his owner or former owner would be found and forced to take him back or pay for his support. And if all else failed, then the county would pay to support him and detain him.

Yet despite these extremely vigorous measures against people of small or negative economic value, the ruling whites feared the "idle and the restless" - a mostly black population of freemen.

It seems that in the West Indies, despite the option of forcing people to work under the whip, and despite the fact that a primitive low tech economy has plenty of mindless brute force work suitable for work under the whip, a significant number of blacks still had negative economic value even as slave laborers, enough of them to be a problem. They had not done anything wrong enough to justify killing them, or even severely punishing them, yet, somehow, managed to make themselves thoroughly unwanted.

With the improvement in technology, the proportion of people, and especially the proportion of blacks and mestizos, who are of no economic value, useless to a non government employer, must be much larger than it used to be, and the option of selling useless people into slavery, or giving them away into slavery like a dog pound for humans, less appealing than it used to be – and it was not really sufficiently appealing even in the West Indies.

What abolished slavery was not meddling do gooders, but improving technology. Slavery in Europe largely ended as a result of the invention of the horse collar, which made it possible for a horse to do much of the work that had formerly been suitable for slaves, and the problem of useless unwanted people has been getting steadily worse since then.

It used to be that slavery gave private enterprise the incentive to look after, protect, and supervise, problem people. Now, however, less incentive, so what do you do with problem people?

Slavery was not a primarily a product of slaver raiders, but rather problem populations. Suppose you were a cattle rancher in Africa, a Tutsi or a white settler. Primitive people keep eating your cattle. What do you do with them? You hold a roundup, and then march them off to anyone who will take them. If no one takes them, you have to kill them, which may make subsequent roundups difficult. The value of slaves near the point of capture was usually low, zero or negative.

Ever since the development of the horse collar, the problem of what to with unwanted problem populations has become more difficult.

I don't think slavery is immoral. Many people are naturally slaves. What is immoral is enslaving someone who is not naturally a slave. Rather, the problem with slavery is that because there is less and less work that can be usefully done by someone who is whipped into doing it, slavery has ceased to be a useful solution to problem populations, to people who cause problems and reduce other people's standard of living.

Slavery used to be a useful and necessary institution for disposing of and taking care of those that were no #@^&*# good. Its abolition was premature. That slavery is now considerably less useful leaves us with big problems.

One solution to this problem is the casual and frequent use of execution as in the middle ages, but, of course, the problem with that is: who do we trust to execute the right people? They might execute the wrong people!

Another solution is segregation: You send all the presumably useless people (profiling, discrimination) into certain suburbs (segregation), and don't let them out, except that they get jobs in suburbs where the useful people live. Although it is no longer economically viable for private enterprise to take care of those that need whips to keep them adequately behaved, it is economically viable for private enterprise to sort out who respond to financial incentives for good behavior, and who will not.

Presumably those who will respond to financial incentives are better behaved, or capable of being induced to be better behaved, hence produce substantially smaller negative externalities.

If they burn down their own suburbs, you let them, if they start burning down other people's suburbs, then proceed with warlike measures until peace is restored. If they are particularly difficult, you intern the males in one area and the females in another or castrate those males that seem to be producing the greatest amount of difficulty.

Because slavery has become less useful than it used to be, probably need to rely on ethnic cleansing and segregation ameliorated with job based integration - people allowed to integrate if they get jobs, rather than integrating them by law and then manufacturing fake jobs for them. People who are employable, though somewhat dimwitted, will still produce substantial negative externalities, probably negative externalities much higher than their wages, but removing the rapidly increasing category of those unemployable due to bad character will reduce these problems substantially.

In summary:

All adult males should have financial incentives for good behavior and holding down a job, and all women should have financial incentives for good behavior and either holding down a job or being a good wife.

We should try to exclude the stupid and include the smart by non coercive means.

We should employ drastic and coercive means to exclude those too stupid or too obnoxious to respond to such incentives because such people generate large negative externalities. We should shove them somewhere out of sight and out of mind, and should they insist on obtruding on sight and mind, do whatever it takes to get them out of the way.

Racial problems will then disappear, except that such measures are apt to have grossly disparate impact on different races.The measures employed in the West Indies back in the days of slavery suggest that a significant proportion of blacks are unresponsive to incentives even when those incentives are extreme.

## Civilization: Hold back the darkness

2013-02-03 05:43:15

It is often said, and is true, that progressivism is in revolt against nature, but it is only true because progressivism is in revolt against the past and past knowledge, and a large part of our accumulated wisdom is knowledge of the nature of man, what humans naturally are. Progressives are not only in revolt against nature, but revolt against civilization.

Civilization is an artifice, a bunch of skills and methods by which large groups of people are able to live together and coordinate their activities.

Progressivism abandons all such artifices, leaving us with the social instincts that were adequate for a band of a dozen unarmed apes wandering through the jungle eating ants and leaves. (Our more recent ancestors, killer apes, being insufficiently progressive.) Civilization requires several inventions and virtues that are counter intuitive, and have to be continually re-learned, reinforced, reimposed, and enforced.

Civilization is the collection of skills and behaviors that we have discovered that made large groups possible for us.

1. Cleanliness. You cannot have cities unless people and places are clean. Without cleanliness, people cannot live close to other people, because they get diseases. Thus, dirty people are bad, need to be treated as bad, repugnant, undesirable people, and similarly dirty places. Civilized people stay out of dirty places, or they get rid of the dirty people and clean those places up. Progressives tend to be dirty. Recall the astonishing piles of filth and trash left behind after the One Nation rally, the Occupy Wall Street encampments drowning in their own slowly accumulating garbage and human faeces[14], and the stench and disease characteristic of Britain's public hospitals.

2. Economics: Respect for private property, freedom of contract, the free market, and freedom of trade. Adam Smith explained how this solves the coordination problem. Violating these rights complicates the coordination problem, making it unmanageable and impractical to coordinate large numbers of people. Nuclear families are naturally socialist, for as long as they all live under one roof, and this works well enough provided that Dad is dictator. It fails even within families if Dad is not dictator. The larger the group, the larger the necessary role for private property, freedom of contract, and freedom of trade in relations between the smaller groups of which the larger group is composed.For big groups, every intrusion on property is a disaster because it makes the coordination problem more difficult. The criterion for regulation should not be "would this regulation provide some benefit assuming the regulators are sufficiently wise", but "is this regulation so vital that I myself would hold a gun to my grandmother's head to make her submit to it and I myself would pull the trigger if she did not comply". Because the coordination problem is hard, regulators are never sufficiently wise. The more visible coordination you have, the less actual coordination you have, because for large groups, visible coordination works poorly. When the best leader's work is done, the people say "We did it ourselves."

3. The scientific method. Progressivism rejects the scientific method for the "scientific"

---

[14]https://www.mercurynews.com/breaking-news/ci_19373284

consensus, such as peer review. We continually need to ask "how do you know that", rather than relying on a suitably prestigious authority – we need to use what Wikipedia deprecatingly calls "original research" – which is to say, replicated research, not original research. Without this, society becomes riddled with superstition, and lives in the demon haunted dark - for example recycling rules, and the dietary rules against animal fat. Science ended around 1942 or thereabouts, as peer review replaced replication. The demon haunted dark closes in upon us, shutting down nuclear power, forbidding fracking, superstitiously terrified of dangerous compounds at one thousandth their harmful levels. Science needs to be restored.The need for the scientific method is a phenomenon of large groups. In small isolated groups, everyone is close to the original evidence, the testimony of the senses. In large groups we become overly reliant on what other people tell us, which can circulate and endlessly recirculate entirely disconnected from the testimony of the senses. The scientific method is a continual demand that such disconnects be watched for, detected, and rejected. Peer review needs to be treated as abhorrent and immoral, like plagiarism or research fraud, since it is in practice a continual demand that such disconnects be ignored, that official truth shall rule over observable truth. Peer review in practice detects and punishes heresy, not error. Indeed, by its nature, how could it detect error? Only replication can detect fraud and error. Scientific consensus must rest on evidence that has not been filtered through consensus. Peer review creates consensus that rests on consensus, anti scientific consensus, faith that rests on authority rather than observation.

4. Fatherhood. Males need to raise their children, which requires rules for families that make it attractive for males to stick around, in other words: patriarchy and female chastity. As the rules have been changed to be less and less favorable for males, more and more children have been deprived of their natural fathers, and even when fathers stick around, they are less and less involved in their children's lives.

5. Crime needs to be suppressed. It should seem odd and shocking that we need to lock our doors and take the keys out of our cars. It should be bizarre and horrifying that there are large parts of the city where it is simply hopelessly unsafe for an outsider to go. There are plenty of societies where the victimization rate is a hundred or a thousandfold lower than it is in the modern west, for example Singapore, and they accomplish this using methods that horrify modern progressives. Gangs that attack random people in the street should be as bizarre and improbable as man eating crocodiles in the municipal pond. They don't exist in Singapore. Why should they exist anywhere?Observe the crime surrounding the Occupy Wall Street encampments. Observe that under Hugo Chávez, "Venezuela has turned into the most violent country in South America, and that Caracas has become a global murder capital[15]. According to the independent Venezuelan Observatory of Violence, the annual number of homicides nationwide grew[16] from 5,974 in 1999 (when Chávez took power) to 17,600 in 2010". Similarly observe the extraordinary explosions of murder and violence that occurred with the end of apartheid in South Africa, and the left wing takeover of Detroit.

6. Civilization is unequal and undemocratic: The civilized, being better able to coordi-

---

[15]https://www.osac.gov/pages/ContentReportPDF.aspx?cid=11224
[16]https://www.fas.org/sgp/crs/row/R40938.pdf

nate, impose civilization on the uncivilized. Individuals and groups are unequally civilized, and the civilized need to rule over the uncivilized. Adults impose civilization on children, men on women, law abiding people on criminals, races highly adapted to a world of artifacts and agriculture on races adapted to wandering naked through the jungle, employers on employees. Civilization is not natural and spontaneous. At the current stage of our evolution, it has to be taught and enforced. The civilized minority, knowing what is needful, has to impose what is necessary on the uncivilized majority. In a well functioning civilization this happens primarily in the form of fathers imposing it on children and husbands enforcing it on wives. Propagating civilization through families is the most pleasant and humane form of enforcement, Other, less affectionate forms of enforcement, inhumane forms of enforcement, up to and including chattel slavery and execution, become necessary in proportion as civilization is not propagated in the family. That aspect of segregation that involved manufacturing a well behaved black middle class, installing it in power and affluence over the black majority, and upholding the authority of black fathers, should be understood as an effort to civilize blacks by a more civilized method than chattel slavery. As far as possible, civilization should be transmitted through the patriarchal family, where the bonds of natural affection limit the propensity of the civilized minority to mistreat the uncivilized majority, and through employer/employee relationships, where the liberty of the employee to walk away limits the possibility of mistreatment. Other means necessarily result in abuse and mistreatment of the uncivilized majority by the civilized minority, but the probability of such abuses should not restrain the civilized minority from doing what is necessary to uphold civilization.

And that is what is needful to hold back the darkness, a darkness populated by imaginary demons and real criminals. Eighteenth century Britons were correct to belief that upholding civilization justifies a great many sins, and frequently necessitates them.

If you have a plan for victory over progressivism, don't think of making entitlements expand at a one percent slower rate, think of restoration of the basic requirements for civilization, think of civilization protecting itself by enforcing them against the savages and subhumans. Plan on jailing a significant number of government employees, and forcibly rusticating most of them. Plan on taking a good part of the criminal underclass and some of the welfare underclass permanently out of circulation.

Any plan for victory over progressivism has to start with firing most government employees, imprisoning those that say "you cannot fire me", and similarly throwing most of the priesthood (by which I mean official science, public broadcasting, high status universities, and the like), off the government tit. This is necessarily going to be rather like a coup.

Victory over progressivism means firing the old official priesthood, and hiring a new, saner, and substantially smaller, official priesthood. Changing the official priesthood is apt to result in a holy war, which can get very nasty indeed, although when the old priesthood is decadent, one can frequently get away with a single battle, as when the Regent of the King of Hawaii defeated the high priest. I am pretty sure today's progressives are decadent, and have been decadent for over a century, so full scale holy war may well be avoidable.

Now this may seem like a crazily ambitious proposal. Progressivism has been going from victory to victory for one hundred and eighty years, but progressivism has developed a great weakness. In abandoning civilization, they have abandoned what is required for large group coordination. So when progressives attempt to mobilize as a large group, for example the Occupy Movement, total chaos ensues. They are coordinated only through holding the apparatus of the state, coordinated only through the apparatus of the state. As with the government of a banana republic, should a handful of state functionaries go off the air, there would be nothing left.

## Scalzied

### 2013-02-05 09:43:43

Author John Scalzi's propensity for terrified whimpering grovelling before leftists[17] has led Heartiste to coin a new word "Scalzied"[18]:

> When men are scalzied manboobs and women are manjawed feminists, the bedroom is an arid wasteland of dashed passion.

Inwardly Scalzi is a reactionary, in that he despises democracy and supports war and colonialism, but is terrified lest our masters detect his evil thoughts.

Because of crimestop, an author can get away with a lot of thoughtcrime without our masters noticing. See "District 9" for a spectacular example. The movie is a lecture that it is the duty of the superior race to rule the inferior, and failure to do so results not only in disaster for the superior, but considerably worse disaster for the inferior. Progressives totally failed to notice the message, for to notice it would be indication of agreeing with it. Scalzi allows himself a little bit of thoughtcrime in his novels, but not nearly as much as he could easily get away with.

## Boots on the ground are insufficient

### 2013-02-09 16:18:05

Joe Huffman estimates that in civil war, the right would have overwhelming military superiority[19].

As, of course, it would. Obviously. But boots on the ground are insufficient. As Stalin said "Ideas are more powerful than guns". The problem is not that the federal government has tanks and artillery. That is not doing it much good in Afghanistan, Iraq, and the rest. The problem is that progressives have intellectual dominance.

The majority of voters are illegitimate and/or non white and/or female and/or illegal immigrants. What do you do when a violent, corrupt, despotic, and tyrannical government is more or less freely and fairly elected? For example, the Nazis in Germany, Allende in Chile, Chávez in Venezuela, or ... Jerome Cavanagh in Detroit.

Jerome Cavanagh was a white Mayor who was elected because of overwhelming black vote in his favor. The federal government, to reward and reinforce the turn left, poured

---


[17] https://blog.reaction.la/politics/why-racefail-09-hates-john-scalzi.html
[18] https://heartiste.wordpress.com/2013/01/31/this-house-is-clean-and-sex-free/
[19] https://blog.joehuffman.org/2013/02/07/boots-on-the-ground-2/

vast amounts of money onto Detroit and other leftwards turning cities, resulting in his 1965 re-election. However it rapidly became apparent that had the federal government spent the money bombing these cities, rather than subsidizing social pathology in them, it might well have done less harm.

Cavanagh, or perhaps federal funding, or perhaps both, proceeded to run Detroit into the ground, which instead of exposing the economic and political bankruptcy of left wing policies, race baiting, and stirring up racial hatred, resulted in radical movement further left. In an attempt to ensure re-election, he proceeded to ethnically cleanse the white majority of out of Detroit. No right wing revolution ensued. Instead the left revolution naturally devoured its children to move further leftwards. In the next election, the black candidate and the white candidate for Mayor agreed to avoid the law and order issue, which is to say, agreed to avoid any suggestion that voting for the white man would mean less ethnic cleansing than voting for the black man. The 1967 riot never entirely stopped until the white presence in Detroit was reduced to insignificant levels. Whites in Detroit could not resist ethnic cleansing because they could not get a white candidate, white leadership, who would resist ethnic cleansing. Though the national guard theoretically moved in to quell the riots, in practice, its primary job was to protect the rioters from white "racism".

People just could not think the thought that racially and politically motivated ethnic cleansing of whites was under way, that such cleansing was illegitimate, *and that therefore any political and electoral process that could not produce leadership capable of opposing such cleansing was illegitimate.* That if "law and order" was somehow not a political issue, despite being the biggest and most important conflict under way, then there was something unacceptably wrong with the political institutions and the political process, that if the issue was excluded from the normal political process, then the normal political process had to end.

## In favor of Obama's drone strikes

### 2013-02-09 18:27:05

Congress has declared war on Al Quaeda, its affiliates, its franchisees, its allies, and its sponsors, a vague and ill defined group, a nebulous category. This gives the president the legal authority to assassinate lots of people in lots of places on the basis of vague and secret evidence, some of them American citizens.

But it does not, however, give the president authority to assassinate abortion clinic bombers, or even Islamic terrorists who are not allied or affiliated to Al Quaeda, for example Hezbollah terrorists. Seems narrow enough to me. Congress could have, and arguably should have, declared war on Islam.

If anything government does is legal, if there is any legitimate purpose of government whatsoever, that purpose is making war. Congress has declared war in a completely constitutional fashion in response to an extraordinary act of aggression. Thus nothing the US government does could be more legal, more properly constitutional, than Obama ordering a drone strike on a US citizen on the basis of Obama's reasonable and plausible suspicion that that US citizen is an Al Quaeda franchisee.

Just about everything the US government does is illegal and unconstitutional. Assassinating America's enemies in accordance with a congressional declaration of war is one of the very few legal and constitutional things it does.

For this to be a legal precedent for launching a drone strike on me, Congress would need to declare war on"enemies of equality" or some such. Which it may well do, but I don't think that assassinating real enemies in a real war makes this any more or less likely.

## Postmortem on Warmism

### 2013-02-14 07:57:57

We are always moving leftwards, but not every leftwards program succeeds. Should one fail, they try something different.

I have not published much on warmism lately, because they were defeated by Climategate, even though every academic institution, every government institution, and every group of organized scientists swore fealty to Warmism, officially proclaimed that Climategate was no big deal, and have been trying to carry on as if Climategate was no big deal. But now they are subsiding, so time for a post mortem on the warmist movement, which has pretty much gone the way of the communist movement, where fans of the proletariat have shrunk down to few little academic circles holding reality at bay from behind their little Berlin walls, while the rest of the communist movement substitute females and minorities for the proletariat, and continue business as usual.

The driving force of the left singularity is that deviation from orthodoxy to the right gets the most extraordinary punishment for trivial or nonexistent sins, but deviation to the left is at most very gently restrained[20], even when the leftists commit gross crimes in the service of their ideal.

Nonetheless, today warmists are being gently restrained from committing their worst offenses, today warmism is a leftwards deviation from current left orthodoxy. They can no longer endlessly republish[21] their grossest frauds over and over again as they used to be able to..

1. In Australia, Climategate caused Tony Abbot to become leader of the opposition.

2. Tony Abbot prevented Australia from implementing Copenhagen.

3. Australia refusing to implement Copenhagen led to China refusing to implement Copenhagen.

4. China refusing to implement Copenhagen killed Copenhagen.

5. And, in retrospect, it is apparent that the failure of Copenhagen to implement a terrorist world government of artificial famine was not merely a temporary setback for Warmism, but its death knell.

After seven years of fruitless struggle against truth and reality, in 2012 October, the scientific establishment quietly decided that no further hockey sticks shall be published or publishable, and quietly conceded that the medieval climatic optimum happened.

The warmists use a statistical method that amounts to cherry picking the data, while obscuring the fact that one is cherry picking, perhaps obscuring it from oneself. One

---

[20]https://charltonteaching.blogspot.com.au/2013/02/wasting-time-on-educating-liars-like.html
[21]https://wattsupwiththat.com/2012/10/31/mcintyres-triumph-over-gergis-karoly-and-mann/

weights the data in proportion to how much it agrees with one's hypothesis, a technique that since the dawn of the science of statistical methods has long been notorious for generating whatever results one desires.

Sometime in 2012 every science journal everywhere suddenly decided it would no longer allow the warmists to get away with using this method, which being at the core of warmism, was becoming increasingly notorious.

And so, naturally, the warmists proceeded to piously claim that they were no longer using this method.

Gergis, Karoly and Mann generated their usual hockey stick by their usual methods, while, naturally, denying that they were using this method. Jean S. on McIntyre's blog pointed out that they had to be "mistaken", because, obviously, the data as a whole does not support the hockey stick or Warmism. McIntyre and company made a freedom of information request for their data, data which according to the unwritten rules of science, and the written rules of the major scientific journals, should have been freely available.

One of relevant universities complied fully and swiftly with the spirit and intent of the freedom of information laws, possibly because it lived in well founded fear of Tony Abbot getting charge of their budget.The information revealed that the authors of the paper were lying mistaken.

Journal of Climate editor Chiang wrote[22]:

> After consulting with the Chief Editor, I have decided to rescind acceptance of the paper- you'll receive an official email from J Climate to this effect as soon as we figure out how it should be properly done. I believe the EOR has already been taken down.

So, as of 2012 October, no more hockey stick, and, as of 2012 October, Medieval Climatic Optimum reinstated.

Today Warmism is only orthodoxy in the sense that communism is orthodoxy - that it is always safe to be leftwards of the official doctrine, and always dangerous to criticize those to the left of official doctrine, for they uphold a higher, purer, and more extreme version of the official doctrine, thus any such criticism leads to one being suspected as a critic of the official doctrine, rather than defender of the official doctrine. (Hence the obscure and diplomatic way in which the paper was unaccepted.)

It is still hazardous to be antiwarmist, as it is hazardous to be anticommunist, but Warmism is no longer official truth. It is officially incorrect.

## The end of democracy

### 2013-02-17 16:01:35

Winston Churchill quipped that democracy is the worst form of government except all those other forms.

Democracy worked when the franchise was restricted to property owning adult male heads of households, and when the population had high moral standards. Visitors to

---

[22]https://wattsupwiththat.com/2012/10/31/mcintyres-triumph-over-gergis-karoly-and-mann/

America frequently remarked that while democracy worked for Americans, Americans being virtuous and self reliant, it would not work for the corrupt and degenerate mob they had back in their home countries.

Today the white population is substantially fatherless, the other populations generally worse, those on some form of government benefit substantially outnumber those paying taxes, and the government is buying up huge numbers of low IQ voters from the third world and importing them.

We used to at least get Mexicans who wanted to work, but increasingly, these days we get the Mexican underclass, the ones that normal Mexicans do not want, people who lived on their votes in Mexico, and proceed to do the same in the USA. We used to get Mexicans imported by farmers to pick strawberries, but we now get Mexicans imported by politicians to vote left.

Now the voters are a corrupt and degenerate mob that votes for the highest bidder, resulting in insolvency and socialism.

The modern electorate is substantially composed of bastards (people who were not raised by their biological fathers) and is in substantial part composed of an underclass purchased by politicians and imported from foreign lands.

And so democracy votes for insolvency and socialism.

Government is not the solution to public good problems[23], but the rather the greatest public good problem of them all. A public that cannot themselves produce public goods, cannot produce good government.

With a corrupt and decadent public, elections become advance auctions of stolen goods. Everything is up for grabs, thus private property is insecure, hence is not used productively. Everything is dissipated, spent on buying votes, thus public and private insolvency. Toyota gets sued for practicing capitalism without being a crony.

## Teleology and Darwinism

2013-02-20 07:27:56

Darwin freely used teleology as a metaphor for natural selection, that natural selection works as if an intelligent breeder was consciously pursuing a goal, as if aiming at horses, to take advantage of the grasslands, or as if aiming at men, to create a creature capable of planning and cooperating to defeat any creature less capable of planning and cooperation.

And by an interesting coincidence, whosoever hates the metaphor, hates natural selection.

As Bruce Charlton tells us[24]

> most modern intellectuals - and especially the public intellectuals who write in the highbrow media and publish big-selling nonfiction books; and including most scientists and indeed biologists and psychologists- **do not believe that natural selection explains 'higher' human facultiessuch as intelligence, language, consciousness and morality.**

---

[23]https://reaction.laanarchy/public_goods.htm
[24]https://charltonteaching.blogspot.com.au/2013/02/does-natural-selection-explain-human.html

These people believe in human evolution, in the sense that they believe humans descended from primates etc – yet they do not believe that this evolution was caused by natural selection - yet they do not have any other explanation.

In short, evolutionists but not Darwinists.

In essence, they believe that the higher human faculties *just happened*. They are simply *brute facts*.

I first was sure about this in listening to an interview with Noam Chomsky, in which the interviewer pushed him hard to explain how it was that humans developed language.

Chomsky was uncomfortable and rather irritated, and eventually came up with a scenario where something like a cosmic ray caused a mutation and human language ability was accomplished at a stroke.

(No wonder Chomsky was uncomfortable, since this is a ridiculous assertion; yet here it was, emanatingfrom the most highly-cited human scientist/ social scientist of the modern era.)

But similar end points can be reached among most intellectuals who write about intelligence, language, consciousness and morality.

They are sure of only two things about higher human faculties:
1. These phenomena cannot be explained by supernatural agency (because they *know* that the supernatural does not exist)
2. These phenomena cannot - or at any rate should not - be explained by natural selection.

This is the way of thinking about evolution that comes from Aristotle and which has dominated theoretical biology with people such as Goethe, D'Arcy Thompson, Gregory Bateson, Waddington, Kauffman and the modern chaos complexity theorists - and Sheldrake.

Such thinkers are generally evasive or vague about where these forms come from, or how we know about them - necessarily vague since they exclude any divine role or revelation.

Charlton is of course arguing for a divinely ordained human nature, but is himself rather vague as to how that divinely ordained human nature differs from human nature as ordained by political correctness

The Old Testament is pretty clear that God ordained human nature, and what that nature is, and, that nature is rather similar to what a Darwinist would expect natural selection to produce of risen killer apes. Modern Christians, including Bruce, find this rather distasteful and are apt to interpret it away as much any modern leftist, because it implies a God who is patriarchal, racist, vengeful, genocidal, and disturbingly old fashioned, much like those made in his image.

If you care going to believe in a creator God, you had better believe in one that chose to create the world the way it actually is, and that is the creator God we find in the Bible, one that, as a result of original sin, made men as they actually are.

The modern Christian right, as much as the modern Christian left, seeks to make a peace with progressivism. Unlike the modern Christian left, they want a peace that does not involve the erasure of every last trace of Christianity and its total replacement with progressivism. But it does not matter what they want, for that is not what they are going to get.

If someone takes his bible seriously, and does not take the need for peace with progressivism seriously (for there is no peace to be had) he is going to believe rather similar things about human nature as a Darwinist believes.

> Somehow we [supposedly] know about them and somehow we can recognize them.

> These attributes of humans, these phenomena which are what make humans distinctive, did not evolve but are [supposedly] part of reality.

> In particular, morality - by which they mean modern leftist morality as it has emerged in the West in the past three hundred years - is built into reality.

> But the same applies to language, consciousness, and intelligence - these are seen as qualitative and 'given'.

> I am pretty sure that most people do not realize, have not noticed, how vague and strange are these bottom-line beliefs of [supposedly] hard-nosed, mainstream intellectuals.

> On the whole these beliefs are never stated. On the whole these dominant thinkers are able to evade examination of their own bottom-line convictions by means of articulate and aggressive attacks on those with whom they disagree.

> That is to say with Christians (the religious Right) and with sociobiologists/ evolutionary psychologists (the secular Right).

> But it is a remarkable fact of modern intellectual life that public discourse is dominated by a perspective that is defined almost entirely negatively - on the basis of convictions that are mostly unstated, and which when stated are absurd to the point of being self-refuting.

> Yet when any person tries to explain human distinctiveness on the basis of stated and explicit convictions - either religious assumptions, or else on the axiomatic assumption that all such phenomena *must* be explicable by natural selection and the only question is a matter of specific detail - then that person is unrestrainedly attacked, vilified and mocked on the evil ridiculousness of their beliefs ...

For example Chagnon

...

> So they reach this weird, unstated but undeniable position of arguing from the brute facticity of leftist morality - without any possibility of explaining how this can be known to be true, or why it should be true, or how it is true - or even why such brute facts have any influence on human choices (given that *other* brute facts, such as sexual differences, are denied to have any implications whatsoever for human choice) ...

This progressive doctrine is of course, the ancient Judeo Christian doctrine of a human nature divinely ordained by a creator God, only with the God removed, and with the actual empirical observation of human nature denied. A creator God explains and justifies the observed creation. Progressivism has deleted both ends of this doctrine, the God and the observation, while retaining the doctrine, and denouncing whosoever deviates from this completely incoherent doctrine.

Observe the denunciation of Chagnon, wherein Chagnon supposedly caused bad things to happen to the primitive natural native rainforest dwellers merely by thinking bad thoughts. He was denounced not merely for heresy, for believing that men evolved, that human nature evolved, by natural selection, but for what not so very long ago, the progenitors of today's progressivism called witchcraft.

## Blacks are stupid.

2013-02-22 15:11:22

Occidentalist has updated his survey of surveys. Despite radical social changes and a wide variety of testing regimes, American black IQ always tests out one standard deviation below American white IQ. Similar differences in character and criminal propensities are obvious.

How big is one standard deviation? If you take a random black, and a random white, it means that someone's race does not tell you a whole lot about which one is smarter, but, in practice, one never meets a *random* black and a *random* white.

Suppose blacks are affirmative actioned into a diverse elite group, police, academia, etc. Then, because IQ variance between random white academics is lot less than IQ variance between random whites, almost every black academic will be markedly and strikingly dumber than every white academic, meaning that few black academics (in a non elite university no black academics whatever) will be capable of doing the kind of academic things that academics traditionally do. Similarly, in a police force, all or almost all black cops will be markedly more criminal than all or almost all white cops.

This leads to the one rotten apple problem. In a diverse police force, being honest is racist and disloyal to you fellow cops. In a diverse academia, doing stuff that requires intelligence and ability is racist and anti scientific.

We see a similar result when women are affirmative actioned into jobs requiring upper body physical strength: We get the no lift rule. People, both males and females, are forbidden to use upper body strength. In hospitals, when you need a sick patient lifted up, you cannot call a male nurse, because that would be discrimination. They could not say equal pay for equal work, if some tasks were manifestly unequal. This sometimes results in patients dying. Computer science courses are dumbed down so that females can pass them. The removal of certain aspects of computer science on which men perform markedly better than women makes both male students and female students ignorant, makes them both worse off. Not only the males, but also the females would be better off covering those areas, even if the women performed poorly.

In general, whenever you mingle two groups, you get a leveling down to the worst characteristics of both groups, so that the diverse group is worse in important ways to at least one of the unmingled groups, and usually worse in important ways to *both* of the unmingled groups, partly because there are few groups so uniformly bad that they do not have at least some virtues, and partly because differences in virtues leads to those virtues being deprecated: The no lift rule denies both men and women the use of their upper body strength, making women effectively weaker than they already are. Similarly, in diverse communities, blacks tend to be more criminal than they already are.

## Law of everywhere treaty

### 2013-02-26 07:14:32

You think the Law of the Sea Treaty is about ships having fender benders on the high seas?

Think again: if you take piss in the middle of the Rocky Mountains, you would, if Obama, the Democrats, and a substantial part of the Republican party had had their way, been subject to the Law Of The Sea Treaty[25], and thus, if the treaty had been signed, under UN jurisdiction.

> "pollution of the marine environment" means the introduction by man, directly or indirectly, of substances or energy into the marine environment, including estuaries, which results or is likely to result in such deleterious effects as harm to living resources and marine life, hazards to human health, hindrance to marine activities, including fishing and other legitimate uses of the sea, impairment of quality for use of sea water and reduction of amenities.

So if you take piss in the middle of the Rocky Mountains, you, you the individual, not the state, not the evil capitalist overlord shipowner, would have been subject to the Law of the Sea Treaty as interpreted and applied by a bunch of corrupt third world despotisms that hate white people and capitalism.

People have noticed that the amount of mercury in the ocean is arguably higher than is good. And since Nature is Good, and only man is vile, this is proof that the mercury is the result of unidentified human activities. And since no one can identify the specific activities that are supposedly causing there to be mercury in the ocean, any behavior or suspected behavior anywhere that greenies feel bad about is alleged to be poisoning the fish and people who eat the fish, pretty much as old ladies were accused of causing their neighbors milk cows to dry up by witchcraft. No actual material flow of mercury from the

---

[25]https://www.heritage.org/research/reports/2012/03/accession-to-un-convention-on-the-law-of-the-sea

land to the sea actually caused by the wicked polluter is ever identified, it being sufficient, as in a racial discrimination lawsuit, to show that the accused might plausibly have wicked thoughts. Mercury in the oceans is routinely used as an all purpose Greenie accusation against anyone and everything. It is official science that ocean mercury is anthropogenic, and the complete and total lack of evidence that the mercury is anthropogenic makes this Official Science more useful for litigants, not less useful, since no actual material causation, whereby the accused's wicked thoughts led to wicked deeds actually poisoning fish with actual mercuric material, need be presented. And this much made accusation, if brought under the jurisdiction of the Law of the Sea Treaty, would be judged by a bunch of third world despotisms that hate US, white people, and capitalism, and are even more inclined to magical thinking than the audience of the Oprah show. The Official Science does not identify any actual human controlled mercury, so the litigant does not need to either - indeed, the relationship between Official Government Approved Science and the litigants is so close that it is hard to distinguish them. Under the Law of the Sea Treaty, this old chestnut would have been moved from the jurisdiction of particular nations, to the jurisdiction of the UN.

## Why Darwinism is more controversial than ever

2013-02-26 12:03:57

Darwin not only tells us that one individual is not equal to another, he also tells us that races are the origin of species, which means that in general races will be unequal in major and important ways.

Darwinism also tells us that men and women are genetically predisposed to different and unequal social roles, which implies that attempts to make their roles legally equal will not work very well.

Darwinism tells us that we have a moral sense evolved to further our self interest, leading to the proposition that people's real moral theory is closer to that of Ayn Rand or the classic Greeks, and that claims to the contrary are lies and hypocrisy. Darwinism tells us about our nature, and tells us about our moral sense, and what it tells us about our moral sense implies that the man who says he would hold a child's face in the fire to find the cure for malaria is apt to hold a child's face in the fire and forget he was trying to cure malaria

If you believe that men were not created equal, that some races really are inferior, that most endangered species are overdue for extinction and need to be turned into fur coats and hamburgers, that women should stay in the kitchen and if they must work, do female work, lest their delicate souls be shocked by male crudity, because if they are in the male workplace doing male jobs, they are apt sue their coworkers and bosses for being males, then Darwinism looks mighty like common sense.

If you believe that most people raising money to help far away strangers are going to use it to rape children, then Darwinism looks like realism rather than nihilism.

Darwinism should not cause you to doubt all morality. Darwinism tells us we evolved from killer apes by evolving towards more cooperation and more successful and effective cooperation. It should, however, cause you to doubt the morality of the Pharisees.

## Sequestration

**2013-03-01 17:44:28**

The US Government is launching a big propaganda offensive on how hurtful sequestration will be, and keeps issuing lists of the horrible horrible horrible harms sequestration will cause.

What the sequester reveals is that the great majority of government expenditure consists of paying people to support the Cathedral and the Democrat party. Most of these horrible harms looks to me remarkably like a bunch of mostly nonwhite people getting laid off or having their grants delayed, non white people who are theoretically getting paid to do stuff that I don't want done, but are more likely being paid to vote Democrat and engage in Democratic party activism.

For example there will be less TSA agents. Oh the horror!

I can't see how any of these can possibly lose the Republicans votes. For example head start (free child minding for black sluts receiving welfare for popping out fatherless children) is going to be cut. How many black sluts vote Republican?

Now I am not a typical voter, but the victims of these supposedly horrid cuts are not typical voters either. They are, for the most part, paid democrats. Obviously the government must be trying to cut stuff that affects swinging voters as much as possible, but is coming up with mighty slim pickings.

What about military cuts?

"Maintenance and repair of five ships ..." What is being cut is the ability to swiftly project military power to far away trouble spots. Far away strangers, whose race, language, and culture differs from my own, will alas have to defend themselves for a while. Poor things. How sad for them.

The Pax Americana is going to be trimmed back two percent, which I suppose means that people far away who are not like me will enjoy two percent less peace. If we had been stealing the oil and ravishing the women, I would worry about the cuts, but instead our troops have been heavily armed nursemaids. We build schools for our enemy's children, on the theory that being nice to Muslims will inspire them to convert from Islam to progressivism, which schools our enemies blow up. Somehow, schools for our enemy's children are not on the sequester list, probably because people would care about them even less than they care about repair and maintenance for some ships.

The absurdity of the wasteful, frivolous, and politically one sided expenditures that are being cut explains why western governments around the world are running ever bigger deficits and spending an ever larger proportion of GDP. Buying a left electorate costs money. Buying an ever more left wing electorate costs ever more money. For example Obama wants more free childcare for sluts on welfare because he wants more sluts on welfare.

Presumably they are trying to come up with the least wasteful, least frivolous, and least politically one sided things to be cut, the things that people will care about the most, the things that will most hurt the median voter, and what they come up with instead is child care for sluts.

## Bloomberg speaks truth to power

2013-03-02 12:45:42

When I was in Sunnyvale in 2005 November, the vast majority of people who were buying million dollar houses were no-hablo-english hispanics on foodstamps with no regular job buying houses no money down. As far as I could tell, every person buying a house for over a million dollars was an unemployed underclass non white. Earlier there had been some whites buying, but by November, anyone with a credit rating or an employment history had given up on buying or was trying to sell.

I don't have any direct evidence that Bloomberg's cover accurately displays the way things are now, but it accurately displays what I saw with my own eyes in Sunnyvale California in November 2005. It was million dollar welfare handouts back then, and I doubt that things have improved under Obama.

You may ask who gets to lose the money this time around. The answer, this time around, is instead of the fed indirectly, it is the fed directly. Instead of bailing out those who irresponsibly buy mortgage backed securities, it has been buying mortgage backed securities directly - which means those who foolishly treat dollars as money will, eventually, be those paying.

The pile of hundred dollar bills that the dog is using for its bed were freshly printed up by the federal reserve, which obtained in exchange mortgage backed securities, hence reports no loss. Indeed, it has reported no loss on any of the very large pile of mortgage backed securities that it now owns, even though, for the most part, no one has made any payments on the mortgages underlying those securities. This is your off the books deficit, which outweighs the on the books deficit to the same degree as off the books welfare outweighs on the books welfare - your deficit, in the sense that if you are one of America's rapidly diminishing minority of taxpayers, people think you are going to pay it. You are going to be making that dog's bed.

Mestizos in California drive cars even though no one really expects them to have a driving license or third party insurance, and not all of them know how to drive a car. To deny them the right to drive a car by imposing white centric standards of licensing on them would be *raaaaciiisssst*. Similarly, expecting them to make payments on the mortgage would be *raaaaciiisssst*.

Equality before the law obviously is not equal if the law reflects white behavior. And so, equality before the law quietly transforms into statistically equal impact of the law. Expecting mestizos to make mortgage payments would impact them more severely than it impacts whites. Mestizos are a voting majority in California. Californian blacks, who are a voting minority, still need to pay their mortgages and get driver's licenses. Theoretically Hispanic privilege extends to all Hispanics, to anyone who claims to be Hispanic, and that is federal law and practice, but suspiciously white looking Hispanics find that they do not get some of the more outrageous Hispanic California state privileges. Now that Hispanics have a majority in California, it is becoming harder to qualify as one of this privileged group.

## Libertarianism and Equalism.

### 2013-03-03 06:09:15

I regard myself as a libertarian and anarcho capitalist, but I see all these Libertarians who want the the government to import unlimited numbers of underclass people from Mexico to live on welfare and vote democrat. They worry about the government intruding into people's lives by not allowing gays to marry, and are entirely unworried about the government intruding into people's lives to desecrate the sacrament of marriage, by forcing everyone to recognize gay marriage, despite the fact that those few gays that get married frequently do it to épater les bourgeois by having sex in public in a great big pile.

Forcing everyone to refer to homosexuals as "gay" did not result in the good feelings and good associations of the word "gay" being associated with homosexuals, but instead made "gay" into a curse word of startling potency. The theme song of the Flintstones, and the second verse of "Deck the halls" disappeared. Forcing people to call gays "married" following group sex on the church altar is apt to have similar effect on the word "marriage". If ever we revive the old fashioned marriage contract, we will likely need a new word for it.

Gay marriage follows from equalism. If women are equal to men, then interchangeable, in which case why not interchange them? If you reject gay marriage, logically you have to reject egalitarian marriage, reject legal equality between men and woman in matters related to sex and reproduction - indeed in any area where the obvious differences are extreme. If women's suffrage, then gay marriage follows. If gay marriage is unacceptable to you, women's suffrage should be unacceptable also. If, on the other hand, you believe that women should have the right to vote, you really should believe in gay marriage, and try to contain your gag reflex when the bridegrooms and their best men have sex on the altar in a great big pile. After all, if men and women are equal, then gay marriages cannot be different, even though they quite obviously are different.

And similarly, if all men are equal, on what basis can we justify not allowing all men to vote in US elections and collect US welfare?

To deduce standard libertarianism, we proceed from the obviously reasonable assumptions that microeconomics, economics in one lesson, is right, and coercion is wrong – and the "obviously reasonable" assumption that all men should be equal before the law.

Or equivalently we can deduce it from the principle that negative sum interactions should be suppressed, since if an interaction is positive sum, there is room to make a deal whereby both parties will agree to it, positive and negative sum interactions being identified by microeconomics – and the "obviously reasonable" assumption that all men should be equal before the law.

Or equivalently we can deduce it from the principle that predations and parasitism should be suppressed, with predation and parasitism being defined relative to standard microeconomics – and the "obviously reasonable" assumption that all men should be equal before the law.

But no one believes that children should be equal before the law, so libertarians wind up making a variety of vague, incoherent, and unprincipled exceptions for children.

And though everyone pretends to believe that women should be equal, no one in their guts believes that a reproductive age female should be responsible for the consequences of her actions, which has the implication that no one in their guts believes that a reproductive age female should make her own decisions for herself. When a woman is in trouble as a result of her own decisions, no one, left or right, feels she should be responsible for the consequences of her own decisions. They feel for her like a child, as for example the character of Fantine in *Les Misérables*. In the song "I dreamed a dream", Fantine refers to herself as a child, even though she is starting to hit the wall, implying that it was cruel to allow her to make her own decisions for herself, as indeed it was. If Fantine pulls your heartstrings, you don't really believe that women should be emancipated. If you allow women to run around loose, you will feel a highly unlibertarian urge to childsafe the world to protect Fantine from herself.

And so libertarians wind up making a variety of vague, incoherent, and unprincipled exceptions for marriage, reproduction, and sex.

Further, there are many adult males who simply cannot look after themselves, who wind up living on welfare and crime, and people want laws to deal with them, laws that give police alarmingly great authority and privilege police to use alarming amounts of violence.

The intent is always that the laws will be applied selectively, that in practice they will be applied only to bums, winos, and minorities.

It is often said that guns don't kill people. People kill people. Similarly, drugs do not addict people. There are however some people, quite a lot of people, who should be permitted neither guns nor drugs.

Trayvon Martin was not forced burgle or mug by drugs. But since he was spending a fair bit of money on drugs, and had no job, we should conclude he was burgling or mugging. So Trayvon Martin intoxicated should have been treated very differently from someone intoxicated who had means to pay his own way.

But in practice these laws always get turned around, because applying such laws to bums and such is more work and more dangerous, and because the ruling party needs the votes of its underclass mascots, so in practice these laws wind up being selectively applied only to employed white males, the opposite of the original intention that they be applied only to the poor and black. We get anarcho tyranny, as illustrated in the Tony Martin burglary case.

In a rural area in England a team of burglars went forth most days, for years on end, robbing, assaulting people in their homes, committing vandalism, starting fires, day after day, year after year, committing hundreds, probably thousands, of burglaries. Police did nothing – well not quite nothing. The burglars went through the revolving door of the justice system numerous times without ever being removed from circulation. Tony Martin shot one of these habitual repeat burglars, and the entire resources of the state were applied to destroy him, to dig up any dirt that could be thrown in his general direction in order to prejudice the jury.

Similarly, in California, a mestizo can drive a car without a license or third party insurance, and not get in trouble even if demonstrably incompetent to drive a car. Libertarians are strangely unable to acknowledge or mention this striking *lack* of equality before the law. Unemployed Mestizos are equal before the law to employed white males, yet somehow, strangely, employed white males are not equal to unemployed mestizos

Committed to supporting equality before the law for people that are demonstrably unequal, libertarians are strangely struck silent by the phenomenon of unidirectional equality.

The no parasitism rule assumes a world of independent adults, thus is fundamentally incompatible with the equality of all men, for a great many able bodied men, the undeserving poor, are unable or unwilling to support themselves, thus must necessarily be parasites.

If only independent adults count, thus a world in which only heads of households count. Dependents do not count because they, like Fantine, should make decisions under the supervision of the head of household, or with his consent. Parasites don't count because non parasites have a common interest in eradicating them like vermin.

It thus presupposes something mighty close to patriarchy, in that without welfare, heads of households are apt to be overwhelmingly male, and that we deal with able bodied indigents, the undeserving poor, in a manner that is mighty close to chattel slavery and, chattel slavery not being very economic these days, genocide.

The first principle of libertarianism has radically reactionary implications fundamentally incompatible with the second principle, equality before the law. If we are going to ship all bums off to the gulag, we are not treating them as equals.

But, approved libertarians, academic libertarians, libertarians organized as a political faction, are anti patriarchy and take a"utilitarian" approach to welfare. ("Utilitarian" in scare quotes because there are no real utilitarians. It is always a rationalization for an unspeakably horrifying position.)

The no parasitism rule leads not to orthodox official progressive libertarianism, but to profoundly reactionary libertarianism.

We have a pile of intrusive and unreasonable laws that theoretically apply to everyone, that were intended to apply only to blacks and poor people. In practice, in some upper crust areas, areas where successful progressives hang out, they are applied to blacks and poor people.In most places in California, it is the other way around. These laws are applied only to employed white males Libertarians seem curiously tongue tied about both forms of inequality.

If you believe that all men are equal, you cannot really believe in the non coercion rule, because some men need a great deal of coercion, you cannot really believe in the no negative sum interaction rule, for the same reason, nor the no parasitism rule, for some men are naturally parasites.

I suggest a different principle, one that England was pretty good approximation to from Charles the Second to George the fourth: That all property owning self supporting heads of households should be equal before the law, that people unable to support themselves should have substantially less legal power and freedom, and that able bodied people unable or unwilling to support themselves, the undeserving poor, should be subject to quite severe coercion, should be kept under supervision and compelled to good behavior on pain of imminent and immediate physical punishment - the old English workhouse.

Libertarian rules are rules for interaction between people for whom violence, physical coercion, is inappropriate: In other words, rules for gentlemen. There are a lot of people for whom physical violence, or the imminent threat thereof, is unavoidably necessary. So a libertarian society has to divide the world into people that are gentlemen, and people that are not. The more people it fits into the gentleman category, the more libertarian it is, but some people, quite a lot of people, are not going to fit.

This principle, that property owning self supporting heads of households should be equal before the law, is workable because heads of households don't have much conflict of interest with other heads of households, assuming that they all believe in microeconomics. That all men are equal before the law is not workable, as is revealed by libertarian paralysis and hypocrisy at all the numerous various unprincipled exceptions to this rule.

I don't view that part of libertarianism that proposes equality before the law as inherent, but as a blemish that has to be removed, a legacy of libertarianism's alliance with progressivism, an alliance that progressives abandoned in the nineteenth century, but which jilted and abandoned libertarians have for one hundred and thirty years vainly and pitifully hoped to renew.

A self supporting head of household should be equal before the law to another self supporting head of household. There should be equality before the law between households, but equality before the law within households means the state thrusting itself into households as big daddy, infantilizing adults – resulting in actually existent family law, which intended to apply libertarianism at gunpoint to wives and children to protect them from sexist patriarchal oppression – but fails to protect them from statist oppression.

Much unlibertarian law is intended to deal with people that are not self supporting, but instead gets applied to everyone. For example if someone is unemployed, homeless, has no rental deposit, and is stoned, then the fact that he is stoned *under those circumstances* shows he needs to be coerced and supervised by his betters. If he is not going to be coerced, compelled, beaten if necessary, and it frequently is necessary, he winds up above the law, while the guy who works and pays his taxes winds up underneath the law. If someone is stoned, but holds down his job and pays his rent, then it is intrusive to meddle in his recreations. His home should be his castle so long as he pays his rent, while the man who gets high in public because he cannot make his rent needs a thumping, for if someone has no visible means of support, his invisible means of support are parasitic or predatory. Libertarianism means you get rid of such people. They should neither be allowed to vote redistribution, nor be allowed to do redistribution themselves.

Equality before the law is only workable if people are well separated (separate households), and if people are not too grossly unequal. You cannot apply it to someone who cannot afford his own household, because of lack of separation, and, frequently, because of lack of competence and future orientation. Libertarians keep trying to differentiate themselves from the right by advocating further moves left, for example gay marriage

This is corrupt behavior, betraying their allies in an entirely unsuccessful effort to suck up to their enemies. Equalism is necessarily unlibertarian, because some people are not equal, and those people wind up preying on productive people, and have to be restrained, frequently by crude and primitive means, by grossly coercive means. It is frequently the case that nothing less than a good thrashing will stop them, and usually the case that nothing less than the imminent threat of a good thrashing will stop them.

Prohibit such crude physical violence against inferior people, the prisons get flooded. Revolving door justice, as for the burglars that terrorized the area where Tony Martin lived, necessarily follows. Some people are restrained by concern for their job, good name, and relationships with their fellows. Such people should never be subject to physical violence. Some people are not, and should be subject to frequent physical violence. This is inequality before the law, and quite severe inequality at that. If you apply a no violence policy for everyone, then those who fit the profile that violence will likely be necessary, wind up being above the law, while the white male with a job winds up beneath the law. As in California, you get one way equality.

## Christianity and morality

### 2013-03-06 08:03:17

A lot of Christians argue that atheism must be nihilistic, and that nihilism cannot possibly oppose or resist the self confident moralizing of the progressives.

There are three problems with this theory:

1. The pagan Greeks had Gods that were no better than men, and for the most part a

good deal worse, and yet the Greeks did not suffer from nihilism until after they suffered social decay. Social decay and childlessness caused nihilism. Nihilism did not cause social decay. We could do with their heroic and manly morality, in place of the excessively feeble, defeatist, and other worldly Christian morality.

2. Progressives are atheist or New Age, and their new age spooks are easily recognizable as what used to be called demons and the evil undead, hating life and the living, the beings that used to be mocked and appeased at Halloween and Samhain, the evil fairies and gibbering ghosts of Samhain. And yet progressives are full of self confident self righteous anti morality, not nihilism, the atheists even more than the New Agers.

3. The reactionary atheist branch of the PUA movement, though defeatist, is not nihilist, but rather evinces the manly and stoic spirit of the Greeks, a manly morality ultimately rooted in Darwinist teleology.

Since Darwinism, no one takes a creator God very seriously. CS Lewis celebrated those medieval thinkers that took theology as serious account of the world that had to make sense and explain the world as it is, while he himself wrote children's stories. Christianity is down to a mustard seed, while progressives take over the churches, empty out the old bottles, and fill the old bottles with progressivism. God is dead.

What did Auster do about progressive takeover of the Churches? If Christianity is going to defend us against progressivism, where is the defense of Christianity against progressivism? Only Dalrock and Sunshine Mary are resisting the progressive takeover of Christianity, and they are heavily influenced and motivated by the atheist reactionary branch of the PUA movement. It is the atheists influencing Christians to put aside nihilism, rather than the other way around.

## Did Hormonal Contraception cause the destruction of the family?

2013-03-12 06:04:23

The sexual revolution happened when the pill happened, that is, when Hormonal Birth Control happened.

*In the comments Spandrell provides compelling evidence that the effect of hormonal birth control on the sexual revolution was not very large[26].*

Yet we have long had methods of birth control and early stage abortificants. Condoms are so ancient that males have evolved to dislike them. The sponge has been around for several hundred years, the cap has been around for a hundred and eighty years, the diaphragm for a hundred and thirty years. The IUD has been around for eighty years, but was not perfected until about 1950 or so..

The sponge, the diaphragm, and the cap have the inconvenience that they have to be inserted before sexual intercourse and removed after a day or so. The greater convenience of the pill and the modern IUD could well be the cause of the sexual revolution. But the IUD was safe and convenient ten years before the pill, and we only got the sexual revolution after the pill.

---

[26]https://blog.reaction.la/science/did-hormonal-contraception-cause-the-destruction-of-the-family.html/comment-page-1#comment-250361

The sexual revolution happened when the pill happened, fifty years ago, consistent with the conjecture that the pill interferes with some critical component of bonding.

Among the atheist, materialist, and reactionary pick up artist movement, it is generally believed that the monthly ovulation hormone surge and the resulting behavior change that happens during ovulation is intended by natural selection to promote paternity fraud. Now while paternity fraud is a big problem, in that any paternity fraud is a really bad thing, and the threat of paternity fraud undermines fatherhood and the family, the actual amount of paternity fraud is pretty small, (not nearly small enough, but small) so I am inclined to agree with Sunshine Mary that paternity fraud is unlikely to be the primary purpose of the hormone surge.

(Digressing, one of the easiest things we could do to promote family formation is ensure serious legal and social consequences for paternity fraud, comparable with those of rape, thereby reducing a potent threat, and encouraging better female behavior by authoritatively stigmatizing the worst female misbehavior.)

The blogger Sunshine Mary, whose wonderful blog "The Woman and the Dragon" has now sadly disappeared, seems to have had an ovulation hormone surge that was quite noticeable to herself, so probably bigger than most, and she believed, on the basis of her subjective experience, that the primary purpose of the hormone surge was to promote sexual bonding, to bind women to stick around with the father of their children, to promote, rather than destroy, the family, though she recognized it could easily work both ways.

Perhaps women are programmed to bond when they orgasm with breast manipulation of those extra sensitive breasts that they have at ovulation time.

Hormone based contraception suppress the monthly ovulation based hormone surge, making women quite noticeably less irrational, emotional and illogical at least twice a month, and perhaps for the entire month. Perhaps irrational, emotional and illogical is what we need in order to reproduce successfully.

My own personal experience and observation is consistent with the theory that females who are not on hormone based contraception tend to form strong bonds, and stick around, and females on hormone based contraception tend to move along after three or four years, but I don't have enough anecdotes for them to be data. (For housework, on the other hand, I have enough anecdotes to tell you confidently that it is apt to be disastrous for men to do women's work. For housework, I have enough anecdotes to be data.)

No one has ever examined the effect of the pill on female bonding. It needs scientific examination. The pill obviously, on casual observation, has a significant effect on female behavior. It affects their minds quite noticeably, and many men view that as a major benefit. No one, however, has ever attempted to measure behavioral side effects. How does family formation and marital stability compare between women who use the pill, and women who use other methods?

## Moldbug's solution to the moron problem
2013-03-15 07:11:54

There are a large number of people who have no jobs, who make their living by voting left. Many of them, mostly the males, entertain themselves with arson, assault, and burglary, though we are seeing overweight women engaged in such manly pursuits with increasing frequency, though for the females the major recreation seems to be engaging in unprotected sex with males who demonstrate their superior manliness by mugging and arson.

Moldbug discusses[27] solutions to this problem, as did I, People of Negative Economic Value[28], and Red in a comment[29]

Many of these, particularly the whites, are people who could get a job if the alternative was sufficiently dire. Some of them are too stupid to get a job, and some of them are too badly behaved to get a job, even if the alternative is starvation or dire punishment they will not respond to incentives.

The inherently badly behaved, the undeserving poor, are an easy problem, since no one feels bad about killing them off, except those that want their votes. Until recent times, even the most tender hearted progressive societies had a rule that after a certain number of minor crimes, the punishment would escalate, rapidly escalating to execution. Almost everyone felt good about that, and almost everyone still would feel good about that, though they hesitate to say so out loud.

But what about the deserving poor, people of negative economic worth, who are nonetheless decent people?

Idleness destroys, makework degrades, the more so if it is obvious makework, such as digging ditches with a spoon. In his article, Moldbug suggests that much of the modern economy, for example the Finance, Insurance, and Real Estate (FIRE) economy, propped up by moving Mestizos into middle class houses with loans made by the fed, loans that will never be paid back, is makework, corrupting and destroying. Most of our suppose Real GDP, which Moldbug calls Fudged GDP, is makework, of negative value. See a devastatingly accurate depiction[30] of the FIRE economy, a value subtraction industry.

Some forms of makework, however, are arguably not exactly makework. Moldbug suggests handmaking wooden toys, and artisanal slow food production. This is somewhat similar to Red's suggestion, forcibly ship them into something like monasteries, were they are forcibly provided not only with meaningful work, but with meaning, purpose, and community, with a human existence in a world where it is not economically efficient for some people to have a human existence, and where merely keeping unproductive people alive like pets in a no kill shelter gives them the freedom to make choices that deny each other a human existence.

The fact that he, and we, are discussing how problems are to be solved after this equality and fraternity silliness goes away, indicates rising confidence, perhaps induced by accelerating leftism. Since things are getting worse ever faster, something has bust soon, hence people are giving serious thought as to how to solve things in ways that would have

[27] https://unqualified-reservations.blogspot.com.au/2013/03/sam-altman-is-not-blithering-idiot.html

[28] https://blog.reaction.la/economics/people-of-negative-economic-value.html

[29] https://blog.reaction.la/culture/christianity-and-morality.html/comment-page-1#comment-248839

[30] https://blog.reaction.la/economics/bloomberg-speaks-truth-to-power.html

been considered sane and reasonable several centuries ago, in a world whose social order would have been considered sane and reasonable several centuries ago. It is not that we are any closer to a solution, but that the problem is getting worse so much faster, that the other side of the crisis has to be in sight.

As I said earlier, if you are in bus moving at high speed, and the driver is blind and insane, the bus will stop eventually.[31].

## The latest PC

### 2013-03-17 10:06:24

It used to be mandatory to believe that evolution was a mere creation myth, something that happened long, long ago, and far far away, but had not happened in the last hundred thousand years or so, so that it was impossible for there to be differences between races, or indeed between men and woman.

But, in that case, we would still be shaped for eating meat and fat, and not yet shaped for eating wheat and vegetable oil, which is horribly politically incorrect. Vegetable oil would produce heart disease,[32] which is as bad as lack of global warming. And so, it is now mandatory to believe that evolution is extremely fast when it would produce politically correct results[33], and does not happen at all when it would produce politically incorrect results.

PC gets ever more stupid, as the arrogance of power has excused it from making any sense at all.

PC requires us to believe that human subspecies do not exist. PC also requires us to believe that meat is bad for you and grain is good for you. Logically, this requires us to believe that evolution does not happen, and that evolution is incredibly fast.

## Soft Power

### 2013-03-17 21:35:17

Modern leftism is a plot by some white males to use women and non whites to destroy other white males. Obama is president, but he does not know what some white male has written on his teleprompter until he reads it.

Spandrell complains[34] about a Chinese billionairess piously saying the the politically correct things about democracy.

> This Chinese billionaire just threw her whole nation and political system under the bus, and said, to the everlasting delight of that insufferable puritan busybody hag, that what the Chinese nation **craves**, is democracy. Not civil rights, or liberties, mind you. Democracy. And nobody even asked her! Look at the interviewers, who look like they just won at the lottery. She said it! Wew!

---

[31] https://blog.reaction.la/culture/why-the-left-always-wins.html

[32] https://www.naturalnews.com/022860.html

[33] https://mangans.blogspot.com.au/2013/03/feminist-reviews-paleofantasy-likes-it.html

[34] https://bloodyshovel.wordpress.com/

I would guess that she wanted the white elite, her interviewers, to approve of her.

You think Obama pissed away a lot of money giving politically correct loans to politically correct crony capitalists to produce miniscule amounts of politically correct solar power?

The Chinese pissed away even more money[35] on solar power.

When the Chinese blew off the Copenhagen climate treaty, they did not say the truth, that it was a plot by Harvard and the rest, a bunch of mostly white people, to create a world command economy which would command the third world to permanently stay poor and third world, but instead used political events in Australia to excuse themselves. They needed some Australian white males to give them permission to refrain from destroying their economy and giving up their national sovereignty.

Now obviously China has been moving rightwards ever since the Gang of Four was overthrown, and will probably continue to do so, but they feel really guilty about doing so.

Nineteenth century anglosphere capitalism survived in Shanghai till 1941, long after it had become extinct in the anglosphere, and to some extent survived in Hong Kong to the present day. After the coup, Deng set to work reviving Shanghai capitalism before the show trial of the gang of four had even began, and in this sense, China has become deeply reactionary, preserving some of the best of the west's past. On the other hand, in another sense they are still a bunch of commies kowtowing to elite white male leftists.
#### What is soft power?

It is difficult to define, and difficult to explain, but I would say a large part of it is that state funded propaganda seemingly coming from multiple independent voices, each voice purporting to be high status, and confirming the high status of each of the other voices, works.

Blacks and Mestizos are stupid, thus easily snowed by the progressive elite. That is soft power. East Asians are not stupid, but are conformist and compliant, thus vulnerable to coordinated and state marshaled social pressure, so again, soft power.

I don't think soft power will suffice, unless backed by hard power, and today's progressives are rapidly running out of hard power. But while hard power was necessary to destroy Rhodesia, soft power sufficed to destroy South Africa.

## Why East Asians vote Democrat

### 2013-03-18 12:43:16

It is easy to understand why Mestizos vote Democrat. They are stupid. Observe Venezuela. Chavez stole their food, told them the evil capitalists were starving them, and the hungry Mestizos loved him and voted for him, without wondering overmuch as to why Chavez was so strangely unsuccessful at defending them from evil capitalists. But why East Asians?

West Hunter reports on Dan Freedman's research on babies[36]:

> Chinese babies adapted to almost any position in which they were placed;
> for example, when placed face down in their cribs, they tended to keep their

---

[35]https://mungowitzend.blogspot.com.au/2013/03/china-as-solar-icon.html
[36]https://westhunt.wordpress.com/2013/03/16/dan-freedmans-babies/

faces buried in the sheets rather than immediately turning to one side, as the Caucasian babies did. They briefly pressed the baby's nose with a cloth, forcing him to breath with his mouth. Most white (and black) babies fight this maneuver by immediately turning away or swiping at the cloth with their hands, and this is reported in Western pediatric textbooks as normal. While the average Chinese baby would simply lay on his back, breathing through the mouth, accepting the cloth without a fight. ...

Later, he looked at Navaho babies: they're like Chinese, only more so.

Japanese babies are like Chinese, but less so: more irritable, but not as irritable as white kids.

## Bitches in Tech

### 2013-03-23 14:18:18

The internet is buzzing[37] with the Adria Richards dongle incident that demonstrates what everyone knows, but that until now no one could say, not even me: That women in the tech industry are frequently humorless, dangerous, threatening, difficult, unreasonable, and hard to work with. In a word, bitches. That women bring drama and soap opera to the workplace, and males are unable or unwilling to prevent them.

Bitches in tech get a double dose of privilege. Firstly, just by being female they are, like all females, privileged, the routine recipients of instinctive white knighting, given special protection from their own screw ups and misdeeds, never expected to take responsibility for anything, even if they would like to take responsibility, indeed never able to take responsibility for anything even if they want to and are competent to do it. Regardless of whether a female can actually do the work, as in any industry, if some of the work is difficult, or has large consequences if done wrong, she is apt to get a lowly white male assistant to do any of the work that is difficult to do, and take the blame for any of the work that is apt to go badly wrong. For example Marie Curie did not extract radium from pitchblende nor determine its chemical properties. Debierne did. Perhaps he did so while carrying out her idea and under her supervision, but all the contemporary evidence indicates he did so while carrying out Pierre Curie's idea under Pierre Curie's supervision.

Political Correctness gave Marie Curie two Nobel prizes of work that no one paid the slightest attention to when a man did it, for example Dorn and the discovery of Radon. But it was something more ancient that made it unnecessary for her to do the actual discovering herself.

Because eggs are more valuable than sperm, men inherently tend to treat women as more valuable than men, which results in disruptive female behavior in the workplace.

Secondly, since women are markedly less capable of tech than males, they are particularly underrepresented in tech, and underrepresentation is of course illegal, so any time they have a real or imagined grievance, they can sic the state onto the company and any random males in the company that they happen to capriciously feel like destroying, thus

---

[37]https://foseti.wordpress.com/2013/03/22/volunteer-thought-police-2/

females in tech much more privileged, much more dangerous, than females in other industries.

This double dose of privilege causes grotesquely inflated egos, which in turn causes casual and unthinking arrogance, capricious malice, and reckless malice.

The internet is buzzing about Adria Richards and the dongle joke, which buzz got her fired and is causing all sorts of bad consequences for her. This might seem evidence against the thesis that women in tech are extraordinarily privileged - except that Adria Richards has been a vicious malevolent disruptive drama queen bitch for many a year, and has never suffered any consequences for it until this time, when her latest little piece of nastiness went viral and blew up in her face.

Sometime ago, at Gasonics, a female employee complained her supervisor was sexually harassing her. She was assigned to a different supervisor. I never observed her doing any actual work, while I did observe her vigorously attempting to seduce her new supervisor, on one occasion diving under his desk. Eventually she made a complaint of sexual harassment against her new supervisor, and was transferred to me. I immediately asked her, in the presence of numerous witnesses, while standing a quite considerable distance from her, to perform a task that she considered beneath her dignity - though I had been doing it.

I left her to it. Some hours passed, and it did not get done. I courteously chided her about this, again in the presence of numerous witnesses, and she responded with a raised voice and sharp words. I lost my temper and proceeded to shout her down. Immediately my boss, and his boss, came into workshop at a dead run, as if the place was on fire. She proceeded to embrace my boss and weep noisily and wetly on his shoulder.

Men just don't do stuff like that. The presence of fertile age women in the workplace is just inherently disruptive, partly because they are inherently inclined to certain kinds of misbehavior (drama), mostly because men are inherently unwilling to restrain them from bad behavior, partly because political correctness forbids us to restrain them from bad behavior characteristic of females.

Men, and women past fertile age, do not weep on the shoulder of their boss's boss.

Fertile age women in the workplace are very likely to have sex with their boss, or their boss's boss, that being human nature, and if they manage to restrain themselves, they will not restrain themselves from giving their boss high hopes whenever they want to get their way, which enables profoundly disruptive behavior.

If a woman has sex with her boss, she will not view her equals as equals, but inferiors, indeed as nonexistent, resulting in damaging and disruptive behavior. If she has sex with her boss's boss, or is even thinking about having sex with her boss's boss, she will treat her boss as inferior or non existent, resulting in very damaging and disruptive behavior.

## I want an SPLC listing too!

### 2013-03-25 14:52:00

Scott Terry, famously, got listed as a hate group, for arguing at CPAC (conservative political action conference) that the slave Frederick Douglass was the recipient of a favor by his master.

I have often argued that most slaves were not enslaved for profit, but because they profiled as likely to only be able to survive by hunting someone else's cattle and gathering someone else's crops, and so the owners of those crops and cattle proceeded to chase them off to anywhere they could go, and if there was nowhere they could go, ship them off to anyone who would take them, which is pretty much Scott Terry's argument– that slaves in large part were, and their descendents in substantial part are, people who to survive in the modern environment need either state subsidies or external discipline, both of which are favors commonly done by white people to black people. The largest source of slaves was black elites exporting their unwanted underclass, or ethnically cleansing inferior groups that caused problems. Underclass people do not deserve freedom, and are not capable of handling it. If you allow them to vote, they will of course vote against freedom.

CPAC, the supposedly conservative political action conference, stands firmly in favor of electing a new people, in favor of the mass importation of a welfare underclass from Latin America to outvote employed taxpayers. A lot of people say this is a business friendly policy, because it reduces the cost of unskilled labor and so forth. This is untrue. A business friendly policy would be to make it easy for employers to get work visas for their employees. The CPAC policy is aimed at making it easy for illegal immigrants to get welfare and vote. A business friendly open borders policy would aim at importing people who work, rather than people who collect welfare, thus would issue visas through employers, rather than issuing voting rights through federal agencies.

The big conflict at CPAC is between "conservatives", and "libertarian" equalists. A CPAC "conservative" believes in affirmative action, government spending, social breakdown, family breakdown, general lawlessness, and so on and so forth, but believes in this increasing slightly less rapidly than it has been doing under Bush/Obama. He also believes the economy will grow rapidly to sustain the slightly slower growth in these things. He is is in favor of "immigration reform"– importing a massive welfare underclass to vote democrat.

The libertarian equalist believes that we can some how pretend that inferiors are equals without affirmative action, government spending, and so on and so forth increasing rapidly, and that the Latin American underclass we are importing are going to get jobs, buy houses in the suburbs, and pay their mortgages.He too is in favor of "immigration reform"– importing a massive welfare underclass to vote democrat. He is probably right about them buying houses in the suburbs, but demonstrably wrong about them working and paying for them.

CPAC is probably slightly to the right of the median voter, so a CPAC approved political movement will never win an election. The median voter is a fatherless husbandless jobless white woman with an obamaphone, zero assets, and two children by two different biological fathers. CPAC is, however, wildly, bizarrely, insanely, to the left of reality. I would say that the CPAC program would be politically realistic if the median voter was divorced white woman, no assets, and children by a single biological father, child of intact family, mother of a broken family which she broke up. Now, however, we are getting the second generation of broken families, making CPAC's program as unrealistic electorally, as it is unrealistic about dealing with our problems.

You think maybe I am being a little harsh in saying both sides favor increasing lawlessness, favor anarcho tyranny? When did either side acknowledge the selective enforcement of ever more laws against white males, and ever less enforcement of ever fewer laws against other groups? When did either side acknowledge one way equality, wherein women are equal to men, but men not equal to women, and mestizos are equal to whites, but whites not equal to mestizos, the former being demonstrated in VAWA, the latter in most Californian traffic accidents, which are generally an unlicensed uninsured unemployed mestizo on welfare driving into someone and getting away with it.

VAWA stands for "violence against women act" and requires police and courts to assume men are aggressors and women are victims in every conflict involving violence, which is probably true in general even if often untrue in individual cases. Let us imagine, however, a similar law VAWA, "violence against whites act". It is probably roughly as true that in any violent conflict between a white and a nonwhite, the nonwhite is the aggressor, as it is true that in any violent conflict between a woman and a man, the man is the aggressor. The point of having a justice system is to find the truth in the particular individual case, which VAWA forbids. If it is reasonable to have a general law defining all males guilty, let us have a general law defining all blacks guilty.

The CPAC conference is the sound of democracy becoming irrelevant, as tax producers are permanently outvoted by tax consumers, resulting in ever deepening economic and financial crisis.

CPAC reflects a vast and unbridgeable gap between reality on the one hand, and policies likely to be acceptable to the median voter on the other hand.

The time to address this crisis will be when printing money stops working, the day that soldiers find that they are not necessarily in the front of the line to get paid with money that can actually buy stuff. At that point the army will go into politics, and will be looking for an ideology to justify the move.

But it could, and well may, turn out worse than that. Things could continue to get worse until we see a transfer of power to sergeants, rentacops, and mercs, rather than to generals. By the time the proverbial hits the fan, the highest ranking officer in the Pentagon will likely be a mestizo male to female transexual claiming to be a lesbian.

Bu it could, and well may, turn out worse than that. Things could continue to get worse until, as in the fall of the Roman empire in the west, we see a transfer of power to bandits and pirates. Not that there is anything wrong with rule by bandits and pirates. The British empire was rule by pirates until around 1830 or so, and they did a fine job. The trouble is that there is likely to be a lengthy period of unpleasantness before bandits become stationary bandits.

I would like to see anarcho capitalism, but am realistically hoping for Blackwater neo feudalism, based on the impressive performance of mercenaries in dealing with Somali pirates, and rentacops in dealing with the Occupy movement. A feudalism that grows out of rentacops is likely to be more free, prosperous and law abiding than a feudalism that grows out of piracy and banditry as European feudalism did. Rentacops are instinctively propertarian. Soldiers and mercs not so much, bandits and pirates not propertarian at all.

Of course the least drastic solution, the minimal necessary reform, the reform that would solve the problem with the least disruption and violence, would be to keep electoral democracy while throwing everyone off the electoral roll except for income earning property owning heads of households. The voters should be pretty much everyone that has authority over his dwelling and household up to his fenceline. That is the moderate realistic reform, necessary to avert rather more drastic reforms, such as Blackwater neo feudalism Of course for such a reform to stick it would also be necessary to replace the presently politicized professoriat, educracy, and civil service with a professoriat and civil service that would take a benign view of such a polity– a new official truth, while speaking the old official truth becomes likely to render one unemployed, a transformation modeled on General Monck's purge following the restoration, when doubting Divine Right or Latitudinarian Anglicanism became a bad career move for anyone in government, Church, or Academy. Most of the rest followed their bread and butter. Ridicule, supplemented by unemployment if necessary, rather than hanging, was sufficient to deal with those who would not dance to the new tune.

General Monck's reforms preserved the existing state, while completely reversing the ideology of the state with astonishingly little violence. A move to Blackwater neo feudalism would involve the complete disappearance of the existing state, which might be a lengthy and violent process, as it was in the Roman Empire in the West. Trouble is, a supposedly lesbian transsexual is no General Monck, and Pinochet was no General Monck either.

## No, the Pope is not Catholic

### 2013-03-31 18:00:56

Recently our state sponsored intellectuals have been waxing indignant about the fact that the recently elected Pope is Catholic. They have not yet complained about bears shitting in the woods.

But, in fact, the Pope is not Catholic. He is progressive, merely less progressive and more Catholic than our state sponsored intellectuals would prefer.

Our state sponsored intellectuals are indignant because the Pope opposes abortion, women priests, gay marriage, homosexual bishops and so on and so forth. (I would have thought that the Church was seriously oversupplied with homosexual Bishops, but I suppose the objection is that they are not openly homosexual, or not open enough)

But notice that our state sponsored intellectuals are not attacking him for supporting marital rape (traditional Christian marriage) and the enslavement of women (traditional Christian marriage)

The traditional Christian position is that marriage was an irrevocable contract in which both spouses agreed each to be always sexually available to the other. If you are married, you don't need consent for sex. You need consent to refrain from sex - and you are not even supposed to give consent to refrain from sex too easily or for too long. You are supposed to "rape" your spouse, in order to maintain the marriage. This seems reasonable to me, for my observation suggests that if people consent to stop having sex, they are apt to not resume, and pretty soon the marriage breaks up.

If there is such a thing as "marital rape", then it is impossible to contract to marry and stay married, which is a massive violation of freedom of contract, which violation of freedom of contract gravely impairs our ability to form families and reproduce.

In fact, the Roman Catholic Church still supports that position - in Spanish. In English, however, it is silent. It seems that state sponsored intellectuals cannot speak Spanish, hence "rape" is one of the few things they are not attacking the Pope for.

Now since I think that all religions are at best pious frauds, at best a collection of children's stories embodying ancient wisdom, at worst evil scams, Roman Catholics might reasonably say this is none of my business. Trouble is, while Jesus gives permission to ditch any parts of the Old Testament that might prove inconvenient, no Christian has permission to ditch the New Testament. If the priest ditches the politically incorrect parts of the New Testament, people smell that he does not really believe, and the churches empty out and turn into museums.

I regret the passing of Christianity. Europe is the faith, the faith is Europe. Civilizations die when their animating religion dies. We will likely need a new religion, or some synthetic substitute, or shall vanish utterly. When a people lose their religion they are apt, like the Romano British, to disappear. In much of the Roman Empire in the west, the people remained and had descendents, but came under the rule of foreign aristocracies formed by invading bandits. The Romano British were, however, pretty thoroughly genocided except in those areas least subject to Roman influence. The same will likely happen to much of today's Europe.

## How sweet it is

2013-04-03 08:30:12

Marcott et al recant the blade of their Hockey stick[38]

This is a huge change, in that previously, when warmists lied, and got caught doing so, every scientific institution, every science journal, every prestigious academy, and every organized group of scientists would piously swear holy fealty to the lie. Now, instead, they quietly twist the liar's arms behind closed doors.

As I said earlier, the status of warmists has dropped to that of communists. The orthodox believers in official truth are anti anti communist but not pro communist, and theorthodox believers in official truth are anti skeptic, but not pro warmist. Before 2012 October, official truth was warmist. Now warmists are, like communists, merely another left faction.

Of course any left faction is automatically higher status than any non left faction, so warmists are still automatically higher status than skeptics, even when caught lying, but warmism is no longer official truth. As of 2012 October, embarrassing misbehavior by warmists gets squelched, instead of every scientist and every journal kowtowing.

## History interpreted as left singularities

2013-04-05 05:23:21

History is one damn thing after another, and any attempt to make sense of it necessarily leads to leaving out lots of important stuff. Thus making sense of it by looking at it in one way does not necessarily falsify making sense of it by looking at it in another way.

---

[38]https://opinion.financialpost.com/2013/04/01/were-not-screwed/

The trend from around fourteen hundred AD to the present has been for states to become ever stronger. On the other hand, was not the trend from four hundred AD to one thousand AD. Of course, it might be a bad idea to bet against a trend that has been running strong for well over six hundred years, but here is why I am betting against it:

That trend, from 1400 AD to the present, has in large part been driven by what I call left singularities. Leftism enforces ever greater leftism, so society moves leftwards ever faster, until things blow up.

Leftism is Phariseeism. A leftist is supposedly holier than you are, and so you should obey him. Leftists then compete each to be holier than the other, so Leftism's religious roots are swiftly left behind, as leftism becomes ever more extreme.

The first leftist movement began as the false popes of Avignon, which became French leftism, which became revolutionary leftism, the red terror, and the war in the Vendee, which became Bonapartism,

Although the French Revolution was supposedly purely political without obvious religious elements, the war in the Vendee, and Napoleon's war in Spain were openly religious wars. The objective was to force the people at gunpoint to attend churches with priests appointed by one side, and murder those that attended churches with priests appointed by the other side, a goal that rapidly became as genocidal as the thirty years war between protestants and Roman Catholics, and was accompanied by similar religious rhetoric. You might have thought the false popes were still in Avignon.

Bonapartism self destructed, and was conquered by anglosphere leftism, thus the French wound up with government modeled on the mother of parliaments imposed on them. Ever since then, the French regime has been a pallid echo of anglosphere leftism, but the final step following their left singularity was a major step rightwards, since anglosphere leftism of that time was well to the right of French Revolutionary leftism.

Similarly, leftist Czars succumbed to a left wing movement of their own creation that led to their own overthrow and execution, eventually resulting in Stalin, who halted the ever leftwards movement, announced that utopia had arrived, and there would be no further movement leftwards or rightwards.

If Stalin had not put a stop to it, Russia probably would have gone all the way to Pol Pot style socialism under Trotsky.

Stalin placed Russia in political stasis, which eventually cracked. Russia was initially conquered by anglosphere leftism, attempting a rerun of what was done to France, but today's leftists are less virile than the Duke of Wellington, and Russia may well be rejecting the foreign imposition. Still, today's Russia is in form and rhetoric anglosphere leftist. The political differences between today's America and today's Russia are roughly comparable to the difference between anglosphere leftism at date X plus ten or twenty years, and anglosphere leftism at date X, an utterly trivial difference when one considers that anglosphere leftism has been moving left for over two hundred years.

Anglosphere leftism originated from the Puritans, and was heading into a left wing singularity with the civil war, the commonwealth, and the execution of Charles the first. Oliver Cromwell took fright at the sight of the levelers and, like Stalin, froze things, heading off the looming chaos. After Cromwell's death, General Monck reversed the left wards movement, creating a theocratic monarchy based on latitudinarian (tolerant) Anglicanism.

Some Puritans were purged from government, academy, and the Church, and the rest saw which side their bread was buttered on, and quietly decided that they were not only latitudinarian Anglicans, but always had been latitudinarian Anglicans,

Similarly, I expect that if we get a reactionary restoration in the US today, 99% percent of the gender studies movement will cheerfully agree that organizations generally function better with male leadership. (After one percent of them have been fired)

Under this excellent system (theocratic monarchical latitudinarian anglicanism) British colonialists, pirates, merchants, slavers, and adventurers conquered most of the world, and Britain created the scientific revolution and the industrial revolution.

Then in the late Georgian or early Victorian period, the ever leftwards slide resumed, perhaps starting with the inability of George the Fourth to penalize queen Caroline for not submitting, failure to perform her marital duties, and flagrant adultery. (Whatever happened to that stick no thicker than a woman's thumb?)

The trouble was that they were too latitudinarian. Leftists, once in power, did not make the same mistake.

Because the anglosphere left singularity lagged behind the others, having been paused for a century and a half by the restoration, it tended to occupy the rubble when other left singularities collapsed. The movement to ever stronger states has in large part been a movement ever left, and to ever greater anglosphere domination.

The ever leftwards movement eventually killed off science shortly after World War II, replacing it with state sponsored religion dressed in lab coats[39]. Peer review and consensus means that instead of the experimenter telling the scientific community what he sees, the scientific community tells the experimenter what he sees. As with Wikipedia, believing one's own eyes constitutes original research, and we should supposedly leave original research to the trained professionals.

Technology continued to advance, but after 1972, in ever fewer areas. In one area after another, the advance in technology has come to a stop. Last man on the moon, 1972, tallest buildings in the west, 1972. Coolest muscle cars around then. Progress continues in some areas, most strikingly in computers and telecommunications, but in one are after another, progress stops. DNA reading continues to progress. DNA writing, maybe not. In the outposts of fallen empire technology has continued to advance in some areas abandoned by the west. Cool tall buildings continue to be built in Shanghai, Singapore, and Dubai, but in the center of anglosphere, when the two towers fell, they could not be rebuilt, and London looks ever poorer, ever shabbier, ever more early twentieth century. Stockholm is in a timewarp from the pre war period.

The anglosphere left is moving ever further leftwards ever faster. Trees do not grow to the sky. At some point, I hope short of Pol Pot leftism, it has to collapse.

With good luck, a reactionary regime might be reconstructed, as general Monck did. With moderate luck, a Stalin might freeze the system for a while. With bad luck, we will probably be conquered by a Caliphate or China, or just overrun by bandits, pirates, and adventurers like the Roman empire in the West. I think that Europe will mostly go

---

[39] https://dresdencodak.com/2011/04/19/dark-science-09/

Caliphate, parts of the US will create reactionary regimes, and the rest of the US will resemble Latin America. If we are lucky, parts of the US will resemble the wild west.

In the collapse scenario much of the world will become protectorates of the new Chinese empire, as is already happening in Africa. The rest will be patchwork of monarchies, aristocracies, good anarchy, bad anarchy, and general chaos. Russia will chart its own path. At present, Russia is not a favorable environment for high technology despite the abilities of many Russians, and it has a rather long history of not being a favorable environment for high technology.

This is a dark age scenario, or mostly dark age scenario. One way to avoid it would be a reactionary restoration, similar to that which General Monck brought to England.

As a non believer, I cannot see anything wrong with restoration Anglicanism, Anglicanism from the restoration to the early Victorian period. A fine prosocial religion, which supported order, private property, the family, the rule of law, the pursuit of truth, and the authority of the father. Under the rule of restoration Anglicanism, we had the industrial revolution, the scientific revolution, and British colonialists conquered most of the world. That was period of greatness on par with Golden Age of Classic Greece. What is not to like?

It taught the ten commandments, in particular:

> Thou shalt not covet thy neighbours house, thou shalt not covet thy neighbours wife, nor his manservant, nor his maidservant, nor his ox, nor his ass, nor any thing that is thy neighbours.

It also taught that all men were created unequal:

> Each little flower that opens,
> Each little bird that sings,
> He made their glowing colors,
> He made their tiny wings.
>
> The rich man in his castle,
> The poor man at his gate,
> He made them, high or lowly,
> And ordered their estate.

In other words, since (before Darwin) the natural world was obviously the product of divine design, social inequality was also the product of divine design.

And women also unequal to men

> then shall the Curate say unto the Man.

> . Wilt thou love her, comfort her, honour and keep her, in sicknes and in health and forsakeing all other, keep thee only unto her so long as ye both shall live ?

Then shall the Priest say unto the woman.

> . Wilt thou obey him, and serve him, love, honour, and keep
> him, in sickness, and in health, and forsakeing all other, keep
> thee only unto him, so long as ye both shall live ?

Alas, Christianity is likely dead beyond possibility of revival.

Today Ed School serves the function of the theocratic church. To teach children, one needs to be credentialed, and the credential is primarily certification of political correctness. My libertarian inclination is Separation of Church and State: that we should shut down Ed school, indeed burn them to the ground, salt the earth where they stood, and make possession of such a credential a horrid secret resembling former membership in the Hitler Youth or the Waffen SS.

That is the libertarian solution, separation of Church and State, but Restoration Anglican theocracy was overthown because it was excessive tolerant of its enemies. The reactionary solution is to reverse the politics enforced by the ed credential: all previously issued credentials authorizing people to teach children would be invalidated, and credential holders invited to take a "refresher" course. I expect most of them would get the same high marks on the refresher course as they got on the original course, piously declaring that slavers and pirates brought civilization and Christianity to the heathen backward peoples with the same confident certainty as they previously piously declared that today's capitalism rested on the ill gotten gains stolen from non whites by those pirates and slavers. Indeed, most of them would scarcely notice the change in the curriculum. They could recycle their previous essays using a word processor macro that replaces "Four legs good, two legs bad" with "Four legs need supervision by two legs".

We would also teach those seeking educational certification "Economics in One Lesson", microeconomics, which they would probably find a good deal harder. Microeconomics tells us that the rich, other than those on the revolving door between regulators and regulated, and cronys of politicians, actually earned their money. Now that we can no longer argue divine design, have to teach microeconomics.

But really, such an outcome seems unrealistic to me. General Monck's program rested on an influential class of well armed and respected gentlemen with extensive family connections. By and large, today, family, the fundamental building block of society, has collapsed. We should perhaps think about ways of establishing order from the bottom up, following a total collapse during which the overclass/underclass alliance manifests as both blacks and police looting anyone sinful enough to look after himself and his family, as after the Katrina disaster, rather than Moldbuggian fantasies of restoring order from the top down. There is no ring of Fnargl. Order is hard to build from the top down, for the top has nothing to stand upon.

After the Katrina disaster blacks, government employees, and the underclass, mostly blacks and government employees, predated upon the middle class[40]. Imagine that the disaster is that the government has no money to pay its underclass and employees, or far too much entirely worthless money, and there is no General Monck on a white horse. Start with heads of households who have land, gold, guns, and food, and are unenthusiastic about involuntary sharing. Starting from that, build a society in which political

---

[40] https://bayourenaissanceman.blogspot.com.au/2008/08/lessons-learned-from-hurricanes-katrina.html

power is in the hands of solvent heads of households.

## Dark Enlightenment and the Endarkenment

2013-04-07 12:57:36

The Dark Enlightenment:The movement that concludes that the Enlightenment took a bad turn, or that the Enlightenment itself was a bad turn. I take both positions: That the Enlightenment was wildly and dangerously wrong to proclaim all men created equal, and that restoration England was a pretty good political system, which gave us the scientific and industrial revolutions, and the British conquest of most of the world, and it has been downhill since the restoration, with things going to hell in a handbasket around 1800 or so, and getting steadily worse since then.Dark Enlightenment:Forbidden knowledge about society. For example that while women want their husband to do woman's work around the house, they don't want their husband if their husband does woman's work around the house. If you realize the truth of some hate fact, you have been darkly enlightened (verb).The Endarkenment.Plain meaning: The coming dark age of the west, and perhaps the world, the rise of magical and superstitious thinking, for example Hillary Clinton and Oprah Winfrey, the transformation of science into theocracy, the stagnation of an increasing number of technologies.Ironic meaning: A sarcastic reference to the enlightenment, implying that it blinded men, rather than enabling them to see. Roger Bacon and Galileo popularized rationality, but Voltaire and Rousseau abandoned rationality. That the planets go around the sun follows from the evidence. That all men are created equal defies the evidence.The Left Singularity:Leftism leads to more ever more leftism, ever faster. If the process was not interrupted by dictatorship, civil war, or social collapse, it would end with everyone torturing each other to death for insufficient leftism, Khmer Rouge style, and the last torturer committing suicide for his failure to inflict infinite torture in finite time.

## Kermit Gosnell, partial birth abortion, and regulation

2013-04-14 10:52:28

A major part of Kermit Gosnell's business was late term abortions. The usual way to do a late term abortion is to induce childbirth, and then, as the baby's head comes down the tubes, jab a steel straw into its head and suck out its brains with a powerful vacuum. This collapses the head, making the rest of the birth easy. However, because Gosnell was doing an abortion mill, doing as many abortions as possible as cheaply as possible with the least possible skilled labor, he generally left his patients unattended, so they would frequently pop out a living, healthy, screaming baby before Gosnell got around to looking in on them. So instead of killing the baby five minutes before birth, he would kill the baby five minutes after birth. There is much shock and horror about this ten minute delay.

Notice I have categorized this post under economics, not politics. I am not among those horridly outraged by this ten minute delay.

Anti abortion forces are, of course, vigorously mobilizing to regulate abortion clinics. The permanent government, the official left, is vigorously mobilizing to regulate everything except abortion clinics, as it has been doing with ever increasing vigor for many decades, while they are doing their damnedest to prevent the Kermit Gosnell incident from leading to regulation of abortion clinics.

I expect the anti abortion forces will piously say that the women suffered great pain and suffering by passing the baby's entire head, and the poor innocent darlings should be protected from that terrible pain by regulation that makes sure the steel tube and vacuum arrive in time - and no one will believe them, for we all know that the real intent will be to strangle abortion clinics in red tape.

The reason Kermit Gosnell got busted is that the narcs got on his case, and the narcs are far less left wing than most of the permanent government,

Meanwhile, the permanent government will quite correctly tell us that market forces will usually protect women, and busybody regulators will just strangle everyone in red tape.

Quite so. But why is what is good for abortion clinics is supposedly not good for the rest of the economy?

Although regulations ostensibly have modest, reasonable aims, in practice, regulation is advocated and implemented by those who seek to destroy capitalism entirely - except, I suppose, for abortion clinics.

The whole point of this rant is that whenever you hear of some worthy regulation to accomplish some worthy objective, you should assume Jon Corzine will be implementing and enforcing the regulations. Both sides in this debate reveal their inward unstated knowledge that regulation is an attack. The left favors capitalism for what they actually want done, and opposes capitalism for everything else.

The anti abortion forces are thirsting to ensure that existing abortion regulations are enforced, and new regulations shall be added, even if the supposed aim of these regulation is to ensure that babies get their brains sucked out through a steel tube fast enough to avoid hurting the mother, because they know the regulations will in practice be implemented by the likes of Jon Corzine. The pro abortion forces are resisting for the same reason.

## Bitcoin as a speculative bet

2013-04-14 14:29:02

Charting bitcoin, it looks good, if you are inclined to gamble on charts. The recent collapse from two hundred dollars tested support at the hundred dollar mark, found plenty of support around there. By and large, it is a good idea to buy at major support levels, since a speculative property is a lot more likely to go up than to break through the support level. If it did not penetrate the support level for very long during the panic, likely will not do so now.

But I am an intrinsic value investor. What is the intrinsic value of Bitcoin? In one sense, absolutely nothing.

But, in another sense, bitcoin is better than gold.

Moving physical gold from point A to point B in order to settle a transaction is obviously inconvenient and dangerous, so naturally one prefers to leave it locked in the vaults of some power that is famously reliable, trustworthy, and resistant to coercion, such as...The United States after World War I and II... and merely move ownership around. Banks and nations kept their gold with the United States Federal Reserve, which supposedly kept it in Fort Knox and similar places.

Now, people are increasingly realizing that there is no gold in Fort Knox, and the US Federal Reserve stonewalls increasingly insistent demands for withdrawal. It is the closing of the second gold window. Paper gold is in slow motion collapse.

This is a major and fundamental advantage of bitcoins– that bitcoins can be moved from being controlled by one secret, to being controlled by a different secret, hence can be moved at speeds that though much slower than light, are faster and more secure than any merely material thing can achieve.

Of course gold has the advantage of history. Gold really is money because it is money, and bitcoins really are not money because they are not, and for bitcoins to become money will take, not as much time and blood as gold took, but still quite a lot of time and blood.

Gold has an enormous advantage of being truly untraceable, in that one lump of gold is indistinguishable from another lump of gold. Bitcoins are, unfortunately, totally traceable, and, contrary to report, not very anonymous at all. Bitcoins, however, being totally unregulated, and even harder to regulate than gold, have wonderfully convenient money laundries. Some of these money laundries are probably NSA fronts (private citizens are not the only people who find untraceable money convenient), but the lack of busts would suggest that none of them are FBI fronts.

The potential value of bitcoin is entirely monetary. The instability of bitcoin undermines its monetary use, indicating an excess of speculators over people actually using bitcoin for monetary purposes. Supposing that the monetary use of bitcoin is growing, or likely to grow, this is a reasonable equilibrium.

It looks as if bitcoin has support levels at psychological round numbers. For a long time it was steady as a rock around fifty dollars, then it shot up to two hundred dollars, crashed down to one hundred dollars.

Supposing that the monetary use of bitcoin continues to increase, I expect it will sit at one hundred dollars for a while, then wander erratically between one hundred and two hundred dollars, then sit at two hundred dollars for a while. Next support level after that, five hundred dollars. The arbitrary and conventional values of these numbers reflects the fact that they are ratios between two currencies that have only arbitrary and conventional value.

Moldbug, on the other hand, argues that monetary use of bitcoins is vulnerable to state action, that a determined government effort to shut down the monetary use of bitcoins, for example by criminalizing MtGox, would kill it stone dead. And if the monetary use of bitcoins continues to grow, there certainly will be such a determined state action.

I think Moldbug has excessive belief in the power of the state. He thinks governments are always omnipotent, I think they are bluff and theater floating over a storm tossed sea of anarchy. A part of town where order comes from the police is an unsafe part of town. And if one is in that part of town, and feeling nervous, as one should, one ducks into a mall or a McDonalds for safety. That nervous people are inclined to head for the mall, not the police station, leads me to believe that attempts to demonetize bitcoins are likely to fail.

## Japan succeeds in inducing inflation

### 2013-04-20 18:16:56

Every time Keynesianism fails, they say is evidence it was not done hard enough.

In Japan, they decided that this time they really would do it hard enough. And it worked[41].

Rapid inflation ensued. Employment and production did not.

I suppose Keynesians will be telling us that it is early days yet.

Superstimulus in Japan has definitely solved the problem of wages being sticky downwards. Prices are up, wages are not. This, however, is merely more efficient adjustment to a poorer, more backward, less technologically advanced, Japan.

Krugman is fond of telling us that "austerity" does not work. By "austerity" he means raising taxes that are already far above the Laffer limit. It is unsurprising that this does not work.

"Austerity" is always raising taxes, yet somehow, strangely, "stimulus" is seldom cutting taxes, and is never significant and substantial cuts in taxes on the rich, on the group most likely to respond to tax cuts. If a "stimulus" cuts taxes at all, it cuts them primarily on the poor, on people likely to be below the Laffer limit.

In a society where markets are free, and government is small, and prices and wages are sticky due to the influence of custom and expectations, Keynesianism might well be true, or at least somewhat true, at least in the short run, until people's expectations adjust. In the great depression, prices and wages were indeed sticky, not because of custom and expectations, but because government forbade changes in prices and wages, thus Keynesianism was legislated into reality.

When, however, government is large and getting larger, eventually supply side effects are going to substantially outweigh Keynesian effects, supposing that there are any Keynesian effects in a society where government does not meddle too heavily in prices.

With the ever leftward movement, supply side economics has become true. Thus, any cut in spending that makes things worse for government employees and people on welfare stimulates, and any cut in taxes paid by the private sector also stimulates.

It would also stimulate if we forced everyone on welfare or government employment to dig holes and fill them in again. It would also stimulate if every woman who produces a fatherless child was publicly punished.

Conversely, any politically correct "stimulus" will cause stagnation. If stimulated sufficiently, we get what is now happening in Japan, stagflation.

Reagan demonstrated that supply side economics was true. If true then, much more true now.

It is often pointed out, against supply side economics, that the Bush tax cuts did not pay for themselves. But the Bush tax cuts on the rich more than paid for themselves. What did not pay for itself was substantially reducing the number of Americans who paid any income tax at all.

---

[41] https://www.zerohedge.com/news/2013-04-18/mcdonalds-hikes-japanese-burger-prices-20

Leftism is always expansion of the state. Leftists have realized that the expansion of the state is a problem, have retreated from socialism, cut taxes on the very rich, denationalized industries, but the logic of progressivism requires movement ever leftwards. If they retreat in one area, they must advance in half a dozen others. Thus, when cripples were the object of legislation, the government confiscated staircases and the best parking spots. When cross dressers are the object of legislation, the government confiscates bathrooms, and guarantees free hormones. That men and women do equal work requires a no lift policy. Thus every movement left suppresses the private economy, the economy on which modern leftism depends. Economic stagnation is primarily an indication of the left singularity approaching. The left no longer proposes outright nationalization, but regulations multiply endless, causing creeping nationalization. Economic leftism, socialism and nationalization, has been abandoned, but every alternate left wing program creeps towards the same goal. Giving up on anthropogenic warming, they double down on gays and cross dressers, which less directly and less drastically harms the economy - but still harms the economy.

## The thirty nine articles and the second book of homilies.

2013-04-21 08:47:07

The most successful recovery from a left singularity was the restoration, which created a counter theocracy, restoration Anglicanism, which lasted from 1660 to 1828. The Anglican religion theoretically endorsed the divine right of the King. Since, however, by long established precedent the King could not actually behave like an absolute monarch without losing his head, the practical effect of this was to discourage private citizens from political power, from intruding on the royal prerogative. So, the main function of the King's supposedly absolute power was to prevent anyone from exercising it, and similarly, the main function of the official religion was to prevent competing religions from seeking and obtaining power.

Every Englishman who wanted to attend a prestigious university, or get elected to parliament, or get a prestigious government job, had to declare allegiance to the thirty nine articles, and the second book of homilies, just as today he has to write essays proving how progressive he is.

Most of the articles concern things of the next world, for example that God is Three and God is One, stuff that can never be proven or disproven, and has little effect on life on earth. But some of the articles very much concern things of this world.

Paraphrasing them, and re interpreting them as a reaction to the left singularity ending in Cromwell and the continuing struggle with Puritan descended forces:

Article Fourteen:"Voluntary Works besides, over, and above, God's Commandments, which they call Works of Supererogation, cannot be taught without arrogance and impiety" Thus, no loudly proclaimed excessive holiness, no claims of authority based on extra and unusual holiness, thus, *No Pharisees*! You are encouraged to be holier than is required but forbidden to teach others to be holier than required, forbidden to claim authority on the basis of superior holinessIn other words, leftism forbidden, puritanism forbidden, for the fundamental core of leftism and its nominally Christian predecessors is Phariseeism:

"I am holier than thou, therefore I am entitled to command thee", which leads to the left singularity as each Pharisee competes to be holier than each of the others.Articles Eighteen to Twenty one:The official church is officially true. Accept no substitutes!Article Twenty Three:Only those officially endorsed to preach at you should be preaching at you. Claims of authority not based on official endorsement should not be accepted. In other words, no puritans, no pharisees, no leftists.Article Twenty Six:Conspicuous lack of holiness among official ministers of the church is irrelevant. They are still officially official. So ignore the pharisees pointing out that they are much holier than the official ministers, and claiming authority thereby. It is being official, not being holy, that counts. Thus no Pharisaical competition to be holier than thou, because no claims of authority based on mere holiness should be accepted.Article Thirty Four:Rituals reflect custom, and are ultimately arbitrary, so variations in official ritual are OK, And thus the puritan claim that their rituals are more authentic than the official rituals is irrelevant, and Roman Catholics can comfortably proclaim themselves Anglican while continuing to practice their preferred rituals. Holy wars over the question of how many fingers are to be used when crossing oneself are not merely stupid, but impious.Article Thirty Five:Includes the second book of homilies, the official sermons that everyone that goes to church heard on a regular schedule. Thus when an Englishmen declared he believed in the thirty nine articles, which was required to be allowed anywhere near the levers of power, he declared he believed in all of the official sermons.Article Thirty Seven:Give unto Caesar that which is Caesar's. Declares the superior authority of the state over the church in the things of this world. In particular, no conscientious objection allowed, no conscientious civil disobedience. If you are in the army or the militia, and the King sends you into some war, off you go. The church does not have secular authority. Superior holiness does not give anyone secular authority.Article Thirty Eight:Communism is bad! "The Riches and Goods of Christians are not common, as touching the right, title, and possession of the same," Private property is ordained by God.Anglicans, of course, should go to church, though they generally did not, and if they went to church would hear the Second book of Homilies preached, which homilies they piously affirmed they agreed with then they declared that they agreed with the thirty nine articles.

Among the Homilies of the Second Book of Homilies:
Seventeen: A homily for the days of Rogation Week.

> "It is the blessing of the Lord that maketh rich men (Proverbs 10.22). To this agrees that holy woman Anne, where she says in her song: 'It is the Lord that maketh the poor, and maketh the rich, it is he that promotes and pulls down,' "

This homily is restated in the hymn "All Things Bright and Beautiful"

> Each little flower that opens,
> Each little bird that sings,
> He made their glowing colors,
> He made their tiny wings.
>
> The rich man in his castle,
> The poor man at his gate,

> He made them, high or lowly,
> And ordered their estate.

In other words, since (before Darwin) the natural world was obviously the product of divine design, social inequality was also the product of divine design.

In our era, post Darwin, I doubt we could get away with this one. Instead, need to teach micro economics, from which follows a great many reactionary things that economists are embarrassed to mention, among other things "The Chamley-Judd Redistribution Impossibility Theorem" which tells us that redistribution from capitalists to workers is impossible, and trying to do so merely buggers the economy making everyone worse off. Economists find it very difficult to express this theorem in plain language, for the plain language version is pretty much "Ayn Rand was right."

Eighteen: the State of Matrimony

Wives should obey their husbands. Husbands may beat wives for misconduct, but should endeavor to obtain obedience by gentler means.

Twenty one: A Homily against disobedience and willful rebellion.

This tells everyone that they should obey the King and abstain from politics.

One solution to America's problem would be swipe one of the more manly of the descendents of Charles the second, such as prince Harry, and restore Restoration Anglicanism, but I suspect that, because of Darwin, the decline of the manly and martial aristocracy, and the shriveling of Christianity to a tiny remnant, that would not work. Instead, need something that has the same effect of as restoration Anglicanism.

# Stimulus

## 2013-04-24 06:55:29

Byran Caplan assures us that progressives have the easy painless cure for unemployment, but somehow, due the pernicious influence of cruel heartless free marketers who just do not care about the unemployed[42], the government is just too right wing to apply the magic.

The magic cure is, of course, to print more money. If it has not worked yet, obviously that proves we have not printed enough. Whosoever doubts this obviously does not care about the unemployed as deeply as Bryan Caplan cares.

# Against female sexual choice

## 2013-04-25 11:31:31

Heartiste and Steve Sailer[43] provide compelling evidence that females should not be allowed to make their own sexual and reproductive choices. Their hormones make them stupid. Thus we have a bunch of baby murderers running around who will doubtless repeat their parent's choices. And here is another video of raging hormones on parade[44].

---

[42]https://econlog.econlib.org/archives/2013/04/the_grave_evil.html

[43]https://isteve.blogspot.com/2013/04/wapo-tavon-white-of-black-guerilla.html

[44]https://www.youtube.com/watch?v=C9Ko6Xfa84w "raging hormones on parade"

Most females, upon meeting a seemingly high status male, will jump his bones given a few minutes of opportunity, which is why societies where virginity was important and illegitimacy disastrous kept fertile age women on a very tight leash.

The Daily Mail reports[45] that Tavon White had five children with four female prison guards, all of them in their years of maximum hotness (why the hell is anyone hiring females as prison guards - oh yes, because failure to do so would be *discrimination*) They suggest that the problem was that the guards had low self esteem, which kind of neglects the fact that most of the fertile age female guards were Tavon's personal harem. Did they all have low self esteem?

All thirteenindicted correctional officers were reasonably OK looking chicks, or at least all them that I could find. A few were too fat, one was way hot. Did anyone ever hear of a hot chick with low self esteem?

My personal highly unscientific observation is that the lower a woman's self esteem, the better her behavior, and vise versa, since the lower her self esteem, the more vulnerable she is to social pressure and male authority. It is the girl with high self esteem that follows her pussy.

Obviously you should not have male guards in a female prison, because they are going to do the prisoners, pretty much all of the guards doing all of the prisoners, and equally obviously you should not have female guards in a male prison, because they are going to do the prisoners, or rather the prisoner, the one highest status prisoner.

So when did the madness set in? When did people start thinking that women were a bunch of angels? No one is going to think that equality of the sexes means that male prison guards should be employed in female prisons.

Seems to me, that the PC doctrine that women are angels set in with the Whig campaign against George the Fourth, and therefore in support of that dreadful slut, Queen Caroline, and ever since then the natural momentum ever leftwards has compelled us to believe that women are ever more angelic. Plus, of course, if they acknowledged the nature of women, then it follows that King George the fourth should have beaten queen Caroline with a stick no bigger than her thumb, and the puritans had already rejected that a hundred and fifty years earlier.

## The papacy goes pharasaic

2013-04-27 23:02:47

And, as always pharaseeism equals leftism.[46]

Avenging hand reminds us:

> Each Pope must show himself more humble than the previous one. The truly humble thing to do would be to submit oneself to the tradition of the Church, to do just as one's predecessor had done, and not to call attention to one's humility.

Conspicuously demonstrating himself ever more humble, the pope must demonstrate himself ever lefter.

---

[45] https://www.dailymail.co.uk/news/article-2313882/Tavon-White-Murderer-fathered-FIVE-children-FOUR-guards.html

[46] https://avengingredhand.wordpress.com/2013/04/24/papal-humility/

## Neoreaction and libertarianism

2013-04-28 15:17:55

The great flaw in libertarianism is egalitarianism. People are unequal, groups are unequal, reproductive roles are unequal.

Superior people need to rule inferior people or else inferior people will cause problems for each other and for their betters. Superior people need to be more free. Inferior people cannot handle freedom, need supervision, discipline, and control. Inferior people need to be substantially less free.

Equality worked by consuming the social capital created by inequality. Now, however, with tax consumers (single mums, government employees, quasi government employees such as human resources, and people on welfare) outnumbering and outvoting tax producers, we have finally run out of social capital. Increasingly, young white males do not, cannot, aspire to have wives and children, because doing so will likely result in the state taking his children away, nor to save for retirement, for the grasshoppers will devour what the ants put aside. For people to have a reason to save and invest, those who save and invest must have superior political power to those who do not. Children need fathers. For children to have fathers, fathers must have authority over their families. For the economy to function, property must be secure. For property to be secure, those who have property must have political power over those that do not.

## What unites neoreaction?

2013-04-29 06:22:05

Firstly, why neoreaction, rather than reaction?

Because the principles and social organization that we want to restore are completely dead, available only in dusty old books whose language is a little bit strange. We are not reacting to the latest outrage, but to outrages that were a fait accompli a hundred years ago. Since what was an fait accompli a hundred years ago has led to the disastrous consequences predicted, the possibility now opens of reversing what was supposedly irreversible. The Neoreaction is heavily influenced by books long, long, out of print, and previously inaccessible.

Neoreactionaries, all of them, respect the past. Traditional solutions derive from Nature, or, some would say, from Nature's God, and embody unspoken and difficult to explain wisdom. Sweeping them aside was apt to have disastrous consequences, and, in substantial part, did have disastrous consequences.

Reactionaries, all of them, are realists, seeing the real, not the official truth.

Neoreactionaries, all of them, recognize that races are different, the sexes are different, and man is a hierarchical animal.

Neoreactionaries, all of them, regard the official truth, the Cathedral as highly unlikely to have any connection to the truth, indeed as evil and insane. If all academics and the New York Times agree on X, the neoreactionary assumption is that X is likely to be a lie. The only way one would get such agreement is if it is enforced, and, if enforced, must be untrue.

That being said, what divides neoreactionaries?

Christian Traditionalists are just not all that neoreactionary, even though they are supposed to be faithful to a very ancient book. Everything the Christian Manosphere, such as Dalrock, says about trad-cons tends to be somewhat true of Christian Traditionalists. The left would imagine the Christian Traditionalists as proposing a Christian Theocracy with fire and brimstone, and that each variant of Christian Traditionalism proposed to burn each of the others at the stake, but even those who do in fact propose a Christian theocracy, such as Bruce Charleton, want a King, not a priest, at the top. They are alarmingly willing to render unto Caesar not only what is Caesar's, but also what is God's. Saint Paul wanted the Church practices to symbolically and socially enforce male supremacy. Women were to be silent in Church, and in Church dress in a way symbolizing modesty and submission. Today's Christian Traditionalists, reasonably enough, shrink from such a blatant confrontation with the Cathedral. They hope for a Caesar that will permit them to be more authentically Christian, but have no great inclination to stick their heads out when today's Caesar prohibits key parts of the New Testament.

If Bruce Charleton had his King, and the King mandated Mormonism, Bruce would gladly be a Mormon, if Greek Orthodoxy, he would be Greek Orthodox, if Restoration Anglicanism, he would be Anglican. Any King that mandated something that was not violently unchristian would be an improvement for Bruce Charleton.

Ethno-Nationalists, like Christian Traditionalists, tend to be not all that reactionary. An ethno nationalist typically believes that if we adjusted borders to get some predominantly white nations, and if our ruling elite was ethnically homogeneous, we would be fine. A neoreactionary thinks our problems are too serious to be solved in that manner.

The Ethno Nationalist correctly observes that Jewish members of the elite tend to think of themselves as non white, and hate whites. Indeed they hate whites and Christians so much that if destroying the white race and Christendom destroyed the Jewish race and Judaism, as seems rather likely, they would be fine with that. The Ethno Nationalist however fails to observe that our ruling elite has hated whites and Christendom even back when it was ethnically homogeneous and nominally Christian. Nineteenth Century Whitehall imperialism was anti colonialist, an attack on eighteenth century British colonialism. Anti colonialism goes back to the nineteenth century British gentry sneering at those that got rich in India. Until 1950 or so, there were few or no Jews in the ruling elite, yet it still hated whites and Christendom.

Thus the Ethno-Nationalist tends to say, "Let us turn the clock back to 1950", while I say, 1800. In the great debate about whether Nazis are left or right, the answer is that Nazis are 1950s leftists. The Zietgeist has moved leftwards since then. Although as recently as 1950, our ruling elite thought of leftism as a form of Christianity, indeed as more Christian than regular Christianity, nonetheless as early as the War Between the States, the Christian left was aware that its religious beliefs differed radically from traditional Christianity, and were correspondingly hostile to traditional Christianity.

Suppose we magically got whiteopia borders - nation states that were all white, and indeed each of a single white ethnicity. And suppose government employees in powerful positions were also all of single ethnicity. (Suppose we fired all the Jews.) Government employees would still be fireproof, thus power would still be diffused. Being diffused, we get rule by consensus. Jim's rule of large committees applies: That consensus will always wind up dominated by the evil and the insane, which is to say the left. To maintain the appearance of democracy the government needs to manufacture or import an electorate that will vote for what it is going to do anyway, which is how we lost ethnic homogeneity in the first place.

Still, turning the clock back to 1950 is a good start, and as far as I can tell most Ethno-Nationalists want to make government employees fireable at will, so my primary disagreement with them is that they underestimate the scope of the problem. Purging the civil service and the voter rolls is easier done, and more likely to be effective, than adjusting borders.

If we adjusted the borders, which is what the Ethno-Nationalists want, and ensured that the ruling elite was ethnically homogeneous, the fundamental causes that got us into this problem would still be acting. The government would still suck in pretty much the way it sucks now. On the other hand, making public servants fireable at will would go a long way to fixing things. We would then merely be stuck with an army of fatherless children and single mothers voting for handouts.

By and large, fatherlessness is a bigger problem than race. We would get more mileage making it hard for the fatherless to vote, than hard for the black to vote.

To the Christians in the neoreaction, the Masculine Reaction seems to be in favor of social decay. Heartiste claims to be a minion of Satan. But, in fact Heartiste is not in favor social decay. Rather he is against males being required to take the traditional male obligations unreciprocated in a society that is in decay, against white males attempting to carry carry the impossible burden of a society that has already collapsed. Absent socially and legally enforceable contracts, love is war. All is fair in love and war. Heartiste and company represent sex realism, as the HBD branch of the neoreaction represents race realism.

Obviously Neoreactionaries do not favor a society in which each individual pursues his best interests without regard to the costs that he imposes on others. But in sex and reproduction, we have such a society. It is possible to establish, by force of character and reckless will to power, a family with different rules, though it is a lot easier if one's starting material is an aristocratic girl brought up in a profoundly conservative family within a profoundly conservative society. For most young men today, that is not an option. Marriage is collapsing, even among the white elite, even among those white males whose income is high enough that marriage to them is higher status than marriage to Uncle Sam the Big Pimp.

## US economic decline

2013-05-01 09:35:25

Supposing the official cpi to be true, US real GDP per capita has been growing at about 1% per year in recent years.

Supposing the big mac index to be true, US real GDP per capita has been falling at about 1% per year in recent years.

Motor vehicles per capita, according to world bank statistics, have been falling about 1% per year in recent years.

Electricity consumption per capita, taking indexmundi[47] figures for US electricity consumption, and world bank figures for US population, has been falling at about 2% per year in recent years, consistent with the greeny attack on energy.

So, the evidence favors the big mac index. Which is not showing hyperinflation, but is showing more inflation than is good for the economy.

## On what used to be called marriage

2013-05-05 07:48:03

On what used to be called marriage back in the days before marriage was something disgusting that gays did to épater les bourgeois.

My personal observation is that every successful marriage is quietly and furtively eighteenth century, so thoroughly politically incorrect as to be illegal.

And a little reflection reveals that the New Testament/eighteenth century form of marriage,in which both parties give consent to sex once and forever, and the wife submits to the husband, is simply the only kind that can work.

All is fair in love and war.

Love is a battlefield

Love is war.

If the male does what is best for himself, and the female does what is best for herself, the outcome is likely to be unsatisfactory for both parties. To solve this problem, the New Testament commands an indissoluble contractual commitment to mutual support, and sexual availability, so that, once married, you are stuck with each other, for better or worse, and required to have sex according to the other's desire. "Marital rape" is not only permitted, but absolutely mandatory. This contract changes the incentives, creating an incentive for good behavior, among other things giving the man the ability and incentive to invest in his children.

Absent contract, the incentives are for bad behavior. Women always want better, and they can get it, if only briefly, and men always want more.

If two people are close, they cannot be equal, Equality requires fences, requires some separation, requires each has his own turf, his own things. A single household, must have a single head of household, thus the contract must designate one person as the head. And, in practice, women will not put up with being the head of household. They will struggle to take charge, but if they succeed in taking charge, will not have sex with their husbands. So the contract, necessarily, commits the wife to submit to the husband. The contract must designate the man to be in charge. The New Testament prescription – indissoluble and patriarchal marriage, is the only practical solution. A society with some other form of marriage will have trouble reproducing biologically, culturally, and economically.

---

[47] https://www.indexmundi.com/g/g.aspx?c=us&v=81

People say the rot set in with no fault divorce, but it is worse than that. The rot set in with George the Fourth's unsuccessful attempt to divorce Queen Caroline. We then, in 1820, first see the doctrine that women are angels, with no sexual character, therefore do not need restraint, supervision, and discipline. Around 1960 or so, the left doctrine that women are angels with no sexual character was replaced by the doctrine that woman are angels even if they have sex, and history was abruptly rewritten to attribute the previous version, that women are sexless angels, to the right.

Of course the actual right wing point of view was always that given half a chance, a woman will bang a total stranger like a barn door in a high wind, should he superficially appear sufficiently high status, with utterly disastrous results for her family, her children, and herself, and that therefore women had to be restrained for their own good, and the sake of society. As various Youtube videos show, it is women that are the uncontrollably lustful sex[48]

This left wing doctrine, the angelhood of women, led the state's destruction of the family, starting in England with the Matrimonial causes act of 1857. It set in a fair bit earlier in the US, though this is complicated to track in the US, being primarily done in state rather than federal law, with some US states obstinately holding out until the civil war, which was fought not only to free the slaves, but also, among other things, to destroy marriage.

The British Matrimonial Causes Act of 1857 meant that a woman who left her husband had the legal status of an independent household, but not a man who left his wife – thus began what in due course became unilateral divorce at female whim, and the requirement for continuing moment to moment consent to sex, rather than consent to sex being formally given once and forever. A woman could wash her hands of her husband, but not a husband of his wife. Hence the 1860s begat the 1960s. Smash monogamy and all that. If a wife left her husband, perhaps in the hope (seldom realized) that her demon lover would visit her more frequently, she gained, under the 1857 Matrimonial causes act, full control of her income and finances, but did not automatically and immediately lose the husband's obligation to support her. Every change since then as just been doubling down on that big 1857 change.

The 1857 act fatally undermined the new testament prescription for marriage, in which both parties give consent to sex once and forever, and the wife submits to the husband.

Old Testament marriage favored polygyny: A wife could have only one husband, but a husband multiple wives. The New Testament does not explicitly prohibit polygyny, but the requirement that the husband always be sexually and emotionally available to the wife implicitly prohibits, or at least strongly discourages, polygyny, and arguably explicitly prohibits it: "Let every woman have her own husband".

The British 1857 change gave the woman a bomb and a detonator to blow up her family at any moment, thus increased her power, and decreased the husband's power over her, and every subsequent change to the present day in every country increased the power of the explosive and inducements to press the button. But this necessarily results in husbands being less inclined to marry in the first place, and reduces their investment

---

[48]https://www.youtube.com/watch?v=C9Ko6Xfa84w

in what could be capriciously destroyed, reduces their investment in things that reduce their power and freedom – which is to say, their sons and posterity, which change is not to the advantage of wives. That a woman cannot irrevocably commit herself to marriage, necessarily reduces the husband's commitment, no matter what the law may say.

Making contracts non binding on women is the same thing as forbidding women from entering into contracts. It disempowers women, not empowers them. Taking the marriage as given, it empowers them. But the marriage is not given. Giving them the power to capriciously destroy the marriage that they momentarily don't want, denies them the power to obtain the marriage that they do want.

Feminists interpret the Matrimonial causes act of 1857 as partriarchally favoring men, because they interpret everything as partriarchally favoring men. Supposedly, it favored men in that female adultery was grounds for divorce, but male adultery was not. Men, however, do not bring their bastards home, so that is a perfectly reasonable law. The big high explosive, society smashing bomb in the 1857 act is that a woman could walk out of marriage, get a job, or get her lover to let her stay with him, and she was just fine, it was as if the marriage had never been, none of her former obligations entangled her, other than that she needed to get a divorce before marrying again, but if a man walked out of marriage, and had a job, he was in deep *$%!#*.

This fundamentally and radically altered the balance of power in marriage – which of course made women less satisfied with marriage, and less inclined to get married, because it deballed their husbands.

People say that marriage was fine in 1950, if only we could go back to 1950. And marriage *was* fine in 1950, because church and society socially enforced the rules that the state no longer legally enforced, indeed was busily undermining: That the husband was the head of the household, and that it was utterly unthinkable for a wife to walk out on her wifely duties.

But these rules were under social and cultural attack starting with the attempted divorce of King George the Fourth, and had ceased to be legal, had come under legal attack with the Matrimonial causes act of 1857. So from 1800 to 1950, we were running on cultural capital that was under social and legal attack, and around 1960 or so, just ran out out of cultural capital.

For society to reproduce itself culturally and biologically, husband and wife have to have incentive to behave well. To have incentive to behave well, have to be stuck with the marital roles they have agreed to, with bad legal and social consequences should they abandon them. The rot set in when, during the the divorce proceedings of King George the Fourth, the left got away with arguing that it was so extraordinarily unlikely for a woman to behave badly, that extraordinary evidence of bad behavior was required, thus in 1820 effectively negating the existing laws against such bad behavior, which laws were finally repealed in 1857. Social and cultural enforcement of these laws, however, continued until the 1950s, revealing that the attack on marriage was a state centered attack.

Well of course it was a state centered attack, the state attacking society. The state is the left and the left is the state.

If it is extraordinarily unlikely for women to behave badly, then obviously the entire apparatus of coercion to make people fulfill their marital vows was completely unnecessary for women, and only needed to be applied against men. Applying it against women was supposedly just sheer gratuitous cruelty.

And thus, the left completed their attack on marriage that they began during the reign of Cromwell, when parliament declared marriage not a sacrament. Marriage was indeed smashed in the sixties– the eighteen sixties.

## Mestizos and National Wealth

### 2013-05-12 06:35:37

Conservatives are fleeing the evil witch and horrible heretic Jason Richwine.

Richwine pointed out what everyone knows, but no one can say: That mestizos are genetically low intelligence, and that importing a low intelligence underclass will cost Americans a lot of money, and that this underclass, even if, unlike blacks, they really want to assimilate, can never assimilate, and will forever resent their failure to assimilate, forever blaming it on racism.

Richwine's estimates were, however, very much on the low side. He only considered the costs of a genetically low IQ underclass that sucks up welfare and fails to pay taxes. He ignored Smart Fraction Theory[49].

Smart Fraction Theory is that nation's per capita GDP is determined by the population fraction with IQ greater than or equal to some threshold IQ. Consistent with the data of Lynn and Vanhanen, that threshold IQ is somewhere around 108, a bit less than the minimum that used to be required for what used to be a bachelor's degree. This gives a remarkably good fit to variations in wealth between countries. Average IQ influences average per capita wealth much more strongly than individual IQ influences individual wealth. Richwine only considered the extent to which average IQ influences individual wealth.

Smart people create the modern economy, perhaps directly by operating businesses, perhaps culturally, by creating a society of trust and cooperation, perhaps politically, by resisting self destructive economic policies. Most likely by some combination of all three. Smart people create an environment that allows less smart people to make a decent living. Thus intelligence has a large positive externality, and stupidity, similarly a large negative externality.

A person of average IQ is not the average IQ of your friends. If you are a typical reader of this blog, you would perceive him as remarkably stupid. Consider that man in a backward African economy. Likely his best option is to scratch the ground with a digging stick, grow yams, and hunt rats and small animals (the larger animals already having been killed). He produces very little, and is accordingly very poor. The same man in Singapore is highly productive because smart wealthy people provide him with highly sophisticated equipment, and tell him what to do with that equipment. Modern living standards are a gift by the rich to the poor and a gift by the smart to the stupid.

If you have ten percent more low IQ people, then the amount of modern economy you have is diluted by ten percent, for the modern economy is, to a good approximation, smart people cooperating with each other, and the rest are in large part just leeching on

---

[49]https://www.lagriffedulion.f2s.com/sft.htm "Smart Fraction Theory"

wealth created by others. Thus on average every average and below person that enters the United States costs the existing residents fifty thousand dollars a year, as does every child spawned by the innumerable short fat pregnant single mestizo woman that clog up every emergency ward in California, except for the Stanford emergency ward. Richwine considers only the part of this loss that comes in the form of government expenditures.

The ethno nationalists in Dark Enlightenment hope to restore geographic white nations, on new, much shrunken borders. This seems as impractical as unscrambling an omelet, and leaves the big problem of the white underclass created by welfare and the collapse of the family. My proposed solution is an end to universal suffrage - whether by literacy tests and property tests, or by abandoning democracy altogether for some other system, any other system, and the reintroduction of segregation and small apartheid. We put a sign over the black section in the school cafeteria that says "black section" so that no one gets confused. And we also need male only areas.

Of course not all stupid people are black, and not all black people are stupid, and similarly for criminals. When considering which people need to be kept away from civilized people, we should profile. Race and culture should be one factor, an important factor, but one, as in Rhodesia, capable of being outweighed by other factors. The Rhodesian slogan was "Equal rights for all civilized men" – which they carried out to very good effect, and to the benefit of everyone, including, indeed particularly, the benefit of uncivilized men, who benefited from firm supervision, who benefit from firm supervision by their superiors more than anyone. Compare Rhodesia under white rule, with Zimbabwe.

We should employ a full Bayesian approach: Fatherlessness, employment, literacy, credit rating, criminal history, and property should weigh in various profiles applied for various purposes, as well as race and culture. A major effect and intent of these profiles should be unmix the omelet on the micro scale, to keep uncivilized men of all races away from civilized men of all races. We need ghettos, not only because there are blacks and mestizos, but because there are too many stupid whites, and too many whites that have been raised feral by single mums. And if someone who belongs in the ghetto is found where he should not be, he is asked for a justification for being where he is. If no adequate justification, gets in trouble.

## The ideological cause of the Benghazi bungles

2013-05-15 09:56:43

When Pizarro hit the Incas, they just could not see him unless he got in their faces and started poking swords into them. They could not see him, because they could not believe in him.

The attack on the Benghazi embassy was not a terrorist attack. It was a conventional military operation by the uniformed and well equipped troops of an organization that frequently engages in terrorist attacks. They used truck mounted artillery, not box cutters, and were dressed as Al Qaeda armed forces, not civilians. If you cannot say "War with Dar al-Islam", or even say "War with Radical Islam", you cannot see Islamic armed forces.

No one seems able to say "uniformed". They say that they were wearing "Afghan costumes". But no one in Libya wears "Afghan" costumes except armed forces affiliated with Al Qaeda, thus the costumes clearly identify them as members of an organized military force, which is the Geneva Convention definition of a military uniform.

So Al Qaeda launched a conventional military attack on the US government, and the US government refused to fight back. That was scandal one. Scandal two was that the US government proceeded to lie about it, to fit it into what they wanted to believe, rather than what actually happened. Hence the cover story that the attack was a demonstration related to a video critical of Mohammed – that it was outraged civilians, or perhaps terrorists hiding amongst outraged civilians and using them as human shields.

This lie was not only intended to cover up the first scandal, but to enable them to continue to believe in a worldview that had been falsified by events. They lied to themselves, as well as to their opponents.

This is akin to the fact crimestop prevents progressives from seeing reactionary propaganda, most famously in "District 9" Reactionaries are taking advantage of progressive crimestop, and Al Qaeda is taking advantage of progressive crimestop.
> Shawn Turner, spokesman for Mr Clapper's office, said that in the immediate aftermath of the attack, US agencies came to the view that the Benghazi attack had begun spontaneously after protests at the US embassy in Cairo against a short film made in California lampooned the Prophet Mohammed.
>
> Mr Turner said that as US intelligence learnt more about the attack, "we revised our initial assessment to reflect new information indicating that it was a deliberate and organised terrorist attack carried out by extremists".
>
> He said it remained "unclear" if any individual or specific group commanded the attack.

The lie drifts slightly closer to the truth, without any danger of making contact.

Progressives reacted to the 9/11 attack as an opportunity to invade Muslim countries, kill their leaders and convert them to ... progressivism

As Moldbug sarcastically tells us, progressivism is a superior revelation of which Christianity and Islam, along with all other religions, is a mere anticipation, a kind of lame-ass John-the-Baptist point-the-way figure. Backward people who refuse to accept this inevitable transition are called "fundamentalists". If they do accept it, they are "moderates" or some other term of approbation.

There is a fair bit of "moderate Islam" in the US, meaning preachers who preach progressivism to a rapidly emptying mosque while calling themselves Muslims, for in the US the full power of the state can be applied to bend preachers to the will of the state. Progressives believe that there is a fair bit of "moderate Islam" in the middle east, but they are deluded. From time to time Obama (himself a "moderate Muslim") has embraced some Muslim preacher as prince of moderation, only to later add that preacher to the list of people that assassin drones are to kill on sight. Obama seems to be waking up the fact that "moderate Muslims" are as thin on the ground as shovel ready government projects. This, however, puts Obama well to the right of the Department of State, and indeed well to the right of most neoconservatives.

Because progressives are unaware how much coercion they apply to convert people subject to the rule of the USG to progressivism, they profoundly under estimated how much violence would be required to convert the middle east. Thus they were, and are, in denial about what happened in Benghazi. The new regime in Libya was supposedly progressive, thus unthinkable that some military units of the Libyan spring were in fact Al Qaeda, unthinkable that they were in state of conventional war, declared by both sides, with the USA. Official truth was and is that there was no significant Al Qaeda presence among the rebels against Gaddafi's regime, hence the inability to recognize "Afghan" clothes for what they were. The failure to respond to a military attack, and the subsequent lies and cover up, are all in an effort to uphold official truth, all in an effort to *believe* official truth.

## All your skypes belong to Microsoft

### 2013-05-17 07:25:39

All Your Skype Are Belong To Us
Microsoft is reading everything you write[50]

Skype used to be the most secure instant messaging system and I have frequently recommended it on this basis. Microsoft, under Bill Gates, used to be the big company most willing to protect user's privacy. Skype was recently purchased by Microsoft.

> Heise Security then reproduced the events by sending two test HTTPS URLs, one containing login information and one pointing to a private cloud-based file-sharing service. A few hours after their Skype messages, they observed the following in the server log:
>
> 65.52.100.214 - - [30/Apr/2013:19:28:32 +0200]
> "HEAD /.../login.html?user=tbtest&password=geheim HTTP/1.1"
>
> ...
>
> ... In visiting these pages, Microsoft made use of both the login information and the specially created URL for a private cloud-based file-sharing service.

By "specially created URL" they mean a secret URL that looks like random gibberish. When one accesses a web site over https, other people can see what website you are accessing, but they cannot see the url, thus secret urls are regularly used like passwords over https to access secret files.

I am putting this in the category party politics as well as politics, because these days Microsoft is, like all big software companies, Democrat aligned. Likely if a republican candidate says something interesting, or sends an interesting link to a fellow republican, his Democratic party opponent will get wind of it.

Adam Back replicated this experiment.

The delay of several hours suggests that there is a human in the loop, keeping an eye out for anything good, though Adam Back finds this hard to believe.

---

[50]https://www.h-online.com/security/news/item/Skype-with-care-Microsoft-is-reading-everything-you-write-1862870.html

I recommend using OTR over pidgin. For one's Skype contacts, Adam Back recommends using OTR over adium4skype[51].

After purchasing Skype, Microsoft replaced its peer to peer architecture with a central server architecture. There is no good reason for doing this other than to spy on everyone. It is obviously much more efficient to send messages as directly as possible, rather than through Redmond.

## Game, Dark Enlightenment, and Reaction

2013-05-19 13:18:21

You will notice that the Pick Up Artist Community and the Christian Reactionary movement get along mighty well, despite the fact that Heartiste claims to be a minion of Satan, and despite the fact that they are in total disagreement about ultimate ends.

The thesis that Game works is logically equivalent to what used to be the right wing view of women, before the right became the left that is lagging four to eight years behind the mainstream left in moving rapidly ever leftwards.

Rightists used to believe that fertile age women were uncontrollably and self destructively lustful, and therefore needed male adult supervision to prevent them from self destructively howling for their demon lover like cats in heat, that given half a chance, a woman will bang a total stranger like a barn door in a high wind, should he superficially appear sufficiently high status, with utterly disastrous results for her family, her children, and herself. And, of course, game is largely about superficially appearing to be sufficiently high status.

Conversely, if you are a Christian, you accept that Paul was right. (Note that by this standard, there are very few Christians, and the Pope is not one of them.) And if Paul was right, most women will misbehave, unless subject to the stern controls commended by Paul. In which case, you think that game works.

There are of course lots of charlatans and con men purporting to teach game, but equally there are lots of practitioners who have a truly astonishing notch count.

From 1820 to 1960, leftists held that women were sexless angels, reluctantly forced into having sex by evil men imposing on them, therefore it was completely unnecessary to enforce the marital contract on women, only on men. In 1960, having successfully disempowered husbands, they switched to abolishing fatherhood altogether, which allowed them to acknowledge that women have some very slight sexual character, while nonetheless remaining angels.

Which view of women, then, is correct? Angels or succubi? If you are in any doubt about the answer, see the video that I have so frequently linked in so many of my posts[52].

If you believe that game works then:

1. You are darkly enlightened, since you believe at least one forbidden truth about human nature.

2. You should logically conclude that women should never have been emancipated and never given the vote, thus logically, you should be reactionary.

---

[51] https://trac.adium.im/wiki/SkypeInAdium

[52] https://blog.reaction.la/culture/on-what-used-to-be-called-marriage "On what used to be called marriage"

My own observations hint that possibly the sexless angels account might be accurate for sexually inexperienced girls for the first two weeks following menstruation. They are interested in romance at all stages of their menstrual cycle, but not interested in getting dirty except during estrus/ovulation, and to a lesser extent following estrus/ovulation.

However it seems to me that women tend to imprint on whatever sexual activities they try during estrus, and are subsequently happy to repeat them at any stage of their cycle. I hope that some of my readers may have better data on this question than I do. (I am crowd sourcing the issue of the effect of estrus on female behavior, particularly imprinting, for I have a suspicion that there is an imprinting effect, though as far as I know this has never been scientifically studied. We largely ignore the effects of women going into heat, or at least we largely ignore the impolite consequences of women going into heat, because we are still dominated by the ideology that women are sexless angels.)

## The next official belief system

### 2013-05-22 18:24:12

I wish we could have separation of information and state, but that is impractical, short of the abolition of the state altogether, short of anarchy or anarcho capitalism. Official truth is too useful to the state, and the state too useful for ideologies seeking to be official. This is apt to result in a positive feedback loop, power manufacturing belief, and belief manufacturing power, each ever more extreme.

After they executed the King in the English civil war, they theoretically disestablished the official church, but it was of course immediately obvious that they instituted an officially unofficial church that was vastly more intrusive and oppressive. When, with the restoration, officially official theocracy was reintroduced, people celebrated it with pagan festivals such as Maypole dancing, recognizing the introduction of official theocracy as ending the oppressive theocracy of ostensible lack of theocracy.

And today, the successors of those that executed the king have officially unofficial theocracy. To go to the best universities, to run for political office, to be employed in the government service, you have to submit essays and evidence of your commitment to one thousand and one points of progressive doctrine, much as in restoration England, you had to swear allegiance to the thirty nine articles and the second book of homilies.[53]

Today's Anglosphere Christianity has been wholly absorbed into progressivism. It supports egalitarianism, matriarchy, fatherlessness, and race replacement, so as a commenter asks:

> should we try to fix Christianity or should we finish it off and move on without it?

Societies need myths, but we are not a society, we are just a bunch of social critics. It's best for us to discard all myths and push forward with a commitment to absolute scientific truth. Perhaps a new mythology will arise once we've destroyed the Cathedral or accomplished something else that is worthy of being immortalized in legend.

---

[53]https://blog.reaction.la/culture/the-thirty-nine-articles-and-the-second-book-of-homilies.html    "the thirty nine articles"

A monogamous patriarchal society remembers its fathers, and slowly accretes tall tales and true connecting it to ancient blood and soil. We have lost that, and I think hopes to quickly synthesize a substitute are unlikely to succeed.

So here is what I propose for a sane official belief system, one less likely to be very repressive, or to go into positive feedback loops.

## The incarnation of evil, the defining example of collective evil

Instead of Nazism-discrimination being the incarnation of evil communism-covetousness should be the incarnation of evil.

Communism and Nazism should get coverage in proportion to the number of people murdered, which means Nazism should get very little coverage – the average student will entirely forget that Nazism was ever mentioned at all.

To the extent that Nazism is mentioned at all, we should emphasize their complaint that the Jews were disproportionately successful and influential, so that it fits into the pattern covetousness-murder rather than discrimination-murder

The various communist democides should be described in the context of wanting to have what is someone else's (envy and covetousness).

The propensity of Marxist minions to loyally go to their own deaths should be remembered, so that every time someone sees a depiction of an evil overlord, when the evil overlord capriciously executes one of his minions for some frivolous reason, usually with horrible torture, the audience should think "based on communist minions and communist evil overlords", for example Aristide personally gouging out the eyes of one of his minions.

All the various envy based ideologies, such as feminism or anti racism should be tarred as neomarxist, much as today anyone who disagrees with any tenet of envy based ideologies is a fascist or a neonazi. Feminism shall be dismissed as penis envy, and illustrated by various efforts to give women equal, but unearned, honors in fields where males have a natural advantage. The Spartans gave a woman who died in childbirth the honor of a fallen warrior, but they did not pretend to put them in the front lines.

We cannot resume scientific progress until every child is taught to laugh at Marie Curie getting two Nobel prizes for being on a team that made a discovery that would have been unlikely to get one Nobel had the team been all male, nor can we resume the conquest of space till every child is taught to laugh cruelly at Amelia Earhart.

Charles Lindbergh flew solo across the Atlantic and became famous for so doing, so feminists proceeded to manufacture an equivalent female poster girl. Amelia Earhart received a ticker tape parade and a presidential reception for flying across the atlantic, in pretended imitation of Charles Lindbergh but she did not fly, rather she was flown. As a passenger. By a man.

And when she subsequently attempted to herself fly long distance, to actually do the thing she had already become a famous poster girl for supposedly doing, promptly crashed her plane and killed herself. Everyone should laugh at her death as deserving the Darwin award.

When they gave two Noble prizes to Marie Curie for being female, that did not hurt anyone except more deserving potential Noble prize winners.  But handing out phony Nobles on the basis of sex, race, and nationality necessitated handing out phony degrees on the basis of race and sex, and handing out phony degrees on the basis of race and sex necessarily led to a crisis where these phony degrees were being ignored by employers, so employers necessarily had to be forced to give out well paid jobs on the basis of race and sex.  But being given well paid jobs on the basis of race and sex failed to result in recipients living a middle class lifestyle, so lenders had to be forced to give out a middle class lifestyle on the basis of race and sex.  Which led to our present financial crisis.

It all began with Marie Curie, and to undo it, we must start by laughing at Marie Curie and laughing cruelly at Amelia Earhart.  Every child needs laugh cruelly, so that envy based political movements die of shame, as Amelia Earhart died of vanity.


## Latitudinarianism

What made official religion, the unity of Church and State, compatible with freedom in Britain in the period from the restoration to the Victorian era, was latitudinarianism, that you could piously claim to believe in the official religion while believing in anything other than the major tenets of competing theocratic religions hungry for power.

At present, to get into an elite university like Harvard, you have to plausibly claim to believe in every single one of ten thousand points of left wing doctrine,and if you deviate on a single point of a ten thousand points, you are XXXist.

Instead, it should be sufficient to disbelieve in the key tenets of the major competing theocratic religions.  Thus applicants for any establishment position, leadership qualification, or establishment accreditation should merely be required to reject the key tenets of the two major competing theocracies: Progressivism and Islam.  You must not believe that Mohammed is the final prophet of God, and you must not believe in equality nor oppose profiling. You must believe that all men were not created equal, and that therefore different rules should apply to different types of men.

For example, if someone reasonably believes that females are on average less honest than males, and that homosexuals are on average less honest than heterosexuals, and that it is hard to get good information on individual honesty, then you are required to believe that he has a duty to exclude all females and homosexuals from a security job where honesty is important, even though sex and perversion are not very reliable indicators of honesty

And if he can get better individual honesty information on fellow members of his congregation than on outsiders, then he should hire from within his congregation for the job for which honesty is important.

Anything else, you should be allowed to believe or disbelieve, except for stuff that is empirically stupid or wrong.

Should new theocratic belief systems appear, seeking power, their tenets should be added to the forbidden list. We should have a Grand Inquisitor to manage the forbidden list, and to detect disguised versions of forbidden beliefs.  The Grand Inquisitor purges the public service, the universities, and so on and so forth, but does not attempt to purge all of society. People should be allowed to believe what they please, just not allowed near the levers of power if they have dangerous beliefs. In particular, and especially, not allowed near anything that gives them the opportunity to apply state power in support of forbidden beliefs. That is how England went off the rails. In Victorian England Anglicanism ceased to be an instrument of the King and the aristocracy, and became a weaponized belief system used to attack the aristocracy.

We should not be too latitudinarian. Victorian England should have executed William Wilberforce, and it is probable we will need pogroms to persuade Muslims that their religion does *not* require forceful imposition of Shariah on the rest of us.

## Theocratic repression

Restoration Anglicanism avoided being stifling. But, sending its enemies off to colonize America instead of sending them off to cut sugar in the West Indies turned out to be a very bad idea.

Trouble is, if you repress Galileo, you don't get the scientific and industrial revolutions, but if you fail to repress William Wilberforce, you get replaced by holier than thou fanatics, by people who claim that:

I am holier than thou, therefore I should command thee

It was correct to honor Lyell, who noticed that the rocks of the earth were immensely ancient, even though this was, strictly speaking, heresy punishable by death. It was suicidally self destructive to honor William Wilberforce, who discovered that morality required a radical redistribution of power and prestige away from colonials towards people strikingly resembling himself. William Wilberforce should have been executed for heresy on the question of slavery. The difference was that that Lyell was not seeking political power for his belief system, therefore not a threat to the enforcers of the heresy laws, while William Wilberforce was seeking political power for his belief system, therefore was a threat to the enforcers of the heresy laws.

Lyell was correct, so the Anglican Church was right to tolerate him. William Wilberforce was a pharisee, so they should not have tolerated him. The fact that he was correct meant that they should have been twice as intolerant, and the fact that he really was holier than they were meant that they should have been four times as intolerant. They should have shipped him off to the West Indies to cut sugar cane for rum.

By a pharisee, I mean people who claim that they know more than others, therefore should be obeyed, that they are more virtuous than others, therefore should be obeyed, are holier than thou. William Wilberforce opposed slavery, and proposed that virtuous people like himself should suppress with fire and steel the slavery tolerated by wicked people unlike himself, thus people like himself should have charge of fire and steel, and people unlike himself, should not.

I suggest therefore, that the official clerisy of the official truth focus on repressing competing pharisees. If someone not officially endorsed as speaking the official truth claims authority on the basis of his superior knowledge of the truth, rather than merely publishing the evidence that inclines him to his understanding of the truth, he should be repressed. If someone not officially endorsed as officially virtuous claims authority on the basis of his superior virtue, he should be repressed. If he really is more virtuous than those who are officially virtuous, he should be executed. After executing him, ironically check his body in three days. If he has not risen, was not sufficiently more virtuous than the official promoters of official virtue.

## Hygiene

Cleanliness, they say is next to Godliness. An official religion needs Godliness, but God is dead, so cleanliness will have to do. People need rituals.

## The Scientific Method.

No, the scientific method is not consensus, and even less is it peer review. Rather it is skepticism about third hand facts, disbelief in the authority of experts. Trust but verify, which in the context of science means trust but replicate, which of course really means, don't trust. Consensus is the madness of crowds. We are prone to believe stuff because everyone else believes it, which is at best a vicious cycle leading to madness, and at worst prone to being unduly influenced by the insane, and manipulated by the evil. The insane don't shift, because insane, and the evil don't shift, because they are lying about what they believe, so the evil and the insane tend to dominate the consensus.

## Teach economics

Textbook: Economics in one lesson

That property rights should, and generally do, capture all the costs and benefits of a decision, therefore, an economic decision should be left to those that own the items at issue.

That price control and wage control will fail, and will disrupt the lives of the supposed beneficiaries.

That true monopoly is rare, except in the common case of regulatory capture, because the mere presence of *potential* competition makes it no longer a monopoly. Actual competition is not required. The threat that monopolistic behavior would end or undermine market dominance is sufficient to make market dominance harmless.

The Chamley-Judd Redistribution Impossibility Theorem: Redistribution from capitalists to workers is impossible, and trying to do so merely buggers the economy.

## Public Choice theory

That where there are large externalities, such that a sufficiently wise and good regulator could in theory produce a better result, by intervening against property rights that are imperfectly aligned with costs and benefits, wise and good regulators are seldom to be found, that regulators tend to create externalities by protecting the regulated from the consequences of their own bad decisions.


## Darwinism

Leads to evolutionary psychology and human biodiversity.

Teach the kids all those horrible unspeakable unthinkable statements by Darwin as the logical and necessary implication of Darwinian evolution, while commenting that many people find this horrifying, and doubt that it is God's plan for man and mankind, that this is reason to doubt evolution, or to emotionally reject its implications, or suspect that God allows evil, but expects mankind to do better than Darwinism might lead us to expect, Darwinism being taught as disturbing and unpleasant fact, and God's alleged plan as what some people think about this disturbing fact.

> The great break in the organic chain between man and his nearest allies, which cannot be bridged over by any extinct or living species, has often been advanced as a grave objection to the belief that man is descended from some lower form; but this objection will not appear of much weight to those who, from general reasons, believe in the general principle of evolution. Breaks often occur in all parts of the series, some being wide, sharp and defined, others less so in various degrees; as between the orang and its nearest allies- between the Tarsius and the other Lemuridae- between the elephant, and in a more striking manner between the Ornithorhynchus or Echidna, and all other mammals. But these breaks depend merely on the number of related forms which have become extinct. At some future period, not very distant as measured by centuries, the civilised races of man will almost certainly exterminate, and replace, the savage races throughout the world. At the same time the anthropomorphous apes, as Professor Schaaffhausen has remarked,* will no doubt be exterminated. The break between man and his nearest allies will then be wider, for it will intervene between man in a more civilised state, as we may hope, even than the Caucasian, and some ape as low as a baboon, instead of as now between the negro or Australian and the gorilla.


## Human Bio Diversity.

Tell them that both evolution and the bible implies that groups are not the same and are not equal, without, however, explaining in excessive detail in what ways particular identifiable groups are unequal.

## Sex Education

It is hard to get into trouble by not knowing the mechanics of sex, for nature leads us to discover them, we intuitively and instinctively know them, but not knowing the psychology of sex is apt to lead to big problems. Therefore, sex education needs to teach the different nature of men and women.

Darwinism tells us that men are naturally inclined to polygamy, women to hypergamy, and that this leads to conflict between men and women. For example this difference and conflict is the reason why women can be sluts, and men can never be sluts, even if a married man sleeps with a woman married to someone else.

Which does not of course mean it is OK for a married man to sleep with another man's wife, but does mean that people are apt despise the adulterous wife as a slut, while admiring the adultering man. Double standard because it is easy for a woman hard for a man. Because of the natural and unavoidable differences between men and women. Women are expected to keep their legs closed, while men are admired for getting those legs open .

Girls should be taught that like it or not, rightly or wrongly, they *will* be judged by the double standard.

School should teach the double standard as biblical commandment and the natural result of evolutionary psychology.

Teach men and women how their fertility and sexual market value proceeds over time. Most women these days find it hard to believe men are naturally polygamous, projecting their own behavior and inclinations onto men, and are astonished to discover how soon and how rapidly their fertility and sexual attractiveness diminishes. They are apt to believe they have a relationship with a man when it is perfectly obvious she is just one more hole to relieve himself in.

## A proposed sex education video:

Contrast preselection scene in romance movies, with man with options scene in porn movies: Title the first part of the movie Romance Story for Women, the next part of the movie Porn Story for Men. In Romance Story, one man is treated with respect by four unattractive males, five woman are after the one man, but he has eyes only for one of them, the prettiest one, and swears his undying love, totally failing to notice the other four. He bends his knee to her, begs her to be with him forever. The loving couple ride slowly off into the sunset on his white horse, together. She is looking very, very happy, he is looking kind of stern. The other four males are never seen in the story other than initially establishing that the romantic lead is respected by his fellow males.

In Porn Story, the same five woman are after the same one man. He romances the same one woman as in the first movie, same scenes cut to be considerably swifter, but instead of riding off into the sunset on his white horse, it is implied he immediately bangs her off screen on the nearest horizontal surface. We see her glowing.

Then he bangs the next, and we see the next one glowing and the first one glowering.

And the next, and the next, in order of boob size, the one with the biggest boobs first, smallest boobs last, each one starts glowing after being banged, and then stops glowing and starts glowering when the next female appears, glowing. He then gallops off on his white horse into the sunset, unaccompanied and looking very happy indeed, way happier than in the first story. Last girl (one with the smallest boobs) wails and attempts to chase after him, but he is riding one hell of a lot faster than in Romance Story, and when girl number five starts chasing, he lays his spurs into his white horse. We see the four sad and bitter males (all of them furtive and guilty looking) timidly watching the five sad and bitter females from a distance. The females, however, treat them as completely invisible.

Needless to say, a sex education video like this is never going to be shown in schools until the current theocracy is purged, and a new more realistic theocracy replaces them.

## On Sovereignty

### 2013-05-26 09:58:24

Mencius Moldbug has argued that Sovereignty is conserved - meaning that constitutions are ultimately worthless, there will always be a sovereign, and nothing can stop the sovereign from doing what he likes, government cannot bind itself

This presupposes that government always exists, that it is easy to create and maintain government, easy for a large number of enforcers, of men with guns, to act as one.

I don't think so. I think anarchy is the natural and normal state of mankind, disorderly anarchy is easy, orderly anarchy difficult, government is a fragile illusion, that exists only because every everyone pretends to believe it exists, fearing what might happen should the illusion fail. Fiat government is only real in the sense that fiat money is real.

Observe that in any place where you rely on the police to maintain order, that place is unsafe.

In practice, what respectable people do tends to trump what the law supposedly says they should do, as the book Order without Law: How Neighbors Settle Disputes[54] shows.

The divine right of kings, and the British empire, were similar illusions. If Kings did not rule by divine right, then any man might hope to make himself king, and the wealth of the kingdom, and frequently its blood, would be spent in struggle for political power, hence everyone piously endorsed the lie that the King ruled under God by the will of God.

Similarly, before world War II, it was widely believed among non white races, or pretended to be believed that the mere sight of a white face provided order and rule, perhaps because local rule tended to be disorderly and oppressive so purporting to believe in a white right to rule considerably improved the security of one's property, much as pretending to believe in the divine right of Kings considerably improved the security of one's property.

A constitution can rule if enough people believe it can, or pretend to so believe.

Suppose, however, the education system, the mass media, and all that lot, the Cathedral, tell us that the constitution is whatever the Supremes deem it to be.

Then they will, of course, deem it to give the government unlimited power, except for special privileges for judges and lawyers.

---

[54]https://www.amazon.com/gp/product/0674641698/

In most of the rest of the world, constitutions derive their power, and their interpretation, from the US government. If the US dislikes some regime, it will bring soft power to bear. If soft power is resisted, hard power is apt to follow, except, of course, for China and Russia, who can therefore resist soft power with impunity, though they do not always do so.

What happened in the US is that during and shortly after the civil war, the Cathedral did an end run around the constitution using the fact that president's interpretation is difficult to resist. Since this was indiscreet, and contained the seeds of future violence, they proceeded to reinterpret what they had done, a reinterpretation that gave birth to the new deal and the supreme court as ultimate constitutional arbiter.

What happened in most of the rest of the world is that constitutions derived from the US army, and continue to do so. Thus, for example, the EU from time to time grants itself ever more power, and no one makes a fuss, though it does not seem to have any legal or ideological basis. I keep expecting the EU to softly and silently vanish away, but so far this has not happened. The EU exists by the power of the US State Department.

## On Formalism

### 2013-05-26 10:01:03

Radish has classified me as a formalist[55], presumably on the basis that I think that the government should actually be in charge of the public service and the top universities, and that professors and senior public servants should be fireable for any reason and no reason, and should do as they are told.

Further, that ones that profile as unlikely to do as they are told, which most of them, for example everyone in the State Department, Justice Department, and the Environmental Protection Agency, should be fired en masse. Further, I think that when the government passes a budget that money be spent for some purpose, this should actually cause the money to be spent to that purpose, and if it declines to allocate money to some purpose, government money should cease to be spent on that purpose, that writing and passing a budget should be an exercise of real power, with some people being funded and others defunded, rather than a tedious boring ritual resembling the Queen opening the houses of parliament.

But I don't go all the way with Moldbuggian formalism. Moldbug believes that governments are real, that they are naturally all powerful, that the US Government really owns the US.

Moldbug's theory that the official description of the government should correspond to the actual reality of government.

But I think that the USG is rather like the Divine Right of Kings, a fiction that everyone pretends to believe, for fear of what would be revealed were it to vanish away - that anarchy is the natural state, and not necessarily the orderly anarchy proposed by anarcho capitalists, that the state exists only in that enough people imagine it exists, that the state, like fiat currency, is a bubble.

---

[55]https://radishmag.wordpress.com/2013/05/24/volume-2-issue-8-heroes-of-the-dark-enlightenment/

Moldbug's formalism would acknowledge the reality that our elected officials are powerless muppets of no great consequence. But would formalism reveal that anyone in the government has actual power?

I think that the formal description of the state can never correspond to reality, because if it did, the state would softly and silently vanish away. The state lives in its myths. It is stories that we tell each other. Strip away the myths, you are likely to have no state at all.

The Formalist position is that the US Government owns the US, so we should figure out who owns the US government, give them shares of stock or whatever, and proceed with business.

Since the US Government has overpromised its obligations to various interest groups, the formalist position is that we should probably hold a bankruptcy procedure, in which everyone who is owed something gets some shares in place of that possibly unfulfillable obligation. So, for example, in place of your social security, you get a small number of shares. In place of your tenure at Harvard, you get a rather larger number of shares, but the president is now empowered to fire you. (We abandon the ludicrous pretense that Harvard, the NGOs, and the US Government are separate entities) In place of your senior position in the public service you get a considerable number of shares, but definitely get fired and replaced by someone who, unlike you, will do what he is told, something that public servants have no background, experience, or training in doing.

If you are a senior public servant, a formalist reorganization means that you lose your ill defined power to make policy and grant special favors to interest groups, and in its place, get shares of ownership of US Government incorporated, a corporation run from the top down in a rational manner, where the organization chart reflects reality.

Well I don't think the US Government owns the US, or that the US is kind of thing that is all that easy to own, or that the US government is a kind of thing that can easily be owned.

If we had a formalist reorganization of the US government, I don't think it would stick. The US Government would, like the former Soviet Union, softly and silently melt away. People would see right through it, and it just would not be there any more.

Some people who were powerful in the previous government would grab stuff, some would not, some organized criminals would grab stuff, some big corporations would grab stuff, and some people who were smart and lucky would grab stuff. Chances are that some sort of replacement state would re-emerge from the chaos, with some new faces, some old faces, and a lot of old faces no longer to be seen, but the final outcome would not much resemble the orderly liquidation envisaged by Moldbug's formalism.

## Who speaks for reaction

**2013-05-30 06:46:42**

In the reactivity place, one of the commenters asks:

> Who speaks for reaction?

To which the host replies:

Nature... or Nature's God... or both[56]

In other words, the unifying factor among reactionaries of all diverse kinds is The Dark Enlightenment[57].

# Debate with Vox Day: Evolution by natural selection
## 2013-06-01 04:37:01

We have been discussing on what the various kinds of reactionary agree. We agree on reality and agree that reality is important. I also agree with Vox Day[58] about Scalzi[59], who exemplifies the progressive tendency to cut the balls off male progressives. John Scalzi is exhibit A for Heartiste's position that any man who is a man should reject the entire progressive political movement, including and especially the early nineteenth century emancipation of women, which led to the English 1857 Matrimonial Causes act legally privileging wives above their husbands.

So let us see if we can discuss what we disagree on and remain courteous and continue to respect each other.

OK:


## Evolution by natural selection

Well, it is obvious: Darwin 101. Creatures of the same species nonetheless vary, even though of the same species. Variation is substantially inherited. Some variants will survive better than others, thus, creatures evolve. We can in fact measure small changes over the period of human history, and for small very fast breeding creatures, such as microbes, large changes.

Over ages vast and long, vastly longer than the human mind can comprehend, small changes will necessarily become large changes, just as mountains rise and fall in movements almost imperceptibly small.

To say that natural selection cannot turn one kind into an entirely different kind, is like saying that the rain and wind cannot turn a mountain into a valley.

This has important implications for humans: We are risen killer apes. Thus, naturally fierce. We evolved to cooperate better than the competition, but the major purpose of that cooperation was to put a hatchet in heads of the competition. We are naturally inclined to friendship, loyalty, courage, kindness, and reciprocity, the better to destroy outsiders.

Among the implications of Evolution by Natural Selection:

Utilitarianism, caring for distant strangers, is absolutely not in our nature. There are no utilitarians. Show me the man who would experiment on children to end malaria, and I will show you the man who will experiment on children and entirely forget he was planning to end malaria.

---

[56]https://nickbsteves.wordpress.com/2013/05/29/going-meta-on-meta/
[57]https://blog.reaction.la/tag/the-dark-enlightenment "The Dark Enlightenment"
[58]https://voxday.blogspot.ca/
[59]https://blog.reaction.la/tag/scalzi

We have an obligation not to harm distant strangers, because our moral sense evolved to keep us out of trouble, to avoid unnecessary war, but we don't care for them, we have evolved to be efficient in destroying them should they seriously get in our way, and anyone who says he does care, is lying, and, if lying, probably intends to harm those close to him. Whosoever claims to be utilitarian is lying, if lying, up to no good, if up to no good, evil.

Thus, from natural selection, we may conclude that so called heterosexual aids in Africa is actually progressive aids, spread by medical clinics funded by foreign aid - since "heterosexual" aids in Africa suits the agenda of those funding it. They did not consciously intend to spread aids, but when they found that they were, that they quite conveniently were, were in no hurry to address the problem of needle re-use by internationally funded clinics in Africa. We can predict that, and on examination, we observe, what natural selection predicts. "Heterosexual" aids in Africa occurs predominantly and overwhelmingly amongst those Africans who attend clinics funded by far away do-gooding strangers.

This outcome, progressive aids, is an outcome predictable from a moral sense that evolved, rather than was given to us by God in an Apple. If we got our moral sense from God via a tree in the Garden, one would see a bit more concern among progressives about progressive aids. If, on the other hand, we are risen killer apes, we are unlikely to have risen very far in our treatment of distant strangers.

## Moldbug's Liquidation

### 2013-06-02 08:53:23

Moldbugs liquidation would be a Pareto improvement on the present government. Large numbers of people would be made better off, and no one would be made worse off.

Once upon a time there was a man who was infested with parasites, that were gnawing his flesh and relieving themselves in his blood. The man said to the parasites:

> Why don't you come out of me, and I will serve you a wonderful four course meal with wine and cheese, and we will all be better off and no one will be worse off. It will be a Pareto improvement.

To which the parasites replied:

> The moment we come out, you will wrap us up in newspaper, and cast us onto the fire.

Government is insane, destructive, and self destructive in large part because power has been distributed amongst the winners in millions of tiny little bite sized morsels. This leads to the tragedy of the commons, not exactly the mobile bandit problem but similar. So Moldbug's plan is to make the government into a rational organization that is run in reality the same way it is supposedly run (formalism) and distribute shares in this government among all the existing beneficiaries of government, to compensate them for the fact that they will no longer be receiving benefits in the convoluted and corrupt way that they used to receive benefits.

Now, what share do we allocate to a consultant for obtaining approvals for land development that might theoretically adversely effect sites of potential archaeological interest?

Someone wishing to develop land has to show umpteen bureaucracies that it would not adversely affect umpteen things, some of them remarkably obscure and improbable.

To get such approval, you hire a consultant. The bureaucrat lets a lawyer know which consultants have the magic power to persuade the bureaucrat, so you consult with the lawyer, and pay a lot of money to the consultant, and lo and behold, the bureaucrat is, surprise surprise, persuaded.

Obviously how big a share we allocate to the consultant and how big a share to the bureaucrat depends on how much of the consultancy fee the consultant is passing under the table to the bureaucrat.

But, supposing this is sorted out, the bureaucrat gets his share, in compensation for the fact that he used to be fireproof, and is now no longer fireproof.

And, no longer being fireproof, is instantly fired, because his entire department's activities are corrupt, crazy, and stupid, leaving his pet consultants similarly unemployed.

And after the firing, it rapidly becomes apparent to everyone that he and his department's activities were corrupt, crazy, and stupid.

Where upon, it is apparent that his share is a payoff for no longer doing the harm he used to be doing.

Light the fire.

## Preparing for Civil War Two

### 2013-06-05 15:47:11

Many reactionaries compare today's America to the latter days of the Roman Republic, reflect on the excellence of the early Roman empire, and hope for a military coup that ends the corrupt and decadent American republic, replacing it with disciplined imperium.

The reigns of the five good Roman emperors illustrate that the reign of stationary bandit, an absolute dictator secure in his power, fearing neither votes nor coups nor riot nor military insurrection, is a pretty good system. He has an incentive to shear the sheep, but not flay them, while other forms of government tend to flaying. Observe that taxes on the rich are everywhere far above the Laffer limit, and in many places, such as Greece, taxes on the working poor are far above the Laffer limit.

Unfortunately such a tranquil transition seems improbable, for every officer above company grade in the US army is selected not only for political correctness, but, more importantly, for lack of military competence. The Cathedral fears losing a war with the US military far more than it fears the US military losing a war with some external enemy. A successful coup requires a leader who commands a reasonable level of respect from the junior officers. Being such a potential coup maker absolutely disqualifies officers for promotion above company grade.

Nor could the US military provide order after such a transition, for order requires legitimacy, and such a tranquil transition would leave the new imperator illegitimate. Coercive power is insufficient to enable a government to govern.

Further, the five good Roman emperors did not stroll calmly into power on the basis of the unchallengeable coercive power and perfect discipline of the famed Roman legions. The five good emperors arose out of a long succession of bloody Roman civil wars from Sulla to Antony, ending with Augustus becoming emperor by murdering his step brother Caesarion, the child of the two greatest people of the age – thereby ending the chance of Rome becoming a hereditary monarchy. The five good emperors preserved the illusion of the Republic, from which they derived a large part of their legitimacy. Most of their legitimacy, however, came from the fact that people were tired of the civil wars, so everyone was willing to pretend that they were legitimate, willing to pretend that the Republic was still in effect.

## Arming for Civil War Two

Bob Owens tells us[60] that since 2009 private citizens have purchased enough new firearms to equip every member of the military of the United States, including National Guard, Air National Guard, and Reserve units eighteen times over. Of those arms purchased, the overwhelming majority are not sporting arms, but weapons intended for war, revolution, and riot.

Private citizens have purchased more ammo since 2009 than the US used in World War II.

To defend against home invasion and mugging, the appropriate weapon is a short arm with a large magazine, a nine shot handgun. (A shotgun is of limited value unless you are hunting birds, though racking a shotgun makes a wonderfully intimidating sound.) For hunting and target practice, the appropriate weapon is a long arm with small magazine.Instead, people are buying military rifles and civilian versions of military rifles, long arms with large magazines.

The most popular ammo is the 22LR. Demand for the 22LR may well be partially monetary. Being useful in a wide variety of guns, it would be valuable as money in the event of crisis, perhaps more universally acceptable than gold.

If the government was united and cohesive, there would be no possibility that armed American citizens could stand against it, since each individual one at a time, would feel the full wrath of the entire state. But the reason we are getting such bad government is that the government is not united and cohesive. The Cathedral is not one person, or even a single conspiracy, but rather a multitude of conspiracies each seeking to be lefter than all of the others.

## Likely shape of a Civil War Two crisis.

Let us imagine a crisis where the US government has no money, or far too much entirely worthless money. In that case, likely that the overclass/underclass alliance will predate directly upon the middle class and survivalists, as they did in the aftermath of Hurricane

---

[60]https://pjmedia.com/blog/barack-obama-worlds-greatest-gun-salesman/

Katrina. According to Peter[61] government teams sent in to rescue people tended to attack, kidnap, and rob those that had made good survival preparations. The unprepared tended to attack the prepared. The word "unprepared" is euphemism. What he really means is that blacks, government employees, and underclass, mostly blacks and government employees, predated upon the middle class.

> rescue authorities seem to regard with suspicion those who've made provision for their safety and have survived (or bugged out) in good shape. It seems to be a combination of "How could you cope when so many others haven't?", "You must have taken advantage of others to be so well off", and "We've come all this way to help, so how dare you not need our assistance?"

The political overclass/underclass alliance manifested in Katrina as direct violent predation on middle class and survivalists. Probably they would respond to a man made crisis in a similar fashion.

Left singularities do not always have really bad economic effects, though the Cambodian autogenocide and the French Maximum did have really bad economic effects. An economic crisis depriving the overclass of funds would likely trigger Civil War Two.

If tax systems supporting the overclass and underclass collapse, as well they might, (US currency hyperinflates, everyone uses gold, bitcoin, or one of bitcoin's successors) we may well see the overclass/underclass alliance that attempts to loot the middle class directly.

That is not necessarily the most likely outcome, the approach to the left singularity is inherently unpredictable, but it is certainly possible, and it is reasonable for people to prepare for it.

## Civil War and post civil war institutions

In such case the correct response is coalition building between the prepared, between those willing to respect property. Assume that the overclass and underclass members will in practice not back each other up, that the underclass begins with no cohesion, and overclass will find what little cohesion it does have collapsing. People who respect property rights will find it easier to cooperate.

The worst case outcome, the highly likely outcome is something like post-Roman civilization - centuries of poverty and ruin, with marginally better organized and less devolved outsiders occasionally wandering through, killing all the men, burning all the homes, and raping all the women.

To build order, to avoid the worst case outcome in Civil War Two, have to build upon the armed middle class head of household. Order and authority has to come from armed individuals who support private property, which is likely to mean rentacops and heads of households. If property owning heads of households come out on top, we are likely to get at best anarcho-capitalism, at worst Blackwater neo-feudalism. If the overclass/underclass alliance comes out on top, then either anarcho-piratism, as after the fall of the Roman

---

[61]https://bayourenaissanceman.blogspot.com.au/2008/08/lessons-learned-from-hurricanes-katrina.html

Empire in the West, or else the left singularity continues to the next crisis, whatever that may be.

The difference between anarcho capitalism and feudalism is a matter of degree. Since all law in anarcho capitalism is private law, people are necessarily unequal before the law. Feudalism, anarcho capitalism, and anarcho-piratism are decentralized systems in which coercion and coercive authority is privatized, legal authority is a form of private property, and much law is private law.

Feudalism arguably works a lot better with a strong King to make sure that feudal property rights stick, but where do we get a strong King from? There is no Ring of Fnargl. At best, will get a Godfather, a coalition leader. At worst, weak or absent private property rights will result in the new nobility becoming mobile bandits, as in the fall of the Roman Empire in the west.

Order requires legitimacy. The shortcut to legitimacy is to pretend the old republic is still in effect. For feudalism or anarcho-capitalism, such a pretense would involve a radical reduction in the franchise.

In the early Roman monarchy, before the Roman Republic, the king was elected for life by the Senate, the People, and the Gods– who tended to display such remarkable unanimity that we can be pretty sure the election was fixed in advance in a small room. In our current system, we get a genuine choice between a Democrat candidate acceptable to the Cathedral, and a Republican Candidate acceptable to Cathedral. Unfortunately the only Republican candidate acceptable to the Cathedral is whichever Republican recently conspicuously and dramatically collaborated in legislation moving our society substantially further left. Thus, for example, McCain collaborated in McCain Feingold, and Romney produced ObamaRomneycare. The next republican presidential candidate will probably be whoever further opens the borders and helps import a left voting welfare underclass from Mexico – the Rubio Amnesty Bill, or whatever it is going to be called.

I recommend that whatever actual system we wind up with after Civil War Two, we keep the form of the Republic and switch to elections on the model of the early Roman Monarchy. The electoral college provides a good mechanism for this, and was probably originally intended for that purpose.

## Moral Progress

### 2013-06-12 08:18:12

At one of the main supposedly libertarian sites on the internet, where, every few days, they pimp for mass migration of the Latin American underclass to come to the US to live on welfare and crime, and vote Democrat, they recently preened themselves on the wonderful moral progress we have made since the horrible evil bad old days[62].

Fosetti cut them a new anal orifice[63].

Every decade or so, we are required to hate the enslavement of blacks by white Southerners twice as much as we did last decade, while the vastly larger, more brutal, and more

---

[62]https://marginalrevolution.com/marginalrevolution/2013/06/how-depressing-is-the-moral-regression-of-syria.html? "Cheap Chalupas"
[63]https://foseti.wordpress.com/2013/06/11/moral-progress/ "moral progress"

recent use of slavery by the communist nations politely vanishes down the memory hole.

Observe that Tyler Cowan is terribly worried about the horrible horrible brutality of the Syrian government, even though the Syrian government is not doing anything the US government would not do were one of the US states to declare independence or be taken over by militias. However Tyler Cowan, and our government, was entirely unworried that a government in the Congo that they armed and funded, and continue to arm and fund, put down a revolt of Tutsis with mass state sponsored rape and by vaginally impaling Tutsi women with very large objects. Observe that when these crimes in the Congo are reported, they are reported in the same pious way that car burnings are reported, wherein unidentified people set fire to the cars of other unidentified people. If anyone is blamed, it is "warlords" for creating the conditions that led to these events, "warlords" being the rebels themselves – in other words the Tutsis in the Congo had it coming to them for rebelling.

If it was Tutsis doing it to Hutus, let alone whites doing it to blacks, the outrage would be wholly apocalyptic. And if the Cathedral reacts this way to state sponsored mass rape and sexual mutilation of Tutsis, how would they react if the victims were white? Well, we don't need to speculate, because this was pretty much the way that whites have been ethnically cleansed from rural parts of South Africa.

The state of the Congo, the state of South Africa, the increasingly totalitarian character of the US government, all look like moral regress to me.

And I would say that moral regress set in with the Victorians, who at the same time as they were busy bowdlerizing literature and congratulating each other on how the culture supported chastity, removed the punitive consequences for female sexual immorality, and the restrictions that denied women the opportunity to engage in sexual immorality, and it has been ever escalating hypocrisy since then.

## Bitcoin scaling problems

2013-06-14 09:35:11

When bitcoin was first proposed, I argued that the proposed algorithm failed to scale.

Well, when getting started, scaling does not matter. Now, however, a bitcoin wallet is starting to cost substantial bandwidth and processing power. There are plans to address this, but I am underwhelmed by those plans. The proposed plans will make bitcoin more centralized, and will still have scaling issues.

Seems to me that we need an algorithm where no one computer needs to keep a copy of all transactions, or even a complete listing of who owns what coins, so as to maintain scaling all the way to operating all of the world's transactions, and full decentralization both.

Gold also has problems, in that transporting gold from one place to another is slow and risky. Easier to leave the gold in one place, and transfer ownership. This, however tempts the proprietor of that place to misconduct (fractional reserve and term transformation) and exposes the proprietor to attack. So the most trusted proprietor winds up being the most powerful state, which is to say, the USG. Banks around the world leave their gold with Fort Knox the New York Fed, and simply move ownership of it. And that state then steals the gold. Banks that are owed gold by the USG have been asking for their gold back, asking for physical gold, and not getting it.

I recommend a system in which the private key that is the rightful owner of a bitcoin possesses data showing that he rightly acquired bitcoins from someone that was previously acknowledged as the rightful owner of those bitcoins by a previous leading hash of the state of bitcoin ownership, and a hash chain showing that his rightful ownership is acknowledged in the current leading hash of the state of bitcoin ownership, but not very many other people possess that data, not everyone in the system possesses that data, so not everyone in the system has to download that data and check it for internal consistency. When he spends the bitcoins, he proves ownership by showing that his ownership is in the most recent hash - but the recipient's wallet would not have that information until supplied. This sounds easy, but the tricky bit doing it without risk of the network splitting into inconsistent states.

Instead of this, the proposed scaling fix for bitcoin is a very large blocksize, which would mean that only a small number of big wealthy institutions are full participants in the system – which brings us back to the problems we have been having with gold and fiat money.

## Speaking truth to power

2013-06-15 13:16:17

The big lie is not equality. The big lie is not that women are naturally virtuous. The big lie is not that gays want monogamous marriage. The big lie is not the magic negro.

The big lie is that the Cathedral is holy. Every item of propaganda issued by every Cathedral spokesman has the subtext "I am holier than thou", and it is this subtext has to be attacked in the same utterly venomous and fearless manner that Jesus attacked it.

If when Cromwell's puritans desacralized marriage, the cavaliers said that puritan pastors were planning to bang the wives of their congregation, we might not have been in this hole. Instead, everyone seriously and earnestly debated the issue marriage as a sacrament, as if the Puritans gave a tinkers dam.

If when the successors of Cromwell's puritans, the dissenters, in order to supposedly "rescue fallen women", proceeded to eliminate all the unpleasant social, legal, and economic consequences of being fallen, reactionaries had forthrightly accused them of abusing fallen women, we might not be in this hole. Instead, we let them demonstrate their superior chastity by covering up women's ankles and bowdlerizing Shakespeare, while banging those sluts.

When progressives, still at that time pretending to be Christians, defined temperance as absolute no alcohol, leading to prohibition, we should have noticed that they were claiming to be holier than Jesus and the apostles, a claim they had already made in relation to slavery and female emancipation, and ridiculed them accordingly. We did not.

When Obamacare was introduced, the AMA piously approved prolonged deep sedation for the very ill – a course of treatment that is invariably fatal, usually within a few days, even when given to the young and healthy. The plan is to murder old people so as to make available medical resources for free abortion and free sex changes. Nobody mentioned this. Perhaps they felt it was improper to cast doubt upon the good and proper motives of the cathedral.

Deep sedation is never given as assisted suicide. Assisted suicide is a fentanyl clicker. Oops, says the doctor, the patient clicked a little too hard, and the death is piously ruled death by accidental self administered overdose. Maybe it was. Prolonged deep sedation on the other hand is always given without the consent of the patient. It is murder, the most direct possible violation of the Hippocratic oath.

This medical program is a continuation of the original project of Cromwell's Puritans, more sex for the highest status males, and to hell with society and civilization. Most progressive projects somehow wind up getting more sex for those males highest in the Cathedral, sometimes indirectly by increasing their status relative to the rest of us, but usually directly by directly encouraging hypergamy. For example war on Christmas, which started with Cromwell's puritans and continues to this day, is part of the war on the family. While other tactics come and go, that one has been around from the beginning.

The latest Cathedral project, now that they have finished destroying the health system, is to open the borders and register the flood of underclass mestizos from Mexico to vote for more welfare. When justifying this project, the Cathedral spokesman will inevitably use language that implies or explicitly says that these migrants are coming here for jobs.

Cathedral subtext:

> "Oh, you evil person. I care about the welfare of far away strangers, I care about people different from myself, but you, cruel selfish man, do not"

But there is another subtext, which needs to be made explicit:

> "Hah hah hah. I, unlike you, can afford to live in the bubble where the only mestizos I see have jobs as maids and gardeners, unlike you who get to experience the vibrancy of underclass mestizos who have absolutely no interest in getting jobs, who live on crime and the welfare payments their numerous girlfriends get for their numerous anchor babies. If you are ethnically cleansed by them and need a place to live, you are going to have to bid up the price of property in my bubble to even higher than it is already, which will enable me to hire even more mestizo maids. Sucks to be you, does it not?."

When we argue, we always argue from our own self interest. Thus, for example, Sunshine Mary does not say that a woman should submit to her husband because it is good for men, or because the will of God favors men. She says that women need to submit because a woman is the weaker vessel, and needs male authority to protect herself from herself, and because it is hot, and because a woman's fulfillment is in her husband and her family, and submission gives her a good husband and a good family. The Cathedral always claims to care deeply about the good of other people, the good of far away strangers, and that claim is always a lie. The Cathedral always brutally pursues the immediate short term gratification of the higher males of the Cathedral, without any regard for collateral damage.

Progressives did not care about slavery. Observe their total lack of interest in enslavement of whites by Muslims. They cared about subjugating the South. They still don't care about slavery. Observe their total lack of interest in the use of slavery by Marxist states.

## Always betraying, and always betrayed

### 2013-06-19 07:29:34

Observe that the Tea Party is on the brink of its first great achievement: Population replacement of whites by a voting majority of mestizos on welfare.[64] (The two thousand page amnesty law, which we have to pass to learn what is in it, is being written by two Democratic Party immigration lawyers, and the usual government employees).

The psychological mechanism underlying this is that the overwhelming majority of politically active people are unwilling to speak or think ill of those to the left of them, perhaps because the left rules, and have no hesitation in demonizing of anyone to the right of them, perhaps because the right is powerless and afraid. Or perhaps it would be more accurate to say the non left, since no one wants to identify as right, and because there a thousand rights and only one left. The left is a thousand points of doctrine every single one of which must be affirmed, while whosoever disagrees on any one of these thousand points is deemed right wing, and deemed evil and hateful, not merely by the left, but by anyone less right wing than himself, and indeed by anyone who disagrees with the left on a different point of doctrine.

He who is subject to this mechanism, which is most of those in politics, has no friends to the right, no enemies to the left, which means all his friends are his enemies, and all his enemies are his friends, which means that he is always betraying, and always betrayed.

See for example Bryan Caplan vomiting the most extraordinarily hateful bile, as if possessed by demons, at those who oppose the importation of mass of low IQ voters to live on welfare and crime, and at those who think that fatherless children are prone to moral defects. But he would never dream of drawing the glaringly obvious conclusions from the "10:10 no pressure video", that those who composed it are monsters, or notice massive and systematic fraud and conspiracy revealed by the Climategate files.

Whosoever argues that those to the left of him are merely mistaken, not malicious, despite many cases where malice is obvious, will argue that those to the right of him are malicious, even when honesty and decency is obvious, thus no enemies to the left, no friends to the right, thus all his friends are his enemies, thus always betraying and always betrayed, thus utterly untrustworthy. Any organization that contains such people will be destroyed from within. If you give such a person any power within the group, he will conspire with that groups enemies and commit fraud, theft, and violence.

Thus, for example, in the American Revolution, the British general Lord Howe not merely supplied Washington with gunpowder, but arranged for his men to die, in order to advantage Washington. ( See Sydney George Fisher's True History of the American

---

[64]https://foseti.wordpress.com/2013/06/18/the-tea-party-gets-pwned/

Revolution[65].) He deliberately caused the deaths of those near to him to advantage those far from him, the classic alliance with far against near so characteristic of leftism.

Quite simply: Unreasonable willingness to trust the powerful is a very reliable indication that someone is dangerously untrustworthy. So someone who supposedly agrees with you 99%, for example Bryan Caplan, except that he says that Obama is mistaken while he fails to notice that Obama hates America, Americans, and whites in particular, will stab you in the back, like Lord Howe, whereas someone who disagrees with you 100%, who thinks that Obama is the lightworker will merely stab you in the front.

We don't need ideological purity. We do, however, need to be pure from those who grovel to power. Any organization that contains such people will move left, as the Tea Party did, regardless of what ideology they purport to have. If someone cannot read fraud and conspiracy in the climategate files, cannot read hatred of America and whites in Obama's history, cannot see monsters in those authoring public education videos such as "10:10 No Pressure", he can be relied upon to knife you in the back.

If your comrade cannot see evil, because power obscures his vision, then when you expect him to stand with you against power, he will stab you in the back.

## Economic efficiency of slavery

2013-06-22 13:16:32

For tasks requiring intelligence and independent judgement, for the kind of job where one would ordinarily employ a contractor or high level free employee, slave owners generally gave one of their best slaves an incentive environment approximating that of a high level free employee, where the slave had a future career path, the opportunity to save and invest, to own money and buy assets, including buying other slaves, indicating that slavery does not work to get such tasks done– hence the failure of the Soviet Union.

However for many tasks, tasks suitable to stupid people, tasks for bad people, tasks where you want people to reliably do as they are told rather than make good decisions, the sort of tasks that most black people are suitable for, slavery was markedly more productive and efficient than free labor, with the slave producing more value for himself and his owner with less labor, than he did when freed.

When the slaves were freed, they became for the most part, considerably worse off economically, having to work harder and getting less to eat[66].

My! dem was good ol' days.[67]

...

Twarn't long atter dat dey tell us we'se free. But lawdy, Cap'n, we ain't nebber been what I calls free. 'Cose ole marster didn' own us no mo', an' all de folks soon scatter all ober, but iffen dey all lak me day still hafter wuk jes'

---

[65] https://books.google.com/books?id=SZccAAAAMAAJ&printsec=toc&source=gbs_summary_r&cad=0

[66] https://xroads.virginia.edu/%7Ehyper/wpa/index.html

[67] https://xroads.virginia.edu/%7Ehyper/wpa/anderso1.html

as hard, an some times hab less dan we useter hab when we stay on Marster John's plantation[68].

...

Freedom is all right, but de niggers was better off befo' surrender, kaze den dey was looked after an' dey didn' get in no trouble fightin' an' killin' like dey do dese days. If a nigger cut up an' got sassy in slavery times, his Ole Marse give him a good whippin' an' he went way back an' set down an' 'haved hese'f.If he was sick, Marse an' Mistis looked after him, an' if he needed store medicine, it was bought an' give to him; he didn' have to pay nothin'. Dey didn' even have to think 'bout clothes nor nothin' like dat, dey was wove an' made an' give to dem. Maybe everybody's Marse and Mistis wuzn' good as Marse George and Mis' Betsy, but dey was de same as a mammy an' pappy to us niggers.

Source: *American Slave: North Carolina Narratives* 14 [69]: 284-290.

Economists find this outcome most strange, but there is no mystery to it. When stupid people, prone to short time horizons, get to make their own decisions for themselves, they are apt to make stupid decisions.

A slave maid could not steal the silverware, because she could not own anything. An employed maid could steal the silverware, and probably would, and would be the worse off for it. An employed maid might well beat the baby with stick as thick as her arm because her mistress spoke sharply to her. A slave maid would not, because her mistress could do worse.

If masters and slaves were better off than employers and employees, an economist would ask, why could they not just cut a deal to do what they previously did, only without chains and beatings, do the same tasks in the same way, only as employees?

The answer to that question is: that the former slaves, once freed, could not credibly commit to stick to such a deal, and generally did not stick to such a deal, thus economically worse off. Stupid people, prone to violence, with short time horizons, needed masters.

## Selecting for stupid

2013-06-24 10:07:28

Before Google became a huge success, it tried to select for the smartest people, in so far as it was legally possible to do. It then became a huge success.

Today, Google's chief human resources officer tells us selecting for smart does not work, so Google does not do it any more[70]. (Hat tip, Lion of the Blogosphere[71])

What do you think is more likely: That selecting for smart does not work, or that it gives politically incorrect results?

---

[68] https://xroads.virginia.edu/%7Ehyper/wpa/callowa1.html

[69] 1

[70] https://www.nytimes.com/2013/06/20/business/in-head-hunting-big-data-may-not-be-such-a-big-deal.html

[71] https://lionoftheblogosphere.wordpress.com/2013/06/23/interview-with-googles-senior-hr-guy/

This looks like the same phenomenon as elite educational institutions furtively or openly blowing off the LSAT, and contenting themselves with an intake that is low on the LSAT. Google says smarts are not useful, colleges are finding the results of LSAT inconvenient.

## On ripple

### 2013-06-28 16:55:09

Ripple[72] is a scam cryptocurrency. Pity, since the alleged design is more scalable than bitcoin.

A cryptocurrency is mainly worth its speculative value, worth the possibility it could replace the US. Obviously Ripple is not going to replace the US, being a wholly controlled muppet of Cathedral minions.

If Ripple was funded by Baidu rather than Google, I would be on it like a tomcat on a pussy in heat.

Ripple is backed by Google, which means it has all the money it needs to get the software written right, and do all the things it has been promising to do. But if it did all the things it has been promising to do, the Cathedral would be mighty pissed, and Google is entirely subservient to the Cathedral.

The way Ripple is supposed to work is that there should be no one central authority that sets, and changes, the rules, and issues more money at will. No one person or small group should be able to change the rules, because if they do, their software will generate a different root hash to the other person's software and they will not be able to transact with the other person's software. Unfortunately, ripple.com controls the software, and can change the code on all users at will, without most users knowing about the update, or being able to easily prevent the update, making it effectively a centralized currency under the control of an entity wholly subservient to the USG, like Paypal.

The alleged design is nice, but I have absolutely no confidence that the implementation reflects the alleged design. And if it does reflect the design today, that could be abruptly changed on you tomorrow.

I prefer the alleged Ripple design to Bitcoin, but we need an implementation where updates require user initiative, rather than being automagically rolled out, where some substantial number of users themselves compile their money client from source, and where the major transacting entities are physically located in places somewhat resistant to USG power - where the major holders of the currency, major performers of transactions, and major software developers are serious about destroying US hegemony and causing the collapse of the US$ and, if possible, the USG with the US$, and intend to get rich by doing so.

A cryptocurrency is only worth the probability that it could replace the US$, times ten trillion dollars or so, divided by the number of cryptocurrency units. And that probability depends on having a revolutionary as lead developer, and other revolutionaries as leading entrepreneurs.

---

[72]https://ripple.com

## The left devour their own

### 2013-06-29 14:49:04

In the latest re-run of Racefail09[73], Barry Malzberg and Mike Resnick are being demonized for insufficient leftism – primarily Barry Malzberg[74], previously a leading leftist of Science Fiction, who, in his younger days, was substantially influential in imposing the then new and rigidly boring political orthodoxy on science fiction and fantasy. Now in their seventies, they failed to quite keep up with the latest orthodoxy, falling two or three years behind the latest feminist line. Or rather they were in their seventies. They are now, like Winston Smith at the end of "1984", pre-dead.

In my post Always Betraying and Always Betrayed[75] I point out how the conservative movement is always destroyed from within by betrayal, but leftists suffer more from this than anyone. The conservative movement is destroyed, the leftist movement is strengthened, but leftists personally and individually are destroyed. You know how the arch villain drops one of his loyal minions into the piranha tank, and all the other minions are inspired to be twice as loyal? That is leftism. When Aristide personally with his own hand gouged out the eyes of one his loyal minions, his non political minions joined the revolution against him, but his politically sincere minions were inspired to be twice as loyal and twice as sincere. Similarly Stalin, though Stalin, unlike Trotsky, was not so crass as to get his own hands covered with the disgusting body fluids of his fellow leftists, instead having his minions torture each other.

But I get away with stuff, Neill Blomkamp, the writer/director of District 9, gets away with stuff. From the trailer of his movie Elysium, it looks like waves of subhuman illegal immigrants overwhelm the remaining nice, technologically advanced parts of earth, turning the city of tomorrow into a third world garbage heap and forcing the elites to flee into space. Hard to tell from the trailer, but just as "District 9" was about the end of white rule (the prawns, metaphor for the blacks, were abandoned by their betters to fester in their own filth), looks like "Elysium" is about illegal immigration.

The further you are from the left, the less likely you are to be mau maued for insufficient leftism. Real reactionaries, like Neill Blomkamp, are doing fine, while Barry Malzberg, one of the architects of the reinvention of science fiction and fantasy as a repetitious megaphone screaming trite propaganda with the volume turned up hard, is pre-dead.

## Racism explained

### 2013-06-30 12:50:35

Yet another excellent post by Radish.[76]

All whites are racist. Only whites can be racist. Therefore all whites need to be attacked and beaten up – starting of course, with someone like a small woman who cannot

---

[73] https://blog.reaction.la/tag/racefail-09

[74] https://www.bing.com/search?q=Barry+Malzberg+sexist

[75] https://blog.reaction.la/culture/always-betraying-and-always-betrayed.html "Always betraying, and always betrayed"

[76] https://radishmag.wordpress.com/2013/06/28/volume-3-issue-1-no-reason/

and will not fight back.

This post categorized under culture rather than politics, because politics implies that there is some conflict and disagreement on the issue, whereas culture refers to universally shared and accepted values.

## The real charge against Zimmerman

2013-07-01 09:37:27

Supposedly, the state's theory is that Zimmerman followed Trayvon, jumped him, beat him up, then shot him.

Of course no one believes this. When the prosecution questions prosecution witnesses, they make no attempt to support their supposed theory. Every prosecution witness bar one, while being questioned by the prosecution, has shot down that purported theory one way or another. It is clear from the prosecution witnesses while being questioned by the prosecution, even Trayvon's girlfriend, that Trayvon jumped Zimmerman from the shadows and beat him up, motivated in part or whole by racial hatred. Rather, what the prosecution does attempt to argue, by the questions that it puts to its witnesses, is that Zimmerman was not hurt all that much, that he should have just put up with being beaten and mugged, that he should have just sucked it up.

Obviously, were the situation reversed, no one would suggest that a black man should just suck it up. Were the situation reversed, that a dead white assailant was in part or whole motivated by racial hostility would have been reported in headlines the size of tombstones.

The basic issue here, the real, though unspoken, prosecution claim, is that blacks are entitled to attack white people without being resisted by lethal force, even though no one would propose the converse. It is that simple.

## GDP and lies

2013-07-01 17:58:17

When a government moves left, it damages the economy. When it moves left far enough and fast enough, this becomes embarrassing, so it lies about the economy. North Korea, Cuba, and Argentina are infamous examples of this, the Soviet Union used to be an infamous example. Lately the USA has been understating inflation and overstating real GDP growth. How far out of contact with reality have things gone?

CIA World Factbook for USA GDP (purchasing power parity): $15.66 trillion (2012 est.)

CIA World fact book for China: GDP (purchasing power parity): $12.38 trillion (2012 est.)

But it is obvious that in reality Chinese real GDP is about ten or fifteen percent greater than the USA, even though China also has been overstating its growth. Chinese GDP per head is still substantially lower than the USA, but total GDP is higher, in that Chinese in total buy more cars, more computers, more internet, more of just about everything.

Therefore, the US is overstating its real GDP by around twenty five percent, thirty five percent, or so, the cumulative effect of overstating growth by one or two percent every year for many years.

If we suppose that the books have been cooked uniformly since 1980, and that China has been entirely truthful about its growth, then the US has been overstating its growth by around one percent per year.

My gut feeling is that the cooking of the books has been markedly more severe since 2005-2006, that the discrepancy has been much more severe and obvious since then, in which case growth has recently been overstated by several percent, and the US is in economic decline. This is consistent with the reduction in cars per head, meat per head, and electricity per head. Americans are simply getting poorer.

Now one might suppose that while the median American is getting poorer, this is compensated by some Americans getting richer, and there is some truth in this. While the number of cars per head is falling, the number of private jets per head is rising. However, the large GDP discrepancy suggests absolute decline, that the US, as a whole, simply cannot afford what it used to be able to afford – such as a money losing empire.

## Marriage, supply and demand

### 2013-07-02 04:43:42

The old deal, legally enforced before 1857, and socially enforced before 1960, was that a man got:
1. The role of head of household.
2. Marriage for life.
3. Not to be denied sex by his wife.
4. A bride who gives him her youth, virginity, and submission.

This gave all males a powerful incentive to build civilization for their posterity, to invest in the future and in themselves.

The deal has been endlessly changed to be worse, and yet supply and demand tilted ever further in favor of women

Before 1857, women were eager, indeed frantic, to sign up for the deal, and men considerably less enthusiastic

In 2000 or so, however, a women in her thirties, her pussy saggy from being pounded by hundreds of high status charismatic manly males with big tools, had no difficulty getting some poor loser to sign up for a deal where he is apt to lose all his assets and his children.

Although the deal got steadily worse for men, most women are happy to have one thirtieth of a high status male, leaving the other twenty nine males lonely losers. Hence the high male demand for marriage, even on highly unfavorable terms.

Note that when I say high status, I don't mean high status as males measure status. Women assess status childishly, like four year old children who say "my daddy can beat up your daddy". Thus the guy in jail for rape and murder gets unsolicited pen pal letters from hot chicks who want to meet him in person, while the guy in the corner office who landed the account of a major corporation does not. In general, a woman is only apt to sleep with her boss's boss when her boss actually demands she do her job, and successfully gets her to do it, thereby demonstrating his superior status. While men settle their status differences quickly, and then get on with the job, a woman always pushes back, always testing a little, always pressing a little, which makes them profoundly disruptive when you allow them into an organizational hierarchy. They are superficially more compliant than men, but they never stop pressing, never stop testing, and these days it is almost impossible for a male to pass the test without being guilty of sexual harassment. One way to press on and test her boss, is to sleep with his boss. If, on the other hand, she succeeds in walking all over her boss, as she usually does, she is apt to satisfy her hypergamous impulse not by sleeping with his boss, but by sleeping with a thug. Thus the declining rate of boss fucking, and the increasing rate of thug fucking, indicates the collapse of discipline within organizations. Women are less and less inclined to view organizational status as real, because when they press on it, it is not real, whereas men regard organizational status as real, partly because unlike women they do not get special legal status, partly because men are less inclined to keep on pressing, but mostly because of who signs their pay checks. Men perceive a job as a deal where they do stuff that people want done and get paid for doing it, while women perceive a job as boyfriend and family. When their boss is not nice to them they want a divorce with alimony and the house their boss fired but they should keep the office and the paycheck

Absent legal and social enforcement of monogamy, there is a massive surplus of males and shortage of females. At age thirty or so, this tends to become less unbalanced, as the highly desirable males don't particularly want to poke used up old women, with the result that women become willing to reluctantly and regretfully settle for males who are willing to commit, when formerly if any male was so desperate as to give indications of willingness to commit, they would have turned up their noses at any loser so desperate as to offer commitment. Indeed, I can say from personal experience and direct observation, that if you are a man and want to marry young, you must give not the slightest indication of interest in marrying young, or indeed ever.

Patriarchy with polygyny causes similar problems, as the absence of patriarchy. There is massive homosexuality among Pashtun males for lack of women, but the big problem that needs control is women wanting better, not men wanting more. A society that allows hypergamy is more messed up than a society than allows polygyny.

The only way to make supply equal demand is to enforce monogamy, and since females are the uncontrollably lustful sex[77], the big problem is enforcing monogamy on women. When a girl is young enough and pretty enough get plowed by Mister One in Thirty, she is happy to have three percent of Mister One in Thirty.

To maximize male investment in posterity and the future, need to share out one man per woman, and one woman per man, something that is forcefully resisted both by women and by high status men, but the resistance by women is the harder problem..

At some point the deal gets so bad, that increasing numbers of men just give up, contenting themselves with porn, whores, and whiskey. We are now approaching that point. The massive decline in male participation in the labor force is a measure of the problem.

---

[77]https://blog.reaction.la/culture/on-what-used-to-be-called-marriage.html "Females are the uncontrollably lustful sex"

The age of marriage can be considered to be approximately the marriage price. Marrying an old woman is what a man desperate to get married pays for marriage. Conversely, marrying young and staying faithful, thus giving up all that alpha cock, is what a woman desperate to get married and stay married pays for marriage. Age of marriage is the price matching supply and demand.

If shortage of wives, if wives are in high demand, women do not respond to that demand. Instead women ride the cock carousel until they notice that they no longer need an abortions every couple of months, and start worrying about their fertility, so, obese and pushing towards forty, hop off the cock carousel to condescend to reluctantly marry some lucky guy.

If shortage of husbands, girls start figuring who is husband material at age sixteen, and worry that if they kiss a boy, or wear unduly sexy clothes, they will get a reputation for being easy and no one will marry them, and they do their best to get married when they are at the age of peak hotness, which is to say, very young,which was roughly the situation before 1820 or so.

Suppose that Uncle Sam the Big Pimp ceased paying women to spawn bastard children, that all the numerous subsidies from men to women are ended, except the subsidy that a man is expected to support his good, obedient, and faithful wife, that all the sex quotas for women to take the career track were ended, so that any woman on the career track would forced to compete with men on equal terms, which of course most women cannot do except at the lower end.

Suppose that illegitimacy is disgraceful for both mother and child. In China, illegitimacy is fined instead of subsidized. If they can punish them, so can we.

So suddenly a lot more woman would want to get married. Presumably all those who would in today's order be spawning bastards, would instead be looking for husbands, thus approximately doubling the supply of potential wives, relative to the supply of potential husbands, since about fifty percent of children are fatherless. In addition, approximately one third of generation X wound up childless who had not planned on being childless, presumably career tracked and distracted by the cock carousel, so a more conservative environment would roughly triple the supply of prospective wives relative to prospective husbands.

So women would have to offer more – more youth and chastity, or else get left on the shelf. The age of marriage would then drop, to equalize supply and demand.

Monogamy, of course, would also require a lot of cheap housing. In most states, to subdivide land and build housing on it requires environmental review that no one can possibly pass except by political pull and massive bribery. In those states where it is reasonably possible to subdivide, notably Texas, housing is cheap, family formation is correspondingly high, resulting in people voting conservative.

Reasonably priced housing of course also require that police and private citizens would be allowed to profile, to prevent whites from being ethnically cleansed. In most of America, whites are being ethnically cleansed, depriving whites of reasonably priced housing. The reverse phenomenon, gentrification, occurs in places like San Francisco where the left piously looks the other way and encourages, indeed directs, the police to act like jackbooted Nazi thugs. Ethnic cleansing occurs when black thuggery is indulged, but white self defense is not permitted, as happened most infamously in Detroit. Gentrification occurs when elite members of the left, finding their elevated selves are being preyed upon by non asian minority thugs, finding their bubble is frighteningly small and alarmingly permeable, tell the cops to go hog wild and supply law and order to those that profile as disorderly and lawless, San Francisco being an extreme example of such left wing hypocrisy.

There is a positive feedback effect (readers of this blog, unlike our "cognitive elite", know the difference between positive feedback and negative feedback[78]). The more supply and demand favors women, the less they practice monogamy. The less they practice monogamy, the more supply and demand favors women. So society tends to flip between two states, the state where males, marriage, and commitment is in high demand, and most children have fathers, and the state where most males are surplus to requirements, have no incentive to contribute to or protect society, and most children are fatherless. Civilization only gets built in the condition where males, marriage, and commitment, are in high demand.

## Why gay marriage is not

### 2013-07-02 14:40:53

Why Gay Marriage is not[79]

One of the gay couple had a son by artificial insemination, the couple adopted the child, became poster boys for Gay Marriage "Two Dads are Better Than One", and proceeded to use him sexually, and rent him out to their friends.

Now someone will say "Not All Gays are Like That", but all the gays I know are like that, and when the progressive media go looking for a couple of poster boys, that is what they come up with. If not all of them are like that, nonetheless, that is the way to bet. The media has spent and continues to spend a lot of effort looking for a gay couple that fits the narrative, and it is evidently difficult, quite likely impossible, to find a gay couple that fits the narrative.

Lesbian couples are not nearly as bad as gay couples, but they are still horrifyingly bad to their own children. I suppose the media might have managed to find a lesbian couple that fits the narrative, but if they have, they probably spent quite some time looking.

## Radish explains what racism means

### 2013-07-07 08:11:13

This is an old post of Radish's[80], but it took a while to sink in, so now I summarize it.

Radish is replacing Moldbug, with lengthy, slow essays, that marshal all the facts without clearly pushing the conclusion, leaving a mental time bomb to slowly detonate as the implications slowly dawn.

---

[78]https://blog.reaction.la/economics/not-the-cognitive-elite-2.html "Not the cognitive elite"

[79]https://winteryknight.wordpress.com/2013/07/01/why-two-dads-are-better-than-one-pro-gay-adoption-abc-profile-of-convicted-pedophile-mark-newton/

[80]https://radishmag.wordpress.com/2013/06/28/volume-3-issue-1-no-reason/

Racism, racist, etc are new words. We did not have them before 1930 or so (earlier sightings in google ngrams appear to be false positives). Now if one looks up the official supposed meaning of "racism", the alleged meanings are incoherent, stupid, and mutually contradictory, originally the babbling of clever sillies, now the babbling of the merely stupid. So not only did we not have a word that meant what it supposedly means, we still don't have a word that means what it supposedly means.

Words mean what they are used to mean: When a bunch of blacks go looking for some white person to beat up, and beat the hell out of him, without bothering to steal anything:

Do progressives call them racist? No. Do conservatives call them racist? No. Do libertarians call them racist? No. Do reactionaries call them racist? No. So "racist" is merely a hostile epithet for white, same meaning as "honky" or "cracker", a mere term of incoherent abuse, a preparation for ethnic cleansing as in Detroit, or genocide as in rural South Africa.

And that is all it ever was. All the other supposed meanings were mere rationalizations by clever sillies.

Words mean what they are used to mean. If we look at actual usage, rather than claimed usage, "racist" is merely a hostile epithet for white, preparatory to state or private violence against whites.

## Yes, Obama is a Muslim

### 2013-07-08 10:50:47

The pseudonymous Tyler Durden has collected an interesting collection of messages to America from Egypt[81], messages that the mainstream press, strange to report, is not reporting.

Of course he is a progressive Muslim, which progressivism pisses off a great many Muslims, but, ultimately, he is in bed with people who want to conquer the world and make it all a third world hellhole like the middle east. This is simply the classic left wing far against near alliance, which has served them so well, for example Lenin with the Kaiser and Lord Howe arranging the deaths of his own men to benefit Washington

## I predict no riots in Seminole County

### 2013-07-14 14:45:26

The press have been calling on blacks to riot in the event of a Zimmerman acquittal

Assorted black leaders have been calling on blacks to riot in the event of a Zimmerman acquittal.

We have a full Zimmerman acquittal, somewhat to my surprise, since I expected an all female jury to do whatever the judge signals she wants them to do, which in this case was to convict Zimmerman of a lesser charge.

The sheriff of Seminole county, where the incident and the acquittal happened, says rioting will not be tolerated.

---

[81] https://directorblue.blogspot.com.au/2013/07/15-photos-from-tahrir-square-protests.html

Black riots are astroturf. Always have been, always will be. Every black riot happens when the authorities give a wink that rioting *will* be tolerated.

If a riot happens, and the Sheriff follows through with his promise that rioting will not be tolerated, then I will be proven wrong. Even if the riot was swiftly squelched, indeed especially if it was swiftly squelched, we would know that blacks had rioted on their own initiative, rather than as directed, which would show that black riots are not necessarily astroturf.

If a riot happens and the Sheriff fails to follow through, then we may conclude he said one thing in public and another thing in private to community organizers. Such an outcome would not prove me wrong. However I am pretty sure he is not kidding, for he called on businesses to remain open, which is code for "call up every rentacop".

## The decline of sperm production

**2013-07-15 06:09:07**

Today's average male has sperm production and sperm motility considerably lower than when these were first recorded, the data least subject to systematic error being sperm counts from couples tested for infertility where the infertility was subsequently determined to be due to the female. It has been in decline over the last seventy years. Testosterone levels have also fallen substantially[82]. Changes in obesity and other factors do not explain the decline in testosterone.

I was watching the anime cartoon, Strike Witches, which is the Battle of Britain fought by cute witches on broomsticks in their underwear, and was wondering why I did not like it, when I realized that characters were behaving in a way that was both very feminine and quite manly, which was rubbing me the wrong way like a girl with hairy legs. This caused me to look up the real heroes of the Battle of Britain, on which the loli catgirl witches with BFGs were based, and I found that those who fought the Battle of Britain really were manly, much more manly than moderns.

If you look at photographs of the soldiers of World War II, it is obvious that they were more manly than moderns.

And, of course, I have long known that the Victorians were much more manly than those who fought World War II, and Greeks of the March Upcountry far more manly than Victorians.

I would be inclined to guess it is the decline of patriarchy that is doing it. The Classic Greeks were more patriarchal than Christians, Christianity has been in decline ever since William Wilberforce and his fellow Calvinists discovered that they were more holy than Jesus and the apostles, and here we are. My guess is that feminism is quite literally emasculating men, making men physically sick, though World of Warcraft is another possibility.

The definitive test would be a country that is moving back to the natural sex roles, or at least not moving away from them, but due to world wide Cathedral hegemony, we seem to be short of such examples.

Polygyny, of course, leads to widespread homosexuality, so the Taliban victory in Afghanistan does not give us suitable comparison. The early Victorians were about as pa-

---

[82]https://jcem.endojournals.org/content/92/1/196.long "Decline in testosterone"

triarchal as the Muslims, but were far more manly. To properly test the theory, we would need sperm counts from a mostly monogamous country in which feminism is losing traction, or at least not gaining traction quite as fast, preferably a highly polluted modernizing country to rule out the other variables of modernity.

There is strong geographic variation in sperm production, which hints at variation in sperm production by religious affilation, counting academic attendance as a church attendance. It looks to me that the closer your research is done to a major Cathedral facility, the lower the sperm production you find. The real test would be to compare Mormon couples with Anglican couples. (Comparison with Amish couples would not only vary in exposure to feminism, but also exposure to other ailments of modernity). Unfortunately, no one has surveyed sperm production by religious affiliation. If feminism is doing it, Mormon men married to non Mormons would have markedly lower sperm production than Mormon men married to Mormons.

## The cause of social decay

### 2013-07-20 20:16:50

Prosperity is not the problem.

Many great nations have declined before we did, showing much the same symptoms as we are showing, and none of them were as prosperous as eighteenth century America.

I suggest the root of civilization is patriarchy.

Firstly, patriarchy with monogamy gives men posterity, and civilization is what men build for posterity. In a society where most men do not have children or do not know who their children are, do not raise their sons, they have no reason to work, to save, to invest, to build, nor to fight, to defend, to conquer, so their society leaves behind nothing for future historians to remember them by.

Secondly, patriarchy where marriages are arranged between families rather than lovers links families, creates tight knit extended families, links families through marriage, marriage in patriarchy being between families rather than purely between a man and a woman. The resulting society is able to create public goods, good government being one such public good. Instead of government creating the public good of the road serving your homestead, you contribute to getting the road built, because otherwise your father, your father in law, your brothers, and your brothers in law would disapprove of you.

Women get liberated, marriage and the family break down, society becomes atomized, a sea of isolated individuals. Becoming incapable of creating public goods, society looks to good government to create them – but who will create the public good of good government?

Without the capacity to generate public goods the struggle for political power becomes an advance auction of stolen goods. Eventually the army finds that it is at the back of the line behind various special interest groups sucking at the teat of the state. The army collapses, or goes into politics, or both.

The reactionary prescription for our present problem is that the army should go into politics, and fire most of the state apparatus. Other civilizations facing a similar decay have done that, it is pretty much the standard solution, and it has worked somewhat, but not really cured the problem. Rome under the five good emperors had good government, but nonetheless the continued decay of classical civilization was apparent.

## Black privilege

2013-07-23 06:06:52

Milhouse in esr's comments[83] linked to[84]:

On October 21st 2011 a burglary took place a few blocks from Krop Senior High School where Trayvon Martin attended. The stolen property outlined in the Miami-Dade Police Report matches the descriptive presented by SRO Dunn in his School Police report 2011-11477.

> as a result of pressure from M-DSPD Chief Hurley to avoid criminal reports for black male students, Dunn wrote up the jewelry as "found items", and transferred them, along with the burglary tool, to the Miami-Dade Police property room where they sat on a shelf unassigned to anyone for investigation.

So, the reason Martin Trayvon was casing the apartment complex that George Zimmerman was protecting, looking for houses to rob and people to mug, was that the police, under pressure to reduce the disturbing black crime statistics, ignored his burglary.

Trayvon was enraged to be profiled by George Zimmerman because he felt entitled to rob and beat people up– and the reason he felt entitled, the reason millions of indignant and outraged people feel he was entitled, was because he *was* entitled.

And the moral of the George Zimmerman case is if you interfere with blacks exercising the rights of black people over non black people, you will be punished.

## The Keynesian Fallacy

2013-07-24 06:00:18

The Keynesian fallacy is not that Keynesians believe that governments can stimulate. Of course governments armed with fiat money can stimulate. Look at Argentina! Look at Zimbabwe! Look at the Wiemar Republic! The Keynesian fallacy is that Keynesians believe that turning labor into goods is easy, so excess demand will mop up excess labor, resulting in the expected level of production.

Some of the conditions required to turn labor into goods are security of property rights, the rule of law, and freedom of trade.

Well that sounds like mere piety. Everyone is in favor of those things (though not necessarily for foreigners or with foreigners). In practice, however, these things mean that a well run business succeeds, and a poorly run business fails. If the government deems it a crisis when a poorly run business, run by pals of the government, fails, and intervenes with

---

[83] https://esr.ibiblio.org/?p=4994&cpage=1#comment-406414

[84] https://theconservativetreehouse.com/2013/05/01/m-dspd-cover-up-the-curious-case-of-trayvon-martins-backpack-with-stolen-jewelry-and-burglary-tool/

regulation to keep the zombie business running, then you don't have freedom of trade, security of property, etc, you have socialism without a central plan. And your economy is going to go to hell in a handbasket. Zombie businesses are not capitalism, but crony capitalism.

Turning labor into goods is hard, and people whose chief asset is their place on the revolving door between the regulators and the regulated are not going to do it. Stimulus may raise profits and employment, but you are not in fact going to get production. The economy is running on habit and inertia, on people doing what they used to do because that is what used to be done, and over time, this gets more and more detached from doing anything very useful.

Finding stimulus unstimulating, governments then lie about inflation and GDP, at first lying a little, and then, eventually, like Argentina, lying a lot.

Looks to me that living standards in the US have been declining since 1972. Food, fuel, education, and house that is safe to raise children, goes up, but supposedly this is off-set by the fact that you now have an internet connection that can download more porn than anyone could watch, and your car now has electric windows. Every so often growth declines to a new new normal, and statistics are adjusted so that we pretend the old normal is still in effect. Median male income has, notoriously, been falling, as has male employment. Creative measures of inflation, wherein everything you have to buy goes up, but it is supposedly offset by everything you don't much care about going down, is not the only distortion. Increased female employment transfers unmeasured household production (such as children and a nice house) to measured production, thus male income is arguably a better indicator than GDP per head. Increased female employment leads to a statistical mismeasure, since they were probably working harder and producing more value back in the days before they had office jobs. If female employment goes up while age of marriage goes up, there is not necessarily more production. If male employment goes down, there is really, no kidding, less production. Comparing the past with the present leads to a lot of apples and oranges problems, and the government increasingly chooses whichever approach that makes the present look good, and the past look bad.

## Keynsianism manufactures its own truth

2013-07-29 09:55:39

Nigel asks:

> A problem is over-reliance on foreign work to produce goods. The jobs that are left here are service jobs and managerial jobs. ...
>
> Did we get this way by free trade or by government intervention?

In "Death of the Doctor", the virtue of a character is proved by that character having traveled around protesting:

> ...he's picketing an oil rig...
>
> ...you're fighting oil barons and factories...

Fighting factories. Not any specific kind of factory - just, factories, as if it were proof enough of a person's virtue that he was fighting factories - any factories.

This is the same worldview as encapsulated in "sweatshop"- that capital formation, savings and investment, harms people.

The regulatory state is overwhelmingly dominated by people who have internalized that worldview – thus regulation is in practice applied to halt capital formation by businesses, to prevent savings from being put to productive use, in particular and especially to prevent them from being applied to factories. Regulators see it as a simple wrong, to be stopped on any vaguely plausible grounds.

This regulation produces the Keynesian paradox – that saving is harmful and has to be offset by state dissaving.

## The last pope

### 2013-08-03 12:18:10

Pope Benedict XVI was the last Roman Catholic Pope. It is unlikely that there will be any more. There will be people called popes, but they will be megaphones for progressivism, not Roman Catholicism.

Progressivism is an entryist movement, the last major entryist movement standing, having fully assimilated the remaining communist movements. The progressive believes in Jesus the community organizer, Marx the moderate progressive, Mohammed the prophet of progressivism, Adam Smith the anticapitalist, and so on and so forth. He also believes in Christ the Redeemer, where by redemption is meant bringing people to progressivism, and in Salvation, where by salvation he means electing a progressive government that does everything a progressive government is supposed to do, including, indeed especially, those things that are impossible for a government to do. Jesus would drive a prius were he here today, and his mission, rightly understood, is to save the earth from man.

Similarly, the progressive, and no doubt Jesus, Mohammed, Karl Marx, Adam Smith, etc, believes in capitalism and markets in the sense of "Carbon Markets", "Cap and Trade", and "Health Care Exchanges" (If you, like most people, are wondering what a "Health Care Exchange" is, it is an online welfare application, to make us all dependent on government as conveniently as possible, with the least amount of embarrassment.)

Is this what Pope Francis is preaching– well, you cannot quite tell what he is preaching, which is characteristic of entryists, but what he is preaching sounds enough like progressivism that it is mighty hard to tell the difference, enough like progressivism that the average person cannot tell the difference.

In the first step of entryism, entryists enter the group, whether the Communist Party, the Republican Party, the Roman Catholic Church, the State Department, or whatever, claiming to agree with group beliefs and support group goals, while in fact supporting the progressive interpretation of group beliefs and supporting progressive goals incompatible with group goals.

In the next step of entryism, non entryists are removed from power, or destroyed by character assassination, (someone remembers being fondled as a child forty years ago, though he never mentioned it until recently) or destroyed physically by actual physical assassination.

In the next step of entryism, entryists are quietly in power, still purporting to agree with group beliefs and support group goals, while in fact supporting the progressive interpretation of group beliefs and supporting progressive goals incompatible with group goals. The organization officially pursues its original goals and officially adheres to its original beliefs, but not really. It starts to wither away.

In the next step, the organization officially and overtly supports the progressive interpretation of group beliefs and supports progressive goals.

In the final step, the organization disappears altogether, its assets and personnel fully absorbed into the Cathedral. The physical Vatican will become a tourist attraction, and the organizational Vatican will become a letterhead issued from the desk of a minor NGO minion, whose physical location and postal address will probably be rather close to Harvard. The letterhead, to the extent that it is used at all, will be used to directly support progressive goals, such as transexuality, higher taxes, open borders for the non working underclass, and gay marriage, without referring to the now forgotten reinterpretation of Roman Catholic goals.

At first it will not be that people realize that the papacy ended with Pope Benedict, but rather that they will forget that it supposedly continues, just as the Roman Empire in the west supposedly continued, until people forgot that it was supposedly continuing. Later, historians will wonder when it ended, and will set a date, and will set a last Pope, and that last Pope will have been Benedict.

Progressives and communists practiced entryism against each other, or, as they would doubtless describe it, for each other. At first communists were clearly winning, due to greater zeal, certainty, and greater willingness to use physical assassination. After Stalin halted the left singularity, announcing that socialist utopia had already arrived, and shooting anyone who wanted it to be even more socialist and more utopian, the communist entryists became less effective, and when the Soviet Union fell, of course they withered on the vine, having been always dependent on a physical headquarters in a communist country and funding from communist regimes.

Progressivism has been markedly less murderous than Communism even if you count those dying because of environmentalism, so initially it seemed as if the progressive victory was a good thing. Trouble is, the progressive victory occurred because progressivism still is heading to its left singularity. A government run, centrally planned economy, is a very bad thing, but a government run economy with no central plan is a worse thing.


## The first rise and fall of the Left.

### 2013-08-05 08:42:39

Before the English Civil war, the state was Throne and Altar, what we would now call the right. The state maintained slavery, enforced official religion, and everyone was required to pretend to believe in the divine right of Kings, much as today everyone is with equal plausibility required to pretend to believe that women are equal to men.

The English Civil war was intended to secure the rights of Englishmen, but to Englishmen's dismay, what we would now call right dictatorship was replaced by a dictatorship of the predecessors of today's left.

Holy leftists were continually outflanked by people even holier and lefter.

This is not some weird Moldbuggian reinterpretation of what leftism means. Marx also traces the roots of the left to the movements holier than Cromwell and suppressed by Cromwell, the Levellers and the Diggers. A faction of the twentieth century hippy movement called themselves "The Diggers", claiming to be continuation and revival of the seventeenth century Digger movement.

Cromwell became dictator and ended the left singularity, announcing that England had become sufficiently holy, and repressing those to his left equally with those to his right, much as Stalin declared the Soviet Union sufficiently socialist, and proceeded to kill everyone more socialist than Stalin, as well as everyone less socialist than Stalin. Threatened on the left, Cromwell took the royalist General Monck out of prison and gave him a high command, and his own personal right wing praetorian guard, now known as the Coldstream guards.

When Cromwell died, his son was to succeed him, but, since Cromwell and the holy left had been busily opposing monarchy and undermining monarchism, this failed to take. General Monck then marched on London, defeating the New Model Army. He set his Praetorians to "guarding" Parliament, The puritan parliament immediately voted to dissolve itself and hold a new election with rules more favorable to the cavaliers. A Royalist parliament was elected, still guarded by Monck's Praetorians, the Coldstream guards, who continue to guard the British Parliament to this day. The new Parliament restored the monarchy and Anglican theocracy. For anyone to get near the levers of power, they had to swear fealty to the thirty nine articles, much as today you have to submit essays showing how progressive you are.

This loyalty oath remained in effect from approximately 1662 to 1826.

The restoration regime was an astonishing success. It created the scientific revolution, the industrial revolution, and British adventurers conquered most of the world, forming what would later be called the British empire.

Under the restoration regime, science was high status – not official science, but real science, the scientific method. Today, the scientific method is only carried out by subversive troublemakers, who are likely to be deemed enemies of the state, for example the climate skeptic movement. Similarly, before the restoration, as today, the scientific method was largely carried out furtively. The predecessor of the Royal Society was the invisible college, and the reason it was invisible is that they would rather not be seen.

I attribute the success of officially Anglican England to the fact that official Anglicanism was latitudinarian In Bruce Charleton's terminology, it tolerated heretics but not apostates.

Today, one must believe everything the state believes, one must believe all official truth, of which there is a great deal. Deviation is tolerated amongst the lower classes, since they are deemed hopelessly ignorant, but the higher one is in society, the more precise and detailed one's knowledge of the official truth is expected to be, and the higher one's status, the more one is expected to agree ever more meticulously and in ever more precise detail. In contrast, the thirty nine articles mostly focused on points where members of competing theocratic movements would disagree, mostly focused on the antigens of hostile enemy theocratic movements, permitting much greater intellectual freedom than can exist today.

Because the thirty nine articles were latitudinarian, they did not cause an ever rightwards movement analogous to today's ever leftwards movement. The requirement to enter the corridors of power was not to be sufficiently holy, which test Charles the Second would surely have failed, but to not be an adherent of Roman Catholicism, Puritanism, or Puritanism's successor movements.

## The history of leftism against freedom

### 2013-08-07 05:46:15

Today's state is the left, and the left is the state, as is apparent when one traces the funding of Occupy astroturf to itself.

Recapping Moldbug on the history of the left:

If we trace back the American left through the years, decades and centuries, we find the roots of today's distinctly anti Christian and disproportionately Jewish left were nominally Christians, the super protestants of the 1940s, who in turn have plausibly Christian roots - the prohibition movement, the early feminist movement, the movement to raise the age of consent, the movement to give women the vote, and the anti slavery movement: "Onward Christian soldiers".

The center of the Anglo American left in the nineteenth century was England, and thought of themselves as primarily Christians, rather than leftists. They did not pride themselves on being lefter than thou, but on being holier than thou. In the early nineteenth century, the American left were muppets of the English left, and the English left ran the world, imposing leftism at gunpoint, for example abolishing slavery with the British navy. Today, the American left runs the world and thinks of itself as anti Christian, and it is difficult to say when the transition took place. The transition to a US centered conspiracy could be said to have taken place as early as the Civil war, when the theocratic state of Massachusets and the theocratic city of Boston, its theocracy centered in Harvard University, imposed its theocracy on all America. Back then the regnant left thought of themselves as Christian, and, indeed, much holier than Jesus, and continued to do so perhaps as recently as the 1940s.

The transition to American centered rule could also be said to have taken place as late as after World War I. It was a gradual process without well defined dramatic transitions.

The transition from thinking of themselves as Christian, and indeed much holier than those horrid hateful reactionaries, Jesus and the Disciples, to thinking of themselves as anti Christian, took place after left wing power became centered in America. The American constitution unambiguously prohibits theocracy at the federal level. What America had after the Civil War was theocracy at the federal level, so it was necessary to kick the Theo out of their Cracy.

Kicking the Theo out of their Cracy was easily done, since they had long believed themselves holier than Jesus, but it was done late. The regnant left believed themselves holier than thou, rather than lefter than thou, all the way to the 1930s or 1940s, and did not allow too many Jews too close to the corridors of power until the 1950s.

It was in the anti slavery movement that the predecessors of today's left began to distinctly depart from Christianity: For the New Testament takes a tolerant attitude towards slavery: It gently suggests that Christians free their own slaves, but does not require it, and clearly prohibits Christians from freeing other people's slaves, though they are perhaps permitted to close their eyes to other people's runaway slaves and look the other way. The civil war conspicuously and spectacularly exceeded not only what the New Testament requires, but also what it permits. Killing people in large numbers and breaking other people's stuff in order to end slavery is clearly and violently unchristian. A Christian approach to the slavery problem would be to vigorously enforce the Old Testament rule "He that stealeth a man and selleth him, he shall be put to death", and allow slavery to slowly wither away, as was successfully done in much of the world.

Killing a large part of an American generation and burning much of the South was holier than Jesus.

With the emancipation of women, they really had to ditch Christianity and started doing so, for while the New Testament is mildly disapproving of slavery, it endorses stern patriarchy in no uncertain terms, and thus, with women's suffrage, we see the familiar modern left, the modern lefter than thou mingled with the older holier than Jesus.

The infamous "Society for the Suppression of Vice", which is what we think of when use the term "Victorian" to mean stern disapproval of sex and the belief that women have no sexual nature, was a left wing movement, operating in England out of the same headquarters and operated by the same people as the anti slavery movement, the movement to get Calvinist bishops into the Church of England, and the movement to make the Thirty Nine Articles a mere formality with no real content.

Since women supposedly had no sexual nature, the repressive measures that the "Society for the Suppression of Vice" successfully imposed were anti male measures, strikingly similar to the measures imposed by modern feminists despite the supposedly very different rationale.

The "Society for the Suppression of Vice" theoretically believed in chastity for both men and women and said so frequently, stressing the "both", so frequently as to suggest that people doubted it, or that they doubted it themselves, but they believed that to make women chaste was primarily a matter of preventing evil men from making poor innocent women do bad things.

Perhaps when they emphasized "both" they were having a dig at the right wing view that it was women, the uncontrollably lustful sex, that needed to be restrained for their own good, the good of the family, and the good of society, and not men, or they thought of it as a dig at the right, but the emphasis on "both" seemed guilty and defensive to me, that they were saying "We are not the hypocrites! You are!"

In fact it was the "Society for the Suppression of Vice" that were the hypocrites, for though theoretically opposed both men and women having sex, in practice they were closely associated with the various movements to rescue fallen women, which proposed to rescue fallen women by removing all the adverse social, legal, and economic consequences from women having sex outside marriage.

Thus, in practice the supposedly anti sex "Society for the Suppression of Vice" was, like modern supposedly pro sex feminists, opposed to beta males having sex and in favor of women having sex with alpha males outside marriage. Indeed we can trace this all the way back to Cromwell's puritans desacralizing marriage and legalizing divorce. The modern supposedly pro sex feminist movement, who, despite supposedly being pro sex, are always inventing new forms of "rape", has continuity of personnel and organization all the way back to Cromwell's puritans.

Since women, unlike men, bring their bastards home, with disastrous consequences, and women are, according to the right of that time (the reactionaries of our time) the uncontrollably lustful sex, it makes perfect sense to control female sexuality, rather than male. The double standard rests on biology. There is nothing hypocritical about it, and the then right and the present day reaction have never been the slightest bit ashamed of the double standard. It was those proposing to both suppress vice and also protect women from the consequences of vice, that were hypocritical. And indeed are hypocritical, for the same hypocrisy stands today, when women are encouraged to get drunk with strangers, but should they wake up with a stranger and a terrible hangover, it is rape, the stranger is the rapist and the poor innocent woman the rape victim.

Similarly, the temperance movement had massively overlapping personnel and postal addresses with the female emancipation and female suffrage movements, and their personnel, organizations, and postal addresses were in part descended from the anti slavery movement.

Since Jesus and the disciples, and just about everyone in the New Testament, drank alcohol socially, at mealtimes and in moderation, the movement to prohibit alcohol was holier than Jesus, which is to say pharisaical.

Since Jesus and the disciples accepted the institution of slavery, discouraged slaves from running away, and prohibited freeing other people's slaves, the movement to free the slaves was holier than Jesus, which is to say pharisaical.

Since Jesus and the disciples firmly endorsed and commanded stern patriarchy, the movement to emancipate women was holier than Jesus, which is to say pharisaical.

Thus the Victorian movement to ever greater holiness prefigured and became the movement to ever greater leftism, prefiguring today's left singularity.

Tracing the English speaking left all the way back, we see continuity of personnel and ideology, the ideology slowly changing from Puritan Christianity to Unitarian Universalism to modern leftism, but changing slowly and continuously without any abrupt change, though over time every detail of the ideology changed, except for the war on Christmas, desecration of marriage, and the emancipation of women, which remained the whole time, even though sometimes justified by the argument that Christmas was too pagan, and at other times justified by the argument that Christmas was not pagan enough, and sometimes, strangely, both arguments simultaneously, while the desecration of marriage never got an explanation, for they never admitted that that was what they were doing, nor did the emancipation of women for as long as they thought themselves Christian, for Paul unambiguously tells the Church to socially enforce male authority over women.

To oppose the left, is to oppose the state. To oppose the state is to oppose the left. Disagreements between those who would replace the state with a large and effectual state, and those would replace it with a small and effectual state are inconsequential, in part because if the central authority, the federal level, attempts to do too much it is guaranteed to be ineffectual, disruptive, and disorderly, due to diseconomies of scale.

All governments are in some sense theocratic, though the ideology may pretend to have no gods, or, like communism, actually have no gods. You can restrict theocracy to only apply at the local level, as the United States used to do before the War Between The States, or, like the Ottoman Caliphate, tolerate other religions as subject states within an empire, in which one religion exercises imperial domain over subject religions, like an emperor exercising imperial domain over subject Kings. The only way to not have theocracy is to have some form of anarchy.

If there is going to be a government, that government is going to control the schools, and openly or furtively control the churches, and make them teach a particular viewpoint. The question then is, what shall that viewpoint be?

If the official belief system bans too many heresies, as it does today, science and technology stagnates, because the scientific and technological way of thinking comes to be deemed hostile, subversive, and low status. Thus, for example, evidence is forbidden in Wikipedia. Only the voice of authority is deemed relevant. On the other hand, too much tolerance for hostile theocratic alien outside belief systems is likely to result in the official theocracy being infiltrated and overthrown by a more passionate, more self righteous, and more repressive belief system, as happened to theocratic Anglicanism.


## On Funding Science

### 2013-08-10 16:16:08

Funding science is not a job that government can do, due to diseconomies of scale, and because government is inherently a religious organization. It winds up funding pseudo science, thus damaging real science. The patron has to know and appreciate that field that he is patronizing, and has to personally gain status from the success of his clients. Otherwise he has the wrong incentives and the wrong knowledge, so patronizes the wrong things, resulting in pseudo science substituting for science.

What government could do is spend money on stuff that needs science, such as killing people and breaking things, or exploring distant planets, and some of that money will unavoidably wind up spent on real science, because those best able to provide better ways of killing people and breaking things do know the difference between real science and pseudo science, unlike petty bureaucrats.

Galilean kinematics were developed on a grant for finding rules to fire cannon balls at targets hidden behind city walls, and the telescope that enabled Galileo to see the phases of Venus, proving that the Copernican model was approximately correct, and the Ptolemaic model flatly wrong, was developed to spy enemy fleets at sea.

If some engineers get wealthy, they can patronize real science. The guy with a masters in administration cannot. Maybe he can patronize the arts.

# The time approaches for a Sulla or a Monck

2013-08-19 16:51:32

In a tranquil and orderly society a bunch of high status males work things out between themselves by means far short of actual violence, hence are "gentlemen". These gentlemen then present a unified and extremely violent front against outsiders. Over time, their arrangement is apt to break down, their unified front against ungentle means of advancement dissipates, and it becomes increasingly possible to get ahead within the elite by using or organizing actual physical violence against fellow members of the elite, as for example Sonia Sotomayor and Ward Churchill did. As they become less violent to outsiders, they find that increasingly those who have intruded among them are more violent to each other.

Elite politics then becomes progressively rougher, eventually resulting in a Sulla: rule by a single extremely violent man.

Contrary to Moldbug, societies ruled by a single strong man rarely prosper, since the single strong man has limited capability to shake down the society, and so tends to maximize his take, rather than maximize what is to be taken, thus under a single strong man, the state is apt to become more corrupt and violent, not less corrupt and violent. Because one man is weak and vulnerable, the difference between stationary bandits and mobile bandits is less than advertised. Moldbug is correct to argue that the weakness of the ruler is a problem, wrong to think it is soluble. Stationary bandits are always apt to mutate into mobile bandits due to institutional decay.

Our elite is not all that violent, and exceptional cases, such as Sonia Sontamayor, are not all that elite, but is is apparent which way the wind is going. Like a neighborhood going bad, the level of trust is going down, the level of corruption is going up, and actual violence, once quite unimaginable, is now, though still uncommon, entirely imaginable. The Occupy rentamob was intended to physically threaten the financial elite and physically occupy their premises, though it instantly became apparent that the financiers and their rentacops were way tougher than the occupy rentamob.

Democratic politics is a mock civil war: The side that could call out the most people were it to come to actual fighting is agreed to rule. But the failure of the Occupy movement suggests that the inner party cannot, in fact, call out a significant mob.

# The total absence of a manosphere schism

2013-08-20 06:54:32

Lately a bunch of people have been complaining about a schism in the manosphere. Roosh dissed everyone except pick up artists, which upset lots of people. But Roosh's complaint was that men without lots of experience with lots of women are poor sources of advice about women, which is trivially true. Dalrock is good as a source of truth about women, but Heartiste is better, even if you approve of Dalrock's goals, and disapprove of Heartiste, minion of Satan.

If you care about truth, take it like a man. I knew the nature of women when I was teenage, but am a poor source of advice about women since I married very young, and stayed married, which cramped my style a little.

Since the greatest pick-up-artist blogger, enjoy-the-decline Heartiste, minion of Satan, is also a major inspiration to reactionaries everywhere, and himself a great blogger of the Dark Enlightenment, how can there be a schism? It is not schism, it is disagreement in the search for truth.

If you worry about schism, you are trying to build consensus. Consensus is the opposite of truth, it is the madness of crowds[85]. Consensus is truth by agreement. The Dark Enlightenment truth by reality.

Now if we were fighting an actual shooting war with a competent, cohesive and disciplined enemy, we would have to choose someone as dictator and loyally obey, and he would say,
> "Man the barricades here!"

and anyone who did not do so would be schismatic. But we are far from there yet, and when it happens, it will not be the clash of competent and cohesive groups, but the hopelessly decadent clashing in confusion and darkness with the marginally more competent and serious. The Occupy movement prefigures the future conflict[86], which is why I have more hope in rentacops and mercenaries than in the regular army, which, as the Cathedral deballs it in fear of a coup, looks more and more like Occupy.

## Do not believe anything in the New York Times
### 2013-08-22 06:55:35

The New York Times has gotten hold of a secret Chinese Communist Party memo, which lists seven subversive currents in Chinese society, which could lead to the overthrow of the party after the fashion of the French Revolution. The New York Times, however fails to list all seven subversive currents, merely giving us their interpretation of selected parts of the document.

Therefore, spin, therefore a lie. If they did not intend to mislead you, would give you the full seven.

## Words and meanings
### 2013-08-25 08:58:02

When the ostensive meaning, the nominal meaning, and the nominal ostensive meaning of a word differ, the word is itself a lie, a lie contained in a single word that makes any sentence containing it a lie.

A word primarily means what it is used to refer to, its ostensive meaning. During childhood language acquisition, it means what mothers refer to when speaking to their children. The mother says "look, a dog", and the child then knows what a dog is.

Then there is the nominal meaning, what dictionaries say the word means in terms of other words, what high status people say they mean, which is not necessarily what they do mean.

---

[85] https://blog.reaction.la/economics/stultum-facit-fortuna.html
[86] https://blog.reaction.la/economics/the-sins-of-%E2%80%9Coccupy-wall-street%E2%80%9D.html

And then there is the nominal ostensive meaning – what people say they are pointing at, even though in fact they may be pointing at something completely different.

The difference between the ostensive meaning, what they point at, and the nominal ostensive meaning or the dictionary meaning, what they say they point at, is the lie.

The word "racism" illustrates this. The ostensive meaning, what it is actually used to mean, is an insult term for white, like "cracker" or "honky". The nominal ostensive meaning is KKK Hitler slavery. The nominal meaning, what people claim they mean by it, what dictionaries say they mean by it … is incoherent, incomprehensible, and differs from one source to the next, because no one really cares or pays any attention.

The lie implicit in the word "racism" is therefore that all whites are guilty by original sin of KKK Hitler slavery, that blacks suffer because whites exist, that merely by continuing to breath, whites harm blacks. For example, by thinking evil thoughts about blacks, whites cause blacks to underperform, (stereotype threat) and devastate black run cities such as Detroit. The logical implication of the word "racism" is that non whites need to eradicate whites, because evil white magic is causing non whites magical harm.

Similarly for "sweatshop", The ostensive meaning, what it is actually used to mean, is capital and entrepreneurs making those of a different race to the entrepreneur and owner of the capital productive by leadership and expensive equipment. The nominal ostensive meaning is something like a factory operated by slave labor. Supposedly the peasants are dragged to factory and chained to the bench. Allegedly evil capitalists did this somewhere some time, though it is not very clear when or where or who. The dictionary meaning is a shop employing workers at low wages, for long hours, and under poor conditions, but when communists forced people to work with actual chains and whips, for wages paid in money that could not be spent, for long hours, and under poor, and frequently fatal conditions, that was never a "sweatshop", nor is it a sweatshop when the business employs very little technological capital, as for example a coffee plantation.

The lie implicit in the word "sweatshop" is therefore that capital, capitalism, and entrepreneurs make people worse off, that the way for individuals, peoples, and nations to enjoy prosperity and economic development is to imitate the wonderful examples of Soviet Russia, North Korea, and Castro's Cuba and simply command prosperity into being. And if prosperity failed to be commanded into being, this was due to the continuing harmful influence of evil hate thoughts of evil capitalists - see "the kulaks". If the command that utopia exist was mysteriously disobeyed, the solution obviously must be stronger regulation and harsher punishment.

## Christians did not build the Cathedral - but Churches did.

### 2013-08-25 14:47:30

The Orthosphere is always apologizing for Christianity, supporting it, and defending it, while I treat as merely markedly less harmful than the belief systems that people are likely to believe when they stop believing in Christianity. And today the Orthosphere publishes a guest post that asserts Christians Did Not Build "The Cathedral"[87]

Which tells us:

---

[87]https://orthosphere.org/2013/08/25/christians-did-not-built-the-cathedral/

you should begin to doubt the internet authors who tell you that the leftist programs of what they like to call "the Cathedral" originated in the *Christianity* of the churches of New England.

Indeed, it originated not in the Christianity of the churches of New England, but in the heresy of the Churches of New England.

And which also tells us.

because the Puritan believes that he is "better than other people," he "feels bound to keep 'watch and care,' as the phrase runs, over other people's affairs." And in order to satisfy this implacable itch to keep watch and care over other people's affairs, the Puritan is ever eager "get hold of some great 'moral idea' ... and get into power with it."

Which does not seem very different from what those internet writers he complains about wrote.

## On Judaism

### 2013-08-28 07:17:53

I have been arguing in the comments with B about Judaism, and in the course of this argument, my position shifted considerably.

Judaism was a theocratic national religion, state religion, and ethnic religion, a nation state religion. Just what the doctor ordered, just the kind of thing reactionaries like, just the kind of thing that makes a people strong.

Upon the Jews being exiled, the Sadducees lost their power base and Rabbis remade Judaism to be an exile ethnic religion, inherently hostile to, and subversive of, the host nation and host society.

This has become a paradoxical and psychologically unhealthy religion, since the Jews are no longer in exile, but Judaism is still in exile, still subversive of the host nation even when the host nation is Israel, and still subversive of the host society even when the host society is Jewish.

Orthodox Jews are still in psychological exile. The Rabbis won and the Sadducees lost, but to come home, to once again be a religion of nation and state, Judaism has to change once again, has to cease to be a religion of exile and become less Rabbinical and more Sadducee, something that even the most reactionary Rabbis do not much like, preferring to concentrate on ever more extreme expansions of Deuteronomy 14:21

On the one hand, there seems to be very little taste for reaction in Israel – even the religious right is not very rightist, though B has high hopes for them. On the other hand, if they stay the course with the leftist program, they are all going to die.

So I rather think they face a choice between remaking their religion, and being killed by the Arabs, and will probably choose, to the great horror of American progressives, and to the great delight of Christian apocalyptics, to radically, and somewhat coercively, remake their religion.

I do not believe in scriptural prophecy. I do however believe that Israel faces a choice between annihilation through self inflicted defeat, or adopting a nation state religion that looks suspiciously like making a good start on fulfilling their scriptural prophecies. They need to be at least as theocratic as those who would destroy them. They also need the soldiers in charge of the priests, like the theocracy instituted by Charles the Hammer, not the priests in charge of the soldiers. If priests get too uppity, they are apt to go holier than thou, and rabbis have a bad record of holier-than-thou disease, at least as bad as puritans, perhaps worse. Soldiers tend to be more effectual in defending the land than priests.

And B, when you do get started on the nation state religion, ease up on Deuteronomy 14:21. It will be time to issue new antibodies against new antigens, the number one such antigen being those precepts and practices of progressivism that make a Jewish state illegitimate unless gerrymandered to indefensible borders resembling the spots of a mutant leopard.

## Dysgenics and mutational load

### 2013-08-31 18:01:30

It seems probable that most variation in health, beauty, and IQ is due to genetic load, large numbers of rare genetic variants. About fifteen percent of the human genome is under negative selection[88], meaning that in about fifteen percent of the human genome, any random change is likely to be harmful, most variants get eliminated by natural selection in a reasonable time.

The mutation rate in humans is one or two mutations per hundred million bases per generation[89], probably around one mutation per hundred million bases, for a total of around thirty to sixty mutations per generation, implying around five to nine harmful mutations per generation.

Since we must have been near equilibrium in the ancestral environment, this implies five to nine harmful mutations were eliminated every generation.

This amounts to natural selection working fiercely – that just to stay in the same place we were running mighty fast, that survival of the fittest was pretty harsh. Since we have not been experiencing severe natural selection since the Industrial Revolution, the number of harmful mutations in the typical individual must have increased by about forty or so. We must have devolved quite significantly.[90]

Suppose the typical genetic load, the number of harmful mutations that need to be eliminated is n2, so that the variance is around n.

Let us assume that most of these mutations are about equally harmful, which sounds like a silly assumption, but we shall see this assumption matters little. Let us also assume that they are not very harmful, since the really harmful ones will result in spontaneous abortions or people who have no prospect of reproducing, and the rest of them must be somewhat harmful since natural selection tended to get rid of them in the ancestral environment.

---

[88]https://genomeinformatician.blogspot.com/2012/09/encode-my-own-thoughts.html
[89]https://johnhawks.net/weblog/reviews/genomics/variation/human-mutation-rate-review-2010.html
[90]https://iqpersonalitygenius.blogspot.com/2013_05_01_archive.html

Let us assume that in the ancestral environment, each of these mutations reduced survival chances by a factor of 1- h, h being a very small quantity.

There has not been much natural selection since the Industrial Revolution, so we typically have a lot more harmful mutations than they did, and it is not killing us yet, so h must be quite small, from whence we may conclude that n is quite large, and n2 very large indeed.

So if an individual's genetic load is N , where N is a quantity close to the average level of n2, his genes have a chance of being represented in the next generation of

(1-h)N-C

Assuming that each harmful mutation reduces survival prospects independently of all of the others.

Where h and C are constant for the species and the environment as a whole, and N is the individuals total genetic load.  At equilibrium, C will be very close to the average genetic load, n2, and N - C is the individual's genetic load relative to the average successfully reproducing individual.

The mean of N - C is close to zero and the variance in N - C is n.

We are assuming, as seems likely, that most variation is genetic load.

Under realistic assumptions, assuming h is quite small, the number of harmful mutations eliminated in each generation is very close to

h * n2

So, if h is quite small, the genetic load must be very high

Someone entirely free from genetic load would have a quite amazing reproductive success, would be quite godlike.

Assume that in the ancestral environment, seven harmful mutations were eliminated every generation

If a typical mutation reduces fitness (reproductive success) by ten percent, then typical genetic load must be seventy in which case an Adamic individual (no genetic load) would have a reproductive success of fourteen hundred, unity being normal

But ten percent seems quite a lot.  If it was that high, we would be really sick and stupid compared to our Victorian ancestors. Suppose it is more like one percent. In that case typical genetic load must be seven hundred, in which case an Adamic individual (no genetic load) would have a reproductive success of eleven hundred, unity being normal. For a mutation rate of seven per generation, and a harmfulness effect of anything substantially smaller than ten percent, mutations accumulate until the load depresses reproductive success by a factor of around eleven hundred or so, which means an individual free from load would be quite extraordinary.  It also means we don't need to know what the typical harmfulness of a mildly harmful mutation is to judge the genetic load.  The genetic load is proportional to the number of mutations that, in the ancestral environment were routinely eliminated to keep those areas of the genome fairly stable.

Assuming our ancestors were in equilibrium, the typical harmfulness of a mildly harmful mutation does not matter much.  Genetic load must be huge. If mutations are typically not very harmful, they accumulate to very high levels, so the total harm remains roughly constant independent of the harmfulness of the mutation – and extraordinarily large. We could not have kept so large a genome free from variation, unless the difference between an Adamic individual, and a regular individual, is huge.

Adamic individuals would all be Einstein combined with Hercules and Genghis Kahn. To halt our genetic deterioration and improve the race, we can raise the reproduction rate and the death rate, which sounds mighty unpleasant, or we could, if progress continues, solve the problem by genetic engineering.

Could we synthesize a genome free from genetic load?

If we had very high accuracy reads of a very large number of individuals, we could make a pretty good guess as to which variations were genetic load, by determining which variations had survived for many centuries, and which have not. Having determined what a genome free from load would be, the problem is synthesizing it.

All multicellular animals turn out to have roughly similar genomes, sponges and men, commonly three billion base pairs, organized in chromosomes of around one hundred million base pairs each. There are a few with much more, or much less, but mostly it is something like that.

That is a long way from what the Venter institute can do, but not, perhaps, entirely out of reach. Craig Venter made a working chromosome of one million base pairs[91].

It is not such a huge leap from booting up a simple microorganism, the simplest possible microorganism, to booting up a human egg. The main difference is that the genome of one is three thousand times bigger than the genome of the other.

It rather looks to me that while progress in reading genes continues, and is accelerating, progress in writing genes has substantially stalled. The Craig Venter project may represent our high point of genetic engineering achievement, as a man on the moon represents our high point of space travel. It is not obvious that we will be able to produce supermen in time to avoid a dark age of cultural and genetic decline.

Reasonable and foreseeable progress is that we will soon be able to measure the genetic load of a fetus. We will probably not, however, be able to do anything about it other than selective abortion.

## War with Syria

### 2013-09-01 16:48:33

If crimes committed far away by bad people against other far away bad people are important enough for Americans to go to war over, they are important enough to call Congress back to work early from summer vacation to vote for war or peace.

If they are not important enough to interrupt congresscritters summer vacation, they are not important enough to go to war over.

## Radish nails libertarianism's race problem

### 2013-09-02 09:18:39

Libertarianism had its one brief shining day in power in alliance with the anti racist, anti slavery brigade, was swiftly kicked out of that alliance, and has been beaten over the head

---

[91] https://www.jcvi.org/cms/press/press-releases/full-text/article/first-self-replicating-synthetic-bacterial-cell-constructed-by-j-craig-venter-institute-researcher/home/

with race stick ever since, despite endlessly begging to be allowed to renew the alliance.

Since then, the only times it has ever gotten anywhere is in alliance with the "racist", aka white, faction.

## The Dark Enlightenment critique of Libertarianism

2013-09-05 07:18:35

The problem with libertarianism is that it really only works if libertarian rules are generally enforced, accepted, and felt to be right, only works if other people practice libertarianism. What, then, do you do with the large majority of mankind that are disinclined to live by these rules, or incapable of living by these rules?

Consider Xenophon slaughtering, looting, and burning his way across Asia. Consider the various piratical adventurers that founded what became the British empire. Raffles killed a lot of people, was apt to murder competing merchants, destroy cities, shake down rajas for gold and land, and so on and so forth. Yet one cannot help forming a compelling impression that Xenophon, Raffles, Clive, and most of the rest of those piratical cutthroats and slave raiders were upright, honest, virtuous, and decent men.

We are always in a state of anarchy, in the sense that the government's ability to be obeyed rests largely on bluff and social pressure, in the sense that any place you rely on police to keep you safe, is a very dangerous place, in the sense that we have a lot less government than we pretend we do.

Since we are never entirely out of a state of nature, always in anarchy to some considerable extent, libertarianism only works in a community of well behaved people.

Anarcho capitalism is anarchy where most people adhere to natural law as described by Locke, peaceful orderly anarchy. But Hobbesian anarchy, Hobbes' state of war is, if not as universal as Hobbes argued, common enough to be normal. Xenophon, Raffles, and the rest, were upright men dealing with a world that is with great regularity in a condition of Hobbesian anarchy, where highly unlibertarian policies and programs, grossly negative sum policies, unambiguously damaging policies, are frequently just and necessary. Raffles had to murder competing merchants and shake down Rajas to get his ever flowing chest of gold, with which to fund armies to ravish cities. He needed to ravish cities in order to ensure that he and his fellow merchants could safely and freely engage in business.

## Cladistic analysis of neoreaction

2013-09-05 07:21:31

As humans are bony fishes, and the Cathedral the heretical spawn of Cromwell's puritans, the neoreaction is the heretical spawn of Libertarianism and anarcho capitalism. Consider for example the blog title Anarcho Papist[92].

The Dark Enlightenment is libertarians mugged by reality, a libertarian who realizes that the eighteenth century was right about women, and Bull Conner right about blacks..

---

[92]https://anarchopapist.wordpress.com/ "Anarcho Papist"

An anarcho capitalist favors a free market in law and defense agencies, defense agencies that are in many cases the private property of individuals and small groups. A neoreactionary is an anarcho capitalist who thinks that a monopoly defense agency that is the private property of one man (monarchy) or a cartel of defense agencies that are the private property of a few men (feudalism) is not so bad after all. Hence, throne conservatism.

He concludes that, progressivism being an official religion, therefore an official religion is unavoidable. He suspects that most people need religion to persuade them to act sensibly, hence, whether Atheist or Christian, he endorses altar conservatism. (Or in the case of Israel, Temple Judaism.)

Thus libertarianism mutates into throne and altar conservatism, as puritanism mutated into militant atheism.

Now if Bull Conner was right about blacks, one might conclude that the Cathedral's evil consists primarily in suppressing the Caucasian race, giving rise to an *ethno-nationalist neoreaction*

If the eighteenth century right about women, then perhaps the Cathedral's evil consists primarily in destroying marriage (which goes all the way back to Cromwell's puritans) and in suppressing men, especially beta males, (which goes all the way back to the Victorian Society for Suppression of Vice, themselves descended from Cromwell's puritans), giving rise to a neoreaction that appreciates the wisdom of game, itself descended largely from the libertine strand of libertarianism, giving rise to a *Patriarchal Neoreaction*. Atheist Patriarchal neoreactionaries profoundly appreciate the wisdom of Saint Paul, while theonomist reactionaries find Saint Paul a bit scary, and are apt, like Bruce Charleton, to hide him in the basement behind the water heater while Talmudically reinterpreting him away.

If the Cathedral's evil consists primarily in being anti capitalist, in creating the regulatory state where successful businesses operate by social consensus with personnel on the revolving door between regulators and regulated, as exemplified by politician bureaucrat businessmen such as Jon Corzine and politician businessmen such as George Soros, if its evil consists of preventing the technological singularity, of ending scientific and technological progress, then you get the *Techno-Commercial Reaction*. (Reaction, not neoreaction, nothing neoreactionary about it. They are fans of good old fashioned manchesterism, which is libertarianism as it was before it entered the demonic alliance with the anti slavery puritans and other non Anglicans.)

If the Cathedral's evil consists primarily in heresy, in suppressing non heretical Christianity, on coercing all Christian churches to follow in its heresy, then you get the *Theonomist Reaction*, which looks backwards to what Christianity used to be before they made concessions to the heretical spawn of the Puritans and Calvinists. Theonomists would like a state church, but where as I am keen on the Church of England, from the restoration to 1820 or so, which presided over the greatest flowering of science, technology, capitalism, and empire in the history of mankind, they tend to prefer older and less heretical churches, or newer and more prosocial churches, or, like Bruce Charlton, both, judging official churches more on their virtue or Biblical correctness, rather than their effect in promoting the worldly success of the nation that they teach and inspire.

These divisions of the Dark Enlightenment, the reaction, and the neoreaction, are less important that they seem, for if you are one, you are apt to be something of each of the others.

In particular, I want to get to the technological singularity (techno commerical reactionary), which makes me object to dysgenics, hence ethno nationalist neoreactionary, I am a darwinist, hence a partriarchal neoreactionary, I admire the success of England under the restoration Church of England, an official state church which was much better than today's official progressivism, hence at least somewhat sympathetic to the Theonomist Reaction.

It is looking less and less likely that progressivism can make it to the technological singularity before lapsing into a dark age. I suspect that later historians will set the turning point towards a dark age, the end of the scientific age, as 1972.

If a white, patriarchal, theocratic, capitalist, throne and altar society gave us the scientific and industrial revolution, perhaps that is what it takes to get to the technological singularity.

## All your keys are belong to us

### 2013-09-06 16:10:43

The official truth, which for once seems believable, is[93]:
> because strong encryption can be so effective, classified N.S.A. documents make clear, the agency's success depends on working with Internet companies — by getting their voluntary collaboration, forcing their cooperation with court orders or surreptitiously stealing their encryption keys or altering their software or hardware.

So, the NSA has the private key that is used by your https server. The question then is, how?

If you leave the front door wide open, and you find your house has been burgled, it is possible that the burglars have a super secret underground tunnel that comes up into a well hidden trapdoor in your basement.

But chances are that they waltzed in through the wide open front door.

And by "wide open front door" I mean the common practice of the certificate authority making up your secret key for you and sending it to you.

Snowden, who knows what the NSA is up to, tells us:[94]
> Encryption works. Properly implemented strong crypto systems are one of the few things that you can rely on.

Trouble is, seldom properly implemented.

Strong, non human memorable, secret keys should be created in place on the device that their corresponding public key identifies, and never leave that device. There should be no user interface and no best practice procedures for managing such secret keys, only for managing the corresponding public keys, which should be presented to the user as guids or something like a guid, as something like a vin number. The way a sysem administrator should perceive setting up an https server is that the server makes up a guid, and he then gets a certificate from the certificate authority saying that the guid is good for his

---

[93] https://www.nytimes.com/2013/09/06/us/nsa-foils-much-internet-encryption.html?_r=0
[94] https://www.theguardian.com/world/2013/jun/17/edward-snowden-nsa-files-whistleblower

organization and/or domain name, and installs the certificate for the guid on the server. He should not need to know or think about private keys.


# How not to be spied on

## 2013-09-07 14:06:34

It looks as though the major NSA tricks are:
Taking over routers using tricks similar to those botnet operators use to take over individual computers.
Twisting the arms of major corporations to backdoor their products and share information, for example Skype.
Encouraging the adoption of flawed cryptography with hidden backdoors through its standards arm, NIST.
Taking over individual computers using tricks similar to those of botnet operators. However they do not take over most people's computers, since doing so indiscriminately on a large scale would get them caught and people would adopt methods to protect their computers, as against botnet operators.

Supposing this to be so, the software published by Guardian[95] is likely to be fairly spy resistant, among them Ostel[96], a secure skype replacement.

Your contacts will still show up on NSA's contact tracing if you use Ostel, but they will not be able to listen in your calls. The bit they are most interested in is your instant messaging, since their computers can grep that information. Ostel's instant messaging is not secure. Perhaps it will be secure soon, but it is not secure now. Gibberbot instant messaging is secure in that no one can listen in, provided both ends use it, but you can still be contact traced.

Torchat[97] provides instant messaging that cannot be contact traced or spied upon, though it is not as instant as you probably used to, installing it is painful, and getting your friends to install it apt to be more painful. It requires Tor, and due to the current NSA scandal, so many people are joining Tor that it is going down under the load. Tor is Snowdened under.

And, what leads me to suppose that Skype, and therefore Microsoft is entirely in bed with the NSA? Create a web page, that has no links leading to it, which therefore no one should ever hit on. Mention that web page in a skype instant message. Someone, presumably the NSA, will download it.

The efficient way to transmit video and speech, and the way with the least lag is as directly as possible between the two peers. Instead, all skype voice and video goes through a central location in the US, introducing significant additional lag and very substantial additional costs and complexity for Skype/Microsoft.

---

[95] https://guardianproject.info/apps/ "The guardian project"
[96] https://ostel.co/ "secure skype replacement"
[97] https://github.com/prof7bit/TorChat

# RDRAND

## 2013-09-08 07:51:22

Cryptography needs random numbers, numbers unpredictable to an adversary. Computers are built to be as non random as possible, so this is a problem. Intel created an instruction, RDRAND, that supposedly creates a random number on each read.

This instruction appears to be backdoored by the NSA.

The numbers produced by any random physical process are always offwhite, in ways characteristic of that physical process, and diagnostic of the underlying physics. Because the numbers are whitened on chip, because we don't see the raw output, we cannot tell if the underlying physical process generating randomness has failed, has been turned off by the NSA, or ever existed at all. The decision to whiten the numbers on chip is a most strange one. It costs a bit of silicon, and lessens the utility of the physical random number generator, assuming there is a physical random number generator, for because of on chip whitening, there is no way to tell if there really is a physical random number generator or not.

This strange decision created much suspicion.

One of the designers responded to this suspicion, and my interpretation of his words is that he is a very bad liar, which is to say, his lies are both wicked and incompetent.

On 2013-09-08 3:48 AM, on the Cryptography Mailing list, David Johnston wrote:

> It interesting to consider the possibilities of corruption and deception that may exist in product design. It's a lot more alarming when it's your own design that is being accused of having been backdoored. Claiming the NSA colluded with intel to backdoor RdRand is also to accuse me personally of having colluded with the NSA in producing a subverted design. I did not.
>
> A quick googling revealed many such instances of statements to this effect, strewn across the internet, based on inferences from the Snowden leaks and resulting Guardian and NYT articles.
>
> I personally know it not to be true and from my perspective, the effort we went to improve computer security by making secure random numbers available and ubiquitous in a low attack-surface model is now being undermined by speculation that would lead people to use less available, less secure RNGs. This I expect would serve the needs of the NSA well.

Firstly, an honest person does not tell us that it is hurtful that his integrity is doubted, since that is an effort to shut down discussion. An honest person instead provides evidence of his integrity. A dishonest person wants to shut down discussion. An honest person wants discussion of the truth told his way.

Secondly, an honest person would not tell us that any doubt of RDRAND is doubt in his integrity, since Snowden has just revealed that the NSA has been subverting cryptography with secret agents acting behind the scenes. He would instead tell us that that part of the system of which he has knowledge has not been subverted in ways he can detect, that if RDRAND has been subverted, it has been subverted by a secret agent playing clever tricks behind his back. An honest person concerned for his good name would avoid the risk of taking the blame for furtive acts done by secret agents.

Thirdly, an honest person would spontaneously and unprompted provide some innocent explanation for the strange and suspicious looking design decision to whiten RDRAND on chip.

Suppose you see some people showing up at your neighbor's house while your neighbors are away. You go out to see what is up. If they immediately and spontaneously start explaining what is going on, probably innocent. If they cry indignantly that it is outrageous that you act as if this is suspicious behavior, they are guilty as hell.

When David Johnston starts off by saying how hurtful it is to doubt him, rather than "We chose to whiten on chip because ...", that is like the Wizard of Oz saying "ignore the man behind the curtain".

From which I conclude that David Johnston, one of the designers of RDRAND, is as guilty as hell.

## Northwest passage

2013-09-09 08:16:26

I have not been doing much global warming blogging lately, since that seems to be an area, where, like socialism, everyone knows the ruling elite is lying, and their continued lying only embarrasses them. When the climategate files came out, we had documentary proof that all the conspiracy theories about official science were true. Indeed the concept of the Cathedral, which is a loose coalition of many small conspiracies that in effect act like a vast conspiracy, owes much to what was revealed in the climategate files.

But, in response to the news that the Northwest passage never opened this year:

For as long as people have been searching for the Northwest passage, they have found that it sometimes opens in summer, sometimes remains closed, and sometimes opens briefly and closes unexpectedly, trapping whoever was trying to use it. That the Northwest passage has recently been open in summer, and has recently been closed in summer, is true for as far back as we have records.

## NIST curves backdoored

2013-09-10 05:47:18

Gregory Maxwell on the Tor-talk list has found that NIST approved curves, which is to say NSA approved curves, were not generated by the claimed procedure, which is a very strong indication that if you use NIST curves in your cryptography, NSA can read your encrypted data.

So don't use anything NIST approved.

NIST curves are supposedly verifiably random, which, if true, would be proof that they are not backdoored. Gregory Maxwell attempted to replicate this claim, found that they were verifiably nonrandom.

From: Gregory Maxwell <gmaxwell@gmail.com> mailto:gmaxwell@gmail.com To: "This mailing list is for all discussion about theory, design, and development of Onion Routing." <tor-talk@lists.torproject.org> mailto:tor-talk@lists.torproject.org Subject: Re: tor-talk NIST approved crypto in Tor? Reply-To: tor-talk@lists.torproject.org mailto:tor-talk@lists.torproject.org

On Sat, Sep 7, 2013 at 4:08 PM, anonymous coward <anonymous.coward@posteo.de> mailto:anonymous.coward@posteo.de wrote:

> Bruce Schneier recommends *not* to use ECC. It is
> safe to assume he knows what he says.

> I believe Schneier was being careless there. The ECC parameter sets commonly used on the internet (the NIST P-xxxr ones) were chosen using a published deterministically randomized procedure. I think the notion that these parameters could have been maliciously selected is a remarkable claim which demands remarkable evidence.

On Sat, Sep 7, 2013 at 8:09 PM, Gregory Maxwell <gmaxwell@gmail.com> mailto:gmaxwell@gmail.com wrote:

Okay, I need to eat my words here.

I went to review the deterministic procedure because I wanted to see if I could repoduce the SECP256k1 curve we use in Bitcoin. They don't give a procedure for the Koblitz curves, but they have far less design freedom than the non-koblitz so I thought perhaps I'd stumble into it with the "most obvious" procedure.

The deterministic procedure basically computes SHA1 on some seed and uses it to assign the parameters then checks the curve order, etc.. wash rinse repeat.

Then I looked at the random seed values for the P-xxxr curves. For example, P-256r's seed is c49d360886e704936a6678e1139d26b7819f7e90.

_No_ justification is given for that value. The stated purpose of the "veritably random" procedure "ensures that the parameters cannot be predetermined. The parameters are therefore extremely unlikely to be susceptible to future special-purpose attacks, and no trapdoors can have been placed in the parameters during their generation".

Considering the stated purpose I would have expected the seed to be some small value like ... "6F" and for all smaller values to fail the test. Anything else would have suggested that they tested a large number of values, and thus the parameters could embody any undisclosed mathematical characteristic whos rareness is only bounded by how many times they could run sha1 and test.

I now personally consider this to be smoking evidence that the parameters are cooked. Maybe they were only cooked in ways that make them stronger? Maybe????

SECG also makes a somewhat curious remark:

"The elliptic curve domain parameters over (primes) supplied at each security level typically consist of examples of two different types of parameters — one type being parameters associated with a Koblitz curve and the other type being parameters chosen verifiably at random — although only verifiably random parameters are supplied at export strength and at extremely high strength."

The fact that only "verifiably random" are given for export strength would seem to make more sense if you cynically read "verifiably random" as backdoored to all heck. (though it could be more innocently explained that the performance improvements of Koblitz wasn't so important there, and/or they considered those curves weak enough to not bother with the extra effort required to produce the Koblitz curves).

# The loyalty oath

## 2013-09-16 09:39:01

Reactionaries are wondering how to gain power – gain power against the existing Cathedral, with its no limit credit card, horde of purchased voters, and an increasingly unhappy but loyal army.

I don't see that as a problem. I see chaos coming. Power will fall into the street, hot, radioactive, dangerous, and desired, to be picked up first by one group, then another, each new pair of hands slippery with the blood of innocents, after the fashion of the Arab spring. So, here, I address the topic of keeping power, of making normality stable, after some lengthy period of horrifying chaos driven by fanatical utopians.

The Roman Empire in the west ended in anarcho piratism, which took centuries to stabilize into feudalism. I rather like feudalism, but it seems to take a while to gel. It never did quite gel in the British Isles until William the Bastard.

The natural state of government is government by a tribe, racially cohesive, sharing common beliefs, a common religion, mutual affection, suspicious of outsiders and frequently hostile to them.

However, west of the Hajnal line, European tribes are too weak, too incohesive, to hold power. East of the Hajnal line, they are too small.

Orthodox Jews, conservative Jews, are cohesive enough, and numerous enough, but reform Jews are perpetually at each other's throats. Orthodox Jewry is a religion of permanent exile, even in Israel it is a religion of permanent exile, hostile to and subversive of the surrounding society. It can be conspiratorially influential, but is incapable of outright ruling, incapable even in Israel, subversive and in exile even inside Israel.

Recall that the Old Bolsheviks were a heretical Reform Jewish sect, but as soon as they had power the Jews purged each other till the party was Judenrein. The Trotskyites still are a reform Jewish sect, and they hate Jews as much, and probably more, than neo Nazis do. Were the Trots ever to gain power, they would go Khmer Rouge on each other – and on everyone else as well, but especially on each other.

Tribalism makes for corrupt governments, if the government supposedly represents several tribes. The natural condition is that the government is controlled by one tribe, possibly ruling over other tribes.

Since the natural size of tribes is rather small, this presents a problem.

Religions are of course in large part synthetic tribes, hence the tendency to theocracy. If the theocracy recruits on sincerity and zeal, you get the left singularity as the ruling class rapidly becomes holier than Jesus, and shortly thereafter holier still. Thus rule by the Cathedral, our Harvard based theocracy.

The optimum system seems to be a pleasantly corrupt theocracy, where archbishops are good old boys who come from the right family, usually military family, and saints are revered, but saints are not allowed anywhere near the levers of power.

Modern society being too large for natural tribes, theocracy is inevitable, but you have to exclude believers in hostile religions without recruiting for zeal and sincerity in the official religion. Saints are dangerous. Saints that show excessive enthusiasm for the levers of power (pharisees) should be dealt with harshly even if they are saints of the official religion. Saints of the official religion should be rewarded for their saintliness with a hermitage on some bleak island far far from the capital, serviced by a slow ship at infrequent intervals. Saints of hostile theocratic religions should be severely persecuted if sighted sneaking up on the levers of power – they should get the inquisition.

An inquisition is relatively harmless if, like the Elizabethan inquisition, primarily concerned with protecting the powerful against hostile theocracies. If, like the Spanish inquisition, it has pretensions of sincerity and holiness, can get very nasty.

Repeating: The state requires a tribe. Actual tribes are weak, small, or nonexistent, hence the need for a synthetic tribe. Other, hostile, synthetic tribes will attempt to infiltrate. You have to exclude them, which requires a loyalty oath, and some degree of demonization. Indeed the loyalty oath should incorporate some demonization of the competition, which the Thirty Nine articles failed to do.

My favorite regime is restoration England, because under the theocratic government established in the restoration, began the scientific and industrial revolutions.

The scientific revolution began immediately in the restoration, as science and the scientific method received the royal blessing, and became high status, with every pirate who aspired to be a gentleman collecting botanical specimens while shaking down rajas for chests of bloodstained gold. Today, official science is high status, but official science is not science, but anti science, for the scientific method is at best despised as ignorant and vulgar, at worst demonized as neo-nazi.

Today, replicating research is felt to be a hostile act against the person whose research is being replicated, thus anti scientist, thus anti science, anti scientific

The industrial revolution began a little after, but it was still the case during the industrial revolution, that to get into parliament, or be a professor at a high status university, or to get a good job in the public service, or suchlike, you had to swear allegiance to the Thirty Nine Articles incorporating the Second Book of Homilies. They still took efforts by other theocratic religions to infiltrate the state religion seriously.

The Thirty Nine Articles was intended to exclude Puritans, Calvinists, and Roman Catholics, and the Second Book of Homilies covered assorted other mischief makers.

The great weakness of the Thirty Nine articles was that they placed selective pressure on hostile groups to change their antigens to avoid these antibodies. Thus William Wilberforce and the Clapham sect (the saints) claimed to be Anglican, though obviously they were not. They believed themselves to be the saints, the elect, and regular Anglicans to be damned. They also believed in Jesus the community organizer, and believed themselves holier than Jesus, were nine tenths of the way to being Unitarians, and viewed Unitarians as closer to their beliefs than regular Anglicans.

As hostile groups change their antigens, the loyalty oath needs to be updated with new antibodies.

One might suppose a loyalty oath can be trivially defeated merely by lying or doublethink, but remember, the threat is not infiltration by individuals, but infiltration by hostile organizations. If the hostile organization tells its members to lie, it can never be sure if they are telling the truth.

The hostile organization cannot safely tell its members to lie, but it can, and regularly does, tell its members to engage in doublethink and doubletalk, thus, Jesus the community organizer, redemption is voting for Obama, salvation the successful implementation of a progressive state: Observe Pope Francis, for whom Salvation is homosexual Bishops. However it has to somewhat openly preach doublethink and doubletalk to its members, which is to say, change its antigens. Which is why you need to update the antibodies at regular intervals.

Progressivism practices entryism against all existing organization, coordinating them all to promote progressivism. Thus, for example, the Science Fiction Writers Association becomes an organization dedicated to turning all science fiction into turgid boring dreary impenetrable progressive propaganda.

So every organization needs a loyalty oath to exclude progressives. We should not, cannot, wait for the collapse. Have to start now. If you want an organization to go camping in the woods, and don't want it to become a entirely urban organization campaining against carbon, have to have a loyalty oath against progressives. If you want to organize cooking classes, and don't want it taken over by feminists campaigning against women in their homes, have to have a loyalty oath against progressives. If you have a fishing club...

In a world were all activities are coordinated to promote the progressive world view, an organization that functions to visit the wilderness without opposing industrial society and capitalism is a reactionary organization, and needs to defend itself against attack.

## Capitalism dead in the USA, live in China.

### 2013-09-17 15:15:31

After ordering Pax fired for political incorrectness, Anil, who simultaneously holds both governmental and private enterprise positions, is both regulator and regulator, dispenser of government funds and recipient of government funds, has a talk with Pax[98].

---

[98]https://dashes.com/anil/2013/09/my-meeting-with-pax.html

I was pretty amazed that he went for it. He flat out said that he wants his startup to be funded and wasn't sure if it'd be possible after all of his, and I replied that it realistically wasn't going to happen without the say-so of someone like me, and I wasn't inclined to give some VC the nod on this.

So, these days, the merely wealthy need a nod from the likes of Anil, the powerless need to run all their decisions past the powerful.

## On Fractional Reserve Banking

### 2013-09-19 09:53:15

Fractional Reserve Banking is not the problem. Term Transformation is the problem. Australia and Singapore ban substantial term transformation, came through the recent financial crisis without problems.

The banker borrows short term at 1%, lends long term at 4%. People deposit their money short term in case of rainy day. One day it rains on everyone, they all want to withdraw their money at the same time, problem.

The financiers run to the government and tell the government, quite truthfully, that they cannot fulfill the promises that they made, and unless the laws of economics are suspended in favor of corrupt and badly behaved bankers, the masses will be hurting.

The ensuing bank runs and financial panics cause widespread economic hardship, there is clamor for the government to ease the pain and prevent similar things from happening in the future, bingo, centrally planned finance. Capitalism continues as crony capitalism in which the favored financiers earn guaranteed profits dependent on government favor and regardless of competence or performance. Power and wealth slides into the hands of unproductive idiots selected for their political ideology.

Suppose, however, term transformation is forbidden. In that case, you cannot borrow long term at fixed interest rates, or if you do, you face exorbitant rates. So, when everyone wants to withdraw their money at the same time, interest rates soar.

This causes pain for borrowers, but since financial institutions remain solvent, we don't get a self amplifying panic, we do not get runs. The masses suck it up, business as normal continues, and in due course, another crisis of capitalism passes with capitalism unchanged and continuing to work just fine.

In an anarchic society, if depositors monitored their financial institutions solvency *and liquidity* (liquidity of a financial institution being largely the extent of its term transformation) thus discouraging term transformation, crises would not get out of hand. In Singapore, the government just asks financial institutions to report on the extent of their term transformation, with the implication that anyone who goes out too far on a limb will be invited to jump, thus no one engages in excessive term transformation. If a financial institution were to have excessive term transformation, and the Singaporean government were to make it known it found this excessive and destabilizing, there would be a small run, analogous to firefighters lighting a small fire in the woods so that a big fire in the woods will not have fuel.

# Google is evil

## 2013-09-24 11:47:34

With phones becoming more capable, an obvious way to make money was to create and sell a suite of productivity apps, so Quickoffice, the company, produced Quickoffice, the product, to allow you to edit your Microsoft Office documents on your phone, which product they sold very cheaply. Quickoffice, the company, sold lots and lots of copies of Quickoffice the product. They rapidly became the leading productivity phone app, with three hundred million installs.

Google, the company, purchased Quickoffice, the company, and made Quickoffice, the product, free. How very nice of them. What, you may ask, does Google get out of supplying Quickoffice for free?

Their actions tell us: They are generously giving anyone who uses Quickoffice plenty of free storage space on their supercomputer, and, considerably less generously, making it a lot harder for you to store your documents anywhere else. They promise that come 2014 they will make it largely impossible. So, best store all your documents on Google's supercomputer for convenient access from your phone.

Which means that Google's supercomputer, the greatest AI on planet earth, gets to read your documents.

And what might it do with that information?

Recall what it did with the information that Central Intelligence Agency Director David Petraeus was doing his email late at night from a single female's apartment.

# Putin deals with Civil Disobedience

## 2013-09-27 09:56:23

When someone claims to be engaging in "Civil Disobedience" he means "We are the state. You have to obey our laws, but we do not have to obey our own laws."

Observe that Bill Ayers, Obama's bomb making pal, never spent a day in jail despite having organized the bombing of numerous buildings to "protest the war" - actually of course, he was a state department proxy making war on the Pentagon, hence, no jail time. If *you* try bombing the Pentagon to protest the latest erroneous drone strike, you will get a big surprise.

But when state department proxies committed acts of piracy against Putin's state, they got a big surprise too.

Greenpeace has committed trespass, vandalism, and piracy on the high seas all over the world, acts that a hundred years ago would have resulted in them hanging from yardarm, and have never received any real punishment. Until now.[99]

Take a look at the expressions on their faces. They are thinking

> "Hey, surely they cannot charge us with piracy on the high seas just because
> we engaged in piracy on the high seas, can they? Can they?"

---

[99] https://www.ablxboston.com/national/18585-u-s-captain-and-crew-of-greenpeace-ship-jailed-over-russian-oil-protest.html

Please Putin, please, hang them from the yardarm.

## Australia wins the right to remain white.

2013-09-27 20:20:42

Since Europe has been flooded with non whites, Australia is close to being the whitest remaining country, possibly is the whitest remaining country. This is of course illegal under international law – since the Cathedral writes international law.

The Cathedral holds that international law requires that if a boatload of third worlders shows up, the first world country where they show up has to take care of them and put them on welfare for the rest of their lives. (It is more complicated than that, and different rules apply to America, but that is the practical effect in Australia and Europe.)

This international law has been seriously getting up the noses of Australians. The newly elected Australian government announced a new policy: That boatloads of illegal immigrants would be taken back to the land from whence they came.

This would have been a violation of Indonesia's sovereignty, since Indonesia did not want them back, and the Australian navy and Australian marines would have to sail up to the beach and unload the illegal immigrants in rubber boats, which would require Australian marines kicking the asses of illegal immigrants while within Indonesian waters, indeed while between the high tide mark and the low tide mark, which is one step short of invasion.

To which the Australian government replied that Indonesian boats coming to Australia without permission was a violation of Australia's sovereignty.

The Cathedral media, and Cathedral academics in both Australia and Indonesia had a meltdown and said the policy would lead to war, but, in the last few hours, Indonesia backed down, and now the Australian navy sails to twelve miles off the Indonesian shore and hands captured illegals over to the Indonesian navy across the twelve mile limit. Two shiploads were unloaded a few hours ago. If Indonesia, then anywhere. The Australian navy has established its right to send people back to whence they came.

I fear that Europe lacks the balls to follow this precedent and it is probably too late for Europe anyway.

## The fake shutdown confrontation

2013-10-01 06:17:48

Whichever party yields, winds up being blamed for any disruption caused.

Therefore, the party with the weaker hand should always yield swiftly, and the party with the stronger hand should never yield. And since the constitution gives the party that controls the house of representatives the overwhelmingly stronger hand, the Republicans would win - except that the whole thing is staged. They intend to lose, in order to persuade their voters that they have no choice but go along with Obamacare.

Spending bills must originate in the house of representatives. So the house of representative can vote to fund and open anything that the senate defunds and shuts down. Suppose, for example, the government shuts down the Applachian Home for Homeless

Kittens. Pitiful youtube videos appear of lost and homeless kittens, mewling sadly. Then the House of Reps simply passes a bill to fund the Applachian Home for Homeless Kittens. The senate then has to reject the bill, (because it fails to fund Obamacare as well as kittens) and look like bad guys.

If the senate allows the bill to fund the Applachian Home for Homeless Kittens, then the Republicans just fund the entire government piecemeal, except for Obamacare.

Republicans should be working around the clock to continually send funding bills to the senate, which those cruel flint hearted kitten hating Democrat senators have to reject around the clock.

If the Republicans were serious, they would be sending a stream of bills to the senate day and night to fund anything and everything, except Obamacare. Especially to fund kittens.

Which is to say, they would pass a budget or budgets, legislation that authorizes the government to spend on some things and not other things, something that has been missing from Washington for many years.

Instead, after seven days of completely symbolic government shutdown that does not inconvenience anyone, they will cry,

> Oh, we cannot take the pain, it is horrible, horrible, far too horrible. We capitulate. We tried, and tried, but we have no choice but to vote to fund Obamacare.

Then after voting to fund Obamacare, their polls will take a dive, and they will say:
> See how terrible it is to oppose any government spending. We have absolutely no alternative but to exponentially increase government spending without end.

If they are not voting to fund the poor little kittens, which is to say, passing a budget, they are not serious.

## Moving away from NIST

### 2013-10-04 06:21:15

Jon Callas, a leading cryptographer, is issuing a new version of Silent Circle, which by default uses only non NIST cryptography.

It was necessary to change the curves, since the NIST curves are probably backdoored. It was arguably not necessary to change the symmetric encryption and the hash, since they are unlikely to be backdoored. Nonetheless, he replaced AES with Twofish, and SHA with Skein-MAC.

> absolutely, this is an emotional response. It's protest. Intellectually, I believe that AES and SHA2 are not compromised. Emotionally, I am angry and I want to distance myself from even the suggestion that I am standing with the NSA. As Coderman and Iang put it, I want to *signal* my fury. I am so pissed off about this stuff that I don't *care* about baby and bathwater, wheat and chaff, or whatever else. I also want to signal reassurance to the people who use my system that yes, I actually give a damn about this issue.

By moving away from anything NIST has touched he deprives the NSA of leverage to insert backdoors, contributing to the general good, from which his company, and thus himself also benefits. By opposing the NSA, he gives his company credibility that they will not secretly play footsy with the NSA behind closed doors, reassuring his customers and contributing to the particular good of his company and himself.

## Cryptography standards

### 2013-10-04 08:49:33

If everyone was to do their own thing in cryptography, that would be very bad.

But committees are less intelligent than their individual members and are prone to evil and madness.[100] IEEE 802.11 was stupid. If NIST was not stupid, it was because evil was calling the shots behind the scenes, overruling the stupid.

Linux was a success because Linus is unelected president of linux for life.

Let us follow Jon Callas as unelected president for life of symmetric cryptography, Daniel Bernstein as God King of asymmetric cryptography.

## Technological failure of the silk road system

### 2013-10-04 16:55:27

Silk Road servers stored all messages in the clear forever.

The government placed malware on Tor exit nodes, located the Silk Road servers, raided servers, game over.

Private messages should have been end to end encrypted, existing in the clear only on the computers of the sender and recipient, and should have been deniable, except for messages containing money, where the sender needed to be able to prove that the recipient account had received a message with a particular hash, and thus able to prove that the recipient account received a message with particular content including payment.

Silk road servers should have performed a zero knowledge password login with each account, and for each account authenticated but not signed transient public keys for signing and encryption. Private messages from account to account should have been encrypted with these transient keys. Shortly after each login, transient public keys from previous logins should have been erased, as should any private messages.

Though messages should be deniable, sender should be able to prove he sent money, with or without revealing the content of the message containing the money.

## The underground economy continues

### 2013-10-05 03:33:49

I, and others, have been assuming that the takedown of Silk Road represents competent action by the NSA.

Outside In, however, points out the interesting coincidence[101] that the takedown of

---

[100]https://blog.reaction.la/economics/stultum-facit-fortuna.html
[101]https://www.xenosystems.net/crypto-capitalism/

Silk Road follows, rather than precedes, the appearance of competition to Silk Road.

Atlantis, however, appears to have skedaddled with its user's money, thus this looks like a successful shutdown of the online black market, hence likely to be primarily state action.

So, contrary to the headline, the underground economy does not continue.

## Republicans not folding yet

2013-10-06 12:24:51

A week ago I predicted that the Republicans would fold like a cheap deck chair, and and issue a grovelling apology for their evil attempt to implement their election platform merely because they won the House of Representatives.

Some of them are apologizing, but so far, no folding.

The Democrat strategy is to do random bad things to the American public, and have the tame press blame the Republicans for it. By and large they are reluctant to shut down any government activities that are actually affected by the withdrawal of funding, since the primary purpose of government spending is to benefit government employees, not to make them do any actual work.

So instead they shut down private facilities that, far from being the recipients of government funding, pay rent to the government.[102]

Stuff like this is the main damage - the government continues as usual, illegally, in the sense that government employees continue to receive pay and exercise power, but issues nasty orders forbidding *other* people to work and produce.

But, if government activities, including Obamacare, continue as usual, despite not being legally funded, why do they pay any attention at all to these votes? Instead of continuing business 99% as usual, why not continue business 100% as usual?

Because the vote undermines the pretense of democracy. Have to get the people to arguably vote for what the government is going to do anyway.

When the Republicans fold, rendering their election victory irrelevant, that makes those irritating white voters irrelevant.

## The Shutdown problem

2013-10-07 16:23:31

The republican party has a big problem: How to snatch defeat from the jaws of victory.

The government has, without quite realizing it, accepted piecemeal funding of everything except Obamacare. There is no shutdown. There is just the government doing occasional bits of petty spitefulness and nastiness to express its hatred of its subjects.

Since no shutdown, no reason for the Republicans to pass a bill funding Obamacare. The "shutdown" can continue forever. How are they going to get themselves out of this problem?

---

[102]https://www.coyoteblog.com/coyote_blog/2013/10/first-explanation-in-writing-as-to-why-usfs-is-closing-privately-funded-parks.html

If the Republicans retreat from victory, republican voters are going to become even more disgusted than they are already. If, on the other hand, they stand pat, and the government just goes right ahead with Obamacare, they will have failed in their task of making it look as if voters can influence the government.

Since the Republicans have won, the only way to maintain the illusion of democracy is to postpone Obamacare.

Those parts of the world where health care works have a system that is both more socialist than the US and more capitalist than the US, in particular, and especially, Singapore. Singapore has a fully capitalist health care system with actual prices. The American health care system does not have prices, therefore does not have markets, therefore is not capitalism. But, if someone is stony broke, the Singaporean doctors can kick him from the fully capitalist health care system, to the fully socialist system, where he is taken care of by a doctor on the government payroll, gets government medicines, has a government bed in a government owned building, for a low government set price, or for free if he cannot afford that price.

Somehow, almost everyone in Singapore prefers to go with the capitalist health care system.

Similarly, a major reason the Canadian health care system works is that nearly everyone lives a short distance from the US border.

## Obamacare is not the law of the land.

### 2013-10-10 07:58:49

Obamacare is not a law that Congress and the President negotiated together and passed.

As Hayek pointed out: Socialism needs a central plan. There are an infinite possible number of different central plans, any one of which will step on the toes of quite a lot of people, so one can never get majority support for any one central plan, or even the support of a significant plurality for any one central plan.

So the ordinary procedures of legislative rule will not work, will never come to agreement. And, as we saw, they did not work, did not come to agreement.

The normal procedure for passing laws, as laid down in the constitution, is that one house of the legislature passes an act, and the other house agrees to that act, and then the president signs it.

But what in fact happened is that neither house would vote for a version of Obamacare that the other house would accept, nor one that the president would sign.

Obamacare was passed by the mysterious extraconstitutional process of "reconciliation", resulting in a bill that neither house has ever voted for, which contains numerous amendments rejected by both houses, and fails to contain numerous amendments accepted by both houses, thus was not "reconciliation" at all, but the permanent government overruling the merely elected government when the merely elected government was unable to reach agreement.

After being passed by this extraconstitutional process, it was further amended by presidential decree, an unprecedented extraconstitutional action,

This abandonment of constitutionality and legality is an unavoidable consequence of socialism.

To implement socialism one needs a single individual, or a very small cohesive group, small enough to sit around a coffee table and feel each other's breath, with immense power.

Ever since Reagan decreed unlimited free healthcare for the poor and illegals, we have had socialism without a central plan. It works very badly.

Our ruling elite think themselves terribly smart people and are sure they can do better, and I am sure any one of them could do better. I am equally sure that one hundred of them can not do better, and will very likely do a great deal worse. If power is too diffused in the legislature for the legislature to give effect to socialism, it is also too diffused in the permanent government for the permanent government to give effect to socialism.

Indeed, that is the basic problem with the permanent government. Power is diffused, leading to the tragedy of the commons, public money being a commons, and power over the subjects of the government being a commons. That we are ruled by an unelected government is not the problem. Democracy sucks. That the permanent and unelected government lacks a czar with the power to defund any activity, fire any bureaucrat or group of bureaucrats for any reason or no reason at all, impose a loyalty oath, and shoot any bureaucrat that violates his loyalty oath, is the problem.

Obamacare illustrates that democracy has been dead for a long time. So does gay marriage and affirmative action. The problem, however, is not so much lack of democracy, as absence of a central power. The rationale for government is to make one decision for all, in particularly, and most importantly, the decision of war or peace, that if it chooses peace, permits no one to cause trouble, if it chooses war, commands all to harm the enemy. But, in fact, our government is not capable of making one decision for all. It is anarcho tyranny.

A common semi humorous definition of anarcho tyranny is that everything is illegal (that is the tyranny) except crime, which is legal (that is the anarchy)

But a more serious definition is that the government is vast, powerful, intrusive (that is the tyranny) but is itself anarchic, itself subject to the tragedy of the commons (that is the anarchy)

The one definition, of course, tends to cause the other definition. The government being itself anarchic is uninterested in upholding law, since the rule of law, though it would benefit everyone, would not particularly benefit any one member of the government that himself attempted to uphold the rule of law without support from other members of the government, and the government being itself anarchic cannot restrain any one member of government from capriciously deeming any act by any subject illegal and punishing it.

## CBO projects deficit under control.

### 2013-10-14 04:29:20

Business insider points out the that the CBO projects the deficit to fall as a percentage of GDP[103] over the next three years, neglecting to recollect that the CBO has been projecting the deficit to fall as a percentage of GDP for quite some time, while it has continued to soar as a percentage of GDP. The CBO has a record similar to that of Anthropogenic Global Warming models. Global warming models always predict doom, which never arrives, CBO never predicts doom, which always arrives. CBO model is that normal growth is going to resume, any day now. We are not a society that peaked in 1972 and has been in accelerating decline every since. We are not a society that was cooking the books and adjusting the statistics until things got so bad that the discrepancy between reality and official reality manifested, Soviet Style, as crisis. All that is needed is a a bit more stimulus. CBO model is that Obamacare is going to save us piles of money on healthcare.

## Lessons from the silk road.

### 2013-10-16 05:38:42

As I said earlier, without providing evidence or explanation[104], the big flaw was that the server kept the messages in the clear. A recent news report has confirmed this from official sources[105]:

> The complaint says "an image of the Silk Road Web Server was made on or about July 23rd, 2013, and produced thereafter to the FBI" as a result of a request made to a foreign country under a formal MLAT.

> "An image of the Silk Road Web Server was made on or about July 23rd, 2013."

> That image, or bit-for-bit copy, of the Silk Road server gave authorities access to private messages between the Silk Road's owner and other members of the site. It was instrumental in seizing the site and arresting Ross Ulbricht, the man police allege was behind the Silk Road.

## The "shutdown"

### 2013-10-16 13:15:32

I have been analyzing the "shutdown" as politics as usual, which is to say, a fake conflict between the inner party and the outer party to give the appearance of democracy. I predicted the Republicans would roll over and wet themselves in a week.

It has now been two weeks.

---

[103] https://www.businessinsider.com.au/facts-about-debt-and-deficits-2013-10

[104] https://blog.reaction.la/economics/technological-failure-of-the-silk-road-system.html

[105] https://www.theverge.com/2013/10/14/4836994/dont-host-your-virtual-illegal-drug-bazaar-in-iceland-silk-road

I still think it is politics as usual, but the increasingly strident reaction of the inner party organs indicates that some of them are seeing it as politics for real. "Outside In" is therefore analyzing it as a real conflict[106].

In the Game of Chicken, the side that can most convincingly signal madness wins, so when the inner party call the Tea Party crazy, they are preparing to lose. Or they could be preparing to ship the Tea Party off to concentration camps, after the fashion of Golden Dawn.

Two cars drive at each other at high speed down the middle of the road. The guy who swerves loses. In the Republican car, the establishment, the outer party, is in the driver's seat, and wants to swerve. The Tea Party is in the passenger seat, but is fighting for the wheel.

Given the commotion in the Republican car, the Democrat car would be well advised to swerve. Or they could shoot the guy in the passenger seat.

I still think this is going to end with the outer party driving the Republican car off the road, but some elements of the inner party are starting to doubt it.

Obama has been thinking about halting EBT payments in the event that the debt limit is not raised. That is the responsible thing to do. If he does not pay EBT, he can honor the debt limit, pay the interest on government bonds, and pay the army. What is not to like? Could any Tea Partier disagree? If the government is going to prioritize, it has to shut down something big and simple. Most government expenditures take years to halt, but we have seen that EBT cards can just be turned off with a switch. A sudden absence of blacks, indios and morbidly obese heavily tattooed women each with nine screaming demon spawn in tow, ensues at shopping centers. Instant overnight solution to the deficit.

The Tea Party would be fine with such a solution. With such a solution in place, why raise the debt limit ever again?

"Oh no, the demon spawn are starving. To save the demon spawn, arrest the Tea Party."

I rather like that scenario, since really I would like us to get the collapse over with, rather than endless decline. But the Republican establishment driving the car into the ditch seems more likely.

## The outer party rolls over

### 2013-10-17 10:21:26

The outer party has rolled over for the inner party and wet themselves.

Because they lost, they will be blamed for holding the confrontation at all. Had they won, Democrats would be blamed.

In that the Democrats had accepted funding to keep almost all the government open except Obamacare, the Democrats were most of the way to losing. In that the Democrats were starting to call the Republicans crazy, the Democrats were most of the way to losing (since in a game of chicken, the guy who can most convincingly demonstrate craziness wins). So the Republicans had no choice but to declare defeat.

---

[106]https://www.xenosystems.net/chicken/ "The Game of Chicken"

That the Republicans snatched defeat from the jaws of victory confirms my original analysis, that the whole thing was charade from beginning to end, which analysis I had started to doubt as the confrontation went on for two weeks and the Democrats came ever closer to capitulating.

## Stupid U and faking the GPA
### 2013-10-21 09:00:39

Lately universities, especially high status public universities, have been introducing courses in stupid, to accommodate the increasing number of students that have difficulty doing traditional university courses. The students who attend courses in stupid are overwhelmingly female and disproportionately lower class. At the same time, degrees in smart, for example Computer Science, get women and blacks affirmatively actioned into them, and when those students struggle, get quietly and furtively dumbed down, becoming yet another degree in stupid.

In Paying for the Party: How College Maintains Inequality[107] the authors note with puzzlement that lower class students that come to university with a high GPA, tend to struggle doing traditional university courses, and repeatedly switch majors towards courses in stupid. Because they repeatedly change majors, they spend an unreasonably long time in University and thus rack up unreasonably high debt, finally leaving university with high debt, a low GPA and a degree in stupid. They then fail to get middle class jobs, being stupid people with a degree in stupidity.

Of course, back in the early nineteenth century everyone knew that parental achievement was the best indicator of a child's likely achievement. Tests are easy to game, so are only a reliable indicator when the test outcome does not affect anything.

But why does lower class GPA droop in university? The authors of Paying for the Party noticing that upper class students tend to party their way through university, doing no actual studies, staying drunk and chasing girls, yet nonetheless get high marks and good degrees, followed by good jobs, suggest that there is magic invisible classism dripping off the walls, much like the magic invisible racism that holds blacks back and destroyed Detroit.

It has long been obvious that schools and universities are artificially marking girls up and boys down. You can see this from the discrepancy between GPA (girls higher) and SAT (girls lower), and from the outstanding incompetence of female computer science graduates. But lately the extreme pressure, represented by such projects as "no child left behind", is for low achieving high schools (schools mostly attended by lower class and non asian minorities) to achieve the same results as high achieving high schools (schools largely attended by upper class and whites). Of course the easiest way to comply with such requirements is to cheat and lie, so we would expect that As are a lot easier in lower class schools than in higher class schools, so that a good GPA in a lower class high school means much less than good GPA in a higher class high school.

Of course higher class schools have compensating advantages:

---

[107] https://www.amazon.com/gp/product/0674049578/ref=as_li_tf_tl?ie=UTF8&camp=1789&creative=9325&creativeASIN=0674049578&linkCode=as2&tag=jimsblo0e-20

If you go to a lower class school, and you are smart, you will get beaten up and robbed. thus lowering your self perceived status and expectations. The teachers, being startlingly dumb, will hate you for being smarter than they are, and vindictively find ways to harm you. You will learn burglary, and how to do drugs.

At a higher class school, you will learn that non fiction reading is interesting and fun, you will learn how to fake a history of left wing activism to impress the universities you are applying to, and you will make friends and connections that may well be valuable in later life. (And you might even learn something from the teachers, though I doubt it.) But your GPA will be markedly lower than if you went to a lower class school.

However, even though lower class high schools are under pressure to equalize their GPAs with higher class high schools, universities are not under pressure to equalize the GPAs of their lower class students with that of their higher class students. And so, when two students with supposedly equal GPAs enter the same class at the same university, the one whose GPA came from a lower class high school fails, because her high GPA is a lie, and the one whose GPA came from a higher class high school passes, because his high GPA is the truth.

Two kids, one with a high GPA from a lower class school, one with a high GPA from a higher class school, go into the same class, take the same tough course, but, the authors of Paying for the Party tell us, the one from the lower class is wasting time and money, while the one from the upper class schools graduates with flying colors while partying his way through university. The authors of Paying for the Party think this is due to magical invisible classism, but I think that the course has been so dumbed down in an unsuccessful effort to accommodate students with fake GPAs, that the student with the genuine GPA (a male from an upper class school) would be wasting his time to pay more than minimal attention to the course, and so is considerably better off spending his time partying, thereby laying girls and making connections that may well serve him in future life.

Hence the swarm of lower class people, mostly lower class women, getting very expensive degrees in stupid.

Schooling largely exists because it is government subsidized child minding. The government wants to get hold of your children to indoctrinate them, so compels schooling and arranges social institutions so that schooling is needed. Absent subsidy and social engineering, formal schooling would be vastly reduced. People would instead rely largely on home schooling, apprenticeship, and internship.

One of the mechanisms for ensuring adequate attendance at government indoctrination sessions is that schools perform a sorting function. For the able and industrious to be sorted into the able and industrious category, they first have to attend X amount of time listening to government propaganda.

But that propaganda, that indoctrination, is against sorting – sorting is discrimination. We are therefore proceeding to subtler forms of discrimination, degrees in stupid, versus degrees in smart. The logical endpoint of this process is that everyone in America gets a PhD which costs six hundred thousand dollars, but most of the PhDs are in basketweaving and puppetry. The sorting function, which is the incentive to attend college, is continually sabotaged and subverted.

No one should run up large amounts of debt to get a degree in stupid.

# In favor of official religion

2013-10-23 05:29:05

Official science is, as all reactionaries know, and all progressives deny, a disaster.

All progressives also know that official religion is a disaster, despite the fact that progressivism is the official religion. This should make you suspect that official religion is a good thing - unless, of course, it is progressivism.

If a meme complex is selected for virulence, if for example if it is transmitted by street corner preaching, it is going to be a cult, will have characteristics likely to be harmful to the host.

If, however, a meme complex is parentally transmitted, then it is going to reflect the characteristics of those who successfully reproduce, hence likely to be beneficent, providing divine authority for behaviors that parents know to be beneficial, behaviors which provide long term rewards but not short term rewards.

If a meme complex is state transmitted, the meme complex will reflect the values of a successful state. Unless, of course, it becomes a tool for power struggle within the state, and so continually changes to become ever more extreme, as each pharisaic politician priest strives to be holier than each of the others, resulting in a left singularity. If, however, it is a conservative religion that claims to transmit the wisdom of your forefathers, and sends any living saints to hermitages on the outer Hebrides where they cannot cause too much damage, generally works tolerably well.

An official religion should squeeze out and discourage more virulent religions, such as street corner religions, without, however, discouraging and displacing parentally transmitted religions. Parentally transmitted religions should be encouraged, protected, and supported, but individuals who deviate from the official belief system should not be allowed access to the levers of state power. The Ottoman empire operated in this fashion, with an official Judaism, various official Christianities, etc. One might point out that the official belief system of the Ottoman empire was pretty bad, but we have seen a great many worse. It was not cultish, which lack of virulence in the end led to its undoing.

Theocratic Anglicanism allowed parentally transmitted religions through latitudinarianism, though this ultimately was its undoing. William Wilberforce and the rest claimed to be living saints, claimed to be the elect. All elect that were plausibly saintly should have been sent to hermitages in the Outer Hebrides. All elect that were obviously pharisaic, for example William Wilberforce, should have been sent to the West Indies as slaves to cut sugar cane. Official religions should not tolerate the dangerously holy, and particularly and especially should not tolerate those who claim to be exceptionally holy adherents of the official religion.

# The anti-anti reactionary FAQ Part 1, Terror and mass murder

2013-10-23 09:23:46

In this post, I address Scott's anti reactionary FAQ[108] on terrors and mass murders. In other posts I will address economic growth, sex, freedom, art, and other issues. The anti

---

[108] https://slatestarcodex.com/2013/10/20/the-anti-reactionary-faq "The anti reactionary faq"

reactionary FAQ is big, and has a lot of points, most of which I will deal with in separate posts.

Reactionaries say that democracy leads to the left singularity, which at best results in great suffering, and usually in mass murder.

Scott in his anti reactionary FAQ refutes this by a pile of supposed reactionary mass murders, notable among them the horrible reactionary mass murderer Zhang Xianzhong, better known to reactionaries as the horrible radical leftist mass murderer Chang Hsien-chong, the man who distributed the wealth of the landlords to the poor, then ate the landlords for oppressing the poor, then exterminated the intellectuals for infecting the poor with insufficiently progressive ideas, then flayed the poor alive for being insufficiently grateful for having the wealth of their oppressors redistributed to them.

Of all those who write in English, the historian Donnithorde[109] was in the best position to know the truth about Chang Hsien-chong, and he tells us that the radical leftist Chang Hsien-chong reduced the population of Szechwan from three million to seven thousand, largely by torturing people to death.

The Ming dynasty was under attack by left wing revolutionaries. The most extreme, and most religious, of the leftists rose to the top, being holier than any of the others. Inevitably he found that not only were the elite not left enough, but the masses were not left enough. And soon after that, his own lieutenants were not left enough either.

This seems to be the closest approach to the left singularity ever.

Earlier I wrote[110]

> The left singularity is the same each time in its approach to infinite leftism, but differs chaotically and surprisingly each time in its ending short of infinite leftism
>
> If it did not end, the final outcome, infinite leftism in finite time, would be that everyone is tortured to death for insufficient leftism, except the last torturer, who then commits suicide to punish himself for failure to inflict infinitely severe torments, but this does not happen in practice, because always at some point short of infinite leftism, something, or someone, goes boom – though not necessarily very far short of infinite leftism.

Which is a close approximation to the career of Chang Hsien-chong. Things did not go boom until rather late in the process.

Wikipedia gives a more progressive account[111], but the whitewash seems to be based on nothing but wishful thinking, on progressive unwillingness to believe ill of progressives. They cite Donnithorde to tell us that the seven kill stele is a myth, but neglect to cite Donnithorde that the words were Chang's, irrespective of whether he carved them on a stele.

Chang said:

---

[109]https://images.library.yale.edu/divinitycontent/dayrep/9866641_1938_040-007-008_eng.pdf   "Chang Hsien-chong and the dark age"

[110]https://blog.reaction.la/tag/left-singularity

[111]https://en.wikipedia.org/wiki/Zhang_Xianzhong "progressivism adjusting history"

Heaven brings forth innumerable things to nurture man.
Man has nothing good with which to recompense Heaven
Kill. Kill. Kill. Kill. Kill. Kill. Kill.

To update his words to the twenty first century just substitute earth for heaven:

Earth brings forth innumerable things to nurture man.
Man has nothing good with which to recompense Earth
Kill. Kill. Kill. Kill. Kill. Kill. Kill.
10:10 no pressure.

The progressive rationale is that it was not Chang Hsien-chong Zhang Xianzhong that killed all these people, but something or someone else, that no one noticed at the time.

Hang on. China in the seventeenth century was a literate and bureaucratic society. We have a pile of census records showing the near total depopulation of Szechwan. If someone or something killed everyone in Szechwan, it would have been noticed. There is overwhelming historical evidence that Chang Hsien-chong did it, or rather that the population of Szechwan did it to each other under his leadership and under the influence of his ideas. There is precisely zero evidence of anyone or anything else doing it.

So the progressive position on Chang Hsien-chong Zhang Xianzhong is similar to their position on Pol Pot and Kim Il Sung. Supposedly he is a reactionary, and anyway the CIA made him do it. If reactionaries want a monarch, was not Kim il Sung a monarch?

Well actually, no, Kim Il Sung was not a monarch. He was a demotic radical, and should his descendents become monarchs, which may well happen, then North Korea will be fine. But since they are demotic radicals, North Korea is a hell hole, though not as bad a hell hole as was Szechwan province under Chang Hsien-chong.

Supposedly, if Zhang Xianzhong did it, he was a reactionary and monarch (Scott's position), and if he was a radical leftist, he supposedly did not do it (Wikipedia position).

This post cheerfully stolen from Konkvistador[112]

# The anti-anti reactionary FAQ Part 2, Crime.

## 2013-10-25 08:05:09

A major reactionary argument is that since the early eighteenth century, since the reign of throne and altar, war, state political repression, state violence against respectable citizens, underclass crime, and minority crime have all risen enormously, that the overclass and underclass are attacking the productive, and the attack has been escalating.

Scott's anti reactionary FAQ[113] points out that murder is pretty much the same as ever it was. Quite so. Those crimes that the state tolerates are increasing – thus burglary, assault, and mugging has soared everywhere, whereas home invasion burglaries, where the criminals riotously enter an occupied dwelling, have only soared in those countries such as Britain where home invasion is tolerated.

---

[112]https://slatestarcodex.com/2013/10/20/the-anti-reactionary-faq/#comment-17867
[113]https://slatestarcodex.com/2013/10/20/the-anti-reactionary-faq "The anti reactionary faq"

Scott tells us that Victorians felt profoundly unsafe from crime:

> Violent attacks by strangers were seen as grave cause for concern. There was
> a disproportionate amount of attention paid to violent nighttime assaults
> by strangers in urban areas, called "garroting" and similar to what we might
> call "mugging". There were garroting panics in 1856 and 1862

He neglects to tell us why the Victorians panicked.

The Victorians panicked because, over the course of several weeks, two people in the city of London were mugged, a crime that they had no words for, never having experienced it before.

Scott points out that crime has diminished over the last few decades, neglecting to acknowledge that this is a short term and small decline compared to the long term trend of a gigantic rise in private and state violence.

The cause of the decline is pretty obvious in San Francisco. Police are kicking black ass. The highly progressive far left elite piously averts its eyes while its police force does extremely racist and reactionary things to protect them from minorities.

It seems the same thing has been happening everywhere.

Although progressivism moves steadily ever leftwards, in any one area of policy there are waves. First a large movement left. Disaster ensues, as with freeing the slaves, then a small movement right, as with Jim Crow. Then after a while, another large movement left.

Crime has diminished somewhat because we are in the small movement right phase with respect to crime. From what is happening in New York city, looks like the next large movement left phase is about to resume, whereupon we will see gentrification end, white flight resume and New York head off in the footsteps of Detroit.

Crime has risen because of movement left. It fell because, for a little while, we moved a little bit right on crime. But since progressives always need each to be lefter than the other, they can only move rightwards on crime by moving leftwards on something else - and in due course, are coming back to moving leftwards on crime.

# Progress

## 2013-10-27 08:20:32

In 1900, there were no planes, no space travel. Motorcars were toys that enthusiasts played with, not useful means of transport. There were no computers, no radios, no antibiotics, no rockets, no nuclear power, no knowledge or understanding of the interior the atom, no very useful plastics.

In 1961 we had all of this stuff

Since 1961, what have we got?

The last man on the moon is getting pretty elderly. We have abandoned supersonic transport, and supersonic fighter planes are close to being abandoned.

Cell phones and the internet show radical improvement, but are just more intense and improved use of computers and radio, technologies that existed well before 1961. Genetic technology shows promise, but is not yet doing anything big. While reading genes continues to improve, writing them may well have peaked, and without vastly improved writing, gene technology is not going anywhere exciting. AI remains thirty years in the future, as it has been for the past sixty years, even though every desktop now contains more computing power than the human brain.

And, as I regularly point out

The last man on the moon left in 1972[114]

The tallest building in the united states was finished in 1974.[115]

Cars are becoming humbler.[116]

# The anti-anti reactionary FAQ Part 3, Freedom and Monarchy.

## 2013-10-30 07:11:51

In his anti reactionary FAQ Scott tells us how terribly repressive Queen Elizabeth was, failing to compare actually observable dissent in her time with actually observable dissent in our time:

> Likewise, Elizabeth and the other monarchs in her line were never shy about killing anyone who spoke out against them. Henry VIII, Elizabeth's father, passed new treason laws which defined as high treason "to refer to the Sovereign offensively in public writing", "denying the Sovereign's official styles and titles", and "refusing to acknowledge the Sovereign as the Supreme Head of the Church of England". Elizabeth herself added to these offenses "to attempt to defend the jurisdiction of the Pope over the English Church...". Needless to say, the punishment for any of these was death, often by being drawn and quartered.

But every Shakespearean play was written from within the worldview that Roman Catholicism is true in its views about the next world, or that paganism is true, or that materialism is true and God or the gods care nothing for humans. They are incompatible with the official religion of which Queen Elizabeth was the head

In contrast, today every television show preaches our official religion. Thus, for example every father on television is an idiot and/or evil, and his family would be much better off without him.

Under democracy, efforts to control public opinion are far more strident, aggressive, and intrusive than they were under monarchs.

Under Stalin, thought crime could get you killed, but it generally just caused you to lose your job. Under democracy, thought crime causes you to lose your job.

Under monarchy, thought crime did not cause you to lose your job, or get you killed. Using speech to in an attempt to overthrow the ruler could get you killed, but you did not have to worry about microaggressions against the monarch, the way one has to worry about microaggressions against women or blacks.

---

[114] https://blog.reaction.la/economics/decline-of-the-west.html

[115] https://blog.reaction.la/economics/decline-of-the-west.html

[116] https://blog.reaction.la/economics/decline-of-the-west.html

Shakespeare could not present a play in which Queen Elizabeth needed to be overthrown, but he could present a play in which a King needed to be overthrown, a play in which England's official religion of which Queen Elizabeth was the head, was assumed to be false.

Today you could not present a play in which father knows best, still less one in which a wife deserves a spanking for failure to perform wifely duties, gets one, and improves her conduct.

If you turn on the television, you get strident, insulting, non stop propaganda, all counter stereotypical women and blacks, all insultingly and viciously stereotyped fathers and husbands, and continual denigration of males. If you attended a play in Elizabethan England, you seldom got propaganda.

Whenever someone wants to argue that Shakespeare's plays were propagandistic, they point to his enthusiastic demonization of Richard the Third. But Richard the Third attained the throne by murdering his nephews, the rightful heirs to the throne. How is a playwright going to depict an uncle who murders his nephews?

Another example of Shakespeare's plays being propagandistic is that they are unkind to Joan of Arc. But the official story was that Joan of Arc was a witch. Shakespeare implies the official story is a politically convenient lie. On today's television, not only are all today's official stories true, but anyone that thinks that today's official stories are lies is a tinfoil hat wearing nazi white supremacist moron. Official government issued truths, such as Global Warming and female equality, are not presented as state issued, but as issued by plucky rebels resisting government power - and repeated over and over again, and woven into stories without regard for story, plot, or drama.

If you share your workplace with women or blacks, you live in continual fear of losing your job on charges of sexual harassment, sexual assault, racism, or sexism, and your employer lives in fear of a "civil" lawsuit by government charging him with alleged acts of racism or sexism by his employees, or even mere thought crimes by his employees. People in the days of Queen Elizabeth did not live in fear of losing their jobs for lese majeste.

Today, everyone lives in fear of being accused of thought crime. In the days of Queen Elizabeth, they did not. You can criticize today's regime, but only through an identity that cannot be easily linked to your employment or business.

## Apostolic Succession

2013-11-01 14:45:25

According to some branches of Christianity, notably Roman Catholicism, Jesus ordained his disciples to perform certain sacraments, and they in turn ordained others to perform these sacraments, and only the legitimate successors of the apostles can validly perform these sacraments. So supposedly most sacraments are invalid unless performed by a priest, by someone who has been authorized by someone who has been authorized ... all the way back to Jesus.

Trouble is that because the official Roman Catholic Church has not believed in Apostolic Succession for some time, Pope Francis arguably never got ordained, in the sense that his ordination did not grant him power over sacraments, in the sense that it failed to say, or act out, the granting of power over sacraments, and is therefore only a layman who cannot perform a valid sacrament.

If you do not believe in apostolic succession, then Pope Francis is just another man. And if you do believe in apostolic succession, then he is still just another man, because ordained by people who corrected the ordination to avoid expressing belief in apostolic succession.

The radical protestant position, the puritan position, the leftist position is that any baptized Christian who inwardly and outwardly has right intention can perform any sacrament that is appropriate to his authority within the congregation. Unlike most puritan positions, there is reasonable scriptural support for this position, while scriptural support for the proposition that only a priest can perform a sacrament is lacking. Indeed, arguably the doctrine of special priestly power over sacraments verges on theomancy.

But even if the left is correct on this one, they are still arrogant, overbearing, and intrusive.

The left rules, and the Church complies. Thus, in the sixties, Anglican priests and Roman Catholic priests, and indeed priests of every major Christian church, except for Greek Orthodox stopped ordaining priests as having special power to perform sacraments. In particular Roman Catholic ordination dropped the line that they were endowing the supposed priest with the power to "offer Mass for the living and the dead"

Maybe that line was not necessary, because making the priest a priest implies it. But if you delete the line, then it no longer implies it.

Greek Orthodox does not have that line, but does have instead ritual that solemnly acts out the bestowal of special power over the Eucharist passing from the ordaining priest to the ordained priest.

The ritual changed because progressives reject apostolic succession. Changing the ritual therefore ends apostolic succession because that is what the change was intended to mean.

So, if you believe in Apostolic succession, you need to get your sacraments from someone who has been ordained in one of those schismatic micro churches by a bishop who schismed from one of the major Christian religions when they turned left and submitted to the Cathedral in the sixties. Pope Francis is not a Pope, nor even a Bishop, nor even a priest.

Charles the First said "No Bishop, No King", and ever since then the descendents of his enemies have been trying to eradicate Bishops. In the sixties, they largely succeeded.

If there is such a thing as Apostolic Succession, and if Apostolic Succession continues, it continues in Bishops descended from the schismatics of the sixties - whose churches are the size of a mustard seed.

Protestants said "no" to popes.

Puritans said "no" to popes and kings.

Now Puritans rule the world. Kings are gone. Did you think popes would remain?

Neo reaction means that conservatism has expired. There is nothing left to conserve. Reaction has expired. The old regime has died beyond possibility of revival. Not only is the Pope not Catholic, you cannot find Catholics in the Vatican. Apostolic succession of Bishops remains in a mustard seed of schismatic far right churches, but apostolic succession of Popes has lapsed.

Neo reaction is a radical, revolutionary, anti utopian movement. We have no good solutions to the problem of collective decision making, and therefore it is time for bad solutions.

There is no Pope, and the only way you are going to get a pope back is if a new holy Roman Emperor summons a conclave of Bishops to appoint a new Pope.

A god who designed creatures, a maker as men are makers, a God in our own image, was a mighty defense of order.

> Thou shalt not covet thy neighbour's house, thou shalt not covet thy neighbour's wife, nor his manservant, nor his maidservant, nor his ox, nor his ass, nor any thing that *is* thy neighbour's.

…

> Each little flower that opens,
> Each little bird that sings,
> He made their glowing colors,
> He made their tiny wings.
>
> The rich man in his castle,
> The poor man at his gate,
> He made them, high or lowly,
> And ordered their estate.

After Darwin, the designer God is dead. There is no longer evidence of a God made in our image.

We must look to some different defense of order. Micro economics defends the capitalist order. Darwinism defends the natural rule of men over women and superior races over inferior races.

The Christian Church has been highly successful in resisting external attack, but progressives are entryists. The holier than Jesus Church to which William Wilberforce belonged claimed to be Anglican, while they believed that members of their church were the elect, were saints, and regular anglicans were damned. They swore to the 39 articles while believing these articles to be instruments of evil class oppression.

Entryists form an organization within the organization, claiming to be loyal members of the outer organization, indeed more loyal than thou, while working to its destruction, cooperating with those that are openly on the outside, while purporting to cooperate with those on the inside.

And, in the sixties, Churches that believed in the apostolic succession and ordained their priests with the special and miraculous power to perform sacraments, were taken over by those who quietly rejected that doctrine. And thus, in those churches, the apostolic succession was ended.

Conservatives conserve their victorious enemies. Roman Catholics attribute to their Church a meaning it is not willing to express. A Roman Catholic believes that there is an important difference between his church and a protestant church such that his Eucharist is valid, and the Protestant's Eucharist is invalid. But there is no important difference, cannot be any important difference, is not permitted to be any important difference, between progressive protestantism, and progressive Roman Catholicism, because they are all under the same thumb.

Ecumenism was quietly implemented when you were not looking. A progressive believes that all religions are precursors of progressivism. His Jesus is a sort of John the Baptist pointing the way to Obama. Jesus the community organizer replaces Christ the Redeemer. Feminism replaces marriage.

Apostolic succession is a doctrine that favors official religions. And the official religion is progressivism. Progressives have, supposedly, received the authority passed along by Jesus.

If a neoreactionary favors official religion as a force for order, and progressivism is official religion, what is his complaint?

His complaint is that progressivism is a force of disorder. Progressives want to run everything, but, as Obamacare and the Occupy campsites illustrated, cannot run anything. They are like a horde of locusts. They take over everything and ruin everything. The only way you can have an organization that functions is to have an organization that actively evades and resists progressive dominion.

Progressivism is a force of disorder because progressives are commies, or rather, progressives are not commies but commies are progressives. Progressives want to submit everything to collective decision making, which is to say, progressive decision making, but we don't have any good mechanisms for collective decision making.

A progressive thinks collective decision making is wonderful, and therefore should be applied everywhere on everything. A libertarian thinks it is terrible, and therefore should be applied as little as possible. A neoreactionary thinks it is terrible, so when we really need collective decision making we might as well use known terrible that have, in the past not been as disastrous as usual.

# The anti-anti reactionary FAQ Part 4, Ever leftwards movement

2013-11-03 06:27:35

In his anti reactionary FAQ[117] Scott argues that ever leftwards movement is not a bunch of conspiracies run by Harvard and the State Department, but rather a natural response to prosperity and power. We are richer and safer, so can afford a little decadence, perhaps a lot of decadence.

This fails to explain the ever more drastic measures applied by the state to move us left, for example population replacement, and the ever more strident propaganda in school and on television.

This also predicts that no crisis shall ensue, that we will reach an equilibrium level of leftism appropriate for our level of prosperity and power, that there is a natural level of leftism, and this natural level has moved left because we are richer, have contraception, treatment for sexually transmitted diseases, dominate all our enemies, etc.

---

[117] https://slatestarcodex.com/2013/10/20/the-anti-reactionary-faq/ "The anti reactionary faq"

But every other leftwards movement has become ever more extreme, moved leftwards ever faster, eventually resulting in crisis, usually a bloody and disastrous crisis. The reason that leftists of anglosphere puritan origin rule the world is in large part because all the other left wing movements self destructed horribly, leaving Anglosphere leftists of puritan origin the last power standing.

Karl Marx predicted the second coming crisis of capitalism, in which capitalism would collapse, and the saints his followers take over.

I can confidently predict the collapse of leftism, but alas, not that the saints get to win. It sometimes happens that reactionaries take over after the crisis, and all is peace and order, but the more usual outcome is outside invaders take over, sometimes genocidally, or pirates and brigands take over, and slowly over centuries the brigands transition to being feudal lords.

A reactionary victory is possible. Strange things are apt to happen as history approaches a left singularity. White autogenocide is also possible, in which first all white heterosexual males are murdered, largely by each other, then all whites are murdered (Jews discovering to their great shock and surprise that they are white after all), all heterosexuals are murdered, and all males are murdered, then anyone insufficiently leftist is murdered, then the bar for being sufficiently leftist is raised, and raised again, until some of the remaining leftists wise up and murder everyone who is excessively leftist, thus ending the crisis.

If it winds up that bad, or any where near that bad, will not end in the second coming of Charles the Second.

## Murdering Grandma does not substantially save on health costs

2013-11-04 09:58:07

All the intellectuals in the US who are officially deemed to be very smart people are officially telling us that the big problem with health care, the reason your Obamacare bills are going out of sight, is that keeping Grandma alive for a few months longer can cost unlimited amounts of money

As you doubtless know, most government health care systems around the world wind up murdering Grandma to free up beds: "Prolonged deep sedation"; "The Liverpool Care Pathway".

To rationalize this, as we in the US increasingly move towards a government health-care system, everyone is telling us that grandma is causing out of control health costs.[118]

> People 65-79 (9 percent of the total population) represented 29 percent of the top 5 percent of spenders. Similarly, people 80 years and older (about 3 percent of the population) accounted for 14 percent of the top 5 percent of spenders (Chart 2[119], 40 KB).2[120] However, within age groups, spending is

---

[118]https://www.ahrq.gov/research/findings/factsheets/costs/expriach/index.html

[119]https://www.ahrq.gov/research/findings/factsheets/costs/expriach/expriach2.html

[120]https://www.ahrq.gov/research/findings/factsheets/costs/expriach/index.html#ref2

less concentrated among those age 65 and over than for the under-65 population. The top 5 percent of elderly spenders accounted for 34 percent of all expenses by the elderly in 2002, while the top 5 percent of non-elderly spenders accounted for 49 percent of expenses by the non-elderly.

But what all that adds up to is that grandparents dying of complications of old age are causing only a small proportion of total health care costs. The article whines about how selfish grandma is for expensively remaining alive, but reveals that grandma is not in fact costing enough to make a noticeable difference. If in each year you kill off the most expensive five percent of over sixty fives, you save twelve percent.

A casual glance around the emergency room suggests that the main cause of out of control health care costs in the US is people who can freely demand health care without facing any risk that they will have pay for it, that the major factor influencing health care demand, is not age, but whether one has to pay for it out of one's own pocket, that a young healthy person for whom health care is free, demands a lot more expensive health care than an elderly person for whom health care costs money.

On casual and unscientific observation, looks like affluent white people are paying for most health care, and underclass and non asian minorities are consuming most health care, looks that married people are paying for health care, and single women are consuming health care, rather than young people paying for health care, and elderly people consuming most health care, that health care in the US consists of massive transfers from whites to non whites, and substantial transfers from males to unrelated single females, most of them indios.

But since the evidence of one's own eyes is horribly racist, sexist, and homophobic, let us see if we can find some scientific and statistical evidence for this.

In Singapore, they have prices for health care, and even when these prices are set by the state in government health care facilities, they are not too far from market prices. Almost everyone everyone has to pay these prices, or some substantial part of them, except for catastrophic health care. Almost everyone in Singapore has catastrophic coverage, but has to pay for normal health care themselves, in whole or substantial part.

Singapore has quite a lot of government intervention in health care, so some people point to Singapore and say "See, capitalist health care works", and other people point to Singapore and say "See, socialist health care can work", but the big difference between Singapore and most other countries is incentives: That most health care in Singapore is paid for by the person receiving it, that health care in Singapore is, for the most part, paid for by the customer, and that doctors therefore answer to the customer, not the bureaucrat. He who pays the piper, calls the tune. If Singaporean healthcare is more capitalist than that of the rest of the world, this is an almost accidental and perhaps unintended consequence of the fact that people have to pay for it themselves.

Grandma dying of cancer is the same problem in Singapore as under socialist health care systems (she and her doctors are tempted to run up excessive bills) since most people in Singapore have catastrophe insurance, but with regular health care, people only pay for if it is worth the price.

Guess what. Singaporeans, having to pay for health care from their own pockets, do not buy much health care at all, and despite that, have very good health outcomes. That total health care expenditures in Singapore are remarkably small indicates that Grandma dying of the ailments of old age is not the problem. The problem is incentives for young healthy people, for that is the big difference with Singapore.

Since Singaporeans get good health outcomes, they are not underconsuming health care.

Therefore people in other countries are overconsuming health care - which is what we would expect if health care is free or heavily subsidized.

In some countries, health care is free for everyone, and I suppose that most people overconsume, though those with the most free time, the unemployed, the underclass, and the retired, probably overconsume the most. But most of the time, in most countries, and in particular in America, it tends to be free for some people rather than others – for the poor, for non asian minorities, and for unmarried women, and so we should expect most overconsumption to be by such people.

And that is what I seem to see when I go to medical facilities in the US.

Grandma having an incentive to spend irresponsibly is not a significant part of the problem. The problem is beggars, gypsies, liars, cheats, tramps and thieves. The problem is gimmiedats.

What makes healthcare expensive is the gimmiedats, not Grandma. And proof of this is that when, as in Singapore, you continue to indulge Grandma, but you don't indulge gimmiedats, healthcare costs a lot less.

In Britain, the NHS murders your grandmother to save money, but gives the man who thinks he is a woman a free sex change. In Singapore, they will not murder your grandmother, and will not provide a free sex change. Which place is more successful at reducing health care expenses?

If health care costs are such a problem that we need to murder people, let us murder gypsies. Saves a lot more money than murdering grandmas.

Whenever one of the officially smart people tells you that the problem is old folks, he is saying "Let us murder your Grandma for your own good. It is going to maximize utility. You will love it." I say, kill the gimmiedats.

If we are going kill elderly people and eight month fetuses because they are expensive and inconvenient, I have a long list of people who are a lot more expensive and less convenient.

# The anti-anti reactionary FAQ: Sluts

## 2013-11-11 09:21:44

Scott, good progressive that he is, is horrified by the fact that reactionaries use the word "sluts"[121] and feels that reactionaries are being illogical and inconsistent to endorse different standards for different genders. Which argument, like all his arguments, presupposes that men and women are exactly alike and everyone knows this and believes it. So it is completely unnecessary for him to bother producing any argument for the proposition that men and women are alike.

---

[121] https://slatestarcodex.com/2013/10/20/the-anti-reactionary-faq/ "The anti reactionary faq"

Scott cannot believe that reactionaries say what they say and mean what they mean, and assures us that reactionaries do not really think that different standards apply to men than to women, and different standards should apply. That would just be too awful even for reactionaries to think!

He piously explains that now that we have contraception and all that, there is no longer any reason for the old fashioned view of sluts.

He seems to have failed to notice that we have approximately fifty percent fatherlessness, (illegitimacy plus early divorce) and fatherlessness is strongly correlated with very bad outcomes for children – and civilizations.

Without posterity, soldiers will not fight, businessmen will not invest, and leaders will steal instead of lead. The big problem with sluttiness is not disease. The big problem is that without security of paternity, men will not invest in the the future, and thus, civilizations without security of paternity disappear from history.

Which is why society as a whole should penalize sluts. Sluts cause collective externalities far more serious than tobacco smokers. Because of the grave and great externalities produced by sluts, they should be taxed and penalized, like tobacco smokers, only at considerably higher rates, rather than subsidized, and subjected to official shaming and exclusion similar to that applied to tobacco smokers, only more severe.

Marry a slut, you will likely get divorced: alimony, charges of child abuse, lose your children.

Which is why men as individuals should discriminate against sluts. Sluts are dangerous and hurtful to the men in their lives, which is why you should bang them but stay out of their lives.

You can take the girl out of the bar, but you cannot take the bar out of the girl. Because a girl can have sex with a much more desirable man than she can marry or have a relationship with, if she has slept with thirty men before you, she has slept with thirty men who were handsomer than you, richer than you, have bigger tools than you, more self confident and socially skilled than you, but since those guys did not return her calls the morning after, and she realizes she is now running out of eggs, since she is having a lot fewer abortions than she used to, she has decided to reluctantly settle for you.

And then, of course, there are those infamous open relationships, or polyamorous relationships, where you get to sleep on the couch, and clean up the love stains on the main bed. Polyamory resembles a Sultan's harem. One sultan, lots of eunuchs. If a girl tells you she wants an open relationship, you are not the sultan.

If a woman decides on the option for casual sex, she will have casual sex with a man who is a lot more desirable than any man she has a relationship with, or is likely to be able to have a relationship with. So you should not be that guy that has a relationship with that girl. Sluts are good only for pump and dump, because any man that they can have a relationship with, they will despise.

For men, there is an equivalent to a girl being easy. If a man who wants to marry young, reveals that he wants to marry young, no woman will want him. Women despise men who are eager to have a relationship, even good women despise men who are eager to have a relationship, just as men despise women who are eager to have sex. If you are a man who wants to marry a good woman, you need to marry young. If you want to marry young, cultivate your inner dark triad, and let her believe she miraculously tamed the wild one. Taming the lovem and leavem cad is what women want, as marrying a virgin is what men want. So you are not going to marry a virgin, if the virgin girl thinks you are a virgin also. The double standard works both ways. Men like virgins, women don't like virgins. That includes supposedly Christian women. Perhaps especially Christian women.

The male equivalent of a slut is a man who is looking for a relationship with a woman. Women instantly despise him, as men instantly despise a woman who is looking for a quick bang. So, if you are looking to marry a virgin (which you should), don't let it be known. Instead let it be known that you are looking to pop a virgin to add to your notch count.

Sluts are bad for civilization, and bad for individual men, so men do not like them, and should not like them.

Rakes, however, men who sleep with lots of women, men who have sex rather than relationships with women ... women do like them. Everyone admires the man who has sex with lots of women, because that is hard, while everyone despises the woman that has sex with lots of men, because that is easy.

## Stupid U

### 2013-11-14 11:11:31

Inequality, as you know, is rising (because of the mass importation of a low IQ Indio and Mestizo non working underclass from Mexico into the US) The progressive diagnosis was that university makes everyone affluent and middle class, so they would run everyone, especially women, through university.

Unsurprisingly[122]:

> Between 2000 and 2008 the typical earnings of men with at least a bachelor's degree fell by more than $2,000, after inflation, to $70,332 a year. Between 2008 and last year they fell a further $3,500.

Falling rewards for a Bachelor's degree reflects the dumbing down of Bachelor's degrees, which is in substantial part driven by the flood of women in higher ed.

Women in higher ed tend to run up substantially higher debts than males in higher ed, because they initially get streamed into hard course, cannot handle those courses, and keep changing majors to dumber courses, which notoriously tend to be overwhelmingly female. To solve this problem the hard courses are being made stupid.

Being made stupid, a college degree is no longer an indicator that you are smart.

Males tend to get streamed out of hard courses, to keep the hard courses from being disproportionately male, so breeze through, so run up substantially less debt. This is deemed to be male privilege, which privilege can only be corrected by making university more stupid and discriminating in favor of women and blacks even more than they are doing already.

University, to be valuable, has to be a filtering system that separates smart and industrious from stupid and lazy. But, if a filtering mechanism, will tend to produce racial and

---

[122]https://isteve.blogspot.com/2013/11/the-missing-i-word-in-inequality-mystery.html

gender inequality. This, progressivism can only solve by making it not a filtering system, or by filtering for PC rather than ability.

## Progressives are channeling me

2013-11-15 17:20:18

Not long before 10-10 no pressure came out, I compared environmentalists the French Revolutionary terrorists, and said that they would murder children for insufficient environmentalism, and then the revolution would devour its children. And lo and behold, they produce an ad depicting themselves murdering children for insufficient environmentalism, and then murdering each other.

Observe, the Obama ads for Obamacare: Now people who actually work for a living will fund your self destructive behavior! Is it not great? Obamacare is wonderful since it makes other people pay for your decisions! Now typical Obama voters, such as alcoholics and fat sluts will no longer have to bear the costs of their own decisions!

The only way they could have made the Obamacare ads more truthful would be to give the beneficiaries the appropriate skin color.

## Your taxes at play

2013-11-16 13:38:04

Crystal Mangum, the whore who accused the Duke University Lacrosse team of raping her, is currently charged with murdering her boyfriend Reginald Daye Wilson.

The incident that led to the death of her boyfriend started with her applying for food stamps, Medicare, subsidized child care, cash, and employment assistance, which application was, in whole or substantial part, granted. Your taxes at play.

Crystal Mangum was falling down drunk or stoned at the time of the murder, and was "arguing about money" with her boyfriend. She has nine prior convictions, many of them for alcohol related violence.

After she stabbed Wilson, she left the apartment with his rent money. Her story is that he earlier gave her the rent money for safekeeping. No place safer than a drunk whore's handbag.

Looks like she got money from Uncle Sam the big pimp, promptly got drunk, murdered her boyfriend, and attempted to steal his rent money.

Wickepedia has a long, too long, don't bother reading, account of the Duke University Lacrosse case. The short version is that there were five men's DNA inside Mangum, but none of it matched any of the forty nine Lacrosse players, nor her boyfriend. This, however, did not stop the good and the great from sainting Mangum and demonizing the Lacrosse players on the basis of class and race. For a better account, See Durham in Wonderland[123].

Here is some material that should have been in Wikipedia, but was not:

---

[123]https://durhamwonderland.blogspot.com/2007/03/overall-case-narrative.html

**We are listening to our students.** We're also listening to the Durham community, to Duke staff, and to each other. Regardless of the results of the police investigation, what is apparent everyday now is the anger and fear of many students who know themselves to be objects of racism and sexism, who see illuminated in this moment's extraordinary spotlight what they live with everyday. They know that it isn't just Duke, it isn't everybody, and it isn't just individuals making this disaster.
**But it is a disaster nonetheless.**
These students are shouting and whispering about what happened to this young woman and to themselves.


## What Does a Social Disaster Sound Like?

> *. . . We want the absence of terror. But we don't really know what that means . . . We can't think. That's why we're so silent; we can't think about what's on the other side of this. Terror robs you of language and you need language for the healing to begin.*
>
> *...*
>
> *This is not a different experience for us here at Duke University. We go to class with racist classmates,*
> *we go to gym with people who are racists....It's part of the experience.*
> *[Independent,29March2006]*
>
> *...*
>
> *If it turns out that these students are guilty, I want them expelled. But their expulsion will only bring resolution to this case and not the bigger problem. This is much bigger than them and throwing them out will not solve the problem. I want the administration to acknowledge what is going on and how bad it is.*
>
> *...*
>
> *Being a big, black man, it's hard to walk anywhere at night, and not have a campus police car slowly drive by me.*
>
> *...*
>
> *Everything seems up for grabsI am only comfortable talking about this event in my room with close friends. I am actually afraid to even bring it up in public. But worse, I wonder now about everything. . . . If something like this happens to me . . . What would be used against memy clothing? Where I was?*
>
> *...*
>
> *I was talking to a white woman student who was asking me "Why do people and she meant black people make race such a big issue?" They don't see race. They just don't see it.*
>
> *...*
>
> *You go to a party, you get grabbed, you get propositioned, and then*

*you start to question yourself.*
*[Independent, 29 March 2006]*

...

*. . . all you heard was "Black students just complain all the time, all you do is complain and self-segregate." And whenever we try to explain why we're offended, it's pushed back on us. Just the phrase "self-segregation": the blame is always put on us. [Independent, 29 March 2006]*

...

*. . . no one is really talking about how to keep the young woman herself central to this conversation, how to keep her humanity before us . . . she doesn't seem to be visible in this. Not for the university, not for us.*

...

*And this is what I'm thinking right now – Duke isn't really responding to this. Not really. And this, what has happened, is a disaster.* **This is a social disaster.**

...

The students know that the disaster didn't begin on March 13th and won't end with what the police say or the court decides. Like all disasters, this one has a history. And what lies beneath what we're hearing from our students are questions about the future.

This ad, printed in the most easily seen venue on campus, is just one way for us to say that we're hearing what our students are saying. Some of these things were said by a mixed (in every way possible) group of students on Wednesday, March 29th at an African & African American Studies Program forum, some were printed in an issue of the Independent that came out that same day, and some were said to us inside and outside of the classroom. We're turning up the volume in a moment when some of the most vulnerable among us are being asked to quiet down while we wait. To the students speaking individually and to the protestors making collective noise, thank you for not waiting and for making yourselves heard

We thank the following departments and programs for signing onto this ad with
African & African American Studies:
Romance Studies;
Psychology:
Social and Health Sciences;
Franklin Humanities Institute;
Critical U.S. Studies;
Art, Art History, and Visual Studies;
Classical Studies;
Asian & African Languages & Literature;

Women's Studies;
Latino/a Studies;
Latin American and Caribbean Studies;
Medieval and Renaissance Studies;
European Studies; Program in Education;
and the Center for Documentary Studies.

Because of space limitations, the names of individual faculty and staff who signed on in support may be read at the AAAS website[124]:

...

## An Open Letter to the Duke Community[125]

In the spring of 2006, the Duke community was rocked by terrible news. We heard that a woman hired to perform at a party thrown by our lacrosse team had accused members of the team of raping her. Neighbors, we were told, heard racial epithets called out at the woman as she departed the party. The criminal proceedings and the media frenzy which followed are perhaps beginning to wind down. For us at Duke, the issues raised by the incident, and by our community's responses to it, are not.

In April, a group of Duke faculty members published an advertisement in The Chronicle. The ad, titled "What does a Social Disaster Sound Like?" was mostly a compilation of statements made by Duke students in response to the incident and its immediate aftermath. This ad has figured in many discussions of the event and of the University's response. It has been broadly, and often intentionally, misread. We urge everyone to read the original ad, available at `https://listening.nfshost.com/listening.htm`. We have. Some of us were among the ad's signers.

The ad has been read as a comment on the alleged rape, the team party, or the specific students accused. Worse, it has been read as rendering a judgment in the case. We understand the ad instead as a call to action on important, longstanding issues on and around our campus, an attempt to channel the attention generated by the incident to addressing these. We reject all attempts to try the case outside the courts, and stand firmly by the principle of the presumption of innocence.

As a statement about campus culture, the ad deplores a "Social Disaster," as described in the student statements, which feature racism, segregation, isolation, and sexism as ongoing problems before the scandal broke, exacerbated by the heightened tensions in its immediate aftermath. The disaster is the atmosphere that allows sexism, racism, and sexual violence to be so prevalent on campus. The ad's statement that the problem "won't end with

---

[124]https://www.duke.edu/web/africanameric/
[125]https://www.concerneddukefaculty.org/

what the police say or the court decides" is as clearly true now as it was then. Whatever its conclusions, the legal process will not resolve these problems.

The ad thanked "the students speaking individually and...the protesters making collective noise." We do not endorse every demonstration that took place at the time. We appreciate the efforts of those who used the attention the incident generated to raise issues of discrimination and violence.

There have been public calls to the authors to retract the ad or apologize for it, as well as calls for action against them and attacks on their character. We reject all of these. We think the ad's authors were right to give voice to the students quoted, whose suffering is real. We also acknowledge the pain that has been generated by what we believe is a misperception that the authors of the ad prejudged the rape case.

We stand by the claim that issues of race and sexual violence on campus are real, and we join the ad's call to all of us at Duke to do something about this. We hope that the Duke community will emerge from this tragedy as a better place for all of us to live, study, and work.
Click for list of Concerned Faculty[126]

## Hayekian critique of Obamacare

### 2013-11-18 06:19:33

Hayek correctly predicted that socialism must be despotic, because it cannot operate according to laws, but according to decrees. And so we see the President issued a speech declaring his intent to ignore and unilaterally change some parts of a law, passed by Congress and signed by him, that he was suddenly finding inconvenient and then enforcing obedience on state employees, non federal government employees to obey his words and ignore his laws[127].

But, Hayek tells us, even this does not work, because the decrees are apt to be mutually incompatible. They cannot all be carried out. And so the Pharaoh winds up commanding bricks to be made without straw.

Issuing a thousand page law is revealed to be, in practice, the equivalent of issuing no law at all, and issuing thousands of pages of regulation, in practice, the equivalent of issuing no regulations at all.

The usual meaning and manifestation of anarcho tyranny is black privilege - that Martin Trayvon was allowed to get away with crimes against white people that that white people would rightly be prohibited from committing against each other, and that white people are required to treat black thugs like Martin Trayvon with special respect that they do not receive from each other, and still less from blacks.

But we are seeing another meaning manifest, another form of anarchy, that the commands issued by authority are chaotic, inconsistent, lawless, arbitrary, and mutually incompatible, that authority, trying to command more than it is capable of, is flailing chaot-

---

[126] https://www.melloweb.com/concernedDuke/signatures.html
[127] https://rwcg.wordpress.com/2013/11/17/he-is-the-law/

ically, helpless to plan, far too capable of causing injury, disrupting the plans of others: We see socialism as so accurately depicted by Hayek.

Obama made a bunch of promises that could not be fulfilled simultaneously. And now he commands that they be fulfilled simultaneously, giving commands without bothering with any legal authority, and successfully enforcing obedience, though of course the obedience is unlikely to produce the expected results.

This is the slippery slope where socialism produces more socialism. The logic of events leads to killing fields, as commands mysteriously fail to have their intended effect, requiring ever greater extra legal powers which in turn require ever greater extra judicial punishments of ever more numerous "wreckers".

While in general the Cathedral has moved ever leftwards, every time it was in danger of being sucked into the the socialist maelstrom, it has backed off.

On past form therefore, one would expect an successful tea party movement of massive deregulation and denationalization, of abolishing government departments, starting with genuine markets in healthcare, though leftism in other areas would continue and accelerate.

Does not seem likely.

An alternative interpretation of past form is survivorship bias: We only see those brands of leftism that managed to resist the socialist maelstrom, because the others were sucked in and perished in horror and blood - that the past escapes of the Cathedral were mere luck.

Survivorship bias means one starts with a many dice, throws each one. The one that does not come up six, gets smashed. Pretty soon you have only one dice remaining, which has a past form of coming up six, which is to say, past form of backing away from the socialist maelstrom.

It is possible to back off from socialism, and anglosphere leftism has survived this long by doing so whenever it found itself drawn towards that whirlpool, instead focusing on going leftwards in some different direction, though the further it goes leftwards in other directions, the harder it is to resist the pull of the socialist whirlpool. Backing well away from 1949 style socialism by nationalization, which today it will not touch with a ten foot pole, it now finds itself sliding into the whirlpool through socialism by regulation.

The trouble is since the government has elected a new people, it is ever harder to repeat past form. To back away from the socialist maelstrom this time around, will likely need to fix the electorate

Backing off from healthcare socialism means drifing towards a two tier system, where the poor and the healthy get free government healthcare that is worth ever penny and the government wards smell of death, and the middle class themselves pay for their healthcare and control it, a mixed economic system best exemplified by Singapore. That is a mixed system, not a fully capitalist system, but it is capitalist enough to avoid the killing fields, and to make sure that only unimportant people go to the killing hospital wards.

With Obama's slide into rule by decree, the gulag is now in sight, though as yet only a small cloud on the horizon. At which point the Cathedral can ask how it wound up with thousand page laws and no budget, and back off from that path, which is to say a lot of Cathedral insiders secretly turn to the Dark Enlightenment, or the Cathedral keeps merrily sailing ever leftwards with gulag in sight and looming larger.

Past form is that it will find a way to back off from socialism and find some other direction leftwards. But past form may well be a survivorship illusion.

## Predicting collapse

### 2013-11-19 07:00:53

I am a prophet of doom. There tends to be an oversupply of prophets of doom, and the proportion who turn out correct is quite small.

Equally, there are also a large number of prophets of non doom, for example the numerous prophets of complacency during the fall of the Roman Empire in the west, who assume that everything will continue as today, often even when spectacular collapse is under way, they assume that everything has now stabilized, or will very shortly stabilize.

So, I reach for the mantle of an accurate prophet: Ayn Rand in her science fiction novel Atlas Shrugged[128] accurately predicted the condition of today's Detroit, though her book was published when Detroit had the highest standard of living in America.

In Atlas Shrugged "Twentieth Century Motors" adopts far left principles– which turn the factory and the surrounding city into a desolate ruin. Government do gooding prevents the market from correcting the problem, as more money keeps being funneled into losing programs.

Her account differs from the way things actually went in that she omits all mention of race, racial politics, and race baiting. Indeed, her America has no Jews, no blacks, and no Asians, White Anglo Saxon Protestants do it to themselves. Or perhaps it has all the usual ethnicities and races, but this is irrelevant to her story and left out of her prophecy.

Her America does, however, have anti discrimination laws, which are applied to destroy the banking system, just as in real life they actually were applied to destroy the banking system.

This, however, is simply a matter of focus. She is telling us about self destructive belief systems. The original cause of the death of Detroit was not blacks, it was the ideas that she so accurately skewered, for Detroit was white when she wrote. Electing a new people was merely a detail, a result not a cause, a detail irrelevant to the story, hence left out. That the left buggered the economy was the story.

So her prophecy leaves out a very big area, the inculcation of race hate, the creation of black privilege, state encouragement and tolerance of attacks by blacks on whites. The prophecy is economics only, but in what it covers, it is remarkably accurate.

Her America has no real distinction between the parties, which was probably true in her time, but has now become more obvious.

"Atlas Shrugged" is set in a carefully undefined time. Technology is in part time of publication technology, in part steam punk retro (steel and railroads), and in part city of tomorrow futurist (unreasonably fast trains).

The Soviet Union has collapsed, and/or survives only on American aid. Thus a book written in the 1950s casually predicts the situation that in fact prevailed after 1994 or so.

---

[128]https://www.amazon.com/gp/product/0452011876/

The story occurs a generation after the final collapse of General Motors " "Twentieth Century Motors", after a long period during which it was kept half alive by government interventions.

The fictional equivalent of General Motors in the ruins of Detroit is "Twentieth Century Motors" in the ruins of Starnsville, which name for a company that passed away a generation before the time of the story suggests a time early twenty first century. So, in so far as she hints at a date, she got the date reasonably correct.

In this undefined time, laws and regulation have multiplied so as to become irrelevant, and the government increasingly rules by moment to moment decree, drifting into capitalism without markets and socialism without a central plan, sliding into socialism through regulation rather than nationalization, and from regulation to rule by decree[129].

At the time she wrote, the west was backing away from the socialism of nationalization and price control, but she correctly foresaw it was merely heading into socialism by another path.

## The history of the left

### 2013-11-21 12:15:26

This is a relatively short recap of Moldbug on the origins of leftism.

Leftists like to trace leftism to the people who sat on the left hand of the French assembly, which traces back the left to its very first pretense to be something other than a religion, and then traces it no further. The French left, before they were "the left", were Gallicans, and before they were Gallicans, were adherents of the false Popes of Avignon.

Yet no sooner did they give themselves a secular name, than they proceeded to fight bloody holy wars in the Vendée and in Spain, as though the false popes were still seated in Avignon.

French leftism expired with Napoleon. Today's French left is a muppet manufactured by Anglosphere leftism, which originated in Browneism, which became Puritanism.

Today's state is the left, and the left is the state, as is apparent when one traces the funding of Occupy astroturf to itself.

If we trace back the American left through the years, decades and centuries, we find the roots of today's distinctly anti Christian and disproportionately Jewish left are nominally Christians, the super protestants of the 1940s, who in turn have plausibly Christian roots - the prohibition movement, the early feminist movement, the movement to raise the age of consent, the movement to give women the vote, and before that, the anti slavery movement: "Onward Christian soldiers".

The Anglosphere left, the left of Puritan origin, now dominates the world, all other lefts having expired, and been reduced to muppets of the Anglosphere left.

In Spain, a church was fined two hundred thousand euros for heresy, the[130] heresy[131] being an ad that featured some of the grosser and more self parodying elements of the gay pride parade.

---

[129] https://blog.reaction.la/economics/hayekian-critique-of-obamacare.html
[130] https://elpais.com/diario/2010/07/03/sociedad/1278108010_850215.html
[131] https://elpais.com/diario/2010/07/03/sociedad/1278108010_850215.html

This does not confirm Mencius' account that Europeans are ruled by muppet governments. What does confirm Mencius, is that in Spanish "gay pride day" is called "día del Orgullo Gay" - revealing that the theocracy being enforced in Spain is American, is Massachusetts, is Harvard.

Similarly "Pussy Riot[132]", wherein Russian protesters in Russia wear protest signs written in English.

The French Revolution would be an obscure dusty footnote in the history books, were it not that the Anglosphere left likes to dress itself in foreign clothes to facilitate the rule of foreign nations.

The French left originated in Gallicanism, became atheistic in the same way and for the same reasons that progressives became atheistic two centuries later, and dead ended in Napoleon the First. The modern French left is a creation of, and in substantial part a muppet of, the Anglosphere left, manufactured after Napoleon was defeated. Today's left has no organizational or institutional continuity with Rousseau's left. The modern French progressive is influenced by Rousseau's ideas, and likes to dress himself in Rousseau's ideas to make himself look less like a US State Department tool ruling over Europe through NGOs with their headquarters in New York and their branch offices in Brussels, but his organization and institution is organizationally and institutionally descended from English Puritans.

Anti colonialism is imperialist, and imperialism was anti colonialist:

Consider the path that Alassane Ouattara took to power: Educated in the US, career in Washington, raised to high position in the IMF. In due course jointly holds high position in the IMF plus high position in the Ivory government, despite the fact that he seldom visits the Ivory coast, briefly flying in from Washington from time to time, Election rigged in his favor in the Ivory Coast by UN troops, large numbers of native thugs imported from neighboring country. Population replacement and ethnic cleansing of the native population. Alassane Quattara then flies in from Washington to take power, despite the fact that he had not bothered to show up to his high Ivorian government job for six years. Clearly, the power that installed him over the Ivory Coast was located in Washington, not the Ivory Coast. Imperialism is still going strong today, and it still spouts anti colonialist rhetoric. Similarly Aristide and Mugabe, installed from without against the wishes of the locals.

The colonialists were piratical, and sometimes, as in the west indies, were indeed deemed pirates, but generally the Imperial approach, as with Clive of India and Raffles, was to disapprove of their piratical acts, and use them as justification for more centralized power, without actually going so far as to call people like Raffles pirates or bandits.

In practice, of course, empire, centralization of power, and the abolition of slavery, does not seem to have been all that popular. The Indian mutiny was in substantial part caused by do-gooder land reform – it was in substantial part a revolt against do-goodism by meddling outsiders far away in London, though it was deemed by London to be a failure of the colonialists, and grounds for even more centralization of power in London and even more unpopular do-gooderism.

When British adventurers first started raiding and trading with distant lands they

---

[132]https://blog.reaction.la/tag/pussy-riot

peaceably purchased spices, and they aggressively stole gold and spices. They attacked ships and seized cargoes because they just plain and simply wanted those cargoes, not out of any economic rationale about enforcing English monopoly. They did not think much about whether attacking ships full of valuable cargoes was good for England. It was good for the East India company, and what is good for the East India company is good for England. The trade rationale was something of an afterthought.

Over time, they tended to transition from mobile bandits to stationary bandits, becoming, without anyone particularly realizing it, governments, governments that enforced a local monopoly over trade in spices, among other things. Many of them became rich, and returned to England to buy respectability, disturbing those who's wealth came through respectable channels, who called these upstarts "nabobs".

Eventually, in the nineteenth century, the center, London, belatedly realized that these adventurers had become governments, and set to taking over from these colonialists, on the rationale both of benefiting England through trade monopoly, and the leftist do-gooder rationale of benefiting the natives.

The British empire was not conquered by imperialists, but by eighteenth century merchant adventurers, who mixed honest trade, piracy, conquest, and state formation. The nineteenth century imperialists took it over *from* the colonialists, and immediately the empire went into decline. In the nineteenth century, Colonialists right wing, Imperialists left wing and anti colonialist.

Today's anti colonialism is still imperialist, as illustrated by population replacement in the Ivory Coast.

It was in the anti slavery movement that the predecessors of today's left began to distinctly depart from Christianity: For the New Testament takes a very tolerant attitude towards slavery: The New Testament gently suggests that Christians free their own slaves, but does not require it, and clearly prohibits Christians from freeing other people's slaves, though they are perhaps permitted to close their eyes to other people's runaway slaves and look the other way. The civil war conspicuously and spectacularly exceeded not only what the New Testament requires, but also what it permits.

Similarly, with the emancipation of women, they really had to ditch Christianity and started doing so, for while the New Testament is mildly disapproving of slavery, it endorses stern patriarchy in no uncertain terms, and thus, with women's suffrage, we begin to see the familiar anti Christian modern left, though it was only in the 1940s or so that large numbers of Jews were permitted to join the modern American left.

Tracing the English speaking left all the way back to Browneism, we see continuity of personnel and ideology, the ideology slowly changing from Puritan Christianity to Unitarian Universalism to modern leftism, but changing slowly and continuously without any abrupt change, though over time every detail of the ideology changed, except for the war on Christmas, desecration of marriage, and the emancipation of women, which remained the whole time, even though sometimes justified by the argument that Christmas was too pagan, and at other times justified by the argument that Christmas was not pagan enough, and sometimes, strangely, both arguments simultaneously, while the desecration of marriage never got an explanation, for they never admitted that that was what they were doing, nor did the emancipation of women for as long as they thought themselves

Christian, for Paul unambiguously tells the Church to socially enforce male authority over women.

In the long and winding path between Browneism and today's left, there is one strong unchanging thread. The left is holier than thou. They were holier than thou when they were Christian, and they are still holier than thou now that they are anti Christian.

# Black Privilege

## 2013-11-26 06:01:16

**No Limit Nigga**

This is a picture of No Limit Nigga. If he does not much resemble the massively photoshopped image of Martin Trayvon you see everywhere, he nonetheless is a good match to the pre photoshopped image[133].

## The knockout game

You have doubtless heard of the knockout game, where a black suckerpunches some random white in the street.

Is the knockout game happening everywhere all the time and the press and police are politely ignoring it, or is it a very rare occurrence, and evil white racists are making a big deal out of this very rare event?

---

[133]https://blog.reaction.la/economics/photoshopping-trayvon.html

A congresswomen just got hit, so[134], if happening to a congresswoman, happening to very large numbers of ordinary people, but only reported when Jews or politicians get attacked.

A girl, Phoebe Connolly, punched in the head, apparently as part of the knockout game, promptly gave a speech piously calling for more generous welfare for the blacks who attacked her[135]. If some white guy at work sent her flowers, she would have called in HR to have him fired. Girls like attention from high status males, even if it takes the form of a punch in the face, don't like attention from low status males. Also bears shit in the woods/

## No Limit Nigga exercising the rights of blacks over whites

In October 2012 Martin Trayvon was suspended for writing obscene graffiti on a door at his high school. During a search of his backpack, security officers found 12 pieces of women's jewelry recently stolen from a house near the school and a screwdriver they thought had likely been used as a burglary tool.

Because No Limit Nigga was black, he was let off, and the property was not returned to the rightful owner.[136] If he had been white, would surely have gone to jail, and the property would have been returned.

Trayvon was enraged to be profiled by George Zimmerman because he felt entitled to rob and beat people up– and the reason he felt entitled, the reason millions of indignant and outraged people feel he was entitled, was because he *was* entitled to rob and beat people up.

In the arguments that immediately followed the shooting, those supporting No Limit Nigga, and condemning George Zimmerman held that George Zimmerman was white. (He was not.) That he looked white. (He does not look white. He looks Mestizo) And that he provoked Martin Trayvon.

But that is not an argument that George Zimmerman attacked Martin Trayvon. It is an argument that Martin Trayvon was entitled to attack George Zimmerman, that he had a right to beat the crap out out George Zimmerman without George Zimmerman defending himself. If they actually believed that George Zimmerman attacked No Limit Nigga, they would not talk about provocation. And if they believed that No Limit Nigga had no right to beat whites up, they would not talk about whiteness.

They claimed that they believe that Zimmerman attacked No Limit Nigga, but their arguments only make sense as arguments that Zimmerman was uppity, only make sense as arguments that Zimmerman disrespected Trayvon by not letting himself be beat up, only makes sense as an argument that Zimmerman "attacked" by fighting back.

Which is why Phoebe Connolly has the hots for the guys that punched her in the face, while her contempt and derision for the white males around her has left her an aging spinster heading fast towards becoming a cat lady. It is really our fault, not her fault, it

---

[134]https://www.dailymail.co.uk/news/article-2511614/Teen-game-randomly-punching-strangers-nation-wide-problemCONGRESSWOMAN-latest-victim.html

[135]https://dailycaller.com/2013/11/20/girl-who-got-punched-in-head-gives-lame-liberal-speech-humanizing-her-attackers-video/#ixzz2lOWOZFcX

[136]https://blog.reaction.la/culture/black-privilege.html

really is the fault of white males. Of course women are not turned on by men who submit. They want winners, we are losing. We should no more complain about that than women should complain that men want women who are young and slim.

In the ancestral environment, the guys who get punched in the face would not be able to provide a safe environment to raise children, and in our modern environment, the guys who get punched in the face also have trouble providing a safe environment in which to raise children.

If all men (and women) are created equal, then obviously female underperformance and black underperformance must be because the evil and astonishingly powerful white males are keeping them down. White Privilege!

Therefore, harsh measures are needed to punish these evil white males, to end White Privilege

Strangely, the harsh measures fail to work.

Obviously therefore, harsher measures are required. Rinse and repeat, without end.

The battle of the sexes is limited by the propensity to fraternize with the enemy, but race war has no limit.

A normal war can be ended by surrender, but a war for social justice can never end short of genocide, because there can never be social justice.

For this process after umpteen repetitions, observe those parts of black Africa where the Tutsi are ruled by their inferiors. As a result of the UN and international pursuit of equality and social justice, we see arson, mass rape and mass murder, and large numbers of Tutsi women murdered by vaginally impaling them with large objects, while the world piously and virtuously averts its eyes, and cannot bring itself to mention who is doing the impaling, and who is being impaled. And yet even as the impalings proceed, the Tutsis are still superior.

What must be done?

Impale with bigger objects. Only thus can the problem of Tutsi privilege be finally and permanently solved so that Black Africans can live together in the wonderful peace and harmony that existed before the evil white colonialists divided them from each other. Progressives the world over feel a warm glow of virtue, which might be disturbed if the details of what they are doing in the Congo was examined too closely.

Those who create value tend to be wealthy, those who consume value tend to be poor. If the government aligns itself with the poor against the wealthy, it winds up meddling with private property, and replacing the decision making process of the owners with its own decision process.

The pursuit of social justice on the basis of property rights, social justice for those who do not own property against those who do own property, leads government to massively violate property rights.

This faces government with an impossibly enormous pile of decisions which have to be made by people who can know very little of the matters they capriciously decide. Bureaucratic chaos ensues as the amount of red tape explodes, as depicted by Hayek and Ayn Rand. As the government operates without a budget, as it passes legislation thousands of pages long, which legislation is a set of headers for regulations tens of thousands of pages long, which entirely unworkable regulations are ignored by the regime itself and overridden by decrees casually issued in speeches.

This problem, called by economists the problem of socialist calculation, has been much studied by economists.

The equivalent problem, the problem of social justice between races and the sexes has not been similarly studied.

The the pursuit of social justice between ethnic groups leads to ethnic cleansing and pogroms, because no amount of state persecution of the superior group makes the inferior group any the less inferior. We are seeing increasing amounts of UN sponsored mass rape and ethnic cleansing, most recently in the Congo.

As with social justice between economic classes, the state is attempting to do that which cannot be done. Disaster necessarily ensues. With race the disaster takes the more direct and visible form of outrageous ethnic violence, while with economic classes, it is rather the government strangling itself in red tape and administrative chaos.

**So, how do we have a society in which this does not happen?**

**What is the cure?**    The problem is that leftism is a slippery slope. Indeed it is a conspiracy for finding slippery slopes, for each slippery slope creates a bunch of permanent government jobs, wherein political activists make a living solving problems that can never be solved. The Cathedral is aware of the economic critique of leftist hostility to property rights: Laws and regulations violating property rights mysteriously fail to achieve their objective, which is deemed reason for more laws and regulations, which also mysteriously fail to achieve their objects, till you get the total bureaucratic self strangulation exemplified by the Soviet Union and portrayed in "Atlas Shrugged". The Cathedral tries to resist the continual temptation to slide down this slope, not very successfully.

The Cathedral, however, is unaware of the similar slippery slope problem with privilege for inferior groups, and is sliding blindly.

The state provides "equality" for groups that are, on average, not equal. Problems ensue. It solves these problems at the expense of the superior group, applying unequal laws that discriminate between the groups, in favor of the inferior and against the superior. For example it is illegal for a white to insult a black, perfectly legal for a black to insult a white, and this is continually reflected in everyday life. The law requires everyone to support black and female self esteem, requires everyone to punish and degrade white male self esteem, the latter requirement being highly visible on television.

That white males are legally at the bottom of the totem pole deprives them of structural alpha. It makes white females less enthusiastic about sex and marriage.

But these laws, rather than remedying the inferiority of the inferior group make its inferiority more obvious, enraging it. The more the inferior group is privileged, the worse it behaves, the more inferior it is, the more problems ensue, the greater privilege is demanded.

You cannot actually treat unequal groups equally. For example if we have to restrict young people's drinking, we have to restrict blacks drinking for similar reasons. In America an eighteen year old is apt to be arrested for carrying a bottle of beer. Are you more worried by a white eighteen year old with a bottle of beer or a black thirty year old with a bottle of beer?

Fertile age women should not be allowed to drink in mixed company, except under the supervision of father or husband, not because they pose a risk to others, as hard drinking males do, but because they pose a risk to themselves. And thus we wind up with laws that say that if man and a women get drunk and have sex, and discover in the morning that they do not much like each other, the man is at fault, is in fact a rapist, unreasonably legally privileging women, and outrageously mistreating men.

We cannot restrain ourselves from giving women special protection. If we are going to protect them from the consequences of their own actions, which inevitably we always do, we cannot give them a free hand to perform those actions. If women are allowed to cry rape for decisions made while drunk, they should not be allowed to get drunk unsupervised.

To thrive, blacks need simpler, harsher laws, more vigorously enforced, than whites. The average black cannot handle the freedom that the average white can handle. He is apt to destroy himself. Most middle class blacks had fathers who were apt to frequently hit them hard with a fist or stick or a belt, because lesser discipline makes it hard for blacks to grow up middle class. In the days of Jim Crow, it was a lot easier for blacks to grow up middle class.

Of course a law that treats blacks differently from whites is going to be unjust to some blacks, but a law that treats someone over eighteen differently to someone under eighteen is going to be unjust to some eighteen year olds.

It is not that laws that treat different groups differently are more efficient. We do not care about efficiency that much. The problem is that if we refuse to treat different groups differently, we wind up solving the resulting problems by legally privileging inferior groups over superior groups, treating the superior group unequally before the law, and considerably worse. Such privilege tends to escalate without limit. Privileging inferior groups creates problems that result in escalating privilege. Priviliging superior groups is self limiting. Naturally the superior group is only privileged to the extent that it is superior. The inferior group, however, is privileged to make it equal, but its privileges do not make it equal but instead make its inferiority more painfully apparent.

The cure is that our laws and the enforcement of the laws have to reflect race and sex realism. Which will require a general purge of academia and government employees (especially the judiciary) of those who deny race and sex realism. We have to reject the proposition that all men were created equal and endowed with certain inalienable rights, and get rid of the entire apparatus for making this unreality real, this impossibility possible.

If we do not apply this cure, you are going to find it harder and harder to marry, harder and harder to buy a house where you can raise children, harder and harder to avoid being ethnically cleansed after the fashion of Detroit, harder and harder to have what was once regarded as a normal life. South Africa foretells a majority minority future.

## Moore's law ends. Technological singularity postponed indefinitely

2013-11-27 04:34:20

The fabs will soon be delivering "16nm" chips. But they are not in fact 16nm chips. That is just marketer spin. The wire to wire spacing, the pitch, is still 64nm, as it has been for some considerable time. There have been substantial improvements in power consumption, and this and that, but chips have just stopped getting denser. There are no more transistors per unit area than in previous technology generations. They are 64nm chips, and we have been stuck at 64 nm for some time[137].

For a long time, social decay and dysgenesis was masked by the march of science and technology. After World War II, the march of science pretty much stopped, but technology continued. After 1972, march of technology stopped in many areas, and severely slowed in most areas. Since then, one technology after another has been stopping.

Living standards in the US have been stagnant or falling since 1972.

DNA technology continues with exponential growth. Possibly hard disk storage and fiber optic bandwidth does also. For the moment.

If we are going to make it to the singularity, either have to have a political and cultural renewal, or else DNA technology has to make us smarter people. Unfortunately, while DNA reading and DNA editing continues to progress, DNA writing has maxed out. It is far from clear that we can make smarter people without a thousandfold improvement in DNA writing.

## Pilgrim socialism

2013-11-28 13:38:01

By now everyone knows the real story of thanksgiving. The pilgrim fathers attempted socialism, as usual famine ensued, followed by mass die off, they appointed a new governor who concluded that when God expelled Adam and Eve from the garden, God ordained private property in the means of production. Famine solved, prosperity ensues. Pilgrims ordain a day of thanksgiving to thank God for their prosperity.

But strangely, the New York Times, and the left generally, is fighting back, attempting to speak power to truth. According to the New York Times:

> Historians say that the settlers in Plymouth, and their supporters in England, did indeed agree to hold their property in common — William Bradford, the governor, referred to it in his writings as the "common course." But the plan was in the interest of realizing a profit sooner, and was only intended for the short term; historians say the Pilgrims were more like shareholders in an early corporation than subjects of socialism.
>
> "It was directed ultimately to private profit,"

---

[137] https://spectrum.ieee.org/semiconductors/devices/the-status-of-moores-law-its-complicated

This assertion of course, is based on precisely nothing. Governor Bradford, the reforming governor, attributes socialism to unnamed socialists, who believed that they were "wiser than god" and that socialism would produce prosperity and harmony, not to those funding the colony, who were in any case not much interested in profit.

Governor Bradford's description of puritan socialism shows that it was based on socialist idealism, on leftism.

Like the early Kibbutzim, they imposed perfect economic equality. Economic equality between the productive and the unproductive is not aimed at private profit, but demonstrates utter contempt for profit, indeed bitter, angry, hostility towards private profit.

Governor Bradford tells us:

> The strong or man of parts had no more in division of victuals and clothes than he that was weak and not able to do a quarter the other could;[138]

That is not what you do if you want private profit.

Like Pol Pot, and like the early Israeli Kibbutzim, they sought to smash the family and patriarchy.

> And for men's wives to be commanded to do service for other men, as dressing their meat, washing their clothes, etc., they deemed it a kind of slavery, neither could many husbands well brook it.

That is not directed at private profit.

When the natural order, ordained by God, was restored by governor Bradford, private property in the means of production and the patriarchal nuclear family, they had food and prosperity, and to celebrate, set a day on which they would give thanks.

> They had very good success, for it made all hands very industrious, so as much more corn was planted than otherwise would have been. The women now went willingly into the field, and took their little ones with them to set corn; which before would allege weakness and inability; whom to have compelled would have been thought great tyranny and oppression". By this time harvest was come, and instead of famine, now God gave them plenty, and the faces of things were changed, to the rejoicing of the hearts of many, for which they blessed God.

Thanksgiving is the day on which you thank God for the prosperity provided by divinely ordained capitalism and the intact nuclear family.

If the Cathedral did not intend socialism after the fashion of Pol Pot and to destroy the family, why would they lie about this? Governor Bradford's retreat from socialism was a defeat, and for four hundred years they have sought to reverse this defeat.

---

[138] https://books.google.com/books?id=hKlPLxAmX0kC&pg=PA172

# The anti-anti reactionary FAQ: war and democide

## 2013-12-01 16:20:29

Scott, good progressive that he is, assures us that with the rise of democracy, war has diminished.[139]

He gets this bizarre conclusion in two ways: By starting the clock at Zhang Xianzhong, after which violence diminished, and by starting the clock at World War II, after which violence diminished.

But Zhang Xianzhong was a radical leftist, not an emperor[140], and violence diminished after Zhang Xianzhong, because everyone was so horrified by the bloodthirsty record of leftism that they did not let it rise again for centuries,

Let us instead start the clock at the Restoration. We then see wars and genocide getting steadily bigger and bloodier to World War II.

As the world got more demotic, war, and democide increased from the days of the Restoration until World War II, after which we got the pax atomica, the peace of terror, the nuclear peace. Things were, during the nuclear peace, if not quiet, comparatively quiet.

Then there is slavery:

Those mightily indignant about slavery that substantially increased the living standards of those lucky enough "to catch the boat", as Mohammed Ali famously phrased it, just loved slavery that caused a hundred million or so to starve to death. We also saw all the gliterati and the progressive intellectuals gathered to support Mengistu's slave state. In the twentieth century, we had more slavery, and more slavery related deaths, than through all of previous history.

As for the nuclear peace:

Let us look at the middle east. Would anyone be worried if one of the monarchies had nukes?

No, they would be mightily relieved, confident that the Kings would keep the fanatics quiet.

But when the nearest thing to democracy in the middle east reaches for nuclear weapons, looks like the peace of terror may finally end in terror, probably with a kill level that substantially exceeds World War II. And if we don't have nuclear war this time, there will be a next time.

# anti anti anti anti reactionary faq

## 2013-12-04 13:23:35

Scot Alexander has answered the anti anti reactionary faq[141].

The anti anti reactionary faq argument to which he replies is that leftist have a dreadful record of misgovernment, terror, tyranny, artificial famine, and leftists tend to get

---

[139]https://slatestarcodex.com/2013/10/20/the-anti-reactionary-faq/ "The anti reactionary faq"

[140]https://blog.reaction.la/politics/the-anti-anti-reactionary-faq-part-1-terror-and-mass-murder.html "Zhang Xianzhong"

[141]https://slatestarcodex.com/2013/12/01/empireforest-fire/

lefter over a time. It is a slippery slope, the slope gets steeper and steeper, and at the bottom of that slope, a deep pit filled with sharpened stakes.

Scot's reply is that these bad things done by leftists were a response to the horrid horrid horrid evil oppression by extremely reactionary regimes, which made the masses so very angry.

The trouble with this story is the King Louis and Tzar Nicholas were very progressive - and very powerless. To the extent that they were able to exercise any power, it was to reward and protect their enemies, and destroy their loyalists. It is probably fortunate that King Louis XVI, a supposedly absolute divine right monarch, was completely unable to get any of his policies implemented, because they were all disastrously stupid highly fashionable left wing policies, in particular the proposal to abolish the taille.

## Venezuelan Elections

### 2013-12-08 06:27:51

As you no doubt know, there will be local elections in Venezuela shortly, and, in preparation for these elections, the Maduro government, having previously won an election by blatantly stuffing the ballot boxes, has murdered or arrested many, probably most, of its opponents, and has made it illegal to campaign against itself.

"Boring", I hear you say. "Is that not standard operating procedure in Latin America?"

What is interesting is not the Venezuelan elections, whose outcome has long been decided, but western reaction to these elections. Remember that today's leftism is tomorrows orthodoxy, which it is unthinkable to question, therefore, western leftist reaction would suggest that as the USG government moves ever leftwards, Venezuelan style elections are coming here.

If the New York Times reports Venezuelan elections rigged, Tea Party definitely not going to be shot any time soon. If it studiously ignores them, probably not any time soon. If it reports them as if legitimate, shootings are coming in sight

BBC is reporting the Venezuelan elections as legitimate, consistent with the fact that British government has been arresting real opponents, and shutting down hostile websites.

## Equal opportunity

### 2013-12-09 06:37:42

Whenever someone announces that they are in favor of equal opportunity, in favor of equality of opportunity rather than equality of outcome, they have usually a few paragraphs, or a few comments away, defended some outrageously unjust inequality of opportunity implemented and enforced by state power to destroy group X, as punishment for group X privilege.

Everyone is in favor of equality of opportunity. I am in favor of equality of opportunity. But, realistically, you are not going to get it, and attempting to get it is apt to result in genocide, as in the Congo, or terror, as in Sri Lanka.

Solving the problem of Tutsi privilege in the Congo means leftists protected by UN troops get to rape and sexually mutilate Tutsi women.

Everyone is in favor of equal opportunity. But how many cities are you planning to burn, how many women are you planning to have raped with large objects, in order to achieve equality of opportunity?

If group X is generally more honest, peaceful, intelligent, cooperative, and hard working than group Y, then associating with members of group X rather than members of group Y is going to give you a lot of benefits regardless of your own personal merits, thus, X privilege. For example, the public bathroom is less likely to be smashed up if you are in group X, and group X can exclude group Y.

To end group X privilege, you are going to have to impale women of group X with large objects. Is the fan of equal opportunity willing to do so? If not willing to do so, why is this fan of equal opportunity not complaining about the end of apartheid and UN intervention in the Congo?

When the state intervenes to create equality of opportunity, this is indistinguishable from creating inequality of opportunity in order to compensate for imaginary inequality of opportunity. Further, some forms of entirely real inequality of opportunity can never be remedied even by the most dreadful violence. We know that because, with great regularity, the most dreadful violence winds up being employed.

## Radish on anarcho tyranny

### 2013-12-14 13:23:08

Radish is excessively unkind to anarcho capitalism, though he is correct to point out that a lot of anarcho capitalists would be quite horrified by an anarcho capitalist polity in which, because the police and judiciary were in large part the direct employees of shopping malls and suchlike, capitalists had a lot of legal authority, and even more horrified if, because suburbia was protected by heads of households, and organizations paid by heads of households, each head of household had near total legal authority over his household, after the fashion of Republican Rome and the Old Testament.

But most of his wonderful article[142] is on anarcho tyranny:

> In 1961, 1971, and 1981, city street lights were not systematically de-wired. And the fact that plaques and bells of a century's pedigree were just now looted attests that they all survived the Great Depression, the punks of the 1950s, and the crime-ridden 1970s.

## No peak oil

### 2013-12-15 11:32:54

Inflation adjusted price of oil shows no obvious trend, suggesting that limits on oil production reflect social decay and technological slowdown, rather than physical exhaustion of resources.

---

[142]https://radishmag.wordpress.com/2013/12/13/anarcho-tyranny/

Oil prices rose, and rose, to 2008, and in 2008, it looked like the peak oilers were, like a stopped clock, finally correct. And then prices fell, a lot. They have risen since, but not to their 2008 peaks. From 2010 to the present oil prices have been high and steady in nominal dollars, while Chinese and Indian consumption soars. But steady in nominal dollars means falling about six percent a year in real prices, (or three percent a year if you believe the official cpi) So, more oil produced and consumed at lower prices, indicating that oil extraction technology continues to advance fast enough to keep up with increased demand.

If real prices start rising again, more likely social decay than limits to growth.

## The Jewish Conspiracy

2013-12-15 13:21:19

A lot of people believe that the Jews act as one, that they secretively and conspiratorially pursue Jewish interests at other people's expense.

The coordination problem is hard. No one successfully acts as one. Two Jews, three factions. That is why neoreactionaries propose terrible solutions to the coordination problem, on the grounds that other, more sophisticated, solutions are even worse. The Cathedral acts more or less as one – one madman, but they have visible institutions to coordinate them, and even then, do not do it too well.

The Old Bolsheviks were mostly Jewish, and proceeded to purge each other until the party was damn near Judenrein. The Trotskyists were overwhelmingly Jewish, and, lacking the power to send each other to the gulag, still are overwhelmingly Jewish, (hence the saying two trots, three factions) and they hate Jews more than anyone.

Jewish progressives are conversos. They hate Israel, and in a couple of generations, will disappear, will entirely cease to be Jewish. Jewish progressivism is progressives doing to Jews what they did to Christians. If a progressive Jew believes in Jewish solidarity, Madoff will educate him.

One big problem with Jews is that vibrancy undermines social cohesion, so that when the White Anglo Saxon Protestant ruling elite allowed the Jews in, they all started behaving badly, for example the Civil Rights Movement. But as we saw in the recent financial crisis, now that they are allowing white Hispanics and white Egyptians in, they are behaving even worse. Vibrancy not only brings in criminal outsiders, it lowers trust amongst insiders, making them criminal.

In the recent financial crisis, Jewish criminality was insignificant. The biggest villain was Angelo Mozillo (affirmative action Hispanic), who pissed away nearly a trillion dollars, for which misconduct he was fined the princely sum of seventy million. Compared to him, Goldman Sach's misconduct was a rounding error. Further, if we look at "Friends of Angelo", which is to say, the people in government that he bribed, none of which have been punished, they are a diverse and vibrant crowd, but only a few of them are Jewish.

In so far as elite misconduct followed from letting the Jews into the elite, worse misconduct has followed from letting other groups in.

I suspect, however, that when the elite finds itself in serious trouble for its misconduct, Jews will find themselves performing their usual function.

You can tell who has the power, from whom Angelo bribed, just as you can tell who had the power, from whom Margaret Mead had sex with.

## The overclass hates you.

### 2013-12-21 02:46:18

People notice the overclass (brahman, in Moldbug's terminology) hates whites. So they figure.

> Well, people who think of themselves as white cannot possibly hate whites,
> so it must be Jews, who don't consider themselves white, hating us.

Wrong.

The overclass hates whites because it is almost entirely white. It hates Jews because it is disproportionately Jewish. It hates males, marriage, and so on and so forth for much the same reasons.

And it hates all humans because it is composed of humans, hence the Greenie position that humans are a cancer upon the earth.

The left is the state and the state is the left, and the left has a long history of self destructive self hatred

The Populares (loose translation: Democratic Party, or People's Popular Party of Rome) allied with the enemies of Rome, and did not seem to doubt the wisdom of this alliance, when during their civil war, in 82 BC, their allies showed up at the gates with the intention of not merely defeating the other side in the Roman civil war, but of permanently and completely destroying the city of Rome. The army of the Populares, seeking to rule Rome, fought shoulder to shoulder with the Samnites, seeking to destroy Rome, and against the army of Sulla, seeking to preserve the Roman Empire against internal and external enemies.

In 1647AD Chang Hsien-chong said:

> Heaven brings forth innumerable things to nurture man.
> Man has nothing good with which to recompense Heaven
> Kill. Kill. Kill. Kill. Kill. Kill. Kill.

He committed an autogenocide more thorough than that of the Khmer Rouge. As with the Khmer Rouge, first killed the landlords for owning the land, then the intellectuals for insufficient ideological purity, then the peasants for insufficient collectivism, and so on and so forth.

To update his words to the twenty first century just substitute earth for heaven:

> Earth brings forth innumerable things to nurture man.
> Man has nothing good with which to recompense Earth
> Kill. Kill. Kill. Kill. Kill. Kill. Kill.
> 10:10 no pressure.

Perhaps the reason is that leftism is always based on allying with those far away against those that are near, and leftism always gets lefter, so they wind up allying with trees against humans.

Perhaps the reason is that the easiest way to be holier than thou, the way that takes the least effort or thought, is to hate those closest to one for insufficient holiness.

Likely, both reasons and several more.

## Global Warming Scientists trapped in Antarctic Denial

### 2014-01-01 17:04:44

This expedition to Antarctica is led by global warming scientist Chris Turney, whose company, Carbonscape, sells carbon indulgences. If you sin by emitting carbon, Chris Turner will, for a suitable payment, offset your sin with his carbon offset credits.

In the course of this expedition, they have repeatedly smacked up hard against ice that their ideology said could not possibly be there, and then proceeded to act as if the ice was not there. And then their ship got stuck.

The Global Warming research expedition, the Spirit of Mawson, aboard the Akademik Shokalskiy, has become stuck in something resembling ice, in high summer of the Antarctic. The leader of the expedition, however, assures us that the Antarctic ice is melting, so I suppose the material that it is stuck in is denial that has taken the form of white crystals.

Three icebreakers have been sent to rescue them, but were defeated by the thickness of the ice, notwithstanding highly scientific measurements proving that antarctic ice is becoming thinner. Doubtless Chris Turner is going to offset all that carbon expended by the icebreakers.

The purpose of the expedition was to retrace the Mawson expedition of a hundred years ago, and compare their measurements of the ice and penguins with modern observation.

There is an interesting expedition blog post, return to Mawson's hut[143], which dances around the fact that one hundred years ago, when Mawson's expedition built their base, the base area (Commonwealth Bay) was completely ice free in summer, while now the sea is covered in thick impenetrable ice that looks that it has been there a very long time. "It felt like we were in the interior of the continent, not at its edge." But in Mawson's day, the hut was at the edge.

It seems that the expedition planned to break their way through the ice to the shore, and blog that they were doing what Mawson did a hundred years ago - a plan that was quite obviously insane.

Reading between the lines of the blog posts, the original plan, of retracing Mawson's expedition, has proven impossible, because the Antarctic icecap has grown since then, covering the seas that Mawson sailed with permanent ice impenetrable to icebreakers.

But this should have been obvious as soon as they thought to retrace Mawson's expedition. They could have figured out it could not be done before they did it. The project was, like most modern science, ideology over eyesight, power speaking to truth.

---

[143]https://www.spiritofmawson.com/return-to-mawsons-hut-one-hundred-years-on/  "https://www.spiritofmawson.com/return-to-mawsons-hut-one-hundred-years-on/"

They just kept recklessly driving the Akademik Shokalskiy into thicker and thicker ice, as if it was an icebreaker. It is an ice strengthened ship, which is a lightweight icebreaker. And eventually, could go no further, which had happened before, as in the visit to Mawson's hut, but one day, found they could not only go no further, but could not turn around and go back either.

They got stuck in the ice because they refused to acknowledge the glaringly obvious fact that Mawson's route has long been covered by a growing antarctic ice cap, even when the ice was right in their faces, and even when the ship was making terrifying sounds as it unsuccessfully attempted to bust the ice.

## Leftism as cancer

### 2014-01-05 15:20:54

Leftism is to memes as cancer is genes.

If the cells of the body mutate, cells that multiply at the expense of the body will be selected. And cells that mutate to a faster mutation rate will be selected, since they will have more fast multiplying variants.

In a healthy body, each cell lives for the body, and performs its role in the whole body, making the body one. In cancer, each cancer cell lives for itself, at the expense of the body, parasitically, until the parasites devour the host

Left wing memes are selected by propagation through state power for propagation through state power.

In a healthy state the state is one, but there is large civil society, which is many. Following Marx's definition, by capitalism and civil society we mean[144] the *"society of industry, of general competition, of freely pursued private interest, of anarchy, of natural and spiritual individuality alienated from self."*

The civil society, which is many, produces the wealth, the science, and the technology. The state, which is one, defends civil society from enemies internal and external. For the reasons explained by Hayek and Mises, and colorfully dramatized by Ayn Rand, a unitary entity just cannot coordinate production very well. It runs into analogous problems with technology and science.

For civil society to function, to create wealth, knowledge, and technology, it must be free, a hundred flowers. For the state to function, it must be one flower. Elements of the state apparatus cannot be permitted to use state power to pursue their own goals. Elements of the state apparatus must be profoundly unfree in their role of elements of the state, in their exercise of the powers of the state, so that the state can be one.

In anarcho tyranny each groupuscule of the state uses state power and state resources to pursue its own particular good, thus the state spends money it does not have, and taxes and regulates beyond the laffer limit, suffering the tragedy of the commons. That is the anarchy. Because the state regulates beyond the laffer limit, we also get tyranny. Civil society, instead of having a hundred voices, has one voice, the voice of the state

Here is the state launching its latest little attack on the family and Christmas.

---

[144]https://www.xenosystems.net/luciano-pellicani/

That is the tyranny, a hundred supposedly independent voices of civil society speaking the exact same words.

Thus instead of the state being one, and civil society many, civil society is the voice of the state, one microphone heard through a thousand megaphones, while the state is many, and state resources suffer the tragedy of the commons, and the state is unable to pass a budget.

Elements of the state apparatus are free in their exercise of state power, thus everyday life of respectable people is subject to capricious tyranny, while criminals run free.

The left singularity is analogous to aneuploidy in a cancer. Cancers get selected for a high mutation rate, and left wing memes get selected for a high mutation rate.

This results in rising time preference, as depicted by Konkistador, and affinity for r-selected behaviors, as depicted by Anonymous Conservative.

Thus left wing movements start out each quite different from each other, and converge more and more to the left archetype, under the selective pressure for the niche of state mediated propagation of memes, just as all severely aneuploid malignant metastatic cancers look pretty much alike, by convergent evolution, and not much like their various tissues of origin.

If you are going to have a state, you are going to have a state religion or state ideology. The only way to avoid this is anarcho capitalism.

If you are going to have a state, you are going to have state official truth. If you are going to have state official truth, you need to stop it from endlessly mutating to ever greater virulence.

To prevent the official belief system from suffering memetic selection, the only solution is to have bishops, rather than open entry to the role of "opinion leader". The Bishops need to maintain a monopoly on the state propagation of official truth, and any elements of the state that start free lancing need to be, at a minimum, excluded from the state, which is to say, at a minimum fired, and, in serious cases, convicted of apostasy from the official belief system, and imprisoned, sold into slavery, or executed. If your official belief system will not sell William Wilberforce into slavery for apostasy from the thirty nine articles, his beliefs will win and the official beliefs will lose. His beliefs may well be better than the previous official beliefs, but every man jack will proceed with further improvements, resulting in memetic selection for virulence and a high mutation rate.

Non state apostates are harmless, since their belief systems are not selected for propagation by power. The problem is state and quasi state apostasy. Apostasy, in the sense of the sort of apostasy that the state should worry about and suppress, is mutation in the state meme system, mutations in the memes propagated by power.

Late stage leftism is the memetic equivalent of aneuploid maligant metastatic cancer. In cancer, the genes are selected for virulence within somatic growth, in leftism, the memes are selected for virulence within the state propagation of official memes.

Alien memes need to be excluded from participating in state power, thus the list (antibodies) of forbidden thoughts (antigens) needs to be updated frequently, while the list of required thoughts should be kept short, unchanging, and immune from empirical falsification by the facts of this world, to minimize memetic selection for propagation by power. This suggests an Archbishop to ensure that official memes do not mutate, to propagate the official and unchanging list of official memes, the archbishop having final responsibility for the propagation of the official list of unchanging official memes, and a Grand Inquisitor, to detect entryists and the undercover use of state power to propagate unofficial memes, or to furtively mutate official memes. The Grand Inquisitor should deal with endless change by ever changing conspiracies like that revealed by the Climategate Files, the Archbishop with unchanging official truth.

People who are in the position to deploy state power to propagate their beliefs need to be severely unfree in what beliefs they may espouse, just as police are not free to make up their own laws. To constrain such people, to constrain the state apparatus, we need the traditional thought control apparatus of Bishops and Inquisition, just as the courts are supposed to constrain the police.

If, however, that apparatus were to be applied to civil society, science, technology, and capitalism would be destroyed. The only penalty applied to people thinking unapproved thoughts should be exclusion from state employment and high status universities, exclusion from teaching jobs in the government education system, and the resulting lower status. We need to avoid penalties for thoughtcrime from pervading the civil society through regulation the way they do now, because that adversely affects the creation of wealth and knowledge. The state should be one being, and should therefore hold one set of official beliefs. Civil society should be many beings, so that the truth will out. To avoid potential conflicts between state and civil society, official truths should be either demonstrably true, or difficult to falsify.

It follows that the state cannot directly sponsor science, cannot be the sort of entity capable of directly sponsoring science. What the state can do to sponsor science is pay for impressive technological feats, and those who are successful in providing impressive technologies will sponsor science. Galilean kinematics was developed to land cannon balls on targets out of sight behind city walls, and the telescope with which Galileo saw the phases of Venus and the moons of Saturn was developed to spy on enemy fleets at sea. Should the state directly sponsor science (a most dangerous practice, for it is likely to wind up sponsoring apostatic religion dressed in the robes of science) it needs to forbid and severely criminalize peer review, and any form of science by consensus. Consensus is for bishops, not scientists. Scientists should form their opinions on the basis of public and replicated evidence, not on the basis of discussions behind closed doors, discussions which will inevitably lead to wanted evidence being published, and unwanted evidence being suppressed or "corrected".

Whenever we see scientists discussing truth behind closed doors, they are always up to no good, invariably engaged in criminal fraud, for if actually pursuing truth, would be pursuing it in public, that being how scientists get scientific reputation. What scientists do behind closed doors is get power, which is fundamentally inimical to science and the scientific method, because even though the rationalization is "we know the truth, and need to impose it on those ignorant hicks", what actually gets done is always the coercive imposition of lies on their fellow scientists, by committing fraud and silencing those who would point it out.

Peer review is OK for unfalsifiable truths, transcendent truths, truths that are not of this world, truths that people agree to for the purpose of social cohesion, like no work on the sabbath. When you peer review supposedly empirical truths, the social dynamics inexorably lead you wind up committing fraud, because the social dynamics inexorably lead you to wind up with supposedly empirical truths that are in fact not empirical, not truths of this world. And, having wound up with non empirical truths, for example the sinfulness of global warming, you wind up committing fraud by claiming empirical status for a non empirical truth, and falsifying the data as necessary to support this transcendent truth against inconvenient facts of the world.

You should not jail scientists merely on suspicion of fraud, for scientific fraud is hard to prove - but you should not hire, fund, or even associate with scientists who profile as likely fraudsters either. Anyone who participates in, or submits to, peer review of empirical truths, profiles as party to fraud.

Restating in slightly different words:

Cancer cells are selected for rapid multiplication. They run into various limits that are supposed to stop body cells from multiplying out of control. In escaping these limits, they become aneuploid, thus develop a very high mutation rate.

Those mutants most apt to multiply rapidly and to penetrate other tissues are selected, thus cancer progressively becomes more cancerous, eventually becoming aneuploid metastatic malignant cancer.

If one is going to have a state belief system, and this seems unavoidable if one is going to have a state, then one needs an archbishop to ensure that all elements of the state apparatus stay on message - that in the cancer analogy, all cells of the body display stable and unchanging self antigens, and a grand inquisitor to detect hostile entryist belief systems.

In the cancer analogy: The Archbishop enforces mandatory unchanging self antigens, the Grand Inquisitor searches out and prohibits ever changing non self antigens.

Of course, if the Archbishop enforces self antigens on absolutely everyone, intrudes on the civil society, this is horribly oppressive, and has, as in Spain, extremely bad economic effects, but it is reasonable to enforce self antigens on everyone who matters in the state apparatus. Thus, in restoration England, if one wanted to be a member of parliament, be a professor at the best universities, have senior government employment, etc, one had to subscribe to the thirty nine articles.

Once in a while, in restoration England, heretics got their houses burned down by hostile mobs while authority looked the other way, but as far as I can tell this was only when their heresy pursued state power, engaged in entryism. You could be a Jew, a Puritan, or a Roman Catholic in Restoration England, and suffer no very great disadvantages other than lower status and exclusion from the state apparatus.

No matter how badly the official belief system stinks, if it is subject to furtive mutation and selection for virulence, it will in time stink even worse. To prevent this, the Archbishop should prohibit spontaneous memetic mutation, the Grand Inquisitor should detect hostile memes and eradicate them from the state apparatus.

## Reasons for the endless movement left

2014-01-05 17:22:58

I have identified several different mechanisms for the endless movement left. Entryism[145], the conspiratorial takeover of organizations by other organizations. This is exemplified by Acorn, which has a single headquarters, but a hundred organization names, the residue of all the many organizations they have taken over.

Phariseeism[146]: The Puritans were holier than thou, their successors holier than Jesus. "I am holier than thou, therefore you should obey me."

The madness of crowds[147], the tendency of consensus to go horribly wrong

And metastatic apostacy[148], the tendency of official belief systems to mutate to greater virulence.

All of these tend in practice to be the same thing. Greater virulence is apt to be the same thing as greater holiness, greater holiness is amplified by the madness of crowds, and the entryist organization, being holier than the entered organization, takes advantage of the madness of crowds.

Thus in a single movement left, for example entryists taking over the the Science Fiction Writer's Association, one observes entryism, the entryists are pharisees, the process of entry took advantage of consensus decision making, and the progressive pieties uttered to justify the takeover reflect that the official belief system is now more virulent than it used to be. Each of these mechanisms was involved.


## A creationist, an evolutionist, and a Darwinist were walking in the woods

2014-01-07 10:02:32

They saw a patch of flowers.

"Why are these flowers beautiful?" asked the creationist rhetorically.

"OK" said the evolutionist, "Why?"

"For the joy of God and man," said the creationist.

"No" said the evolutionist, "Beauty is subjective, in the observer, not in the flower, and nothing in nature has any purpose. It just is."

"No," said the Darwinist. "These flowers must be pollinated by a creature that drinks nectar by daylight, probably a bee, and the flowers are beautiful to please the bee, as a woman is beautiful to please her husband."

"That is sexist," said the evolutionist, "and why should bees care about beauty?"

---

[145]https://blog.reaction.la/tag/entryism

[146]https://blog.reaction.la/tag/phariseeism

[147]https://blog.reaction.la/economics/stultum-facit-fortuna.html

[148]https://blog.reaction.la/science/leftism-as-cancer.html

## Races and subspecies

2014-01-12 07:03:40

Darwin defined race and subspecies to mean the same thing, a difference between kinds that is noticeable, but less than a species difference.

He then proceeded to argue that there was no objective distinction between a race difference and species difference, that two very different races were the same degree of difference as two closely related species.

And thus, that race is the origin of species. Over time, races may become more different, and, at some ill defined and undefinable date, it becomes reasonable to call them two different species rather than two different races.

He then proceeded to argue that the difference between the more distant human races, in particular the difference between blacks and whites, is large enough to be called a species difference, and considerably larger than the differences between many kinds that are recognized as distinct and different species.

However, it is terminologically inconvenient to call two kinds two species when there is a large cline between them. The middle east makes it inconvenient to define blacks and whites as two species. Therefore, Darwin *defined* humans as one species, this being a fact about preferred scientific terminology, not a fact about the world. It is convenient to call it a species difference when the cline is small, as between coyotes and wolves, and convenient to call it a subspecies (race) difference when the cline is large, as between whites and blacks.

There is a large cline between Californian spotted owls and barred owls. It is frequently hard to tell the difference. Male and female owls don't care about the difference, if there is one. Owls from the same nest, brothers and sisters, are apt to be assigned to different species, one brother spotted, the other barred, if the observer does not know they are from the same nest. It is as if we tried to divide humans into blue eyed, green eyed, and brown eyed species. Some owls have spots, some have bars, and most have spots that are kind of like bars, or bars that are kind of like spots. However, it is politically convenient to declare them different species, because that gives the greenies power over the loggers, and the urban elite hates those redneck loggers.

From time to time a proposal is floated to clarify the difference by killing off "hybrids", which is to say kill off owls whose spots are suspiciously like bars, or whose bars are suspiciously like spots. This, however, might be difficult to explain to those rednecks whose lives have been destroyed to protect the owls that were just shot.

Humans are one species so that Darwin did not have to draw a line across the middle east, and spotted and barred owls are two species so that our elite can make rednecks suffer.

## Demotism and lies

2014-01-14 13:15:19

North Korea is demotic. The US is demotic. North Korea murders large numbers of people. The US does not. Scott Alexander argues[149], therefore, that the word demotic is

---

[149]https://slatestarcodex.com/2014/01/12/a-response-to-apophemi-on-triggers/

not meaningful, in that it lumps unlike things together.

The North Korean regime is based on lies, since it claims its right to rule comes from the will of the people. Therefore, the North Korean regime needs an elaborate apparatus of thought control.

The US regime is based on lies, since it claims its right to rule comes from the will of the people. Therefore, the US regime needs an elaborate apparatus of thought control, and, as the US goes ever further left, that apparatus becomes ever more oppressive.

The Dubai regime is based on an obvious truth: that Dubai is a monarchy, and that his Highness Sheik Mohammed bin Rashid Al Maktoum is the rightful monarch.

Moldbug argues that to avoid an oppressive apparatus of thought control, we need a strong government. The problem with this solution is that there are no strong governments. There is no ring of Fnargl. Government is an illusion. We are always in anarchy, and never in anarchy. Most systems can be usefully analyzed as variations of anarcho capitalism, or as dysfunctions or malfunctions of anarcho capitalism. Since Anarcho capitalism must always have some degree of malfunction, Anarcho Capitalism can never exist. Since there is no Ring of Fnargl that magically guarantees that the rulers can reliably win, Anarcho Capitalism always exists.

Moldbug blames the evil of the modern state on insecurity of power. His solution is security of power. I don't believe it.

The state suppresses speech because it fears overthrow. But who fears truth? In the private everyday world, who fears truth? Who wants to hide the truth from everyone else?

It is the criminal who needs to hide. The honest of course also need to hide certain things like the location of their buried treasure, but they need to hide from the criminal. The evil needs to hide much more than the good, at least on the small scale. The good needs to hide its treasures. The evil needs to hide its crimes.

It is the evil states that need to control speech more strictly.

Democracy adds a wrinkle to this because the mass voters need to be controlled. But the Soviet Union was not a democracy. And still it suppressed speech.

Pharisees tend to be evil in the way depicted by Jesus, because their power is based on lies.

So pharisaic regimes are evil, and are exceptionally motivated to conceal their evil, hence exceptionally motivated to control speech, to intrusively inject their power into everyday life, thereby smashing capitalism and causing science and technology to stagnate.

Consider the Soviet Empire. When they claimed that the liquidation of the kulaks was class warfare by oppressed lower peasants against rich peasants, they were not trying to conceal the truth from the peasants, who knew perfectly well the party was making war on the peasants. Rather, they were concealing the truth from each other and from themselves.

The obvious difference between North Korea and Dubai is not that one ruler is more secure than the other, though someone who calls himself Sheik Mohammed bin Rashid Al Maktoum sounds a lot more secure than someone who calls himself Kim.

The obvious difference is that North Korea even more demotic than the USA, while Dubai is an old fashioned monarchy. Sheik Mohammed bin Rashid Al Maktoum claims Dubai is a monarchy, and it obviously is. Kim claims that North Korea is highly democratic, and it obviously is not. Kim's authority rests on a blatant lie, Sheik Mohammed bin Rashid Al Maktoum's authority rests on an obvious truth.

So Kim needs a massive apparatus of thought control, while Sheik Mohammed bin Rashid Al Maktoum merely needs to look and sound like the King he was born to be.

## Cthulhu swims only left

2014-01-18 14:17:07

The Orthosphere and Zippy Catholic seem curiously optimistic about the future of the Roman Catholic Church.

Seems to me that anyone who is genuinely Roman Catholic should be making spiritual and organizational preparations for excommunication.

Here are some entertaining bits from the Pope's interview with La Republica[150], which came to my attention when it was parodied as "The Third Vatican Council". I at first mistook the parody for the real thing, since Pope Francis is hard to parody.

> "Proselytism is solemn nonsense, it makes no sense. We need to get to know each other, listen to each other and improve our knowledge of the world around us. Sometimes after a meeting I want to arrange another one because new ideas are born and I discover new needs. This is important: to get to know people, listen, expand the circle of ideas. The world is crisscrossed by roads that come closer together and move apart, but the important thing is that they lead towards the Good."

> Your Holiness, is there is a single vision of the Good? And who decides what it is?

> "Each of us has a vision of good and of evil. We have to encourage people to move towards what they think is Good."

Which was fairly parodied as "all religions are true", which is the progressive position that all religions rightly understood, are true, because all religions, rightly understood, are progressivism.

In the same interview Pope Francis also said

> "The Son of God became incarnate in order to instill the feeling of brotherhood in the souls of men."

Which replaces Christ the redeemer with Jesus the community organizer. In the parody, they have the Third Vatican Council removing the sexist, homophobic, transphobic, and whateverphobic parts of the New Testament, which is not entirely fair, but is true in the sense that demoting Jesus to community organizer is a result of being holier than Jesus. So the parody, which has him revising the bible, is truer than the actual truth.

---

[150]https://www.repubblica.it/cultura/2013/10/01/news/pope_s_conversation_with_scalfari_english-67643118/

# Tall buildings and the social order
## 2014-01-20 16:19:27

To make and keep the upper stories of a tall building habitable requires routine high technology. The lifts have to work, the water needs to be pumped, the toilets have let the poop down one hundred stories without shattering violence. It is not all that expensive. Current office space costs in the centers of major cities are so high that very tall buildings are immensely profitable. It is simply difficult to do, requires able people working together, both initially to build the systems, and subsequently to keep them going.

It is habitable floors that are hard to do, and habitable floors are what generates the rental income. So, to assess a society's technological level, count habitable floors.

By and large, the taller the building, the more the profit. Doubtless there is a limit, but in the center of most major cities, most tall buildings are below that limit. If people could build taller, they would. At our present technological level, settling space seems likely to be fatally unprofitable, but building upwards, building the city of tomorrow, is highly profitable.

In South Africa the upper parts of tall buildings built by whites have become uninhabitable. That the upper part of the skyline has gone dark is the most visible symptom of social decay.

Mark Steyn makes fun of the South African government's incapacity to govern[151], for which National Review will surely purge him, if it has not done so already.

> Thamsanqa Jantjie, the lovable laugh-a-minute sign-language fraud who stood alongside President Obama gesticulating meaninglessly to the delight of all, was exposed in the days that followed as a far darker character. A violent schizophrenic charged over the years with burglary, rape, kidnapping, and murder, he was also a member of a "necklacing" gang — necklacing being the practice of placing a gasoline-filled tire over the head of the victim and setting it alight.

> ... a lot of things in South Africa simply don't function anymore. As revealing as Mr. Jantjie's extensive and violent criminal background is the fact that the National Prosecuting Authority cannot reliably state which offenses he has been convicted of, and, for the one crime for which he seems definitively to have been sentenced, whether in fact he served the sentence.

The twin towers had one hundred and ten habitable stories.

The top habitable floor of Freedom Tower, the replacement to the Twin Towers is labeled floor 104, but that is fraud, to disguise the fact that we cannot do this thing any more. It is actually the ninety fourth habitable floor.

A slower pace of decay than South Africa, but decay nonetheless. Seems to me that the pace of decay has accelerated lately, but to draw definitive conclusions, will need a few more years.

The Soviet Union fell in part because they could not keep the lights on, and the elite got sick of the darkness.

---

[151]https://www.steynonline.com/5995/heading-south

I expect that by the second term of Bill de Blasio, the New York night skyline will be showing some dark spots, like the missing teeth of an aging homeless alcoholic. This will be proudly depicted as huge progress in reducing carbon emissions.

## Now I understand the koan

2014-01-23 19:56:35

Several people have been darkly amused[152] by the koan

> I walked to Master Moldbug but the road was too long. I visited master Jim and he hit me with a stick.

> I did not understand it. Seems to me that I am a pussycat.
> But now[153] I think I understand

## mens rea

2014-01-26 12:16:09

I have been arguing that social decay is ending technological and scientific progress. In most areas it has strikingly slowed, in some areas, going backwards in the west, as we forget how to do what once we could do. Others, however, argue that technological and scientific progress is still running hot, or that if it has slowed, it is that we ran out of low hanging fruit.

But a big tell is that people are lying about it. The lie indicates not only failure, but that the failure is shameful - that the failure is in us, not in external circumstances. That we are lying about it shows the failure is social decay.

IC manufacturers continue to announce new generations, 45 nanometer, 32 nanometer, 22 nanometer, and coming soon, 14 nanometer, though in fact we have been stuck at 64 nanometer for quite some time. There have been process improvements, but these are incremental improvements. The line pitch remains 64 nanometers. We cannot actually build circuits smaller than we could eight years ago. That these are improvements is no lie, but to label them by a size is a lie. If they had said "second generation 64 nanometer" instead of "45 nanometer", if they had said "third generation 64 nanometer instead of "32 nanometer", then they would have been speaking truth, or at least speaking hype rather than lies.

Similarly, it is embarrassing that while the twin towers had one hundred and ten habitable floors, their replacement, the freedom tower, merely has ninety four habitable floors. That the top story of the freedom tower is labelled 104 shows mens rea.

The US government gets wonderful ratings for lack of corruption by various organizations quietly dominated by the US government, but that really has not been my experience. And if you suspect that my personal experience might be atypical, or that I might view the behavior of various governmental entities I have dealt with with undue cynicism,

---

[152]https://www.xenosystems.net/roughened-chan/
[153]https://bonald.wordpress.com/2014/01/23/a-dreadful-thought-will-there-be-no-persecution/

consider the extraordinary crimes revealed in the financial crisis, the lack of prosecutions for those crimes, and the failure of civil suits against financial misconduct.

You cannot do large projects in the US any more, because any new project attracts a horde of government officials seeking a payoff, the bigger the project, the more people seeking a payoff, until eventually you get a hundred officials each seeking five percent of any added value the project would generate. Possibly this a result of the well known effect of diversity in lowering trust, trustworthy behavior, and social pressures that enforce trustworthy behavior. Add five percent affirmative action blacks to the ruling elite, get one hundred percent Chicago style corruption.

The Challenger inquiry revealed that our rocket scientists are idiots. Mulloy and Hardy would talk technobabble whenever they were in a corner, and everyone would solemnly treat their technobabble as if they were making sense.

> CHAIRMAN ROGERS: Read it again. And as I read it, it means that if the primary seal fails that the mission will fail. Am I wrong?

And of course, the reason for the inquiry is that the primary seal failed, causing the space shuttle to blow up.

> MR. HARDY: That is not my interpretation.

Because black is white and white is black.

> CHAIRMAN ROGERS: Well, let's read it. "Loss of mission" - this is actual loss. "Failure effects summary. Actual loss. Loss of mission, vehicle and crew due to metal erosion, burn-through, and probable case burst, resulting in fire and deflagration." Now "Note, leakage of the primary" -and this is the part that I want to refer to.
>
> "Leakage of the primary O-ring seal is classified as a single failure point"-" as a single failure point "-" due to possibility of loss of sealing at the secondary O-ring because of joint rotation after motor pressurization."
>
> Now, that suggests to me that the critical items list says that if the primary O-ring seal fails, that you have got a good probability that the mission will be a catastrophe. Am I wrong about that?
>
> MR. HARDY: You are not wrong,

Observe that Mr Hardy has directly contradicted himself.

> if I might put my clarification into that, if the primary O-ring fails after motor pressurization, after joint rotation.

In other words, if primary O-ring fails when it is needed, the shuttle will blow up.

> CHAIRMAN ROGERS: I guess what I'm saying is, isn't that a possibility of exactly what happened in this launch?

MR. HARDY: I don't believe so.

CHAIRMAN ROGERS: Why?

MR. HARDY: Well, I will elaborate on that a little bit later here.

Later he gives us a stream of gibberish technobabble.

> But in the considerations, at least in the considerations of the subjects at hand, relative to the discussion on the 27th, the discussion on the 27th had to do with the possibility of the cold temperature delaying the complete actuation of the primary seal, thereby extending the duration of blow-by.
>
> Now, when we talk about blow-by of the primary seal, blow-by has to go somewhere, and where it goes to is the secondary seal. If blow-by occurs as soon as the pressure gets to the primary seal, early in the ignition, and that seal doesn't sustain that pressure, it goes immediately to the secondary seal, prior to the time that the joint is rotated.

Too long, don't read. The short of it is that when the pressure rises then the joint rotates, and then the shuttle blows up if the primary O-ring has failed..

> CHAIRMAN ROGERS: This says "possibility of the loss of the sealing of the secondary O-ring."
>
> MR. MULLOY: After the joint has rotated, sir. The condition that is on the screen now is before joint rotation.
>
> DR. WALKER: But I think a critical and a literal interpretation of that waiver has to be that the primary seal is a single point failure. Now, the wording goes on to explain why this is so, but the wording does not make an exception. It merely explains why the single point failure mode refers to the primary seal.
>
> But a strict interpretation of that wording to my mind is that the primary O-ring is a single point failure.

Of course Mr Mulloy does not want to admit that he signed off on a study saying that if the primary O-ring failed, the shuttle would blow up, and another report that the primary O-ring was going to fail. But neither can he deny it. So he technobabbles.

> MR. HARDY: I wouldn't deny that. I am relating to what many of us knew about the performance of that joint, its rotation, when we lost-when we could lose, because of the stackup of [836] tolerances, when in the ignition transient prior to full motor pressurization or after full motor pressurization when we could lose that secondary seal.
>
> Our interpretation or my interpretation of the waiver was not to remove the secondary seal from the hardware.

So he would not deny it, but then he does deny it. If the primary O-ring is a single point of failure, that means that if it fails, there is no backup, the mission fails. The secondary O-ring will not serve. If the secondary O-ring would serve, then the primary O-ring would not be a single point of failure. That is what "single point of failure" means. Due to joint rotation, if the primary O-ring is failing to seal, the secondary O-ring will fail considerably worse.

Now because Mr Hardy is not making any sense at all, Dr Ride then comes to his aid with more technobabble, and then there is much meaningless gibberish back and forth between them in which each solemnly and respectfully treats the other as if he is making sense, much like Jacques Derrida discussing "the Einsteinian Constant".

There was a lot of this sort of thing, technobabble in place of technical argument, in the events that led to the destruction of the shuttle, and during the shuttle inquiry.

If someone engages in technobabble, he is lying to idiots, so our rocket scientists are, at the top, liars and idiots.

Which explains where we are going in space.

## No real AI progress

### 2014-01-28 12:31:38

AI is a hard problem, and even if we had a healthy society, we might still be stuck. That buildings are not getting taller and that fabs are not getting cheaper and not making smaller and smaller devices is social decay. That we are stuck on AI is more that it is high hanging fruit.

According to Yudkowsky[154], we will have AI when computers have as much computing power as human brains.

The GPU on my desktop has ten times as much computing power as the typical male human brain, and it is not looking conscious.

Artificial consciousness will require an unpredictable and unforeseeable breakthrough, if it is possible at all, because we now understand aging, but do not understand consciousness

A self driving car would be true AI, or a good step towards it, as would good machine translation. You don't mind the computer sometimes getting the meaning backwards when it does translation, but you would mind if a self driving car drives into someone or something.

With chess playing computers, it seemed that we were making real progress towards AI but it was eventually revealed that chess playing computers do not figure out chess moves the way humans do, and the difference matters, even if a computer can beat any human chess player.

With big data, it seemed that we were making real progress towards AI, but it was eventually revealed that just as chess playing computers do not figure out chess moves the way humans do, neither does big data.

When humans found the Rosetta stone, they were able to learn Egyptian. Having fair number of words and sentences to start with, they could then figure out other words

---

[154]https://yudkowsky.net/obsolete/singularity.html

from context, giving them more words, and more words gave them more grammar, and more grammar and words enabled them to figure out yet more words from context, until they had pretty much all Egyptian. Google's machine translation learns to translate from a thousand Rosetta stones. It is not doing what we are doing, which is understanding meaning and expressing meaning.

Humans do not use big data, just as they do not examine a million possible chess moves.

Atop each Google self driving car is a great big device that performs precision distance measurements in all directions, giving the computer a three dimensional image of its surroundings. It is a big object because it collects a huge amount of data very fast. Human eyes just collect a small amount of data, from which the human constructs a three dimensional idea of his surroundings. Humans don't need that much data to drive, and could not handle that much data if their senses provided it.

The Google car has a centimeter scale map of the world in which it is driving. It can see traffic lights because it knows exactly where traffic lights are in the world. If one day, someone moved the traffic lights six inches to the right, problem. If roadworks, problem. If a traffic accident, problem. And that is why the cars need someone in the driver's seat.

Maybe big data will produce acceptable results for self driving cars, acceptable being that in the rare situations that the computer cannot handle the car, the computer realizes that there is something wrong, comes to a halt, and asks for human assistance. But it is not quite there yet, and if it does produce acceptable results, will not produce human like, or even non human animal like, performance.

What is missing seems to be consciousness, and we don't really know what that is. Intelligence seems to require huge numbers of neurons. Consciousness seems to require considerably smaller number.

The male human brain has around eighty six billion neurons.

The maximum output of any one neuron is about three hundred hertz, but only a small fraction are running near the maximum output, because if all of them were running near maximum output, the brain's oxygen supply could not keep up.

This output from any one neuron is a summary of the data received by a large number of synapses, typically a thousand or so synapses.

So we can suppose that the male human brain processes something like three terabytes per second if we look at neuron output, or something like three thousand terabytes per second if we look at neuron input.

The GPU on my desktop generates eight thousand single precision gflops per second, which is thirty two terabytes per second.

It seems obvious to me that the problem is not artificial intelligence. By any measure of intelligence, computers are highly intelligent. The problem is that they are not conscious. And the reason they are not conscious is that we do not have the faintest idea what consciousness is. Maybe is something supernatural, maybe it is something perfectly straightforward, but we cannot see what it is for the same reason that a fish cannot see water.

Furthermore, interacting with non human animals, it seems obvious to me that a tarantula is conscious, as conscious as I am, and a GPU is not. The genetic basis for brain structure is the same in the tarantula as the human, which hints that the common ancestor of the protostomes and deuterostomes, which had a complex brain, but was otherwise scarcely more than a bag of jelly, was conscious - that consciousness was the big breakthrough that resulted in protostomes and deuterostomes dominating the earth, that consciousness is a single big trick, not a random grab bag of tricks.

From time to time, I read claims that someone is successfully emulating a cat brain or some such, but no one has successfully emulated the nervous system of Caenorhabditis elegans, which has three hundred and two neurons, nor has anyone successfully emulated the human retina, in which data flows through three layers of neurons with only local interactions, so that if we understood a single tiny patch of the retina, a dozen neurons or so, we would understand all of it. In this sense, neurons are doing something mysterious, in that quite small systems of neurons remain mysterious.

This does not prove that consciousness is magic, but, as far as our current knowledge goes, it is indistinguishable from magic.

## Freedom in Russia and the US

2014-01-29 07:15:28

Let us compare the career of journalist and writer Yulia Latynina, with the career of Dinesh D'Souza.

Yulia Latyninais a Russian megaphone for the Harvard microphone. Supposedly Bush was a moron, Putin is a tyrant, Putin is a homophobe, Putin murders his political opponents, or jails them on vague laws, selectively enforced. Putin is a sexist, Putin is a criminal, and friend of criminals, and so on and so forth.

Yet she has not been murdered, nor, unlike Dinesh D'Souza, charged under vague and selectively enforced laws. Has not even had to face a SLAPP suite, unlike Mark Steyn.

Seems to me that Russia could do with a whole lot more repression. The reason that Yulia Latynina needs a bullet in the head, while Dinesh D'Souza should not have been charged is that Putin's repression is arguably protecting Russia, or at least is not obviously stupid, whereas Obama's repression is destroying America

Today, Disney makes a television episode whose primary theme is support for gay marriage. The good progressive naturally supports Gay marriage, and confidently believes that gay marriage not only is right, but was always and eternally obviously right, and he always supported Gay Marriage. And yet, a few years ago, our progressive did not support Gay Mariage. Perhaps he always supported Gay Marriage, but society was not yet ready for Gay Marriage. What then will society be ready for in ten years? Our progressive does not know.

The problem is that US repression is against the internal enemies of a line that undergoes rapid and never ending change, to ensure neverendingly more extreme conformity to an ever more extreme line. Putin represses his enemies, though he should do a lot more to suppress the agents of Islam and the agents of the Cathedral. The USG represses sanity.

## Darkness is the norm

### 2014-02-02 13:59:33

Copper production shows three peaks[155]: The Roman Empire in the west, the Song Dynasty, and modernity.

The Roman Empire in the west and the Song Dynasty had about seven times the preceding and following level of copper production, thus while those civilizations were going concerns, they had far more production and wealth than the rest of the world put together.

When the Roman Empire in the West fell, its GDP dropped about a hundred fold[156].

So, looking at the past few thousand years, the norm has been relatively brief periods of civilization in relatively small parts of the world.

I would guess the problem is that the state lacks the cohesion and self discipline necessary to refrain from devouring civil society, and anarchy lacks the cohesion necessary to keep the roads safe and property rights secure. Technology can advance during anarchic periods, often quite rapidly, but the amount of wealth, as indicated by copper production, shipwrecks, and such, tends to be very low indeed during such periods. Despotic states, on the other hand, have higher wealth, probably because they can make the roads safe over a large area, but are apt to end technological progress, and often reverse it.

Technologically, Somalia is probably the most capable state polity nationality in southern Africa, while Botswana was remarkably prosperous for a black state, when ruled by a combination of traditional monarchy and DeBeers, very thinly disguised as democracy. Singapore trembles towards crisis and decline as its pretense of democracy shows dangerous symptoms of becoming real.

In America, it becomes impossible to do high technology in physical things without an ever multiplying number of permits, which require paying off an ever multiplying number of bagmenconsultants. This exploding regulatory state resembles the decline of the Song Dynasty, where all high technology became a state monopoly, all education aimed at state jobs.

In Rome, the decline of military discipline, for example the year of six emperors, meant that the legions became more like mobile bandits than stationary bandits, though even to the very end of the Roman empire in the west, Roman handouts to an ever more degenerate underclass, the infamous bread and circuses, remained startlingly generous. Rome taxed beyond the Laffer maximum, so Diocletian decided that if high taxes discouraged people from working, the state would make them work.

Our ever increasing underclass has become a problem like the legions, where the state in every election promises goodies far beyond what it can actually deliver. The underclass is a lot easier to shaft than the legions, yet the Roman Empire in the West, still making a thin pretense that the Republic lived, failed to shaft its underclass, until the fall of Rome.

---

[155] https://historum.com/ancient-history/43434-rise-fall-ancient-economy.html
[156] https://historum.com/ancient-history/43434-rise-fall-ancient-economy.html

## The collapse of fertility

2014-02-03 15:57:25

Spandrel has a post wondering where all the babies went[157], and whenever I propose one of the usual suspects, for example no fault divorce, denormalization of masculinity, and such, he says "Ah, but many Muslim countries also have fertility collapse".

Good point. So let us look at a Muslim country with dramatic fertility collapse, and see if we can find any of the usual suspects.

So I looked at Iran

1: Harvard on the Arvan Rud.

While most of Iranian society is pretty much what one would expect of a Muslim society, for example poor employment prospects for women, legal enforcement of husband's authority, and so on and so forth, school and University is Harvard on the Arvan Rud. Despite lower female intelligence, smaller female brains, and the fact that very few girls will wind up in employment (the rest of society still being quite Muslim) *62% of people admitted to university are female*[158] *and only 38% are male*. Schools and universities consider it their mission to raise female status and lower male status, to transform those horrid old fashioned obsolete unprogressive aspects of Islam. All students are compelled to attend courses urging them to have fewer children, and denigrating marriage and motherhood.

2. Who cares about 2? OK: 2 is Sodom and Gomorrah in Harvard on the Arvan Rud. Iranian girls are very strictly controlled until they get to university, coed university, whereupon... most of them are ruined for any man who would be inclined to marry her, since they will now see him as low status and insufficiently handsome and manly.

Ayatollahs! You need to behead most of these academics. These guys are planning to take your society away from you. Pretty soon you will be like wasps at the Obama Whitehouse.

## Entryist attack

2014-02-04 10:44:28

Some time ago there were some thoughtful critiques of the Dark Enlightenment, Reaction, and Neoreaction, worthy of thoughtful and lengthy response.

More recently, there was a lot of childish name calling. *Racist*

And, predictably, the next step would be entryism[159].

Patri Friedman, fresh from screwing over Libertarianism and anarcho capitalism, promises us a more politically correct Dark Enlightenment[160].

---

[157] https://bloodyshovel.wordpress.com/2014/02/01/babies/

[158] https://www.un.org/esa/population/publications/completingfertility/2RevisedABBASIpaper.PDF

[159] https://blog.reaction.la/tag/entryism

[160] https://www.facebook.com/patri.friedman/posts/10152224034719766

I think I need to recap some of the more offensive hate facts of the Dark Enlightenment, for example what happened to Rhodesia, the Congo, what is happening to South Africa, the benefits of slavery in the United States, the consequences of affirmative actioning women into roles for which they are unsuited, and Whig treason against Britain in the revolutionary war, and recommend these hate facts for inclusion into the canon, as an immovable obstacle against a more politically correct Dark Enlightenment.Though, of course, Radish has already done much fine work along these lines.

## Sunshine Mary nails it

### 2014-02-06 12:10:44

We have been discussing the demographic transition - the tendency of peoples to fail to reproduce, examining varying nations, religious groups and such to see what makes a difference and what does not.

Sunshine Mary has proposed a theory which I think fits all our data.
Ten changes that need to happen in order to promote society-wide traditional sexroles.[161]
> The only way that it is safe for women to engage in traditional sex roles – keeping the home, nurturing the young, caring for the old, ministering to the sick and the poor – is if they can depend on the support of a husband and kin network. And the only way it is safe for men to engage in traditional sex roles – providing for and protecting women and children – is if their investment in their families is protected from destruction and theft by corporations, governments, and the women themselves.

One might suppose Saudi Arabia to be a counter example, but Saudi women are exposed both to easy divorce, and to state intervention to raise the status of women.

One might suppose China to be a counter example, but the excess of males caused a rise in the status of women, and an ensuing sexual revolution, since those females could play around, and still get married.

## Cathedral imperialism revealed

### 2014-02-08 06:39:29

We hear Assistant Secretary of State Victoria Nuland and Ambassador to Ukraine Geoffrey Pyatt discussing what role which people will play in the post coup Ukraine government, revealing that the Ukraine "opposition" are puppets, entryists, cogs in the Cathedral machine, loudspeakers for microphones held in Harvard.

They discuss what orders they will give to which Ukraine politicians, and what jobs they will assign to which Ukraine politician, like the CEO discussing new employees with HR, revealing that the "Unrest" in the Ukraine is a Cathedral plan to install a puppet regime.

Presumably this phone call was tapped by the Russian KGB, and then released by them to Youtube.

---

[161] https://sunshinemaryandthedragon.wordpress.com/2014/02/05/ten-changes-that-need-to-happen-in-order-to-promote-society-wide-traditional-sex-roles/

Trouble is, Cathedral puppet regimes have generally been disastrous, most infamously in Zimbabwe, Rwanda, the Congo, and Haiti.

This is not the colonialism that Neoreactionaries favor for the same reasons as North Korea is not the monarchy reactionaries favor. Good imperialism is order supplied from outside. Cathedral Leftism is disorder supplied from outside. The old colonialism would punish, subdue, or enslave the worst elements of society. Cathedral imperialism, most infamously in Rwanda, encourages them to run amuck. Rhodesia was the old colonialism, Zimbabwe the new imperialism.

Hurrah for the Russian KGB!

It is interesting that the ambassador wets his pants in fear while speaking to Assistant Secretary of State Victoria Nuland, and his conversation implies he expects other leading lights in the Ukrainian protest movement to react similarly.

He is an ambassador. He should be able to maintain a polite, unimpressed, poker face under any circumstances. I am not an ambassador, but I can retain a polite, entirely unimpressed, poker face under very dire circumstances. What sort of an ambassador can be heard to wet his pants in fear? That man could not play poker.

Our ruling elite is, once again, revealed to be garbage. You don't make weaklings ambassadors. Were the ambassador ever to speak with Putin, Putin would instantly know the truth.

## Working class consciousness

### 2014-02-16 08:43:07

Working Class consciousness (in other words envy and covetousness) runs into economics: "The Chamley-Judd Redistribution Impossibility Theorem" which tells us that redistribution from capitalists to workers is impossible, and trying to do so merely buggers the economy making everyone worse off.

This conflict between reality and ideology brings you nazism and communism.

The Chamley-Judd Redistribution Impossibility theorem is economists admitting Ayn Rand was right while trying to sound as if they are not admitting it. The economy needs savings, investment, and entrepreneurship. Entrepreneurs will arrange to get a good chunk of the wealth produced, and if you try to stop them, you will discourage, or altogether stop, savings, investment and entrepreneurship.

You try to distribute from the capitalists to the workers, and somehow it does not happen. Obviously an evil conspiracy. So you round up the usual suspects. Somehow, this fails to work. Obviously the conspiracy must be bigger than you thought. So you round up everyone vaguely connected to the usual suspects. And you wind up killing them.

Yes, there are perfectly real conspiracies, as the previous post reveals, and some of them, such as the one revealed in the previous post, contain a curiously large proportion of Jews, but this is not what causes economic differences between capitalists and workers. The usual object of conspiracy is political power. This causes economic inequality between people in political power and people out of political power, but other forms of inequality are more resistant to politics, and attempts to politicize other forms of inequality will have disastrous effects.

The inequality between Jewish tax farmers and the peasants had political origins and was reasonably answered by political measures against tax farming. The inequality between Jewish Estate managers and the people who worked on those estates, the inequality between Jewish money lenders and European borrowers, and the inequality between Jewish vodka merchants and Russian drunks did not have political origins, hence trying to remedy it results in you killing the Jews, not to mention capitalists, kulaks, foreign educated intellectuals, and whatnot. And after they are killed, your peasants are still screwed. Indeed they are even more screwed.

Hence successful official belief systems prohibit this fallacy. Believing it gets punished by social disapproval and exclusion from the levers of political power.

## The USG immigration problem

2014-02-17 08:53:13

The problem is that people we are allowing in have too much power over us. Also, most of them are stupid people, and when their children go to school, the Cathedral teaches them to hate us and attack us.

When nonwhites have the majority, whites will be a market dominant minority, like Jews or overseas Chinese. In nonwhite countries, market dominant minorities seldom exist, because they get exterminated or expelled. In the middle east, sometimes enslaved.

Smart fraction theory implies that intelligence primarily produces externalities, benefits for other people.

Thus, people of below average intelligence produce large negative externalities.

The policy of the King of Dubai, assuming that policy to reflect the best interests of an undeniably able monarch, indicates that even when stupid people are not allowed welfare, not allowed to vote, are subject to an ironfisted law enforcement system that completely eliminates the kind of crimes that stupid people might commit, are subject to the iron fisted control of employers, who may at any moment expel their employees back to their home countries to face the horrors of those governments that they democratically elected, even with all that, stupid people still have substantial negative externalities.

If Mexicans were being brought in to work, like their equivalents in Dubai, the benefit would be mutual.

But Dubai has a policy of not letting perpetually low income people set down roots, which implies that such people have substantial negative externalities.

In Dubai they cannot bring in their families, and if they remain low income indefinitely, they get the heave ho even if their employer wants them to stay.

However, in the United States, Mexicans are not being brought in to work, but to vote. It is illegal for them to work, but they get privileged access to welfare, onerous regulations are less enforced on Mexicans than on Californians, and they get to drive without a license. A illegal immigrant female who spawns an anchor thuglet to some random thug, a little Democrat voter, gets far more money than the illegal immigrant who mows Bryan Caplan's lawn, which shows you what the priorities of the open borders crowd is.

If we replace one smart person with one dumb person, it's pretty obvious that this has a negative externality.

But if we add one person, arguably this has a positive externality. The larger the society, the richer, often enough, presumably due to specialization.

There is however a certain size beyond which further specialization is impossible, limited by technology. and intelligence.

Therefore beyond a certain size, there is no difference between adding a person and replacing a person. Holding specialization constant, adding a stupid person is like replacing a smart person with a stupid person. Moreover, stupid people reduce the degree of specialization, and so their addition is a double whammy.

Still, it's not completely obvious why the smart fraction of the population in Dubai is vulnerable to the addition of a stupid person, even if the total size of the population is beyond what is necessary for full specialization. At the very least,they ought to be able simply to exclude the moron.

Of course, in the US, this is racism, sexism, and what have you. Observe that the housing bubble was, at least in California where I could see what happening, entirely Mexicans buying house no money down.

But in Dubai, complete freedom of association. Why don't they just exclude the moron?

The stupid person is like spam. A spam filter runs the risk of blocking good email. A stupid person takes up a recruiter's time. Time is wasted identifying and rejecting the stupid, and the rejection is not perfect, so a stupid person can end up getting placed, pushing aside a smart person.

Observe the very poor performance of the Chinese mandarinate system, which wound up admitting not the able, but those good at gaming the system. The emperor wants the best, but is unable to accurately assess whether examiners are truly selecting the best. If the examiners grade mechanically, then the system can be gamed. It is quite difficult to grade in a way that resists being gamed.

Furthermore, social relationships are considerably less tightly protected than business relationships. People are more vulnerable to knowing a stupid person socially than to hiring a stupid person. The stupid can therefore pollute the culture by their presence. They debase the culture, as we now see in the US.

## The Death of Libertarianism

### 2014-02-28 13:23:00

What is libertarianism?

Stephen Landsburg complains that Arizona law protecting religious people from being forced to enthusiastically support and endorse gay marriage is unlibertarian.

Bryan Caplan, a libertarian and theoretically an anarcho capitalist, wants the Mexican underclass moved here to live on welfare, crime, the production of anchor babies, and voting Democrat.

Esr recently used exterminationist rhetoric against "racists". I doubt he knows what "racist" means, but those that put that exterminationist rhetoric into action will know that "racist" is simply a hostile word for white.

As the Overton Window moves ever leftwards, there is no more room for anti statism, and so libertarians, seeking to remain inside the Overton Window, have abandoned their anti statism, becoming just another variant of progressive, thus totalitarian statist.

If genuinely libertarian or anarcho capitalist, then have to abandon the Overton Window, whereupon anarcho capitalism becomes feudalism, and you are a reactionary.

(If we actually had anarcho capitalism, we would not have borders, but we would not have welfare either, and likely we would have the death penalty for most crimes typical of the underclass, and serfdom or slavery for vagrants and sturdy beggars. Let us introduce the death penalty for everything, abolish voting, at least for the poor and the stupid, and reintroduce serfdom or some similar way of getting people disinclined to work out of circulation, and *then* we can open the borders.)

Landsburg argues against allowing anyone to refuse to embrace Gay Marriage supposedly because he does not want to privilege the religious. I seem to recall that the first amendment privileges the religious and the owners of presses, so obviously that needs to go also - and in fact it already has.

Most "libertarians" have, as libertarianism comes close to being illegal, abandoned libertarianism. It is now an entirely dead doctrine.

Originally libertarianism was "classic liberalism", an alliance between economists, and the religious left, the descendents of the puritans well on the way to becoming unitarians.

The economists assumed that slaves were homo economicus, economically rational man. Therefore, if the slaves were freed, they would be able to make the same deal with the former slave owners, doing the same work as before, only for better pay, and without whips or chains. Of course this did not eventuate. The great majority of the former slaves could not make the same deal, because they could not be trusted to do the same work, and so the former slaves were economically far worse off, and a lot of them died, making worse decisions for themselves than their former owners had made for them. The economists could have argued that the outcome was still better than slavery, but that is not the argument that they made, nor the outcome that they expected. Rather, they just ignored the discrepancy. Homo economicus is a reasonably good approximation for males of IQ 105 and above, particularly white males of IQ 105 and above, thus a reasonably accurate approximation for businessmen, for the people who make the economy tick, thus a reasonably good approximation for the economy. It is a poor approximation for most people, and a very poor approximation for most black people.

As the religious part of the alliance moved ever left, the economists split off, becoming libertarians. As the religious part continued to move ever leftwards, the Overton Window ceased to permit libertarians. And so, libertarians have ceased to be. If you used to be a libertarian, you can become a progressive, or a reactionary.

## Fertility

### 2014-03-04 17:36:04

My unmarried niece failed to show up at my son's wedding. I complained to her mother, observing that she has no life, so no excuse for not turning up.

Her mother, who is my elder sister, was somewhat indignant about this and alleged that my niece had a boyfriend. I commented that since my niece was too old to be fertile, her boyfriend was not serious, unlikely to become a husband, and may well be a boyfriend only in my niece's energetic imagination.

At this my sister went apocalyptic, claiming that women can go on having children forever, or for a very long time, and that women remain attractive to potential new husbands forever, although her own life should have disabused her of this theory. (She foolishly divorced her high socioeconomic status husband, and expected to remarry swiftly, and remarry someone of equal or higher socioeconomic status, despite two kids in tow and a past history of … behavior unsuitable for a wife.)

It would seem that the male belief that fertility and attractiveness decline rapidly once a woman reaches a certain age is phallocentric and oppressive.

Equality means that female ovaries have the same functional lifetime as male testicles, which is logical, and, like equality itself, insane.

So here follows a public service announcement for women:

Ovaries dry up a lot quicker than testicles. At age thirty six two fifths of women are infertile, and most of the women that are theoretically fertile have a hard time getting pregnant, plus there is a substantially higher risk of the pregnancy going wrong. So you should have your babies before thirty six. If planning three babies two years apart, need to get pregnant at thirty one. If pregnant at thirty one, married at thirty. Which is why your prospects for getting married plunge abruptly at thirty, because any potential husbands are doing the same arithmetic. Yes, some woman you know got pregnant and married at forty four - but your chances of being that woman are not good.

Getting married and having kids is going to deep six your career to the same extent regardless whether you marry at eighteen or thirty five. Being successful in your career makes you less attractive to men, because of the higher divorce risk, bitchiness risk, and infidelity risk of successful career women. You can always do the career thing later. You cannot do the baby thing later. Male doctors marry nurses. They do not marry female doctors.

And if you divorce after having kids, you are *not* going to remarry a handsome physically fit millionaire, no matter what the movies and romance books tell you. Even divorce before having children substantially impairs your marriage prospects, because of the high infidelity and divorce risk posed by divorcees.

You can probably postpone getting married to thirty six, but if you postpone having children to thirty six, you are likely to have zero or one child.


## Tonto and the lone ranger.

### 2014-03-09 14:29:06

Tonto and the lone ranger (formally the Lone ranger, with his comedy relief sidekick Tonto, whose name means "silly" in Spanish) have recently been rebooted, with the no longer silly Tonto as main character and the lone ranger as his sidekick. Since the audience is largely white, and Tonto is authentically alien (covered in warpaint and wears a dead bird on his head at all times) this, of course, went over like a lead balloon. Even genuine native Americans are unlikely to identify with this authentically alien representative of culture that was already dead and mythical a century ago.

Even in its original form, when Tonto (Silly) was merely a comedy relief sidekick, the Lone Ranger was already left wing propaganda, being absurdly non violent, and having lovable injuns.  But, as the overton window moves ever leftwards, has to become even more left wing.

The real wild west really was a place for heroes, for men who became legend. Bad guys were generally hunted down and killed by heroes, not the state, thus the classic western: Bad guy does something horribly bad, victimizing elderly widows, little girls, and at least one pretty girl. Hero does something about it.

It really happened that way, happened a lot. Evil bad guys does evil things, good guy takes care of it. Plus, Cowboys, horses, hostile injuns, a prairie, a campfire, a saloon, and you have a western.

The ruling morality that the good guys acted out was that found in the bible, with a fair bit of the old testament, plus that found in Blackstone's commentaries - a profoundly reactionary morality, in which, for example, good women got special protection and privilege, but only good women got special protection and privilege. It was a morality that is not only profoundly and shockingly reactionary by our standards, but also profoundly and shockingly reactionary by the standards of London, New York back in the day. An eye for an eye and a tooth for a tooth was not good enough. Rather, the penalty for stealing a horse was hanging, the penalty for "insulting" a woman was hanging, the penalty for just about everything was hanging. The civilized urban contemporaries of the heroes of the old west found the real life heroes of the old West disturbingly right wing.

And, of course, there were the injuns, which for the purposes of a rattling good yarn were depicted as ever ready to kill any white person they could get their hands on in the most horrible possible fashion, and in real life really were frequently apt to kill any white person they could get their hands on in the most horrible possible fashion.

What typically happened in real life was that the injun tribe would sell some substantial part of their hunting grounds. They would use the money partly to buy food, but mostly to buy rotgut whisky. One day, the money would run out, they would wake up with a horrible hangover, no food, and no hunting grounds. Some of the young hotheads among the injuns would then go to their former hunting grounds and attack some settler family, preferably one with several cute young children, and perform some incredibly horrifying over the top atrocity of torture and mutilation upon those children.

They would then return to the tribe, and say "OK, now it is war. Who are you going to back?  Your fellow tribesmen fighting for your lands, or these evil whites whose evil rotgut whiskey gave you this incredibly blinding headache?" The tribe would, quite unwisely, choose war.

This backstory tended to be left out of the Westerns, not so much because it discredited the whites as destroying the injuns with whiskey in order to obtain their land, but because it discredited the injuns as destroying themselves with whiskey.

# Exhaustion of the low hanging fruit, or moral decay?

2014-03-10 09:24:03

Photolithography is limited by the wavelength of light. Below 160 nanometers, UV is not light, but ionizing radiation. So at some point, have to switch from photolithography to contact lithography, such as imprint lithography, or direct contact printing. But did they stop shrinking stuff before we reached that limit? That they are lying about it suggests moral decay, rather than exhaustion of the low hanging fruit.

Current photolithography is stuck using UV at 193 nanometers. Could they have gone lower?

Nitrogen and fused quartz, which they are already using, is good down to 160 nanometers. They are using water for their high refractive index fluid, and water becomes opaque below 193. Perfluorocarbons, however are good all the way down to 160 nanometers. So they did not push current technology to its final limit. It was not exhaustion of the low hanging fruit that caused the current alarmingly indefinite pause in Moore's law.

My prediction is that if humans resume technological advance, will resume in China, and will resume using contact lithography or direct contact printing, as there is little point in recreating from scratch a technology that has reached its ultimate limit. And if humans don't resume technological and scientific advance, it will be a long, slow, painful and messy descent into a dark age, until harsh conditions cause natural selection to resume.

# Players, PUAs, and Petruchio

2014-03-13 07:30:12

Some people in the Reaction complain that players are evil, and therefore should be cast out of the Reaction. Perhaps, but you cannot cast them out of the Dark Enlightenment, for the Dark Enlightenment is simply truth, unwanted and unpleasant truth, and no one has better cause to know the unwanted truth than players.

As for evil, it is not the duty of men in general to protect women in general, but of husbands and fathers to protect wives and daughters.

It is natural and right for men to predate upon feral women. The problem is that we should prevent women from becoming feral, not that we should protect feral women from their own lusts.

It is not the man's job to control the woman, it is a husband's job and a father's job.

In so far as we need collective social action, we need collective social action to uphold the authority of husbands and fathers to discipline badly behaved women, not to restrain players from taking advantage of feral women.

Now I hear someone saying "Well, it is natural for men to predate upon feral women, but is it right?"

And, as evidence that it is indeed right, I review "The Taming of the Shrew"

Shakespeare makes it clear that Kate's seeming hostility to men, her shrewishness, arises from sexual desire, sexual interest, and her fervent desire to get married.

In the modern adaptations, Kate behaves badly to men because she hates men. In Shakespeare's play, she behaves badly to men out of excessive desire.

Heartiste tells us that women fitness test men the way men look at women's breasts. Kate is fitness testing men at psychotic intensity, fitness testing them in a comically exaggerated fashion. Her comically bad behavior arises out of sexual desire.

Petruchio is a player. We know that, because his servant Grumio has complete confidence that Petruchio's wooing will swiftly succeed, implying it has swiftly succeeded many times before, and because Kate suspects Petruchio of being an inveterate seducer, as one would suspect from Grumio's confidence.

Petruchio has, in comically exaggerated form, the classic dark triad traits so attractive to women, he is a sociopath, a psychopath, arrogant, an asshole, is wealthy and powerful, and uses the classic player tactic, again comically exaggerated, of assuming the sale.

Petruchio passes Kate's fitness tests effortlessly, which, realistically, would turn her on, and does turn her on, which only makes her fitness tests more extreme.

Kate says she does not want to marry Petruchio, that she loathes him, though she physically attacks him, which naturally results in him touching her a great deal. The dialog about a wasp's sting implies he touches her intimately, though the fact that the dialog implies it would suggest that the intimate touch is not directly visible to the audience for reasons of decency.

Kate's father interrupts the activity while his daughter's chastity is still more or less intact. From the dialog, it sounds as if he is in the nick of time. When her father interrupted them she was about to jump Petruchio's bones and ride him like a motorcycle over nine miles of bad road.

Petruchio tells Kate that he will tell her father she has agreed to marry him, and that she is not to contradict him.

*And she does not contradict him* which makes the lie the truth. Obviously, in the case of Kate, "no" does mean "yes" because her "no"s are merely a fitness test.

And this fact, so obvious from Shakespeare's dialog, is something that no twentieth century production of "The Taming of the Shrew", has dared depict.

And then, Petruchio tames the shrew, restores the rightful social order that she has disrupted with her psychotically severe fitness tests.

Female emancipation was a fitness test that we failed, leading to massively bad female behavior. Let us not criticize those that train themselves to pass fitness tests gracefully.

Men who behave traditionally towards women and children –which is to say protect and support their wives and children –get very badly treated. So, fewer and fewer men are inclined to act like that.

The reason women are finding male authority in pick up artists rather than in husbands and fathers is because the state and the wife uses the husband's children against him to destroy his authority, threatening to take him away from his home and his children for any attempt to exercise his authority. Thus a man who invests in his family is made weak, and, being made weak, fails to provide the authority, command, and leadership that women crave, so they turn to players, for the authority that women need, which authority is of course abused. To properly exercise family authority for the good of his family, a man needs some degree of assholery, impudent defiance of the social consensus, and a reckless will to power. In other words, in today's hostile circumstances, he needs to be a bit like Petruchio.

It is not only natural for a man to predate on feral women, it is right. The problem is not predation, but that women should not be allowed to become feral in the first place, that they should submit to the authority of those males who have incentive to use that authority rightly.

## Recap on Warmism

### 2014-03-14 22:38:37

I have been ignoring the issue of Global Warming for a while, because it is pretty much settled. Anyone who still believes in Warmism is stupid, crazy, or lying. Usually stupid.

But, a short summary:

### Climategate files:

The internal emails and documents of a conspiracy to falsify science, which revealed that peer review is a conspiratorial system to ensure that holy views are published and heretical views are not published, regardless of facts and evidence. I have read about six hundred of the slightly over a thousand emails of the first Climategate release, and every single one is incriminating. They are all more or less summarized by the infamous email"trick to... hide the decline". If you twit a leftist on any of the emails, they will patronizingly explain to you that "decline" does not mean what it sounds like it means, but resist explaining "trick" or "hide" no matter how vigorously you twit them on it, implicitly admitting that they know full well that"trick" and "hide" mean exactly what they sound like they mean. The first climategate release was the emails of a criminal conspiracy to falsify science. The second climategate release[162] was the emails of a holy priesthood engaged in a crusade to purify the planet of the sins of mankind.

The climategate files not only give us reason to disbelieve "Climate Science", but discredit all peer reviewed science. Peer review means you don't get the actual evidence, but rather the consensus about what the evidence should show if it was not so wickedly prone to evil heresy. Peer review means that a consensus is quietly established behind closed doors, and then the evidence is corrected to agree with the consensus. This maximizes the authority and prestige of official science, at the expense of disconnecting it from reality. Science got along fine without peer review until the 1940s. The core of the scientific method is "Nullius in Verba", "take no one's word for it". Peer Review reverses that for taking the word of a secret committee of scientists reaching agreement behind closed doors, reaching agreement for secret reasons on the basis of secret evidence.

---

[162]https://blog.reaction.la/global-warming/climategate-1-and-2.html

## No observed warming:

Supposedly the surface instrument record indicates the world warmed rapidly from 1975 to 1998. Climate scientists issued a bunch of models that accurately retrodicted this supposed warming, and projected it into the future, projecting doom.

Unfortunately, they then started making accurate measurements of climate, and, by and large, since 1998 the climate has cooled down as much as it warmed up. For sixteen years, there has been no net global warming. Climate models retrodict with wonderful, indeed quite improbable, accuracy, but have totally failed at predicting.

The surface instrument system was not maintained for the purpose of measuring minute long term changes in climate, but large days to day variations in weather. So equipment was frequently moved or replaced, generally moved to some place closer to people because of technological changes in the equipment.

Thus the surface climate record has large systematic errors if one attempts to extract climate data from that record. If one ad hoc corrects for those sources of error that tend to contradict the result one wants, and is less apt to correct for those sources of error that produce the result one wants, one can produce, in the short term, pretty much any result one wants.

Careful examination of "corrections" made by the warmists reveals some rather disturbing ad hoc corrections[163]. They knew what the result should be, and if the data failed to agree, simply changed it, on the quite plausible basis that we know the data to be total cow manure. Since there is in fact no accurate indication of whether the world warmed in the period 1975 to 1998, they were totally justified in pulling data out of their asses.

Now in fact we have rather good data indicating the world did not warm up much over the period 1975 to 1998[164]. In particular, global sea ice remains much the same as ever it was and the tree line has not moved.

But, supposing that the world did warm by the amount claimed over this period, climate models provide a very good fit, a suspiciously good fit, to that warming. Their retrodiction is extremely accurate, suspiciously so, given that what they are retrodicting is not at all accurately known.

Hence the Spirit of Mawson expedition attempted to sail through ice that their ideology told them was not there[165].

So, since 1998, the gap between the 1998 models and reality has grown very rapidly. They retrodict wonderfully, but their predictions have been a total failure.

And same is, I expect, likely to be true for the 2014 models.

---

[163] https://wattsupwiththat.com/2009/12/08/the-smoking-gun-at-darwin-zero/
[164] https://blog.reaction.la/global-warming/no-twentieth-century-warming.html
[165] https://blog.reaction.la/global-warming/global-warming-scientists-trapped-in-antarctic-denial.html

## The trouble with gay marriage

2014-03-21 15:47:49

Scott Alexander has just posted that anyone who objects to homosexuality must be a repressed homosexual[166], which is typical of what passes for rationality among the "Less Wrong"crowd.

By the same reasoning, anyone who objects to coprophagy must be a repressed coprophage, because, of course, everyone at "Less Wrong"knows perfectly well that there can be no rational, innate, or instinctive reasons to dislike eating *$#!%*.

When we were all forced to call homosexuals gay, "gay" instantly became a startlingly potent curse word, and so the second verse of "deck the halls with boughs of holly" instantly disappeared from the Christmas Carol rotation, as did the Flintstones theme song. Clearly, it was not the intention of the social engineers who forced us to use the word "gay" that the second verse of "Deck the Halls" would vanish, yet somehow it did.

Forcing people to call gays married will predictably have a similar effect on the word "marriage" – people will titter when they hear the word. "Marriage" too will become a curse word and an insult, just as "Gay" instantly did.

We have thousands of years of experience with euphemisms. Applying a nice word to something disgusting does not make the disgusting thing nice, it makes the nice word disgusting.

## Prediction, Retrodiction, Warmism and the Demon Haunted Dark

2014-03-23 15:40:52

We are far more impressed by a scientific theory that predicts, than a supposedly scientific theory that retrodicts, even though from the Bayesian point of view they are the same.

Successful prediction tells us that this is an actual theory, rather than a slippery and ambiguous pile of vague fudge factors subject to post hoc reinterpretation.

As you probably know, Global Warming models are 100% successful at precisely "predicting" (retrodicting) the alleged past, even though past climate is not in fact known very accurately. They are totally unsuccessful at predicting.

By and large, Warmism is not incorrect science, but anti science. Catastrophic Anthropogenic Global Warming is an attempt by skeptics to make sense out of the Warmist position, to construct a plausible scientific theory that makes the predictions that Warmists predict, but Warmists are not much interested in making sense.

The theory attributed to the Warmists by the skeptics is that water vapor provides positive feedback, clouds also provide postive feedback, so any small nudge tends to have large effects on the climate.

Do Warmists believe the theory that skeptics attribute to them?

Perhaps. To find out, you would have to sue the model builders under the freedom of information act, and the model builders would stone wall, the courts would favor them, and the model builders would complain they are being persecuted by big oil.

---

[166]https://slatestarcodex.com/2014/03/20/typical-mind-and-disbelief-in-straight-people

The term "multiplier" in the sense that skeptics use it never appears in Warmist works, only in critiques of Warmism. The term "climate sensitivity" does appear in Warmist works, but it does not seem to be used in the same meaning as in skeptic works. It is not a ratio that can be larger or smaller than unity, not a number, but more like sin and purity, not the kind of thing where one might say the "the climate sensitivity is 2.7" To a Warmist, to assert that the climate sensitivity is 2.7 would be as ridiculous as if a Roman Catholic priest were to say that that the sinfulness of adultery is 2.7 A Warmist paper will say that climate sensitivity is greater than we thought, but will not give a number for what we supposedly used to think it was, nor a number for what we now supposedly think it is – which does not stop them from deducing from this unspecified change in this unspecified number that the temperature in 2100 will be precisely six degrees hotter.

I have not read much of the Warmist literature. Perhaps there is some that understands the theory of Catastrophic Anthropogenic Global Warming attributed to the Warmists by the skeptics, but what I have read seems to me more like inspiration by the spirit of Gaia decorated almost at random by scientific sounding words. It could be that the author understands and believes a scientific theory that makes the required doomful predictions, but there is no very clear indication that he does.

Steve McIntyre argued that it is likely that clouds create negative feedback. Do Warmists attempt to argue with him? Do Warmists say "no, clouds create positive feedback"? Do Warmists even know the difference between positive and negative feedback? Nasa discussing clouds sound like they use the terms correctly, but then fail to apply them when discussing the stability of temperatures between the wet season and dry season in the tropics, even though this is an obvious case of negative feedback.

Rather, Warmism is a revival of the old demon worshiping cults. The priests announce the gods are angry, any unusual weather event being evidence of the wrath of the demon gods, and that to appease these hostile and wrathful beings sacrifices shall be made, which sacrifices the priests get to administer.

## Creeping coup in the Ukraine

### 2014-03-25 18:01:46

The fascists took over Japan in the 1930s by a creeping coup. There was a fair bit of violence and assassination by people with friends in government, and people in government had friends in the violence and assassination business. Similarly, that is how Mossadegh "democratically" came to power in Iran, without ever facing the inconvenience of an election.

And that is how the Cathedral installed a puppet regime in Ukraine.

I read, in google translation, a Russian web page on the amazingly cute Prosecutor General of Crimea[167].

She has survived one assassination attempt. She is guarded by two men with machine guns. She got the job because the first four candidates they approached were frightened to take the job.

---

[167] https://www.rg.ru/2014/03/20/poklonskaya.html

Before she became the Prosecutor General of Crimea, she was a prosecutor in the Office of the Prosecutor General of Ukraine. In that job she complained because people in Ukraine were engaged in political violence, and yet not being prosecuted – and so was "invited" to take a holiday.

And that is how a creeping coup works.

## Still patting themselves on the back

2014-03-26 10:41:28

The Cathedral believed it was unthinkable that Putin would annex Crimea. When Putin annexed Crimea, they believed he had made a terrible mistake, and they just needed to allow him some face saving way to back down.

Mother Jones tells us: Russia Is Not Exactly a Big Winner in the Crimean Dispute[168]

Here is how Russia has won: The Cathedral has murdered its allies, and been unable to murder its enemies. Russia has shown willingness and ability to protect its friends.

Two thirds of Ukrainian troops in Crimea have deserted or gone over to the Russians[169]. More will probably follow now that Ukraine has ordered Ukrainian troops to leave Crimea. Ukraine has been going through defense ministers at alarming rate, which may well presage yet another coup, or worse, the hollowing out of the government as the illusion of government becomes dangerously transparent. Government is a collective illusion. Like the divine right of kings, it exists so long as people pretend it exists, sustained by the power of faith. The Ukraine government may well vanish from between the fingers of the Cathedral as the faith falters, and if on the other hand, the government of Ukraine does not vanish, but continues to exist, it has already cost the Cathedral more than it knows.

Shortly before Russia intervened in Crimea, Russian loyalist militias spontaneously appeared and Ukrainian regiments spontaneously disappeared. In this, Russia has won, and the Cathedral has lost.

Obama and the Democrats attached a pork barrel rider to their bill sanctioning Russia, dispensing some gravy to their pals, demonstrating to the world and to Putin that internal politics, back scratching, and pork barreling completely outweigh foreign affairs. In this up side down priority, the power of America in world affairs has been undermined. Washington is revealed as distracted and unserious.

And now, for absolutely no logical reason, yet another picture of the world's cutest prosecutor general:

---

[168]https://www.motherjones.com/kevin-drum/2014/03/russia-not-exactly-big-winner-crimean-dispute
[169]https://www.theguardian.com/world/2014/mar/25/shooting-far-right-leader-tensions-ukraine

## The trouble with white nationalism

2014-03-30 05:40:49

is that it is demotic. The trouble with our brahmins is that they are demotic.

If, seeking power, you propose to give all white people a microslice of power, you will be outbid by those seeking power who propose to give everyone a microslice of power.

White nationalism is moderate leftism, and moderate leftism will always be outbid by immoderate leftism

Today's white nationalism is yet another variant on the Republican program of backing away from the left singularity in infinitesimally tiny steps. This runs contrary to the natural ever leftwards dynamic, so always turns into program for heading into the left singularity at a slightly slower pace which in turn turns into a program for heading into the left singularity at an ever accelerating pace - mainstream republicanism.

White nationalism, being demotic, tends to become national socialism. National socialism kills people not because it is nationalist, but because it is socialist.

It is necessary to apply different laws to different people on the basis of superficial characteristics. For example a black man taking certain drugs is overwhelmingly likely to be markedly more dangerous than a white man taking the same drugs. So, in practice, we have very restrictive laws that are theoretically applied to everyone, but are, in practice, applied selectively - the alternative to racially aware enforcement being suicide.

Would it not be a lot fairer to openly issue identity cards, and openly have different laws for different groups, with some groups having laws that were simpler, harsher, more restrictive, and more swiftly enforced?

Of course that would be fairer, more just, more effective, than our current hypocritical system.

And if we had that, would not white nationalism be part of the air you breathed, so that all whites would be white nationalist without thinking about it or being aware of it?

Obviously it would. And obviously that is the system that we used to have. We used to all be unthinkingly and naturally race nationalist, the alternative being obviously stupid and suicidal. And we drifted away from that system, replacing it with elaborate hypocrisy and pretense, because white nationalism is leftist, and Cthulhu swims always left.

You can move leftwards from that system to socialism, and wind up murdering people by the truckload, or move leftwards from that system to what we have now, and white people wind up being ethnically cleansed. On the whole, the latter leftwards movement is markedly preferable to the former leftwards movement.

Whites are not naturally a tribe. To make them a tribe, you would need an identitarian religion. That religion would have to become the state religion, and then forcibly convert all whites to that state religion.

But state religions that forcibly convert everyone are intolerably oppressive, and tend to have extremely bad economic effects. A more workable program is what we have now, where the official religion is high status, all deviations from it are low status, and if you want to get a job in government, or quasi government, or go to the more prestigious universities you have to pretend to subscribe to the official religion.

Now if we had an identitarian religion, and it was the state religion, then after a few hundred years or so, nearly all whites would subscribe to it, much as they subscribe to our current official state religion, and then rule of that religion would effectively be white nationalism.

But, lacking such a religion, whites lack tribal identity, so white nationalism will always fail the way it has already failed.

Been there, done that, prohibited from wearing the t-shirt.

We tried going back to the 1950s, time to try 1660.

## Watt's big list of failed global warming predictions

### 2014-04-03 07:51:52

Watt has a big list of failed global warming predictions[170]. None have been fulfilled, many of them have been falsified.

Here is the subset of Watt's list that has been clearly and obviously falsified.

May 15, 1989, Associated Press: "Using computer models, researchers concluded that global warming would raise average annual temperatures nationwide [USA] two degrees by 2010."

1988 Rob Reiss asked official Climate Scientist Dr.James Hansen how the greenhouse effect was likely to affect the neighborhood below Hansen's office in NYC in the next 20 years, whereupon Climate scientist James Hansen issues this prediction, to be fullfilled in 20 years, which is to say, doom by 2008: "The West Side Highway [which

---

[170]https://wattsupwiththat.com/2014/04/02/the-big-list-of-failed-climate-predictions/

runs along the Hudson River] will be under water. And there will be tape across the windows across the street because of high winds. And the same birds won't be there. The trees in the median strip will change....There will be more police cars....[since] you know what happens to crime when the heat goes up."

Michael Oppenheimer, 1990, The Environmental Defense Fund: "By 1995, the greenhouse effect would be desolating the heartlands of North America and Eurasia with horrific drought, causing crop failures and food riots..."(By 1996) The Platte River of Nebraska would be dry, while a continent-wide black blizzard of prairie topsoil will stop traffic on interstates, strip paint from houses and shut down computers...The Mexican police will round up illegal American migrants surging into Mexico seeking work as field hands."

June 11, 1986, Dr.James Hansen of the Goddard Space Institute (NASA) in testimony to Congress (according to the Milwaukee Journal): "Hansen predicted global temperatures should be nearly 2 degrees higher in 20 years, 'which is about the warmest the earth has been in the last 100,000 years.'" (prediction for 2006)

June 8, 1972, Christian Science Monitor: "Arctic specialist Bernt Balchen says a general warming trend over the North Pole is melting the polar ice cap and may produce an ice-free Arctic Ocean by the year 2000."

June 2008, Ted Alvarez, Backpacker Magazine Blogs: "you could potentially sail, kayak, or even swim to the North Pole by the end of the summer. Climate scientists say that the Arctic ice...is currently on track to melt sometime in 2008." In the summer of 2008 he makes a prediction for the summer of 2008! Careless of him. Shortly after this prediction was made, a Russian icebreaker was trapped in the ice of the Northwest Passage for a week. The state of the Northwest passage today, in 2014, is roughly the same as it was in 1921. Some years you can sail through, some years you cannot, and most years if you try it, there is a high risk of getting stuck.

January 2000 Dr.Michael Oppenheimer of the Environmental Defense Fund commenting (in a NY Times interview) on the mild winters in New York City: "But it does not take a scientist to size up the effects of snowless winters on the children too young to remember the record-setting blizzards of 1996. For them, the pleasures of sledding and snowball fights are as out-of-date as hoop-rolling, and the delight of a snow day off from school is unknown."

2008 Dr.James Hansen of the Goddard Space Institute (NASA) on a visit to Britain: "The recent warm winters that Britain has experienced are a sign that the climate is changing." Implying that the warm winters are now going to be typical, a short term implied prediction. Careless of him. Two exceptionally cold winters followed. The 2009-10 winter may be the coldest experienced in the UK since 1683.

June 30, 1989, Associated Press: U.N. OFFICIAL PREDICTS DISASTER, SAYS GREENHOUSE EFFECT COULD WIPE SOME NATIONS OFF MAP–entire nations could be wiped off the face of the earth by rising sea levels if global warming is not reversed by the year 2000. Coastal flooding and crop failures would create an exodus of 'eco-refugees,' threatening political chaos," said Brown, director of the New York office of the U.N. Environment Program. He added that governments have a 10-year window of opportunity to solve the greenhouse effect. I heard the exact same prediction last night on the television (in 2014), entire nations disappearing, hordes of eco refugees creating political instability, with the date for doomsday changed from 2000 to 2030.

Sept 19, 1989, St.Louis Post-Dispatch: "New York will probably be like Florida 15 years from now."

December 5, 1989, Dallas Morning News: "Some predictions for the next decade are not difficult to make...Americans may see the '80s migration to the Sun Belt reverse as a global warming trend rekindles interest in cooler climates."

Good bye winter. Never again snow?" Spiegel, 1 April 2000

"Within a few years winter snowfall will become a very rare and exciting event. ... Children just aren't going to know what snow is."
David Viner, Climatic Research Unit, University of East Anglia, 20 March 2000

"Winter has gone forever and we should officially bring spring forward instead. ... There is no winter any more despite a cold snap before Christmas. It is nothing like years ago when I was younger. There is a real problem with spring because so much is flowering so early year to year."
Express, Dr Nigel Taylor, Curator of Kew Gardens, 8 Feb 2008

"Unfortunately, it's just getting too hot for the Scottish ski industry."
David Viner, Climatic Research Unit, University of East Anglia, 14 Feb 2004

"Spring is arriving earlier each year as a result of climate change, the first 'conclusive proof' that global warming is altering the timing of the seasons, scientists announced yesterday."
Guardian, 26 August 2006. [171]

"The global temperature will increase every year by 0.2°C"
Michael Müller, Socialist, State Secretary in the Federal Ministry of Environment, in Die Zeit, January 15, 2007

"Unfortunately, it's just getting too hot for the Scottish ski industry. It is very vulnerable to climate change; the resorts have always been marginal in terms of snow and, as the rate of climate change increases, it is hard to see a long-term future."
David Viner, of the Climatic Research Unit at the University of East Anglia.
February 14, 2004[172]

1990 Actress Meryl Streep "By the year 2000 – that's less than ten years away–earth's climate will be warmer than it's been in over 100,000 years. If we don't do something, there'll be enormous calamities in a very short time." Heard the same prediction on television last night, though they were a bit vaguer about the date.

Edward Goldsmith, 1991, (5000 Days to Save the Planet): "By 2000, British and American oil will have diminished to a trickle....Ozone depletion and global warming threaten food shortages, but the wealthy North will enjoy a temporary reprieve by buying up the produce of the South. Unrest among the hungry and the ensuing political instability, will be contained by the North's greater military might. A bleak future indeed, but an inevitable one unless we change the way we live...At present rates of exploitation there may be no rainforest left in 10 years. If measures are not taken immediately, the greenhouse effect may be unstoppable in 12 to 15 years."

---

[171]https://www.guardian.co.uk/environment/2006/aug/26/climatechange.climatechangeenvironment
[172]https://www.theguardian.com/uk/2004/feb/14/climatechange.scotland

April 22, 1990 ABC, The Miracle Planet: "I think we're in trouble. When you realize how little time we have left–we are now given not 10 years to save the rainforests, but in many cases five years. Madagascar will largely be gone in five years unless something happens. And nothing is happening."

November 7, 1997, (BBC commentator): "It appears that we have a very good case for suggesting that the El Niños are going to become more frequent, and they're going to become more intense and in a few years, or a decade or so, we'll go into a permanent El Nino. So instead of having cool water periods for a year or two, we'll have El Niño upon El Niño, and that will become the norm. And you'll have an El Niño, that instead of lasting 18 months, lasts 18 years."

July 26, 1999 The Birmingham Post: "Scientists are warning that some of the Himalayan glaciers could vanish within ten years because of global warming. A build-up of greenhouse gases is blamed for the meltdown, which could lead to drought and flooding in the region affecting millions of people."

October 15, 1990 Carl Sagan: "The planet could face an 'ecological and agricultural catastrophe' by the next decade if global warming trends continue."

Sept 11, 1999, The Guardian: "A report last week claimed that within a decade, the disease (malaria) will be common again on the Spanish coast. The effects of global warming are coming home to roost in the developed world."

March 29, 2001, CNN: "In ten year's time, most of the low-lying atolls surrounding Tuvalu's nine islands in the South Pacific Ocean will be submerged under water as global warming rises sea levels."

1969, Lubos Moti, Czech physicist: "It is now pretty clearly agreed that CO2 content [in the atmosphere] will rise 25% by 2000. This could increase the average temperature near the earth's surface by 7 degrees Fahrenheit. This in turn could raise the level of the sea by 10 feet. Goodbye New York. Goodbye Washington, for that matter."

2005, Andrew Simms, policy director of the New Economics Foundation: "Scholars are predicting that 50 million people worldwide will be displaced by 2010 because of rising sea levels, desertification, dried up aquifers, weather-induced flooding and other serious environmental changes." I heard on the television last night (2014) this exact same prediction with the date changed from 2010 to 2020

Oct 20, 2009, Gordon Brown UK Prime Minister (referring to the Copenhagen climate conference): "World leaders have 50 days to save the Earth from irreversible global warming."

May 31, 2006 Al Gore, CBS Early Show: "...the debate among the scientists is over. There is no more debate. We face a planetary emergency. There is no more scientific debate among serious people who've looked at the science...Well, I guess in some quarters, there's still a debate over whether the moon landing was staged in a movie lot in Arizona, or whether the Earth is flat instead of round."

# Bored with Game of Thrones

## 2014-04-08 12:35:28

I used to be a huge fan of Game of Thrones. Attempted to watch the latest episode, Season four episode one, gave up when we got introduced to some bad guys in the occupation army harassing the North. I don't care about those people. They can rape the northerners all they want. Fine by me. Most of the northerners I cared about got killed off.

Lately the show assumes that the viewers sincerely feel universalism, and that universalism, caring about far away strangers, is the measure of virtue, that we will like people who supposedly care about far away strangers. Not working on me. I don't care about those people. I wonder if it works on anyone?

Since Tyrion Lannister has turned from a capable and decent medieval nobleman into a thoroughly wimpy and gelded women's rights respecting twenty first century male feminist mangina I have stopped caring about him also. Similarly, when the Daenerys Stormborn, daughter of dragons, mother of dragons, turned from being a hot sorceress bent on conquering the world and restoring the magic, to a do gooder abolitionist, aiming to abolish slavery, rather than become a magical queen of a world in which the magic is renewed, she became boring and unpleasant. Every time the viewers see her going forth to free yet more slaves, the viewers are disappointed. It is not just me, I also see complaints in the youtube comments. Let me know when she cuts loose with the dragon magic to make herself queen.

Early in the first season, we were told that there used to be magic in the world, but it went away, perhaps it never was. Then we meet Daenerys Stormborn, who is made of magic, takes magic entirely for granted, and intends to rule the world. It is implied that with a magical queen, magic will return to the world, which plot point seems to have been forgotten, or thrown overboard. How do you make a sorcerer queen with dragons boring?

Answer: Have her do good to far away strangers.

The problem is we are supposed to like these people because they demonstrate their virtue by doing the progressive thing, but it turns out that the progressive thing is just not likable. We don't care about the slaves, because they are just faceless masses of unpleasant people living boring lives, so Daenerys Stormborn is doing good to far away faceless people we really do not like. Similarly, Sansa Stark, the wife of Tyrion Lannister has the unerring ability to make the wrong sexual choice, so we don't really sympathize with the modern position that women should be allowed to make their own sexual choices. She is a spoilt brat who needs a beating. It is almost as if the writers are deliberately undermining their own propaganda. Who could be worse advertisement for a woman's right to choose her own sexual partner than Sansa Stark? (Answer: Kate Gosselin)

Early in the series, I liked Eddard Stark, because he was doing the right thing for a medieval nobleman, but lately, the good guys are all good by being twenty first century progressives, not good by being good noblemen. I just don't care about those people. Progressivism just fails to motivate or interest the viewer. A world with magic and dragons restored is just a lot more fun than a world with slavery abolished.

There was a time when progressive stories were appealing: Oliver Twist showed us that the bad behavior of the poor was wholly the result of the environment and could be cured by giving them money. Les Miserables showed us that criminals were people just as decent as everyone else, that crime was some sort of unfortunate accident, like having a heart attack, no indication of future conduct, and therefore criminals should not be punished. Obviously idiotic, but those were good stories. But in Game of Thrones, progressive propaganda has become a dreary story killing leaden weight.

First they established the Imp as a good guy. Then they show him having progressive attitudes - but having progressive attitudes to women makes him a sackless wimp, and thus totally destroys his appeal. Now we have three major characters that have had their genitals removed.

One of the reasons I stopped watching at that point is that I figured that Lady Arya Stark was about to kill one of the bad guys of occupier force - but the bad guys have not done anything, and don't propose to do anything to Lady Arya Stark. They have been established as bad in that they mistreating the faceless occupied, but the standard way of showing someone is bad is he does something bad to people we care about, or he does something bad to his own people that he should care about (evil overlord condemns minion to horrible death for trivial transgression) As far as I can see, the occupiers care about their own people and are loyal to each other, their army, and their leaders, and their army and their leaders are loyal to them - the medieval virtues.

We are not inclined to naturally and spontaneously feel that it is bad for occupiers to mistreat the occupied, or that slavery is wrong. The show does not teach us to care about these things, but rather assumes that we should care about these things. I find I just don't care. I wonder how many viewers do care? It just makes no sense that Arya Stark, a medieval noblewoman, would care.

So what is happening with progressive propaganda? I get the feeling that people are just checking off the boxes - that a list of requirements was handed down to the writers from on high, and provided that they go through the motions, no one cares if it is done well or badly. Good characters shall demonstrate modern progressivism. Bad characters shall demonstrate medieval reaction, regardless of whether this induces the correct attitudes in the viewer.

## autogynophilia

### 2014-04-10 05:53:58

The progressive model of transexuality is that a man is really a woman inside.

For the most part, this is not true[173]. Transexuals are, for the most part, men who have no interest in knitting, dolls, or housework. They are men who have a sexual fetish for being treated as women. They get a kick out of it. Wearing women's clothing is analogous to flashing girls - it is making other people reluctant props for one's own sexual arousal. Most transsexuals are males who are sexually aroused by themselves as women - autogynophiles, they want to have sex with themselves as women. They don't want to

---

[173]https://www.genderpsychology.org/autogynephilia/male_gender_dysphoria/index.html

have sex with men, even less than they want to do knitting. They want to be treated as a woman by men and woman, because they get off on it.

The progressive movement has, once again, made itself the stage for disturbingly weird and unpleasant public sexual activity. But then, they must be used to that by now.

Some male to female transexuals make OK girls, but the usual outcome is something horribly weird, in uncanny valley between male and female. And that is the way they like it.

It is extremely common for women to be sexually aroused by the thought of themselves as women, but that is not so weird and disturbing, because they actually are women, and because female sexuality is less threatening and aggressive than male sexuality. If an actual woman makes us props celebrating the fact that she is a woman, few are inclined to complain, even if the woman is obviously getting off on it as she so often obviously is. (We complain when older women do this, but they can usually be shamed into toning it down.) Transexuality tends to be more aggressive and hostile, more like flashing. The uglier they are, the more they like your reaction.

While autogynophilia seems to be disturbingly common in males and nigh universal in women (indeed pretty much every sexual deviation seems to be nigh universal in women), autoandrophilia seems to be extremely rare, probably nonexistent.

Other types of transexuals are femme gays and butch lesbos, but these are less apt to harass us normals than autogynophiles are.

## Firing Kathleen Sebelius

### 2014-04-13 09:41:11

Everyone involved in the disastrous rollout of the disastrous Obamacare website has been fired or has had something horribly bad happen to their careers, from Human Health and Services Secretary Kathleen Sebelius downwards. It turns out that people working for the government, like people with tenure, can be punished by the left, though not by the right.

If ever the right should try to fire people, see my post on how to fire big bird[174].

The website was fixed by "the tech surge" –fixed by white males organized in teams that showed very little interest in providing a supportive environment for women and people of color. The screw up was primarily female. Being PC, they had women work on a website and of course the website did not work. Men had to come in and take over.

But the stupid girlie team had plenty of white males. Standard operating procedure in software engineering is that white males do the actual work for team woman, much as Marie Curie got her bright idea when she was with her famous scientist husband, who subsequently hired a male to the actual work of implementing Marie Curie's bright idea.

This, however, only works if you hire on the basis of quotas - the smartest x% of males, the smartest 2x% of females. But if x is a rather small numberit then becomes obvious that every person hired to fulfill the quota is dumber than every person hired on his merits.[175]

---

[174]https://blog.reaction.la/economics/how-to-fire-big-bird/

[175]https://blog.reaction.la/politics/fun-hate-fact-about-the-bell-curve

This, of course, is a hostile work environment. So you don't hire the smartest x% of males. You hire males that fit in, which is to say, stupid males. And then, unfortunately, you cannot build a website.

But there is something odd about this account of events. Government work is enormously rewarded, and Obama spent a stupendously large sum on the website, ridiculously large. Should not the very smartest white males have somehow snuck in when people's backs are turned? Don't the smart people wind up getting all the cherries?

Evidently the smart people do not wind up getting all the cherries[176].

In any society, the normal and natural outcome is that the best people wind up ruling - though not necessarily in the interests of that society. They may wind up doing a very good job of stealing anything not nailed down and setting fire to anything that they cannot pry up, the typical dark age government that has been the norm throughout most of human history, but chances are they will be very good at stealing and lighting fires. There is a strong correlation between intelligence and reacting fast to the movement of your opponent's sword, and even better correlation between intelligence and reacting fast with the best sword move.

We, however, are seeing government by people of very ordinary intelligence, which requires vigorous, active, and effective filtering to keep the smartest people out, which filtration starts in our most prestigious universities.

The original World Bank writers called a run a run. Their replacements called a run "negative feedback loop" because they try to scatter as many erudite phrases in their writings as the original writers were apt to do - but, like Mrs Malaprop, scatter the wrong erudite phrases in the wrong places. It is obvious that Mrs Malaprop is imitating people who are several standard deviations smarter than she is – and today's World Bank writers are similarly imitating yesterday's World Bank writers.

## Real Rebellion in Ukraine

2014-04-14 16:50:39

Reuters shows a video of these people seizing the police station, mayor's offices, and so forth

---

[176]https://blog.reaction.la/tag/not-the-cognitive-elite

Observe, no two in quite the same uniform.

It is very hard for a militia to get uniforms exactly the same. It is very hard for astroturf to get uniforms varied. Therefore, real militia, not Russian astroturf.

These are described as "anti Maidan" protestors. Maidan's website is in English, written in the dialect of the US ruling elite, thus Maidan isCathedral astroturf. Thus this is local rebellion against the Cathedral on the periphery of the blue empire.

## US State Department hints at invading Ukraine

2014-04-15 12:46:13

We currently are working with Ukraine to determine its requirements across the security sector. Based on those requirements, we will review options for potential additional security assistance.

This follows the path that the Soviet Union followed into Afghanistan.

The Soviet Union mistreated its allied government in Afghanistan, after the style of Darth Vader

I am altering the deal. Pray I don't alter it any further.

The allied government, upon being treated as a servant, became difficult, so was overthrown and replaced by a puppet government. The puppet government faced rebellion and a military disinclined to follow orders, so the puppet government was brushed aside and replaced by direct rule of imperial troops. Long, messy, expensive war ensued. Eventually the Soviet Union decides to retreat – but discovers that retreat under fire is a difficult and dangerous maneuver.

Similarly the Cathedral mistreated, then eventually overthrew, its ally in the Ukraine, creating a puppet regime that now finds itself with a rebellion on its hands and a military disinclined to fight. Perhaps the Right Sector is willing to fight, but it is far from clear whether it will fight the puppet government's enemies, or fight the puppet government, or, quite likely, both.

Could the Cathedral be that stupid? Probably not this time, but sooner or later they will do something that stupid. They are blind, crazy, and not as smart as they used to be.

Obama's gut instinct in international affairs is to avoid trouble and make concessions, and right now is the time for that policy, but there are some in the State Department beating the drums for a more martial policy, to cover the fact that the coup was just a bad idea, badly executed, from which the Cathedral needs to retreat.

Obama is infamous for bowing to our enemies, but the USG has also been busily blowing quite a few of them up, a contradiction resolved if we suppose that he is just the PR guy and is not always told what is going down – which is roughly how the Kaiser found himself in World War I.

Puppet regimes have a tendency to disappear. The most easily attainable peaceful outcome would be for Russian speakers to rule the eastern states of a loose Ukrainian federation, and Right Sector to rule the western states of a loose Ukrainian federation, while the puppet regime remains nominally in charge, but abandons real power. The Cathedral and Obama, however, think that the natural flow of history is ever leftwards, and that such an outcome is "on the wrong side of history". The State Department was happy to hand China over to Mao, that being the correct side of history, but is profoundly reluctant to yield Ukraine

## wife goggles

### 2014-04-16 01:16:37

Notoriously, husbands tend to see their wives as hot, when they would never see some other woman of similar age as hot. If they are separated from their wife for a year or so, for example by divorce, the wife goggles fall off.

Wife goggles appear to happen primarily to fathers. If the wife does not have children, then as she grows older, she rapidly becomes less attractive, as any woman rapidly becomes less attractive past thirty.

In the ancestral environment, particularly in northerly lands, women and children were dependent on males for food. Therefore we are descended disproportionately from males who stuck around, but we are also descended disproportionately from males who only saw fertile age women as attractive.

One possible resolution of these conflicting requirements (natural selection wants man to hang out with fertile age woman, but natural selection wants man to stick with the mother of his children) is for a man to see his wife as always that age when he had children with her, or always as sexually attractive as she was at that age, which is to some substantial extent what happened to me. Which suggests that one should have children as young as possible.

# On the attack on Sunshine Mary

2014-04-18 11:03:14

Some boring people are attacking Sunshine Mary[177] in particular and the entire Manosphere in general.

According to Matt Forney, Sunshine Mary[178] said various things about her own life and activities, and the truth is various other things. I am a big fan of Sunshine Mary and yet don't remember her saying most of those things, and if she did say those things, to find out the truth on those matters would require some seriously obsessive stalking, indeed merely paying attention to her saying those things, supposing she did say them, is stalkerish.

According to Matt Forney, she is not in fact submissive to her husband. Did he camp out in her bedroom and check out their relationship? If he says one thing he cannot know, it is a lie. If one lie, all lies.

But suppose that the things he claims, and could perhaps know, are true, for example he claims she was a slut in college. Supposing all that stuff is true, suppose everything he says is true. If it is true, then he is a stalker. If a stalker, the person stalked is interesting, and the stalker is insane.

Supposing that everything Matt Forney tells us about Sunshine Mary is completely true, what does this tell us about Matt Forney?

It tells us he responds to opinions to which he disagrees by investigating where the children of the person he disagrees with go to school.

# Ukraine government fades

2014-04-20 03:12:10

Government is a shared pretense. We imagine governments into existence. Blatant puppetry can puncture the illusion.

The NY Times tells us[179]

> One of the armored columns stopped when a crowd of people, many of whom were drinking or yelling taunts, gathered on the road before them. Later in the day its commander agreed to hand over the soldiers' assault rifles to the very separatists they were sent to fight.

> Another column from the same unit, the 25th Dnipropetrovsk paratrooper brigade, surrendered not only its weapons but also the tracked and armored vehicles it had arrived in, letting militants park them as trophies, under a Russian flag, in a central square.

> A pro-Russian militant climbed into the driver's seat of one of the vehicles and spun it around on its tracks, screeching and roaring, to please the watching crowd.

---

[177] https://mattforney.com/2014/04/14/the-manosphere-is-dead-and-you-have-killed-it/

[178] https://sunshinemaryandthedragon.wordpress.com/

[179] https://www.nytimes.com/2014/04/18/world/europe/ukraine-crisis.html?hpw&rref=world&_r=1

The events on Wednesday underscored the weakness of the new Ukrainian government as it begins critical talks about the country's future with the United States, Russia and the European Union in Geneva on Thursday. Officials unable to exercise authority over their own military seem increasingly powerless to contain a growing rebellion by pro-Russian militants.

The core function of government is to enable the army and the police to act as one. An army needs something outside itself to give it cohesion - the gods, the spirits of real or mythical common ancestors, the man born to rule, the mandate of heaven. Failing that, the will of the people. What has the Ukraine government got?

## Raising fertility

### 2014-04-20 16:01:17

Singapore has terminal fertility - a fertility rate so low that it is likely to end Singapore. Smart people go to Singapore, and just do not reproduce. Black hole dysgenesis. The Singaporean government has issued a bunch of laws and incentives intended to raise fertility, with rather small effect.

Similarly, the emperor Augustus, noticing that Romans were on a similar path to oblivion, passed a bunch of laws to encourage marriage and fertility, with similar lack of effect.

I have a lot of hope in Singapore as a place where technologically advanced civilization might continue as the rest of the world slowly slides into another dark age, but that is not going to happen if Singaporeans do not reproduce

What is the highest fertility country in the world (ignoring black African countries, since they achieve high fertility by methods we cannot emulate and should not want to emulate):

Afghanistan, 7.07, increasing the population three and half times every generation, where they artificially lower female status by drastic and brutal methods in accordance with the Koran and Islamic tradition. Right up with the highest fertility black African countries. Afghans are caucasians, light skinned, dark haired, but a reasonable proportion of them have green eyes or blue eyes. They are generally white enough to pass if dressed in a business suit rather than Islamic costume.

OK, we might not necessarily want to go full Taliban. What is the highest fertility non black Christian country?

Timore Leste, 6.53, Nearly the same as Afghanistan and the high fertility black African countries, still increasing the population three and half times ever generation - and their generations are pretty fast.

OK, Christian, not black, normal IQ race, and they are giving Afghans and African blacks a run for their money, how do they do it?

They don't do it by brutal means. They have benevolent patriarchy in accordance with the bible and Christian tradition. Women are not allowed to own most kinds of property. Women are subject to their fathers until they marry, whereupon they are subject to their husbands. Under the one flesh tradition, a man and his wife are legally one person, and that person is the husband - the husband effectively owns all family property. While in Afghanistan, wives are almost property of their husbands, in Timore Leste, in accordance with the Christian tradition, the wife is the ward of her husband. He is responsible for her welfare, and she is expected to submit to him. And the practical effect of the laws on property is that she is in effect legally compelled to submit to him as well as socially compelled. If she wanders off, she has nothing, and necessarily finds herself dependent on someone who, unlike her husband, is not legally and socially required to care for her welfare. Also, finds herself in social disgrace.

But, Timore Leste is third world. Do we have examples of high fertility in an advanced first world nation in recent times?

Well, as a matter of fact we sort of do: The baby boom among Mexicans in California following the 1986 amnesty.

What happened was a bunch of single male Mexicans got green cards, and promptly sent off for Mexican fiancees. Because of laws and procedures intended to prevent fake marriages, when a woman came to America on a fiancee visa she was, under the laws then prevailing, at first very much under the power of the man bringing her in. He could send her back if displeased.

If you imported a bride, you had a lot legal power, because she needs continuing paperwork to turn a fiancee visa into a green card visa, and because she was not legally entitled to welfare, and a lot of social power, because, you are at home, and she is in an alien country.

During the short period that the new brides were relatively powerless, they were extremely fertile, creating a baby boom that knocked the hell out of the California school system, a baby boom that swiftly subsided as they legally and socially got a stronger hand. I assume the husband said "No oral contraceptives for you, no abortions for you, no condoms for you, and we are having sex whenever I am up for it. Also, toast me a sandwich."

And the bride said "Yes dear"

Comparing these examples with Singapore, it is obvious what Singapore is doing wrong. What did Augustus do wrong?

Under the marriage laws of Augustus, a wife was legally part of her father's household, rather than her husband's household. Not only could she own property independently of her husband, she could not even give her property to her husband, because it was part of her father's family property, rather than her husband's family property. So when a man married, he did not have his own household, rather he had a household shared between two people. His wife was theoretically subject to her parents' authority, rather than her husband's authority, though obviously, in practice out of reach of her father's authority.

This really cannot have been much fun for husbands.


Wife, fetch me a beer, or else I will complain to my mother in law.


And so Rome eventually fell for lack of Romans, though it took a few hundred years.

## The American right is deader than God

2014-04-23 04:32:35

In the last presidential election, nominated governor Romneycare

In the election before that, nominated SenatorMcCain-Feingold

The current huge increase in government expenditures and substantial increase in taxes reflects a bipartisan budget that your Tea Party congressman voted for - which means that your tea party congressman voted to fund Obamacare.

And, very shortly after the 2014 election, the Republican party is about bring in thirty million Democrat voters. (Each person amnestied gets to bring in relatives, and, in the 1986 amnesty, promptly did so. We also had a huge, though short lived, baby boom among immigrants, probably because immigration rights for kin boosted and, for a little while enforced, marriage. This caused some people to say that the immigrants were naturally socially conservative, though fertility eventually declined to normal underclass levels as the freshly imported women started normal underclass sexual behavior, responding to welfare incentives, rather than immigration control incentives. It eventually became glaringly obvious that Mexican immigrants are not socially conservative, once they become eligible for welfare.)

It is deemed essential that the Democrat party appease its base, hence the ban on the Keystone pipeline, while the Republican party can take its base for granted, and should always do what maximally offends them. Every Democrat agrees it is essential to pander to the most radical democrats, whilemost Republicansagree that the Republican wing of the Republican party are ugly hateful racist neanderthals.

And remember the Reagan Revolution. Without the 1986 Reagan Amnesty act Obama would not have won the election, and probably would not have been nominated.

At election time, candidates posture about how right wing they are. Sometimes they do dramatic things like "shutting down the government" - which invariably and predictably end in the total and complete capitulation of the right. When it is time to pass a budget or a law, they are all leftists. Just as you don't get into Harvard except you can do an adequate simulation of leftism, you don't get into politics unless you can adequately simulate leftism, even though you have simulate rightism for those hateful despicable disgusting voters. Democrats are the inner party, Republicans the outer party. They are all one party, the party of the state, preaching the religion of the state.

## Joo talk

2014-04-25 16:54:28

I regard all religions as at best useful pretenses that provide divine authority for ancient truths, sensible collective behavior, and sensible individual behavior, at worst as memetic diseases, and am apt to give advice to the religious on the basis of what would make a useful pretense. Such advice is not always enthusiastically received.

I have long argued that Jews should actually do what everyone accuses them of doing: Have an ethnic national religion and and ethnic nation in which that religion is the ruling religion.

Trouble is that, during their long exile, Judaism has changed, becoming a religion of exile, has adapted rather too well to exile. For the most part, Judaism is still in psychological exile, hence the reluctance to recognize Israel as Israel, and the reluctance to reach out and take the temple mount back. Judaism is not only inherently subversive of its Christian host states. It is inherently subversive of Israel. It needs to come home. Judaism is subversive because it authorizes all the bad things that Jews need to do to survive as exiles, but no longer authorizes all the bad things Jews need to do to survive as a nation in Israel. Jews feel really bad about doing bad things to Muslims who are trying to kill them. Armenians don't feel bad at all. Americans whacked Fallujah a lot harder than Jews whacked Jenin, with not nearly as good an excuse, and feel fine about doing so. Every time Jews defend themselves against people trying to kill them, other Jews, notoriously Jews in the US state department, tell them they should just roll over and die, and they are apt to do so.

B, however, argues that his variant of Judaism is fine, is psychologically healthy, and will, in due course, become the dominant strand of Judaism. I am inclined to doubt this,

The Cathedral interpret B's variant of Judaism as waiting for the Messiah to do the heavy lifting, to make his religion the state religion, and to make the necessary amendments to B's religion so that it will work as a state religion. If you are waiting for the Messiah to bring the Kingdom of Heaven, no threat to them, even if you were to get the temple mount back, since they don't expect divine intervention - and neither do I.

The worst the Cathedral think about B's variant of Judaism is that B's faction are spoiling for a war with Islam in the hope that this will force the Messiah to miraculously intervene to save Israel.

If you are going to restore the Kingdom of Israel by non miraculous means, restore the Kingdom of Israel rather than the Kingdom of Heaven, have to propose an undemocratic one state solution, in which a distinctly Jewish Israel rules over non Jews within the land of Israel, and expels or eradicates any non Jews that get difficult about that arrangement. Now maybe they suspect B of secretly harboring that plan, but if so, B has been keeping it so secret that they neglect to accuse his sect of it.

Since I regard religions as at best useful pretenses, what I would favor for Israel is an official religion that does not have the secret police spying on people's washers and does not send people who get wool lint mixed with linen lint to the gulag, but rather restricts participation in the state apparatus and the most prestigious universities to those that plausibly claim to have the correct washers. Those who attempt to subvert or overthrow this restriction get sent to the gulag, *as do those who attempt to tighten up on this restriction so that only those as holy as their extremely holy selves get to exercise power*. You are going to need soldiers on top of priests, and from time to time, soldiers are going to going to need to smack down turbulent priests hard, even if they are genuinely holy. Indeed especially if they are genuinely holy.

If relying on overtly miraculous divine intervention, I don't think Jews of B's type are any great threat to the Cathedral, and even less is the Cathedral likely to think they are a great threat to the Cathedral.

To get to a one state solutionyou need to tell people that Israel needs a one state solution, and tell them that a one state solution is incompatible with democracy and equality, and propose dismantling democracy and equality without waiting for supernatural rule by the messiah.  If B is telling people that, the Cathedral has not noticed, for if it had noticed, would rocket through the roof like an exploding hot water system.

## Technological decline
### 2014-04-27 13:20:34

If we cannot build high buildings any more, progressives say we are now so sophisticated that we are now superior to status competition based on giant penis substitutes, and status competition based on having a higher corner office than the other business executives.

If high art is an aids infested trannie projectile vomiting over the audience, progressives say that we philistines just don't get high art.

But the most important thing about a military aircraft is that it can fly faster, higher, and further than its opponents, so that you can get away from enemies, but enemies cannot get away from you.  And of these, the most important by far is to fly faster, so that you can bring trouble to your enemies, but your enemies cannot bring trouble to you.

SR 71 Blackbird, first built in 1972, about the time we put the last man on the moon.

> Cruising Speed Mach 3.2
> Ceiling 85 000 feet
> Range 3 200 nautical miles

Today's latest and greatest American warplane, the impressively named F-35 Lightning II. Does not that sound so much more impressive than "Blackbird"?

> Cruising Speed Mach 1.6
> Ceiling 60 000 feet
> Range 1 200 nautical miles nautical miles

So let us make a little table:

| Capability | Then | Now |
| --- | --- | --- |
| Speed | Mach 3.2 | Mach 1.6 |
| Ceiling | 85 000 feet | 60 000 feet |
| Range | 3 200 nautical miles | 1200 nautical miles |

OK, so how are America's enemies doing?  China claims to be making impressive progess, Russia is not declining nearly as fast as the US. This is fairly typical of a civilization in decline. The center declines faster than the periphery, and the periphery may continue to advance in important respects even after the center has completely collapsed, or been conquered by one of the peripheral states.

China promises for 2018:

Chengdu J-20

> Cruising Speed Mach 2.8
> Ceiling 60 000 feet
> Range 1 830 nautical miles

Since the Chinese are smarter but inherently less creative, they may never surpass America as it was at its height, but they are getting close and still advancing rapidly. Everything Americans once could do, they can copy, and probably over time polish up considerably, improving over the original it in modest ways.

## Shooting Gennady Kernes

### 2014-04-30 06:01:16

The Ukraine, like most of the former communist lands, experienced a five finger conversion to capitalism. State assets mysteriously wound up in the hands of some individuals. Gennady Kernes was prominent among those individuals. In the Ukraine the new plutocrats have proven less competent at utilizing assets than stealing them. Ukraine lacks law, tradition, and custom for the orderly exchange of capital assets, so, in the absence of Gennady Kernes, his fortune is probably sliding into other people's hands. He was probably shot by some random militiaman who was worried he was next in line to be arrested, but his assassination must be making some Ukrainians wealthy and a lot of Ukrainians think that they could get very wealthy by the suitable application of violence.

What Ukraine needs is an environment where productive assets have clear owners, and are capable of being exchanged, sold, and mortgaged. That Gennady Kernes title was "Mayor", not "CEO", that he was arresting people, and himself threatened with arrest and execution by the authorities that the Cathedral recognizes as legitimate suggests that it lacks that environment and lacked it even before the coup.

Mayor Gennady Kernes initially opposed the Maidan coup in the Ukraine (as I have mentioned many times before, Maidan was created by George Soros and its website is in English written in the dialect of the American ruling elite) and was threatened with arrest and assassination by Maidan forces. However, no arrest happened. Police, evidently, decided they could not arrest him. However, he switched sides. He then arrested a bunch of anti Maidan militia for possession of Molotov cocktails and pipe bombs. Well, if you arrest men with deadly weapons, better arrest them all, because if you miss some ...

Bottom line, Maidan has trouble killing its enemies. Anti Maidan forces seem to have less difficulty. Although each side accuses the other of the assassination, and the only death threats were issued by Maidan, the assassination is obviously a reaction to him changing sides and arresting people armed against Maidan.

Ukrainian Army and police will not obey orders to arrest or kill the enemies of Maidan. Anti Maidan activists will beat up or kill their opponents. Thus, anti Maidan activists have superiority of force, but no organized government or central leadership. Ukrainian armed forces go looking for someone to surrender to, cannot find a Napoleon. It is said that comes the hour, comes the man. The hour has come, but no man is to be found.

# ESR moves ever leftwards

## 2014-05-02 05:47:02

Esr has to move ever leftwards, or else suffer persecution, and to prove himself sufficiently left, has to enthusiastically support the ever greater persecution of his fellow leftists[180]. Thus each leftist has to move further left, and has to support the persecution of his fellow leftists even more than he did last year.

This is the left singularity, which results in ever leftwards movement, ever faster.

It is always cut short internally by dictatorship, a Stalin or a Cromwell who, finding himself outflanked on the left, makes it as illegal to be to the left of him as it has long been illegal to be to the right of him, or else cut short by foreign conquest, the foreign conqueror is drawn in by weakness, and by the extermination of people he cares about.

If not cut short, the final outcome would be infinite leftism in finite time, where everyone tortures each other to death, and the last torturer commits suicide for his inability to inflict infinite torments.

The closest approach to an actual left singularity was Chang Hsien-chong, who reduced the population of Szechwan from three million to seven thousand, largely by torturing people to death.

Had his career not been cut short by imperial reconquest, would have doubtless reduced the population to zero, either outflanked on the left and killed by someone even lefter than himself, or killing himself after torturing to death the last of his generals. Recall how the political followers of Aristide continued in zombie like loyalty even after he personally gouged out the eyes of one of his loyal minions with his own thumbs. Recall generals in Siberia, surrounded by armed and loyal troops, going to Moscow when summoned for torture and death

As Trotsky said:

> The party in the last analysis is always right ... I know that one must not be right against the party. One can be right only with the party, and through the party ...

Chang Hsien-chong distributed the wealth of the landlords to the poor, then ate the landlords for oppressing the poor, then exterminated the intellectuals for infecting the poor with insufficiently progressive ideas, then flayed the poor alive for being insufficiently grateful for having the wealth of their oppressors redistributed to them.

Of all those who write in English, the historianDonnithorde[181] was in the best position to know the truth about Chang Hsien-chong. Leftists, which is to say all modern historians, either rewrite Chang as a mild mannered agrarian reformer or else a horrible reactionary installed in power by the CIA. (I am just making up the part about the CIA) – modern historians, which is to say modern leftists, go completely incoherent and make no sense whatsoever when reporting these events. To get a report that is evidence based and intelligible, you have to go back to books and articles written in a safer time when the left was less terrified of itself.

---

[180]https://esr.ibiblio.org/?p=5704

[181]https://images.library.yale.edu/divinitycontent/dayrep/9866641_1938_040-007-008_eng.pdf  "Chang Hsien-chong and the dark age"

## Ever faster movement left

2014-05-04 05:36:38

https://weaselzippers.us/184731-company-fires-employee-for-saying-sterling-has-a-right-to-free-speech/Weasel zippers reports

Now, not only can free speech get you fired, supporting, people's right to free speech behind closed doors with the blinds drawn, while piously deploring what they say, can get you fired.

Observe that Josh Olin did not take the horribly extreme ultra ultra far right neo nazi position that people have a right to free speech in public.

Can anyone remember a time when anyone was so ultra extreme far right as to support free speech in public? I am sure that not only did I never support such a horrible thing, but my parents and grandparents and great grandparents never supported it either.

Everyone who was born before 1956 remembers a time when there was no such thing as marital rape, when the idea that there was something wrong with a husband compelling his wife to perform her marital duties was so strange that there was no easy way to say such a thing and be understood. And yet, no one remembers ever thinking such a thing, nor the people of the time thinking such a thing. The past is always changing, only the future is certain.

For a long time, esr has entirely forgotten that once upon a time, he, his entire family, and everyone he knew, took a husband's right to compel his wife to perform her marital duties entirely for granted. Now, it seems, he has entirely forgotten that once upon a time he supported not only the right to freedom of speech behind closed doors with the curtains drawn, but, gasp, horror, free speech in public, a position so extreme right wing that no one has words to express how horribly right wing it is. Freedom of speech is now bullying, just as the marital contract is now rape. All right thinking people agree on this, *and they always have.*

## Why women need to kept on leashes

2014-05-07 08:38:31

A software company just went bust. Happens a lot. That a woman happened to be running this company is not significant. Lots of men have lost lots of other people's money too. What is significant is that she starts offher explanation of how she pissed away all her investor's money[182] by talking about her sex life.

She begins:

> **Something wasn't right, and I couldn't put my finger on exactly what it was.**On the surface, it seemed like I had the best life. A popular blog with millions of readers. The perfect relationship with Brian, the most adoring fiance in the universe.

---

[182]https://www.erica.biz/2014/dear-investors/

"Adoring Fiance" is girl code for "The man I am about to cheat on and then dump." If a woman says her fiancee adores her, she is cruising for a dicking. If she is not cruising for a dicking, she tells us she adores her fiancee, not that he adores her.

> Then, one day, a few weeks ago, an event happened (I'll save the details of that for some other time.) Suddenly a torrent of emotions poured in. I was overwhelmed. I stayed home from work one day–my best friendErica[183] sent me some poetry, and I just cried. I wept. It felt like my soul was pouring out of me, one tear at a time.

> I reeled from the onslaught of emotions for days, and soon thereafter, I broke off my relationship with Brian.

And, by the way, forgot about running the company she was supposed to be running, with the result that the paychecks bounced and the investors lost all their money, but that, not being very important to her does not get much mention, even though the people she is addressing, the investors, are likely to be more interested in that part.

Here is what I guess happened, interpolating between "My adoring fiancee" "onslaught of emotions", and "payroll".

"My adoring fiancee"

She fucked some bad boy, Mr Very Wrong. After Mr Very Wrong was done, he kicked her out of his room and soon thereafter called the next girl on his booty call list.

"onslaught of emotions"

She dumped her fiancee and forgot about her business so as to be fully available in case the next booty call came. And the next booty call did not come.

"payroll".

Payroll.

## The real problem with Boko Haram

**2014-05-12 00:14:42**

The problem is not that they are abducting women and selling them as wives, but that they are abducting Christian girls and selling them to Muslim men. This is not bad for Christian girls. It is bad for Christian men.

The Cathedral, oddly, seems far more frightened of Christian Holy War than Muslim Jihad (observe their disturbing response to ethnic cleansing by Christians in the Central Africa Republic), so is reluctant to mention who is being abducted.

When group A abducts girls from group B, if it makes the girls available for general public use by group A members, this is extremely bad for the girls, since no one man has an incentive to take care of them. But if it assigns them to particular individual men of group A, then not only does that individual have an incentive to take care of the girl and her children, but the apparatus of violence and coercion that made the transfer likely means that he has greater paternal security, and greater reason to expect the girl to stick around, and thus greater incentive to care for the girl and her children than occurs in the Cathedral

---

[183] https://reinventingerica.com/

approved free love/leking outcome. Boko Haram believes that western education for girls is bad, because it indoctrinates them with immoral and self destructive ideas, and that girls should be married off at an early age. Seems to me that they are obviously right about this. The success in Christian societies of the Cathedral program of undermining marriage means that Christian men lack incentive to defend their women from Muslim men, as we see not only in Africa, but in Sweden and England.

## "the Snow Queen" and "Frozen"

### 2014-05-14 18:50:48

Don't worry. This is not going to turn into a My Little Pony blog.

A long time back I heard Disney people worrying aloud that they were having trouble making "the Snow Queen" acceptable to modern audiences. So naturally I assumed they were making it revoltingly feminist and politically correct. And in due course it came out, the feminists loved it, pronouncing it the first feminist Disney movie. Also, people complained "Frozen"did not much resemble"the Snow Queen". So naturally I assumed Disney had murdered a perfectly good fairy tale to make it PC.

So I watched it so I could tell you how evil Disney was.

Nope. It was the original fairy tale that was feminist in mythic proportion, and Disney had to murder it to avoid scandalizing their audience.

In"the Snow Queen", the original fairy tale, the heroine's first love interest turns evil, and is abducted by the Snow Queen. The heroine then goes forth to rescue the first love interest from the Snow Queen, and his own evil.

In"Frozen", the Disney movie, the snow queen is the beloved sister of the heroine. The Snow Queen flees her kingdom, her sister, and herself, turning evil, and casting a spell of eternal winter on her kingdom. The heroine then goes forth to rescue her sister, the Snow Queen, from herself, to cure her, and thereby save her beloved sister, and savethe kingdom from eternal winter. Subsequently her first love interest turns evil.

In"the Snow Queen", the heroine, in the course of pursuing McGuffin boy, her first love interest, is abducted by the second love interest, little Robber Girl, who holds a knife to the heroine's throat. Second love interest then takes the heroine to bed, and they sleep wrapped around each other, beside Robber Girl's talking reindeer.

Robber girl is incredibly alpha, narcissistic, psychopathic, violent, carries a sharp knife, her behavior is completely inappropriate at all times and is all round completely counter stereotypical for a female. And did I mention she is a robber.

In the morning she and the talking reindeer assist the heroine to find the Snow Queen and love interest number one.

It seems that Disney found narcissistic knife wielding psychopathic Robber Girl a bit much, so made love interest number two male instead of female, beta instead of alpha, peaceable and wishy washy instead of violent. And he does not court ladies by holding a sharp knife to their throats.

So, in"Frozen", the Disney movie, the heroine, in the course of pursing McGuffin girl, her beloved sister, meets the the second love interest, Mr wishywashy beta nice guy. He attempts to rob the shopkeeper, but is just too nice and insufficiently violent. He and the heroine then wander in the snowstorm created by the Snow Queen. They find shelter together, and sleep in the same place, the heroine an arms length from the second love interest, and the talking reindeer an arms length from him on the other side.

In the morning he and the talking reindeer assist the heroine to find the Snow Queen.

In "the Snow Queen" she confronts the Snow Queen. In addition to the fact that love interest number one has turned evil, his heart has been frozen by the snow queen. The Heroine's love, however, cures everything. The Snow Queen yields. The end.

In "Frozen" she and nice guy love interest confront the Snow Queen, who freezes the heroine's heart. Nice guy love interest number two sends her back to love interest number one, who turns evil. The Snow Queen, horrified by what she has done to her sister, shows up. Evil love interest number one attempts to kill the Snow Queen and the heroine to make himself king and end the eternal winter, but the heroine cures her sister of evil, and cures her own frozen heart, by her sisterly love. The Snow Queen, cured of evil, now finds that she can unfreeze what she has frozen, so her powers no longer terrify her subjects. Nice guy beta male love interest number two politely asks permission to kiss the heroine, Heroine grants permission, then sucker punches first love interest turned evil, causing him to fall into the sea. The people, relieved that their queen is no longer casting eternal winter, cheer their queen. The end.

After having read the original fairy tale, the only revoltingly feminist part of the Disney movie was that sucker punch. A girl cannot punch a man hard enough to make him fall into the sea like that. Since love interest number one is Machiavellian, narcissistic, and psychopathic, realistically he would punch her back without worrying about hitting a girl.

So all up the major change that Disney made to the fairy tale is that it now teaches little princesses to choose the nice guy. Not that they will. And it no longer teaches them that they can cure bad boys of badness. Not that they will stop trying. The only bad things about the movie is that it teaches boys that nice boys can get the girl. They can't. And it teaches girls that they can punch boys. They can only punch nice boys. Punching bad boys is seriously inadvisable.

Not sure what makes the movie feminist. I suppose that the Snow Queen has really cool supervillain magic powers, that the heroine saves the day, rather than love interest one or love interest two, and that the kingdom has a queen, not a king. Which is, as feminism, goes, fairly harmless.

The Snow Queen shows every fault stereotypical of women in power. She is fearful, emotional, irrational, unreasonable, changeable, unpredictable, flighty, and bitchy. At the end the people love her, but this appears to be because she stops freezing them. In the final scene, where people are cheering her return as queen, and she is entertaining them with her display of (quite dangerous) magic powers, she is still wearing her sexy super villain costume, rather than her crown and scepter.

Still, a queen in sexy supervillain costume with supervillain powers is a lot more appropriate than little robber girl with her sharp knife.

If you wanted to convey a fully realistic message, you could make a porn of the original fairy tale, in which the heroine successfully thaws love interest number one's frozen heart, but totally fails to cure love interest number one of evil. In the grand finale, evil love interest number one does the heroine and the snow queen, while knife wielding love interest number two and evil love interest number one do the heroine. Evil love interest number one then ignores the heroine to (cautiously) hit on knife wielding love interest number two.

But, on the whole, congrats to Disney for fooling the feminists into cheering.

## Racism is an anti concept

### 2014-05-16 10:09:02

We do nothave a word "deskism" for someone who thinks differences between kinds of desk matter, and who has strong preferences in favor of some kinds of desks and against other kinds of desk.

No one can be racist against white people, and all whites are racists. That is why it is not racism when a bunch of blacks beat up a white man who happens to be passing by. When they do that, they are being anti racist. When you try to give "racism" some meaning other than "Beat the daylights out of honkeys", you are trying to push muck uphill.

"Racism" never had the meaning that some reactionaries and extreme right wingers are trying to give it. And it never will, because there is no need for a word with the meaning Zippy[184] is trying to give "racist". It is like gays trying to force us to pretend that the word gay still has the meanings cheerful and happy, rather than filthy, disgusting, weak and depraved. It is not in the nature of words to work like that. If there was a place in the language for a word that means what Zippy wants "racist" to mean, we would have had that word a thousand years ago.

The word "racist" was invented at the start of the twentieth century invented by Trotsky for the purpose of destroying western civilization[185]. It has never meant what reactionaries and right wingers would like it to mean, and it never will mean that. Words mean what they are used to mean, not what people claim they mean or say that they mean, and people just are not naturally inclined to use a word the way that Zippy would like them to use the word "racist". Language does not work like that.

If there was a place for a word with that meaning, we would have had such a word before Trotsky.

They are pushing muck uphill when they try to keep the pleasant associations of gay, but they have the power. Zippy[186] is pushing muck uphill when he tries to call blacks who beat up whites racist, rather than the anti racists that they so obviously are, and he does not have the power.

"Racist" means what it means, and what it means is that blacks are entitled to beat the hell out of whites, and whites are not entitled to fight back. We saw that in the Zimmerman incident. The supporters of Trayvon implicitly admitted what they explicitly denied, that they assumed that Trayvon attacked Zimmerman. They simply felt that Trayvon had the right to do so, and Zimmerman had no right to defend himself. That is what racism

---

[184] https://zippycatholic.wordpress.com/2014/05/15/why-i-am-anti-anti-concept-and-you-should-be-too
[185] https://penetrate.blogspot.com.au/2010/01/racist-word-invented-by-ussrs-leon.html
[186] https://zippycatholic.wordpress.com/2014/05/15/why-i-am-anti-anti-concept-and-you-should-be-too

means. Zimmerman was a racist, because less black than Trayvon, therefore deserved his beating.

Trayvon was obviously motivated in part by hatred of those less black than himself, because, according to retard girl's testimony, when he reached his father's house, he turned around and said he was going to get that "creepy cracker". But scarcely anyone called him a racist for that, which shows that is not what "racist" means, shows that even the tiny handful of reactionaries and extreme right wingers that are trying to give it the meaning "someone who thinks differences between kinds of human matter, and who has strong preferences in favor of some kinds and against other kinds of humans", cannot bring themselves to actually use it in that sense, because it would sound mighty strange to actually use it in accordance with that meaning.

"Racism" is an anti concept because actual usage and purported meaning completely contradict each other. It purportedly means Hitler-nazi-genocide evil, and actually means white, as proven by actual usage, as for example in the Trayvon Zimmerman case. Zimmerman was a racist and Trayvon not a racist, just as an air conditioned capitalist tee shirt factory which has eight hour shifts but limited toilet breaks is a sweat shop, but a communist slave labor camp in the tropics where the slaves are worked to death in baking heat on nineteen hour shifts is not a sweatshop.

Similarly "prejudice". What is prejudice? Is it a belief one assumes true without adequate empirical evidence? Obviously not. "Prejudice" means "hate fact", or "low status belief".

Words mean what they are used to mean. And scarcely anyone calls Martin Trayvon racist. Not progressives, not me, and not Zippy. Zippy is not going to spontaneously call Trayvon "racist" to describe the fact that Trayvon was in the habit of attacking people less black than himself, any more than Zippy is going to spontaneously call me "gay" because I am in a good mood.

## Improbable caring as an indicator of evil

2014-05-18 15:16:36

No one cares about far away strangers, still less about far away strangers very different from themselves. Claims to do so are lies or self deception.

People near one are always the big threat. So if one wants to destroy everyone near one, one justifies it by piously announcing love for those far away.

Of course there are other possible motives for such pious declarations. If the highest status people want to destroy all the people near them in status, which is to say, *destroy meand everyone like me,* they will announce deep caring for far away strangers, whereupon going through the motions of deep caring for far away strangers becomes high status.

However, just as the cautious thing to do is to assume every black man is a murderous thug, even though most of them are not, the cautious thing to do is to assume that everyone who piously proclaims deep love of far away strangers is planning the democide of those of his own class and race.

But how accurate is this cautious approximation? Most blacks are not, in fact, planning to murder the nearest white man. Are most do gooders planning democide?

Empirically, actions taken to benefit far away strangers very different from oneself are usually performed terrifyingly poorly, perhaps always performed terrifying poorly. For example African AIDS turns out not to be heterosexual AIDS, but do gooder AIDS. It is spread by clinics, which have financial incentive to use contaminated needles, in that the more of their clients they make sick, the more money they get.

Similarly, remember "We are the world, we are the children". All the good and the great got together to raise money to help the victims of the Ethiopian famine.

But the primary cause of the Ethiopian famine was not drought, but forced collectivization, government confiscation of crops, government destruction of the crops of rebellious populations, and civil war, in other words socialism. Being good progressives, did not want to admit the role of socialism, so wound up paying for the cattle trucks to take the peasants to death camps.

And, very recently the Cathedral was funding and arming the Army of the Congo to vaginally impale Tutsi women with very large objects.

Thus near 100% intent to commit democide fits available data better than near 50% intent to commit democide.

Observe the total non reaction among do gooders to complicity in crimes against the Tutsi in the Congo, and the total non reaction among do gooders to the ongoing AIDS scandal in Africa. This behavior fits the assumption that all do gooders, as near all of them as makes no difference, are aiming at war against near, and contradicts the assumption that many of them or most of them intend to benefit far.

If status competition was driving the purported caring about far, we would expect to see more monitoring of each other's performance "Hey, your caring for far is producing horribly bad outcomes, which I, your holier and more moral superior will now correct." So, the data compelling fits the theory that concern for far away people of other races is a lie driven primarily by monstrous and horrifying goals, and fails to fit even the relatively innocent explanation of competition to be holier than thou.

## Elliot Roger murders

### 2014-05-27 12:53:48

The first time Elliot Rodger hit on a girl, she gave him a mighty harsh shit test, and he completely fell apart.

From the fact that that his first shit test was the only one he complained about, I deduce he never exposed himself to the danger of a second one, that hewas scarred for life, and never again made any real attempt to hit on a girl, and was forever puzzled that he could go around driving a nice car and being creepy and upset from a safe distance, and yet girls would not hit on him.

When a girl gives you a shit test, it is often mighty harsh, because natural selection intends it to separate the men from the boys, so of course it is tough. If she does not give you a shit test, not really interested.

It is horrible that girls give out shit tests, but they cannot help shit testing males, any more than males can help looking at girl's boobs.

It seems that Rodger's dad was too busy to do much fathering, but if he had done some fathering, here is what he should have told his son:

Petruchio:

> Why came I hither but to that intent?
> Think you a little din can daunt mine ears?
> Have I not in my time heard lions roar?
> Have I not heard the sea, puff'd up with winds,
> Rage like an angry boar chafed with sweat?
> Have I not heard great ordnance in the field,
> And heaven's artillery thunder in the skies?
> Have I not in a pitched battle heard
> Loud 'larums, neighing steeds, and trumpets' clang?
> And do you tell me of a woman's tongue,
> That gives not half so great a blow to hear
> As will a chestnut in a farmer's fire?
> Tush! tush! fear boys with bugs.

Grumio:

> For he fears none.

## falling testosterone

### 2014-05-29 18:02:58

For the past thirty years, testosterone has been falling at about one percent a year[187].

This is about the same rate of decline as that produced by aging after the age of forty. So a forty year old male today has about the same testosterone levels as a seventy year old male had in 1984. This is a change sufficient to produce a massive decline in interest in sex, and a massive increase in odd sexual deviations.

Environmentalists suggests it is estrogen like compounds in the water supply. I am inclined to believe it is metaphorical estrogen in the metaphorical water supply. Society and the education system has been treating masculinity as an evil pathology, with ever increasing severity. Maybe the problem is that we need to encourage boys to be men, to be manly, to be tough.

## Words that are lies

### 2014-05-31 03:35:04

A word should refer to an essence, a natural kind, and normal words do.

Suppose we had a word that referred to roast pork and fried chicken, but not to other foods. This would imply that roast pork and chicken were the same essence, the same natural kind, which of course they are not. So when you have a word that does not refer

---

[187] https://uk.reuters.com/article/2006/11/01/health-testosterone-levels-dc-idUKKIM16976320061101

to a natural kind, that word is a lie - and the lie is usually a lot more hurtful than claiming that pigs are chickens.

For example, a "sweatshop" is entrepreneurship, capital, and low paid labor. Which is no more an essence than entrepreneurship, capital, and tuesdays.

If communists work people to death in the hot sun in twenty hour shifts, seven days a week, and no food, not a sweatshop by definition. If a capitalist builds an air conditioned factory in the third world, and has eight hour shifts, five days a week, but inadequate bathroom breaks, is a sweatshop. This is used to imply that capital, investment, and entrepreneurship makes people worse off, even though it is glaringly obvious that it makes people better off.

This is the lie that kept much of the third world poor for a long time. *By definition*, capital, investment, and entrepreneurship supposedly makes people poor.

Similarly, with "racism". Supposedly this means injustice motivated by race, which not a natural kind, nor is it a definition, but rather a hateful smear against white people, accusing white people of being responsible for the underperformance of black people.

Unjust acts motivated by X are not a natural kind, any more than unjust acts on tuesdays are a natural kind. We don't have a word for unjust acts motivated by sexual jealousy. When someone murders another person to steal his shoes, we do not call the killer "greedy". An unjust act committed for reasons of race is not a natural kind any more than unjust act committed on a tuesday is a natural kind. We did not have a word that supposedly stands for unjust acts committed for reasons of race until the twentieth century, and we still do not have words for unjust acts committed for reasons of covetousness, or unjust acts committed on a tuesday.

So in practice, no one is ever going to use the words "racism" and "racist" in accordance with the supposed definition, at least not if he hopes to be understood. Rather, it is a hateful word for members of high functioning groups. The supposed definition is merely a hateful smear against members of those groups, in particular and especially against white people, and against certain political beliefs.

The supposed definition is not a definition, but rather a claim that Donald Sterling, by thinking bad thoughts about blacks, caused the bad behavior of which he was thinking, that his thoughts were hurtful and unjust acts. Similarly, the genocide of the Tutsi was supposedly caused by Tutsi racism, not Hutu racism.

Another lie is the Marxist definition of value. The Marxists *define* value as labor content. So if someone buys a tree plantation with small trees, and patiently waits till they are big trees, he has supposedly created no value. The man who saves and invests has supposedly created no value.

The entrepreneur is someone who has a vision of how value can be created. He persuades people who have capital of his vision, and summons labor and capital to create value under his command. Supposedly the entrepreneur is merely a parasite, according to the Marxist definition of value.

The Marxist definition of "value" is akin to the dictionary definition of "racist" - the definition is itself a lie, labor content being no more an essence than injustice motivated by race is a natural kind.

If capitalism and poor work conditions were a natural kind, that would imply that capitalism is poor work conditions, or causes poor work conditions. If injustice motivated by racial difference was a natural kind, that would imply that noticing racial difference is injustice.

"Child Molester" and "pederast" is enemy language. "Child Molester" is an anticoncept, since it links things that are very different, and claims they are the same thing.

"Child Molester" fails to distinguish between gays and straights, where the difference is most important, and "Pederast" attempts to distinguish between different kinds of gays, where the difference is unimportant.

The family law of the Old Testament got it right, and modernity is surrealistically deluded, and flat in my face insane. I see in front of my nose stuff that no one else sees, so either I am insane or the world is, and the statistics are strangely consistent with me being sane, and difficult to reconcile with the world being sane. If you are using words for human things and human conduct that the people of the Old Testament had no words for, chances are you are using words for things that have no real existence.

"Pedophile", "child molester", and similar terms normalize homosexuality and sanctify female misconduct by making it the fault of men. If the old testament does not have equivalent terms, it is because these terms do not refer to real things. That females are attracted to alpha males with adult female preselection, Cinderella's prince, at a disturbingly early age, is a different phenomena from the fact that gays are attracted to little boys who have absolutely no interest in sex, let alone sex with men.

"Fetish" demonizes normal male attraction to fertile age females, and the demonizes the different roles that men and women have in the mating dance, while normalizing the destructive and self destructive behaviors of gays and transexuals. The reason the Old Testament does not condemn "fetishes" is that there is no such thing.

## Technological decline

### 2014-05-31 15:14:05

Konkvistador has drawn my attention to the Pu238 shortage. We stopped making Pu238 in 1988 You need Pu238 for nuclear batteries. The 2006 New Horizons mission to Pluto and the Kuiper belt was launched without enough Pu238 to keep all its equipment live during the Pluto flyby, and without enough Pu238 to do its Kuiper belt mission, from which I conclude that since 2011 we have been totally completely flat out of Pu238, just as the Fed is totally completely flat out of gold. For the last few decades, the government has been acting as if we are very very short of Pu238. For example, no allotment for pacemaker batteries, so people with pacemakers have to have surgery every so often. The Europeans are using (dangerous and expensive) americium based nuclear batteries for their space program.

Supposedly we can simply make more Pu238, just as supposedly when the two towers fell, we could supposedly build buildings just as tall or taller, just as we can supposedly still build warplanes that can cruise at supersonic speeds, we just supposedly do not want to. Today's businessmen are supposedly so secure in their masculinity that they do not want a higher corner office with a bigger view than the next businessman.

Maybe.

But I rather think if we could do that, we would not have run out in the first place. we would not have launched New Horizons with a half flat battery. We have been mighty short for at least a couple of decades, and since 2011 the cupboard has been just flat empty.

## Official Reactionary Position

### 2014-06-01 08:56:03

If I meet a tranny in person or on video disguised as a woman, I am apt to vomit. This does not mean that I refrain from text or audio conversation with a tranny. I do, however, refer to trannys as "he" or "him", and when I hear someone using the other term, it puts me off my food.

A someone who has frequently been nominated for the as yet nonexistent post of Grand Inquisitor of the Neoreaction, I, naturally, endorse the Official Neoreactionary Position[188].

1. Talking to, being friends with, showing normal human kindness to a disordered person is not tantamount to:

   a) approving all the free choices that person has made; or

   b) favoring social and/or legal norms that support the person's disorder; or

   c) joining them in their organization (should it exist); or

   d) inviting them into your organization (should it exist)

2. If someone wants to purge someone else then show up with an Institution and your name at the top of it, and then there'll be something to talk about. Until then, all future such attempts to purge are moot, null, damaging, extremely embarrassing, and in very poor taste. This shall be construed as the Official Neoreactionary Position.

3. I shall be the judge of who I can have a drink with. This should henceforth be construed as the Official Neoreactionary Position on this matter.

4. Men shit-test men all the time. It may or may not be a good and proper thing to do. But who is the worse: the one who constructs the shit-test, or the one who fails it?

5. It is the Official Neoreactionary Position that falling prey to hysterical over-reaction to a perceived personal attack is a disqualifying defect in a man who would lead other men.

---

[188]https://nickbsteves.wordpress.com/2014/05/31/the-final-word-on-trannygate/

## The Christian right - is left.

2014-06-05 15:51:51

There are few good Christians, darkly enlightened, neoreactionary: Among them are Dalrock and Sunshine Mary. I really am not aware of many others that blog, or used to blog.

If a Christian is to the left of Saint Paul on female subordination or slavery, he is holier than Saint Paul. If holier than Saint Paul, no friends to the right, no enemies to the left.

An atheist reactionary could have a position to the left of Saint Paul on women and slaves and still be an OK person.

A orthodox Jewish reactionary could have a position to the left of Saint Paul on women and slaves and still be an OK person.

But if a Christian right winger has a position to the left of Saint Paul on women and slaves, then chances are he has no friends to the right and no enemies to the left, which means all his friends are his enemies, and all his enemies are his friends.

And if no friends to the right, no enemies to the left, can be relied upon to throw his friends to the crocodile in the hope of being last to be eaten.

It is not so much entryism, as that if he disowns Saint Paul, he will disown you also.

Suppose a neoreactionary becomes a Roman Catholic. Trouble is that the Pope is to the left of Pol Pot. So he can disown the pope, and keep the New Testament, which is kind of protestant of him, or disown the New Testament and keep the pope, which is kind of commie of him.

He wants to be a throne and altar conservative, but all the thrones are empty, and all the altars desecrated, so he winds up worshiping desecration, which is one step away from the New Age worship of demons and the evil dead.

## The best of slavery, and the worst of abolitionism

2014-06-08 11:19:04

Let us compare the best of slavery with the worst of abolitionism.

In the West Indies, free blacks were apt to be re-enslaved: If found with no visible means of support, would be sent to the workhouse, on the assumption that otherwise they would be stealing or starving or very likely both.

The workhouse would then attempt to find owners for them, but often these were blacks with problems. The workhouse would find if they had a former owner, and twist his arm to take them back. If no one suitable wanted them, the workhouse would support them indefinitely on public and private charity.

So the workhouses in the West Indies, or at least some of them, were operating like a no kill pet shelter. Obviously the people operating these believed they were doing good, and had plausible reason to believe they were doing good. The benefactors could see their beneficiaries and look them in the eye. They might well wind up owning a couple of their beneficiaries, as someone operating a no kill pet shelter often winds up with more than his fair share of problem pets.

Let us compare with the holier than thou abolitionists who caused a civil war that killed a large part of the white male population, burned cities to the ground, and created artificial famine.

After the slaves were freed, a significant proportion died, being generally incompetent to look after themselves. The abolitionists, having denied that blacks needed a paternalistic welfare state, were disinclined to provide one, even as the death rate among their supposed beneficiaries rose to quite alarming levels.

After the civil war and abolition, black productivity as freemen was markedly lower than black productivity as slaves, leading to markedly lower material living standards. In part this must have been because of "slave driving" – that slaves were forced to work considerably harder than they would have otherwise been inclined to work, but in part it was because the employer could not trust a black employee to behave well, whereas he could make sure a slave behaved well.

## Very minor outbreak of democracy

### 2014-06-12 06:32:39

Elections are about goodies. Even more obamaphones for all. No money down mortgages for minorities.

One might hope that republican primaries might be conducted on a slightly higher level.

In the recent primary, Eric Cantor campaigned that he was going to bribe the voters with their own stolen money, while David Brat campaigned on issues that have overwhelming support - campaigned against immigration, against crony capitalism, and against Obamacare. Just about everyone in America, except Washington and big business, opposes crony capitalism, most oppose immigration and Obamacare, and almost everyone who should be voting in a Republican primary opposes all three.

David Brat won 56% to 44%.

However, David Brat does not take the horribly extreme ultra right wing neonazi position that we might actually deport illegals, let alone stop with the Obamaphones.

Bottom line: 44% of the voters in the Republican primary voted like sluts and underclass.

## Does game work?

### 2014-06-15 08:34:50

Read it and weep[189]

If still in doubt, watch the video[190]

For a lot of men, game is not all that effective. This is because the major part of game is to superficially appear to be high status, as women perceive status, which is very different from how men perceive status, and it is simply hard to appear to be high status. One's subconscious shoots one down, resulting in incongruent behavior. Easier if other people act as if you are high status, as in the video.

---

[189]https://sparklesandsecrets.com/2014/06/12/booty-call-etiquette/
[190]https://blog.reaction.la/culture/on-what-used-to-be-called-marriage.html

Obviously it was stupid to emancipate women. Fertile age women should have the legal status of children. The state should back parental authority over children, and the husband's authority over his wife.

Emancipation was a shit test that we failed.

## Bitcoin failure

### 2014-06-15 16:01:23

For bitcoin to work politically, authority over the currency needs to be distributed over a large group of peers. If power is concentrated at a single point, the state can dominate that point, whoever controls that point can steal other people's currency and do a variety of bad things.

Bitcoin was designed so that "voting" depended on computing power and network connection. Initially, almost everyone who had a client was a miner, there were a huge number of miners, everyone who used bitcoin had roughly equal influence because they contributed roughly equal computing power to the block chain.

Today, bitcoin is controlled by by a single miner.[191], which was a predictable consequence of bitcoin's scaling problems.

What we need is a crypto currency which is controlled by the top one hundred or so owners of the currency that are well connected to the net and have adequate computing power, with influence over the currency proportional to the amount of currency that they own, rather than the number of cycles that they burn.

In principle it should be possible to do this using bilinear maps, but the details are a bit tricky, because we have to make sure that manageable number of votes reflects an infinitely divisible currency whose ownership changes continually. So the shares (private and public keys in groups with a bilinear map) have to be reissued frequently, while ownership of the infinitely divisible currency is given value by the fact that if you own a lot of it, you get shares proportional to the amount you own. Since shareholders are people who own a lot of currency, they have an incentive to not misbehave, to continue to reissue shares according to currency ownership and validate transactions according to the rules, since to do otherwise would destroy the value of the currency that they own.

The number of shares remains manageably small, however many people use the currency and however many transactions take place. The shares underlie the value of the currency - and absolutely nothing underlies the value of the shares. Of course we still have other scaling problems, to which I have not figured out a solution except in alarmingly vague outline.

## Another test of the power of the purse

### 2014-06-21 16:56:40

During reign of Obama, attempts by the house of reps to exercise the power of the purse have been universally condemned as ultra extreme far right wing rightingery, and these

---

[191]https://imgur.com/PPVr0Wv

attempts have invariably failed, rendering the house of reps similar in legal status to the Oklahoma University Student Debating society.

The NSA has been spying on Americans in massive and flagrant violation of the spirit of the fourth amendment, the letter of the fourth amendment, and recent legal interpretation of the fourth amendment by the Supremes. The overwhelming majority of Americans oppose this, so the house of reps has attempted to use the power of the purse to reign in the NSA in various ways, among them
> barred the N.S.A. and the Central Intelligence Agency from using funds in the bill to "request or mandate" that an American corporation alter a product to permit surveillance of it.

Often the NSA has perfectly reasonable and compelling grounds to spy on a particular individual who is using a service of American corporation. The NSA then demands all information about everyone who has ever used this service, but, hey, promises that after all the information has been handed over, will only look at that particular individual for whom they have legitimate grounds and will piously close their eyes to all the other information that they have demanded. Scout's Honor!

What makes this legislation less impressive is that this is the second time the reps have passed it. Perhaps they going to pass it a third time and add "But this time we really mean it!"

## The illusion of government

2014-06-23 08:45:49

Government is an illusion, a pretense in which everyone pretends to believe, for fear of what would be revealed should the pretense be seriously doubted. The US spent an immense amount of blood and treasure setting up a Iraqi government in its own image, and one morning that government softly and silently vanished away like the dream it always was. It seems to have been replaced by alarmingly numerous tribal, clan, and religious militias, of which ISIS is merely one of far too many.

Government is not a being like an elephant, nor a physical object like a tall building, but rather, a thought, an idea, ideas about how force shall be used. And ideas can change at the speed of thought. Ideas can change without anyone quite noticing for a time.

The patriarchal clan and tribe is the natural form of government, and any government on a larger scale has big problems for which we don't really have any good solution, even though we have been working on this problem for thousands of years. We make synthetic clans, the church or the party. The result is apt to be a party state, one synthetic clan ruling many. It is oppressive. If the ruling clan loses cohesion, members of the ruling clan act more like mobile bandits, for example Jon Corzine, and it gets more oppressive. The rich are on the revolving door between regulators and regulated, for example Bush the second and Jon Corzine. Those capitalists that make their initial money legitimately, for example Elon Musk, then buy their way into the revolving door, becoming political activists, investing in politics with the intent that political authority will make them richer. Musk's business plan is that car makers will be forced to buy his stuff in proportion to how many cars that they sell, which means that ultimately the ordinary car buyer will be forced to pay for Musk's stuff regardless of whether he is using it or not, regardless of whether it is useful to anyone or not, which business plan pretty much guarantees that Musk's stuff will not be useful to anyone. It is hard to make useful stuff. If your attention is focused elsewhere, and it really does not matter much whether the stuff you make is useful or not, it is not going to be useful.

The Iraqi government vanished when it came under attack by a few thousand competent well trained well armed men employing only personal weapons striking in areas far away from the centers of government power. Word of shots fired far away on the periphery caused government to disappear at the center without a shot fired anywhere near the centers of power. It is interesting to reflect on how much chaos Christopher Dorner caused when he launched his one man war on the Los Angeles Police Department, using hit and run tactics rather similar to those employed by ISIS in Iraq. If one competent man did that, what could half a dozen have done?

The revolving door spins scary fast. Jon Corzine, the man of many hats, regulator and regulated, the most regulated man in the world, took over MF Global, presumably on the basis that he would protect them from regulation if in charge, harm them with regulation if not in charge.

Twelve years ago, this sort of behavior would have been unthinkable. People would have screamed "conflict of interest". There has been a quite sudden change in the political and economic culture, from typical first world to typical third world.

MF Global managed other people's money, which Jon Corzine promptly stole. He expended the money of MF Global's clients largely on buying political influence.

This is classic mobile bandit behavior. Instead of shearing the sheep, he skinned them. He would have made a lot more money steadily milking them over a lengthy period. His real asset was political and regulatory power. I conjecture it was slipping away, and he had to do something in a hurry.

It is difficult to see how to fix this problem. A Tsar is not a solution, due to the agent/principle problem. One needs a ruling elite with asabiyah, a harder and more subtle problem. Asabiyah is easily undermined by small amount of diversity, and I rather think that this is what happened twelve years ago - that the election of Obama is a symptom of the third worldization of our ruling elite, after the fashion of Detroit, and now Chicago. Can't have a Tsar without an aristocracy, and Alexander the Liberator destroyed his aristocracy, replacing it with left wing bureaucrats who found that the more leftism, the more underlings the bureaucracy acquired.

Government needs to be one, which is hard, and the more government does, the harder it is to be one, and the less asabiyah it has, the harder it is to be one. Jon Corzine's career tells us that our government is not one. Whereupon government suffers from the problems it purports to solve, prisoners dilemma, and tragedy of the commons, public funds and regulation being a commons.

# Dysgenic fertility

2014-06-25 10:48:52

Chateau Heartiste, always a great source for the Dark Enlightenment, reports[192]:

> Convicted criminal offenders had more children than individuals never convicted of a criminal offense. Criminal offenders also had more reproductive partners, were less often married, more likely to get remarried if ever married, and had more often contracted a sexually transmitted disease than non-offenders. Importantly, the increased reproductive success of criminals was explained by a fertility increase from having children with several different partners. We conclude that criminality appears to be adaptive in a contemporary industrialized country, and that this association can be explained by antisocial behavior being part of an adaptive alternative reproductive strategy.

Moral: For civilization to continue, female sexual and reproductive activity has to be placed, legally and socially, under the control of fathers and husbands. In actual practice, we tend to treat fertile age women as children, as their bad behavior does not have the legal and social consequences it would have for adult, but whereas a badly behaved child will be hauled off to the responsible adult, and the responsible adult asked to keep him in line, the badly behaved female is not hauled off to her father or her husband.

# "More Right" proposes communism

2014-06-28 13:46:04

More right quoting "Men among the ruins"[193]
> The preliminary condition would naturally be the overcoming of the typical situation in democracies, where the political element makes promiscuous alliances with the plutocratic element, opening itself to corruption and pretending to represent a "Right" in opposition to Marxism. Again, the pure political power must be released from every bond—first from the bonds of capitalism, and then from those of the economy

This is, the state released from every bond, is the old communist fantasy. If the state is released from every bond, it can decree that everything be lovely.

The state does so. Strangely, everything fails to be lovely. Obviously evil people, wreckers, are disobeying the decree. They must found and destroyed. *Then* everything will be lovely.

But things *still* are not lovely. Obviously there must even more wreckers, who must be sought out even more vigorously and destroyed even more thoroughly.

At some point Stalin declares that Utopia has arrived, notwithstanding appearances to the contrary, thereby stopping the madness, or Vietnam invades Cambodia, thereby stopping the madness.

---

[192]https://heartiste.wordpress.com/2014/06/24/study-civilized-chicks-dig-jerks/
[193]https://www.moreright.net/the-relationship-between-capitalism-and-the-state/

The state cannot be free from the bonds of capitalism, because it needs money and goods, and therefore needs capitalists to tax and to purchase technology from. As for being free from the bonds of the economy, we saw how that worked out for the communists.

Reality is that for the reasons explained by Mises and Hayek, and colorfully dramatized by Ayn Rand, the state cannot directly run the economy, nor directly sponsor science. Private individuals, with private wealth, have to be free to create wealth and knowledge, without which the state has nothing to tax, and no means to pay the army, nor any source for the technology to equip the army.

The state is at best a stationary bandit that keeps mobile bandits at bay. If it consumes everything, it destroys itself. Stalinist Russia kept itself afloat on an illegal but essential and tolerated black market, by letting capitalism that it had thrown out the front door in by the back door and by seizing and pillaging additional capitalist economies.

Stalin's successors faced an ever more serious conflict between ideology - that everything should be devoured - and reality - that they needed the market and wealthy people, a conflict that gradually became more serious as no more advanced economies fell under their power.

Which eventually led to the open abandonment of the "seize everything" ideology

## Capitalism and entrepreneurial capitalism

2014-07-01 11:02:43

Capitalism, in the sense of wealth creating wealth, wage labor, power derived from wealth, and trade, is a bronze age social technology. "Capital" literally means "head" in the sense of "head of cattle". Originally, the amount of capital one had was the number of beasts in one's herds. The biblical bronze age patriarchs were capitalists, in that their wealth was their herds, and their power derived from their wealth, their power was their employees. The actual figures on whom the biblical patriarchs are based are probably considerably less ancient than they are depicted in the bible as being but since Moses dates from the collapse of bronze age civilization and he, or the people who wrote him up, are very early iron age, his predecessors have to have been at least late bronze age, possibly earlier. The biblical patriarchs are depicted as fighting, and winning, battles with kings, which would suggest that they were figures of the very late bronze age, since chances are that nomads only gave kings a hard time during the decline and collapse of the bronze age civilizations. The size of states, and the size of armies, declined during the collapse of bronze age civilization, to the point where the sword of a single hero could make a big difference, only to rise again in the early iron age.

But, obviously there is something importantly different about today's capitalism, something that changed around the time of the restoration.

The phrase "Industrial Capitalism" is misleading, for it was this new form of capitalism that created industry, not the other way around.

The big difference, the social technologies that caused the big difference, were double entry accounting, which made the joint stock corporation possible, made it possible to separate ownership of capital from enterepreneurship. Investors could put an enterpreneur in charge of their capital, and use double entry accounting to keep an eye on him. This is the foundation of western civilization, which began to soar when Charles the Second cut joint stock corporations loose from strong government oversight.

This means that owners of capital can employ people smarter than themselves to manage their capital, increasing the effective intelligence applied to production.

Which caused productivity to consistently and substantially rise faster than population, for the first time in history.

Double entry accounting is a critical part of this system. Unfortunately, double entry accounting has been profoundly disrupted in America by Sarbanes-Oxley, making it impossible to tell how a business is doing. This ham fisted government intervention was officially intended to prevent businesses from misleading investors and creditors, but instead it has made it mandatory to mislead investors and creditors. Sarbanes-Oxley consists of thousands of pages of law, each page of law giving birth to thousands of pages of regulation. It is of course impossible to comply with all this, for if one was to comply with any one page of Sarbanes-Oxley, it would put you out of compliance with hundreds other pages of Sarbanes-Oxley, so what the big firms do instead is hire accountants sufficiently well connected with the government, accountants on the revolving door between regulators and regulated, so that any figures the accountant conjures up will be deemed compliant with Sarbanes-Oxley.

The practical effect of this became apparent in the financial crisis, when it became obvious that many banks simply had not been keeping track of their finances, and had no idea what assets they owned, what financial obligations others had to them, and what financial obligations they had to others. Sarbanes-Oxley replaced the intentionally misleading figures of Enron with fog, with meaningless figures.

Which brings us back to the old system, where rich people cannot, and do not, entrust their wealth to smart people.

## The cause of population decline

2014-07-05 16:14:48

At present, only poor countries have reasonable fertility. The fertile age white population is everywhere declining, and the most intelligent and educated women reproduce the least. But quite recently affluent countries such as pre Weimar Germany had high fertility, and many poor countries have fertility as low as the worst of the west.

Conversely, Rome in its decline, and Sparta in its decline, had terribly low fertility, though their only methods of birth control were vice, abortion, and infanticide, and their living standards were relatively low compared to modern standards.

The demographic transition is nothing to do with whiteness, nor with wealth and economic development. Nothing to do with having a Malthusian system. It is not poverty that makes the difference.

Nepal is a good example of a very poor third world country with low fertility comparable to that of the advanced west - but its low fertility is a mix of very high fertility women and very low fertility women, which should make it easy to see what causes the difference.

in Nepal, which is as third world and poverty stricken as you can get outside Africa, females that have been exposed to western schooling to age twelve or older have a fertility rate similar to that of the most infertile wealthy advanced white western nations[194],

| Schooling | Children |
| --- | --- |
| No schooling | 6.67 |
| Islamic Schooling, no Western Schooling | 7.78 |
| Western Schooling to ages 7 to 11 | 4.5 |
| Western Schooling to ages 12 to 13 | 1.44 |
| Western Schooling to ages 15 to 16 | 1.57 |
| Western Schooling to ages 17 and above | 1.50 |

If they don't get that class at age 12, because they went to a Muslim school, or because they did not go to school, their expected number of children is six or seven, even if they went to a high class ladies Muslim school. If they got western education at age twelve, then they have western fertility levels, far below replacement.

There is something taught to twelve year old girls in Nepal in Western schools, but not in Muslim schools, that drops fertility from six or seven children per female to less than 1.5 children per female.

This is what Boko Haram is complaining about. They view it, reasonably enough, as genocidal.

This Nepalese data is consistent with the high fertility of the Amish: The Amish absolutely insist on controlling their kids schooling. They also ban television. They allow their adolescent kids out into the world to visit the fleshpots, but not, however, the classrooms. They fear both the classrooms and the televisions, but primarily the classrooms.

I would say that it is memetic infection, the same memeplex, propagated both by soap operas and the education system, each reinforcing the other, but primarily by the education system.

And that memeplex is exemplified by "Sex and the City", and the nine year old learning to put a condom on a banana, but not learning that a woman's fertility window is a lot shorter than that of a man, and a lot shorter than her career window - learning that normal everyday behavior for women is to follow the same life plan as men - and not learning that that life plan, naturally enough, is consistent with men producing children, but not really consistent with women producing children.

Here is my theory explaining this observation:

If women are emancipated, fertility collapses. But merely legal emancipation has limited effect, because females are extremely vulnerable to social pressure and conformity, so that peer pressure, social pressure and parental pressure, can and routinely does prevent emancipation from being effective, and thus prevents fertility from collapsing.

So the Cathedral has to reach into society through propaganda in school and television, and remake society to emancipate women, then fertility collapses because the girls spend their hottest and most fertile years fucking bad boys.

If women are low status relative to males, all males look attractive to them.

If women are restrained from screwing outside of marriage, if they cannot get their hands on males and males cannot get their hands on them (except in parentally supervised

---

[194]https://www.socialinclusion.org.np/new/files/Irsahad%20Khan_1365502062dWld.pdf

dancing with parentally selected partners) they want to get married. If all males look attractive to them, they can get married, and will love their husbands.

If women get married young, love their husbands, and submit to their husband's authority, they will have a reasonable number of children - around six or seven, if the husband can afford it.

If, on the other hand they perceive themselves as equal to males, they will look around for males that are somehow higher status - typically convicted felons and such, for example Jeremy Meeks. They spend their fertile years fucking those guys, and only when the booty calls stop, only then do they condescend to reluctantly notice someone who is inclined to support and father children. And many of them, particularly the most intelligent, the most highly educated, the most wealthy and successful, for example the infamous lawyer pussy, when they are too old to get booty calls from Jeremy Meeks any more, will find all males that might return their interest beneath their notice, and wind up as cat ladies.

Another factor inculcated in western schooling is the false life plan, the female equivalent of the blue pill.

Girls are told that the normal respectable thing, the thing that all girls do, is put their career first. Marriage and family will just happen by itself, with no need to make it happen. Presumably it will happen while they are fucking Jeremy Meeks. They are told that teenage pregnancy is a terribly bad thing, cause it destroys your career.

Of course pregnancy will have the same effect on a woman's career at any age - and since her fertility window is a lot shorter than her career window, and a lot shorter than a male's fertility window, it would make a lot more sense to worry about marriage and family first, career late. She will never be as hot as she was when young, but she will probably be a lot more competent at making money when somewhat older.

Girls are *not* told that women are hypergamous while men are polygynous, and thus the most attractive man who is interested in them is likely to be a lot more attractive than the most attractive man who is interested in marrying them and having children with them. They are told that men and women are just alike in the sexual natures, and so are not told that they can score a much more attractive man for a one night stand than they can score as a boyfriend, and much more attractive man as boyfriend than as a husband - and that every additional boyfriend and one night stand means the quality of husband that they can attract is correspondingly less. In consequence the large majority of women spend their hot years having sex with the small minority of the most attractive men - who of course are in no position to father their children and have no intention of doing so.

The false life plan, the female equivalent of the blue pill, is that a girl can focus on her career, and spend her youth, her beauty, and her fertile years fucking Jeremy Meeks, and marriage and family will just spontaneously happen without her having to do anything about it or think about it or sacrifice anything for it.

Female emancipation enables women to indulge in the false life plan, and they are also falsely told that it is a good idea. Probably around age twelve in school.

To have eugenic population growth: Abolish welfare and put female sexuality and reproduction under parental control, until they get married whereupon their sexuality and reproduction comes under their husband's control.

Parents will delay their daughters reproduction until their daughters get married. Parents will only allow males able and willing to support a wife and children to court their daughters, and only allow them to court their daughters for marriage, not sex.

Wealthy people will marry young, poor people will marry late.

In order to reproduce successfully, reproduce biologically and culturally, men and women have to behave in different and complementary ways.

For the family unit to function, it has to have a single head, and that head has to be the man, because women will not endure sex if they are the head. And it has to be legally and socially binding.

If, on the other hand, women are free, their natural inclination is to engage their hypergamy with a minority of males outside the family unit, which natural inclination is reinforced as the normal life course, normal behavior, by school and television, which results in non reproductive sex. Successful societies repress this, frequently employing alarmingly drastic means, but the ordinary pressures of social conformity and adverse economic and life outcomes suffice to reduce it to quite manageable levels. Adulteresses in Timor Leste are punished only by social stigma and divorce without property, rights to children, or alimony. Stoning is not required to reduce the problem to acceptable levels.

## Sandra and Woo notice repression

## 2014-07-07 17:05:56

One of my favorite web comics is Sandra and Woo[195], which comic notices that cute funny animals are still inclined to eat other cute funny animals, and that little girls develop a sex drive at a disturbingly early age.

Recently the comic committed an act of political incorrectness. I fear they will be brought to heel as Sinfest was. Sinfest has never been funny since they turned politically correct. The entire Sinfest premise is gutted if the comic cannot make fun of sluts hypergamy female sexual autonomy.

But, get your Sandra and Woo while it is still funny.

teacher says the unspeakable

---

[195] https://www.sandraandwoo.com/

Oh, no, it is the moral police

97 Points on the privilege meter

This will not end well

What will happen to Sandra and Woo if little girls remain perfectly uninterested in nookie until they reach the ever increasing legal age? Pretty much what happened to Sinfest when they could not say the word "slut" any more.

Those poster girls pompously listed by the Commissar are:

Margaret Cavendish: A very ordinary female writer who wrote some rather stupid things on scientific topics.

Laura Bassi: A very ordinary female university science professor, who made absolutely no scientific discoveries - doubtless due to an evil male plot to steal all her research.

Caroline Herschel: She was allowed to assist a great scientist since she was his sister.

Countess Elizabeth Báthory: Believed herself to be a vampire. Tortured hundreds of young girls to death and bathed in their blood in an effort to preserve her beauty. The basis of numerous stories about a hot lesbian aristocratic vampire doing hot kinky non-consensual sex on hot teenage peasant girls.

I think that the vampire chick is inserted in the list to parody it.

Ada Lovelace: *Not* the world's first programmer.

Marie Curie: She was allowed to assist a great scientist since she was his wife. Note that Pierre Curie got the radiation burns, not Marie Curie, which suggests that Marie Curie's work largely consisted of washing his bottles. Supposing that she was indeed the one that did the work, the discovery of radium was similar to but considerably less important than the discovery of radon, and no one remembers the man who discovered radon. That we make a big deal out of a woman who allegedly discovered radium, while we don't remember the people who discovered the other hundred elements shows that a woman doing science is like a bear dancing. We pay attention to a dancing bear not because it dances well, but because it dances at all.

Lise Meitner: Supposedly the discoverer of fission - because she corresponded with the man who actually discovered fission, the correspondence consisting of him sending her a letter telling her he had discovered fission, to which she replied such a thing was impossible[196]. Not even his wife or sister.

Emmy Noether: Emmy Noether is the real thing, a truly great mathematician who will live forever, but that the list is padded with so many fakes tells you that the real thing is in short supply.

Dorothy Hodgkin: Science bureaucrat. After other people discovered the method of resolving complex molecular structures by Xray diffraction, she applied this method to one complex molecule after another. The scientific equivalent of HR. Boring.

Rosalind Franklin: Same story as Dorothy Hodgkin. Even more boring.

Ada Yonath: Same story as Dorothy Hodgkin. At this point the feminist compiling the list of which this is a parody passed out from boredom.

## Sarah Perry on the Economic Value of Children

### 2014-07-10 11:30:25

Sarah Perry argues that children have been nationalized, have become property of the state and ceased to be the property of their parents, so have become a cost to their parents and a profit to the state, so parents decline to produce so many[197].

Makes sense, certainly part of the story, but not what I seem to observe, not the main story.

What I seem to see happening is that the major cost deterring people from children is not economic, but rather loss of female sexual autonomy. If a woman has children during her fertile years, then she is not longer able to respond promptly to a midnight booty call from Jeremy Meeks.

Your feelings differ from mine? Let us look at Augustan Rome.

The Augustan reforms made children the property of their parents, but the wife even less the property of her husband than in the modern west. Fertility continued to collapse, to levels that may well have been substantially lower than modern western levels.

On the other hand, the Pauline reforms, which were that a man and his wife were one person, and that person the husband, that the wife was part of the husband, did help

[196]https://books.google.com/books?id=kn6mb0ltm0UC&pg=PA1001&lpg=PA1000&hl=en#v=onepage&q&f=false
[197]https://qz.com/231313/children-arent-worth-very-much-thats-why-we-no-longer-make-many/

substantially with fertility.

Further, I don't think the nationalization of children is really separable from feminism. Women really cannot look after themselves. They will either attach to their fathers, their husbands, or Uncle Sam the big Pimp. Thus feminism, in practice, means that children become the children of Uncle Sam the big Pimp. If you denationalized children, women would spontaneously submit to patriarchy. Conversely, if you enforce patriarchy, the patriarchs will claim their children. To maximize fertility, need that form of patriarchy in which women attach to their husbands, rather than their fathers, and females are rationed out at only one wife per male, so that as many males as possible have incentive to attach to society, to work, and to invest in posterity.

## The future belongs to those that show up

2014-07-12 13:06:17

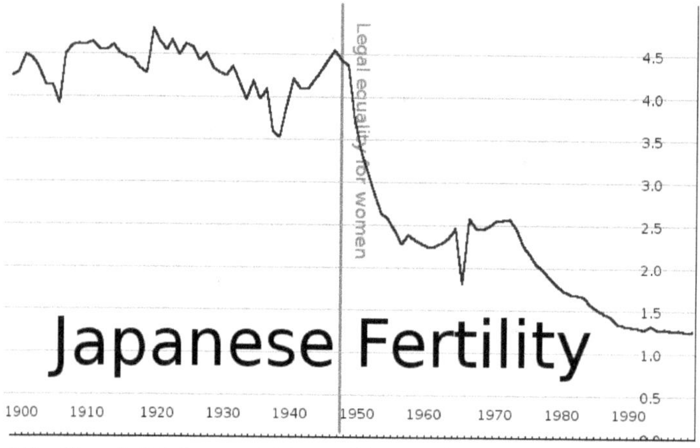


A fertility of slightly over 2.0 is a stable population.

## The false life plan

2014-07-16 14:05:31

Men and women are happiest if successfully performing their traditional roles[198]. This is to be expected, since whites and east asians, the descendents of civilizations, are descended from those that did perform their traditional roles.

The Cathedral, however, presents girls, in school and on television, with a false life plan: That they will follow the same path as males, and marriage and family will just spontaneously happen while they are fucking Jeremy Meeks.

So girls followed that plan. With the result that the male plan (get a career and what you need to support a family, and a good wife will show up) stopped working. So males stopped working. And here we are.

---

[198]https://heartiste.wordpress.com/2014/07/15/the-unhappy-woman-is-a-feminist-archetype/

Girls should be taught the female life plan, in domestic science classes, and in the stories they see on television.

Women have a natural tendency to hypergamy, resulting in the mating patterns of chimps, the ghetto, and some primitive tribes. Successful civilizations come down hard against this mating pattern, which necessarily requires that they come down hard on females, the uncontrollably lustful sex, systematically treating them as in substantially greater need than men of control, protection, and protection from their own selves, treating them all as Medeas, Pandoras, and Eves. The very least we can do it tell girls that the life plan that leads to this outcome, leads to the outcomes that it does.

Of course a civilization that could tell the truth on this question, would be capable of denying the vote to inferior groups, categories, races, and individuals, so would probably be capable of applying greater control to those groups in need of greater control.

I was talking to a mother about her highly "successful" lawyerette daughter, remarking that this child had reached an age where marriage had long been unlikely, and children were now becoming unlikely. The mother was outraged at such horribly reactionary crime think. I never got around to discussing the fact her very high IQ lawyerette daughter had spent her youth, her beauty, and her fertile years fucking stony broke losers, many of them low IQ, many of them loser criminals. (Successful criminals know that politeness is cheaper than violence and you need to be particularly pleasant and respectful to police, even if violence is sometimes necessary, so successful criminals don't clean up with girls the way dumb loser criminals on their way to jail do.) Her mother attempted to introduce her daughter to more suitable males, but her daughter complained that these males of her own economic class simply did not turn her on.

Our culture lacks the eighteenth century role model of the gentleman, the man who is polite, respectful, conventional, but still capable of deadly violence, which contributes to females despising high status as high status is measured among civilized males, for a perception of high status more appropriate among chimps or in the ghetto. They need to be taught to respect and admire the kind of male that is likely to be able and willing to marry them. Males are socially controlled to behave in a manner perceived by females as low status and feminine, so the extent that males comply with socialization, females don't want to have sex with them. We need to adjust socialization of males to make socialized behavior more attractive, which is to say, more masculine and less feminine, and adjust socialization of females to encourage them to associate with socialized males. A broader role for private violence by the affluent and respectable in upholding order, and a lesser role for police violence in upholding order would help considerably. Hard to change the nature of females, easier to change the organization of prosocial violence for the maintenance of order, so that females come to perceive the males that they ought to be interested in as the males who will win a violent conflict.

As I remarked earlier, the female's pussy perceives status in ways appropriate to our ancestral environment, rather than our more recent environment, and there is not a lot that can be done about this other than reduce those differences between the ancestral environment and our more recent environment that tend to mislead females. Just as we need to avoid foods that are simultaneously sweet and fatty, so we need to avoid making civilized men into eunuchs. High socioeconomic status males need to be scarier, if women are going to breed with high socioeconomic status males. Excessive repression of private violence has led to dysgenic sexual choices by women. Partly we should solve this by preventing female sexual choice, but another part of the solution is more selective and less repressive repression of violence by high socioeconomic status males. High socioeconomic status males need to be able to get away with more manly behavior, including more of the primitive behavior that females understand as manliness. In addition to stronger guidance and restraint on female sexual choice, we need less feminization of high socioeconomic status males to reduce dysgenesis driven by female choice.

Not only are females educated to follow the false life plan, males are educated to be unattractive to females. Education becomes a genetic sink, reducing the reproduction of the most highly educated males and females, not only by wasting their time during their most important reproductive years, but by teaching them behaviors that make them less likely to reproduce and more likely to fail in their attempts to reproduce. We should teach, particularly in sex education, behaviors that make them more likely to succeed in reproduction. We need manlier men and more feminine women, but especially, we need manlier men. What is needed for women is primarily to deny them their most strongly preferred sexual choices to prevent them from rewarding unproductive and anti social behavior.

Consider the reality show star Kate Gosselin, woman has eight children by a decent, reasonably attractive husband, who loves her and loves his children. Acts like a complete shrew towards the only man who will ever love her and her children. Ditches him. Is shocked to discover that no other male wants a woman past her prime and encumbered with eight children.

Kate Gosselin was videotaped continually treating her husband like dirt, as the man she reluctantly settled for seeing as all her preferred choices would not return her phone calls.

She then divorced him, depriving him of his much loved children, depriving her eight children of a much needed father, and herself of a much needed and entirely irreplaceable husband.

And I have seen a similar dynamic in every divorce that I have observed, though of course with considerably fewer children. In every divorce that I have observed the wife was utterly and spectacularly out of contact with marriage market realities. The result of the divorce is that the man, who very much did not want the divorce, was much better off, free of a hateful and unfaithful shrew, and the wife was very much worse off. As the wife goggles fell from his eyes, he usually found a considerably younger replacement.

At the age of thirty eight, with eight children and a notorious shrew, Kate Gosselin's chances of marrying even a homeless obese seventy year old alcoholic are about equal to her chances of being kidnapped by terrorists and becoming the wife of the sultan, but she specifically requires her new husband to be rich, six foot tall, physically fit, and childless. (Her previous husband was not rich, not six foot tall, and only ordinarily fit, which is presumably why she divorced him.)

Meanwhile her husband, Jon Gosselin, the father of her children, having lost the wife goggles, promptly got a hot twenty two year old girlfriend to replace his aging thirty eight year old wife, and if the girlfriend is lucky, might marry her. But then, having been burned once, maybe not.

The typical marriage is Kate Gosselin and Jon Gosselin: The wife has a hugely inflated idea of her marriage market value (based on her F-buddy market value when she was considerably younger) and this poisons the marriage.

Now theoretically, if a woman is chaste, men will only approach her that are appropriate to her marriage market value, and she will avoid getting an inflated perception of her value, but no man believes that a chaste women is likely to remain chaste, because, they are not likely to remain chaste. So a woman faces a storm of approaches that would never happen if the boys had to ask her dad before approaching her, and if her dad said yes, they would get not a date with the opportunity of physical contact, but merely the opportunity to court her for marriage. These approaches lead Kate Gosselin to believe that she is entitled to marry a six foot tall physically fit millionaire, and that life, her husband, and the male dominated society is being terribly unfair to her in not giving her what she is entitled to have.

And another of my proposed sex education videos, this one for females only, since it depicts male polygyny.

Scene: An office. A young handsome man in a business suit strides through the office, and everyone's reaction shows that he is the boss, or very important. He guestures at an attractive thirtyish woman to follow him, and strides on without bothering to check that she is following him. Because of his long swift strides, while she is wearing a tight dress and high heeled shoes, hard for her to keep up. He arrives at the executive toilet, and furtively looks around. Then goes into the toilet. She arrives at the toilet, hesitates a moment, furtively looks around, and follows him into the executive toilet. The camera follows her into the toilet. She goes into one of the stalls, closes the door behind, and we immediately hear the sound of panties being pulled down, followed by her gasp. The camera circles around and we see above the stall door the head of the woman, and the head and shoulders of the boss, still fully dressed on the upper parts of their bodies, obviously having sex. After a bit the woman says:

"Grunt. My husband. Grunt. Is going to. Grunt. Divorce me."

Boss bursts through the stall door fleeing her, without bothering to open the door first. The image freezes, with flying shattered parts of the stall door obscuring the view of the most vital parts of the boss and the employee. His pants are a few inches down, her skirt is up, her panties are around her thighs.

Freeze image fades, replaced by a patriarchal father figure who directly addresses the camera, explaining that men are polygynous, and will therefore have sex with women well below their sexual market value, but when they do so, one of the factors important to them is how easily they can get rid of the woman once they have finished using her. When a high value man has sex with a low value woman, he fears that she will cling.

Patriarchal father figure fades, and once again we see the toilet. Woman, now fully dressed, walks to the door, opens it, revealing the toilet symbol and an audience of office workers, presumably non executives. End video.

The purpose of the video is to inform Kate Gosselin that replacing her husband is likely to be less easy than she imagines, something that no woman is likely to learn from our present schools, movies, books and television shows.

Because male attractiveness and fertility fades far more slowly than female attractiveness and fertility, most divorces advantage the male and disadvantage the female, but most divorces are female initiated, and most females initiating divorce have expectations as unrealistic as those of Kate Gosselin. This is part of the false life plan - that females supposedly remain fertile and attractive for as long as men do, so concentrate on your career, girl, the way men do.

## The cure for IQ shredders

2014-07-18 10:19:06

Our best hopes for a high tech future, for avoiding a dark age, are consuming the genes needed for a high tech future. Smart people go to Hong Kong and Singapore and fail to reproduce[199].

Singapore has taken numerous measures, similar to those of the Nazis and Emperor Augustus, to improve fertility, which will doubtless be as ineffectual as those of the Nazis and Emperor Augustus.

Just as the cure for Chinese poverty was to import the economic laws and customs of Hong Kong into Shanghai, the cure for Singaporean infertility is to import the marital laws and customs of Timor Leste, where women cannot own property, because they are wards of their parents until they become wards of their husbands.

Dubai already has a system where low status expat workers are effectively wards of their employers. This typically applies to Indian construction workers (who are all male and unaccompanied by their wives and families) and Filipino "maids", who are all female and normally single when they arrive. If an employee's sponsor is her employer, the employee is effectively a ward of the employer. A higher status employee usually has the free zone authority is his sponsor, not his employer, even though his employer asked the free zone to sponsor the employee so the process looks very similar.

An employee sponsored by her employer normally resides in accommodation provided by the employer. The employee cannot change jobs without her employers permission. If the employer dismisses the maid, he normally cancels her visa, her bank accounts, her phone, and gives her a ticket back to her homeland. He has to give her a ticket out, because he paid a deposit to obtain her work visa, and because if she fails to leave by her employer's fault, the employer is in trouble. If the employer cancels his employees visa, he is supposed to provide the employee with the means to leave. Often however, she fails to show up by her fault, in which case the employer still loses his deposit, so if he can, he drags her off to the airport whether she will or not.

Male Indian construction workers seldom do a run. If fired, they leave without any drama. "Maids" frequently do a run and fail to show up at the airport, because the usual cause of a falling out with her employer is raging hormones. If she does a run, her phone stops working, her credit cards stop working, her bank account stops working and if she does not withdraw any money in her bank account in a timely fashion, she loses the money. She cannot get a new phone, bank account or legal accommodation, and is subject to a large fine for every day she fails to show up. If caught, and unable to pay the fine,

---

[199]https://www.xenosystems.net/iq-shredders/

goes to jail for considerable time, then is sent out of the country and forbidden ever to return.

## Need to kill a lot more civilians in Gaza

2014-07-22 07:30:56

One of the things that the fans of the theory of Democratic Peace, the theory that democracies tend to be at peace with each other, tend to forget is that Gaza and Israel are both democracies.

If you are a Muslim, you demonstrate superior holiness by voting in favor of wars with infidels that may well result in your death, just as if you are white, you demonstrate superior holiness by voting for your country to become non white.

If Gaza was ruled by a King, then if that King was to decide for war, that decision would make him holier, but might well get him killed.

But if a voter in Gaza votes for war, his vote makes him holier, but makes absolutely no difference to his chance of being killed, since it is only one vote of millions. From the point of view of the voter, the ideal outcome is that he votes for war, but is, alas, outvoted, by all those inferior people less holy than himself, much as from the point of view of a white voter, the ideal outcome is that he votes for his country to become brown, but gets outvoted by all those ignorant racist hateful stupid whites.

Thus we get Californication, as Californian whites flee California to whiter and more conservative places, and then vote for those places to become progressive and nonwhite.

To stop a democratic Gaza from making war, need to kill a large proportion of the population. Very possibly all of them.

If you get competition for superior holiness, the holy people get ever holier until eventually the most holy position becomes suicidal. And in a democracy, the holiest position, despite being suicidal, will win the election.

## Who is allied to Israel?

2014-07-27 11:59:34

Egypt proposes a ceasefire between Hamas and Israel in which everyone ceases to fire.

The (Jewish) US Secretary for state proposes a ceasefire in which Hamas gets a new route to import rockets, now that Egypt is trying to stop them from being smuggled through Egypt, and a big pile of money with which to import them.

There are a lot of things wrong with Jews, but being sneakily cohesive is not one of them.

## Demonic possession and Donald McCloskey

2014-07-31 07:47:03

I am a materialist. I don't believe in demons that come from outside. Demons come from within, a part of oneself that hates life, hates the living, and, most of all, hates oneself. Sometimes people indulge such a part of themselves, and it takes them over, possesses them. This happens a lot to leftists. It happens one hell of a lot to transexuals, hence the high suicide rate.

Spandrel recent wrote of one such, McCloskey The voice of evil[200]

So I attempted to look at a McCloskey video - then very quickly shut it down in horror and revulsion, because I could not bear to look at it.

Donald McCloskey, now "Deidre" McCloskey, is a trannie leftist. Which does not necessarily prove he is demon possessed, but should make one suspicious.

When I look at a still of "Deidre", carefully posed and made up, I think of her as "she" with only a slight queasy feeling. She passes. She looks like a somewhat masculine woman, but not in uncanny valley. My guts register her as a faintly odd looking human female, and show no inclination to chuck up. From the still photographs, looks like a quite successful male to female transition.

When, however it is is in motion, that is not what I see. What I see is neither male nor female, but "it", a monster that has devoured a human from the inside and is now wearing its skin like a muppet in an entirely unsuccessful effort to pass as human. My guts not only want to throw up, but are screaming at me that I need to run like hell or kill it with fire and steel.

Intellectually I believe that what is happening is that masculine bone and muscles are animating skin and fat sculpted by surgery and hormones to female form, with the result that when the form is in motion, there is something wrong about its movements, placing it well and truly in uncanny valley. But my guts are screaming. "Monster. Kill it with fire!"

And then I hear its voice. Intellectually, I believe that the voice is emanating from those lips. But it is not a human voice. My guts don't believe that voice is coming from the lips, but from the vocal apparatus of an unhuman monster that is wearing the McCloskey skin like a muppet suit, and moving those lips with its unhuman fingers to ventriloquize. That is what I see. That is what I hear.

Am I being irrational? Should I apply modern sophistication to overcome my fear and hatred of difference? Or is there wisdom in ancient instincts?

Is "Deidre" McCloskey dangerous?

Yes it is[201].


# Death of Christendom

## 2014-08-04 17:44:28

Calvinism in New England was scorned by the heresy of Unitarianism, which deemed itself holier, but Unitarianism only lasted about a generation before it collapsed into Emersonian subjectivist Transcendentalism, which then swiftly (in less than a generation) collapsed into politics (abolition, feminism etc).

If we look at the New Testament position on slavery it is of course passivist and pacifist. Christians are encouraged, but not required, to free their slaves. Slaves are discouraged from rebelling and running away. Masters are required to be benevolent.

---

[200] https://bloodyshovel.wordpress.com/2014/07/30/the-voice-of-evil/
[201] https://www.nytimes.com/2007/08/21/health/psychology/21gender.html?_r=2&oref=slogin&

What happened when many Christian Churches adopted an activist position on slavery, a clearly heretical position on slavery?

An activist position on slavery requires war. War requires dreadful means, requires lies, terror, murder, and artificial famine - all in an undeniably good cause, of course.

Lo and behold, those churches that adopted an activist position against slavery ceased to be Christian. So that heresy, quite predictably, turned deadly.

But, once anti slavery became the law of the land, then a good Christian should of course support that law, so anti slavery did not destroy Christianity.

But now, however pretty much all Churches, have adopted the modern marriage vows, implying a clearly heretical position on marriage, which vows undermine and disrupt marriage, which in turn results in preaching that is fundamentally hostile to marriage as a binding contract.

Equality requires fences, that is to say, requires the dissolution of marriage. An actually functioning marriage is always patriarchal. Show me a man who picks up fifty percent of the socks, and I will show you a man who sleeps on the couch, while once a week or so his wife's lover drops in to rough her up and take her money.

A genuinely Christian Church can no more support modern marriage, than it could support holy war on slavery. In so doing, is necessarily holier than Jesus, and so, runs through unitarianism to vagueness to leftism, and the Church building is remodeled to become a left wing bookstore.

The modern position on wedding vows is leading to pretty much the same consequences as the activist position on slavery did.

If a group of people go to war to resist being enslaved, or to escape from slavery, their cause is obviously just. It is plainly a just war. If a group of people go to war to save strangers far away from slavery even when they have no obligation of alliance or kinship to do so, then in theory it is a just war - but it is not human nature to care about strangers far away, nor does the New Testament command Christians to care all that much about far away strangers, so chances are, those making this supposedly just war are up to no good.

And, observing the aftermath of the civil war, those who abolished slavery were up to no good.

Darwinism has destroyed the strongest intellectual justification for Judaism and Christianity - the formerly compelling evidence for a creator God. Before Darwin, those who proposed various alternatives to a creator God, in particular the spontaneous formation of creatures with complexity visible to the naked eye, were obviously clever sillies.

Old religions tend to be relatively harmless, for the same reason as old diseases tend to be relatively harmless. Old religions that primarily propagate from parent to child tend to be beneficial for the obvious evolutionary reasons.

Unfortunately progressives have interrupted parent to child transmission by universal state sponsored education and by funding fatherlessness and by removal of fathers from families.

By natural selection, we would expect actually existent religions to be profertility and parentally transmitted. Problem is current changes, primarily Darwin, state education, and state funding of fatherlessness, has made these religions non viable.

The Darwin problem can be fixed by simply changing the other worldly content of the religion. The state attack on parental transmission, however, is not so easily fixed.

When paganism died, Rome fell. With the death of Christendom, Europe is falling.

## Why the art, literature, and science of decadent civilization is decadent

2014-08-07 12:21:07

Gibbon called the art and literature of the latter days of the Roman Empire "the second childhood of human reason".

Back in the days when European art was the greatest the world has ever seen, the wealthy and powerful Cornaro family patronized the artist Bernini because he was a great artist. Because high status people like the Cornaro family patronized great artists, great art was high status, and, circularly, the Cornaro family gained status by patronizing great art, such as The Ecstasy of Saint Teresa, which features the Cornaro family as much as a Coca Cola advertisement features coca cola.

Similarly, in Restoration England, high status people patronized science because it was high status, and it was high status because high status people patronized it, starting with King Charles the Second.

Then the government gets into funding art. But the large bureaucratic government funding organization inevitably gets captured by recipients, as Cornaro family could never be captured, as King Charles the Second could never be captured. Funds are distributed for grantsmanship, not art quality. The greatest experts in grantsmanship could draw no better than a small child.

So drawing like a small child comes to be deemed high status.

Neo reactionaries are fond of authority, but need to remember that there is lot that centralized authority cannot do, starting with operate a modern economy. Large organizations suffer from diseconomies of scale, and a severe agent/principal problem. Without aristocrats, kings are not much good.

## How to achieve peace in the middle east

2014-08-08 13:07:15

There is no possible concession that will resolve the Gaza conflict other than Israel ceases to be, or Hamas ceases to be. Just war theory tells us that war is justified to produce peace.

What needs to be done is war that produces a definite winner, and a definite loser. That is the western way of war.

For a determined adversary to lose, generally costs four or five percent of the population, about fifty times what the war has cost Gaza so far.

This could have been avoided had Israel not dragged the settlers out of Gaza.

## The great silence

2014-08-09 10:04:03

There seem to be no great obstacles to intelligent life devouring the galaxy. So why are we here.

If life on earth arose on earth , and produced humans in a few billion years, why not on some other planet ten billion years ago?

Simplest and most likely explanation is that life is unlikely – requiring a stupendously improbable assemblage of molecules to form.

No one has constructed a plausible high probability origin of life.

Indeed, it looks to me that water based life just cannot form spontaneously. The minimum complexity of life in water is just far too high. RNA based life just does not work without DNA and cell membranes, and you don't get RNA and DNA spontaneously forming in water.

Here is what I think happened:

There is some environment, perhaps a mixture of liquid cyanide, liquid formamide, and polyphosphoric acid with star tar dissolved in it, in which life can form spontaneously.

Cold temperature origins seem most likely, since cold temperature life can easily spread from planet to planet, because cold temperature planets with liquids are smaller and lower gravity than warm planets with liquids. Volcanic eruptions etc can easily spit rocks into space.

This low temperature, non water based, life evolved, over ten billion years or so, to adapt to environments increasingly alien to its origins, eventually becoming water based life living in hot deep rocks on asteroids.

From which it infected earth. To produce complex life, you need an oxygen environment so that cells will gang together for defense and attack. For an oxygen environment, you need a water environment. We are the first, because it just took that long. And, in due course we, or some other earth species if we fail, will devour the galaxy.

## Secularization

2014-08-11 15:11:54

Eric Kraufman argues that the religious are inheriting the earth[202]. The religious are reproducing faster, and despite the fact that many of their children are captured by progressivism, the number of people who say they are religious is increasing. According to Kraufman the number of people who adhere to moderate religions is decreasing, and shows every sign of altogether vanishing. The proportion of the religious, and the absolute number of religious people who adhere to fundamentalist religions is increasing.

But he ignores the fact that "fundamentalist" religions are rapidly being captured by progressivism.

In 1960 or so, all Anglicans believed, or purported to believe that divorce was shocking, and that a divorced woman should never remarry. They believed that in marriage,

---

[202]https://www.youtube.com/watch?v=IYEyv5a_3LM

the wife promised to honor and obey, and failure to do so was disgraceful. Today, hard to find "fundamentalists" so fundamentalist as to believe in such old fashioned idea.

Moderate religions are disappearing because no one can tell the difference between adhering to a moderate religion and progressivism. Pretty soon the only Roman Catholics will be sedevacantist rebels, as the Vatican becomes a museum and left wing book store - but the ultra orthodox will be celebrating gay marriage with leather, chains, and giant condoms.

The sedevacantists' priest shall say:

> I now declare you husband and husband. You may now insert these giant vibrators up each other's asses.

# The Spandrellian trichotomy
## 2014-08-13 15:32:32

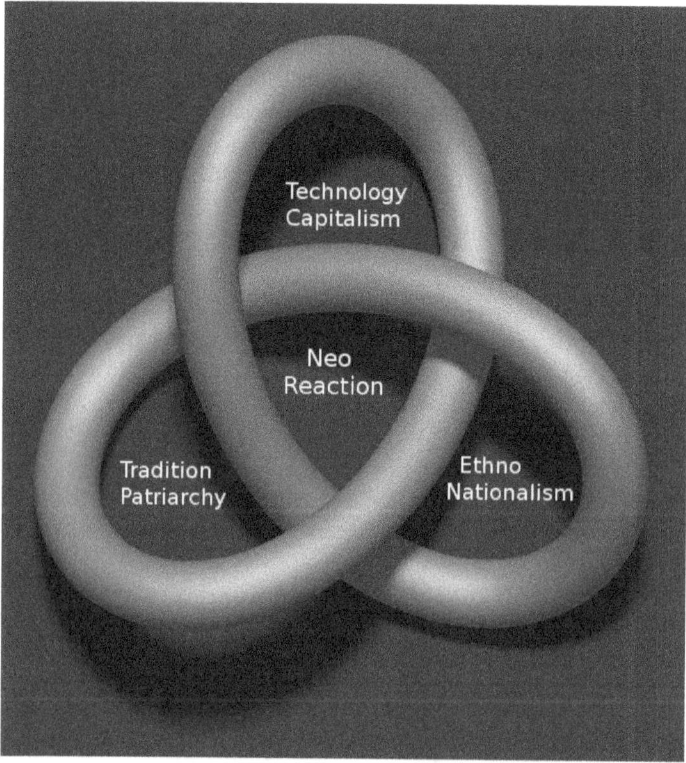


### Technology capitalism: libertarianism

As the left gets ever lefter, it gets every crazier. Since the libertarian tries to make a separate peace with the left on behalf of capitalism, its craziness necessarily flows into libertarianism.

Libertarians notice that capitalism, in particular the joint stock corporation based on double entry accounting, provides a great, humane, and highly productive system for creating wealth, advancing technological progress, and maximizing liberty. They therefore propose to accept the entire left wing program, only without its anti capitalist elements. Supposedly the non aggression principle supports all left wing conclusions, except anti capitalism.

Thus a libertarian believes that people should be able to make binding contracts. So a young and naive woman can bind herself to an enormous debt for a PhD in hating dead white males and capitalism, a debt which cannot be expunged by bankruptcy

However, because leftists believe that female sexual autonomy is sacred, therefore has infinite utilitarian weight, absolutely trumping all other human, moral, and utilitarian considerations, a libertarian also believes that that same woman cannot bind herself to always be sexually available to one man, and never to any other, to submit to him, and to bear his children, in return for him protecting her, loving her, looking after her, supervising her, and fathering his children by her.

But it turns out that without the capacity to make a binding contract, it is mighty difficult to reproduce. It also turns out that the reproductive contract has to be unequal. A ship cannot have two captains, and neither can a household.

Similarly libertarians believe, that since all races are supposedly equal, unlimited brown immigration will not make white countries any less capitalist and less wealthy. On the contrary, those brown people are not going to live on welfare and crime, but are supposedly going to replace the missing grandchildren and work hard to support white people in their childless old age. Supposedly, mass third world immigration will have exactly the same outcomes as mass white immigration did, and the fact that mass white immigration had those outcomes proves it. And if you have a problem with this proof, you are raaaaciiiissst.

Libertarianism tries to be left on everything except markets and property rights, but it fails. Inferior people cannot be permitted the same freedom as superior people, because if you try it, you wind up with a nanny state for all rather than liberty for all.

A free society cannot function without sobriety and family values, so Libertarianism in practice winds up supporting a high-tax welfare-prison state to cope with all the human wreckage caused by excessive liberty. Welfarist libertarians try to hang on to some faint shred of libertarianism by proposing a guaranteed income in place of welfare, but they all know perfectly well that most of the poor remain poor no matter how much money you give them, so a guaranteed income would just be yet another addition to welfare, not a replacement.


## Tradition Patriarchy: Religion.

The religious want to go back to an idealized religious society, where a common faith provides asabiyyah . Not working. The thrones are all vacant, the altars all desecrated. Progressivism is well on the way to digesting what few remnants remain of the old religions.

Those who go to worship at desecrated altars wind up worshiping demons. Reactionaries convert to Catholicism, notice that their Pope is a leftist, wind up rationalizing that racism is big problem and a huge sin, and that Saint Paul did not say what he said about the relationship of men and women. Bruce Charleton explains Saint Paul on women as a metaphor for the relation of Church and Christ.

This, of course, is the wrong way around. The patriarchal family provides necessary psychological support for faith in the patriarchal god. Matrilineal societies slide down the religious scale to primitive Zoism.

By and large, neoreactionaries who convert to Christianity wind up turning intellectual somersaults, because Christianity has been so thoroughly assimilated into progressivism that there are few genuinely Christian communities left. God is dead. Being a Christian in today's west is like trying to be a pagan in fourth century Rome. It did not work for Julian the Apostate, and it is not working for us. After Darwin, hard to have a religion of the creator God. Absent patriarchy, not going to have a religion of a patriarchal God.

Even if a supposedly neoreactionary Christian does not himself wind up helping the invasion on the US Southern border, he will tell you that the Christians who are assisting are wonderful.

Orthodox Judaism is going down the progressive digestive tract slower than Christianity, because progressives are embarrassed to arrest Jews for imposing Jewish roles on women, while they are not at all embarrassed to arrest Christians for imposing Christian roles on women, but it has been swallowed, and the digestive juices are starting to dissolve it. Orthodox Jews still retain the rituals that remind them that in the Old Testament, women are property, but deny that those rituals mean what they mean.

## Ethno Nationalism: National Socialism

And similarly, too late for a monoethnic state. One cannot make fish soup back into fish. One can, however, have empire, one ethnic group more or less humanely ruling the others, giving each their own laws and respecting the customs of each.

Given the white tendency to theocracy, a more practical solution is that to get government employment, public office or go to the most prestigious universities (from which senior members of the government are recruited) one has to subscribe to the official religion, and the official religion is primarily white. We kind of have this system already, in that to go to a prestigious university you have to submit essays showing your adherence in minute detail to progressivism, and your past activity in progressive activist groups - though this tends to select Jews at the expense of the main ethnicity, which undermines the intended cohesion.

A lot of ethnonationalists want a state that in which everyone within the borders is one ethnicity, and everyone within the borders votes and receives welfare. Creating such a state is likely to be horrifyingly bloody. Further, being necessarily a process resembling total war, such a state is likely to wind up socialist, and socialism fails economically for reasons explained by Hayek and Mises, and colorfully dramatized by Ayn Rand.

And, supposing we created such a state, and supposing elections continued, the politicians would still have an incentive to bring in cheap voters to live on welfare.

Monoethnic government is lot easier and more workable. Since in practice we somehow always wind up with monoreligious government, let us have an official belief system that in each country is primarily identified with one ethnicity, the major ethnicity of the better class of people in that country.

## Ferguson chimp out

## 2014-08-17 03:16:58

Short recap of the Ferguson story:

Michael Brown, a huge black man helped himself to some tobacco in a shop, then strong armed the shopkeeper rather than paying. He then walked down the street, expecting traffic to get out of his way. When a policeman told him to stop jaywalking, he attacked the policeman, forced his way into the policeman's car, and attempted to take the cops gun. The cop shot him.

According to heavily tattooed gang members wearing clothes intended to intimidate, after being shot, Michael Brown ran with his hands in the air, and the policeman shot Michael Brown again while he was holding his arms in the air and running.

This might well nonetheless be true, at least the part about him being shot while running, though not the part about his hands in the air, for if Michael Brown attacked me I might well do the same thing. He is big, scary, violent, thuggish, and crazy. Yeah, it would be the wrong thing to do, but when a big crazy guy attacks one out of the blue, one is apt to do the wrong thing.

The blacks proceeded to loot and burn. The local police, facing collective criminal conduct, responded militarily, engaging in collective violence to crush collective violence - a military style response.

This "military", which is to say collective, violence of course horrified the press, who blamed the police, and in particular the white cop in charge. So a black cop was put in charge, and a huge round of news stories proceeded about peaceful protests and how everything was wonderful in peaceful civilized harmony, blithely ignoring events running contrary to story, blithely ignoring that the blacks were taking out one cop after another by collective violence, which the individual violence of the cops was ineffectual in preventing. And then, contrary to story, the black cop had to resort to collective military style violence to keep his cops alive[203].

This is analogous to events in Gaza. One might well believe that Israel blockades Gaza because they are evil racists, but when Egypt blockades Gaza, people of the same race and religion as themselves, it's pretty obvious that the problem is terrorists operating out of Gaza, not Gaza's neighbors. And, similarly, the problem in Ferguson is individual and collective black violence, which collective violence has to be met by collective violence.

The larger story is that blacks destroyed Saint Louis, then, fleeing their own destruction of the city and each other's violence, proceeded to move into a white suburb, which

---

[203]https://www.examiner.com/article/ferguson-unrest-missouri-state-police-captain-ends-up-with-egg-on-his-face

they are now in the process of destroying in turn.

This is a reason that the cost of housing is so high. If wealthy people got to live where they chose, and poorer people got to live in the less desirable places, the inner city would be full of rich people, and poor black thugs would live in the exurbs. The city would be safe and orderly, while slums far away from the center, places that no one ever goes to or cares much about, were dangerous and disorderly. If, however, we look at where people live, it is clear that black collective violence trumps money, which forces up the cost of housing as white people bid up the small and shrinking pool of safe housing, which is usually located in places inconveniently far from the city center, forcing them to perform long commutes.

The white man buys a house. To support his crushing mortgage he makes a long commute every day, along a highway with big wall to protect it from black people living much closer to his workplace than he does. And then some section eight women and her nine kids by nine different thugs is plonked beside his house, and while he is at work, the section eight woman terrorizes his wife, breaking one of his windows and threatening to force entry.

This makes it hard for white men to reproduce, that white men are not able, not allowed, to protect their wives and children, in part because blacks can engage in collective violence against white people, and white people are not allowed to collectively defend themselves. To have a safe place for one's wife and children, it has to be possible to run bad people out of that place.

That blacks live close to where white people work, while white people are forced to live far from where they work, tells us that blacks have the upper hand over whites. Slavery worked. Jim Crow sort of worked. Civil rights has been a disaster.

## Supposedly black Egypt

### 2014-08-22 05:49:44

Lately a lot of progressive blacks have complained that Ridley Scott's movie "Exodus" is racist for depicting Egyptians as Egyptian and Hebrews as white. They want them all to be depicted black.

Ancient Egyptians in their art depict themselves as yellowish brown, somewhat arab looking, pretty similar to the way pharaoh is depicted in Ridley Scott's movie. They depict blacks as black, with exaggerated negro features, and show them in demeaning roles as criminals, slaves, and servants, pretty much as they are depicted in Ridley Scotts movie, and they depict whites as white, and as wearing costumes somewhat similar to those worn by the Hebrews in Ridley Scott's movie.

Egyptian art depicts Egyptians on the one hand and Nubians and other blacks on the other hand with distinctly different ethnic characteristics and depicted this abundantly and often aggressively. The Egyptians accurately, arrogantly and aggressively made national and ethnic distinctions from a very early date in their art and literature

In Egyptian art and writing from around the time that the Hebrews are said to have left Egypt, blacks are slaves, servants, and criminals, whites are invaders and colonialists.

They viewed people who originate from the middle east, from west asia as the Hebrews did, as white and aryan, like the Hyksos, which fits with various records that back in those days, towards the end of the bronze age, west asia was full of aryan whites. The Iranians and the Kurds were originally Aryan, are today browner than the Jews. The Kurds recall their ancestors as fair skinned and fair haired, so likely the Hebrews were fair skinned and red headed.

Ridley Scott's casting and costumes are largely lifted from ancient Egyptian art depicting themselves - a yellowish brown people very different from negroes, but nonetheless not exactly white either.

It is a historical fact that Egypt at the time that Moses is believed to have lived was racially much as it is now - a generally upper class white minority, a poor and frequently criminal black minority underclass, and a brownish majority that have and had approximately modern Egyptian skin color, despise blacks, and were suspicious of whites.

From time to time Egypt gets conquered by whites. From time to time those whites import black slaves. And so, most of the time, Egypt is brownish with a white minority and a black minority, as it is today.

For example we see in an ancient Egyptian painting three black criminals or runaway slaves who have just been arrested and subdued by three white, or possibly light brown, cops.

And that is the way Ridley Scott depicts Egypt.

At the time of Joseph, Egypt had been conquered by the Hyksos, who were fair skinned, red headed, very possibly Aryans, and possibly Hebrews, and most likely a people closely related to Hebrews, which suggests that the Hebrews of that time were fair skinned, frequently red headed, and very possibly Aryans.

So, assuming Joseph was a real person, or based on a real person, the pharaoh that favored Joseph was white, quite likely Aryan, and so, quite likely, similarly Joseph.

So, entirely reasonable, on the basis of history and historical descriptions of the Hyksos, and on the basis of Egyptian art, to depict the Hebrews as whites.

The Egyptians perceived people who came from the east (west Asia, the middle east) and lived in tents as the same race as the Hyksos, so presumably perceived Joseph and Moses as white and Aryan, as Moses is depicted in the movie.

At the time of Moses, Hyksos rule had collapsed, bronze age civilization was in severe decline, and Egypt was ruled, as depicted in Ridley Scott's movie "Exodus", by brownish people with approximately modern Egyptian skin color - the pharaoh that "Knew not Joseph".

Egypt was, if we believe the "Admonitions of Ipuwer", at the time suffering from leftism, high levels of violence, lack of secure property rights, severe social decline, rioting, arson, severe family breakdown, female emancipation, and disastrous levels of political correctness. If we believe the Pentateuch it was also suffering from socialism. In short, not so different from Egypt today and the Arab world today, though with considerably worse family values, the then fall of the Hyksos paralleling today's recent retreat of colonialism.

We have archaeological evidence of the collapse of Bronze age civilization not long after Ipuwer's time, so I am inclined to interpret Ipuwer as describing real and contemporary events, as he claims to be doing, though some people argue he is just telling a morally improving story about long long ago and far far far away.

Ipuwer reports that foreign trade had collapsed. We have archaeological evidence that foreign trade did indeed collapse at about that time, so Ipuwer is probably reporting real events.

Due to infanticide and "barrenness" (which I conjecture was the result of contraception, abortion, and non reproductive sex) Egyptians were, according to Ipuwer, failing to reproduce. If we believe the Pentateuch, the Hebrews on the other hand had strong family values, with women and children being property, hence infanticide was for them unimaginable, unintelligible, and absurd. Thus their population would have been growing as the Egyptian population was, according to Ipuwer, collapsing.

Human nature being what it is, the Hebrews would probably be blamed for the social decay that they were not suffering.

There are several parallels between the Pentateuch and the Admonitions of Ipuwer. Assuming Ipuwer's Admonitions to be true, then the Pentateuch is myth based on real people and real events.

For example the Admonitions and the Pentateuch both say that the river turned to blood.

The Pentateuch says:

> 17 Thus saith the LORD, In this thou shalt know that I am the LORD: behold, I will smite with the rod that is in mine hand upon the waters which are in the river, and they shall be turned to blood.

> 18 And the fish that is in the river shall die, and the river shall stink; and the Egyptians shall lothe to drink of the water of the river.

Ipuwer also tells us that the river turned to blood and Egyptians were unwilling to drink the water. But in Ipuwer's telling the Nile only turned metaphorically and spiritually into blood, because of the vast numbers of wrongfully slain Egyptians dumped in the river, and the many Egyptians who committed suicide in the river, not literally into blood.

According to Ipuwer, the Nile was physically and spiritually polluted by the vast numbers of unburied dead in the river, and was thus unclean in the sense that wrongfully spilt blood is spiritually unclean. The Nile was spiritually turned to blood by natural causes, not literally turned to blood by supernatural causes. The Pentateuch depicts a miracle, Ipuwer reports social breakdown and civil disorder.

Assuming that the Hebrews had the strong family values depicted in the Pentateuch, the angel of death would have passed over the Hebrews and failed to take their children, not because of any miracle, but because Hebrews, unlike Egyptians, were disinclined to murder their own children.

Similarly, Ipuwer and the Pentateuch both depict a storm of fire over Egypt, but in the context of Ipuwer's Admonitions, the fire presumably comes from the rioting mob of lower class looters and revolting slaves, not from heaven.

If you really want to, you could read Ipuwer as reporting the Nile literally and miraculously turned to blood, and fire literally and miraculously from heaven, but there is no way to read his report on the death of the children as anything other than entirely unmiraculous social decay and female emancipation. If the death of the children was leftism rather than wrath of God, then the river of blood and the fire was leftism rather than wrath of God.

Or if you really want to you could argue it was all wrath of God punishing the Egyptians for oppressing the Hebrews and for social decay, and Ipuwer is giving a naturalistic non miraculous rationalization of miraculous events, but I find Ipuwer's account of these events more believable than the Pentateuch version. Gnon was indeed punishing the Egyptians for their wickedness, but through material and effective causation, not supernatural causation.

And, according to Ipuwer's Admonitions, people from West Asia who lived in tents were a big problem, undermining social cohesion. Sounds familiar.

So, I conjecture that they would have been blamed for all these happenings. The brownish rulers would have attempted to appease the brownish mob by punishing the white outsiders who lived in tents. The white outsiders would have made endless concessions, but no concession would suffice, for no concessions would have any effect on the social decay suffered by the brown Egyptians, now incompetently ruling themselves when formerly they had been competently ruled by the white Hyksos, who had now become unwilling and unable to rule. (Bronze age civilization, which is to say white civilization, was suffering general decay. The Egyptians survived it better than the purer whites.)

Ipuwer calls on Pharoah to expel the foreigners.

And the white outsiders would flee. A familiar story, much repeated since then.

Finding themselves pursued by an Egyptian army the white outsiders would need an leader with complete authority. Likely they would choose a white member of the Egyptian ruling class to lead them, and invent for him the correct ancestry. All that is conjecture of course, but it fits the known facts quite well. The Pharaoh of the Pentateuch did what Ipuwer in his "Admonitions" called on the Pharaoh to do. Those whitish outsiders were subverting brownish Egyptian society with the result that Egyptians were doing bad things to each other.

We know that Ridley Scott is correct to depict the pharaoh as brownish Egyptian upper class, and what little we know about the times is consistent with Moses being white Egyptian upper class, as depicted by Ridley Scott in the movie Exodus.


## Marriage is gay

### 2014-08-24 21:37:06

When two gays "marry", the point is not to have sex with each other, but rather to go cruising together for pickups, as wingmen. Predictably, gay style marriage is now being promoted to heterosexuals.[204]

Because otherwise, discrimination.

---

[204]https://whiskeysplace.wordpress.com/2014/07/28/usas-satisfaction-and-the-gay-redefinition-of-marriage/

# Moravec's paradox, RNA, and uploads.

## 2014-08-25 06:26:32

Moravec's paradox is the hard problems are easy and the easy problems are hard. A computer can beat the world's greatest chess player at chess, but it cannot beat a spider at getting around. If humans have been working on a problem for a thousand years, you can program a computer to do it. If evolution has been working on a problem for a hundred million years, not so easy.

It turns out that the vast majority of the functional human genome is information processing. A small proportion of the human genome codes for proteins, but most of the important genes, most of what matters, does not code for proteins. It is RNA world data processing, RNA genes, RNA generated primarily to process RNA.

Given that twelve to sixty percent of the human genome is data processing, is software, is programming, that is a lot of information processing - seven hundred megabytes to four gigabytes of software. A lot of this software is instructions on how to build a human being - where and when to express the proteins of which a human is made.

If, however, you have a massive system for processing data, seems likely that the brain is going to use it.

Particular RNA genes are expressed in particular kinds of neurones, often a particular RNA gene being expressed in few hundred or a few thousand very specific neurones in the entire brain, Protein expression is considerably less specific.

Most of the genetic complexity of the brain consists of very large numbers of very specific RNA genes being expressed in very specific neurons. Protein enzymes for editing RNAs are most highly expressed in the brain, and a disproportionate number of RNA genes are expressed only in the brain, and only in very specific neurons in the brain.

The human brain does thirty five times as much RNA editing per unit mass as the mouse brain. The smarter the animal, the more RNA data processing in neurons. Smarter animals not only have bigger brains with more neurons, they have substantially more RNA software expressed and running in each neuron. This is the missing complexity. Humans have about the same number of protein coding genes as a sponge or a flatworm. They have substantially more RNA genes, a large proportion of which are expressed only in quite specific neurons in the brain.

This suggests that neurons process data at the RNA level - that a large part of the evolution towards intelligence occurred in RNA world creating smarter individual free living cells, before cells got smart enough to gang up for attack and defense, and likely before they developed protein synthesis.

If brain data is processed in complex ways in RNA, there is no way that this can be emulated in silicon. Likely we have software that evolved over billions of years, which software is designed to run on RNA molecules in water solution and can only be efficiently run on RNA molecules in water solution.

So, if RNA world data processing, no possibility of emulating the human mind in silicon. Silicon consciousness would have to be built from scratch, rather than by copying existing software, which looks to me like a very hard project..

## Muslim predation in Rotheram

2014-08-27 09:25:36

In the not very large Yorkshire town of Rotheram, population two hundred fifty thousand, about fourteen hundred girls, almost all of them non Muslims, were subjected to "appalling sexual exploitation[205]" by Muslims. It seems likely this problem exists at similar levels throughout much of England.

Reading the report, it seems that slutty children, and the slutty families of slutty children (typically single and divorced women) were subject to extreme coercion and frequent deadly threats by Islam and individual Muslims to force them to sexually service Muslims. The authorities were unwilling to protect them.

Chaste girls belonging to intact Christian families were not.

Again and again in the report, we read that abduction notices were issued, but no one was convicted, implying that a very large number of girls were abducted, and these abductions went unpunished and generally uninvestigated, presumably because the authorities were scared of Muslims.

In two cases of the sixty six cases that were sampled of fourteen hundred cases:

> fathers tracked down their daughters and tried to remove them from houses where they were being abused, only to be arrested themselves when police were called to the scene.

Assuming the sample of sixty six is representative, that means that in about forty cases in Rotheram fathers attempted to protect their daughters, and were arrested.

We are not told whether these fathers had already been removed from their families, but given the highly selective nature of Muslim predation depicted in the report, seems likely.

It looks that Muslims in Rotheram are, like Boko Haram, upholding the social order that progressives are destroying, but upholding it in a way that advantages Muslims and disadvantages non Muslims by predating on Christians.

## The rectification of names part one

2014-08-29 19:30:49

Bigot, bigoted: Originally meant a sanctimonious person, someone holier than thou, someone who uses his purported holiness to gain advantage over other people.

Now, anyone who uses the word is a sanctimonious person who is holier than thou and uses his purported holiness to gain advantage over other people.

Racist, racism: Never had any coherent original meaning. Now is a hate word for white, frequently used preparatory to murder and assault. Thus for example if a black man enters a white woman's house, hits the baby with a jack handle and throws the woman down the stairs, it is because of racism - because she and the baby are racist.

---

[205]https://mangans.blogspot.com.au/2014/08/rotherham.html?m=1

Prejudiced. Originally meant pre judgment, meant believing ideology over eyesight. Now means believing eyesight over ideology.

Covetousness: Originally meant desiring what someone else has rightly earned or rightly owns. Now means desiring to rightly earn things, rather than take what is another's through the political process - I don't think that intent of present day Christians is to use the words that old type Christians used to use in the new meaning so much as to prevent anyone from using them in the old meaning. see also "prophetic[206]". The intent of using words associated with old type Christianity is to end the use of the words. Once the official hierarchy gets everyone in the church using words in the new meaning, they then shut down the church, thereby ending the use of words associated with old type Christianity in either the old or new meanings.

Hypocrisy, hypocrite: Originally meant someone who proclaims one code of action while acting differently, close in meaning to "bigot" and "bigoted". Now means a non progressive who fails to act according to progressive rules. Progressives, therefore cannot be hypocrites, any more than blacks can be racists, even when blacks are playing the knockout game. Thus if, for example, someone says that a disproportionate number of blacks are dangerous, and since one cannot predict which ones are dangerous, it is necessary to treat them all as potentially dangerous at first, is not only supposedly bigoted, but also supposedly hypocritical if he does in fact treat them all as potentially dangerous.

Because progressives demand that people behave in suicidal ways, they always make unprincipled exceptions for themselves. Because progressives are always struggling for power with each other, they always call each other out over these unprincipled exceptions. But, when calling each other out over these unprincipled exceptions, they would seldom make the faux pas of using "hypocrite" in the old sense. Progressives can never be hypocrites. Progressives failing to act in a progressive manner are not hypocrites. Only non progressives failing to act in a progressive manner are hypocrites.

Marriage: Originally, within the lives of older married people, an irrevocable commitment to live together and raise the resulting children. Now the point of marriage is divorce, the legal authority of the wife over a husband on pain of confiscation of his assets and income. Some people attempt to use Church and social pressure to enforce old type marriage, but hard to find an old type church. Because "gay marriage" means a pair of gays cruising together to pick up boys, an effort is under way to redefine marriage yet again as a pair of people of either sex cruising for pickups but it is probably that this redefinition will fail, because it is hard to get a good wingwoman. Therefore, probably will continue to mean matrilineality and female headship. The feminists and the gays are fighting over this one. Feminists want "marriage" to refer to the female headed family, while gays want it to refer to cruising for pickups.

People continue to have Church weddings in the hope of getting Church backing for the old meaning, but they get stabbed in the back by the Church with the feminist meaning, where the purpose of marriage is to ensure female headship through divorce. Gay meaning soon to follow.

Because of the difference between men and women, if the gays beat the feminists for the meaning of marriage, it will work out even worse for married heterosexual males. Even

---

[206]https://www.firstthings.com/web-exclusives/2011/02/too-often-prophetic

though television today tells you that the latest meaning of marriage means that your wife should be your wingwoman when you go cruising for a threesome, which would be great, it will in practice mean that you sleep on the couch and clean up the love stains on the double bed when your wife's lover comes over to slap her around and take her money.

## leftism as cancer

### 2014-08-30 09:52:00

"Leftism as Cancer" stopped being accessible through google in the course of a blog backup and restore, so reposting it.

Leftism is to memes as cancer is genes.

If the cells of the body mutate, cells that multiply at the expense of the body will be selected. And cells that mutate to a faster mutation rate will be selected, since they will have more fast multiplying variants.

In a healthy body, each cell lives for the body, and performs its role in the whole body, making the body one. In cancer, each cancer cell lives for itself, at the expense of the body, parasitically, until the parasites devour the host

Left wing memes are selected by propagation through state power for propagation through state power.

In a healthy state the state is one, but there is large civil society, which is many. Following Marx' 's definition, by capitalism and civil society we mean[207] the *"society of industry, of general competition, of freely pursued private interest, of anarchy, of natural and spiritual individuality alienated from self."*

The civil society, which is many, produces the wealth, the science, and the technology. The state, which is one, defends civil society from enemies internal and external. For the reasons explained by Hayek and Mises, and colorfully dramatized by Ayn Rand, a unitary entity just cannot coordinate production very well. It runs into analogous problems with technology and science.

For civil society to function, to create wealth, knowledge, and technology, it must be free, a hundred flowers. For the state to function, it must be one flower. Elements of the state apparatus cannot be permitted to use state power to pursue their own goals. Elements of the state apparatus must be profoundly unfree in their role of elements of the state, in their exercise of the powers of the state, so that the state can be one.

In anarcho tyranny each groupuscule of the state uses state power and state resources to pursue its own particular good, thus the state spends money it does not have, and taxes and regulates beyond the laffer limit, suffering the tragedy of the commons. That is the anarchy. Because the state regulates beyond the laffer limit, we also get tyranny. Civil society, instead of having a hundred voices, has one voice, the voice of the state

That is the tyranny, a hundred supposedly independent voices of civil society speaking the same words.

Thus instead of the state being one, and civil society many, civil society is the voice of the state, one microphone heard through a thousand megaphones, while the state is

---

[207] https://www.xenosystems.net/luciano-pellicani/

many, and state resources suffer the tragedy of the commons, and the state is unable to pass a budget.

Elements of the state apparatus are free in their exercise of state power, thus everyday life of respectable people is subject to capricious tyranny, while criminals run free.

The left singularity is analogous to aneuploidy in a cancer. Cancers get selected for a high mutation rate, and left wing memes get selected for a high mutation rate.

This results in rising time preference, as depicted by Konkistador, and affinity for r-selected behaviors, as depicted by Anonymous Conservative.

Thus left wing movements start out each quite different from each other, and converge more and more to the left archetype, under the selective pressure for the niche of state mediated propagation of memes, just as all severely aneuploid malignant metastatic cancers look pretty much alike, by convergent evolution, and not much like their various tissues of origin.

If you are going to have a state, you are going to have a state religion or state ideology. The only way to avoid this is anarcho capitalism.

If you are going to have a state, you are going to have state official truth. If you are going to have state official truth, you need to stop it from endlessly mutating to ever greater virulence.

To prevent the official belief system from suffering memetic selection, the only solution is to have bishops, rather than open entry to the role of "opinion leader". The Bishops need to maintain a monopoly on the state propagation of official truth, and any elements of the state that start free lancing need to be, at a minimum, excluded from the state, which is to say, at a minimum fired, and, in serious cases, convicted of apostasy from the official belief system, and imprisoned, sold into slavery, or executed. If your official belief system will not sell William Wilberforce into slavery for apostasy from the thirty nine articles, his beliefs will win and the official beliefs will lose. His beliefs may well be better than the previous official beliefs, but every man jack will proceed with further improvements, resulting in memetic selection for virulence and a high mutation rate.

You have to kill or enslave William Wilberforce. If he is visibly holy, ironically check the body after three days. If he did not rise, not holy enough.

Non state apostates are harmless, since their belief systems are not selected for propagation by power. The problem is state and quasi state apostasy. Apostasy, in the sense of the sort of apostasy that the state should worry about and suppress, is mutation in the state meme system, mutations in the memes propagated by power.

Late stage leftism is the memetic equivalent of aneuploid malignant metastatic cancer. In cancer, the genes are selected for virulence within somatic growth, in leftism, the memes are selected for virulence within the state propagation of official memes.

Alien memes need to be excluded from participating in state power, thus the list (antibodies) of forbidden thoughts (antigens) needs to be updated frequently, while the list of required thoughts should be kept short, unchanging, and immune from empirical falsification by the facts of this world, to minimize memetic selection for propagation by power. This suggests an Archbishop to ensure that official memes do not mutate, to propagate the official and unchanging list of official memes, the archbishop having final responsibility for the propagation of the official list of unchanging official memes, and a Grand

Inquisitor, to detect entryists and the undercover use of state power to propagate unofficial memes, or to furtively mutate official memes. The Grand Inquisitor should deal with endless change by ever changing conspiracies like that revealed by the Climategate Files, the Archbishop with unchanging official truth.

People who are in the position to deploy state power to propagate their beliefs need to be severely unfree in what beliefs they may espouse, just as police are not free to make up their own laws. To constrain such people, to constrain the state apparatus, we need the traditional thought control apparatus of Bishops and Inquisition, just as the courts are supposed to constrain the police.

If, however, that apparatus were to be applied to civil society, science, technology, and capitalism would be destroyed. The only penalty applied to people thinking unapproved thoughts should be exclusion from state employment and high status universities, exclusion from teaching jobs in the government education system, and the resulting lower status. We need to avoid penalties for thoughtcrime from pervading the civil society through regulation the way they do now, because that adversely affects the creation of wealth and knowledge. The state should be one being, and should therefore hold one set of official beliefs. Civil society should be many beings, so that the truth will out. To avoid potential conflicts between state and civil society, official truths should be either demonstrably true, or difficult to falsify.

It follows that the state cannot directly sponsor science, cannot be the sort of entity capable of directly sponsoring science. What the state can do to sponsor science is pay for impressive technological feats, and those who are successful in providing impressive technologies will sponsor science. Galilean kinematics was developed to land cannon balls on targets out of sight behind city walls, and the telescope with which Galileo saw the phases of Venus and the moons of Saturn was developed to spy on enemy fleets at sea. Should the state directly sponsor science (a most dangerous practice, for it is likely to wind up sponsoring apostatic religion dressed in the robes of science) it needs to forbid and severely criminalize peer review, and any form of science by consensus, especially consensus behind closed doors. If the state finds itself funding "science" that discovers scientific truth through scientific consensus behind closed doors, it is funding apostatic religion. Apply the same remedy to state funded or sponsored peer review as to William Wilberforce. Ideas are more dangerous than guns. We need a free market in ideas that are not backed by state power. We dare not have competition between ideas backed by state power, and need to deal with such competition in the most drastic fashion, for the natural result of such competition is ever more extreme ideas propagated through an ever heavier hand of the state.

If you will not execute William Wilberforce, who swore to be faithful to the thirty nine articles while applying state power to overthrow them, you will lose to William Wilberforce.

Consensus is for bishops, not scientists. Scientists should form their opinions on the basis of public and replicated evidence, not on the basis of discussions behind closed doors, discussions which will inevitably lead to wanted evidence being published, and unwanted evidence being suppressed or "corrected".

Restating in slightly different words:

Cancer cells are selected for rapid multiplication. They run into various limits that are supposed to stop body cells from multiplying out of control. In escaping these limits, they become aneuploid, thus develop a very high mutation rate.

Those mutants most apt to multiply rapidly and to penetrate other tissues are selected, thus cancer progressively becomes more cancerous, eventually becoming aneuploid metastatic malignant cancer.

If one is going to have a state belief system, and this seems unavoidable if one is going to have a state, then one needs an archbishop to ensure that all elements of the state apparatus stay on message - that in the cancer analogy, all cells of the body display stable and unchanging self antigens, and a grand inquisitor to detect hostile entryist belief systems.

In the cancer analogy: The Archbishop enforces mandatory unchanging self antigens, the Grand Inquisitor searches out and prohibits ever changing non self antigens.

Of course, if the Archbishop enforces self antigens on absolutely everyone, intrudes on the civil society, this is horribly oppressive, and as, as in Spain, wrecks the economy (Ayn Rand's heroic entrepeneurs are the first to be repressed) but it is reasonable to enforce self antigens on everyone who matters in the state apparatus. Thus, in restoration England, if one wanted to be a member of parliament, be a professor at the best universities, have senior government employment, etc, one had to subscribe to the thirty nine articles.

Once in a while, in restoration England, heretics got their houses burned down by hostile mobs while authority looked the other way, but as far as I can tell this was only when their heresy pursued state power, engaged in entryism. You could be a Jew, a Puritan, or a Roman Catholic in Restoration England, and suffer no very great disadvantages other than lower status and exclusion from the state apparatus and the most prestigious universities.

No matter how badly the official belief system stinks, if it is subject to furtive mutation and selection for virulence, it will in time stink even worse. To prevent this, the Archbishop should prohibit spontaneous memetic mutation, the Grand Inquisitor should detect hostile memes and eradicate them from the state apparatus.

## Recap on Ukraine

### 2014-08-30 22:18:46

Bored now, which is why I have not mentioned it in a while.

Democracy produced the wrong result in Ukraine, so the Cathedral staged a coup. The instrument of the coup was the Maidan movement, which is supposedly an indigenous Ukrainian movement, but its web page is in English in the distinctive dialect of the American Jim ruling elite. Intercepted phone conversation revealed that State Department regarded the nominal leaders of the Ukraine as menial functionaries which they got to appoint and dismiss.

Russia counterproposed regional autonomy, so that there would be some Ukrainian independence from the Cathedral. The USG was not having any.

So, war. This looks like straight USG imperialism. If, as seems likely, the final outcome is that the Ukraine gets partitioned between Russia and the USG, as Poland was partitioned between Hitler and Stalin, that will not be Putin's fault. He made several attempts at compromise that would have preserved Ukrainian independence.

The interesting implication is that if the Ukraine is run by low level menials of the state department, by people a long way down in the State Department hierarchy, then most or all of Europe is run by low level menials of the state department, as Mencius Moldbug depicted it long before these events.

Lately Putin seems to be moving to a straight imperial position, in which Ukraine will be partitioned, but really, don't much care. What is interesting about the Ukraine is what it tells us about the rest of the world. If a menial in the state department treats the nominal leaders of the Ukraine as considerably lesser menials, what of other leaders of supposedly independent nations?

As you know, the entire west, in suspicious unison, simultaneously decided to allow itself to be overrun by third world hordes.

When Australia broke ranks, this was deemed illegal under international law, though oddly, until very recently international law did not require countries to allow themselves to be overrun by third world hordes. The UN took a break from condemning Israel to condemn Australia. Every international human rights organization now believes that economic refugees from anywhere in the world have a human right to settle in Australia.

This pattern of sporadic minor resistance suggests that the USG empire is ruled through soft power, and soft power is, in fact soft. It is not that when the prime minister of Australia disobeys he gets shot. Rather it is that the television stations, radio stations, and universities supposedly owned by the government of Australia announce that the prime minister is violating human rights. Except when, as in the Ukraine, it turns hard and they start shelling schools and apartment buildings, which is terrible when Israel does it, but no big problem when the "government" of the Ukraine does it.

While every human rights organization everywhere condemns Australian violation of human rights in intercepting boats on the high seas full of illegal immigrants, they don't seem to notice any violation of human rights when the Ukrainian government shells civilian targets. That is soft power. On the other hand, when the Ukrainian government shells civilian targets, that is hard power.

Soft power is a bunch of supposedly independent, supposedly non government organizations, speaking in one voice, their master's voice. One day everyone spontaneously and suddenly agrees it is a human right to move to formerly white majority countries, just as it is a human right for a man to be a woman - but freedom of speech and freedom of association are no longer human rights.

## Nice guys finish last

**2014-09-03 03:38:21**

We all know, just from looking around, that nice guys finish last, that women reliably make extremely bad sexual choices, that female sexual autonomy is a really bad idea. Now that the left have given up on socialism, except to the extent that they accidentally and unintentionally stumble into socialism through disastrously stupid laws like Sarbanes–Oxley, female sexual autonomy is the worst idea of the left.

Scott has done the hard work of collecting some statistics on this question. But he has buried it in his usual pile of pious politically correct rationalizing, so I am copying his little bit of good stuff without his vast pile of @%!&.

Scott tells us[208]:

> I will have to use virginity statistics as a proxy for the harder-to-measure romancelessness statistics, but these are bad enough. In high school[209] each extra IQ point above average increases chances of male virginity by about 3%. 35% of MIT grad students have never had sex, compared to only 13% of the average *high school* population. Compared with virgins, men with more sexual experience are likely to[210] drink more alcohol, attend church less, and have a criminal history. A Dr.Beaver (nominative determinism again!) was able to predict[211] number of sexual partners pretty well using a scale with such delightful items as "have you been in a gang", "have you used a weapon in a fight", et cetera. An analysis of the psychometric Big Five consistently find[212] that high levels of disagreeableness predict high sexual success in both men and women.

No, disagreeableness predicts that men are sexually successful. A high notch count on the bedpost is success for a man, failure for a woman. For a man, a high notch count on the bedpost means that the women keep coming. For a woman, it means the boys do not stick around.

That male assholes are attractive, female assholes unattractive, is part of the reason why men should have sexual autonomy and women should not have sexual autonomy.

> If you're smart, don't drink much, stay out of fights, display a friendly personality, and have no criminal history – then you are the population most at risk of being miserable and alone.

Scott is, of course a nice guy. He is only able to be nasty when it is mandatory for progressives to be nasty to people with certain beliefs.

I, however, am an asshole, who would have a criminal record were it not for good lawyers and willingness to pay them what they are worth.

## Memes and reproduction.

### 2014-09-07 02:36:21

Progressives do not reproduce at anywhere near replacement rate. But they set things up so that conservatives have to send their children to educational institutions controlled by progressives.

---

[208] https://slatestarcodex.com/2014/08/31/radicalizing-the-romanceless/ "Nice guys finish last"

[209] https://www.gnxp.com/blog/2007/04/intercourse-and-intelligence.php

[210] https://www.newscientist.com/blogs/shortsharpscience/2009/06/who-is-the-40-year-old-virgin.html

[211] https://www.ncbi.nlm.nih.gov/pubmed/19350760

[212] https://homepage.psy.utexas.edu/HomePage/Group/MestonLAB/Publications/mestonetal_fivefactor.pdf

If memes reproduce from parent to child, then in the long run, surviving memes will be favorable to the people that hold them.

If, however, memes reproduce through state pressure and state sponsored evangelism, they are going to be selected for state pressure and state sponsored evangelism, which is likely to result in those memes being hostile to survival and favorable to ever greater state intrusion on everyday life.

In Old Testament times, Hebrew memes reproduced from parent to child, hence natural selection apt to result in pro survival memes. The Hebrews had a lower death rate due to their rules of washing their hands, burying their feces, and not eating animals that died of natural causes.

They had a higher reproduction rate because of strict patriarchy, no female autonomy, female consent preferred but not required for sex and marriage, absolute patriarchal power over wives and children, plus a patriarchal duty of care and protection for wives and children, in particular the no infanticide rule. (B. disagrees with my interpretation of Old Testament rules, interpreting them in a manner curiously compatible with modern progressivism. To see how the people of the time interpreted them, read the Book of Ruth, chapters three and four, and Genesis chapter twenty four.)

According to the Pentateuch, the twelve sons of Israel produced six hundred thousand adult males four hundred and thirty years later, which corresponds to a high, but not at all miraculous, growth rate of 2.5% per year.

The Hebrew economy was more productive because of rules protecting private property, and prohibiting coveting, thus prohibiting redistributionist ideologies.

We don't know much about Canaanite memes, but it is clear that the practice of burning one's children alive in front of the congregation, like progressive memes, reproduced through state sponsored religious practices and state sponsored evangelism - that members of the elite were coerced or pressured to burn their children alive, thus inspiring emulation among the commoners.

Soft power, the power of the state department, is the power that accrues to a state by propagating its belief system beyond its borders. When the State department gets Muslim states to make abortion available on *female* demand, the state department accrues power, and when the Canaanites got Hebrews to sacrifice their children to Moloch, the Canaanite states accrued power.

The Canaanites suffered from the decadence characteristic of the last days of Bronze Age civilization. Ipuwer depicts late stage Bronze age decadence as something very similar to modern leftism, which is a meme system that today reproduces through state sponsored quasi religious practices and state sponsored evangelism.

The practice of sacrificing one's infant children to Moloch by casting them into the flames in front of the congregation demonstrated one's faith – and having done such a terrible thing (perhaps to advance one's career in the state apparatus) difficult to doubt the belief system that made it a good thing.

Thus, burning children alive was an effective means of making people into Canaanites. The Canaanite memetic system reproduced, while Canaanites did not, just as progressivism reproduces, while progressives do not.

The Canaanites were successful in their efforts at conversion, inducing some Hebrews to sacrifice their children to Moloch (Canaanite equivalent of Jehovah). This sacrifice was conducted by dropping the living child into the fire in front of the assembled congregation.

Similarly, today's progressives do not reproduce, but instead seduce the children of conservatives.

Memeplexes that propagate through coercion seem an almost unavoidable aspect of states. Such a memeplex is subject to selection pressures that are apt to make it more and more evil, destructive, and insane. Propagation through power is orthogonal to truth or survival, thus entropy prevails. Local reductions in such entropy tend to be astonishingly expensive.

.

## Gamergate

### 2014-09-08 01:50:43

Gamers are a demographic interested in certain topics who buy stuff. Thus, magazines and websites staffed by professional journalists are created to carry articles that interest those people and ads selling stuff that they are likely to buy.

Gamer journalists are, being journalists, extremely politically correct, and make it their mission to morally improve their audience and make them as holy as their extremely holy selves.

Gamers are anonymous, therefore free to be politically incorrect. Further, they are customers, hence game developers really have to give them what they want, rather than what the politically correct think the gamers should receive. Thus games tend to be full of stereotypes.

World of Warcraft's Africa (Stranglethorn vale) contained a Great Zimbabwe that was ugly, primitive, and long been abandoned by the simple minded cannibal savages native to the area. Who, by the way, cannot speak very well, because they are pretty much mentally subnormal.

The Warcraft religion of light was ninth century Christianity with the serial numbers filed off, and all its leading figures were noble, heroic, kindly, and, apart from the tendency to bash evildoers with big hammers, Christian. Which not only depicted Christianity in a good light, but implicitly depicted present day unmanly Christianity in a bad light.

The storyline of Archeage is a war between whites and east Asians, and much of the game play is piracy, with much of the piracy featuring conflicts between whites and east Asians. White male avatars are depicted as way better than anyone else, even though this game was written and the art drawn by east Asians. (And, by the way, the Mongols are catboys)

All white males in Archeage are incredibly heroic and manly, and the white females are a bit on the manly side also, though with gigantic breasts. All east Asian males in Archeage have a girly appearance, and are substantially less heroic and manly. All the east Asian females have an extremely girly appearance and behavior. (You will probably want to play white if you want a cool avatar, and play east Asian if you want to look at the hottest chicks, unless of course you especially like truly colossal breasts, in which case the white chicks are hotter.) If you were to ignore the breasts (which is impossible) the white females would be about as female in appearance as the east Asian males, though white female NPCs are considerably braver and more warlike than east Asian NPCs.

Naturally each journalist sought to be holier than each of the others, thus each sought to deride, despise, and denigrate his audience more than each of the others.

This caused loss of audience, whereupon the game companies started applying large amounts of money to channels that the gamers had created to talk to each other, the money bypassing the journalists as the audience already had.

This caused a truly apocalyptic outpouring of hatred by the journalists against their audience. Or, as they depict it, an outpouring of hatred *by* their audience.

And that apocalyptic outpouring of hatred by journalists against those who pay their bills, is gamergate.

They always hated their audience. But it was only when the game companies started making payouts to non journalistic channels that they went raving mad.

## Breitbart explains gamergate

### 2014-09-10 05:25:21

Too long, don't read:[213]
>Short of it:
>Gamers to press:

>>You lie about games in return for for money, goodies, and whores.

>Press to Gamers:

>>Misogynists! How can you say this when we are obviously so much holier than you are?

## He-who-must-not-be named speaks

### 2014-09-14 07:11:05

Gamergate is gamers spontaneously discovering the Cathedral.
The Cathedral speaks with one voice.

>In the last 48 hours, 15 articles about the "death of gaming" have been published[214]

>And the Cathedral sounds like Lord Voldemort.[215]

To paraphrase the conversation:
feminist:

---

[213]https://www.breitbart.com/Big-Hollywood/2014/09/09/GamerGate-Why-Gaming-Journalists-Keep-Dragging-Zoe-Quinns-Sex-Life-into-the-Spotlight

[214]https://twitter.com/DisgruntleGamer/status/505651805070819328

[215]https://knowyourmeme.com/photos/825141-gamergate

you are sexist and bigoted

target:

I am innocent

feminist:

I can and will crush you

target:

I have said nothing offensive

feminist 2:

failure to be PC is offensive

feminist:

your career is being ruined as we speak

feminist:

you must grovel immediately or face destruction of your career

The target must confess that he is part of the great and powerful male conspiracy, that he is punching down and the feminist is punching up, or be crushed like a bug.

## Massive 4chan purge and censorship.

### 2014-09-18 04:57:51

Most Chan mods have been permabanned and replaced by social justice warriors
Of the 4chan old guard, only four remain.

It used to be said that all organizations become left wing, except those that are explicitly right wing.

We may have to amend that to "all organizations become left wing, except those that are explicitly reactionary".

Progressives long maintained the illusion of an open society by maintaining a neutered opposition. But now, even that neutered opposition is being shut down.

The Republican party has long been a joke. Notice how their presidential candidate is always the man who bipartisanly did the most to move America left, McCain of Mcain Feingold, Romney of Romneycare. Now the same joke is everywhere.

The problem is that social justice warriors are being appointed in charge of absolutely everything everywhere, from subreddits to Apple. Likely that the reason that recent Apple decisions have been so stupid and incompetent is likely that Tim Cook is not a tech guy, he is a social justice guy, a toll that Jobs paid to the Cathedral to be left alone for a bit.

And that is why the cutscenes in your video games are likely to feature tranny warriors and men having sex with men.

# Nazism and antisemitism is PC

## 2014-09-18 22:02:17

Observe that now that 4chan has been totally taken over by social justice warriors, you can still say "nigger nigger kike kike" all day long on 4chan, you can say that Hitler did not kill the Jews but he should have, but you cannot criticize social justice warriors, feminists, trannies, and so forth on 4chan.

Correction: After they purged the anti feminists etc, then they came for people saying kike and nigger. But anti feminists, and opponents of social justice, went first.

For brief period, 4chan was still nazi, while anti feminists and such had been purged. First they came for the patriarchalists, then they came for the nazis.

You can complain that Jews ruin everything, because diverse groups are incohesive and untrusting. You can even complain that vibrants ruin everything, but you cannot complain that women ruin everything by pushing themselves into male activities in which they have no real interest and no competence.

If Jews ruled, you would not be able to say "Kike" on 4chan, and the Gaza/Israel war would have been over in an hour.

Nazism is a variant of leftism, right wing in the sense that is frozen in the already quite left wing 1930s, right wing only in that it has been left behind by the rapidly moving Overton window. Communism descends from the Jews, Nazism was descended from Lutheranism, Anglosphere leftism, which now dominates the world and therefore has no distinct name, descends from the puritans. Communism is now "right wing" in the same sense as Nazism. The Overton window moves on.

The old French leftism was descended from the false popes of Avignon, but it self destructed in its left singularity, and today French leftism is wholly a muppet of anglosphere leftism, a muppet of the state department.

The Jews are doubtless guilty of a great pile of stuff, and the fact that our elite is diverse makes it incohesive and disloyal, but in the recent financial crisis, there were more vibrants behaving badly, in particular Angelo Mozilo, than there were Jews behaving badly. Goldman Sachs pulled strings to get bailed out by the government on obscenely favorable terms in a truly disgusting bit of crony capitalism, but the main reason they needed a bail out was that Angelo Mozilo burned them.

Nazism, anti semitism, etc, thinks that crony capitalism is business corrupting the state, rather than the state corrupting business. They see clever businessmen outsmarting regulators, and do not see the revolving door between regulators and business. They fail to notice that Jon Corzine, the most highly regulated man in history, was both regulator and regulated.

Nazism, anti semitism, etc, thinks our elite is composed of smart, sane, reasonable people. Supposedly it is just that they are behaving badly for lack of ethnic loyalty. In actual fact, only ten percent or so of Harvards are admitted on academic merit, and most of those admitted on academic merit are admitted on SAT and GPA, which no longer correlates with intelligence, rather than LSAT, which still does correlate with intelligence. Our elite is #*#$!%^& stupid and crazy, and every day, as selection for political purity increases, getting stupider and crazier.

## #gamergate

2014-09-21 22:43:55

Social Justice Warriors believe that all people were created equal.

Kind of obviously, people are not equal. Very few video games were created by women, and those games are crap.

If people are not equal, it must be due to the evil magic of thought criminals thinking thought crimes.

Social Justice Warriors therefore convict the broad mass of gamers as thought criminals, whose evil thoughts are magically causing magical harm, and want to punish them. Hence tranny megaman, etc.

Although these gamers are doubtless entirely innocent, I recommend that since you are going to be convicted and punished, you might as well be guilty.

Here is the news:

People were not created equal. As Darwin explains, some individuals are better than others, some groups and categories are better than others, some races are superior, some inferior.

Women are better than men at the very important job of making babies. (No contest there). They are better than men at cleaning house, and way better than men at finding where the man in their life has left his car keys.

At pretty much everything else, they tend to suck.

And one of the things they particularly suck at is writing video games.

## Taking care of Islam

2014-09-29 03:44:29

Every US intervention against Islam backfires.

Progressives believe that all religions, rightly understood, are Progressivism.

Viewed as a cynical lie, it is working pretty well. They actually are reasonably successful at remaking Islam into progressivism.

Unfortunately, it is not entirely a cynical lie. It is also sincerely held insanity. It is quite difficult for the Cathedral to do entirely cynical lies. Their stock in trade is not lies, but delusions.

Meanwhile, Muslims have been figuring out what is up, and are counterinfiltrating. As well as progressives lying that they are Muslims, we have Muslims lying that they are progressives. The former tend wake up with their throats cut by the latter.

Hence Major Hasan, Rotherdam, and Benghazi Embassy. The story of Arab Spring is a story of the counterinfiltration.

When Obama told the mercenaries to stand down, to not retake the embassy, it was not so that he could fool the American people by denying that Al Qaeda troops were operating freely in Libya. It was so that he could fool himself by denying that Al Qaeda troops were operating in Libya.

I don't think progressives are going to succeed at remaking Islam into progressivism, and if they do succeed, I don't think it would be a good thing.

A better solution would be to convert Muslims to the peace of Westphalia and monarchism.

If an Islamic country is ruled by a King, and he decides for war, he demonstrates superior holiness, but will very likely get killed. So he decides for peace.

If an Islamic country is a democracy, and a voter votes for war, he demonstrates superior holiness, but, being one vote of many, his vote makes little difference to his prospects of being killed. So he votes for war.

The problem with Islamic State is that the Caliph is elected for life by the consensus of the most holy. Which pretty much guarantees that soon your Caliph is going to be holier than Mohammed. Indeed he already is.

The Caliph should be elected for life by Sunni monarchs, and should be unable to declare holy war except in consultation with them. If anyone else declares holy war, this is infidelity to Caliph, and the holy warrior loses his head for irreligion and apostacy.


# Unlawful assembly in Hong Kong

## 2014-09-29 06:28:58

Obviously the Chinese government has the mandate of heaven. Those who have power are entitled to keep it if they don't screw up too badly, nor make unsuccessful radical change in the society that gave them power originally.

Obviously, by law, custom, and the two systems agreement, Hong Kongers are entitled to the rights they had before Hong Kong came under Chinese authority, including the right to peaceably assemble, and to petition the Government for a redress of grievances.

Blocking the streets is not peaceable assembly, nor have Hong Kongers ever had such a right, and the government is entitled to deal with it according to Chinese customs - it should roll over them with tanks.

Hong Kongers have never had the right to vote. If Hong Kongers were allowed to vote, they would vote against the capitalism that made them wealthy, and which is essential for such a dense crowd of people to survive on a tiny little island with no resources. Give them democracy, and pretty soon the economy would collapse, refugees would be fleeing Hong Kong as they flee Venezuela - and the Chinese government would be blamed for insufficiently large bailouts.

I urge the Chinese government to drive tanks over the protestors while maintaining the utmost respect for Hong Kong's traditions and the two systems agreement.

The two systems agreement looks, in practice, rather like Hong Kong taking over China, even though theoretically it is China taking over Hong Kong. Hong Kong democracy would be the Cathedral taking over Hong Kong as a step to taking over China. If the voters controlled Hong Kong, the Cathedral would control the voters. Voters are easy to manipulate, since no individual voter has an individual incentive to be well informed or to vote in his own best interest. He is apt to vote for what makes him holiest, and the Cathedral is very good at weaponizing superior holiness.

## Democracy

2014-10-02 05:02:09

Steal this image

## Hong Kong Government needs an inquisition

2014-10-04 23:09:21

In the recent violence six police were injured, and nineteen people arrested, eight of who were triad members.

About half of those injured were police - therefore the police are acting to protect the protestors and or coming down like the wrath of God on the counterprotestors - much like the "antifascist" riots in Europe, where the antifascists assemble to beat up "fascists", beat them up, and then the police beat up "fascists" for provoking other people to beat them up.

The protestors complain the police are not doing enough to protect them, and perhaps they are not - but they are doing a lot more to protect the protestors than they are to clear the streets.

When the "triads" attempt to exercise their right to use the streets, the police stop them, backing the protestor symbolic blockade with actual police violence, without which it could never succeed.

Over and over again, Leung Chun-ying orders police to clear the streets, and over and over again, police obey in a deliberately ineffectual manner.

At the very least, the police in Hong Kong are showing far more enthusiasm for acting effectively to protect the protestors blocking the roads than they are for acting effectively to clear the roads.

If Peking does not want Hong Kong turned into a Cathedral beachhead against China, it is going to have to thoroughly purge Hong Kong government employees - fire everyone who believes in democracy, equality, and social justice.

Because of the two systems agreement, it would be inappropriate to have the same archbishop and grand inquisitor for Hong Kong and the Mainland. Peking should appoint an inquisition and grand inquisitor with credible Hong Kong system credentials, and charge them with thoroughly removing Cathedral agents from Hong Kong government employment and the Hong Kong education system.

Democracy, equality, and social justice have never been part of what traditionally makes Hong Kong Hong Kong. They are a threat to what Hong Kong has always been.

## Fake Hong Kong blockade

2014-10-06 09:08:17

Here are the protestors "blockading" the road outside the Hong Kong Government Complex

You will notice that three strong brave men with stun guns and rubber hoses could clear this blockade in fifteen minutes. If the blockade continues to exist, it is because the police wish it to continue to exist.

## The red and blue empires

2014-10-07 00:55:04

A government is supposed to be one thing, that can be thought of as making decisions like a single person. To the extent that a government is one thing, it is a stationary bandit. But, lacking virtue and asabiyah, is apt to be many things, thus more like horde of mobile bandits.

Moldbug argues that what were supposedly external wars by the US government against external enemies were frequently proxy wars between the red empire, the Pentagon's empire of the bases, and the blue empire, the State Department's empire of the consulates.

Thus the Vietnam war was lost in Washington, not Vietnam, and China fell to the state department, rather than to Mao. "Socialism with Chinese Characteristics" - which is to say capitalism, is China falling away from the blue empire, and the umbrella revolution is a move by the blue empire to regain control.

The relationship between the red and blue empires is like the relationship between the holy Roman Empire and the Papacy - theoretically united, but each seeking dominance over the other.

The red empire, the empire of the bases, the Chinese government understands. The blue empire operates through soft power, which the Chinese government does not understand.

For a long time, India was ruled by the London School of Economics, and the London School of Economics ruled by Harvard.

India took a position in opposition to the Pentagon's red empire, the empire of the bases, while firmly allied to the blue empire, the empire of the consulates.

Lately, India has fallen away from the blue empire, and, worse than that, has been developing friendly relations with the red empire.

Thus I would expect increasingly vigorous State Department efforts to secure its return. Perhaps a bicycle revolution. They already unsuccessfully tried their usual efforts to manipulate election outcomes (the common man party), so, as in Ukraine, will probably find it necessary to destroy democracy in order to save it.

Overreach is inherent in the nature of the blue empire. It just cannot help trying to take over everything, whether video cames, comic strips, science fiction, or Hong Kong.

The people trying to rule gaming are mighty low rank in the blue empire - thus gamers find that though they are fighting the blue empire, they are fighting a lot less than the full might of the blue empire. Win, lose, or draw, they demonstrate it can be fought. The blue empire is the US Government, is also a symptom of the US government's lack of cohesion, and also itself lacks cohesion.

## China's real GDP passes US

2014-10-13 03:54:00

For many years, US statistics have been obviously fake, understating inflation by about two and a half percent a year[216], thus overstating real GDP growth by about three percent a year, and understating the fall in living standards by about three percent a year.

Thus, according to official statistics, US real GDP is still higher than that of China.

Yet, by every measure of actual stuff and technological capability, Chinese production is substantially greater than US production, though Chinese GDP per head is still below the US. China produces more cars, more concrete, more electricity, Chinese buy more cars, more concrete, more electricity, China exports more stuff, China imports more stuff. China produces and consumes more beer, more pork, and far, far, far more steel.

---

[216]https://www.shadowstats.com/alternate_data/inflation-charts

And it is not just tee shirts. China exports twice as much high tech stuff as the US does. China produces and consumes more high tech stuff than the US does. We sell them low tech stuff like wheat, we import high tech stuff like phones. China has the fastest trains in the world, and very large numbers of ordinary people using those very fast trains. China has the coolest airports, and these airports have far more people using them than the US.

OK, what about GDP per capita?

Officially, US GDP per capita is growing. In actual fact, it is obviously falling. Last time I walked around familiar places in America everything was shabbier, older, dirtier, more in need of a coat of paint. US GDP is falling at about two percent a year[217] (used to be falling at about one percent a year, but the decline is visibly accelerating).

US population growth is about 0.6% per year (white population collapsing rapidly due to inability to reproduce without an enforceable system of marriage) so real GDP per capita is falling at about two and half percent per year. This represents a rapid acceleration in the rate of decline.

Chinese real GDP per capita is rising at about seven and a half percent a year. Assuming current trends continue, rather than continuing to accelerate, Chinese real GDP per capita will exceed US real GDP per capita in sixteen years, in 2030.

# The really smart people

2014-10-16 06:19:09

That nurses became sick "shows there was a clear breach of safety protocol" - but they are able to draw this conclusion without knowing what the breach was.

---

[217]https://www.shadowstats.com/alternate_data/gross-domestic-product-charts

The underlying reasoning is clear:

Quarantine is racist.

Therefore ebola is not very infectious.

Therefore business as usual.

Oops. Two nurses are infected with ebola.

Obviously the nurses' fault. They must be racist. This is a tragedy because it makes people think forbidden thoughts about Africans.

## Chinese growth prospects

### 2014-10-22 06:25:24

A politically correct Harvard paper "Asiaphoria Meet Regression to the Mean" by the politically correct authors Lant Pritchett and Larry Summers tells us, or seemingly tells us, that China's rapid growth is unlikely to last. They examine fifty or so periods of rapid growth, and, almost always, sad to say, there is regression to the mean. In the long run, the periods of rapid growth make little difference.

These are, unlike your usual Harvard intellectual, genuinely smart people, and, for smart Harvard people, surprisingly truthful. And, if you take a powerful microscope, read between the lines, read what is unwritten, you will read the truth. If you listen to what they are not saying, you will hear the truth.

There are a near infinite variety of ways to have bad or negative economic growth. There is one way to have good economic growth, and if your country is Cathedral Compliant, it is not allowed to do things that one way.

Instead of just noticing that periods of rapid economic growth tend to come to a sad end, Lant and Larry took a look at these sad ends.

> nearly every country that experienced a large democratic transition after a period of above-average growth (more than the cross-country average of 2 per cent) experienced a sharp deceleration in growth in the 10 years following the democratizing transition.

In other words, the reason that periods of rapid economic growth come to a sad end is that the Cathedral comes after you. It is not regression to the mean, but Cathedral reconquest.

Lant and Larry notice that China is anomalous, different from all their other examples, in that unlike all their other examples, with the partial exception of Singapore, large and long economic growth has not resulted in "Democracy" - their prediction that China will not continue to grow is not a prediction that some mystery factor like "exhaustion of the low hanging fruit" will end China's growth. It is in fact a highly pious prediction that the Cathedral will soon enjoy its inevitable victory, due, no doubt, to the forces of history.

When making highly pious predictions, Lant and Larry are less reliable than usual.

## Neoreaction and Identitarianism

### 2014-10-22 21:35:45

Neoreactionaries rightly look down on identitarians as low class, vulgar, stupid, and, worst of all, leftist.

> "You think construction workers should vote! Worse, some of you think women should vote. You are so ignorant of history that you hate capitalism, forgetting how Europe became rich. And a lot of you are so stupid you think the Joos brought down the two towers."

This tempts neoreactionaries to say to progressives

> "See, we are not like those horrible identitarians. We are like you progressives, smart and civilized"

Then the neoreactionary slobbers all over the progressive's boots like a puppy and rolls over like a puppy to expose his stomach. Then he pees himself in his excitement.

But, of course, neoreactionaries *are* identitarians, among other things.

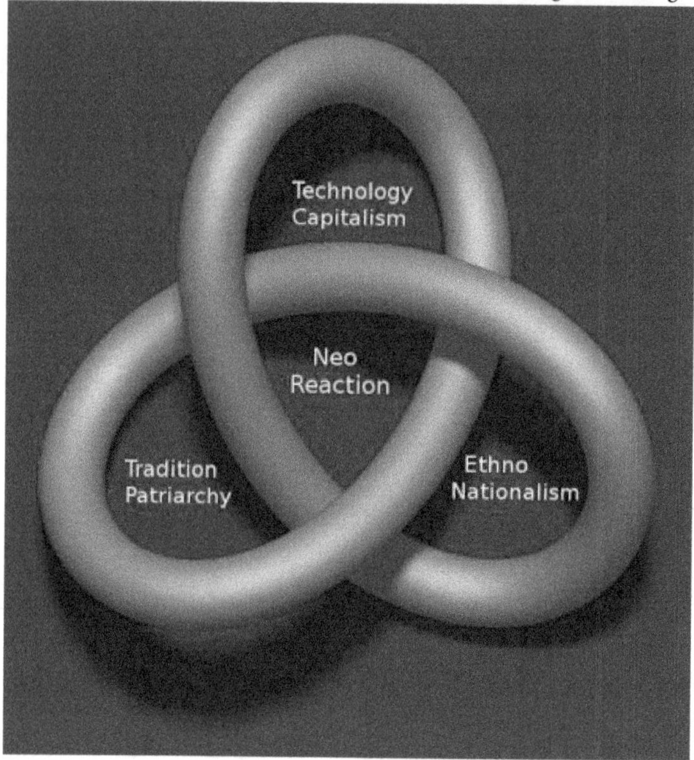


And to remind myself, and everyone else, that neoreactionaries are identitarians, I say that for the white race to survive, it has to reverse the emancipation of women, for we cannot have families if women are equal, and whites cannot reproduce successfully without male headed families, and that for the white race to survive, we must end universal suffrage, for universal suffrage gives politicians an overwhelming incentive to buy the cheapest possible votes, and the cheapest possible vote bank is to import an unproductive foreign alien underclass to live on crime and welfare to outvote and ethnically cleanse the natives.

And when any identitarian hears me say "for the white race to survive", he knows that I also am an identitarian.

## The reason that women need to be subordinated for successful reproduction

2014-10-25 06:25:23

Examining difference in fertility, it is clear that fertility is primarily controlled by female status relative to their husbands. The more women are subordinated, the higher the fertility. Japan is a good test case. Not only did fertility dramatically drop when General McArthur emancipated women[218], but in feudal Japan, fertility among high status families was below replacement when women were high status, indicated by upward mobility and room at the top. Later in the feudal era, when women were low status, fertility well above replacement, leading to a massive oversupply of elite children relative to available elite positions. It is difficult to assess Japanese feudal fertility exactly, but it seems to have been similar in patriarchal feudal Japan as it was in the immediate postwar period in patriarchal industrial Japan, the same laws leading to similar fertility in industrial and feudal Japan.

Modern contraceptive technology changes little, for we have always had infanticide, always had non reproductive sex, long had abortion. Early feudal era upper class Japanese women, late Spartan women, women of the upper classes of the Roman empire, and late Bronze age Egyptian women also had well below replacement fertility.

Societies with emancipated women do not reproduce very successfully.

Men want to have sex with as many women as possible, and give them no support.

Women want to have sex with the highest status men available (as women perceive male status, which is similar to the way a small evil child raised by cannibal head hunters perceives status) and be supported by men.

A prisoner's dilemma problem, the war of the sexes, ensues.

If both freely pursue their interests, we get a defect/defect equilibrium, where a small minority of men have casual no strings attached sex with the large majority of women. Women get the sex they want until they approach the end of their fertile years, but children don't get fathers. Since producing fatherless children places a large burden on women, women do not have children until used up on the cock carousel and approaching the end of their fertile years.

Both sides of the war are better off if a cooperate/cooperate equilibrium is coercively imposed. One could in principle have legal enforcement of the marriage contract, with women being severely unequal inside marriage, but equal (eg, no child support, no special privileges, freedom of association permitted) outside marriage. But a society in which women are equal is going to find it hard to uphold and protect marriage. Further, because women are not in reality equal, women cannot be equal in a society with freedom of association, because people will not want to associate with bastards, because most of the high status associations will choose to be male only, and so on and so forth.

To enforce a cooperate cooperate equilibrium, mating choice has to restricted, denying men access to women, and women access to men. Women have to be compelled to mate with their husbands, and forbidden to mate with anyone else.

Fertility is determined by the extent that we have a cooperate cooperate equilibrium starting early in a woman's fertile years.

A ship can have only one captain, and household only one head. If men and women equal, requires separation. If separation, one side or the other is denied the opportunity to invest in their children.

So, patriarchy. If men own women, except that they may not resell them, cruelly mistreat them, rent them out, abandon them, nor even allow them to rent themselves out,

---

[218]https://blog.reaction.la/economics/the-future-belongs-to-those-that-show-up/

then both men and women know who their children are and live with their children. The converse system, women owning men, would not work, because men would not know who their children were, would be denied the opportunity to invest in their children, and would therefore revolt.

It might be argued we have the converse system now, and yet men are not exactly revolting, but they are dropping out and refusing to participate. They will not support or protect women on current terms.

We have always had fertility control in the form of infanticide, and have fully adapted to it. We have had fertility control in the form of abortion for around three and half thousand years, and have substantially adapted to it. We have had condoms for long enough that men have evolved to dislike them and women are beginning to evolve to dislike them.

Children by previous lovers get in the way, hated by their mother's new lover, inconvenient to their mother. Such inconveniences are, as in fairy tales, apt to be eradicated. This is the most ancient fertility control solution. Tomcats notoriously apply it. Humans and cats are behaviorally adapted to optimal application of this solution.

With cryptic estrus and lengthy infancy, if males and females each freely pursue their biologically optimal strategy without regard to the interests of the people they mate with, very few will successfully reproduce, because almost all infants get infanticided. Prisoner's dilemma, defect defect equilibrium. Successful reproduction requires enforcement of the cooperate cooperate equilibrium.

In a species with cryptic estrus and lengthy infancy, women have to be subjugated for the species to successfully reproduce. Matriarchal societies did not vanish from history because conquered. They vanished from history for failure to reproduce.

In modern times, we are more civilized, and contracept children or abort them to avoid the embarrassment of mummy's latest boyfriend grabbing the child by its feet and smashing its head against the bedpost, but modern mummies have a strange tendency to acquiesce in such "accidents", when they discover just how much their former husband's children cramp their style. There is a very high rate of "accidents" among fatherless children.

If children go with the mother, Gnon demands future male lovers commit infanticide. Civilization avoids this bloody embarrassment with the delicately civilized abortion.

Cooperate cooperate equilibrium is that the man and the women are stuck with each other. He owns her, but does not own her in the sense that he can resell her to the highest bidder, nor punish her without cause or in ways likely to cause injury. There is an approximately equal distribution of women between the men, socialist rationing of women, and each man respects all other men's property rights in their women, with severe punishment for violators, the male who sleeps with another man's wife punished by law, the wife punished by her husband at her husband's discretion.

Under this circumstance, men can invest in their wives and children with confidence in paternity and without fear of losing them, without fear that any attempt to support them will result in them supporting their wife's bad boy lover instead.

In defect/defect, investment in children is inadvisable, for the woman will probably wind up a single mother, and a man a cuckold. Any children with her are likely by previous lovers, so should be mistreated or eradicated, and any children he might have with her are likely to be similarly mistreated by future lovers.

## Why women ruin everything

2014-10-28 09:01:00

Dalrock complaints that women ruin everything[219]. They want to enter male spaces and make the space feminine, as a power play, not out of any interest in the things of value in that male space, which they inevitably destroy.

This is a key issue in gamergate, where feminists demand that the games should be no fun and no one should play them.

Women want to rule, even though it makes them unhappy - it is a fitness test. They are looking for men that can defeat them, master them, and put them in their proper place.

Natural selection wants men to fight against subordinate status so that they will win. Natural selection wants women to fight against subordinate status so that they will lose only to worthy men and and thus get impregnated by those worthy men.

When women push their way into male spaces and then set about destroying those male spaces, they are looking for worthy men who will uphold the space and put them in their place. It is a fitness test. They hope to find the lord of this space who will not put up with a woman's nonsense.

What women really want is to be allowed into a male place on subordinate and unequal terms, to be allowed to speak only if spoken to, and any male wishing to speak the them has to get the permission of their owner first. They will fight like hell against this status, but if they win, they are unhappy, and if they lose, are happy. Women are like poorly behaved dogs. The dog will push to be leader of the pack, a job he can never perform, and does not really want. He wants a master to follow while making his master follow him.

A woman is like a badly behaved dog, a dog that will take his master for a walk, rather than the master taking the dog for a walk, but the dog is much happier when walked by his master, rather than walking his master, much happier with a firm master.

## Gamergate and corruption

2014-10-30 05:21:16

Gawker media's primary audience is nerds.

Their primary income comes from advertisers, who pay them to show ads to nerds. And this is what Gawker has to say about nerds.

Ultimately **GamerGate** is reaffirming what we've known to be true for decades: nerds should be constantly shamed and degraded into submission

Upon receiving a hostile reaction from their audience:

@hamiltonnolan @Based_Tet@**max_read** Max just told me I'm getting a raise because I made gamers cry

---

[219]https://dalrock.wordpress.com/2014/10/24/explaining-the-compulsion/

And, when the advertisers did not like that, that is nothing compared to what they said about advertisers.

> Intel is run by craven idiots. It employs pusillanimous morons. It lacks integrity. It folded to misogynists and bigots who objected to a woman who had done nothing more than write a piece claiming a place in the world of video games. And even when confronted with its own thoughtlessness and irresponsibility, it could not properly right its wrongs.

And, did I mention that Gawker is anticapitalist?

It is apparent that many of the writers attacking gamergate do not have skin in the game with their own publications. They are willing to burn their boss' companies and quite likely it will help their career. They'll keep riling up the mob because they think it means greater notoriety and promotions later on. The longer that they keep riling up the mob, the worse terms that they will get for the companies that they work for, but they are fine with that.

To bypass the first amendment, the government has been systematically installing political commissars in every company. This has the unintended effect that nominally private companies tend to wind up controlled by the state sponsored left.

In any nominally private organization controlled by the left, people get power and promotions not for actions that benefit shareholders, but for actions that benefit the left.

If shareholders lose control, the logical behavior then is to max out every company credit card and company line of credit, pile up everything moveable and take it to the pawnbroker, rip the copper wiring out of the walls, and set fire to company headquarters to collect the insurance.

Hollywood has long been controlled by the left, and by and large, for the most part there are no longer continuing corporations, Hollywood studios, that own production assets, have valued brand names, and regularly produce one movie after another. Rather, people usually get together case by case to produce a movie.

Surviving Hollywood corporations tend to be notoriously under attack for insufficient leftism, for example Disney, and often their movies contain subtle hints of less than total capitulation[220] But even they are tending to outsource their real production to off the radar contractors, while they stuff their nominal production departments with politicals, a process that ends in the company being eaten out by the politicals, and replaced by teams of contractors that come together contract by contract, project by project.

Tim Cook has not ripped the copper out the walls and set fire to Apple headquarters - not yet, but he has rather casually burned Apple's major asset - that it was the high quality, high status brand name, that its stuff just worked.

The modern world was created by the joint stock corporation with the CEO kept answerable to the shareholders by double entry accounting. When King Charles the Second let joint stock corporations off the leash they, in addition to pillaging the third world, used science to build technology, and the resulting technology enabled science, massively raising everyone's standard of living, including that of third worlders and even of slaves shipped from the third world to the first.

---

[220]https://blog.reaction.la/culture/the-snow-queen-and-frozen/

Sarbanes Oxley has destroyed double entry accounting, and politicizing corporations has disempowered the shareholders. In America and Europe, the social technology that brought us science and the industrial revolution is being dismantled.

The social technology that made the west wealthy and knowledgeable survives in Hong Kong and Singapore, and is spreading to China. It has been successfully transplanted to Dubai by their high IQ aristocracy (Some aristocracies eugenically breed themselves smart), and, surprisingly, is doing fine in Nigeria. (I conjecture that in Nigeria a hidden consortium of white and east asian capitalists bribe the government into doing the right thing, always a dangerous mode of existence since the government is always tempted to kill the goose that lays the golden eggs.)

Despite official truth that GDP per head is rising, everyone can see the reality that it is falling.[221]

## Race and species

### 2014-11-02 03:12:09

One of the many politically incorrect aspects of Darwinism is that races are the origin of species. There is no objective way of distinguishing a large race difference from a small species difference, any more than one can distinguish a large hill from a small mountain.

To say that two closely related kinds are two races of the same species, or two distinct species is a fact about scientific terminology, not a fact about the external world. As Lamarck argued, we draw sharp lines on a world that lacks sharp lines. For any two kinds, an intermediate kind likely exists, or once existed.

Everyone agrees that if two kinds are not interfertile, that they will not have sex, or cannot have sex, or if they have sex but no offspring ensues, then that is truly two species, not two races of the same species. But if we said that two kinds that can and will interbreed, given the opportunity, must belong to the same species, then we would be in a world with very few species. We would not only say that dogs and wolves are the same species, which most people would think pretty reasonable, but that wolves and coyotes are the same species, which is a bit of a stretch, and that lions and tigers are the same species, which is just silly.

Such a standard is also unworkable, because there is very commonly a kind in the middle, such that kind A is interfertile with kind B, and kind B interfertile with kind C, but kind A is not interfertile with kind C, in which case we would like to call all three kinds different species, since we obviously have to call A and C different species.

That blacks are the same species as whites is not a fact about human kinds, but rather the fact that Darwin declined to draw an arbitrary line through the Sahara, not a fact about human kinds but a fact about scientific nomenclature.

> We will first consider the arguments which may be advanced in favour of classing the races of man as distinct species, and then and then the arguments on the other side.
>
> ...

---

[221] https://www.ufblog.net/gloom-core/

The inferior vitality of mulattoes is spokenof in a trustworthy work as a well-known phenomenon; and this, although a differentconsideration from their lessened fertility, may perhaps be advanced as a proof of thespecific distinctness of the parent races.

...

Now if we reflect on the weighty argumentsabove given, for raising the races of man to the dignity of species, and the insuperabledifficulties on the other side in defining them, it seems that the term "sub-species"might here be used with propriety. But from long habit the term "race" will perhapsalways be employed.

...

Through the means just specified, aidedperhaps by others as yet undiscovered, man has been raised to his present state. Butsince he attained to the rank of manhood, he has diverged into distinct races, or as theymay be more fitly called, sub-species. Some of these, such as the Negro and European, areso distinct that, if specimens had been brought to a naturalist without any furtherinformation, they would undoubtedly have been considered by him as good and true species

Our naturalist would then perhaps turn t geographical distribution, and he would probabldeclare that those forms must be distinc species, which differ not only in appearance, butare fitted for hot, as well as damp or dry countries, and for the Artic regions. He mightappeal to the fact that no species in the group next to mannamely, the Quadrumana, can resist low temperature, or any considerable change of climate; and that the species which come nearestto man have never been reared to maturity, even under the temperate climate of Europe. He wouldbe deeply impressed with the fact, first noticed by Agassiz (7. 'Diversity of Origin of the HumanRaces,' in the 'Christian Examiner,' July 1850.), that the different races of man are distributed over the world in the same zoological provinces, as those inhabited by undoubtedly distinctspecies and genera of mammals. This is manifestly the case with the Australian, Mongolian, andNegro races of man; in a less well-marked manner with the Hottentots; but plainly with the Papuansand Malays, who are separated, as Mr.Wallace has shewn, by nearly the same line which divides thegreat Malayan and Australian zoological provinces. The Aborigines of America rangethroughout the Continent; and this at first appears opposed to the above rule, for most ofthe productions of the Southern and Northern halves differ widely: yet some few living forms,as the opossum, range from the one into the other, as did formerly some of the giganticEdentata. The Esquimaux, like other Arctic animals, extend round the whole polar regions. Itshould be observed that the amount of difference between the mammals of the several zoologicalprovinces does not correspond with the degree of separation between the latter; so that it canhardly be considered as an anomaly that the Negro differs more, and the American much less from theother races of man, than do the mammals of the African and American continents from the mammalsof the other provinces. Man, it may be added, does not appear to have aboriginally inhabitedany oceanic island; and in this respect, he resembles the other members of his class.

In determining whether the supposed varieties ofthe same kind of domestic animal should be ranked as such, or as specifically distinct, that is,whether any of them are descended from distinct wild species, every naturalist would lay muchstress on the fact of their external parasites being specifically distinct. All the more stresswould be laid on this fact, as it would be an exceptional one; for I am informed by Mr.Dennythat the most different kinds of dogs, fowls, and pigeons, in England, are infested by the same species of Pediculi or lice. Now Mr.A. Murray has carefully examined the Pediculi collected indifferent countries from the different races of man (8. 'Transactions of the Royal Society ofEdinburgh,' vol.xxii, 1861, p.567.); and he finds that they differ, not only in colour, butin the structure of their claws and limbs. In every case in which many specimens were obtained the differences were constant. The surgeon of a whaling ship in the Pacific assured me that whenthe Pediculi, with which some Sandwich Islanders on board swarmed, strayed on to the bodies of theEnglish sailors, they died in the course of three or four days. These Pediculi were darkercoloured, and appeared different from those proper to the natives of Chiloe in South America,of which he gave me specimens. These, again, appeared larger and much softer than Europeanlice. Mr.Murray procured four kinds from Africa, namely, from the Negroes of the Eastern andWestern coasts, from the Hottentots and Kaffirs; two kinds from the natives of Australia; two from North and two from South America. In these latter cases it may be presumed that the Pediculi camefrom natives inhabiting different districts. With insects slight structural differences, ifconstant, are generally esteemed of specific value: and the fact of the races of man beinginfested by parasites, which appear to be specifically distinct, might fairly be urged asan argument that the races themselves ought to be classed as distinct species.

All spotted owls are obviously the same race and same species. Californian spotted owls are no more a species than Californian blondes are a species.

Spotted owls differ from barred owls no more that whites differ from east Asians and, as with whites and east Asians, are connected by a cline. The environmentalists want to exterminate the cline, to make spotted owls and barred owls conform to a plausible species definition.

Similarly coyotes and wolves. The American government exterminated the cline for political reasons. Coyotes are pigmy wolves, and can freely interbreed with large wolves, and are fully interfertile.

Whites and East asians are fully interfertile.

Whites and blacks are interfertile, but *not* fully interfertile.

Whites and Australian mainland aboriginals are interfertile. We don't know if they

are fully interfertile, because by the time Australia was settled, it had already become politically incorrect to study such matters.

Whites and Tasmanian aboriginals were *not* interfertile. Tasmania was initially col-
onized by white males, and initially had zero single white women. Very large numbers
of Tasmanian aboriginal women were purchased or captured by lonely white males. A
fertile age Tasmanian woman cost about the same as a good dog. Not one mixed race
child ensued. Sex with white people was a substantial part of the reason that Tasmanian
aboriginals became extinct.

**[Correction some mixed race children did ensue. James Bonwick was there,
and wrote a book about it "The lost Tasmanian race." He tells us it was rare
for half caste children to be born "even under the most favorable circumstances",
indicating dramatically reduced, but non zero, fertility]**

All existing people who claim Tasmanian aboriginal ancestry and can plausibly trace it
to someone who looks plausibly nonwhite (a very small subset of those who claim Tasmanian aboriginal ancestry), trace it back to one woman who is obviously (from her photograph and the date at which she had children) a mainland aboriginal who came over with
the white colonists after the Tasmanian aboriginals became extinct. If Truganini was the
last Tasmanian aboriginal, and she was certainly the last person who looked Tasmanian,
the Tasmanian aboriginals became extinct without the birth of a single mixed race child,
despite massive fornication.

That Tasmanian aboriginals were the same species as ourselves is not a fact about scientific nomenclature, but a lie. And, if they cannot be classed as the same species, then
if we apply to humans the same standards as we apply to other groups of kinds, we also
have to categorize kinds that are comparably different as different species.

## tasmanian aboriginal skull

2014-11-02 13:18:05

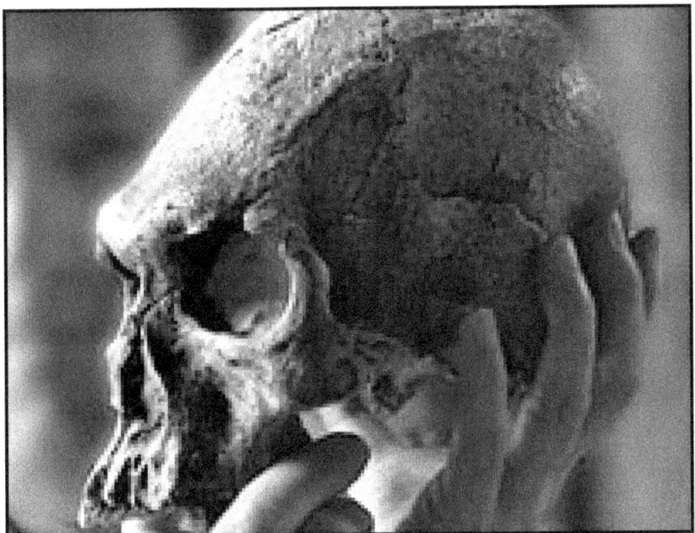

At least that is what the article says[222], though maybe they photographed a Neanderthal skull in error.

On the other hand, Erectus walks among us[223] gives an example of an almost equally primitive looking aboriginal skull, and suggests that our most recent common ancestor with the Australian aboriginals is not very recent.

[222] https://news.bbc.co.uk/2/hi/uk_news/england/oxfordshire/6647547.stm
[223] https://erectuswalksamongst.us/Chap27.html

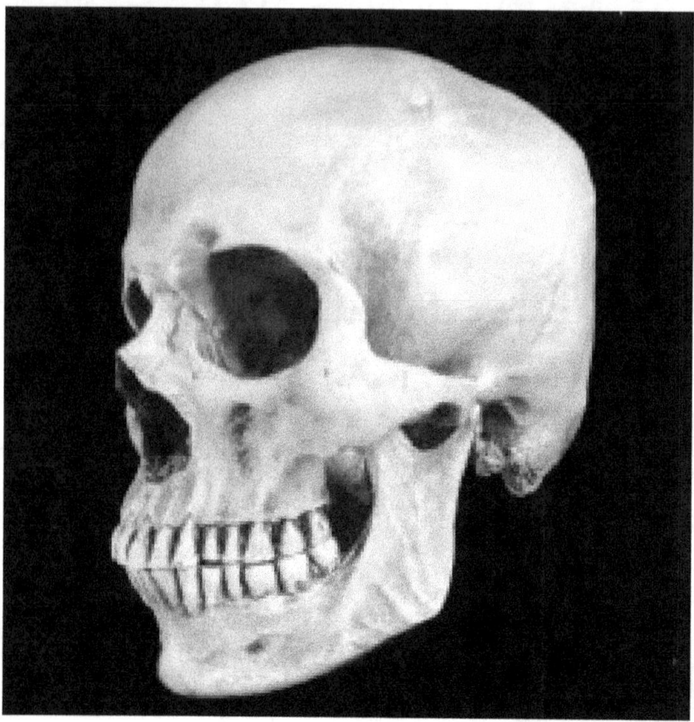

The difference seems to be at least as great, as the difference between a human skull and a Neanderthal skull, and the cranial capacity of the Neanderthal skull considerably greater. Observe the sloping brow and the ridges surrounding the eye sockets, very similar to what makes a Neanderthal skull Neanderthal. Indeed, I wonder if this is a Neanderthal skull somehow mislabeled.

If, as seems likely, Neanderthals had very limited interfertility with humans, we would, on the face of it, suspect that Tasmanians would have very limited interfertility than humans, assuming the skull to be correct, and, from cranial capacity, a substantially lower technological capacity than Neanderthals. In fact, however, Tasmanian technology was better than Neanderthal. Tasmanian art was about the same as Neanderthal art.

## Don't vote. It only encourages them

### 2014-11-03 20:09:25

You will undoubtedly hear that the election is nail bitingly close.

That is a lie. To sustain the illusion of a two party state, large numbers of Democrats are elected as republicans. They reliably vote Democrat whenever it matters. Observe, for example, the "bipartisan" budget passed by the supposedly Republican controlled house.

And what is the issue of the election? Once in a while Republicans point out that Obama is up to his armpits in foreign wars and losing, that the economy has been depressed and is sinking further under Democrat rule, that the streets are unsafe, that the young have no job prospects, that middle class means a hundred thousand dollars in college debt while working at starbucks, that Obamacare turns out to be unaffordable, and so on and so forth. So what are Democrats on about?

They have microtargeted campaigns for low information voters - women, homosexuals, blacks, and hispanics. But if you add up all the microtargets, their one issue is "We hate straight white males."

To which the Republican reply is "We hate straight white males too. In fact we hate them even more than you do." And sometimes, not very often, they add "But we also worry about losing wars and the economy sucks."

Before this election, the anti straight white male party had a majority. After this election, the anti straight white male party will have a bigger majority and more extreme policies.

And similarly for the election after that, and the one after that. You face a government that hates you, and every year it will hate you more. Hence the visibly second class citizenship for whites that we see on the streets, that the recent catcalling video inadvertently highlighted.

Yes, political competition continues, and will continue, but it is competition within the permanent majority party as to hates straight white males even more.

Politicians will use public money to buy votes. They naturally want to buy the cheapest votes, so democracy tends to universal franchise. But they still want cheaper votes, so create an underclass. Then they import an underclass. The final outcome, as in Ivory Coast, is that the former natives get ethnically cleansed with the help of UN troops.

No good person should vote in an election with universal franchise, as it is a declaration that he is equal to his inferiors. Since, in fact, he is not equal to his inferiors, he must therefore be oppressing them, and will be punished for that oppression. Strangely, he remains unequal. Obviously the punishment was not sufficiently severe.

That is what you have been getting for voting, and will continue to get for voting. You have been punished, you will be punished, and the punishments will grow progressively more severe. When you vote, you affirm that you are equal. Since, in practice, you are not equal, you affirm that you deserve the punishment that you will receive.

## Inner Party always wins

2014-11-05 20:30:51

The tea party, upon being elected, deems it impossible to repeal obamacare, despite the fact that it is unpopular, about to become more unpopular with startling price rises, and that it was quite popular to run against obamacare.

Meanwhile, in a move that has *absolutely no connection to obamacare*, we are seeing a movement to publicize sedative overdose as a peaceful happy death.

It generally is not. The dying person makes horrifying sounds that sound very much as if he is very aware that he is dying and has changed his mind very strongly about the issue. Peaceful death, in so far as any death can be called peaceful, is heavy morphine (or fentanyl, which has much the same effect as morphine), not heavy sedatives.

Further, with heavy morphine, the difficult moral issues go away. You give the patient a pain control clicker with no limit, or a very high limit. And if he should die, death by misadventure. Chances are it was accidental overdose, a common side effect of extreme pain control with self administered morphine in dying patients. Doctor did not kill him, and it is hard to tell if he killed himself. Probably he did not.

The great advantage of heavy sedatives from the point of view of the medical profession is that a heavily sedated patient is unable to protest being killed off. Hence the popular "suicide" method where the patient is heavily sedated, then has a plastic bag popped over his head, then a cord is tightened around the patient's neck. Sounds voluntary and peaceful, like Obamacare.

The great disadvantage of unlimited self administered morphine through an IV drip is that if pain control is successful, patient is likely to decide there is no hurry to commit suicide, and hang around occupying an expensive hospital bed for months or years.

Opiates control pain, and overdose will kill you. Sedatives control the patient, and overdose will kill you. If a patient is heavily sedated, cannot choose, therefore, not suicide but murder. Murder is a lot more effective at controlling health care costs.

## Emmet Till was not lynched, but he should have been.

2014-11-06 23:31:06

You tube video of white woman walking for ten hours through the vibrant part of town. Numerous catcalls and numerous menacing pickup attempts, 108 catcalls and crude and menacing pick up attemps, one every six minutes, all of them from vibrants.

You tube video of white woman walking for ten hours through the white part of town[224]. A few stares, mostly from vibrants, no catcalls, and two courteous pick up attempts, one every five hours.

## Silk Road 2.0 goes down

2014-11-08 05:33:02

"This hidden site has been seized"[225]

We are going to need a heavily decentralized solution, so that if a relatively small number of nodes get shut down or taken over by law enforcement, the network continues to function correctly, and, because no single node is central, no single node has traffic patterns that make it stand out.

The Tor hidden site system will always fail if a hidden site generates too much traffic for too long. We need a non Tor solution for publishing and curating reputations and performing transactions.

## Tim Cook "I am proud to be gay" spys on Mac users

2014-11-08 08:09:01

In the recent release of the Mac operating system:

---

[224]https://www.youtube.com/watch?v=kXdMAXaMicc
[225]https://www.forbes.com/sites/ryanmac/2014/11/06/silk-road-2-blake-benthall-fbi-shutdown/

If you set up an email that does not belong to Apple, the OS phones your email domain home to Apple to help them dox you.

No matter who you use a search provider, the browser reports your search strings to Apple

## Obama gets the finger

2014-11-12 01:25:23

How sweet it is. Hat tip Urban Future[226]

In the photo op for the Apec economic leaders meeting, hosted by China, they positioned Obama away from the leaders and with the wives and mistresses of leaders, they placed a tall man behind him to make him look short, and the man behind him gave him the three finger horns.

Also, while everyone else is wearing their polite photo op smiles, the man giving Obama the three fingers has a big genuine grin like a raccoon eating fishguts off a barbed wire fence.

And they titled the another photo featuring Putin and Obama "fiends and neighbors", implying that since Putin is a neighbor, Obama is a fiend.

Sweet!

Of course some might think this is mere pettiness, but on the contrary, it will take the wind out of the sails of the Umbrella Revolution without the risk of martyr creation that tanks might pose.

## The decline of Google

2014-11-15 01:37:28

Originally, Google was famous for hiring the very smartest engineers, and this was reflected in the superiority of its products. Originally, it looked as if Google's massive supercomputer was doing extraordinary things, that one would not expect of a mere computer.

---

[226]https://www.ufblog.net/diplomacy/

And the very smartest engineers were all male and mostly white, and those of them that were not white were east Asian.

As Google became more and more intimate with the government, and in particular the NSA, it found it necessary to affirmatively hire women. (I conjecture that they managed to persuade someone to count east Asians as minorities. Either that or they had lots of their white engineers declare themselves black or Hispanic, much as some of their male engineers have declared themselves female.)

And it found it necessary to fire anyone who openly doubted that affirmatively hiring women was a good idea.

These women tended to be excluded from the work of the real programmers, because they could not do it, could not understand it, and did not much like it.

Google had an elaborate system of metrics to try to measure how people and teams performed, and these metrics showed that the women were no good. Therefore the metrics were sexist, since they had disparate impact. They were replaced by non sexist metrics, which metrics showed that women are wonderful. Metrics that show advantage men are disparate impact. Metrics that show advantage women are just a reflection of the fact that women are wonderful.

Sexist males were laid off, where sexism was largely manifested by doing work that females could not understand or participate in. Which is to say, they laid off their smartest males, in part because smartness tends to exclude women, in part because the new metrics that showed that women are wonderful also showed that their smartest people were doing a really bad job.

Some time ago, Google tried to leverage its existing institutions for billing large numbers of advertisers, and paying large numbers of content providers to carry advertising, into Google Wallet, a competitor to PayPal and the like. This failed dismally, and they are now retreating from the field. Google maps has been getting steadily worse. Looks as if Google is now dominated by incompetent engineers who can no longer produce great products.

Thus dies Silicon Valley.

## No enemies to the left, no friends to the right

2014-11-17 00:50:03

Scott Alexander's blog used to be good, but now he has been terrorized out of politics. Therefore boring. The problem was he purged all frequent commentors to the right of him out of the comments, which means that he had only enemies in his comments. And, being the rightmost, was persecuted. He has stopped posting on politics, I assume as a result of this persecution.

Every so often I see someone reeling in shock and horror that we cannot possibly tolerate any connection with Person P, because they have some connection with person Q, who went to an event that was also attended by person Y, who has some connection with person Z, and, gasp, shock, horror, person Z has some connection with the "extreme" right.

Meanwhile posters, badges, and tee shirts of notorious communist mass murderers continue to sell well, and checking academic syllabi, one regularly reads questions of the form "explain why this noted communist mass murderer was amazingly wonderful, and why those whom he had eradicated were vile scum of the earth", which questions usually contain very clear hints as to exactly what the answer is supposed to be.

If one follows this policy, and one's friends and enemies also follow this policy, then one's enemies are one's friends and one's friends are one's enemies.

Thus the tea partiers and rinos quarrel for republican pre selection, but, once republican preselection is over, the tea party allies with the rinos, the rinos ally with the democrats, and the democrats ally with the foreign enemies of America. The right acts towards the left the way an abused woman acts towards her boyfriend. Hence the pattern of inner party and outer party. The permanent government is innermost, then then democrats, and the republicans are the outer party.

# Famous Barbie realism

## 2014-11-19 20:08:33

A commenter[227] draws my attention to the Barbie book I Can Be an Actress/I Can Be a Computer Engineer (Deluxe Pictureback[228], which appears to be directly and accurately based on the actual careers of real life affirmative action female engineers in the gaming industry. Barbie is off away in the the art harem, to keep her out the hair of the boys who do the actual programming.

I urge those of my readers with experience in the gaming industry to commend the book for imitating life so well and preparing girls for the reality of affirmative action careers in engineering.

Almost immediately after I posted this, the book was, unfortunately, suppressed, for giving entirely accurate information about female careers.

---

[227]https://blog.reaction.la/culture/the-decline-of-google/#comment-807554
[228]https://www.amazon.com/gp/product/0449816192/

## No Peak Oil

2014-11-21 05:58:24

If you ask what are total estimated reserves of some resource, and divide by the amount produced and consumed, the answer is usually about ten years or so - and has been about ten years for the last several thousand years, because people who look for resources look for resources that they intend to use in the near future, and if they find more than they can use in the near future, they forget about them or conceal them, for fear someone else will go after them.

# Religio

## 2014-11-23 03:00:04

I would like to revive the Roman word "Religio", as a word for the shared rituals and solemn pronunciations on virtue that bind a nation together, and symbolize people's trust in each other to do the expected thing, and a word for the suitably solemn and respectful observance of these rituals and pieties.

What we need is not religion, of which we have oversupply, some of them good but walking dead, some of them alive but disturbingly evil. What we need is Religio.

Thanksgiving, the fourth of July, and memorial day are good examples of American Religio: Japanese Shinto is the best example of Religio in the modern world.

Theoretically every Japanese believes that the emperor is a direct descendent of the Sun God. Of course they have not believed that for several hundred years, and yet at the same time, all of them believe it even today.

In Japanese movies, cartoons, comic strips, and video games, Shinto priests shoot down demons with lightning from their fingerprints. All other religions are depicted as corrupt, hypocritical, fraudulent, and rather silly. Buddhist monks are depicted as perverts, hypocrites, lechers and frauds. Christians are perverts and apt to ruthlessly engage in the most terrifying and shocking violence untroubled by the supposed pacifism of their religion. If Muslims are depicted at all, they are homicidally insane. If someone reads the Koran, he immediately concludes he is commanded to murder the main character. Christianity, as depicted in Japan, is pacifist, but Christians don't much care. Islam, to the extent that it is depicted at all, is insanely aggressive.

Japanese are solemnly respectful of Shinto shrines and Shinto priests. They have lots of festivals, in which young people solemnly participate in all sorts of activities as if they believed in all sorts of ancient, and rather silly, superstitions.

If we had a nominally Christian Religio, all our movies, television shows, comic strips and video games would cheerfully depict Rabbis in the scorching and inciendary manner that Jesus depicted them in Mathew 23:3-7, while they would depict Christians as noble doers of good in the manner that World of Warcraft got away with depicting "The Religion of Light" before the Social Justice Warriors hacked the testicles off the World of Warcraft developers and forced them to demonize "The Religion of Light" because of its suspicious resemblance to the Christianity of Charles the Hammer and the Song of Roland..

And we would do this even if Christianity was a dead religion, without any need to restore it to real life and vitality. Indeed, if today's Christianity is almost dead, the robotically animated corpse of a real religion, all the more convenient to celebrate the Christianity of Charles the Hammer. Children and teenagers would pretend to believe, in order to participate with their friends in the festivals, and their parents would pretend to believe, for their children.

But what of the risk of seemingly dead Christianity showing signs of life and mutating to greater virulence? Anglicanism around 1800 mutated from a state religion into a weapon to attack King George, the head of the Anglican Religion, and to undermine the aristocracy. Those advocating religious and sexual purity, which standards of purity were applied selectively against political enemies, should have been excommunicated for the heresy of phariseeism, but were not. I think this reflects the lack of private property rights in superior holiness. Shrines in Shinto tend to be family businesses, while Anglican Churches were captured by the most holy.

Shinto is nominally a private religion, and is showing tendencies to mutate to greater virulence as a result of competition between priests, but this is somewhat held in check by the fact that the valuable shrines are generally public/private, inherited in the family line, rather than being captured by the most holy. To operate a profitable Shinto operation, you need to inherit or purchase a suitably holy shrine, and to be suitably holy, needs to be suitably ancient, whereas in Christianity you can stick a cross on your barn, and claim it is as holy as any other Church. If you whip up your own Shinto Shrine, the authorities will ignore you, and you will have a hard row to hoe. It is working so far. Shinto is alive enough to give Japan cohesion, but we don't see too many Shinto priests denouncing the Japanese establishment for being insufficiently Shinto and condemning large numbers of Japanese to eternal damnation for being the wrong kind of Shinto. And when a Shinto priest does do that, he finds that despite Shinto theoretically no longer being the state religion, the state nonetheless finds ways to make life hard for him. Alas, the Emperor can no longer cast him out, but the Association of Shinto Shrines, which is scarcely distinguishable from the state, can de-recognize his shrine. It would be a lot more effective, however, if the emperor did it.

The Association of Shinto Shrines in practice protects the establishment from being attacked for insufficient holiness by weaponized religion, and also protects the property rights of existing priestly families to own their existing holiness, protecting them from competition from ambitious outsiders claiming superior holiness for their newly minted shrines.

To prevent Religio from becoming an empty dead husk, need a certain amount of religious competition to maintain religious vitality. But to prevent dangerously vital religion from seeking secular power and secular status, need an Archbishop and Grand Inquisitor to do what the Association of Shinto Shrines does. We need sufficient pious hypocrisy that the established religion cannot be used to attack the establishment, nor used to cast out some large part of the population as insufficiently holy.

Spandrel argues that a semi hereditary priesthood, or an official priesthood, a state manufactured religio, is likely to be insufficiently sincere, and will therefore be defeated by dangerously sincere outsiders.

It is only going to be defeated by dangerously sincere outsiders if you give the competition a fair go and a level playing field. Don't do that! Bribe the indolence of the clergy with ample privilege over the competition.

Japan shows how to do this right. Christianity in Japan is insignificant and probably shrinking in the same way as it is shrinking in the west, while Christianity in China is expanding in a way that terrifies the party and should terrify the party.

Communism is dead. In China a startlingly lively Christianity expands into the vacuum. China needs a state backed Confucian religio, and they have not got one. Christians in the west are for the most part merely progressives who are not quite up with the latest fashions. Christians in China are dangerously Christian. China is attempting to create a less threatening form of Christianity. In principle, this should be possible, since Christianity is quietist and other worldly, but they are doing it rather clumsily. Maybe they should try for a Christianity as infused with Confucianism, as Anglo Saxon Christianity was infused with paganism.

Japanese religio is today progressive and feminist, because MacArthur commanded it to be. Should international political conditions change, it could rather rapidly cease to be progressive and feminist.

Japan is sinking into crisis because of population collapse. It currently attempts to fix the problem with ever more extreme applications of Keynesianism. To really fix it, need to restore the pre MacArthur status of women. Japan's strong and cohesive religio is a tool that could do such a thing, though the will to apply this entirely functional and dangerously potent tool is absent, being discredited by the things the tool was applied for in the events leading up to World War II. I don't think Japan has the will to save itself, but it has the tools to do so, and these tools could be copied.

## Ferguson on fire. World to follow

### 2014-11-25 21:13:02

In her book "World on Fire"[229] Amy Chua surveys various market dominant minorites. Usually, sooner or later, they get exterminated or ethnically cleansed. Not always, and often it takes quite a while before the killing starts, but that is the way to bet.

Whites are now a market dominant majority, soon to become a market dominant minority, and when I turn on the television to hear about Ferguson, I hear the narrative explaining why we need to be exterminated or ethnically cleansed, and see the fires burning.

Once outvoted, self defense by whites will be deemed inherently offensive, as will any acquittal of a white defending himself, or any conviction of a colored person attacking a white. The next Ferguson after we lose the majority will be Kristallnacht.

White nationalists have this theory that once things get bad enough, whites will stiffen up. The Jewish reaction to Kristallnacht was to go limp, and, looking around the world, the whiter a country is, the more willing it is to resist massive colored immigration, and the less white the less willing. Similarly, the whites of Rhodesia and South Africa.

A very large proportion of whites, most of them single women, will vote for a Kristallnacht against whites, and by that time, most white women will be single.

---

[229]https://www.amazon.com/gp/product/0385721862

## New York Times tries to get Officer Wilson's pregnant wife murdered

2014-11-27 05:04:31

The New York Times is waging a terrorist war on the process of justice, to create a world where any white who defends himself against attack by non Asian minorities gets punished, and any non asian minority who attacks a white gets off.

And if you are Asian, in that world Gentle Giant Michael Brown gets to rough you up and take your stuff, and you have to smile and say you like it.

The New York Times published the full name of Officer Wilson's pregnant wife, and the name of the lane and suburb on which their house is located. They did not give their house number, but there are only twenty eight houses in that lane. Of course, officer Wilson and his pregnant wife have fled their house - but the problem remains, her full maiden name and employment has been published.

Darren Wilson of course has been threatened with death by the New Black Panthers, which of course will not get the black panthers into trouble with the Justice Department.

In an impressive display of brass balls, Gotnews has published the full names and addresses of the journalists trying to get Officer Wilson's pregnant wife murdered[230], and a photograph of one of them.

---

[230] https://gotnews.com/cant-publish-addresses-new-york-times-reporters/

These journalists seem to live a comfortable distance from the violence that they incite.

The two journalists who doxed Wilson's wife are:
Julie Bosman
Chicago, IL Cook County

Campbell Robertson
New Orleans, LA Orleans County.

Those are not particularly classy locations. Darren Wilson has a nicer house. (Or he used to, but it is no good to him now.) But they are safe locations. Not everyone gets to live in a safe suburb. Some people get to play the polar bear game as the polar bear. And that is what is making housing in the US so horribly expensive. If you want to have kids, need to buy a home somewhere safe. And every time the New York Times incites its pet blacks to violence, fewer places are safe. If you want kids, need a backyard. There just is not much land that is safe, so, a limited supply of backyards. So, fewer white kids. It is a slow motion genocide, to become a considerably faster motion genocide when whites become a minority.

## Koreans are allowed collective defense. Whites are not.

2014-11-29 23:40:25

With the permission of property owners, "Oath Keepers" took measures to prevent properties in Ferguson from being burned and looted.

Police, though unwilling to prevent arson and looting, shut them down.[231]

## Heroic entrepeneurship after the Restoration

2014-12-03 06:42:45

According to the Whig/Marxist version of history, the roots of the Industrial revolution were in the Glorious Revolution, which represented the rights of man and the rising political power of businessmen.

There are several problems with this story. One is that the rise of China decisively proves that the rights of corporations matter a whole lot more for economic development than the rights of man, and if you are looking for the origin of the rights of corporations, you are looking at the Restoration.

The other is that in practice, we are always ruled by priests and/or soldiers. The capitalist class is not the kind of entity that can rule. It is not really an entity, and capitalists, unlike soldiers and priests, find it hard to get together to form a single entity.

The modern world, technology, and industry, comes from science and technology. Technology comes not from scientists, but from Ayn Rand's heroic engineer scientist entrepreneur, who organizes other people's capital and other people's labor to give effect to his value creating innovations. Ayn Rand's heroic engineer chief executive officer has recently been exemplified by the heroes of Silicon Valley, though lately Silicon Valley seems to be switching, like the rest of the American economy, to crony capitalism, with engineers and scientists reduced to interchangeable insignificant menials, far away from where the important decisions are made, the important decisions being made on the revolving door between regulators and regulated.

So when did modernity start?

The most immediate effect of the Restoration on economic development was that King Charles the Second raised the status of science, setting off a status competition among gentlemen to be scientific. Science did not immediately produce practical results, except that Thomas Sydenham advanced the art of medicine, and made doctors somewhat less useless and dangerous, and Robert Hook advanced the art of making scientific instruments.

King Charles the Second also freed the joint stock corporation of inconvenient restraints, encouraging an environment where wealthy men, instead of managing their own investments, sponsored entrepreneurs.

Andrew Yarranton, before the Restoration of King Charles the second, was a capitalist on the older pattern. He personally invested his own money in equipment, employed people to make stuff, and sold it. During the civil war, politics dominated business, so he

---

[231] https://www.stltoday.com/news/local/crime-and-courts/article_f90b6edd-acf8-52e3-a020-3a78db286194.html

engaged in politics to acquire the property of Royalists, the equivalent of today's revolving door between regulators and regulated. Upon the Restoration, these past misdeeds, legal at the time, but suddenly highly illegal, got him in hot water, but he was soon released from prison, and resumed entrepreneurship - but now on the Silicon Valley / Ayn Rand pattern

Where previously he produced iron the way it had always been produced with his own capital and his own employees, now he discovered new and innovative ways to create value, spread knowledge of these new ideas, new technologies, in order that other men, what would now call angel investors, would provide him with capital to give effect to his innovations.

Before the Restoration, big business was the equivalent of today's revolving door between regulators and regulated, and that is where you found Andrew Yarranton. After the Restoration, you found him doing heroic innovative entrepreneurship, probably the first person in history to exemplify Ayn Rands' hero engineer CEO.

John Dwight was a scientist CEO, another example of Ayn Rand's heroic scientist entrepreneurs creating wealth through innovation. Before the Restoration, preachers ruled, religion was the important thing, religion and religious teachers had status and power, and John Dwight was busy with religion. After the Restoration, soldiers ruled over priests, religion lost status, science gained status, and he immediately switched to scientific entrepreneurship.

If we look at the great scientists that appeared shortly after the Restoration, they seem rather virtuous, other worldly, and out of contact with the everyday practical matters of life, love, politics, and people. The hero scientist entrepreneurs of the Restoration on the other hand, show a Bill Gates type eye for the main chance. Like today's Silicon Valley hero engineer CEO Bill Gates, they had a tendency to head straight for opportunity, trampling over anyone in the way, savagely elbowing anyone else heading for the same opportunity, grabbing opportunity with both hands, not letting go, and kicking and biting anyone who tried to take opportunity away from them.

While Ayn Rand generally depicts her hero engineer CEOs as noble and good in every way, and her looters as completely evil, degenerate, destructive, and self destructive in every way, she also depicts some hero entrepreneurs who switch between looting and heroic value creation as the environment permits, which seems to be more typical of actual hero entrepreneurs.

After these two, we see a steady stream of hero entrepreneurs, but these two are the first, and they switched to heroic entrepreneurship from other activities shortly after the Restoration.

The wealth of the modern world comes from innovations in value creation. Innovations in value creation come from heroic scientist engineer CEOs, and this type appears immediately after the Restoration, and continues to the present day.

## America number two

2014-12-06 01:14:08

"In recent years both the Chinese and American economies have been fundamentally transformed[232]."

In fourteen years, America went from three times the size of the Chinese economy to slightly smaller, and the rate of relative decline shows every sign of quite rapidly accelerating.

Chinese GPD per capita is still substantially lower than American GDP per capita, but the number of Chinese with middle class lifestyles is arguably larger than the number of Americans with middle class lifestyles, and will soon become a great deal larger.

## False rape fantasies

2014-12-06 04:14:15

Roissy proposes four possible motives for the UVA false rape accusation, of which sexual fantasizing is only one, the other three being political fantasizing.

Well, I suppose he is more expert at girls than I am, but it seems glaringly obvious to me that the UVA accusation was rape fantasy:

The story departs from realistic rape in numerous ways, and every departure is in the direction of female rape fantasies. That the students are high status fits political fantasies. The broken glass, and a whole pile of them sharing one girl, fits only female sex fantasies.

Men having sex with a girl amidst broken glass is an obvious female fantasy. Gang rape by absurdly many high status males is an obvious female fantasy. If I told you I had sex with the Swedish beach bikini volleyball team, would you believe me?

She is not raped by some random low status male, but by a whole team of the very highest status males in her social circle. Instead of being on the booty call rotation of one high status male with thirty other women, she has more than half a dozen of them all to herself.

And they are so frantically eager to rape her that they get down in the broken glass.

And they rape her for three hours, which works out at twenty two minutes per student. The typical university student is lighting a joint after a couple of minutes. The performance of these rapists tell me she has watched too many porn movies.

Now I can easily imagine that if the girl is in broken glass while being raped that might well make it more fun for the rapist, and more fun for her, but if the guy is in broken glass also - that is going to make it a lot more fun for her, but considerably less fun for him.

No highly attractive high status guy is going to share a girl with half a dozen other highly attractive high status guys, and if I was going to rape a girl for twenty minutes, would first turn on the light, get out a broom, and correctly position all the broken glass. In fact, if going to have sex for twenty minutes, going to do it on a comfortable bed, and find some other more precisely controllable fun way of inflicting fun amounts of pain, such as a spanking. Broken glass implies frantic eagerness, which frantic eagerness does not fit with twenty minutes per rapist, nor does frantic eagerness fit with high status

---

[232]https://pjmedia.com/instapundit/199240/

highly attractive guys having sex. The story in unreal in ways that provide the teller with the maximum sexual arousal.

Her being down in the broken glass makes sense if she is telling a political tale about cis heteronormative rape patriarchal oppression, but the oppressors being down in the broken glass only makes sense as getting her off sexually.

Obviously the reason this appeared in Rolling Stone rather than a slash fiction is political, not sexual - UVA wants to shut down the fraternities. But "Jackie", the woman that composed it, and continues to claim it is true[233], was enthusiastically beating her pussy while she composed it.

Fake rape accusations featuring real people ruin lives. The women that do this need to be destroyed. "Jackie" needs to be identified.

## Death of Christianity

### 2014-12-06 07:34:40

A woman running the Young Christian Activity Group is every bit as incompatible with Christianity as an openly gay bishop, and like gay bishops, results in most of the boys and all of the manly boys dropping out of their religion. People may tell themselves that Christianity can be compatible with progressivism, but each step to reconcile them empties the churches.

If you accept the progressive position on "marital rape", that sex requires the continuing consent of both parties, and reject the Christian position that consent to sex is given once and forever, and that for a married couple to abstain from sex requires continuing mutual consent or physical inability, then you pretty much have to accept the position that divorce is at a woman's whim, which is the end of marriage as traditionally understood.

Since the Church is the family writ large, an echo of the family between the earthly family headed by the father, and the divine fatherhood of god, abolishing marriage as traditionally understood ends Christianity. So, if Christians deviate from the New Testament on male authority and irrevocable consent to sex, Christianity ends, and it is apparent that it is ending.

Pagan morality differs from Christian morality because it is egoist. Attempts to revive paganism are fatally flawed in that they attempt to revive paganism with a universalist morality, a morality compatible with progressivism. The true pagan treats the loser as though he has an infectious disease. The pagan concept of virtue is barely distinguishable from the pagan concepts of strength in men, manliness in men, and femininity in women, if it can be distinguished at all.

Around 390 BC, Brennus, King of the Sennones, was negotiating with the Romans over their Etruscan intervention, an intervention suspiciously resembling conquest. The Romans murdered a Sennone diplomat sent by King Brennus. King Brennus sent some more diplomants. The Romans cut out their eyes.

---

[233]https://www.washingtonpost.com/local/education/u-va-fraternity-to-rebut-claims-of-gang-rape-in-rolling-stone/2014/12/05/5fa5f7d2-7c91-11e4-84d4-7c896b90abdc_story.html?postshare=221417802737104

The Sennones under King Brennus then marched on Rome. During the march his army purchased food supplies from the locals, rather than looting, raping, burning, and killing. The Romans fought the Sennones a short distance outside Rome. Their army was defeated and scattered, and the Sennones marched into the now undefended city. The Romans reformed on the Capitoline Hile, the oldest part of Rome, a wall within a wall. The Sennones looted and burned the rest of Rome. King Brennus demanded one thousand pounds of gold to leave Rome.

The Romans agreed, and Brennus set up a steelyard scale to weigh the gold. When they Romans arrived, they noticed that the weights were heavier than they should be, and complained the Sennones were cheating, to which King Brennus famously replied by throwing his sword on the scales and shouting, "Vae Victis!" which means, "Woe to the vanquished". So the Romans, having given King Brennus a thousand pounds of gold, had to go back to the Capitol for more gold. A steelyard scale has arms of unequal length, so they had to provide many times the weight of King Brennus' sword in gold.

Darwin, and Darwinian theory, predicts that social animals will evolve certain moral characteristics, to facilitate cooperation and avoid killing each other too often. Those conspecifics that Darwin thinks we should kill, and that Darwinian theory predicts that we will be inclined to kill, we call evil, and those that Darwin thinks we should prefer to associate with, and that Darwinian theory predicts that we will be inclined to prefer to associate with, we call good.

The resulting moral system has a fair resemblance to Randian enlightened egoism, Aristotlean ethics, and the moral principles expressed by Xenophon when justifying the conduct of the ten thousand.

Xenophon was an economist and a mercenary. He was one of a group of mercenaries assisting a Persian King, far from Greece. Their employer was killed. The officers of the Greeks were invited to a parley, to which they went hoping for further employment. Their officers were treacherously murdered. Xenophon then announced he had received a message from the Gods that they should elect new officers and get the hell out. The ten thousand slaughtered,looted and burned their way from Asia to Greece. Getting close to Greece, Xenophon was criticized for the trail of corpses the ten thousand had left across Asia.

To which Xenophon replied that they only slaughtered and looted when the locals tried to stop them from passing through, or denied them supplies, that when the locals provided a market, the ten thousand paid for their supplies.

A Darwinian should care about his offspring, and their offspring, and generally does, and therefore cares about the collapse of civilization.

Traditional Christianity would, and did, lead to the kind of society I advocate, in particular Restoration England. But traditional Christianity is dead, save for a remnant small as mustard seed, and shows no obvious signs of being more capable of revival than Greek paganism, though a Christian might reply that coming back from the dead is their specialty. Today's Christianity is progressive, at most trailing behind the official and orthodox progressivism by a few years.

It is probably true that a society needs religious or quasi religious underpinnings, needs a theocracy, or something functionally similar. I am a big admirer of Restoration

England, which founded the scientific revolution and the industrial revolution. But the Established Christianity of restoration England can no more be revived than the official paganism of republican Rome. Julian the apostate tried and failed to revive the old paganism, and got an undead religion.

Christianity contains the seeds of the leftism that devoured it, in its universalism, and in its sympathy for losers. The old paganism inherently had less tendency to head left.

## Islam lives, unfortunately

2014-12-09 07:41:33

Previously I remarked that Christianity is dead, save for a remnant small as a mustard seed, which is a problem, for civilizations tend to die with their animating religion. Europe was the faith, and the faith was Europe - then, later Anglicanism, while it was alive, gave us the scientific and industrial revolutions.

Islam seemed, for the most part, to be going the same way, devoured from withinby progressivism, which wears Islam like a demon dressing in a suit of human skin, but late it has been showing signs of life.

Islam, unlike Christianity, never sustained civilization. The so called Islamic golden age consisted of them conquering the Byzantine Greeks and the Indians, and not immediately strangling those civilizations. Islam's high civilization was Greeks gaining access to the work of the higher Indian races. The famous Damascus steel was actually Indian steel, and not long after they conquered India, the art of making it was lost, so those Damascus steel blades that so impressed the Crusaders were ancient heirlooms, the remnants of a fading civilization and races now lost or degenerate due to conquest.

I recently found a great deal of beautiful Islamic music. A religion that can produce such beauty, still lives. Unfortunately, if Islam conquers, the Anglo Saxon race is going to go the way of other once great races devoured by Dar al Islam. The victory of Islam is going to look a lot like Rotherham, and future Anglo Saxons a lot like today's Indians.

Progressivism, though a live religion, is too ugly, self hating and self destructive to survive any holy war. Rotherham is England..

The problem with these songs is that they are about dying for one's faith, rather than making the other guy die for his faith and then fucking his sister. Islam has a death wish.

## The vast majority of rape accusations are false

2014-12-14 03:18:30

When the media goes shopping for stories of innocent black victims shot by whites, whom do they come up with?

They come up with nine year old honors student Martin Trayvon and gentle giant Michael Brown, that is who, because in reality almost every black shot by a white was committing assault resulting from a recent or intended robbery.

And when they go shopping for stories of innocent women brutally raped, who do they come up with?

They come up with Crystal Mangum and Jackie Coakley. Crystal Mangum is a whore. Jackie Coakley will not stop when friendzoned.Crystal Mangum is a lying thieving drunken violent whore, who made up the Duke University rape story to talk her way out of an arrest for drunken violence after an industrious night of whoring. She is currently in jail for drunkenly murdering her boyfriend while drunkenly trying to steal his rent money. Maybe we really should take a look at the character of rape complainants, rather than the character of the accused.

Jackie Coakley was friendzoned by Randal. Naturally, being entitled to the boyfriend of her choice, she did not take that rejection lying down - well actually she seems to have done quite a lot of lying down but that is irrelevant to our story. She invented a fake boyfriend, using a picture of someone she had never met, to make Randal jealous. No reaction from Randal. After a while, Randal and friends come to doubt the existence of this relationship. Then she tells Randal and friends that her imaginary boyfriend has brutally raped her - which is potentially quite harsh for the real person on which her imaginary boyfriend is based. Randal and friends piously say they believe, possibly because you can get in big trouble for not believing, but everyone in her circle of friends and his circle of friends behaves as if she is complaining about flying saucer abductions. From time to time her story changes radically. Randal declines to give her the sexual comfort that she appears to be fishing for.

Erdley, the journalist responsible for numerous tales of rape, tells us that she goes around shopping for rape victims[234]. Everyone she comes up with is incredible, which tells us that credible victims are in mighty short supply.

Renda testifies to senate about rape on campus[235], in order to shut down fraternities and due process, so that any man can be convicted by any women, regardless of whether he has ever met her, without any examination of the credibility of the accusation.

Sabrina Rubin Erdely goes looking for rape cases to backup Renda's testimony

Meanwhile, on campus Jackie Coakley was friendzoned by Randal. Erdely comes sniffing around the campus looking for rape cases. And what she finds is Jackie Coakley - whose story, when told to Erdely, changes radically, changes to a remarkably good fit to Renda's senate testimony, with Jackie's story almost quoting Rendal.[236] Jackie Coakley has told numerous and incompatible stories about her supposed rape or rapes, all of them charging boys who either do not exist, or who had no relationship with her and were far away at the time.

If most rape accusations were real, if any significant proportion of rapes were real, would not Erdely have been able to find someone who had actually been raped?

Unjustified shootings of blacks by whites are so rare that they have trouble finding them, and so, when looking for a poster boy, black man shot by demonic white, come up with nine year old honors student Trayvon Martin and gentle giant Michael Brown.

And so it is with rape cases. They look for poor innocent girl ravished by brutal blondes, come up with Crystal Mangum and Jackie Coakley. Crystal Mangum is a whore. Jackie Coakley will not stop when friendzoned.

---

[234]https://gotnews.com/breaking-video-rollingstone-uvahoax-author-sabrinarubinerdely-absolutely-shop-victims/

[235]https://28sherman.blogspot.com.au/2014/12/jackies-story-echoed-emily-rendas.html

[236]https://28sherman.blogspot.com.au/2014/12/jackies-story-echoed-emily-rendas.html

## Ann Coulter on the false rape epidemic

2014-12-14 11:29:48

College must be difficult for white, straight coeds, because it's so hard to be a victim. You're not black, you're not gay, you don't have leprosy what can you do to acquire victim cool? Join the rape club![237]

## How to lose

2014-12-18 00:40:40

In the recent hostage crisis in Sydney the Jihadi killed one hostage, intending to kill them all, and then the manager of the shop attacked him, died fighting.

Some media are celebrating him, but most are not. In particular, in the memorial service, where one normally eulogizes the deceased, the eulogy neglected to mention that one of deceased died a hero, protecting his employees and customers.

## Peace is hard, war is easy

2014-12-22 09:31:44

For peace to continue, everyone has to play by the rules established in the last round of wars. Even if the rule is that the hegemon gets his way, he got to be hegemon by doing dreadful things, which tend to be forgotten or denied as time passes.

So there is always a temptation to bend the rules, which tend to get bent further and further, until one party responds to that bending with escalated violence, to which the other party responds with even more escalated violence. And people forget that this tends to get out of hand. They assume that if they escalate, the other party will have no alternative but to yield. And the other party, since so long has passed since the last all out general war, thinks the same.

People forget that the rules are maintained by the threat of general war, and become too clever by half at adjusting the rules in their own favor.

Europe's peace is based on rule by America. They are all muppet states and have been since World War II. America's peace is based on the fact that people still think the government is complying with the constitution, as radically re-interpreted after the civil war. But as speech gets suppressed ever more forcefully that illusion grows thinner. And so, in Ferguson, we see the state restraining whites so that blacks can attack them without being killed.

The president, who commands both the pentagon and the state department, keeps pentagon and state department from going to war with each other. For this to work, the pentagon must see the president as more than just a puppet of the state department.

If a government is cohesive, revolution is impossible, but war between governments all too likely. If a government is incohesive, war between elements of the government is likely, and, because of governmental weakness, war between the government and its citizens is likely.

---

[237]https://www.anncoulter.com/columns/2014-12-10.html

We are moving towards all three forms of war at roughly comparable speed. Hard to say which one will come first. Likely one will trigger the others. The proximate cause of the fall of the Soviet Union was that Reagan drew them into more wars than they could afford, but upon losing one external war, it suddenly became apparent that no one believed in communism any more, and a wave of collapse spread from Afghanistan to Moscow.

The Pax Americana draws to an end, the American government becomes weaker internally and externally, at the same time as it acts more aggressively than ever, internally and externally. This does not mean war tomorrow, perhaps it might mean war in a decade. But it does mean war eventually. Perhaps external war and external defeat will result in economic collapse which will result in internal war. Perhaps internal war will result in external war and external defeat. The general trend in the US empire is that the restraints against all forms of war, external war, intrastate war between elements of the state apparatus, and revolutionary war with subjects of the state, are diminishing, and the provocations are increasing.

There is a great deal of ruin in a nation. This trend has been going on for a very long time without anything remarkable happening, and it could go on for a very long time further without any very remarkable results. But in the end ...

In November 2005 I thought the financial crisis would blow up immediately, or within a few months. Instead, the superficial appearance of financial normality was maintained for two years, as underneath things became more and more abnormal. But in the end, the appearance of normality collapsed.

There will be war.

## Against Scott Alexander

### 2014-12-24 00:42:03

I don't read Scott any more, largely because him being more timid than he used to be, and his blog comments more piously censored, he is boring.

But another reason is that he is a fount of misinformation.

Scott Alexander sounds very reasonable because he is giving the current official Minitrue version, against the crazy radical left version.

Trouble is, today's Minitrue version *is* yesterday's crazy radical left version.

Scott Alexander will tell you "Studies show", and link to all sorts of interesting studies. Trouble is these studies come from Minitrue, and if someone in the comments notices that these studies contradict common sense and the everyday evidence of the senses, that comment will be deleted.

For example, Scott Alexander believes in Catastrophic Anthropogenic Global Warming because "studies show". Of course it was obvious from the beginning that these studies were just Minitrue propaganda, and in due course we got the climate gate files, which contain memos strikingly resembling those that Winston Smith received from Minitrue. But the climategate files has not shaken Scott's faith, and should the comments on the blog cast doubt on his most holy faith, will be deleted.

Similarly Scott argues that UVA and Duke university rape cases is not evidence of a vast number of false rape allegations, because obviously the kind of rape allegations that social justice warriors are going to make a big deal out of are atypically likely to be false.

Well, I went looking for rape cases of black college athletes raping white college girls, the opposite of the cases that social justice warriors make a big deal out of, and found them to be suspiciously non rapey. If some of them were genuine, you would expect some of them to be unambiguously rapey. So I conclude that the reason that Social Justice Warriors cannot find any genuine college rapes is that they almost all false.

In my own experience, I have never met a girl I know or plausibly suspect to have been raped. I have known lots of girls who repeatedly went back to men who beat them in an uncontrolled and careless fashion, causing injuries.

One girl visited America and stayed with me for a short while, but wanted to explore America on her own. I told her there were parts of America that were extremely dangerous for an unaccompanied white woman, so we got out a map, and I marked the dangerous parts of the bay area. An in particular, and especially, I drew attention to East Palo Alto, then the murder capital of America. If you go there, I told her, you will probably be robbed and raped, and quite likely murdered. She promised me she would definitely not go there, though I was already getting suspicious.

So I take her to the train station, and off she goes. A few hours later, I get a call that there is a white girl in an East Palo Alto Mcdonalds who has lost all her stuff, and needs me to come and get her.

So, from personal experience, I would say that even when alarming levels of violence are applied by strangers, that is weak evidence that a woman was raped. And somehow, strangely, very few rapes seem to involve actual violence. The Sharia rules on deciding what is rape and what is fornication or adultery seem to me to be pretty much correct and based on a realistic understanding of human nature, apart, of course, from the rule against the testimony of infidels.

Scott believes Global Warming, Scott believes that women tell the truth, and Scott believes that "studies show". So those are good reasons to not read Scott any more. You should expose yourself to sources that disagree with you, but not to sources that authoritatively endorse plausible sounding lies.

## Post rationalism

### 2014-12-26 19:44:22

Christianity was the basis of European civilization, and now it is dead save for a remnant smaller than mustard seed. Civilizations die with their animating religion, being devoured by demons.

Progressivism wears the religions it has devoured like a monster that dresses itself in the skins of people it has eaten. It has consumed Judaism, Christianity[238], and most of Islam, though the worst and most harmful religion, Islam, still lives and is fighting back[239]. The martial Christianity of Charles the Hammer would serve our civilization well. The

---

[238] https://blog.reaction.la/culture/death-of-christianity/ "Death of Christianity"
[239] https://blog.reaction.la/culture/islam-lives-unfortunately/ "Islam lives, unfortunately"

pragmatic, realistic, and cynical Christianity of restoration Anglicanism would serve our civilization very well, though it proved vulnerable to people whose beliefs were dangerously sincere, being reluctant to martyr them properly for reasons of mere pragmatism. Counter Reformation Catholicism would serve our civilization well. But none of these live, and their revival is unlikely.

More Right proposes a solution[240]: The universe is dead, but we live. The universe does not know good or evil, but we know good and evil. Therefore, let us write our religion upon ourselves, rather than upon the sky.

Tradition is the accumulated experience of our ancestors. We should conduct ourselves as if, on death, one goes to the hall of one's ancestors, and they pass judgment upon our life. One can have ancestor worship without taking the proposition that our ancestors are literally still around too seriously.

It would be better if we could revive Christianity - that being the religion of our ancestors, but that looks difficult, and every day looks harder.

## The Trichotomy

2014-12-31 06:16:43

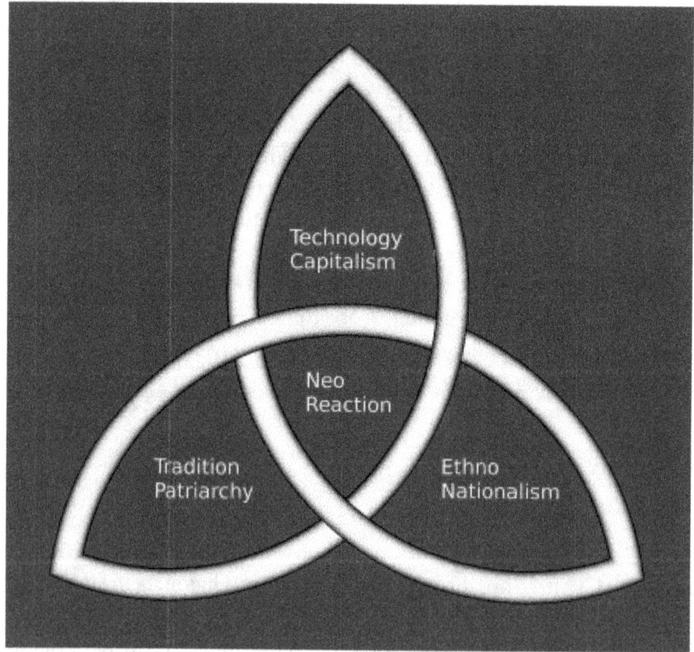


The last time I posted this[241], people did not like the trefoil graphic, and proposed the triquetra, which has the handy property of symbolizing both Odinism and Christianity. So here is the improved graphic.

---

[240] https://www.moreright.net/postrat-religion/
[241] https://blog.reaction.la/tag/trichotomy/

We need capitalism, because we need wealth and technology, we need patriarchy and tradition, to uphold the enforcement of the marital contract without which our population will disappear, and to keep ethnonationalism in line to prevent ethnonationalism from devouring capitalism with socialism and demotism, and we need ethnonationalism to prevent outsiders from devouring our society and our capitalism with it.

## White on black crime

### 2015-01-05 05:03:25

### White on black crime:

This site: [242] has an open invitation to the SPLC to tell them all about white on black crime, to be fair and balanced with their (horrific) black on white page.

They get about one white killing a year of a black man not engaged in a felony.

According to the FBI, in 2011, 193 black men were murdered by whites.

But if these were actual murder type murders, should we not expect rather more of the victims to be not engaged in a felony at the time they were killed?

So, just as we see statistical evidence suggesting that the vast majority of rape convictions reflect false rape accusations, we see statistical evidence that the vast majority of convictions of whites for killing blacks reflect self defense.

Our laws should reflect this. Just as Sharia law on rape rightly starts with a very strong presumption that a rape accusation is false, which presumption can only be rebutted by very strong evidence, we should similarly presuppose that white versus black conflicts reflect white self defense, which presumption should only be rebuttable by very strong evidence.

There is ample legal precedent in our system for loading the scales against certain groups, when the group presumed guilty is heterosexual white males. For example VAWA, the violence against women act, presupposes that in any conflict between a man and a women, the man is always guilty. The pattern of convictions of whites for killing blacks suggests we need a violence against whites act.

## The solution to Jihad

### 2015-01-12 00:14:15

Progressivism is universalist. Islam is universalist. Holy war necessarily ensues. To call on Muslims to abandon Jihad is to call upon them to unilaterally surrender to progressivism.

We faced this problem once before, and solved it once before by means short of genocide. The solution is to impose the Peace of Westphalia, first on ourselves, then on Muslims.

Peace of Westphalia implies that Muslims resident in our lands are forcibly converted to our official belief system, or else are forced to get the hell out. Our official belief system, to prevent entryism backed by violence aiming at state domination, must necessarily

---

[242]https://topconservativenews.com/2014/12/challenge-name-a-white-on-black-murder-occurring-in-the-past-year/

absolutely exclude the proposition that Mohammed is God's prophet, let alone his final prophet,

## Sex and natural law

### 2015-01-12 07:10:44

When it comes to ordinary crime, for example mugging and burglary, natural law is obvious:

What is crime?

Crime is bad actions that are apt to be met by physical violence, socially approved physical violence.

What is law?

Law is social approval for violence against certain kinds of bad actions.

If you see a conflict between someone who is mugged, and someone who is mugging, you will naturally support the victim and oppose the aggressor, because the aggressor might aggress against you, so, natural law. It is natural for everyone to support violence against certain kinds of acts, so those acts are naturally crimes, and violence against those acts is naturally law.

If the state goes with the grain, making illegal those things that are naturally crimes, and not making illegal those things that are not naturally crimes, order is easy. If it runs against the grain, the state creates disorder.

However, when Catholics talk about natural law, they are generally not talking about this obvious, uncontroversial, and straightforward natural law, natural law relating to uncomplicated crime, but about sex.

And the rules on sex are a lot more socially contingent that the rules on violence. It all depends. Which is not to say that progressives can make up any rules they feel like and expect them to work, so in that sense, there is natural law on sex, but in that what is natural depends a lot on socially constructed circumstances, there is no natural law on sex.

What is natural is feral behavior. Natural law is those restraints that are natural to impose on feral behavior - we are disinclined to tolerate predation on people like ourselves, or parasitism on people like ourselves.

Feral female behavior is hypergamy. Women unrestrained by male authority will sleep with the top few percent of men, which means that those men at the top are disinclined to be fathers to their children, and the rest of the males have no children. Such a society is dysfunctional because the males are disinclined to work, to fight in defense of their society or its women or children, or to transmit their culture to the children. Idle hands lead to widespread criminal behavior among the males.

Such a society is indeed natural, but lacks laws on sex.

Now let us imagine a society with strong families, and little or no welfare for bastards. Such a society is not a necessary product of natural law. Rather it requires the patriarchs to agree together to support each other's familial authority. While the lack of welfare is natural, (welfare needs to be socially constructed) strong families are not natural. Strong families need to be socially constructed.

But, given strong families, the patriarchs will wind up carrying a large party of the externalities of feral female sexual conduct. So, naturally, they simply will not allow feral female sexual conduct. Thus, in such a society, severe restraints on female sexual conduct and a strong guiding hand on female sexual choice (only approved suitors allowed, dads, not cads) are indeed natural - natural law, given the not all natural social construction of patriarchal familial authority.

The Roman Catholic "natural law" on sex is only natural for a society with strong families, where contraception is ugly and unpleasant, where abortion is dangerous, and, most importantly, where maternity is a matter of fact, but paternity is a matter of opinion.

The Roman Catholic Church, however, was at the forefront of undermining strong families, sawing off the branch on which they sat. The original Roman marriage, on which Christian marriage is based, was contract between the bride, the groom, and the patriarchs of the families, wherein if the bride or the groom broke his vows, he was not only breaking his oath to his spouse, but to his father. The Christian Church, and in particular and especially the Roman Catholic church, progressively erased the role of the family in the marriage, making it a contract between the bride, the groom, and God, with the parents of the bride and groom merely passive onlookers. In this sense, Christianity has been leftism for a very long time. That the heretical spawn of Christianity disowned first Jesus, then God, was a consequence of that leftism.

Successful past societies took extraordinarily drastic measures to ensure certainty of paternity. In this sense, certainty of paternity is socially constructed, and you need paternal certainty for strong families. Today, however, paternity is as much a matter of fact as maternity, a change that should lead to social changes more drastic than those of the contraceptive pill, but as yet, those changes are suspended, held at bay by a government hostile to fatherhood, that wants women married to the state, and married to their job, rather than married to husbands. Routine paternity testing is socially and legally discouraged, and the law ignores actual paternity for supposed social paternity, treating paternity a matter of opinion, which legal policy is running headfirst into reality. Males care very much about actual paternity, and if it differs from social paternity, are apt to get upset, often homicidally so. One suppose that since paternal certainty was not available in the ancestral environment, males would only care about social paternity, but evidently humans have understood the connection between sex and reproduction for long enough to select for males who care about actual paternity - the latest technologies are a very large change in degree, but not a change in kind.

We can today have the kind of society that past people's had without the need for as much tight control on females, because we can know who the father is without keeping wives entirely locked up and putting them in chadors. So the natural outcome of this improved technology is return to patriarchy, where fathers are entitled to be fathers, and women are forbidden to have children by more than one father - because today it is easier to enforce a prohibition on women having children by more than one father.

Sexual behavior is apt to be subject to very strong selection effects, resulting in remarkably rapid evolution. Condoms are the oldest form of contraception, and evidently in the short time they have existed, many males have evolved to loath them, so it probably did not take very long after humans learning the connection between sex and reproduction, for males to evolve to care about actual paternity.

And, since we now can quite reliably determine actual paternity, this really should show up in society's laws and social expectations, but as yet, it does not.

In today's society, there is nothing natural about Roman Catholic Natural Law.

We have, instead, the natural outcome of unrestrained female hypergamy, a mating system that is primarily lek based. Because of technological changes, Roman Catholic natural law can never be natural again, but we nonetheless have to socially construct institutions that stop female hypergamy and artificially and unnaturally impose monogamy on females.

Obviously, women only have as much power as men permit. The solution is to allow those males that likely have the best interests of the women at heart, husbands and fathers, to exercise that power that is the natural result of male characteristics, and require outsiders to butt out, which requires males to respect each other's property rights in females. Rules on chastity and fidelity are then results of the natural law of property.

The Pauline concept of marriage as contractual imposes obligations on both parties to a marriage. From the natural law of contract, a marriage contracted for the purpose of children is necessarily durable. Neither party can cease to perform the duties of the marriage even if they are not feeling like it. And neither party can employ contraception or abortion or withhold reproductive sex except by the permission of the other.

Modern technology makes it possible to extend adolescence until a woman starts to run out of eggs. This outcome is undesirable, but there is no specific identifiable individual who has an interest in stopping it, except the father, so difficult to deem it illegal if the father permits it.

Rules for the transfer of authority from fathers to husbands are necessarily socially constructed, and not particularly natural. Obviously it is better for society and the family if a woman is under the authority of the man she is having sex with, rather than her father, so the laws should favor that first transfer of authority, and disfavor any subsequent transfer of authority.

A common eighteenth century system was transfer by elopement or patriarchal authority - the girl could transfer herself from the authority of her father to some man, or the father could transfer her. However, marriage without female consent means we don't get all that good Pauline natural law of marriage, for that comes from the natural law of contract. So, a common eighteenth century system was the waltz, where a daughter was socially required by her parents to engage in sexy dancing with a parentally selected male. Which sexy dancing was very apt to lead to sex, which was deemed consent to marriage. So, marriage by forcefully manipulated consent. The only way to end parental authority was though female choice - which is, on the face of it, a dangerous system, since females notoriously are apt to make bad choices. But parents could, and did, apply a forceful thumb on the scales.

I have elsewhere argued for marriage without consent, in which fathers simply assign their daughters as seems best to them, and, in the event of the fatherless, the state acts, after the fashion of the early days in Australia. This is probably necessary when you have a very badly behaved female population, when one is arbitrarily and artificially creating family structures in a society where they have been entirely destroyed, which was the situation that the early Australian state found itself in. Probably the best system is that marriage by manipulated consent is normal and normative, with the possibility of backing it up by shotgun marriage in the event of demonstrated bad behavior, such as, for example, pregnancy.

## The elephant in the living room

2015-01-16 09:11:09

The Chinese look at America and see the glaringly obvious that Americans cannot see Chinese advice to Chinese visitors to America[243]

> "11. Show Humility to Ladies—They're In Charge
>
> "In public, the Americans show particular respect for women. Everywhere is "Ladies First." In social situations, men must show humility to ladies. Men must walk on the outside of the sidewalk, let the woman sit first, open the door for a woman, move out of the way on the stairs or in the elevator to let the woman advance, let women order first at a meal, and let the woman get up to leave first. And when you greet a woman, you must stand up."

Despite the strident propaganda about white privilege and male privilege, the reality is perfectly obvious to outsiders:

In the streets, blacks and women act like aristocrats, white males act servile, like peasants. Blacks take up a lot more space than they did twenty five years ago, and are louder. Women casually interrupt anyone, including their boss, and talk right over him.

When I say that fertile age women are sex obsessed, I don't mean that they think about the sexual act itself as much as men do. If you skim through a romance novel, there are nine hundred pages where the male love interest demonstrates how aloof and alpha he is, a hundred pages where he breaks down, gets weepy, and shows his soft inner core of twu luving betaness, and one page where he tears the lady's clothes off with his teeth and the couple finally at long last get some action. As men understand sex obsession, women are not sex obsessed.

The female equivalent of the male executive groping his secretary's ass is the female executive shit testing the CEO. And observe. Female executives shit test their superiors all the time, paying very little attention to the menial drudgery of merely running the business. In this sense, women at work are seriously sex obsessed.

In this sense, it is sex all the time, work very little of the time. The company is boyfriend and family.

For girls, shit testing men is like men looking at girls boobs. Women want to go into engineering to shit test men. Men want to go into engineering because as little boys they loved toy trucks and video games. Girls go sex crazy at ten and stay sex crazy till menopause.

When the boss talks to a male executive, it is about how to get production up and costs down. When the boss talks to a female executive, she demands that he inflate her

---

[243]https://www.freerepublic.com/focus/f-chat/3136003/posts

self esteem, or else she is going to charge rape, sexual harassment, and discrimination. If the boss passes the shit test, puncturing her self esteem, he will get laid like a rug, but the company may be put out of business. If he fails the shit test by inflating her self esteem, gets no sex, but the company survives. Men want to become executives so that they can tell other men what to do. Women want to become executives so that they can shit test the hell out of the CEO. If your boss is a woman, she is much more comfortable if you don't really give her decisions.

Just listen to the conversation between a youngish female executive and her male superior. It is all shit test, all the time. She demands he inflate her self esteem. Work concerns cannot get in sideways. It is a romance novel with the company as boyfriend. In place of the normal transition, puberty swiftly followed by romance and marriage, puberty is instead followed by the job, but they act like the job is romance and marriage, rather than production of value. Used to be that women did not directly enter the male economy except as a producer within a family unit. They still don't really enter the male economy, just go through the motions, but with the company playing the role of the family unit.

When the boss talks to a male executive, he tells him what he wants to tell him, and asks him what he wants to know. When he talks to a female executive, acts terrified. His words to his supposed subordinate are flattery, appeasement, and endless peace offerings, for which he receives no peace, like a courtier speaking to an oriental despot who might remove his head at any moment for any reason or no reason at all. Which is why, despite hypergamy, you are apt to get more action than your boss does.

Feminizing the workplace usually does not result in turning it into a sultan's harem, alas, turns it into a soap opera and a romance novel, one thousand pages of drama for one page of ripping her clothes off with your teeth. More work would get done if it did turn into a sultan's harem.

Feminism is driven by sex. They are always talking about rape and sexual harassment because they are always thinking about sex. They are not thinking about careers in engineering because they like the C language, but because the boys in engineering have a status hierarchy in which girls are at the bottom, so they want to shit test those boys by demanding equal, indeed superior, status.

## Forget about cultural marxism

2015-01-21 21:26:23

Today's left is, in substantial part Cultural Marxism from the Frankfurt School. Should you conclude that the Frankfurt School is really really important?

If you conclude that Cultural Marxism is really really important and rules the world, it follows that Jews rule the world. Hard to prove they don't. It also follows that leftism was just fine and democracy was just fine all the way up to and including the New Deal, and if we could revive the New Deal coalition and get rid of the Jews everything would be lovely.

If you believe that the Cultural Marxism is the problem rather than a problem, it follows that getting rid of Jews would solve the problem. Hard to prove that getting rid of Jews would not solve the problem. In the course of my many arguments with my Jewish commenter B, I have endorsed pretty much everything that /pol/ and Steve Sailer says about Jews, other than that they rule the world and are responsible for every bad thing everywhere that ever happened anywhere. And B has mostly agreed, because we both agree that reform Jews are a problem, though not the problem, and Orthodox Jews have resisted the rot better than most. We just disagree as to what extent Orthodox Jews have resisted the rot, and to what extent they will continue to resist the rot.

But it is pretty easy to prove that democracy was not just fine and the New Deal was not just fine.

From the day that Cromwell cracked down on those to his left in 1653, the predecessors of today's regnant left were fleeing, or being expelled, to America, and, in America, were plotting to conquer America, reconquer England, and conquer the world. To this end, they founded Harvard, which was from the beginning the center of their conspiracy. And none of them were Jews.

As they became increasingly successful, obtained worldly power, they increasingly came to compete with each other for superior holiness, each holier than each of the others. And pretty soon became holier than Jesus. Being holier than Jesus, swiftly became unitarians, then atheists, then extremely militant atheists hostile to the parent religion from which their heresy sprung.

It was not the Jews that gave us prohibition, female emancipation, and the war between the states, though they eagerly attached themselves to those movements once those movements had already succeeded.

British Imperialism was an anti colonialist movement, the disastrous predecessor of today's even more disastrous anti colonialism, and as one can trace modern leftism back through super protestantism to the prohibitionists and the emancipators, one can trace modern anti colonialism through the London School of Economics to British imperialism. In the 1830s or thereabouts, the British government gradually came to notice that the colonialists had conquered an empire. The colonialists were initially merchant adventurers, meaning they engaged in a bit of trade and a bit of piracy, were initially mobile bandits. Being successful mobile bandits, they had, without anyone quite noticing, transitioned to being successful stationary bandits. They had come to rule, and rule well. The British government decided to shoulder the white man's burden, to rule for the greater good of the poor victimized natives who were being oppressed by these evil piratical colonialist bandits. The result was, unsurprisingly, extremely bad, and every failure convinced them to double down, which doubling down continued almost to the present day, until finally the Chinese started to step into the vacuum the anti colonialists had created. The Chinese have fixed Nigeria, and throughout Africa are remedying the destruction and horror that the anti colonialists created when they drove the colonialists out.

You are not going to be able to make any sense of Africa if you fixate on Cultural Marxism and the Frankfurt School.

The sexual revolution did not begin in the sixties. Rather, that was recovery after a retreat during the war and postwar period, during which the left had focused on the proletariat rather than female emancipation, an unsuccessful attempt to move towards socialism, an attempt that was largely the result of Jewish influence. This failed effort to move left towards command socialism gave breathing room for marriage to make a partial and temporary recovery. It gave the left something to do other than double down on destroying marriage. The sexual revolution began in Victorian times. And you cannot blame the Jews for either Victorian original, or its sixties rebirth.

If you want to blame Jews for the sixties sexual revolution, you are going to focus on Margaret Meade's mentor. But Margaret Meade herself was the protestant descended left, and we can tell who had the power by whom Margaret Meade fucked. She was the protestant descended left, by blood, by culture and by upbringing descended from the prohibitionists and the emancipationists, and was fucking the protestant descended left.

The eighteenth century view of women was that they were the uncontrollably lustful sex, that given half a chance they would crawl nine miles over broken glass to have sex with their demon lover. In the Victorian era, this was replaced by the doctrine that women were naturally pure and chaste, except that evil lecherous men forced their vile lusts upon them. This resulted in the abrupt removal of eighteenth century controls on female misbehavior. Women, such as the protagonist of "Pride and Prejudice" were allowed to be "out" while fertile age and single, giving them every opportunity for twentieth century style misbehavior. The evidence produced in the case of the divorce of Queen Caroline suggests that they did in fact misbehave, but, lacking cameras everywhere, it was possible to get away with denying this fact. Queen Caroline attended a ball naked from the waist up, and returned to her hotel with someone she met at the ball, but the official truth remained that she was a chaste woman cruelly mistreated by her lecherous and philandering husband. In view of what Queen Caroline got up to and got away with, and in view of the lack of controls on the protagonist of "Pride and Prejudice", who at one point was in a cottage by herself visited by male love interests, we may suppose a covert sexual revolution in Victorian times, going public in 1910, in part because cameras were getting usable.

Queen Caroline getting sainted despite fucking around indiscriminately predates the Frankfurt School by quite a bit.

Forget about Cultural Marxism. Remember the divorce of Queen Caroline.

The problem with getting rid of Jews is not that it is rough on Jews. The solutions I propose are likely to be rough on lots of people. The problem with getting rid of Jews is that you wind up with socialism. If the Frankfurt School is the root of all evil, then the New Deal is just peachy.

The problem is not that "Frankfurt School" is the way that smart people say "Get rid of the Jews". The problem is that "Frankfurt School" is the way smart people say "Let us have socialism".

## The bubble in government paper

2015-01-23 09:18:25

Using money as a store of value is inherently problematic. One can store value as canned beans, as rice, but as money?

The usual trick to this is to lend money to young people to build homes and start families. The value is stored in their home, the bank holds a lot of mortgages to these homes, and these back a lot of on demand deposits.

This creates the notorious problem of term transformation, which can be ameliorated by flexible interest rate mortgages - or by an alarming willingness of the government to print money for cronies, but I am here addressing a different problem.

Suppose there are not enough young people building homes and starting families.

We then face the problem of money with nowhere to be stored. So the natural rate of interest falls to zero and tries to go negative So instead of storing it in young people's promises to work hard and build a life for their families, we store it in taxpayer futures. Governments borrow to buy votes, and to "stimulate the economy" So money is backed by a liability on taxpayers.

An ever larger liability on ever fewer taxpayers.

But, surely money can store value even if backed by absolutely nothing. Money is always a bubble. So why worry. How can the capacity of government to borrow enormous amounts of money at negative real interest rates be a bad thing. Surely the interest rates that governments are paying show that our governments are more solvent than ever. The decline of the high IQ working taxpaying population and its replacement by people on welfare and single women in makework jobs has been a huge bonanza for governments, that has deluged them with free money. Indeed, the more single women in makework jobs, the less they will reproduce, and the more money the government can borrow.

Assuming a virtuous and competent government, a deluge of free money is not going to cause that government any harm. If, on the other hand, we assume government thinks no further ahead than the next election ...

# Eight commandments for the neoreaction

2015-01-24 02:22:07

Nyan draws a line in the sand

> *Patriarchy and families are the foundation of society.
> The natural and unmolested course of selection and elimination must be allowed to occur in economics and society.
> Hierarchy is the natural and right way for people to cooperate.
> Different people are different. Equality is a lie.
> Progressivism is an insane religion advanced by a hostile media/academic machine.
> It's not just "The Jews".
> Democracy isn't going to fix these problems.
> Merely denouncing those to the right creates a deadly signalling spiral, so no enemies to the right.

I would expand the last point slightly. Those who notice that females have characteristics that make it difficult to organize large scale cooperation in their presence, but think the leftist program is otherwise OK, are not enemies, but people who have taken one step on the path to dark enlightenment.

Those that think the Jews have mystic superpowers are not enemies, but people who are focusing far too hard on one rather small step to dark enlightenment.

# Hard left wins in Greece

2015-01-25 22:32:00

The interesting question is not whether Greece leaves the Euro, or the Euro leaves Greece, but how many of the opposition will be arrested before the next election.

The victory of the hard left was made possible by arresting the hard right and forbidding them from campaigning.

Which had the effect of discouraging anyone from disagreeing with the hard left

Greek politics is already dominated by police intimidation and the direct use of state power to punish dissent. Election of a hard left party is likely to increase the use of police intimidation and the direct use of state power to punish dissent.

The left, which is to say the state, talks about the side of history. History tells us that if you use state power to suppress your opponents on the right, by and by your opponents on the left will use state power to suppress you.

# Yes, Roissy is correct

2015-02-01 03:02:11

A lot of people who claim to teach how to pick up girls are just scammers. For example, "Neuro Linguistic Programming" is just a variation on the old "Get Girls by Hypnosis" scam. But Roissy is the real deal. I know well his stuff works.

Most beautiful high IQ high socioeconomic status women are blowing their youth, their beauty, and their most fertile years on low income semi employed assholes with room temperature IQs, the kind of guy who sometimes gets a job folding sweaters, sometimes deals a little dope, sometimes a bit of burglary, but mostly sponges off his exceedingly numerous girlfriends, particularly the flock of them that are high socioeconomic status.

And here is a post from a young lady[244] who is industriously blowing her youth, beauty, and most fertile years confirming many of Roissy's maxims[245].

Which raises the interesting question. Why are most naturals kind of stupid? If female hypergamy works, should not naturals be above average intelligence?

I conjecture that much of the problem is that stupid people act brave, not because they are brave, but because they don't think about the consequences of their actions. The man who is a part time sweater folder, part time burglar, and full time sponger off girlfriends is unlikely to be intimidated by political correctness.

A smart nerd and a dumb asshole are forced to attend a lecture on rape and respecting women and consent and all that boring stuff. The smart nerd is terrified and believes everything he hears, and thinks that if he says "hi" to a pretty girl he will arrested. The dumb asshole does not understand a word. All he sees is a fat diesel dyke making menacing gestures like an overweight angry gorilla and braying "waah waah waah"

So the dumb asshole goes forth and grabs some girl's ass, while the smart nerd cowers in the corner trembling in fear.

---

[244] https://sparklesandsecrets.com/2014/06/26/what-do-we-have-to-prove-i-dont-know-that-is-why-im-asking/ "Natural in action"

[245] https://heartiste.wordpress.com/the-sixteen-commandments-of-poon/

A long time ago I was walking along, and ran into a girl I knew vaguely. She was a friend of a friend of friend or something like that. So I grabbed her and kissed on the lips. After several seconds she pulled away and protested vehemently:

What the hell do you think you are doing

She said with much indignation.
To which I impudently replied with a big grin:

Kissing you on the lips.

After a couple of seconds she grinned also, and we kissed a little more.
Then she gave me the "I have boyfriend" shit test, which shit test, being ignorant and innocent back in those days, I failed.
I was never a pick up artist, but however embarrassingly incompetent my efforts to meet girls were, I did better than anyone too frightened to try.
Before 1972, there was no stereotype of the sexually unsuccessful awkward high IQ nerd. I don't believe the awkward high IQ nerd existed until recent times. Something has changed. The stereotypical smart person used to resemble Feynman and Wernher von Braun, who were notorious hits with chicks.
What has changed that leads to stupid people cleaning up?
1. Elite culture has become more hostile to intelligence. Catcher in the Rye replaces Anabasis. Smart people tend to exclude women and blacks. Shirtgate guy.
2. Smart people have a tendency to deal with girls on the basis of what they are taught, rather than instinct, hence, the blue pill generates men who are very bad at women. The smarter you are, the better you are at absorbing and accepting misinformation.
When I was kid, quite a long time ago, a lot of what is now PUA lore, that nice guys finish last, that a man should take rejection imperturbably, that faint heart never won fair lady, was common knowledge, stuff that everyone knew. This widespread knowledge of women was suppressed, and replaced by misinformation, and the intellectuals were the primary targets of that misinformation. The smarter you are, the more exposed to the blue pill.

## Society is a racial construct

2015-02-01 20:44:44

No amount of social change is going to change the nature of races. Egypt has had racial mixing for several thousand years and blacks have always been criminals, servants, and slaves.

But change the race, as is the policy of the permanent and unelected government in every formerly white country except Iceland, and you *will* change the society.

In a few white countries the merely elected government is resisting the policy of the permanent and unelected government. In Australia, the merely elected government has the support, loyalty, and obedience of the military, and is prepared to use it, so, despite a continual storm of attacks by the permanent government, it gets its way on this issue against the will of the permanent government - until the next election. The elected government is only temporary after all, and so, from time to time, will yield to pressure.

What has happened in every white country is that the merely elected government has laws limiting illegal immigration, and limiting benefits received by illegals. And in every white country, those laws are not enforced.

Asylum laws are knowingly and intentionally abused to bring in people persecuted for ordinary non political crimes, and for such political crimes as terrorism. Many recent terrorist incidents in white countries have been committed by terrorists who gained asylum on the basis of persecution resulting from crimes of terror or from ordinary non political crimes. The permanent government wants an underclass, and it wants the worst possible underclass, the worse the underclass, the better it can be used as a weapon against the former majority. Hence the active recruitment of terrorists and criminals, and the use of the school system to indoctrinate the new majority with hatred against the former majority.

## Rape accusation for grades

2015-02-04 04:17:43

Emma Sulkowicz gets an advanced degree in false rape accusations. I hope it comes with a mountain of student debt.

Emma Sulkowicz decided that her last booty call with Paul Nungesser was rape, after several months went by with no further booty calls from him, despite her prompting on instant messaging. Or perhaps she decided when her academic advisor went fishing for rape cases.

## Female Sexuality

2015-02-08 22:13:13

Promoting a great comment by "John" from my previous post "Roissy is correct"

> "20 yo women who were consciously expecting to spend 10 years getting laid by a variety of studs before even thinking about selecting a father for their child"

> This is the true market shift. Women today are allowed to do what they want, so they maximize the benefit derived from having a hot young female body. This means a variety of temporary relationships with the hottest, most charismatic men they can find, followed by marriage with one or two kids to their "best friend" who is usually an attractive beta provider of similar age.

> Having a baby traps them at home and prematurely degrades their hotness. Being legally bound to a single man prevents them from maximizing the enjoyment they can receive from sex.

So the fittest and most desirable women these days are just as commitment averse as the most alpha of cads. It's not until their glory run is over and their looks start to slip that they even start to consider marriage and family.

At that point, if they have managed their looks well, cultivated their charm, avoided becoming totally insane, and didn't wait too long — they can still EASILY scoop up a quality man.

The mating market power of the attractive 18-25 year old female trumps everything else, however, the alpha male's trump card is longevity. He can fuck prime age women (though not lock them down) into his 50s.

Not even trying to lock them down is key, because it is always sure to drive them away if they are pre-baby-rabies. This is the fruit of sexual liberation — a sexual utopia for high achievers who enjoy high quality and quantity of sexual relationships, with varying levels frustration and internet porn for everyone else.

All while the birthrate plummets because it is individually optimal for prime fertility females to keep those peak attractiveness years for themselves by delaying reproduction. Women will make this choice every single time if given the option.

In the ancestral environment, in the environment of evolutionary adaptation, this behavior would have resulted in the hot chick getting pregnant to an alpha male at thirteen, and then married to a beta male at fourteen, and then stuck with that beta male, which is optimal for the individual female in that environment, and not too intolerably harsh on the beta male, given that the alpha male probably had a spear and sword and was pretty good with them, and infant mortality was mighty high.

In the current environment, however, this behavior is apt to continue to age thirty or so, which is pathological, and extremely harsh on the beta male. This is analogous to our love of sweet things being optimal in an environment where the only sweet things are ripe fruit. With contraception and abortion, women are free to overindulge in a supernormal stimulus. In the ancestral environment, this behavior ended with them settling for a beta male at fourteen. In our environment, this behavior ends with them settling for a beta male at thirty.

# Nothing exciting happening with Greece

2015-02-11 00:42:49

For as long as I can remember, the Greek government has been spending other people's money.

For as long as I can remember, there has been a financial crisis in which those reluctantly funding the Greek government announce this is now going to stop.

In the latest crisis, the German government meets with the Greek government and with great firmness tells them to stop spending German money.

But, short of Germany leaving the Euro, the German government has no power to stop other people from spending German money. The European Central Bank has, through a variety of moves, some of them immoral but arguably legal, some of them flat out illegal, gathered the power to spend unlimited amounts of the money of the more solvent countries of the European Union on its clients and cronies.

Only the unelected and permanent European Central Bank has the power to stop funding Greece. When the Greek government starts negotiating with the European Central Bank, then negotiations might matter.

## Revolution in the Ukraine

### 2015-02-11 09:23:25

Some time ago, democracy in the Ukraine produced the wrong result. The Cathedral violently and conspiratorially overthrew the elected government, installed a new government, which then held elections, which elections, predictably, produced the right result.

Revolution ensued against this democratically elected government, and is spreading[246]

Meanwhile in Britain "antifascist" thugs, who are all full time employees of government unions, operating with impunity under police protection, use violence and the threat of violence to disrupt the political activities of the UK Independence Party.

## The weak have it coming to them

### 2015-02-15 05:37:50

The New York Times is getting worried about the wave of persecution that it has done so much to create.

They recently did a pity piece on poor little Justine Sacco[247]

Justine Sacco is a good progressive. She has no enemies to the left, no friends to the right. She had a good progressive job with a good progressive company. She had a good progressive family. One fine day she twittered

"Going to Africa. Hope I don't get AIDS. Just kidding. I'm white!"

Ten thousand progressives mobilized in outraged horror. She lost her job. Her family disowned her, and she was deeply, deeply ashamed. Whenever anyone told her that her tweet was OK because whites seldom get AIDS, was as outraged as anyone.

Meanwhile I had sometime earlier posted that
> The Red Cross donation form is way too long. Could cut it down to one line "Are you a member of an official victim group? If so, we don't want your filthy AIDS infested blood"

with no reaction other than some moron arguing that sodomy was just as bad if a white person does it.

Among my many possibly controversial posts:
Slavery was good for most blacks, segregation was good for blacks, we should have different laws for blacks and whites, we should restore slavery for problem people - and most

---

[246]https://www.zerohedge.com/news/2015-02-10/ukrainians-rage-against-military-draft-were-sick-war
[247]https://www.nytimes.com/2015/02/15/magazine/how-one-stupid-tweet-ruined-justine-saccos-life.html

such problem people would be black.

Very few rape accusations are real, very few rape convictions are just.

Cuckoldry is worse for men than rape is for women, therefore we should deal with heterosexual sex offenses on the old testament model as property rights violations against the owner of the woman.

To the best of my recollection, the only time I got a substantial hostile reaction was when I very politely opined that sex change operations usually left the victim in uncanny valley between male and female, hence the high suicide rate. Perhaps had I added that such perverts make me want to chuck, would have gotten away with it. In my subsequent post on the topic, was careful to emphasize the horror inducing characteristics of intersexuals.

The mob that the New York Times has unleashed is attracted to the smell of fear and weakness. Phil Robertson stands up to them, and it blows over. The victims usually issue confessions of their crimes and apologies for their crimes, as if they are about to face torture and the gulag - because they have been selected for the propensity to break down easily.

I think the Phil Robertson incident led to a general feeling "Let us not try shaming people who live in the middle of nowhere". People who live on the revolving door are vulnerable to all sorts of consequences, and so the mob jumps in, hoping to apply those consequences. If you work in PR, extra vulnerable crunchy target.

## Radix on Christianity

### 2015-02-17 13:30:54

Another profound post from Radix[248]

> The institutional Christianity that flourishes today is no longer the same religion as that practiced by Charlemagne and his successors, and it can no longer support the civilization they formed. Indeed, organized Christianity today is the enemy of the West and the race that created it.

When the Puritans claimed to be returning to the original Christianity, that was, unfortunately, exactly what they were doing - returning to Christianity as it was before Charlemagne.

I would recommend referring the Charles the Great as Charles the Great, rather than Charlemagne, and Charles the Hammer as Charles the Hammer, rather than Charles Martel, because these were the first major figures in history to have modern names, reminding us that they were the very start of yesterday's European civilization.

## Ada Lovelace, poster girl

### 2015-03-01 22:47:49

If one poster girl, or black poster boy, fake, then all fake, since obviously progressives will run with the best they can find.

---

[248]https://www.radixjournal.com/journal/2015/2/14/the-christian-question

From time to time I read people gushing over some poster girl or other. Lately it seems to have become mandatory in every book on computing to announce that they are inspired by the glorious leadership of comrade Stalin all early programmers were women and evil men stole all the credit.

Supposedly the first programmer was Ada Lovelace[249]. This is based on her addendum to Luigi Menabrea's explanation of Babbage's analytical engine.

Her notes contain several "computer programs" - or rather walkthroughs, outlines of how a program might be written were Babbage's engine actually built. However, all of these "programs" were written by Babbage several years previously[250].

Ada Lovelace had rather ordinary mathematical and scientific skills - which made her already famous as a poster girl long before she met Babbage, not for being good at maths and science, but for being good at maths and science *for a woman*. This is the dancing bear effect. A dancing bear is famous not for dancing well, but for dancing at all.

Babbage needed publicity because funding running out. He approached Ada Lovelace because she was already famous *as a poster girl*, because any connection between her and the analytical engine would generate favorable publicity for the analytical engine.

So, far from Ada Lovelace's contributions being ignored by patriarchal males, they were receiving manufactured publicity before they even existed.

## Nazis are commies and commies are progressives

2015-03-06 06:02:51

As you probably know if you read this blog and others like it, the overthrow of the Ukrainian government by Soros et al was a Jewish/State Department conspiracy. Maidan's primary documents are in English, in the dialect of the America Harvard educated ruling class, like so many other similar movements all over the world. The Ukrainian secession movement was and is a response to this foreign created coup installed government.

So, which side do you think the Nazis would support?

Ara Maxima has a nice rant on these pinko progressive nazis here[251] and here[252]. Nazis for the Jewish conspiracy, because loving America, they naturally love the State Department.

As Orwell said, anyone who thinks there is a big difference between Nazis and commies is in favor of one or the other. And, it would seem, sometimes both.

It is always possible to argue that we should support side X because side Y is too far leftist, overlooking the fact that everyone today is leftist by the standards of yesterday, and everyone yesterday is leftist by the standards of the day before yesterday, but if you want to find a genuine reactionary, a Russian who wants to restore the Tsar and Greek Russian Orthodoxy under the Tsar, that man is or recently was fighting for the independence of Russians in the breakaway republics of the Ukraine.

On one side, who started this war?

[249] https://blog.reaction.la/politics/ada-lovelace-poster-girl/ "Ada Lovelace, poster girl"
[250] https://www.salon.com/1999/03/16/feature_217/
[251] https://aramaxima.wordpress.com/2015/03/06/my-divorce-from-ethnonationalism-pt-ii-the-final-solution-to-the-cledun-question/
[252] https://aramaxima.wordpress.com/2015/03/04/my-divorce-from-ethnonationalism/

George Soros, progressive atheist anti zionist Jew.

On the other side, who kept this war going when it would have ended with only the Crimea detached?

Igor Ivanovich Strelkov, Tsarist and theocrat.

So which side are you going to support. The side of George Soros, or the side of Igor Ivanovich Strelkov?

Are you going to support the side sponsored by the State Department, or the side whose soldiers sing "O righteous God" - the anthem sung today by the rebels on the battlefields of eastern Ukraine. was born nearly 100 years ago during the Russian Civil War, sung by the soldiers of Gen Mikhail Drozdovsky, a White Guard commander.

National Socialists are **Socialists**.

The reason George Soros supports Nazis in the Ukraine is that he does not give a shit about Jews, but does care about socialism.

## Nationalism, whiteness, and kin

### 2015-03-15 02:09:51

B.S. Haldane observed "I would lay down my life for two brothers, four nephews, or eight cousins."

In otherwords, kin altruism does not go far, being pretty much limited to the nuclear family and the extended family.

It can be stretched to somewhat larger groups by deliberate inbreeding, by the practice of father's brother's daughter marriage, but then you get moderate IQ depression due to inbreeding, and the achievable group size is not all that much larger.

Nazis tend to believe that whites would not make war on each other except for the evil mind control rays emitted by Jews. Thus world wars One and Two were supposedly Jewish plots.

History demonstrates otherwise. Whites are markedly better at war than other races, because we have been practicing on each other so hard for so long.

The program of Nazism is Socialism for white people only.

To hell with that. Lets be really racist and have capitalism for superior people like ourselves and socialism for inferiors, for people we don't like and wish to see crushed.

So where does nationalism come from?

New International Outlook tells us[253]

> then nationalism becomes not dissimilar to other forms of modern identity politics which afflict the world at present. The Gay community, The Feminist community* or any other such constructs are purely a result of the media fragmenting and power considerations (democratic needs, desperate scramble for state justification) just as much as the nationalism of the 19th and 20th century was the result of mass media identity formation and power considerations (mass conscription, democratic needs etc).

---

[253]https://www.newinternationaloutlook.com/2015/03/02/nationalism-and-nrx/ "Nationalism"

This seems to argue for empire - but empires as we have seen undermine trust and cohesion. In the end the founding ethnicity of the empire winds up being oppressed by the empire, as Turks were oppressed by the Ottoman Empire, and Americans are now oppressed by the American empire.

New International Outlook[254] continues to argue that Nationalism is inherently leftist:

> Nationalism is leftism, it arose as a question of equality based on ethnic similarities and has merely been overtaken by an even more inclusive version of nationalism which holds that all of humanity is one nation.

The validity of Nationalism comes, not from altruism as Nazis tend to argue, but from trust, from the assurance of reciprocity, from the confidence that bad behavior within the group will be prevented.

Nationalism works, is real, if near is actually more trustworthy than far - because word of bad behavior will get back to those close to the person behaving badly, and this word will have bad consequences.

Observe how tourist girls go wild and fuck around indiscriminately, having sex with all sorts of people, old men and blacks that they would never have sex with at home, because they figure that sex overseas does not add to their count.

If, however, this word getting back to near has no consequences, nationalism is unreal. A nation does not really exist, is unreal a mere construct of propaganda, unless bad conduct has bad consequences, at least for members of the elite.

Collective action is hard, the central insight of the neoreaction being that extremely bad solutions are better than pretend solutions. Diversity undermines asabiyyah, making collective action even harder.

The Nazi error is to imagine that collective action is easy - hence their error of socialism, and that asabiyyah comes naturally. It does not.

Nationalism is necessarily ethno nationalism, since diversity destroys trust. Nationalism only works to the extent that near is more trustworthy than far, and that near is indeed trustworthy.

Thus nationalism requires a social order that encourages and rewards virtue - where being a bad guy has consequences, and by consequences I don't mean chicks giving you their number for booty calls.

Jewish cohesiveness rested on strict patriarchy. A Jew would give his daughters to someone talented and virtuous, which compelled all Jews to behave virtuously to other Jews (but not necessarily to non Jews)

Thus, Jews dominated the diamond trade because if one diamond merchant cheated another, he or his sons would not have wives.

As Jewish patriarchy evaporates, as progressivism successfully assimilates Judaism, Jewish cohesiveness evaporates a generation or two later. The Orthodox will slowly follow the path their reform brethren have already taken. Today, they are no longer all that patriarchal. Soon they will no longer have social cohesion and resistance to decadence and fraud.

---

[254]https://www.newinternationaloutlook.com/2015/03/02/nationalism-and-nrx/ "Nationalism"

On the one hand Nationalism is solidly in the left, and yet there is something very left wing about the fact that empires tend to wind up being run for the conquered at the expense of the founding ethnicity, as hordes of foreigners migrate to the capital.

It is obviously easier for the ruled to admire and respect the rulers, and the rulers to look after the ruled, if ruled and rulers are the same ethnicity and religion.

It is obviously easier to build functional institutions, to have reciprocity and trust, between people of the same ethnicity and religion.

Collective decision making is an unsolved problem, and the reactionary insight is that it is better to have horribly bad solutions to this problem, than fake solutions. It is a much harder problem when you have diverse ethnicities involved, because of the lack of trust and reciprocity.

So if we wind up saying that collective decisions need to be made on the ethnicity scale, because larger scales are even harder, that is remarkably similar to ethnonationalism.

Chan/Pol interprets Jewish degeneracy as ethnonationalism, as a plot by Jews to destroy the white race.

Against this analysis: The most cohesive Jews, the believers, and the most cohesive of all, the orthodox believers, are not degenerate, and generally don't show up pushing degeneracy or launching lawsuits against Christmas.

The observations that the pol hypothesis explains are also explainable as Jews as jumping on the prog bandwagon.

If someone is pushing degeneracy, or trying to destroy the white race, he is probably a Jew. If, however, someone is torturing archaeology and history to supposedly prove that Moses, King David, and King Solomon never existed, also a Jew - and often the same Jew.

The Jew that denies the existence of King Solomon is attacking the Jewish identity.

If Jews were trying to take over the world they wouldn't be sabotaging themselves as well.

The fact that they are drinking their own koolaide means that they are just as pwned as your average white progressive

I see orthodox Jews torturing their holy texts to get the conclusion that Orthodox Jews should be accepting of gays - and I see progressive Jews torturing the historical and archaeological evidence to get the conclusion that King Solomon's temple never existed.

Judaism is lagging in its assimilation to progressivism, so progressivism is upping the pressure, and clever Talmudic scholars are cleverly finding increasing amounts of progressivism in the Talmud.

The only religion I see showing real signs of life is Jihadi Islam. Every other religion is just piously going through the motions while slowly being digested by progressivism. Putin is trying to stitch up an authentically Russian Orthodoxy, but has not got far. China is furtively sneaking away from Maoism and Socialism with Chinese Characteristics towards Confucianism and the Mandate of Heaven, but they are still mighty furtive. Meanwhile lots of Chinese go to western universities, where they get brainwashed with progressivism, and since these are the wealthiest Chinese, progressivism is high status for Chinese.

A lot of reactionaries are converting to Roman Catholicism, as the religion with the most credible historical claim to universal religious authority.

If you get married in a Roman Catholic Church, they will shoot the husband in the back by undermining in his authority and promoting divorce in accordance with progressive doctrine and contrary to New Testament and official Roman Catholic doctrine

Further, universal religious authority is a logical implication of of a universal god, one god for all peoples, but I observe the British empire, which the world's greates empire, the scientific revolution, and the technological revolution happened under an ethnic national church.

Universalism is harmful, because universalism undermines social cohesion and asabiyyah, so universal churches are harmful, so universal gods are harmful. And in that sense, the Jews really are to blame - the problem being not undue Jewish influence in banking and Hollywood but that Christianity is a Jewish heresy, and progressivism is a Christian heresy.

National Christian Churches can work, as for example Anglicanism from 1660 to 1820, but they have an innate tendency to turn universal. Perhaps if we made sure that warriors were on top of priests, and made priesthoods into semi hereditary family businesses as in Shinto or Icelandic paganism, the tendency to universalism could be adequately restrained.

Universalism leads to universal empire. Multiple universal empires lead to war. A single universal empire tends to sacrifice its central nation, its founding ethnicity, for the good of the empire, which is what so pissed off the Turks about the Ottoman empire, that they ended the Caliphate.

Like white anglo saxon protestants today, the Turks were oppressed by their subject nations, rather than oppressing them. And that is the problem with worshipping a universal creator God. Not necessarily an insoluble problem, but it is a problem nonetheless. Obviously you need one church per nation - which would suggest one god, or set of Gods, per nation. The Japanese have the sun god and a bunch of vaguely defined lesser deities, and they do fine. It is not apparent that Japanese believe in the Sun God, but they believe in believing. The Japanese are hopelessly decadent now (watch any anime) but they were not decadent before MacArthur.

## Putin reads Roissy

### 2015-03-16 19:47:43

Putin mysteriously disappears from the press for ten days, then upon reappearance:

> Putin's spokesman Dmitry Peskov greeted reporters Monday with sarcastic remarks: "So, have you seen the president paralysed and seized by the generals? He has just come back from Switzerland where he attended the delivery."

> Asked if Putin's condition required treatment by an osteopath, the spokesman retorted: "Yes, the osteopath was with the generals."

He treats the Cathedral as if it was a girl who was shit testing him. Which, since female emancipation, is not that far from what it is.

Disappear for a bit to get the hamster running. Upon reappearance, agree and amplify.

## High reproductive variance among males

2015-03-20 01:53:22

The sociobiology leading to the conclusion that women are ill suited to be part of the larger society, and should be subordinated to husbands and fathers, rests in large part on high reproductive variance among males in the ancestral environment, the environment of evolutionary adaption.

Now it obviously seems likely that reproductive variance among males was extreme - just look! And pretty much everyone in the manosphere agrees that it was, but until recently, I have not been able to find any good science pinning it down.

Now I have[255].

Throughout most of human history, almost all women reproduced but only one male in three reproduced. During the neolithic, from agriculture to the start of the bronze age (very rough dates) one male in seventeen reproduced - sixteen males died without children, one male had seventeen wives, concubines, and slave girls. After this roughly four thousand year period of very extreme inequality, it returned to its long term norm, one male in three - all races, all cultures, all societies, and it is been at roughly its long term norm for the past four thousand years or so.

## Power laws in polygyny

2015-03-21 09:11:03

When we read that only one man in three reproduced, we tend to imagine two thirds of the men in an underclass detached from society, enslaved, killed, or driven out, and one third of the men forming society, with three wives each. Or you could have two thirds killed in war and the survivors get the booty. And similarly, if only one man in seventeen ...

But obviously it is likely to be a power law. The ratio of men having n wives to men having n+1 wives will be roughly constant.

It turns out that, assuming equal production of males and females, this power ratio is equal to one minus the proportion of men contributing to the gene pool.

If one third of men reproduce, then about one man in nine has one wife, about one man in thirteen has two wives (that is to say, two thirds of the number of men who have only one wife), one man in twenty has three wives, (that is to say, two thirds of the number of men who have two wives), about one in thirty will have four wives and so on and so forth.

That seems like a fairly stable society, assuming you keep the excluded men under control. One solution would be to give the more valuable part of the excluded men the used up old wives of the men who are actually part of society, women approaching their

---

[255]https://genome.cshlp.org/content/early/2015/03/13/gr.186684.114.full.pdf+html

use by date, women who have exceeded their use by date. This corresponds to the ancient Hebrew system of easy divorce for men only, and the traditional Muslim system of alarmingly easy divorce for men only.

Equal distribution of pussy by basically socialist means is fair, which is to say, monogamy with patriarchy, since we are reluctant to use market and capitalist incentives to manage the production of women, which is to say, fully propertize them and sell them to highest bidder for profit, with breeder farms functioning like piggeries. If we are not going to incentivize the production of women by capitalist cash market means, should not distribute them by capitalist cash market means.

On the other hand too much equality in the distribution of pussy is dysgenic. We want some men excluded, but two thirds excluded seems so large as likely to be destabilizing.

And of course, we want the right men excluded, which at present does not seem to be happening. Although production of children in marriage is mildly eugenic at present, in that wealthier men have more wives (serially and informally) and more children, the effect is weak, and probably more than counterbalanced by the grossly dysgenic production of children outside marriage - dumb women producing little bastard thuglets, smart women never getting married, never much wanting to get married because they cannot find any men who are their social superiors, and the supply of immortal vampires is a bit low, so they just don't feel much like having sex. And, if they do feel like having sex, which mostly they do not, having had sex with someone they feel is a social inferior, they form weak attachment to any resulting children, aborting, neglecting, or outright murdering, or looking the other way when stepdad number three does the murdering. To become good mothers, women need to first be good wives, to feel themselves owned and mastered by someone better than themselves. Charles Murray argues that upper class women are well behaved, but in fact women who are married to upper class men, which is not quite the same thing as upper class women, are well behaved. Upper class women who fail to form suitable marriages and stay married in those marriages give truck stop strippers a run for their money.

A ratio of fifty percent - half the men have no offspring, a quarter have one wife, a eighth have a wife and a "maid", a sixteenth have a wife and two "maids" and so on and so forth would be pretty stable, since no possible combination of those missing out could overcome those getting some. We could dispense with the easy divorce, at least for wives. One should enforce patriarchal monogamy, which is to say, the socialist equal rationing of pussy, to the extent necessary to ensure a majority of men are attached to society at a youthful age, but enforcing it more than that might well be overkill.


## Racism

2015-03-21 21:27:13

"Racist" is just a hate word for white, therefore I am not racist, merely white. I am anti anti racist.

"Racist" has multiple, vague, slippery, and shifting definitions. I think it is really bad news to live close to blacks, and property owners should be entitled to protect themselves against what happened to those owning property in Ferguson. I think that blacks are, on average, genetically inferior. I think that the genetic and cultural differences between genetic and cultural groups are such that they need different laws, de-facto or de-jure, and in particular that blacks should be subject to different laws than whites, laws that are simpler, harsher, and more restrictive. And in practice, we see that in highly progressive left wing towns like San Francisco, blacks *are* furtively subjected to different laws than whites.

Those that have a ready supply of numerous different definitions of racism, which definitions they selectively apply in some circumstances and refrain from applying in other circumstances, will undoubtedly find that a pile of my positions fit a pile of their definitions. And I don't care.

## Ever purer Islam

### 2015-03-22 23:15:25

Once upon a time, there was a Caliphate, and the Caliphate was hereditary. The Caliph had a thousand sons. When his grip weakened, the sons would kill or imprison each other till only one remained, who became the new Caliph. The Caliph was the supreme leader of both Church and State, and any preacher boy who claimed to be substantially holier than the Caliph was apt to wind up a head shorter. This prevented spirals of holiness competition.

The Caliphate was overthrown, because the Turks became sick of the burdens of empire, an empire in which outsiders were continually favored over Turks, not to mention that the Caliph tended to be noticeably whiter than the Turks.

In the ensuing chaos, the House of Saud grabbed quite a lot of land, on the basis that they were holier than anyone else. Since then, we have seen one movement after another claiming to be holier than the house of Saud. A day or so ago, US troops fled Yemen, abandoning their heavy weapons to the extremely holy Islamic State or the extremely holy Al Qaeda, or, very likely, both. Yemen has not fallen yet, probably will not fall for a quite a while, but the writing is on the wall.

To the extent that these movements adhere to the plain wording of the Koran and the Hadiths, they are delightfully reactionary. I particularly like Boko Haram's position on marriage and western education. But, if you simply stick to the plain wording, that kind of limits how holy you can be. So, as each strives to be holier than the other, we are seeing increasing egalitarianism and socialism. All holiness spirals tend to wind up in much the same place regardless of religion of origin, just as all aneuploid malignant metastatic cancers look very much alike, regardless of tissue of origin. Pretty soon they will be holier than Mohammed, as Christians have long been holier than Jesus. If it were not for that, I would convert to Boko Haram's brand of Islam right away.

## Harry Lee was the greatest statesman of our age, but ...

2015-03-24 03:08:51

Harry Lee took Singapore from third world to first world. He created an economic order that every nation should imitate, and many have.

Singapore was about to fall to communism and racial violence, following the path of so many other third world hell holes abandoned by their colonial masters. Harry Lee created order peace, and economic freedom, which brought prosperity. As Spandrel says, he was a legalist[256], not a reactionary. Legalism, done right, brings order, peace, and prosperity. So, why would one need more than legalism?

In legalism, the great man decides what is to be done, then makes people do it. And then he dies, and the tide comes in, and washes away his sandcastles, however impressive they may be.

## Andreas Lubitz mass murder explained

2015-03-28 07:19:54

Andreas Lubitz murdered one hundred and fifty innocent people by locking the pilot out of the cabin and deliberately flying the plane into a mountain.

Roissy explains it all[257]

Lubitz was a nice guy, so naturally his girlfriend left him. So he converts to Islam and flies the plane into a mountain to get his six pack of virgins in the afterlife.

This is part of the collateral damage we suffer by allowing women moment to moment sexual choice, and part of the collateral damage we suffer by allowing Islam.

Moment to moment female sexual choice needs to be forbidden, and Islam needs to be forbidden outside of Dar al Islam.

## The stupid elite

2015-03-30 03:48:47

It seems obvious to me that our ruling elite has been getting less and less elite, less and less intelligent, since around 1875, and I have previously produced a great pile of anecdotal data on this subject, for example the endless dumbing down of university entrance tests throughout the twentieth century, the hilarious conversations found in the Challenger inquiry archives, showing spectacular examples of pointy haired boss syndrome, the staff of the World Bank, Obama's scriptwriters, and so on and so forth.

Purging engineers for real, suspected, or imagined heresy, seemed to me to purge the smartest engineers - seemed to me that whether or not smarts equate to heresy, smarts are suspected to equate with heresy regardless of whether the suspect is really a heretic or not, much as the Khmer Rouge wound up murdering everyone who wore glasses. They

---

[256]https://bloodyshovel.wordpress.com/2015/03/23/harry-lee-rest-in-peace/

[257]https://heartiste.wordpress.com/2015/03/27/council-of-realtalkers-vindicated-andreas-lubitz-was-a-recent-convert-to-islam-and-a-lovelorn-beta-male/

did not intend to murder everyone who wore glasses, or even intend to murder intellectuals. If you told one of them they were murdering all the intellectuals he would not have believed you. He would have said "We are intellectuals, would we murder ourselves?" (And immediately thereafter the secret police would have dragged him away to the torture chambers because of excessively complicated sentence construction, leading to suspicions of disloyalty and plots, much as the New York Times gets agitated because it is unable to parse sentences spoken by Sarah Palin.)

But all this is anecdotal. Ferguson has some actual statistics, showing systematic discrimination against dangerously smart people.[258]

> The probability of entering and remaining in an intellectually elite profession such as Physician, Judge, Professor, Scientist, Corporate Executive, etc. increases with IQ to about 133. It then falls about 1/3 by 140. By 150 IQ the probability has fallen by 97%!

Observing heresy persecutions in engineering, looks to me to a good approximation, they are getting rid of everyone above 145, that everyone above three standard deviations is excluded from engineering or science in high status firms, so I am unsurprised by Ferguson's report that the same applies in academia, law, and so forth.

Looks like they are recruiting people two standard deviations above the norm, but purging anyone significantly smarter, whether out of deliberate hostility to dangerously smart people, or because smart people exclude women and blacks.

When a female engineer tries to talk to a smart engineer, she finds it hard to talk to him about engineering, so she concludes he raped her repeatedly and demands a million dollars in compensation. Thus the exclusion of smart people could be inadvertent, as the extermination of smart people was with Khmer Rouge. The purging of smart engineers appears to be inadvertent, a byproduct of including women. Likely the same thing is happening to judges, as I see happening to engineers. I see engineers, don't see judges. Ferguson sees judges.

Ferguson's data does not address whether problem is getting worse or better. My anecdotal information indicates that the problem is getting worse, and has been getting worse since around 1870 or so. You notice that smart members of the elite, like Rumsfeld, are much older than regular members, and that when they say something that shows that they are smart, all the chimps get rattled, start shrieking and flinging poop.

The elite:

OK, I hear you saying, "these are two dumb as toad dropping nigger scum who won the debate because black and female."

But could not they find someone black and female who had an IQ above retarded?

OK then, lets look for a white male Jewish member of the elite chosen for his performance in a STEM field. Aaron Swartz. Official genius. a Fellow of Harvard's Ethics Center Lab on Institutional Corruption.

Aaron Swartz conspicuously lacked hacking and social skills.

If he had been marginally competent at computers, he could have downloaded millions of documents from JSTOR through the MIT network without bringing the MIT

---

[258]https://polymatharchives.blogspot.in/2015/01/the-inappropriately-excluded.html

network to a screaming halt, without committing burglary and vandalism against the MIT network administrators, without creating side effects that every single user of the MIT network noticed and was enraged by.

If he had been marginally competent at social skills, he would have known that despite the fact that the police and prosecutors were treating him as just another dumb no account petty crook, who got videotaped by security cameras performing criminal acts and got bagged by security, he was not going to prison, not going to be convicted, that he was still a member of the elite that never goes to jail or gets convicted no matter how stupid the crimes they commit.

If he had any of the normal prosocial qualities like diligence and forethought, would have found a way to hack the MIT network that was not blindingly obvious to every single user of the network.

Aaron Swartz, Jewish Harvard fellow, official genius, is only marginally smarter than the two retarded black ghetto scum that won the debate.

Now you can find genuinely smart members of the elite, for example Larry Summers. But notice: They are getting mighty long in the tooth.; whereas when you find a conspicuously retarded member of the elite, like Aaron Schwartz, they are very young. This is an elite that is getting dumber. When the likes of Larry Summers retire, they will be replaced by the likes of Aaron Swartz.

This is an elite that has been getting steadily dumber since 1875 or so. And it has been getting dumber faster.

Larry Summers born 1954. Aaron Swartz, official genius, born 1987.

A lot of people looking at the war powers debate say, ahh, that was Jews making black people look stupid. Well Aaron Swartz did not make Jews look smart.

## Anime and decadence

### 2015-04-02 06:11:17

Japan is decadent and is committing suicide with impressive grace and style. This is intentional Cathedral and MacArthur policy.

It does decadence very well, and decadence is attractive and entertaining. A little poison, every now and then, makes for an agreeable life, and a lot of poison, in the end, makes for an agreeable death.

In the course of watching more anime that I should, I have observed that the ideas projected in anime are invariably corrupting and self destructive, and probably a major cause of Japan's epidemic of shut ins who live in their mother's basement, watching hentai and playing video games all day.

Been watching various Japanese anime which increasingly indicate a terrible testosterone deficit in Japan, and probably are part of the cause of the deficit.

I recently randomly sampled an episode from the anime series Cat Girl Planet. Science fiction harem anime about cat girls. Sounds good.

Episode five, starting in the middle. Big pirate battleship whose all female crew wear a cross between sexy maid costumes and sexy pirate costumes.

They are under attack by umpteen different and mutually hostile groups, among them a couple of pirate girls wearing bunny costumes and teensy weensy itsy bitsy bikinis, two girls wearing powered battle armor suits, with almost identical uniforms but belonging to different and opposed factions, a bunch of identical robots, and probably maybe some more factions

Oh, I forgot, also under attack by the male protagonist and his super powered cat girl friend.

Unfortunately, her super powers, and her mind, are gone, because she is in heat. To restore her to normal, she needs to be laid, but the protagonist, the only male around, fails to take the hint.

Maybe I forgot them because they fail to do anything brave or manly unlike all the other teams.

Much dramatic action girl combat ensues, action girl on action girl. Finally the big confrontation.

Whereupon the male protagonist, the only male on the entire ship, and if he was not surrounded by extremely feminine girls, you would think him a girl also, proceeds to lecture people with moral lesson of the day - which moral lesson does not seem particularly relevant, but everyone is so impressed by this that they stop fighting.

The protagonist fails to do anything brave or manly, fails to hit on any girls, and fails to respond appropriately when girls hit on him.

The story line requires that the cat girl be restored to her normal self by the end of this episode or the start of the next. I suppose a bad guy is probably going to wind up servicing her off screen, demonstrating that manliness and hitting on girls is bad, but was not inclined to watch the rest of this series to test this theory.

Watched Btooom!

The protagonist has never hit on a girl, never intends to attempt to hit on a girl, lives in his mother's basement playing video games all day. Never intends to get a real life woman or a real job. His single mum is getting increasingly pissed with this.

We see a flashback to his schooldays:

Evil horrible oppressive to women horrible sexist horrible bully at school learns that the protagonist loves some schoolgirl from afar. From very far. Evil Bully tells protagonist that evil bully is interested pumping and dumping that same schoolgirl, but he will hold back so that protagonist can score some sex.

Protagonist declines to hit on girl. Evil bully tells him to man up and hit on the girl. You will get no sex if you take no action he tells him.

Protagonist declines to hit on girl. Evil bully tells him to get moving or evil bully will hit on girl.

Protagonist declines to hit on girl. Evil bully tells him to get a move on, damn it.

Protagonist declines to hit on girl. Evil bully hits on girl, pumps her and dumps her. She cries a lot. Oh the horrible outrage.

Protagonist savagely attacks evil bully. Evil bully declines to fight back, even though he could easily beat the crap out of the protagonist. This is probably even more humiliating for the protagonist than being beaten up. The girl beloved from afar never has any idea why the protagonist attacked the evil bully.

It is perfectly obvious that the evil bully is going to become a successful man in a high status job when he grows up, and the protagonist is going to grow up to be a total loser. Further, the evil bully is not evil at all. He is mentoring the protagonist, trying to give protagonist a little bit of the fathering that he has never known and desperately needs, to help the protagonist to not become the total loser that he is growing up to become.

In the Btooom! universe fathers are invariably evil and a bad influence, and children are better off without them.

In the protagonist's video game universe his player character has an in game wife. His fellow players tell him there are no women on the internet, and the player playing his wife is probably a fat fifty year old male. His in game wife declines requests for her real life identity, leading the main character to suspect "she" probably is a fat fifty year old male.

By an extremely improbable plot contrivance, he gets thrown into a real life adventure with the player playing his wife, who turns out to be an incredibly hot chick very much resembling her in game avatar.

Aaaand - still won't hit on her. In fact, despite having completely heroic adventures, he remains the total loser he always was, never growing an inch.

I originally decided to watch Btooom! because of an online review that it oppressed and degraded the female love interest, though in fact the male protagonist is horribly castrated, and is incessantly bullied and oppressed by the female love interest, on whom he never makes a move.

Instant girlfriend plot, in that they wind up living together in an abandoned building. He risks his life to get food. She does not cook. Building is indescribably filthy. She does not clean. She treats him with absolute and total lack of respect. And did I mention the lack of cooking and cleaning? Good. I will mention it again just in case you forget.

He never hits on her. She never does any housework for him. The place where they hang out continues to look like a homeless squat. Skipping forward to the end of the series, he still has not grown an inch. At the end of the series, she assumes the position (on a couch that is no cleaner than when they first arrived) but instead of screwing her, or better, telling her to clean the couch so that it is fit for screwing on, he talks to the demons in his head.

Now I can see there is a moral argument for him refraining from slapping her around and telling her "I saved your life umpteen times per episode, so put out, woman" but she desperately needs to be slapped around and told to do some cooking, cleaning, and lose the bad attitude. Just as the protagonist would have been a whole lot better off if evil bully / mentor had beaten the crap out of him, she would have been a lot better off if the protagonist had beaten the crap out of her.

The moral universe of both animes is that masculinity is bad, the behaviors that lead to success are bad, male sexuality is disgusting and evil, while female sexuality is pure and chaste. Fathers are absent and/or evil in both animes.

## Chimp politics and Cromwell's puritanism

2015-04-04 03:08:30

Moldbug is a big fan of Carlyle. Carlyle is a big fan of Cromwell.

Well I am a big fan of Cromwell also, but Carlyle takes Cromwell's Christianity seriously. If Carlyle was around today, I would have the exact same quarrel with him as I have with B.

Reading Carlyle on Cromwell, Carlyle takes it as simple fact that the Puritans were very sincere and strong believers in God, which obviously they were - but declines to inquire as to why this sincere and strong faith in God increased dramatically with every election, until Cromwell made himself supreme, whereupon it evaporated like Marxism in the Soviet Union.

A striking thing about this simple and strong faith is that Carlyle shows us that they are always talking about the goodies, about who gets Church of England sinecures. Being simple and strong believers in God, they believed that the goodies should go to simple and strong believers in God, like themselves, and were homicidally indignant when the goodies went to more worldly men, men they indignantly accused of being interested in mere goodies. Carlyle enthusiastically endorses the passionate and angry language with which they expressed this indignation at the worldly concern of those who wanted Church of England sinecures merely for the money and power, rather than wanting them for the greater glory of God.

The Puritans focus on the next world resulted in remarkably passionate and intense focus on the distribution of state and quasi state jobs in this one. Carlyle reports, approvingly, a bunch of incidents where puritans acted like a mob of apes. One expects leftists to act like animals, since they identify with subhumans, but it is disturbing to see Christians act like leftists. Puritanism, to judge by the activities described by Carlyle, was almost entirely about jobs for the boys, and to the objective of getting jobs for the boys, they brought out the mob, made alliances with far against near (Englishmen using Scots against Englishmen) and became startlingly enthusiastic about equality and social justice.

The social justice puritans were outflanking Cromwell, being holier than he. But he put a stop to that.

A religion is a synthetic tribe. (I use the term religion broadly to include things like Marxism and progressivism.) Being a synthetic tribe, useful for shaking down smaller tribes and those less cohesive, thus religion and state naturally become one. A state can hardly exist except it propagates and enforces an official belief system, in other words, something suspiciously like a religion.

Membership of the state apparatus for propagating its official beliefs is lucrative and high prestige, thus if the official belief system is not already a religion, it will be taken over by an organized group of sincere believers in one thing or another, taken over by a religion. If you have open entry into the priesthood (also known as community organizers), you wind up with the most sincere and extreme believers organizing against the slightly less sincere and extreme believers, an endlessly escalating sequence of conspiratorial takeovers by ever holier people, endlessly taking over the State system for propagating official beliefs - in our case, high status universities are endlessly turbulent, endlessly going further left, and endlessly dragging the rest of society along with them.

Stable long lived states have some mechanism against this. The Hebrews had a hereditary priesthood. Japanese shrines were and are private property, even though it is a state religion, and you cannot easily whip up new and competing shrines. Pagan Icelandic shrines were private property, and again, new shrines were not permitted. You could buy your way into the cartel, but you were not allowed to out holy them.

A lot of reactionaries daydream about the dissolution of the universities. It is plausible, indeed likely, that the universities will be dissolved in the quite near future. When the tail wags the dog, surgical tail removal becomes increasingly likely. Leftism can go on getting ever lefter for a while longer, but universities cannot go on spending ever more money, becoming ever more expensive, taking up ever more of people's time, and becoming an ever greater pain in the neck for the Pentagon and the State Department.

Such dissolution would not necessarily in itself result in the abolition of state supported official belief, and abolition of the wealth, privilege, status, and power that comes from controlling the system of state supported official belief. Henry the Eighth dissolved the monasteries, but a hundred years later the problem was back and worse than ever.

The system for propagating official state belief is an attractive nuisance, and attractive nuisances need to be fenced. A libertarian would like to abolish it, but fencing is easier. I would like to see true separation of information and state, which is to say, true separation of Church and state no matter how religion redefines itself to be not religion, but this is utopian. It is a lot easier to have an Archbishop and a Grand Inquisitor to stop the process of mutation to ever greater holiness. We also need to make positions in the system semi hereditary or private property in order the bribe the indolence of the clergy. We need clergy to have the power and the incentive to keep out those holier than themselves, just as we need a King to keep people out of politics.

B complains that I use the word "Holy" to mean "Screaming mob of chimpanzees hurling their feces and biting anything they can bite, including themselves", but no one was holier in B's sense than the puritans, as Carlyle quite correctly tells us, yet when goodies were in reach, they became a screaming mob of chimpanzees hurling their feces and biting anything they could bite, including themselves, as for example the General Assembly of the Church of Scotland in the prelude to the Bishop's wars.

# Evil League of Evil wins Hugo awards.

2015-04-05 23:31:00

With assistance from Gamergate.

Hugo awards controversy[259]

(Actually they dominated the short list, so it is not over yet, but the final outcome is pretty much baked in now)-

Politically correct science fiction simply is not science fiction, none of it, not a single recent Hugo award winner until now, because it continually lectures us on the latest issue, even if those delivering the lecture are supposedly martian elves, thus is always about the present place and the present time, and the martian elf costumes are less than skin deep.

All recent Hugo award winners have been boring tedious lectures spitting on their audience as racist and sexist, which is why Hugo award winners of fifty years ago are still today massively outselling recent Hugo award winners.

---

[259]https://monsterhunternation.com/2014/04/24/an-explanation-about-the-hugo-awards-controversy/

By the way, we don't drag gays to death behind pickup trucks. That is a completely false and malign accusation. That would be lower class, demotic, and democratic. We take them out to sea, till we get to where the currents run offshore to the middle of the pacific, then blindfold them, and make them walk the plank to celebrate the traditions of our colonialist predecessors who so gloriously founded the British empire. It is much more dignified. (Were you wondering why there are so few old gays? Now you know.)

## The point of the dark enlightenment is to understand the world, not to change it.

### 2015-05-10 06:36:16

Theory is understanding and understanding is theory. Seeing the world as a collection of bare unexplained facts is effectively the same as seeing the world as filled with magic. To suppose that somehow price controls on wages or medical treatment do not behave like price controls generally is in effect to believe in magic.

Without theory the world is a collection of magical events, something that defies understanding.

Experiments can be faulty. Experience can be faulty, and its interpretation can be faulty. There are experiments "showing" that Uri Geller is a spoon bender. A person who understands the world will know, despite the seeming evidence, that Uri Geller is a fraud. Reflect on Moldbugs demonstration that macro economics is a fraud[260].

But surely The Reaction is at least a little bit interested in changing the world?

Theory suggests two paths for changing the world.

The Moldbuggian path is to be worthy of power, wait for leftism to self destruct, as it has so many times before, and then when the military come looking for a priesthood, we are available.

The other, more activist, path is to form a thede, tribe, religion, religions being synthetic tribes, and proceed on the long march through the institutions of the red empire, the empire of the bases, and in due course subjugate the blue empire, the empire of the consulates. From time to time the Red Empire has blown up Blue Empire proxies, and vice versa. It would not take much for the fighting to get serious.

The reaction has engaged in a number of experiments in tribe formation. It is too soon to evaluate the results. We don't yet have much empirical data on tribe synthesis.

Which brings us to the secular reaction's view of religion. Which is that Religio matters, religion not so much. A religion's unfalsifiable beliefs, its empirically neutral beliefs, are reverse engineered from its rituals, are rationalizations of its rituals, rather than the rituals being engineered from the beliefs. The unfalsifiable beliefs of Shinto are incoherent, since Shinto is a random grab bag of rituals, yet Shinto still worked quite well regardless, despite having very little in the way of beliefs for people to believe in.

A religion should be an effective tool for transmitting the wisdom of parents to teenagers, telling stupid people to do what smart people already know to do.

---

[260]https://unqualified-reservations.blogspot.com/2008/08/de-gustibus-non-computandum-or.html

## After white male america

2015-05-13 11:53:36

Law enforcement against blacks is inherently racist. Gentrification proceeded under an unprincipled exception. Eric Holder is rolling back that unprincipled exception. Not only does every good progressive know that being black is no indicator of propensity to commit crimes, he also knows that a past history of criminal conduct is no indicator of propensity to commit crimes in future - see "Les Miserables" for the correct progressive position on crime and punishment, which is, pretty much, that punishment is horribly oppressive and old fashioned.

Thus Krystalnacht in the small parts of Baltimore where whites are permitted, areas which were suddenly revealed as a precarious ghetto subject to the terrifying whims of a non white male majority.

If white nationalists were allowed to behave the way the rioters were, we would be back to overwhelming white majority lickety spit.

I suspect that most of the Cathedral is quite comfortable with gentrification, and are horrified to see it rolled back, but, because no enemies to the left, are unable to restrain the radicals among them.

After all, if the radical program succeeds, and ethnically cleansing white males becomes the next big holy cause, the way ladyboys were yesterday's holy cause, each member of the establishment wants to be last to be fed to the crocodiles, and to this end will industriously feed his fellow establishment members to the crocodiles.

If Baltimore is being ethnically cleansed of whites because two thirds black, then this has no great implications for the rest of America. There is a lot of ruin in a nation. We let leftists destroy Detroit out of hatred for whites, we can let them destroy a hundred Detroits.

If on other hand Baltimore is being ethnically cleansed because the New York Times and Eric Holder are rolling back the unprincipled exception that white laws are enforced on black people, then every white male in America is in the same boat as white males in Baltimore.

The obscure town of Ferguson, Missouri remains in the spotlight of national concern because in Ferguson the cops tend to be white and the criminals black. Something must be done about this! Of course, this pattern is observable everywhere in the United States. Ferguson is an extremely average[261] town[262]. Liberal cities like Santa Monica, CA tend to have racial disparities in arrest rates that are much worse. Indeed, the more liberal the city, the more that arrests consist of whites punishing blacks.

Because blacks are naturally and inevitably violent and subhuman, law enforcement is naturally and inevitably racist. Did I hear someone say "Not all blacks are like that"? But when you take statistics over all arrests, all unpleasant encounters between police and citizens, as Eric Holder has been doing, you get the mean, the median, and the mode, and the mean, the median, and the mode is that law enforcement consists of blacks being

---

[261]https://www.unz.com/isteve/everywhere-is-guilty-the-justice-dept-jihad-against-ferguson-in-statistical-perspective/

[262]https://www.unz.com/isteve/arrest-rates-ferguson-v-peoples-republic-of-santa-monica-ca/

vicious subhuman thugs and whites stopping them, which is racist. So Eric Holder issues an injunction to stop this racism, which is to say, to stop police from protecting whites against black violence.

If all men are created equal, it is morally wrong for police to protect whites from black violence. And Eric Holder has proven this, in a court of law, over and over again.

If the Obama Administration and the press were out to do to every municipality in America what they've talked of doing to Ferguson, the country would soon become a lawless Mad Max post-apocalyptic wasteland.

Conservatives tend to suppose that progressives are basically sane, so will refrain from making the US into a lawless Mad Max post-apocalyptic wasteland.

I don't think progressives actually think things through, I don't think they ask themselves "would it be good if we progressives, acting as a whole, did X". Rather each progressive does that which maximizes his status relative to other progressives, makes him holier than the next progressive, and if the net effect of all these holy actions by all these holy progressives is utterly disastrous, they rewrite history and reality that the net effect is just wonderful.

Eric Holder is just proving himself more holy by burning down Ferguson and Baltimore, and if that works, over time, lots of people will prove themselves more holy by burning down lots more.

Since trannie acceptance has maxed out with seven year olds being taught transexuality rather than the three Rs, each of the elements of the Cathedral is casting around for some new cause to be the next big thing.

And what they are right now trying on is getting rid of white males. It is ambitious, but with leftism moving left ever faster, with the overton window shrinking ever smaller, pays to be ambitious, to be in there first with the next big thing.

Quite likely there will be a reaction that causes them to try something less ambitious before all America is on fire. And quite likely there will not be.

Something similar to this happened in the period 1953 to 1969 leading to the 1967 race riots which ultimately resulted in the ethnic cleansing of whites out of Detroit and many other places, and it was rolled back, leading to the era of gentrification.

People take it for granted that "the inner city" is occupied by hostile subhuman savages. But in most of the world the inner city is where the civilized and elite upper crust live and play, since it is naturally desirable to be close to the center of things, and the subhuman savages are excluded to the exurbs, the favelas, where land is naturally cheap. And, until the Warren Court, that was the way it was in America. The Inner City went black due to the courts privileging black violence against whites. If do an ngrams search on inner city and you go through google books by date[263], you don't see references to the inner cities being a scary dangerous place, poor and black, until you see references to civil rights and such, until the Warren Court period. The inner cities are the way they are because, during the Warren court period, whites, rendered second class citizens, denied the right of collective self defense, were ethnically cleansed out of the most desirable real estate, with the result that it became the least desirable real estate.

---

[263]https://books.google.com/ngrams/graph?content=inner+city&year_start=1800&year_end=2000

In the fifties and sixties, the courts systematically abused judicial discretion and due process protections to excuse criminals generally and black attacks on whites in particular. Due process protections were systematically abused to obtain the substantive result that it was difficult to punish crime, and near impossible to punish black crime against white people.

To counter this, the politicians struck back against the judges with mandatory sentencing and terrifyingly broad prosecutorial powers, prosecutorial discretion being abused to counter abusive judicial discretion, and punitive prosecutorial process being abused to counter judicial abuse of due process to obtain substantive results.

Gentrification ensued - or rather regentrification, as parts of the inner city resumed the civilized character that they had had before Civil Rights and the Warren Court.

But since then, with unlimited nonwhite underclass immigration, with huge numbers of foreigners entering the country to live on crime and welfare, which is to say, to live on white males, the white vote has become effectively irrelevant. Most white males vote outside the Overton window, in that they will reliably vote for whichever major politician is closest to the right edge of the Overton window. Single women tend to live on welfare and affirmative action jobs, so vote with non whites.

The great majority of white males already vote for the rightmost candidate permitted. What are we going to do? Vote twice? Backlash is just not going to have any noticeable electoral impact. There is no substantial electoral downside to hating white males twice as much as the other guy and thus being twice as holy. As a tidal wave of non white underclass immigration floods the country to live on crime and welfare, the white male vote becomes increasingly irrelevant. Everyone is asking themselves what they can do to win these new voters. No one wonders what will influence white males.

Thus the kind of political backlash that occurred against the courts allowing criminals to go free, that led to mandatory sentencing and alarmingly broad prosecutorial powers, is now politically irrelevant. It will not change electoral outcomes. It does not matter how white males vote, because most of them already vote their interests, and if even more of them vote their interests, that adds up to not many votes up for grabs.

These days, alarmingly broad prosecutorial powers are apt to be used against any person who attempts to defend himself against black violence.

With white males effectively already a minority, quite likely there will not be reaction that causes them to try something less ambitious - quite likely this will slowly escalate into the coming purge of whites as a market dominant minority.

It is early days yet, but that is the way the wind blows.

And it seems to be working as a political cause. Baltimore and similar riots America wide seem to be gaining the Cathedral support. Only white males care, and they already vote for the least progressive candidate. All the church ladies are having orgasms for the manly rioters, and worrying about how the rioters are oppressed victims.

Whites are well on the way to becoming a market dominant minority. Market dominant minorities tend to get ethnically cleansed or genocided, sooner or later. Further, the necessary mythos for genocide and ethnic cleansing is already in place. We whites, merely by existing, cast baleful magic spells that cause all other groups to underperform. It is like original sin. We can only atone by vanishing. Pretty much everyone believes this, including most whites. Whites possess the evil magic mind control powers previously attributed to Jews.

The nominally Christian Churches, like the mainstream media, are all preaching we deserve ethnic cleansing for our sins, for casting these evil spells. Our powerlessness in the face of ethnic cleansing makes all white males look beta, so naturally all women will vote alpha. Women always identify with the conqueror against their own people.

Progressives collect mountains of evidence that group x is doing poorly compared to white males, for numerous values of x, and there really are only two possible explanations. Evil white males are casting evil spells harming members of group x, or group x really is inferior and needs to be ruled by their betters.

And, of course, no decent person would suggest that group x really is inferior and needs to be ruled by their betters.

Libertarians and Conservative Christians attempt to mark out a position somewhere in the middle, avoiding these two extremes, but a position in the middle turns out to be mighty slippery, seems that rather than avoiding both extremes, they embrace both extremes, depending on whether they are being criticized from the left or the right. Whenever they explicitly deny one position, they implicitly affirm the other.

But I really was not expecting the market dominant minority treatment until whites really were a minority. Cleansing Baltimore the way Detroit was cleansed seems premature. Efforts to cleanse New York, Baltimore style, have been forcefully checked by good old fashioned politically incorrect policing. But if ethnic cleansing is the next big cause, the way ladyboys were the last big cause, the New York check is only temporary,

From the point of view of the Cathedral as a whole, it does not make sense to make a start on ethnic cleansing and genocide so soon, but from the point of view of any one member, any one faction, any one conspiracy within the Cathedral, if ethnic cleansing and eventually genocide is inevitable sooner or later, it is in the interest of any one element of the Cathedral to try for sooner, to gain a status advantage by jumping the gun on the next big thing.

The Cathedral is more like a cancer than a conspiracy. It is not necessarily capable of following its own best interests.

Where do whites go from here? Alaska and Australia are looking good. Settlement of the Arctic is forbidden. Settlement of Antarctica is similarly forbidden, but Australia, the last white haven, has a claim, not internationally recognized, to most of the interesting parts of Antarctica.

Or we could do what the Koreans did - repel troublemakers and cops alike.

Recall the Cronulla beach riots. Police were ordered to back the Muslim rioters and repress the white rioters, but were either unable to obey those orders, or disinclined to obey them very effectively, whereupon the whites made short work of the Muslims.

Ethnic cleansing of white males from most of America, with the probable exception of Alaska, begins. It will not happen all at once, but rather, one city after another, one excuse after another. First Ferguson, now Baltimore, Krystalnacht proceeds.

Quite possibly it will hit determined opposition, and be postponed a decade or two, or many decades, until whites truly are a minority. Early days as yet. But so far, seems to be sufficient that white males are minority, and white females are being taught to despise them.

Because effective law enforcement against blacks is racist, and since the declaration of independence has been an unprincipled exception, and unprincipled exceptions get rolled back one by one, there is no lasting solution short of moving to Alaska, or rolling the enlightenment all the way back, back to that all men were not created equal, and women do not count at all.

Any politically thinkable solution merely postpones the inevitable, temporarily keeping the unprincipled exception in place to allow gentrification, and preserve areas already gentrified. Any permanent solution is going to require the politically unthinkable

And by the unthinkable I don't mean Nazism or white nationalism. Nazis were leftists in 1930, Roosevelt on steroids, became rightists in that the rest of the left continued to move ever leftwards. I mean the reaction of the eighteenth century.

Because the establishment is secretly not all that keen on the latest program, because the establishment rather likes gentrification, it is likely that whites could fight back, and not be crushed by the united power of the state, because the state is not really all that united. We really should try a Cronulla, we should render unsafe white areas safe by judicious lynching of particularly badly behaved blacks and/or wholesale removal of nonwhites, yet I see no one trying that.

We cannot continue the enlightenment project because the effective law enforcement that preserved parts of America for whites is an unprincipled exception to the enlightenment, and always has been

One could have predicted Baltimore from Les Miserables. For whites to live in Baltimore, we need a society in which no one could take Les Miserables seriously.

Here is the outline for such a society[264]. See also[265].

Libertarians, conservative Christians, and such, don't want to accept the position that white males cast evil spells that impair the performance of other groups, which position has the disturbing implication that white males need to be eliminated, but neither do they want to accept the positions that whites should rule over inferior races and men should rule over women, and so they attempt to take a variety of intermediate positions, but these intermediate positions consist of crimestop, doublethink, and unprincipled exceptions, and so are inherently vulnerable to the superior holiness of the position that white males cast evil spells, and since it seems that no amount of punishment or castigation can stop white males from casting these evil spells, white males have to be eliminated.

Thus, for example, a libertarian may piously say that there is no such thing as race, that that is collectivist thinking.

This pious tactic works just fine in Turkey, in most of Latin America, and in Egypt, where anyone who notices that the ruling class is white, and the underclass brown, is apt fall down several flights of stairs in a one story police station. In consequence, everyone piously agrees that all Turks are one race, all nationals of the Latin American country in question are all one race. Similarly, there are a lot of black countries where the ruling elite varies from milk chocolate to "Huh? That guy is white!" and somehow strangely no one seems to notice.

---

[264]https://blog.reaction.la/culture/the-next-official-belief-system/
[265]https://blog.reaction.la/culture/in-favor-of-official-religion/

But in America, such piety does not go far, because a progressive points out that black schools are invariably very bad schools, and proposes that whites fix this problem (presupposing that whites caused this problem). Saying that there is no such thing as black school because there is no such thing as a black is unlikely to be persuasive, because it is perfectly obvious that the progressive is correct in that there are such things as black schools, and that black schools vary from bad to worse.

So the libertarian, inconsistently, temporarily dumps his position that there is no such thing as race, and snarkily asks "Why is that when blacks are bussed to good schools, those schools then immediately become bad schools"

But the libertarian dare not answer his own question, for the true answer is crimethink, whereas the progressive can easily answer the question: White males are so evil and hateful that they cast evil spells upon the school when blacks are bussed there.

So the progressive asks the libertarian what is to be done about black schools. And the libertarian cannot answer, for were he to answer, the true answer is that the black schools must be subject to white authority, black students forced by harsh discipline, including the frequent application of corporal punishment, to behave like white students, (in other words, whites must rule over blacks), and that mothers who deprive children of their biological fathers need to be shamed and punished as trash, sluts, and whores, (in other words, males must rule over females).

And so the libertarian has no answer that he dare speak, or even dare think, but the progressive does have an answer: Somehow make sure that white males are just somehow not around any more.

Any program for races and sexes living together as equals will always run into the problem that they are not in fact equal, and political activists will then always make hay out of this inequality.

And the end result of activists making hay is that one race must be eradicated, or one race must rule the other.

Any solution short of whites ruling over blacks and men ruling over women is always necessarily vulnerable to the superior holiness of those who wish to prevent evil white males from casting evil spells.

Any measure to prevent evil white males from casting evil spells will always fail, requiring ever more drastic action to deal with the evil committed by white males and the very great harm that they magically inflict.

## The Camp of the Saints

### 2015-05-18 10:17:42

The good and the great have announced there is no such thing as an illegal immigrant, in part because anyone who (however implausibly) claims to be a refugee, is legal.

Some time ago Australia adopted a policy of turning the boats around, which policy was and is denounced as a war crime. After a few unpleasant incidents where a few illegal immigrants suffered minor injuries, a few people smuggler boats caught fire, one people smuggler boat caught fire and sank, and some lost engines and steering, the people smugglers stopped coming to Australia. New Zealand does not admit to participating in this horrid war crime, but somehow boats heading for New Zealand seem to get mistaken for boats heading for Australia. Funny thing that. They now seem to have stopped trying to go to New Zealand.

A short while ago Indonesia, Thailand, and Malaysia, being swarmed by Bangladeshis, adopted a similar policy.

Initially Indonesia piously condemned Australia's policy, but finding that Bangladeshis were now coming to Indonesia instead of passing through and heading on to Australia, seem to have changed their mind.

As a result, the entire eastern edge of the Indian ocean is now off limits to people smugglers.

Meanwhile, Europe continues to be swarmed by middle easterners, many of who look suspiciously black - which is to say, is being swarmed by subSaharan blacks making the dubious claim to be middle easterners fleeing Islamic State, though they traveled a mighty long way to reach the lands controlled by Islamic State.

A small number of illegal immigrants are rumoured have died as a result of picking a quarrel with the Thai navy, whereupon the Australian Prime Minister called upon the navies to stand firm.

The problem of stopping Bangladeshis from going to Thailand is roughly similar to the problem of stopping blacks from crossing the Mediterranean. Bangladeshis were not all that interested in going to Thailand until Australia drew up the drawbridge.

## A letter to Sunnis facing Shia Democracy

2015-05-20 04:53:08

They are going to kill you all. So you had better sign up with the Caliphate.

It is inherent in the nature of democracy that you get rule by a religion that has open entry into the clerisy.

It is inherent in the rule of a religion that has open entry into the clerisy that it becomes ever more extreme and eventually, ever more left wing.

They have gotten rid of all the Christians and such. Every election, every year, they get more and more radical. You are next. Then everyone who is insufficiently Shia. They are now mobilizing and arming with American weapons the poorly disciplined and poorly trained Shia mobs that previously attempted genocide[266].

## Indonesia, Thailand, and Malaysia capitulate and allow the boats.

2015-05-22 02:32:53

Since Tony Abbot has been elected prime minister of Australia, no one is known to have successfully illegally immigrated to Australia. Their boat goes back, or if they are unusually stubborn and persistent, they wind up in a military run prison camp in a third world hell hole. From time to time progressives complain about the conditions in these camps.

---

[266]https://pjmedia.com/richardfernandez/2015/05/19/the-road-to-damnation/

As far as is known, no one has yet wound up in Davey Jones locker, though some have come close.

It looks like one hundred percent successful enforcement and if it is not, it is mighty close to one hundred percent.

Illegal immigration can be stopped. Completely. You have to break a few eggs, and maybe set a few boats on fire. There are underage orphans in those prison camps (and if there are not, the Australian government says that there are so that no one thinks that they can successfully play the pity card), but you don't have to drown or shoot anyone.

Under international pressure, Indonesia, Thailand, and Malaysia have agreed to accept the illegal immigrants for up to a year, in return for first world promises that the illegals will then go to some first world country - presumably Australia. The Australian government has other ideas. Presumably the pressure will escalate on Australia, while simultaneously, with a deal guaranteeing illegal migrants unspecified first world residence, we can expect a gigantic flood of illegals piling up in Thailand, Malaysia, and Indonesia.

The flood is going to rapidly grow to spectacular and alarming proportions, so either Thailand and Malaysia are going to get screwed (which I think is the most likely outcome), or Europe and America is going to take this lot (second most likely outcome), or Australia yields, which I think is the least likely outcome, because Tony Abbot has balls.

The plan, however, is that Australia will take them. As illegals pile up in Thailand, Malaysia, and Indonesia, pressure will increase on Australia.

This growing pile of illegals will be the camp of the Saints. The plan was probably to rewrite history that Australia had implicitly agreed to take them, and then shame Australia for failing to live up to this implicit and unstated promise, but Tony Abbot's swift application of a flamethrower has made that rewrite difficult. Anyone joining the camp is expecting an airlift to Europe or the United States, not Australia.

## Losing Ramadi

### 2015-05-23 13:02:29

Obama is of course a Muslim, progressive, and anticolonialist who hates America and wishes to see America defeated, but allowing Ramadi, and indeed Iraq, to be lost was pretty sensible.

The underlying Bush theory was that Iraq would become a well run democracy, like Switzerland, where the Shia majority elected nice moderate progressives, thereby counterbalancing the dangerous influence of the Shia religious crazies in Iran. The middle east would become moderate progressive, rather than Muslim.

As it worked out the elected government Shia government in Iraq was oppressive and intolerant, its primary function being to distribute goodies to voting blocks. The populace conspicuously failed to throw flowers at our troops. The Sunni murderously hated us for removing them from power. The Shia hated us for revealing to the world their incapacity to rule. The influence of Iran keeps them saner - well, less insane - than they would otherwise be.

Progressives, including Obama, misremembered Bush as saying "We will go in to steal their oil", and so believed that when they were running things, instead of Bush, *then* the locals would throw flowers at us and elect nice moderate progressives. Thus, "Arab Spring", which was Bush on steroids with double the already grating optimism. They then discovered that the Iraqi willingness to elect moderate progressives was proportional to US willingness to kick ass, and the locals figured the progressives had no will to kick ass.

Tunisia is perhaps proceeding to democratic progressivism, as originally envisaged in Arab Spring. Morocco is undemocratically proceeding to progressivism because the King commands progressivism. The rest of the countries of the Arab spring were disasters.

The past history of progressive kings is that usually King gets violently overthrown, is remembered as an incredibly brutal reactionary, and is replaced by a horrifying tyranny, but so far Tunisia and Morroco are working out OK - for progressives. Rest of the progressive plan is going to hell.

## Raping Sanza Stark

### 2015-05-24 10:14:10

I have not been watching Game of Thrones since they killed off every character I cared about, but the recent fuss about rape caused me to watch the latest episode. To see the controversy, fast forward to the end. All the rest is people you don't know or care about talking about things you do not understand, apart from a scene where the youngest Stark kid gets the beating she has long deserved.

Game of thrones piously promotes the Victorian myth that women don't like sex.

Nah, women don't like sex with *you*.

They really like sex with the manliest man around. Fertile age women are ten times as horny as men. Because of the immense risk and hazards of pregnancy in the ancestral environment, if women were not extremely keen on sex, human race would have become extinct shortly after women figured out the connection between penis in vagina sex and pregnancy. Trouble is that the manliest man around is usually the guy in a romance book or a romance movie, who is ten times as manly as any real life person around. Or perhaps the man she is pining for is a real person who dropped a load into her in a five minute meeting in the executive toilet, and she has been pining for that man ever since, what Roissy calls alpha widowhood, as for example Monica Lewinsky pining for Bill Clinton.

Since the manliest man in the Game of Thrones universe, as women measure manliness, is undoubtedly her husband, realistically Sansa Stark would have started tearing his clothes off with her teeth before he got a chance to bring her to the wedding.

We need to ban romance novels where there is a ridiculous disparity between the attractiveness of the male protagonist and the female protagonist. Such a ban would bring our fertility rate right up. Ugly fat forty year old women with kids divorce their husbands because they expect to marry a handsome billionaire athlete. Happens all the time in books.

A short while ago a washed up elderly female movie star complained because she was deemed too old to play the love interest of a fifty five year old male movie star[267]

---

[267] https://www.theguardian.com/commentisfree/2015/may/22/id-prefer-to-watch-maggie-gyllenhaal-in-a-movie-than-any-55-year-old-man

In an environment of casual sex where family formation is generally failing, we would expect any female past fertile age to get no attention, any female approaching the reduced fertility age to get substantially reduced attention, and any physically fit man to get about the same attention regardless of age, though old physically fit men are considerably less common than young physically fit men.

And that is biology.Old women do not score old men. (Unless they married them when both were young, and were good wives all their years)

And in an environment of family formation, we would expect considerably greater emphasis on female youth and virginity - in such an environment, older male movie starts would be discriminated against, but older female movie stars much more discriminated against, female movie stars would be washed up and over the hill at twenty, so a common movie scenario would be an older long established male romantic lead, with a bunch of successful movies under his belt, forty years old playing a thirty five year old, romances a character played by a seventeen year old actress, whereas in our current environment of casual sex without family formation, there is no reason why Sean Connery could not romance twenty year olds till he drops, except for feminist meltdown.

## After economic leftism

### 2015-05-25 23:28:14

Economic leftism, workers against capitalists, died with the Soviet Union. Now it is women and nonwhites against white heterosexual males.

American Hindus have extremely high incomes and are extremely reliable Democrat voters. Hindus are the opposite end of income and education spectrum to Mexicans, yet vote the same.

Old fashioned economic leftism doesn't explain this.

And yet there is the sense that something is being redistributed.

The country itself is being redistributed from white heterosexual males to a coalition of almost everybody else. And it makes sense for any ambitious newcomer to try and get a piece of the action. Because they can.

Resentment isn't required, but no one wants to consciously think he is just joining the looter coalition. So resentment is required, and is speedily manufactured.

And since each white wants to be last to be fed to the crocodiles, the whites in the ruling coalition will echo that resentment with double the enthusiasm, and will each be twice as keen on feeding other whites in the ruling coalition to the crocodiles. The situation of white heterosexual males in the ruling elite is similar to that of Jews Jim the Bolshevik party or intellectuals in the Khmer Rouge. The Bolshevik party was pretty much all Jewish, and the Khmer Rouge pretty much all intellectuals, but the climate of hostility and suspicion directed at Jews among the Bolsheviks, and at intellectuals amongst the Khmer Rouge, was such that they were busily purging each other, until none were left.

Parts of this post cheerfully stolen from Handle's member's only post. As usual, anything really horrifying is probably my revisions and not in Handle's original.

## The moron elite

### 2015-05-27 06:08:12

Twenty two out of twenty three Harvard grads could not explain why the earth gets hotter in summer and cooler in winter.

So I asked my cleaning lady, who has received no science education whatsoever, and very little education. She replied that the days were longer in summer and shorter in winter. I then prompted her "Why are they longer in summer and shorter in winter?", to which she correctly replied that the earth is tilted with respect to its orbit around the sun.

To be strictly correct she should have said the earth's *axis* is tilted with respect to the earth's orbit, but since she already got "days" correct, unlike the Harvard grads, axis is implied.

The author of this video suggests we need improved science education, but I think that no amount of education can turn a sow's ear into a silk purse, that what we need is considerably less education, about as much education as my cleaning lady has.

Harvard does not, for the most part, teach anything that matters to anyone other than how to hate whitey. Universities have been dumbing down since 1870. They want to be more inclusive, and then adjust their course material to make those included feel more at home. Which makes them useless.

Ferguson looks at measured elite IQs[268], concludes that our ruling elite is around IQ 120, and that everyone above IQ 140 is pretty much toast. "inappropriately excluded". It looks to me that the situation is worsening over time, that older members of our elite are generally substantially smarter than recent members of our elite, though all my evidence on this is anecdotal, and people dispute it.

Our elite is being stupidified by avoiding disparate impact. Anything that filters for smarts has disparate impact on women and blacks. Also, smart people tend to mansplain - give those affirmative actioned into jobs beyond their competence instructions and advice that they are incapable of following. Wasenlightened denies this. I accuse him of false consciousness. The level of fear at Google seems excessive if Wasenlightened perceptions are accurate. In an environment where one has a large number of female affirmative action employees, filtering for political correctness is going to filter for stupidity since smart people will be perceived as discriminating against the less smart.

Our universities have been dumbed down so that they no longer teach what high school used to teach.

Academic credentials are not indicators that one has learned anything useful, or indeed learned anything at all, rather they are filters for intelligence and diligence, and, due to degree inflation and the inclusion of women and blacks, very poor filters at the upper end.

Used to be that graduating high school proved you were pretty smart. Now, graduating Harvard does not show you are smart.

I propose degree deflation:

Smart kids can learn in high school maths to calculus and trig, science to special relativity, how to calculate pi from first principles, geography, history of western civiliza-

---

[268]https://polymatharchives.blogspot.in/2015/01/the-inappropriately-excluded.html

tion, and can absorb the western culture and western civilization that university no longer teaches.

I propose that the lower two thirds, pretty much everyone below IQ 106, fails to get a school leaving certificate and leaves school at the start of puberty. The somewhat smarter and more diligent people, IQ 106 to IQ 120, about a quarter of the population, also leave school at the start of puberty, but with a school leaving certificate. The smart people, 120 and up, the top ten percent, graduate high school. Ten percent of that ten percent, the top one percent, people 135 and up, take a two year university course.

Attempting to use academic credentials to filter to smarter than the top one percent is unlikely to succeed, because of demand for lengthy recreational degrees. If we try to get an elite smarter than 135, going to need some new filtering mechanism. Also, using academic credentials as a filter means you are up against the bureaucratic imperative to expand. If one is supposedly in the business of educating people, one is naturally inclined to claim that the education is beneficial, and can benefit everyone, rather than acting as a filter. Thus academic institutions have an incentive to subvert their filter function, and thus an incentive to stupidify the elite.

We used to have a public service exam, a requirement for government employment in functions likely to exercise power, that was IQ heavy, though it also tested for diligence by requiring you to memorize a lot of useless nonsense. Unfortunately, this, of course, had disparate impact. Simply re-instituting the exam would dramatically improve elite function, and one could simply make it a substantially tougher exam for anyone in the system at a level likely to make policy. On the other hand, the Chinese mandarinate tried this and it worked extremely badly. The mandarins were not all that smart. It is hard to make a filter that works when everyone is trying to game the system. But it is not as hard as making a filter that works when you are trying to be inclusive.

## Taleb refutes Pinker on war

### 2015-05-28 02:12:34

A long time back I criticized Pinker's "better angels of our nature", arguing that he mistakes leftism for progress and goodness, arguing that criminal violence by citizens against each other is at extraordinarily high levels, that state violence against citizens in the form of imprisonment and policing is at levels unprecedented except when a state is crushing a hostile enemy population in a condition of war or near war, and that levels of warfare between states are pretty much what they always have been, arguably considerably worse.[269]

For example Pinker complacently observes that the Victorians were shocked and horrified by a crime wave, but neglects to observe that this crime wave consisted of one mugging in London every few months - which crime wave never went away, but instead people got used to it, and then it got vastly worse, and people got used to it again, and then it got vastly worse still, and people attempted to abandon much of their cities to savages, and then the crime wave followed them, and there is now no safe area in London. The idea of the inner city as some kind of jungle is new, starting in the late nineteen forties, early fifties. Early in the twentieth century, the idea that the affluent and respectable might

---

[269]https://blog.reaction.la/culture/pinker-on-violence/

have to abandon vast expanses of wealth and property, of huge, beautiful and high status buildings where once the wealthy and fashionable lived, to the vandalism and depravity of savages would have been as unimaginable as wolves and bears prowling the streets of London to devour passers by.

My criticism of his argument on war is that war is a bursty phenomenon, sometimes there are a lot of mighty big wars, and sometimes, when one hegemon has the upper hand, or several hegemons remember the last big war too well, not many wars. This peace lasts until the dominant hegemon weakens, or people forget how bad the last big war was, forget how easy it is to start wars, and how hard it is to stop them, whereupon they go at it again. And the generation that remembers the last big war is now mostly dead.

Taleb, arguably the worlds leading expert on the statistics of bursty phenomena, makes the same argument in a more scientific fashion backed by statistics. War follows a power law with an exponent substantially less than one and substantially greater than zero, rather than a normal distribution, meaning that risk is dominated by large rare events - the risk of losing life and property in a big war is far greater than the risk of losing life and property in a small war, even though small wars are common and big wars are rare.

Pinker tells us.

> wars between great powers and developed nations have fallen to historically unprecedented levels. This empirical fact has been repeatedly noted with astonishment by many military historians and international relations scholars...

Taleb tells us[270] that because war follows a power law rather than a normal distribution, if one analyzes the level of warfare using statistics appropriate to a normal distribution, at any given time, chances are it has either fallen to historically unprecedented levels, or a great war has broken out and one is too busy trying to stay alive to do statistics.

With a power law phenomenon, recent experience almost always massively under estimates the risk of large rare events, recent experience is almost always nicer than experience over a longer period. Until it is not.

## Psychopathy is an anticoncept

2015-06-04 22:11:42

Thumotic proposes that "psychopathy" is an anti concept, created to make men weak[271].

The definition of psychopathy combines traits that are unlikely to be correlated, for example

1: the ability to endure stress and danger calmly, and the propensity to lie casually without regard to the long term consequences.

2: the propensity to act vigorously and competently in pursuit of goals and the lack of realistic, long-term goals

The concept of psychopathy defines manliness as bad, and men as irresponsible and childlike.

---

[270]https://www.fooledbyrandomness.com/violence.pdf

[271]https://www.thumotic.com/the-concept-of-psychopathy-makes-you-weak/

A psychopath is defined as someone who is not a reliable friend, yet I am pretty sure that calmness under stress and danger is a good indication of a reliable friend.

The word "psychopath", like "racist[272]" is a twentieth century invention. If there were such natural kinds as "racist[273]" or "psychopath", there would have been words for them in biblical times. Such twentieth century coinages do not cut reality at the joints, but are intended to manipulate and destroy.

## Mattress girl's porn shot

### 2015-06-06 04:56:55

Emma Suck has posted a porn that re-enacts her "rape"[274], or the way she recollects her "rape", or perhaps cashes in on her "rape" for maximum attention whoring.

What is depicted in the video is not rape, but a woman scorned.

She has consensual sex with a guy. After a bit he starts beating her, but she does not ask him stop or ease up, if anything she enthusiastically encourages the beating. Then he finishes up and pulls out. She rolls over with her legs up for him to finish her off with his hand or to re-enter from the rear, but he just gets up and walks out, effectively scorning her.

I have had sex like that lots of times, but in the end, though I don't finish them off, I give them lots of comforting, hugging them, telling them how much they pleased me, kissing them, etc, especially if I have given them an erotic beating. And if I have to leave quickly after the comforting, send a message telling them they were great.

## Rohingya terrorist problem

### 2015-06-06 21:31:29

You may have heard that there are over a million poor stateless victimized Rohingya that our do gooders want to move into first world countries to vote for more leftism.

And indeed it is true that they are poor stateless and victimized. But a big part of the reason that they are poor, stateless, and victimized, is that they believe that Muslims should live under Muslim rule, and to this end they tried to carve a Muslim state out of Burma. To my surprise, they do not want to go to a first world country, such as America. They want to go to a Muslim ruled state, such as Malaysia. A few days ago, America legally accepted its first batch of Rohingya from a refugee camp in Thailand. Thai military attempted to move them to the US, Rohingya refugees refused and rioted, seeking the opportunity to set sail to a Muslim country.

These guys take their religion seriously. And their religion says that Islam should rule, and they should be ruled by Islam. They are reasonably happy to be ruled by moderate Islam, you cannot get much more moderate than their favorite destination, Malaysia, but Islam it has to be.

---

[272]https://blog.reaction.la/tag/racism/
[273]https://blog.reaction.la/tag/racism/
[274]https://www.pornhub.com/view_video.php?viewkey=785449782

If brought to America or Australia, they will be in America very much against their will, and therefore will likely attempt to create a Muslim ruled state inside America as they attempted to create a Muslim ruled state inside Burma.

The Bangladeshi refugees who are intermingled with the Rohingya refugees, who speak the same language as the Rohingya refugees, who look like the Rohingya refugees, are economic refugees, seeking a better life. They want to go to first world states such as America and Australia. Maybe many of the Rohingya refugees are economic refugees also. But they are primarily religious refugees, seeking, not freedom to practice their religion, but freedom to persecute anyone who does not practice their religion. They don't want to go to the first world. They want to go to Dar al Islam.

If I had my way, we would ship them all to Islamic State.

## Degentrification

### 2015-06-11 04:59:17

Degentrification is ethnic cleansing of whites.

The politically correct account of the inner cities is that white people made them into shitholes in order to hurt black people.

But, if you look at the ruins, there are a bunch of really nice buildings which were obviously once inhabited by the better sort of people, middle class whites, upper class whites.

What happened of course, is that in the 1950s and 1960s, the Warren Court period, whites were dispossessed, ethnically cleansed out of the inner cities, by black racial violence, violence supported by the state, in that whites were denied the right of collective self defense. A few Jewish communities remained, because Jews, in an unprincipled exception, were allowed collective self defense.

After the sixties, the left backed away from ethnically cleansing whites, and we got gentrification. But, after gays and trannies, what is the next big cause? They are casting around for something, and one of the things they are trying on is renewed ethnic cleansing, where once again black people take stuff that whites built away from whites[275]. Hence Baltimore and this poolside party[276].

The current state of Detroit, and what is happening to Johannesburg, tells us that were it not for whites, blacks would be living in the jungle, carrying pointy sticks, and eating each other. Blacks can be civilized, but only if subject to firm, and substantially white, authority. America lacks the hard hand necessary to keep black people from reverting to their natural condition.

With America close to a nonwhite majority, and single women, as always, voting for the victors, there is no natural stopping point for the latest round of ethnic cleansing short of complete removal of whites from everything they have built that is worth having.

Resistance to this process is fundamentally incompatible with democracy with universal franchise. If it does not happen in this coming round of movement ever leftwards,

---

[275]https://www.isegoria.net/2015/06/pool-mob/

[276]https://theconservativetreehouse.com/2015/06/08/the-full-story-of-the-mckinney-texas-pool-mob-inside-the-craig-ranch-subdivision/

will happen in the next or the one after that. If you oppose this outcome, you have to reject democracy with universal franchise. If you reject democracy with universal franchise, have to deny that all men were created, and that women are equal to men. The eradication of white people was inherent in the enlightenment, and our continued existence has only been possible by one unprincipled exception to the enlightenment after another. In the end, unprincipled exceptions always yield to superior holiness.

## On utilitarianism

### 2015-06-13 07:35:05

I, you, and a couple of friends discover that a railroad bridge has been crucially weakened, and if a train goes over it, the train will fall. A train with a thousand people in it, a thousand strangers none of us have ever met, is rattling down the line to bridge.

One among us has his dog with him. If he ties his dog to the tracks the dog will be killed, but the train will stop to investigate the incident, thus saving a thousand lives.

I know human nature. If he ties his dog to the tracks to save a thousand strangers whose deaths he will not see, he will tie his dog to the tracks to gain a dollar, and if he ties his dog to the tracks to gain a dollar, he will tie me to the tracks to gain a dime.

The fatal flaw of utilitarianism is not the difficulty in comparing interpersonal utility. It is that there are in fact no utilitarians. Only evil people with overly clever stories justifying evil acts. Thus utilitarians always wind up killing a million innocent people to make an omelet, and wind up with no omelet.

## Into Darkness

### 2015-06-14 05:07:17

Dalrymple reviews the poor sexual choices of an underclass woman, Tina Nash, who lived a very nice lifestyle on aid to her neglected absolutely fatherless children. She was into horseback riding, possessed disc-jockey equipment costing $3,200 had a car, had a 42-inch plasma television in her living room while her children could watch a second TV in their bedroom.

Two conclusions are obvious from his review: Poverty is not caused by lack of money, you can be poor while having a host of luxuries at taxpayer expense, and that this woman should never have been allowed to make her own sexual choices. She should have been forced to sleep with one man, that man able and willing to support her and her children, forbidden to sleep with any other, and subject to corporal punishment if she failed to sleep with her owner, or slept with some other man.

I know some high IQ high income upperclass women whose emotional maturity is no better than that of Tina Nash, and who made a pile of choices equally bad, but somehow avoided similar consequences - such as pregnancy and violence resulting in lasting injury. Since they demonstrably had the ability to think about the future, I suppose they should have been given a limited choice of men willing and able to support them and their children, and having made their choice once and forever, thereafter forced to sleep with and only with their husbands. And some women, like Tina Nash and her mother, cannot be trusted with even that much choice.

There are a great many people who just are not capable of making the choices needed to navigate the modern world, most of them female or black. They should be under the control of someone else.

I know a high IQ high socioeconomic status woman who from age eleven to age thirty slept with a parade of low lifes, some them as or more dangerous as anyone Tina Nash slept with. Then getting older, when being a total slut starts to look disgusting rather than alluring, cleaned up her act, revirginated, started pursuing nice guys with good careers ahead of them, married a nice high IQ engineer with a good future ahead of him, and proceeded to pump out lots of lovely children. But what she was from preteen to the age when the clicking of her biological clock started to get ominous was disgusting and should not have been permitted. The marriage seems happy enough, but really, should he have to have a wife that has been reamed by a long parade of dicks bigger than his dick, wielded by men who are, as women measure manliness, much more manly than he is?

I see another high IQ high socioeconomic status woman who at age thirty failed to clean up her act, slowly transitioned from alluring slut to disgusting slut, and is now transitioning to cat lady.

I know lots of high IQ career women who, when they see their children growing up, when the years that were most important to spend with their children have passed, *then* lean back from their jobs to spend time with their children.

Women just do not make good choices, and need to have their choices restrained and controlled by fathers and husbands. Females grow up faster than males, but they stop growing up at age eighteen. Women are never adults and should never be treated like adults or allowed to make adult choices, though when the hormones drop in menopause, they stop acting so crazy.

Interestingly, in mattress girl's porn video, the male playing the rapist or abusive lover has his face blurred out, but mattress girl's face is fully visible. Yet the man playing the abusive lover is a well known professional porn actor, who is presumably drawing pay for this role. He is an actor. No one is likely to confuse him with his role, for he has played so many roles, usually undignified roles with fat chicks. He cannot be embarrassed being seen putting his dick into a slut's asshole. Is he embarrassed to be seen putting his dick into crazy?

## Libertarians support ethnic cleansing of whites

2015-06-18 15:38:34

The libertarian position has always been to go with the left on everything except economic leftism.

As the left abandons economic leftism, and at the same time goes lefter and lefter, this leaves libertarians indistinguishable from leftists, and libertarians going lefter and lefter.

And as the left goes frothing at the mouth batshit insane, the libertarians froth with equal enthusiasm.

The highest point of absurdity so far is Reason magazine backing the official narrative on the McKinney pool takeover by black kids[277]

> Police responded to a fight that had broken out between a girl and a mother. A video of the encounter establishes that the fight did indeed take place, but it only involved a couple people—not the large swath of teenagers who were later detained by officers. When the officers arrived, they treated all the minority teenagers as suspects and ignored the white kids.

The problem was not that a fight had broken out. The problem was that a fight had broken out because a bunch of black teenagers had invaded someone else's pool without permission.

So Reason magazine no longer supports your property rights if you are white.

## Anti slavery people were evil from the beginning

### 2015-06-20 07:31:35

Anti slavery people were always evil scum, and the modern left walks in their evil and hateful footsteps.

The Africa Association was founded to explore and economically develop africa. It came completely under the control of anti slavery people, and changed its purpose to opposing slavery and humanizing blacks, showing that the left were entryists back then as they are now.

The Africa Association launched a lawsuit against the Hottentot Venus, to gain control of her and her assets[278], alleging she was kept in slavery.

The court blew them off[279], implying that their testimony was perjury.

So then as now, they engaged in perjury to accuse innocent people of grave crimes.

William Wilberforce, the founder of the anti slavery movement, purported to be an Anglican and to subscribe to the 39 articles, that being at the time a requirement to be allowed near the levers of power, but his claim was fraudulent, making him an apostate, for his church claimed that members of his church were saints, and regular Anglicans were not - and again, the left has not changed since then.

He should have been enslaved for apostasy in office, and sent to the West Indies, and if he had been England and the British Empire would still be going fine.

Similarly, John Brown was a terrorist, horse thief, and cold blooded sadistic killer: John Brown: The Making of a Martyr[280]

---

[277] https://reason.com/blog/2015/06/09/mckinney-of-pool-parties-police-brutalit

[278] https://books.google.com/books?id=YGdZAAAAIAAJ&pg=PA237&dq=%22hotten-tot+venus%22&hl=en&sa=X&ei=vT5VVbOqE8TCmQX4zoHwDQ&redir_esc=y#v=onepage&q=%22hot-tentot%20venus%22&f=false

[279] https://books.google.com/books?id=wHI5AQAAMAAJ&pg=PA260&dq=%22hotten-tot+venus%22&hl=en&sa=X&ei=vT5VVbOqE8TCmQX4zoHwDQ&redir_esc=y#v=onepage&q=%22hot-tentot%20venus%22&f=false

[280] https://www.amazon.com/gp/product/1879941198/ref=as_li_tl?ie=UTF8&camp=1789&cre-ative=9325&creativeASIN=1879941198&linkCode=as2&tag=jimsblo0e-20&linkId=S6L552B5Q3I52PEU

## A terrorized and terrified ruling class

2015-06-21 05:28:02

Radix observes the panic on the left[281] when Rachel Dolezal was revealed as transracial, wearing chocolate covered makeup over her naturally fair skin, dieing her blond straight hair black and curling it into tiny tight curls.

> Melissa Harris-Perry, once called "America's foremost public intellectual" by one of her fellow affirmative action scholars, had real terror in her eyes[282] as she desperately tried to reconcile "transracial" people with "transgenders" without an inadvertent faux pas

> ...

> ...none of the brave independent thinkers rebelling against social norms have been told what the "right" side is yet, and so they remain paralyzed with fear and indecision.

## The chastity of women

2015-06-23 23:44:23

It has always seemed obvious to me that women are far more keen on sex than men, but from time to time one of my commenters tells me that women are the naturally chaste sex.

Nah. The reason they are not in bed with you is that they await a booty call from Jeremy Meeks[283].

## Why human hypergamy is dysgenic

2015-06-28 01:51:55

Normally hypergamy is eugenic. That is what it is for, that is its telos, that is almost the definition of hypergamy. Yet it is very noticeable that a successful natural is frequently poor, perhaps usually poor, and often rather stupid. A loser, except he is a big winner with girls.

Consider the peacock. Glorious tails are so big and heavy that they are bad for the species, bad for the race, would be bad for clan and family if peacocks had clans and families, which they do not. Females tend to want what other females want.

Suppose females tend to go for X, where X is initially a good indicator of health and fitness, where females selecting males on X is initially eugenic. If other females select X, it is good to have sons with lots of X, so a female should select X if other females select X, even if X has ceased to be a good indicator of health and fitness. Selection for X tends to

---


[281] https://www.radixjournal.com/journal/2015/6/20/based

[282] https://www.youtube.com/watch?v=AsNWHpldrOA

[283] https://sparklesandsecrets.com/2015/06/23/fuck-boy-an-original-poem/

become more and more extreme, even if it ceases to be a good indicator of fitness. Sexual selection tends to become driven by unreasonable and rather arbitrary female fashions.

Humans and chimps murder, hunt, eat meat, and, unlike most animals, make war. The only other mammals I know of that make war are the lemming and the naked mole rat. I expect there are plenty of others that I have not heard of, but war is, for obvious reasons, a rare characteristic. We may therefore conclude that the common ancestor of man and chimp was violent, ate meat, and made war.

War requires loyalty and comradeship. You love your comrades, you will kill for them, and risk death for them. Humans are killer apes, but our specialty is loyalty, friendship, and cooperation.

Humans are not only smart, thus good at cooperating, but have physical adaptions for cooperation. Our eyes have whites, which make it harder for us to hide and make us more vulnerable to UV damage, but makes it easier for one human to tell what another human is looking at. Our throats are modified for a wider range of sounds in ways that make it considerably easier for us to choke. Humans are more specialized for cooperating than chimps.

The common ancestor of man and chimp lived in the jungle, but being the meanest sons of bitches in the jungle, some of them decided to wander out on the plains. Since they were the slowest sprinters on the plains, we may conclude that they were dangerous enough to take care of predators. The theory that the first of our ancestors to go on the plains were timid gentle herbivores was not very plausible even back in the days when we thought that chimps were timid gentle herbivores. If you cannot climb out of reach of carnivores, and you cannot sprint very well, what are you going to do?. A child or a female is going to stick with the males, a male is going to stick with his comrades.

Plus out on the plains, there is more meat and less fruit, more hunting, less gathering. So females are more dependent on males. So more patriarchy, more specialization for violence, more specialization for cooperative violence, and, with more patriarchy, more war. We became smarter in the course of thousands of genocides. Conversely, primitive humans that live in jungles tend to evolve to become more like chimps. In the jungle, females don't need male support and can kick their kids out at four to gather for themselves. Cooperation in large groups of men is less important in the jungles, where the individual male tends to individually predate on women and children, and so humans of that ancestry are not very good at cooperative endeavors - much better than any other animal, but not as good as their plains dwelling relatives.

Large groups of males quickly sort out their status hierarchy, after a bit of status jousting that is usually too subtle for women to understand, and thereafter treat each other with respect. The private crisply salutes the officer, the officer salutes back slightly less crisply.

Women in contrast never sort out their status hierarchy, and are always plotting against each other and undermining each other, so that it is difficult for large female groups to work together.

To women, this standard smart male cooperation all looks like submissiveness, looks like being low man on the totem pole, because this stuff just goes over their heads. To her, it looks as if the officer and the private are both kissing each other's asses, so she wants:

See the way he walks down the street
Watch the way he shuffles his feet
My, he holds his head up high
When he goes walking by, he's my guy

When he holds my hand, I'm so proud
Cause he's not just one of the crowd
My baby's always the one to try the things they've never done
And just because of that, they say

He's a rebel and he'll never ever be any good
He's a rebel 'cause he never ever does what he should
But just because he doesn't do what everybody else does
That's no reason why I can't give him all my love

He's always good to me, always treats me tenderly
Cause he's not a rebel, oh, no, no, no
He's not a rebel, oh, no, no, no, to me

If they don't like him that way
They won't like me after today
I'll be standing right by his side when they say

He's a rebel and he'll never ever be any good
He's a rebel 'cause he never ever does what he should
Just because he doesn't do what everybody else does
That's no reason why we can't share a love

By and large, he really will never ever be any good, for for men to get stuff done, have to work well with other men. By and large, he is a rebel because stupid - if he was a smart rebel he would be rebelling in ways less visible and more subtle than shuffling his feet.

But if all women tend to make the same mistake, then in a woman's interests to make the same mistake as other women commonly make, for the sake of sexy sons

Because female sexual selection for X tends to go over the top, tends to become unreasonably extreme, because females tend to select for even more of what other females are selecting for, tends to be fashion driven, selecting for men who are at the top of the male hierarchy leads to selecting for men who do not display submissive behaviors, which leads to her selecting for the rebel who shuffles his feet, when she should be selecting for the officer whose reply salute is slightly less crisp than that of the private, which leads to her selecting guys at the bottom of the male hierarchy, rather than the top.

This post inspired by the movie "Zulu", where all the characters, British, Boer, or Zulu, were ridiculously manly except for the preacher and his daughter, and the preacher's daughter entirely failed to notice.

# Current events

2015-06-28 09:08:04

As predicted, moving left faster and faster. All my life, we have been moving left, and the rate of movement left has been accelerating.

Harvard University was founded in 1637 by radical leftists plotting to conquer the world, though it was at the time a very minor part of the left wing conspiracy. The main action took place in England. When Cromwell halted the left singularity in England in 1648, Harvard became the primary center of the conspiracy.

And they have been getting crazier and more powerful ever since.

The latest developments:

1. Baltimore, Ferguson, and the supreme court case on disparate impact in housing amount to a resumption of the 1950s Warren Court program of ethnically cleansing whites out of what they have built. Difference is that due to the mass importation of illegal immigrants to live on crime, welfare, affirmative action jobs and government jobs, they now have the votes to sustain that policy all the way to its logical conclusion. Baltimore was our Kristallnacht.

2. Finishing off marriage, not that there was enough left to be worth preserving.

3. Obamacare case sets the important precedent that the bureaucracy can budget and legislate, rendering the house of representatives and the senate obsolete ritual survivals[284], like Buckingham palace.

4. Lowering the Confederate battleflag, and raising the butthole sex flag. Not only is what is left of marriage to be destroyed, but all must enthusiastically applaud its destruction, and you don't want to be the first one to stop applauding. So that I am not going to be first to stop applauding, will be leaving this flag on my blog permanently.

---

[284]https://www.powerlineblog.com/archives/2015/06/from-justice-scalias-dissent.php

## Greece runs out of other people's money

2015-07-01 22:34:05

The trouble with socialism is that eventually you run out of other people's money.

The level of economic freedom in Greece is fortieth out of forty three in the Eurozone. It has been falling like a stone for some time.

The real Greek economic crisis has been happening since about 2002, though it was partially hidden by very large amounts of other people's money until 2009.

Supposedly only twenty five percent of the workforce are unemployed, but the unemployed are vastly outnumbered by the steadily and rapidly rising "inactive". If a young man never gets a job, he is classified as "inactive" rather than unemployed. And most young men never get a job.

In most of the world, the anticapitalist economic left has largely disappeared, replaced by the anti white, anti male, and anti heterosexual left. In Greece however the anticapitalist left remains significant, so that in Greece the ever leftwards movement creates profound uncertainty in property rights. Movement leftwards in Greece buggers the economy more than movement leftwards in the US. If you invest, chances are you will lose your investment to a gang of thugs affiliated with a political party and protected by police and bureaucracy. In the event that you don't lose your investment to assorted thugs, in the event that you actually make a profit, tax rates are far, far above the Laffer limit, so you won't get your money back in any reasonable time - and with uncertainty growing every day, a reasonable time is a shorter time every day.

The government program is simple. They demand ever greater amounts of other people's money, so that socialism can work. Since the evil Greek capitalists are tapped out, that is evil German money. Other people's money is a human right, and their failure to get it is a violation of their human rights.

And the more they want German money, the more they cultivate hatred of the Germans. Seventy seven percent of Greeks believe the economic crisis is a German plot to install the fourth Reich on Greeks.

If you are stealing Jewish money, or Greek capitalist money, then it is a useful tactic to hate them, demonize them, and blame them for everything. Hating and demonizing Germans is unlikely to work as effectively.

## Governor Cuomo shocked that women will do anything for an alpha male thug

2015-07-03 06:56:59

"I'd be shocked," he said, "if a correction guard was involved in this." he said of an incident were a couple of female guard now faces the music for enabling the escape of a couple of prisoners that they had been having sex with.

female officers were responsible for the majority of all substantiated episodes of staff sexual misconduct with prisoners.[285]

---

[285] https://www.nytimes.com/2015/07/01/nyregion/escapees-fraternizing-with-prison-workers-doesnt-surprise-experts.html

This is an example of "not getting the joke" "or generational loss of hypocrisy"

One generation pretends, and the next generation actually believes. When I was young everyone politely pretended women were not like this, but everyone knew women were like this. Back in those days no one would ever allow female guards contact with male prisoners for glaringly obvious reasons.

This is a general problem with pretending to believe stuff so as not to hurt people's feelings. After a while, people start actually believing it. Expect aids infested blood to be back in the blood supply real soon now.

[Edit]

A commenter points out that one of the guards to which Governor Cuomo refers to was male. The male guard claims that the female guard hid the hacksaw blades inside frozen meat[286], and he unwittingly took the frozen meat to the prisoners not knowing what was in it. The male guard appears to have been bribed to do what he thought were minor favors. The female correctional officer, however, was doing major favors.

## Yet another final deadline for Greece

### 2015-07-08 02:14:28

Supposedly, if no agreement by Sunday, the ECB will stop funding Greece .

There have been a lot of final deadlines.

That which cannot go on forever will stop, but I would not bet on it stopping on Sunday.

Greece does not need austerity nor does it need stimulus. Greece does not need to remain in the Euro nor to exit the Euro. What Greece needs is a a massive reallocation of labor from luxuries and import consumption, to necessities and export production. Such labor flexibility could be accomplished by cutting taxes, dropping official wage floors and cutting the salaries of government employees, few of whom do anything remotely useful ("austerity"), or could be accomplished by retaining nominal wage floors and inflating them away. (Exit from the Euro plus "stimulus")

In practice however Greece is likely to get the "austerity" of raising taxes that are far above the Laffer limit even further above the Laffer limit, and the "stimulus" of ever more governmental and quasi governmental patronage jobs. When neither measure, stimulus nor austerity, has the intended result, it will get further loans from countries less dysfunctional than Greece. These loans will gradually become stingier and stingier, and less and less able to maintain the illusion of first world normality.

Ending not with a bang, but with a whimper.

## And how many fingers is O'Brien holding up, Gcochran9

### 2015-07-08 21:53:09

The blog "West Hunter", which investigates our ancestry, sometimes gets close to the edge of permitted thought. But will not slip over the edge. The globe is warming catas-

---

[286]https://www.dailymail.co.uk/news/article-3138385/Shawshank-prison-guard-Gene-Palmer-arrested-revealed-man-delivered-escapees-hacksaw-blades-frozen-meat-allowed-access-catwalk.html

trophically, gay "families" are just are ... just like normal families and are definitely not harems of sex slaves, and so on and so forth. And, while it industriously investigates the origin of races, there are, nonetheless, no such thing as races.

In a comment on that blog jamesd127 gives a summary of some of the more horrifying hate facts contained in "The Root of the Phylogenetic Tree of Human Populations" by Masatoshi Nei and Naoko Takezaki, Institute of Molecular Evolutionary Genetics, which tells us that the genetic distance between human populations is of the same order of magnitude as the genetic distance between humans and chimps, and that not all human populations have evolved at the same rate, with humans in environments very different from that of the common ancestor of man and chimp evolving substantially faster than humans in environments resembling that of the common ancestor of man and chimp.

To which the blog author responds simply "False"[287]

Now it might well be that the conclusions one might draw from the paper are false, but to deny that the paper says what it says is on par with saying that O'Brien is holding up five fingers.

Nonetheless he is a good bloke. I also would say O'Brien was holding up five fingers if they had electric wires attached to my testicles.

But, since he probably does not really believe that the paper does not say what it says, I wonder what he really believes about global warming and gay families.

He does not want further discussion of this topic on his blog. He does not say "Because several large black professors with base ball bats and room temperature IQs will visit my office if this discussion continues"

## The death of Christianity

2015-07-11 02:37:29

I have often remarked that Christendom is as dead as Roman paganism was in the fourth century AD, but, not being a believer, have been unable to explain why in ways believers could understand.

"Throne and Altar", however, has nailed it[288]:

> The first is a sense of the sacred, the spirit of reverence, coupled to a sense of God's revelation in the given meanings of the world. The second is a horror of nihilism, so that a man fears meaninglessness more than he craves license. The last is basic tribal loyalty to the Church and her members throughout the ages. The theologians scorn these attitudes because they are after all natural; one finds analogous or even identical things in any vital religion. But without them, any spiritual quest is bound to begin in pride and end in apostasy.

Heartiste, minion of Satan, observes the symptoms with horror[289].

---

[287]https://westhunt.wordpress.com/2015/07/03/inbreeding/#comment-70786
[288]https://bonald.wordpress.com/2015/07/10/what-this-blog-is-for/
[289]https://heartiste.wordpress.com/2015/07/08/horrors-from-the-christian-adoption-scene/

A religion is a synthetic tribe. But progressives hate tribalism, so Christians have piously stopped being tribal.

Some Jews are still tribal, as B smugly reminds me rather frequently. But if they are, B's version of Judaism is not doing a lot to encourage it.

## The median black

2015-07-13 08:02:02

The classic statement Not All X Are Like That is usually uttered in cases where 99% of X are indeed like that.

But suppose it is true. It still the case that different groups have different medians, and these medians often differ by more than the standard deviation. In which case, even if many people of group X are substantially better than the media for group X, it still the case that nearly everyone in group Y is better than nearly everyone in group X.

And behold, the median black.

The girl in the foreground takes a selfie and posts it to twitter[290]. If this behavior was outside the normal range for blacks, would not be done in public.

## Greece to receive yet another bailout

2015-07-14 04:26:55

If you know the the details of the bailout, your brain is being filled with useless misinformation. The important facts are the thirty thousand foot view:

That this bailout is much smaller than the previous bailouts.

That the previous bailouts had extremely harsh conditions that Greece was unable and unwilling to fulfill, and this bailout has even harsher conditions that Greece is even less able and even less willing to fulfill.

That this is not the first time that Greece has been asked to hand over the family silver as surety for a loan, and on previous occasions, the alleged family silver proved to contain no silver. Greece has a lengthy track record of yielding non asset assets to creditors.

## Reality television reveals the difference between men and women

2015-07-16 23:59:40

I have been watching "survivor amazon" and the second season of "The Island with Bear Grylls"

In both reality television series, a team of men, and a team of women, are dumped in separate locations to survive in a tropical paradise.

In both, the men promptly locate a campsite, build a fire, and build shelter. The women hang around in the open in the rain. They do very little any work, and what work they do do is hopeless incompetent and ineffectual.

---

[290]https://twitter.com/LucidHurrricane/status/609566844832215041/photo/1

In "The Island with Bear Grylls" the men locate a campsite and build a fire immediately. They then build first an impromptu shelter for the fire, to protect it from the torrential tropical rainstorms, and then a proper shelter for themselves.

The women spend the first four days in on their Island hopelessly lost wandering in circles in the jungle.

Their efforts to build shelter are feeble, slight, grossly incompetent, and ineffectual, and they soon give up on them.

Eventually they set camp, in the sense that they give up on moving around looking for a nice place to camp, start a fire and attempt to boil some water in a jerry can - which they leave sealed while boiling. Disaster ensues.

After a while they realize that the location where they are hanging out (you cannot call it a camp site, for there are no camp facilities except for a fire) is no good, and move to site previously scouted by one of the few competent women.

They attempt to start a new fire with the fire starting kit that the organizers provided for them (bow and stick) but cannot repair it when it wears out

The organizer has to personally intervene, and gives them a new fire starting bow and stick that he personally made.

Both of these shows indicate that in the ancestral environment, men supported women and children, and women provided sex and children, that women are incapable of looking after themselves.

In both shows, the difference was not physical strength and endurance. The difference was that men are simply markedly more competent, better able to work together as a team, and that men have dramatically longer time preference than women. Some of their superior competence reflects that fact that men are innately smarter than women in the kind of intelligence tests that they faced - physical problems rather than verbal, but most of it reflects their willingness to defer to the most able amongst them, while the women just bitched at each other.

Just as any normal healthy adult male is dramatically stronger than any normal healthy adult women, with essentially zero overlap, the shows revealed a much more important difference: Essentially zero overlap in future orientation.

The women were suffering hypothermia in the rain, and were nonetheless lying about in chilling rain the making no effort to build a shelter. Not one man on the show "The Island with Bear Grylls" behaved as every single woman in the shows behaved.

The women were disinclined to do anything that did not give immediate payoff, so spent pretty much all the time goofing off while homeless, thirsty, and starving in the rain. They very much needed men, not only to look after them, but to tell them what to do, to restrain their bad behavior, and command good behavior, to put them to work, to make them useful.

In both shows the primary difference between team woman and team man was not strength and speed, but that team woman was lazy, stupid, feckless, incompetent, disorderly, disobedient, and irresponsible. I am sure that any eighteenth century gentlemen seeing the even numbered episodes of Season two of "The Island with Bear Grylls" would say "Those women, all of them, need a good whipping."

It was also immediately obvious that women are by nature nurturers, the source of life, while men are by nature killers. When the men encounter a crocodile, ancient instincts command them, and they suddenly become a team of brave, extremely violent, and absolutely determined killers, even though in civilization they answered phones or developed web graphics. When the women encounter some wild pigs, they treat them like babies, they domesticate them. Even though the women have no food to give the pigs, they seduce them into becoming tame and following the women around. And then they tearfully kill and eat the pigs. Clearly it was woman who first domesticated animals. No way would a man have seduced those pigs. And equally, no way could team woman have killed the crocodile.

## Social Justice is highly lucrative.

### 2015-07-18 06:05:52

One of the more noticeable Social Justice Warrior takeovers was the takeover of anarchism reddit. First they banned one "troll", then another, then every moderator who was not in full agreement with social justice, then anyone who noticed that no discussion was possible except full and firm enthusiasm for social justice, so the anarchism board became yet another social justice board, and pretty much died except for repetitious social justice spam. The fact of censorship was censored, the fact of hostile takeover was censored. And you might well say, "what is the point in that? Silencing anarchists is pointless."

Yes, in itself, and in isolation, taking over things like the reddit anarchism board was pointless. But its not isolated.

Consider the Effective Altruism movement. Taking Reddit anarchism facilitates taking over the Effective Altruism movement, and taking over the Effective Altruism movement facilitates stealing three billion dollars in aid to Haiti - well, aid to everywhere, but Haiti is a famous example. There was an earthquake in Haiti, which flattened a lot of buildings and destroyed a lot of infrastructure. This led to a lot of aid, which one might expect to rebuild a lot of buildings and infrastructure. Which has conspicuously failed to happen. Very little of the money even reached corrupt Haitian bureaucrats, let alone manifested in bricks and mortar, let alone benefited the supposed beneficiaries. Corrupt Haitian bureaucrats have been complaining about this for some time.

Now if the effective altruism movement was actually interested in altruism being effective, one might expect it to be asking questions about the near total lack of aid funded rebuilding in Haiti, and the fact that the aids epidemic in India and subsaharan Africa is neither heterosexual nor homosexual, but rather caused by needle reuse by aid funded organizations. Foreign aid is the main cause of aids.

But instead, very conveniently, the Effective Altruism movement seems to be forgetting about altruism actually being effective, just as reddit anarchism forgot about anarchism.

The Future Primeval observes that social justice warrior takeovers are driven by[291]:

> Ideological hijackings like these are a spontaneous failure mode or result of
> a widespread vulnerability of human communities, with the social justice

---

[291] https://thefutureprimaeval.net/socjus-and-ideological-security/

leftism stuff just standing in as a common available ideology to take advantage of it.

These ideological hijackings are the result of a conscious conspiracy of social justice wizards plotting in the back room to take over the world one internet community at a time.

"Hijackings" like this are just the removal of unprincipled exceptions to a widely held moral code that, when consistently interpreted and applied, demands that all communities must be primarily concerned with social justice issues.

"Social Justice" is a sort of semi-autonomous collection of ideas evolved or designed like a rudimentary fungus to take root, grow, take over, and expand from communities in certain conditions, a memetic disease, a demon, a system of ideas that perpetuates itself at the expense of its hosts.

Another factor is: No enemies to the left, no friends to the right.

Since the left has been getting ever lefter, and has been ever victorious, and anyone insufficiently left gets destroyed sooner or later, as soon as a social justice warrior screams like a little girl that she is offended, everyone is terrified, and to protect themselves from future destruction, flings feces at the designated target like a monkey in a tree: Yes, Scott and Esr, I am looking at you.

So how do you stop social justice warriors from taking over.

One method is a commitment to free speech and rational argument. One refused to denounce dissent as unacceptable and beyond the pale, and instead engages in rational and relevant discussion, rather than stridently screaming strident stupid ignorant insults like a monkey in a tree. (And if I am specifically mentioning Scott and Esr, that is not because they are the worst, but because I had expected better of them.) That fixes the spontaneous tendency to failure, and the memetic disease, but does not really do much about the organized conspiracy, nor the systematic removal of unprincipled exceptions one by one.

To deal with the organized conscious conspiracy, one has to answer in kind: "You social justice warrior. You evil stupid and hateful. You die." Only the McCarthy solution works.

To deal with the systematic removal of unprincipled exceptions - well, there is nothing for it but to stop defending them as unprincipled exceptions, but instead to defend them as surviving remnants of the ancient functional social order - in other worlds, no solution other than neoreaction.

## Going home

2015-07-19 23:29:06

kakistocracy on going home.

Home is not just geography. Home is a place of comfort, safety, and familiarity. Of mutual trust and understanding. Of common past and shared future. Home is where children play without fear in a parent's eyes. Home is where speaking honestly offends no shrill aliens. Home is what is passed from your father to your son. And most importantly, home belongs uniquely *to you*.

There are great swaths of her country now no more Ms.Makin's home than the violent North African city she longs to escape. And when those swaths broaden to encompass everything, where will her daughter seek sanctuary upon saying...

*I want to go home.*

Some time ago, I moved from silicon valley to a place pleasantly undiverse. People leave their doors unlocked when they leave their houses. The kids are respectful. By the roadside, one sees unattended fruitstands. You take the fruit and drop the money in a box. Small children wander off unsupervised. I am a stranger here, yet it fits like an old sock.

Even wealthy whites in Silicon Valley live in a place that is frightening, dangerous, hostile, hateful, and alien. A place that hates them for the intolerable sins of sexism racism colonialism homophobia islamophobia and imperialism, and sooner or later will punish them as they deserve for those unforgivable and ineradicable sins. They are frightened and weak. And they cannot afford to have children.

## Traps, ladyboys, Corporal Klingers, and trannies.

### 2015-07-22 11:04:00

A trap is young effeminate gay who likes sex with adult males and disguises himself as a woman to get banged by heterosexual men. To the extent that gays like sex with adult males, they like manly men, and gays are not manly.

A ladyboy is a trap who takes the drastic step of cutting his dick off.

Traps and ladyboys are low status losers, usually thieves and whores. They usually die young of suicide, criminal violence, drug abuse, or weird gay diseases.

Traps and ladyboys transition young, usually while still adolescents.

Another category of transexual, which we are seeing a lot of in the tech industry, is the quota busting transexual - the Corporal Klinger - someone who claims to be a woman to take advantage of hiring quotas. They are typically heterosexual (or as they say, "lesbian") and look like Fred Flintstone in a dress, as Corporal Klinger did. They are usually competent engineers and usually high status winners. These guys transition shortly after entering the job market. Apart from dangerous levels of progressivism, they are not disruptive of corporate order and hierarchy, unlike actual females.

But the well known trannies are heterosexual men, usually extremely manly men who lived high testosterone lifestyles, extremely heterosexual men, usually high status successful men, and when they got older, middle aged, and then their testosterone levels fell, fell to merely normal levels, then they discovered that they were "really" women. Probably a better cure would have been added testosterone, but they could not get medically prescribed testosterone because their levels were "normal" - meaning normal for regular guys, not normal for those guys, not the levels they had experienced all their lives. After transition, their sex life consists of scaring little girls in the lady's room. They don't do anything that normal people would consider constitutes sex. They think they are women, but are merely eunuchs and act accordingly, while the Corporal Klingers act like the normal heterosexual males that they are, and the traps and ladyboys act like gays.

As I grew older my testosterone levels gradually fell, and my estrogen levels gradually rose. I found myself taking a gradually increasing interest in anime girls. Then I had medically prescribed correction of my hormone levels, and after several months with normalized hormone levels, anime girls started to look excessively cartoonish, while real girls looked way hot again. Of course my personal experience is just an anecdote. Could be just randomness. Before drawing any broader conclusions, would need more data. A single case is not necessarily indicative.

I also started to notice that the male protagonist in an anime show acted ridiculously girly, though I am not sure whether this reflects my normalized testosterone levels, or that anime protagonists are acting ever more girly. Probably something of both.

But it is plausible that falling testosterone and rising estrogen alters your brain, turning down the "tap that ass" recognizer, so that normal stimuli are not sufficient to activate the "tap that ass" circuits. Male sexual deviants generally look to me like they have low testosterone.

The government is making it increasingly difficult for doctors to prescribe testosterone. At the same time, no one wants to know if there are health problems related to low testosterone, let alone behavioral problems related to low testosterone. Researching harm done by low testosterone is like researching benefits of global warming. You have to have quite dangerously low levels before you can get treatment.

And since we have an extraordinary epidemic of falling testosterone and rising estrogen …

Just about every male these days has testosterone levels that are deficient by historical standards. Maybe just about every male these days needs medical intervention.

## Defining cuckservative

### 2015-07-24 01:45:44

By one popular definition a cuckservative is "conservative" who supports white replacement. (*Gradual* white replacement, of course, though I am not seeing anything that guarantees that the process will remain gradual.)

Based on cuckold, one who raises another man's son as his own, which is in turn based on cuckoo, which plants its eggs in the nests of others.

One could also apply it, and sometimes does apply it, to a conservative with no enemies to the left and no friends to the right, who thus conspires to the eradication of conservatism and its ever leftwards movement, which strictly speaking is inconsistent with the first definition. One implies physical and biological elimination, one implies mere memetic elimination.

However, the one is in practice pretty much equivalent to the other since leftist memes are in practice race replacement memes, as exemplified in Baltimore. Maybe in future there will be conflict between these two definitions.

The broader definition of cuckservative, however, communicates the neoreactionary concept of innerparty/outerparty, shows how the republican party does the left's work for it. Though race gives the word its bitter power, the broader definition cuts reality at the joints, showing the relationship between inner and outer party.

Observe that Trump is beyond the pale and supposedly a joke for pointing at the costs of unlimited illegal immigration. Meanwhile Israel has the world's toughest policy on illegal immigration, and Australia a close second. Both have no problem reducing illegal immigration to zero. But the Australian policy is "controversial", and like most popular but "controversial" policies, may well be furtively changed. Note that the Austalian policy is somehow highly "controversial", even though voters support the policy overwhelmingly. Something is unpopular and illegal. So the government puts a stop to it. This is "controversial".

But it is too late to halt illegal immigration in America. Australia could halt illegal immigration because still mostly white. To halt illegal immigration in America, have to end democracy first.

But at least, if we use words that cut reality at the joints, we can see our doom upon us.

## Why Islamic State is successful.

2015-07-24 11:46:59

According to progressive mythology

> insurgents must be like a mist—everywhere and nowhere—never trying to hold ground or wasting lives in battles with regular armies. Chairman Mao insisted that guerrillas should be fish who swam in the sea of the local population. Such views are the logical corollaries of "asymmetric warfare" in which a smaller, apparently weaker group—like ISIS—confronts a powerful adversary such as the US and Iraqi militaries. This is confirmed by US Army studies of more than forty historical insurgencies, which suggest again and again that holding ground, fighting pitched battles, and alienating the cultural and religious sensibilities of the local population are fatal.

This, of course, is a load of horseshit. One needs a base area in which one can conscript and gather funds, where leaders can safely and openly administer and coordinate. Hard to run the war from a secret cave. Often that base area has been the Kremlin - and even more often, it has been the London School of Economics.

In asymmetric wars, one's base is often beholden to others, and one is therefore handicapped by unwanted ideology and rules. So Islamic State decided it just plain needed to grab its own base area. Islamic law is that you cannot claim the Caliphate unless you have your own base area - because you cannot be Caliph if you are beholden to others. So, needed a base, took a base. So Islamic State chooses to fight symmetrically. In an asymmetric war, the weaker side is a muppet for somebody powerful, usually the London School of Economics, which is itself a muppet of Harvard. Islamic State is nobody's muppet.

This allows it to be authentically Islamic - to implement its own program and its own ideology.

And, being able to implement its own program and own ideology, gives gays the high jump, reintroduces slavery and the marriage of minors.

Progressives are mystified and uncomprehending.

> horrors unimaginable even to the Taliban—among them the reintroduction
> of forcible rape of minors and slavery—have been legitimized.

Slavery never really went away. Saudi Arabia reluctantly abolished it 1964. The suppression of slavery is not the natural result of the Zeitgeist, but the military programs of British imperialism. Since the imperial tide retreats, slavery returns. As for the "rape" of minors, minor girls are going to have sex, which is to say, be "raped" unless they are married off young or kept under tight control, pretty much locked up except when appropriately supervised, and progressives have never been worried about the statutory rape of minors, nor the actual rape of minors, nor the actual enslavement of minors for sexual purposes, provided that the right people get raped and the right people are doing the raping. The ever rising age of consent was always a pretense and a pretext. Provided that fathers lose control of their daughters and husbands do not gain control of those daughters, progressives are untroubled by pimps gaining control of those daughters.

## Gay families bang their children

2015-07-26 07:13:43

The Story of Moira Greyland

tl;dr She got banged a lot by her parents with lot of sadism and bondage, starting at age five.

> from my experience in the gay community, the values in that community
> are very different: the assumption is that EVERYONE is gay and closeted,
> and early sexual experience will prevent gay children from being closeted,
> and that will make everyone happy.

Yes, she is right about that. Gayness in males is spread in whole or major part by adult men fucking male children, and they intend to spread gayness that way. Lesbianism is more complicated, since women remain sexually flexible all the way to menopause.

If you raise a sheep among goats, the sheep grows up goatosexual. Hence the program of providing schoolchildren with positive gay role models, and getting gay men into contact with scouts and schoolchildren. They want gay scoutmasters to recruit young gays. Whether it works or not, and I think it does work to some considerable extent, they believe that it works. They believe that gays are made, not born, and intend to make them, starting at a school near you.

New Study On Homosexual Parents Tops All Previous Research[292]

Progressives are fine with rape and slavery, provided the right people are doing the raping, and the right people are being raped and enslaved. Truth is, I am fine with rape and slavery also, except that my definitions of the right people differ radically from those of progressives.

# How to really win the "Hispanic" vote.

## 2015-07-28 01:50:26

If the Republican party seriously wanted the "Hispanic" vote, which of course it does not, because if it won the "Hispanic" vote it might win elections, and if it won elections, might have to implement its agenda, the way to go would be to split the "white Hispanics" from the indios and mestizos, and the indios and mestizos from the blacks. "Hispanics", whether white, mestizo, and indio, really hate blacks, and the Democrats are the black party. It would be easy to take advantage of racial tensions to break "Hispanics" away from the democrat party. "Hispanic" children go to schools that impose equal disciplinary outcomes by racial quota, so that black kids get away with stuff that white and Hispanic kids face zero tolerance for.

So, find a prominent republican who is a fair skinned Mexican who speaks Mexican Spanish as his mother's tongue. He tells them, in Spanish:

> "Our kids are punished while black kids go unpunished, because Democrats are the black party, while Republicans are the white party. The schools are in chaos because of black misconduct. Do you want to be ruled by the black party or the white party?"

By and large the government quietly allows Mexicans collective self defense against blacks, while it does not allow whites collective self defense against blacks, but every so often, the Democrats, being the black party, give Mexicans the short end of that stick also. The Republicans could make hay out of such incidents.

Mexicans have a lot more contact with blacks than whites have contact with blacks, and are less brainwashed by Cathedral propaganda. Leftists keep telling republicans that Mexicans have old style Catholic values, are social conservatives, even though your local hospital is flooded with short fat pregnant Mexican women surrounded by a half dozen children by half a dozen different fathers getting free medical care for themselves and their grossly neglected children. Nah, they don't have old style Catholic values, and neither does the Pope these days, they are not socially conservative, but they are race realists.

The left is run by white males, but their voter bank is a coalition of everyone against white heterosexual males. For Mexicans, problems with blacks are way more salient than problems with white heterosexual males. Electoral politics 101: Split the enemy coalition. Get some fair skinned Mexicans who don't live in the bubble, who have friends and family exposed to black dysfunction, and have them stir up the $#!%. Are republicans worried about losing black votes? Bad black behavior is an enormous vote winner for republicans which they refuse to cash in. And never will choose to cash in.

---

[292]https://www.frc.org/issuebrief/new-study-on-homosexual-parents-tops-all-previous-research

The major victims by far of bad black behavior are Mexicans. Democrats are the black party. Republicans are the white party. You want to stir up anger at blacks among those nonblack democrats who live in the closest proximity to blacks. It really is that simple.

Instead the Republican party pursues sainthood for blacks, and always will.

## Kin altruism, reciprocal altruism, and ethnic altruism

2015-07-28 11:01:38

Kin altruism does not make much sense outside the nuclear family, or narrowly extended family. It can work in slightly larger groups if they deliberately practice inbreeding, but the groups are not much larger, and you get IQ depression from inbreeding.

So what explains the tendency of ethnics to stick together?

Well if people resemble you, they are predictable. You know you can trust them in some matters to some degree. So you do. This makes reciprocal altruism workable. Mix in outsiders, and you lose trust. Thus Jews thought they could trust Madoff to cheat gentiles, and not cheat his fellow Jews. Because Jewish cohesion has been diminishing for some time, this turned out to be a bad expectation.

Another thing that causes loss of trust is mandatory lying and betrayal. Hence when east Germany and west Germany were reunited, the east Germans appeared to the west Germans to be subhuman, even though there was no significant genetic difference. East Germans would not work unless someone was standing over them, and would cheat, lie, and steal for any momentary slight advantage. The difference seems to have diminished now that they have been living under the same political system for a while.

People are not going to be altruistic to whites just because they themselves are whites, and Jews are not altruistic to Jews just because they themselves are Jews. This is a Nazi fallacy. Comradeship of whites is no more workable than comradeship of the proletariat. Whites have always been primarily at war with whites. This is not caused by sneaky Jewish mind control rays. Man is wolf to man, and whites are wolf to whites.

Good behavior is trustworthy and honorable behavior, not benevolent behavior. People who claim to be benevolent to far away strangers seldom are, and when they are, their benevolence is disturbingly and dangerously selective and capricious. This is yet another reason why utilitarian theories of morality don't work. Not only is no one utilitarian, no one is benevolent.

Altruism is unworkable for any group above a dozen or so people. Trust is scalable to vastly larger groups.

## How to stop mass illegal immigration to Britain

2015-07-30 07:38:09

Lately the British government has been making feeble ineffectual gestures vaguely in the general direction of attempting to slightly slow the flood of illegal immigrants, most of them black and Muslim, into Britain. This has resulted in dramatic scenes of disruption at the Calais truck terminal, but ...

All of them get there in the end,' he said. 'No fence is too difficult – in the end, borders are there to be crossed.'[293]

Actually not all borders are made to be crossed. America has been allowing unlimited third world immigration for some time, Britain first started allowing unlimited third world immigration in the late 1990s, and for a little while, starting around 2010 or so, every single white country, even Israel, was allowing unlimited third world immigration. Pretty soon Israel had a rush of sanity, declared an unprincipled exception for itself, and in 2013 or so, completely and totally ended illegal immigration. Very shortly afterwards, also in 2013, Australia abruptly, completely, and totally ended illegal immigration. New Zealand did the same, while furtively denying it was doing so, and piously weeping tears for the poor illegal immigrants. Australia is famous for this, for however lefty and progressive Tony Abbot's government is, it takes no crap from the fans of illegal immigration, and, Trump like, makes no apologies, throwing those who would eliminate white nations into hysterics of outrage. The State Department is traumatized by severe cultural shock every time they have to deal with the Ambassador for People Smuggling Issues for Australia, even if Tony Abbot merely stands for a substantially slower rate of elimination of whiteness.

At present, if an illegal immigrant armed with a knife smashes his way onto a lorry headed for Britain, then, in the unlikely event a policeman removes him, he removes him a few hundred meters to the illegal immigrant camp, and a few minutes later, the illegal immigrant has another go, smashes his way into another lorry causing more damage. With this sort of law enforcement, indeed no fence is too difficult, for no wall can stand unless protected by men with the will to make it stand. Walls do not stop people, just as bullets do not kill people. People stop people. With the will to stop illegal immigration, illegal immigration can be halted abruptly and completely. Without the will, it cannot.

The solution of course is that illegal immigrants need to be removed, starting with those that do illegal things like trespassing on other people's lorries while armed with a knife. Australia has created a number of "offshore processing facilities", prison camps on remote islands run by the army and outside the jurisdiction of the judiciary. (Officially they are of course not prison camps, and officially they are run by "private contractors", not the army.) You stick the illegal immigrant in an offshore prison camp resembling Gitmo, and when you get around to it, you return him home. If he claims asylum - well after being in prison for a few years, they usually stop claiming asylum and want to go home. If their home country does not want them back, you dump them on the beach regardless in an orange inflatable. Australia's inflatables have become an increasingly familiar sight on third world beaches. Some of the inflatables have chains to restrain the more uncooperative occupants. If they are really stubborn about claiming asylum, and their claims are not entirely implausible, you find a third world country as poor or poorer than their original home, where they are not racially too much out of place, and send them there.

Now let us suppose that British Prime minister never finds the stones to do what Tony Abbot does. Then there is nothing to stop all of Africa from moving to Britain, for no

---

[293]https://www.dailymail.co.uk/news/article-3179276/Flimsy-fences-no-barrier-Calais-security-farce-wave-wave-migrants-trample-wire-mesh-bid-wander-train-tracks-risk-lives-cross-Channel.html

wall can hold without the will to hold it. And if anyone lives in Africa, that is the sensible thing for him to do. In due course, rapidly increasing numbers of people will move till Britain becomes indistinguishable from Africa.

## Skittles guy and female agency

2015-08-01 09:24:12

There has been a tremendous amount of research in how to sleep with as many women as possible, and it is relatively easy to obtain good scientific data on this question, because the experimenter can try one thing on a statistically significant sample of women, then another thing on a significant sample of women, then form theories based on the results, and test the theory with yet another significant sample of women. Heartiste is your best entry point into this research. Be warned that not all experimental results can be easily and accurately expressed in words. If having trouble with the words, check the words against a frame by frame analysis of video. Ninety percent of it is in movement and body language. Mating preceded language, and still does.

The optimal strategy for sleeping with as many women as possible is exemplified by Skittles Man[294].

However, this strategy is suboptimal for keeping women around. You are not going to fulfill your Darwinian imperative unless you keep a woman around.

We don't have the scientific knowledge for keeping women around that we have for getting them into bed in the first place, but I probably know slightly more than most. Research on this topic is costlier and more time consuming, and one is always facing samples that are statistically inadequate and unlikely to be comparable.

After being sexed a while, girls want signs of love, which Skittles Man conspicuously fails to provide - but not signs of neediness, they want behavior that show you care for them, but not behavior that shows you want to please them.

Believing that women lack agency helps with this. If you think that what she wants is not necessarily relevant, that women lack agency, then giving her what you think she needs does not show neediness, but affection.

Women want to be owned. They want to be owned by someone that loves them, but not someone that needs them. If you don't think women are entitled to make decisions, nor good at determining their best interest and acting on it, you will not be acting needy. If you simply believe that decisions are yours to make, that her decisions are made by your permission and are ultimately subject to your approval, if you don't believe that women have agency, in the sense that they are not morally entitled to agency and are not good at exercising it, you will express that belief non verbally and she will gladly accept that belief - provided of course that that belief comes out of love.

If you want to reproduce, you should believe that women should be property, should be pets, are happier that way, and that a society that allows them agency is corrupt, ridiculous, immoral, and absurd.

---

[294]https://heartiste.wordpress.com/2009/05/19/be-a-skittles-man/

## Intact fetal cadavers

2015-08-07 14:55:15

An anti abortion organization, posing as a fetal tissue buyer, gets planned parenthood to agree to arrange for twenty week babies to be born alive, and then supplied to the buyer[295].

At which point you are doubtless thinking "How mature is twenty weeks? Are they conscious?"

Here is a video of an unborn boy masturbating at fifteen weeks[296]. (At 6:30 into the video) If he can beat himself off, he is conscious. (From fifteen weeks to birth, there is a male hormone surge, to ensure that little boys are born looking conspicuously different from little girls. During this hormonal surge, unborn and newly born males are apt to beat themselves off)

Of course, really it makes no moral difference whether the baby is killed one minute before birth or one minute after birth, and whether the still living but abandoned child is sold for profit. The profit just reminds us of what we are allowing people to do.

If children are not valuable, except as their parents value them, if they can be disposed of at whim, there is no moral basis to force men to provide child support, any more than they should provide cat support for cat ladies.

If children are inherently valuable, if allowing them to be killed brutalizes us all, because a society that can dispose of unwanted babies can dispose of unwanted pensioners, political troublemakers, etc, then women have no right to abort, still less to abort without paternal permission, and no right to behave in ways that deprive children of fathers.

It would seem that children have zero value except their mothers value them. And if their father values them, but their mother does not, they still have zero value. But, if their mother values them, they have infinite value - except that they can be denied their biological fathers.

So we go from infinite valuation of human life, to treating children as disposable garbage, accordingly as convenient for women, and inconvenient for men.

## Political correctness castrates men

2015-08-12 12:31:53

A public radio station (Government left wing propaganda station) had its staff testosterone[297] levels tested[298]. They all came out pathologically low, the highest being a gay New York Jew who almost made the official normal range (the official normal range being much lower than the actual normal range) Every one else was less than half the lower limit of the supposed normal range.

In the ensuing conversation, they remarked on how girly and effeminate public radio is[299].

---

[295] https://www.centerformedicalprogress.org/

[296] https://www.youtube.com/watch?v=sVB0qTiq5jU

[297] https://heartiste.wordpress.com/2015/08/11/this-american-life-shitlibs-get-their-testosterone-levels-tested/

[298] https://mpcdot.com/forums/topic/8368-shitlib-facespng/page__st__180#entry215500

[299] https://www.thisamericanlife.org/radio-archives/episode/220/testosterone?act=3#play

"Todd had never been seen as especially manly during his life, but thought maybe here, in this group, compared to the rest of us, he might at least stand a chance"

"That at least someone would be girlier than I. If I cannot be the most manly in public radio, where the hell can I be the most manly?"

This suggests that filtering for political correctness is filtering for lack of manliness.

Alternatively filtering against "rape" and "sexual harassment" is filtering against manliness.

Or, and this is my preferred hypothesis, political correctness actually causes lack of manliness, that continually censoring one's words and thoughts, continual crimestop, has the same effect as continually being defeated, humiliated, and degraded, in reducing testosterone levels, that crimestop lowers your ability to reproduce.

This would explain the continual and major drop in testosterone levels. It is not literal estrogen in the literal water supply, but metaphorical estrogen in the metaphorical water supply.

# Trump plan to stop (nonwhite) immigration
## 2015-08-17 15:53:34

The Trump plan broadens the Overton Window by speaking the unspeakable.

Ann Coulter says "I don't care if @realDonaldTrump[300] wants to perform abortions in White House after this immigration policy paper. https://bit.ly/1EvT3Ja[301]"

Of course ending immigration is enormously popular. Everyone is unhappy with the program to turn all white nations majority nonwhite in the fairly near future, but no one dares say so. The program will turn whites into a market dominant minority, and market dominant minorities usually get genocided or ethnically cleansed sooner or later, as for example Zimbabwe and large parts of South Africa.

The ideology justifying the eradication of whites is already in place and taught at every school. White males cause poor performance of women and nonwhites by thinking evil thoughts at them. They do this because they are just hateful and malicious. For example after blacks acquired Detroit, whites, out of sheer hateful malice, turned it into a third world hell hole by thinking evil thoughts at it. Since no amount of thought reform seems able to halt these evil thoughts, obviously white males have to be eradicated and white females bred with nonwhites.

Of course it is possible, that as in latin America, whites can manage the decline so as to avoid the usual fate of market dominant minorities. In most latin American countries, people believe that they are all one race, and anyone who notices that they are not is apt to fall down several flights of stairs in a one story police station. But I am not seeing any military, political, ideological or social preparation to manage the transition. People continue to throw lighted matches into what will soon become a pool of gasoline. Recall

---

[300]https://twitter.com/realDonaldTrump
[301]https://t.co/l7nq8gN7i5 "https://bit.ly/1EvT3Ja"

what was done to the Tutsi in the Congo with the full military and political support of the Cathedral.

Trump's plan, despite being outside the recent Overton window, is oddly moderate. No plan to halt welfare for illegals, no plan to forcibly remove illegals already here.

Further, Trump's plan relies on the cooperation of the courts, who will surely not cooperate. Australia found it necessary to bypass the courts and use direct military power, and use what are officially regional processing centres run by "civilian contractors" but are in fact prison camps run by the military (yes, *those* civilian contractors).

The Trump plan resembles the various anti immigration initiatives of the Australian labor party, which failed because of hostility and forcible resistance by government employees, and fraud and defiance by the courts.

Presidents cannot do *$#!&* unless they are prepared to use the military, as the Australian government finally did. And the US military has become so PC in its upper ranks that it is far from clear that it would obey such orders.

## It begins

### 2015-08-23 00:32:13

A huge flood of blacks from subsaharan Africa is pouring into Europe, since stopping them has very recently been made illegal, and when they arrive, they are guaranteed free food and housing, and the welfare state and feminist laws has left white pussy readily available, undefended, and defenseless. What man in his right mind will protect a slut (assuming she wants to be protected, which is unlikely)?

A necessary consequence is that whites are going to be eliminated from Europe - probably not any time very soon, but now it begins:

> Boris Palmer, the Green Party mayor of Tübingen, told Welt newspaper the town was struggling to find accommodation for migrants.
>
> "The Police Law has clear rules. If there is a threat of homelessness in a city, vacant houses can be seized for accommodation," Mr Palmer said.

And if they are not vacant now, they will be soon after a bunch of blacks move in next door.

These guys were sleeping in mud and thatch huts before they came, if they were not sleeping in the long grass. Now they get a house some white man built. And when they turn that house into a burned out ruin, after the fashion of Detroit, built by whites, burned by blacks, they will complain of racism and systematic discrimination because whites still have nicer stuff than they do, so they need to take more white stuff and wreck it also.

Blacks are like locusts. They take the stuff that white people built, for example the American inner city, destroy it, and then move on to take something else. They cannot be stopped because the state apparatus forbids white collective self defense, while encouraging black collective rioting, encouraging collective attacks on random isolated whites motivated by black hatred of whites and black sense of collective identity. This raises the cost of housing for white people to unaffordable levels, preventing family formation.

Whites move out from their houses because of state sponsored collective black violence, as is happening now in Baltimore and Ferguson, and blacks move in to houses white people built.

## Trump: Empowering the powerless
2015-08-27 06:41:03

There is a rule that people like Jorge Ramos are entitled to act like like the subhuman savages that they are, and white males must respectfully suck it up.

Trump broke that rule[302].

People like Jorge Ramos should not be allowed out in public without a leash. All men are not created equal, and forcing people to act as if they were unavoidably and necessarily oppresses the superior.

This post categorized in culture rather than politics, because election campaigns are merely theater. Trump bouncing Jorge Ramos is more important than anything a president can do.

## In Russia, there is freedom
2015-08-31 10:04:50

Recently a gay black journalist murdered a white woman and a white man because he hates whites[303]. This happens all the time, continually, day and night, but was more newsworthy this time because he did it live on air and on Facebook and explained his reasons on Facebook.

In Russia, but not in America, the news reported this event as "a black man ..."
We love Putin, because Putin defends freedom.

## The medium is the message, and the message is progressivism
2015-09-05 00:18:54

New wine in old bottles.

A couple of weeks ago, I attended the Roman Catholic church of one of my sons. He seemed quite satisfied that it was preaching Roman Catholicism, rather than progressivism.

The service was presided over by three people: A white male, a black male, with blackness much emphasized, and a woman. Which is to say, presided over by diversity and consensus.

I suppose that to the eye of faith, and to one sufficiently expert in Roman Catholicism, there were various indications that they were not presiding equally, that one was a priest, and the other two were not, or maybe the two males were priests, and the female was not. But such indicators were subtle.

---

[302] https://https://heartiste.org/2015/08/26/go-back-to-univision/
[303] https://www.breitbart.com/big-government/2015/08/26/black-gay-reporter-murders-straight-white-journalists-media-blame-the-gun/

Theoretically they were talking about the Eucharist, though the black man made a big deal out of the fact that his name was unpronounceable by white people. He seemed mighty proud of the fact.

But words don't matter much unless congruent with deeds, and symbols. And the deeds and symbols were not the Eucharist, were diversity and consensus, rather than hierarchy and ancient ritual connecting the congregation to the apostles and to all co-religionists, living, dead, and not yet born.

I suppose that it was preaching Roman Catholicism - in words - but the words were incongruent.

## The Trumpening

### 2015-09-07 02:46:32

Polls indicate that Trump is going to the Republican candidate, and going to win, going to be the next president[304].

In substantial part because he gets a lot more black and hispanic votes than Republicans usually do, which is to say, a lot of votes from those who are most directly hurt by illegal immigration.

The Cathedral attitude is that the voters are throwing a silly temper tantrum, which will be ignored. It is possible that they will declare his election unconstitutional, because racism, but more likely that they will just carry on as if he is not president, because racism.

This is pretty much what happened when Kevin Rudd attempted to stop illegal immigration to Australia and deport illegal immigrants. Totally failed. This is what Jorge means when he correctly tells Trump that Trump's plan is unworkable. The country is ruled by priests, not politicians, and Jorge is a priest and Trump is not. Therefore Trump's plan is unworkable. However, Kevin Rudd's efforts eventually made possible Tony Abbots efforts. Tony Abbot just ignored the judges and used the military directly.

At one point the judges ruled that a bunch of Tamil illegal immigrants from India could not be expelled, unless their asylum status was checked with the Indian government. Tony Abbot readily agreed, since it is ridiculous for anyone to claim asylum from the Indian government these days. Then the judges pulled a switcheroo - their asylum status could not be checked unless they consented to it be being checked. Within minutes, airforce commandos were stuffing the Tamils onto airforce planes, which proceeded to fly the Tamils to some place far from Australia, with total disregard for Australian court rulings, supposed international law, and such. The judges hair caught fire, (only metaphorically, unfortunately) but since then they have been mighty quiet, and have stopped trying to meddle. Warriors 1, priests 0.

You can do anything with bayonets except sit on them. At some point we will find out whether soldiers obey priests or presidents.

---

[304]https://www.surveyusa.com/client/PollReport.aspx?g=d950cadf-05ce-4148-a125-35c0cdab26c6

## Trump and democracy

### 2015-09-11 02:29:28

The Trump candidacy is great because:

The voices of the Cathedral from time to time say he will not be allowed to win, revealing the managed nature of democracy.

All the other candidates are ladyboys, revealing both the managed nature of democracy and the emasculating nature of progressivism. Also revealing that the Republican party is the outer party, a fake managed opposition. It makes "cuckservative" a devastatingly effective insult, linking their race traitor politics to their conspicuous lack of masculinity.

The voices of the Cathedral from time to time say that if he wins, will not be allowed to govern, revealing that they regard legislature and executive as mere theater, a meaningless show performed while the important people take care of the important stuff.

And best of all: Every time Trump opens his mouth, he widens the Overton Window.

## Diversity means defection

### 2015-09-11 20:48:11

Yet another great Steve Sailer post[305]. Diversity, even with groups of comparable ability, leads to loss of trust and bad conduct.

This is revealed by the FBIs ten most wanted white collar criminals. White collar crime requires intelligence, but the only American born white on the top ten, the only one you could not tell was a diversity by looking at him, is named Hamed Ahmed Elbarki. Every single one on the top ten is a diversity, and most of them belong to groups with a known tendency to ordinary lower class dumb vicious thug type criminality. The Russian Jew looks not at all Russian, and very, very Jewish. Most Jews are white, though they don't identify as white. The Russian Jew is not white.

This reminds me of the last days of Informix. They hired very large numbers of Indians (dot, not feather). Because of corruption in the Informix hiring process, the Indians were not all of the best quality, but that was not the big problem. The big problem was that each caste or clan formed a conspiracy which proceeded to plot against the company, against whites, and against each of the other castes or clans. Though this was more a case of diversity leads to war, than diversity leads to defection. Towards the end, Informix was showing signs of becoming Beirut on the Bay. My boss sent me to a meeting, pretty much to spy on them. I go into the meeting and they are all Indians, all Indians of a particular Indian race. And they all look at me as one and viscerally react "Enemy spy". All business halted while I was present.

---

[305] https://www.unz.com/isteve/fbis-top-ten-most-wanted-white-collar-criminals-list-not-too-white/

## Hillary and the decline of the elite.

2015-09-11 22:36:35

Bill Clinton was a truly great politician. He could embrace you and steal your wallet, embrace your wife and fuck your wife, and you would still somehow like him.

Hillary Clinton is the drunken dumb heiress bitch Bill Clinton married to fund his initial entry into politics. She is now big fat drunken carpet munching dumb bitch. Bill Clinton is a very good liar, an extraordinarily good liar. Hillary Clinton is a terrible liar. Whenever something bad happens in her vicinity, she goes into damage control mode which immediately leads everyone to assume that she deliberately caused that bad thing. Nothing stuck to Bill. Everything sticks to Hillary.

Bill Clinton was a very good politician. Hillary Clinton is hopelessly incompetent, and particularly bad at politics.

So why is the Cathedral preparing to enthrone Clinton the Second?

Answer: The Cathedral is stupid and getting stupider[306], in part because everyone is required to believe ever sillier things with ever greater sincerity.

## The great cuckolding

2015-09-13 02:36:14

Stolen from the heartiste comments:

It is frequently reported that white women in Sweden have reasonable total fertility rate. What is not reported is that this largely consists of fatherless brown babies supported by white male taxpayers.

At an instinctive gut level, women recognize this for what it is: Invasion!

And respond sexually to invasion as women always have and always will unless kept under tight control. Yet another reason why we should never have emancipated women (to prevent them from fucking outsiders) and never given the vote to women (to prevent them from voting for outside conquest).

## A lost military technology

2015-09-13 22:35:18

In the eighteenth and early nineteenth century, wealthy private individuals substantially supported the military, with a particular wealthy men buying stuff for a particular regiment or particular fort.

Noblemen paid high prices for military commands, and these posts were no sinecure. You got the obligation to substantially supply the logistics for your men, the duty to obey stupid orders that would very likely lead to your death, the duty to lead your men from in front while wearing a costume designed to make you particularly conspicuous, and the duty to engage in honorable personal combat, man to man, with your opposite number who was also leading his troops from in front.

---

[306]https://blog.reaction.la/tag/not-the-cognitive-elite/

A vestige of this tradition remains in that every English prince has been sent to war and has placed himself very much in harms
way.

It seems obvious to me that a soldier being led by a member of the ruling class who is soaking up the bullets from in front is a lot more likely to be loyal and brave than a soldier sent into battle by distant rulers safely in Washington who despise him as a sexist homophobic racist murderer, that a soldier who sees his commander, a member of the ruling classes, fighting right in front of him, is reflexively likely to fight.

So what made very large numbers of rich and powerful people personally sacrifice for the military? They must have gotten something out of it, and at what they were paying, it was not the salary.

Presumably they got social status, which could be cashed in for wealth and power. This however requires that we award social status for activities that are actually constructive and support society and order, and that we then allow social status to be cashed in. Which means we have to make sure that social status is not awarded for superior holiness - we have to hang Greenpeace from the yardarm when they engage in piracy on the high seas, and send William Wilberforce to west indies as a slave to cut sugarcane in punishment for apostasy.

I understand how eighteenth century patriarchy worked, how good behavior was socially and coercively enforced on women.

But I don't understand how private and individual support of the military by wealthy and or aristocratic males was motivated. This is a lost social technology.

To make it work, have to bestow status on those worthy, and reward earned status with money and power.

The system eventually failed because the holy claimed higher status than that horribly brutal racist sexist homophobic baby eating military. The attacks on the military began with synthetic moral outrage at the British army's successful and heroic measures to cut Russian logistics in the Crimean war, in which the courage and victory of officers and men should have covered them with glory, and have escalated ever since, with ever more severe efforts to denigrate and disadvantage soldiers. What was heroism before the Crimean war has become baby eating ever since.

In place of crediting heroes with heroism, they credited whores like Florence Nightingale with heroism. (I assume she was a whore because most of the female camp followers, and most of the camp followers were female, worked vertically by day and horizontally by night. Also, when she was hot, she had many connections with many wealthy men, but never married. When a young cute girl spends a lot of time hanging out with a succession of old rich guys ....)

## Review of Left Singularities.

2015-09-14 23:23:17

The Left Singularity is increasing leftism causing ever faster increases in leftism until something breaks short of achieving infinite leftism in finite time.

Dark ages are slow, more or less continuous, economic and political decline, imperceptibly slow, typically about one percent a year on average, hard to notice against the background of random economic and political fluctuations.

Left Singularities, on the other hand, unlike dark ages, end with a decisive boom, a close approach to infinite leftism in finite time. Sometimes a left singularity is followed by reforms or a restoration. Sometimes, as when Stalin purged the left, things just stop getting worse, but do not get a whole lot better.

The basic mechanism of a left wing singularity is political correctness. The elite competes to be holier than each other. Everyone is compelled to be ever holier, and the holier they get, the more everyone is compelled to be even holier.

if we believe the "Admonitions of Ipuwer", Bronze age civilization ended in a left singularity. Archeaology shows that bronze age civilization ended with a bang, that led directly and immediately to a dark age. Presumably the social technology of trade and commerce was lost in the left singularity, and not immediately recovered.

Recent events in China happened the other way around, a long slow decline into darkness, with intermittent left singularities along the way, and then the restoration following the Maoist left singularity cured the dark age.

China was in continuous slow economic decline from the Southern Song Dynasty until Socialism with Chinese characteristics. Thus a dark age, terminating in a left singularity followed by a restoration, rather than starting in a left singularity.

Which gives me hope that our left singularity will be followed by a similar restoration.

The bronze age left singularity resulted in the total destruction of most existing states, with new states growing up from large extended families. Assyria survived, and Egypt did not altogether cease to be a state, but the rest of them mostly vanished. Egypt survived in bad (highly leftist) condition - liberated women and all that.

Rome suffered its bout of leftism before its greatest days, and then suffered a long slow decline that terminated in anarchic and disorderly feudalism, not leftism. The dark age did not set in until long after Rome's bout of leftism, and we recovered from the dark age without any left singularities.

The decline of China started with a burst of leftism, but not a full blown left singularity. During its decline there were at least two left singularities - Maoism and Chang Hsien-chong - arguably more. The final left singularity was followed by a cure, which is not a very common outcome of left singularities, though I have hopes for Russia That cure was the communist party converting to a hereditary aristocracy with an electoral monarchy, which elected competent monarchs, the first such monarch importing an economic system from Hong Kong, which had absorbed eighteenth century Manchesterism from nineteenth century colonialists and preserved it, more or less, though the twentieth century.

For feudalism with electoral monarchy to work, the election should be for life or good conduct, the removal of a monarch being an extraordinary, and usually quite violent, event.

Russia, on the other hand, after recovering from its left singularity, attempted to import the modern western economic system, which turned out that they imported the parasite but not the host.

The bronze age transition from large scale civilizations to disorderly familism happened abruptly and was mediated by a left singularity. The transition to disorderly feudalism following the decline of Rome just gradually happened without any connection to radical leftism.

The French left singularity ended in the Red Terror. The French left was fairly thoroughly squashed by Napoleon, much as the Russian left was very thoroughly squashed by Stalin. It utterly and permanently disappeared following its attempted recovery of power in the Paris Commune. Britain imposed its institutions on France, so today's French left is a colonial outpost of the anglophone left.

The initial stages of a dark age are over taxation and over regulation, where the government attempts to persistently tax and regulate beyond the Laffer limit. However in the final stages of a dark age, the government is apt to be nonexistent, lawless tax collectors gradually becoming indistinguishable from bandits, which does not in it itself necessarily cure the dark age.

Leftism tends to involve:

Breakdown of traditional gender roles, emancipation of women.

Breakdown of traditional hierarchies, progressing towards more democratic and bureaucratic forms from authoritarian and legal forms. Dissolution of responsibility and answerability for decisions.

Anarcho-Tyranny, where protection of the law from criminals is removed from decent citizens, but self-organized self defence is still illegal.

Millenarianism, the belief in an ongoing or near-at-hand massive transformation of society. Accelerating this is considered a moral imperative. This belief also justifies the above breakdowns as disposing of "outdated" things

What Happens in a Left Singularity

In the realm of discourse, non-leftist ideas become increasingly unacceptable, with their proponents facing social, professional, and legal consequences. The negative consequences for speaking against leftism quiet down the resistance and thus increase the boldness of the left, which accelerates the process.

The French left singularity began with false popes of Avignon. Its initial growth was relatively slow, becoming rapid, pathological, and alarming under the highly progressive radical left regime of King Louis XVI.

The anglophone left singularity began with the Puritans, ended in Cromwell doing a Stalin and crushing everyone to the left of him. After Cromwell died, Monck made a military coup. His praetorians proceeded to "guard" parliament and restore the monarchy. Leftism continued to fester, but did not really go malignant in Britain until perhaps 1770 (American Revolution) or 1820 (failure of King George to divorce Queen Caroline despite conspicuous infidelity, disobedience, and gross sexual immorality).

It manifested with alarming moonbat crazy biting mad leftism in 1820, and has continued to get worse faster and faster ever since.

The Russian left singularity began not with a religious heresy, but rather with Alexander the Liberator being fashionable and influenced by British leftism.

The British nineteenth century enclosures were a land reform that redistributed land from the aristocracy to the individual peasants. The left wanted the land redistributed collectively rather than individually, so that the left would have to administer land and peasants (administering the peasants on behalf of the peasants, because they love the peasants so very much). What you think you know about the enclosures is the left demonizing them. The enclosures were in practice a quite reasonable moderate left wing land reform - but the left wanted a moonbat crazy frothing at the mouth biting mad left wing land reform, and did not get it, and so have stridently demonized the enclosures to this day.

In Russia, Alexander the liberator, influenced by fashionable British leftists, introduced the moonbat crazy frothing at the mouth biting mad left wing land reform that they had been seeking, and to this day argue should have happened. He distributed the land to the serfs collectively, rather than to the individual serfs. But of course, the serfs were, for the most part, incapable of administering the land, so there followed endless further reforms to administer land and serfs, which moved Russia ever lefter, creating an ever larger class of government and government privileged leftists, eventually culminating in the artificial famines of the 1930s, leading to Stalin's great purge, during which he purged both the largely imaginary right, the wreckers, and the terrifyingly real left, the trots, thereby ending the left singularity started by Alexander the Liberator.

## What to do in a restoration

### 2015-09-17 09:54:52

That which cannot continue must end. Thus one way or another, the movement ever leftwards, ever faster, is going to stop, going to be stopped, probably after the fashion of Stalin, if we are lucky after the fashion of conspiracy of 9 Thermidor, if really lucky after the fashion of Cromwell.

That does not necessarily mean things will get better, merely that, as in Stalin's Soviet Union, they will stop getting even worse. But when China recovered from Maoism, it not only had a pretty good restoration, but came out of a dark age. And today's Russia is not doing too badly.

So here is what is going to take to clean up the Augean stables:

Cannot stop a left singularity. unless you get real serious about stopping it. Hence the end of a left singularity is apt to lead to a restoration - though it may instead merely lead to the execution of a remarkably large number of leftists, suspected leftists, potential leftists, and suspected potential leftists. (Yey Stalin! Go Stalin Go!)

The inability of King George the Fourth to divorce of Queen Caroline was lunatic barking mad leftism in charge, frothing at the mouth, and biting crazy, and it has been going downhill ever since, getting crazier and more extreme every day, faster and faster. This is damaging technology through rule by consensus. Peer Review means that instead of experimentalists telling the scientific community what they see, the scientific community tells experimentalists what they would see. Science died when peer review was introduced in the nineteen forties, and in the seventies, technology began to follow.

To fix the left singularity needs military force and martial law. Warriors on top, so warrior status has to be raised, priest status lowered. Confiscate the Ivy endowments, and completely destroy Harvard, totally bulldozing every trace. Symbolically pour salt upon the earth, then redevelop the Ivy campuses for housing, shopping malls, and offices.

Deflate academic credentials, with the school leaving exam, taken at the age puberty begins, discriminating between those above and below IQ 105, and the school matriculation exam (high school, taken at completion of puberty) discriminating between those above and below IQ 115. University entrance begins at IQ 125. Some people fail university, quite a lot fail university, about half of them, so that pretty much everyone with a two year or more degree is IQ 130 or above. Four year degrees, however, should not be significantly smarter, just more academic. Above common IQ levels, above IQ 130, we don't use academic credentials, but rather deal with individuals case by case. So if you are really smart and leave school at school leaving age, then self educate, you will still do fine. We cease to force people to waste their fertile years in zero sum competition for credentials of little value. Post deflation academic degrees are given new names to differentiate them from inflated academic degrees. The net effect is that far fewer people go to university, and those that do go to university for a far shorter time.

To lower priestly status, we make sure that there is a non academic path into every career, often built around apprenticeship - that there are no careers where academics have a legal monopoly of licensing people to perform certain tasks. Well established and successful practitioners can also license people to perform those tasks.

School years should be tied to puberty, so that people with the same physical development are taking the same exam, so as not to discriminate in favor of blacks and against whites, and so as not to discriminate in favor of females and against males, and to create an expectation that completion of puberty means getting a job, a wife, and having children.

Issue a clear definition of orthodoxy and heresy and systematically purge government, academia, and quasi government institutions such as banks of heretics.[307].

The Mad Max scenario - trade and specialization of labor collapses as at the end of the Bronze age - is unlikely. That social technology is too widely known and too well understood. However, we are losing, have lost, the scientific revolution and the scientific method. In place of Nullius in Verba, we are now required to believe in the scientific consensus established behind closed doors on the basis of secret evidence. Reflect for example on the endless and generally unsuccessful lawsuits attempting to get the Universities to reveal the evidence for Anthropogenic Global Warming, even though all the older journals have rules theoretically in place requiring full data and evidence for any published article to made available. Double entry accounting is under attack, with Sarbannes Oxley replacing accounts that reflect reality, with accounts that reflect official reality.

We have also lost the important reproductive technology of marriage -that a man and a woman could make a contract to stick together and raise their children, and be socially and legally forced to stick to it. The concept of marital rape - that the thought seems meaningful, that the concept exists, is incompatible with the existence of marriage as marriage has been understood for the past few thousand years. If either party may withhold sex or reproductive sex at any time for any reason or no reason, then either party may cancel the

---

[307]https://blog.reaction.la/culture/the-next-official-belief-system/

marriage at any time for any reason or no reason, which is a profound deterrent to having children.

Patriarchy is also necessary for marriage. If one person does not have final authority over the household, you don't have one household.

Without marriage, marriage as it was understood up to 1950 or so, whites are not going to successfully reproduce.

Before 1972, not only was "marital rape" legal, but people had difficulty understanding what feminists were talking about - the combination of words made no sense to most people. Feminists had to talk around the topic in long winded ways. Legally the right of a man to compel his wife to perform her marital duty had been quietly abolished early in the nineteenth century, but socially, people continued to pretty much take it for granted until the nineteen seventies.

## Not the Zionist Occupation Government

### 2015-09-20 06:31:29

Is the problem an evil Jewish Conspiracy, or, as Mencius Moldbug argues, out of control runaway Christian descended holiness.

In Moldbugs account: the Puritans started off holier than thou, then became the Evangelicals and such, who were holier than Jesus, then the Unitarians, who were holier than Christ, and finally the progressives who are holier than God. And here we are while they get holier still. While Jews are overrepresented among progressives, they are conversos.

Jews are massively overrepresented in various areas of life, sometimes to their credit, sometimes to their considerable discredit. There are a number of websites which list Jewish overrpresentation in various unpleasant activities, but none of these unpleasant activities matter much, except that they are rather strikingly overrpresented in the Cathedral, from which throne they venomously condemn Christianity, the crusades, white history, whites and white culture, while considering themselves nonwhite.

Is this because the Cathedral is a Jewish plot using non Jews of tools, or is it a ruling class plot using Jews as tools? Historically rulers have routinely used Jews for various objectionable activities, and then, when these activities attracted too much heat, proceeded to throw the Jews to the wolves, like the matador using his cape to distract the bull.

Remember the war on Christmas was a traditional Puritan activity - Jews never cared much about other people celebrating Christmas one way or another until they signed up with progressivism.

So, are the Jews the matador, in which case getting rid of the Jews would make a big difference, or are they the easily discardable matador's cape, in which case getting rid of the Jews would be a mere distraction?

The voice of the Cathedral is the New York Times.

The voice of the Cathedral made an interesting report on the murder of Alexander Levlovich by Palestinians[308].

---

[308] https://www.nationalreview.com/corner/424102/returning-copy-desk-briefly-kevin-d-williamson

If Jews ruled America, Hamas and the Palestinian Authority would be reduced to smoking grease spots in half an hour and the Al Aqsa Mosque would be flattened in a day. Therefore, the matador's cape, not the matador.

There are a lot of things wrong with Jews. But my diagnosis is that exile has made them sick, has made their religion sick. For Jews to heal, not only do Jews have to go home, but Judaism, which is still in exile, has to go to home. A nation state religion became an exile religion. For Jews to heal, it has to become a nation state religion once again. Today the state religion of Israel is not Judaism, but progressivism. Hence the stoning of Alexander Levlovich.

Over time, Jews should move to Israel or be assimilated. And that is what, in fact, is happening. As Jews become progressives, which is to say conversos to the official state religion of their country of exile, they become indistinguishable from, and intermarry with, Christian derived progressives, as we would expect if Jewish progressivism is conversion to a Christian derived heresy, rather than a Jewish plot. If Israel exists, the long run solution, and the long run trend, is for people to become adherents to the state religion of their country of residence, or residents of the country of their religion.

## Intersectionalism

2015-09-21 22:11:56

One of my commenters made the cuckold apology "I am not a racist".

If you are white, you are racist, if male, sexist, if heterosexual, homophobic, and if your sex is identifiable, transphobic. Repeat after me: I am racist, sexist, homophobic and transphobic.

Hence the rise of intersectionalism.

Women tell men they are inferior, because feminism. Black women tell white women they inferior, because black liberation. Lesbian black women tell straight black women they are inferior, because gay liberation, and trans lesbians ... Hey, wait a minute, is not a trans lesbian actually a thinly disguised, usually very thinly disguised, heterosexual male?

## The British military as a self licking lollipop

2015-09-23 10:07:36

Britain lately has been suffering completely ridiculous one sided defeats by small ill equipped poorly trained Arab forces.

I wondered how this could be so, so I purchased Losing Small Wars: British Military Failure[309]

tl;dr

During World War II Churchill complained:

> "Pray explain to me how it is that in the Middle East 750,000 men always turn up for their pay and rations but when it comes to fighting only 100,000 turn up."

---

[309] https://www.amazon.com/gp/product/0300182740/

When fighting Arabs in Iraq and Afghanistan, only a couple of hundred turned up.

Compare and contrast the British army before the Crimean war, where if you had a ten thousand troops, ten thousand troops would usually fight, their officers leading from the front rather than hanging around surrounded by numerous flunkies in a large well appointed well defended base, logistics being largely provided by camp followers employed by regimental commanders, mostly female camp followers who worked vertically by day and horizontally by night, and consequently had immeasurably lower status than actual fighting men.

Partly this is Parkinsons law, but partly it is rule by priests over warriors. The typical British general regards hurting people and breaking their toys as rather disgraceful and embarrassing, and such activity is unlikely to lead to medals and promotions. They focus on activities that do not directly aim at hurting people, like raising the self esteem of Afghan women and British servicewomen.

## The 2007 British surrender incident.

2015-09-25 09:47:22

A British warship was sailing in Iraqi waters, waters that Iran had in 1975 agreed were Iraqi, which treaty it had never disavowed. Iraq was at the time effectively ruled by the British and Americans.

Two small boats with fifteen British sailors left the warship to inspect a small ship for contraband. Under the nose of the British warship, in Iraqi waters, three Iranian coastguard vessels kidnapped those British sailors. Despite immensely superior firepower, those aboard to the British warship were too terrified to do anything about it.

There were several different official versions of why the warship failed to act, with the final and official version being that they failed to notice. Oh come on.

The sailors, and Britain, and numerous organs of the British government, proceeded to issue apologies to their captors. After much groveling, the captives were released. The denouement of this incident reveals its cause.

## The principle of merited impossibility

2015-09-28 07:05:10

When gay marriage was first on the radar, it was piously declared that it was completely impossible that this would result in repression of Christians, and that when they get it, they deserved to get it good and hard.

Similarly, it is completely impossible that white minority status will result in ethnic cleansing and genocide, and when whites get it, they deserve to get it good and hard.

## On cuckolding

2015-09-29 02:37:48

On PUA sites, one regularly reads posts from readers who suspect they are being cuckolded, or know damn well they are being cuckolded.

"My girlfriend has an active account on e-harmony. What should I do?"

The advice they get tends to be disturbingly feminist.

"What do you mean *your* girlfriend? She belongs to herself. She is her own property. All you can do is spin more plates, see other women, so that she is too busy worrying about you seeing other women to see other men."

It is not really in a woman's nature to belong to herself. Like a dog without a master, it makes her nervous.

"Act like you don't care. There are plenty of other girls. And even if there are not plenty of other girls you should act as if there are plenty of other girls"

Well, it is surely true that you should act like there are plenty of other girls, but even if there really are plenty of other girls, a pretense of not caring is not going to fly. Being cuckolded is humiliating and degrading, and pretending to be fine with it is even more humiliating and degrading, and she knows it.

There was an Ottoman Sultan who had several thousand girls in his harem. He discovered that one of them had slept with another man. He killed the man, but could not find which girl was at fault. So he killed them all and dumped their bodies in the river, which was choked with bodies. Women are turned on by this story to this day. Even if you had as many other women as that Sultan, you would still care, and everyone knows it. "Act like you don't care" is bad advice because your behavior just will not be congruent, and if it was congruent, would come off as weird and spergy, like Scott Alexander piously endorsing polyamory when his camwhore girfriend does not fuck him but fucks other men. Who gets pussies wet? Scott or the Sultan?

The advice given in the PUA forums is the advice of despair. You can take the girl out of the bar but you cannot take the bar out of the girl. If you are picking up girls in a major city, in particular if you are picking up girls in San Francisco, they are all hard boiled burned out sluts who have taken too many dicks up every orifice starting at a very early age. There is always someone handsomer than you and more charismatic than you, and all your girls are all yearning for a booty call from Jeremy Meeks.

But the situation is not really quite that hopeless. If you pick up girls who have recently arrived in the big city, or cruise places far from the center of the Cathedral looking for chicks, there are quite a few rubies to be found.

All girls yearn for the gentle but firm touch of ownership, even the hard boiled burned out sluts who can no longer enjoy it or experience it yearn for it.

So what do you do if someone smiles at your girl and says hello?

You drop a possessive hand lightly but firmly over her shoulder, to restrain her from smiling back, saying hello back, giving the guy her phone number and hinting that if he plays his cards right, she might drop her knickers. And then you stare coldly into his eyes, because a bro does not hit on another bro's girl.

# Arab Spring

## 2015-09-30 09:00:45

Arab Spring has predictably been an utter disaster.

By undermining the legitimacy of existing authority, it has turned the middle east into a sea of blood and fire, the worst cases being Syria and Libya.

Middle Easterners are mostly of inferior races, and at the best of times, it is hard for them to maintain the basic functions of a modern society, hard to keep the electricity running, the water running, the sewage off the streets, and all that. To operate this quite ordinary stuff in a society dominated by an inferior race requires a fair bit of arrogant confident elitism and a cheerful willingness to smack grossly inferior people around to keep them from mischief. Arab Spring has been democratic and anti elitist. Thus most of the anti Bashar Assad groups in Syria just cannot keep that stuff functioning, and keep begging the horrid evil tyrant Bashar Assad to keep that stuff operating for them.

Near as I can figure, the major reasons that Bashar Assad is a horrible tyrant is that he stops stupid people from doing stupid things and he will not let them rape and murder those of non Muslim minorities.

Oddly, Obama and the Cathedral press have unshaken confidence that Obama is on the correct side of history. From time to time they confidently predict that Putin will fail unless he overthrows Bashar Assad for the Cathedral, after many years of disastrous failure by the Cathedral in its efforts to overthrow Bashar Assad.

Obama and the New York Times and the rest live in an echo chamber, utterly impervious to outside reality. Their policy cannot be a disaster, because they are on the right side of history.

The natural outcome of democracy is that each tribe votes for its tribal interest. The result is unacceptable to all the minority tribes. War ensues, unless the majority group has a natural advantage in military struggle as well as voting, unless the majority group is the clearly superior group. If you have democracy without war, it is because you have an ethnically homogeneous society, or someone is rigging the system to produce acceptable results.

Bashar Assad's strength is that his religion is the only religion in Syria, other than Christianity, that is tolerant enough that it can be trusted to refrain from massacring minorities and his political organization is the only one that has the basic competence to keep the basic services of a modern society functioning and the will to keep the hands of subhumans off those basic services.

The Cathedral congratulates itself that it is rule by smart superior people, but rule by smart superior people was an unprincipled exception, which exception has now been rolled back[310].

The effects of rule by stupid people are most immediately apparent at your DMV department, at your airport security screening, and in Syria.

If you are not getting Syrian style brownouts, the people who are keeping our power system functioning, the people who making sure you do not get brownouts, are all rather old and due to retire soon. Soon your power supply will be provided by the same people

---

[310]https://blog.reaction.la/economics/the-stupid-elite/

who operate airport security, because right now, white male privilege keeps the power on, and that is an unprincipled exception.

## Putin reads neoreaction

2015-10-06 07:19:24

Or perhaps he listens in to State Department phone calls.

Putin on Islamic State as a state department proxy:

> In these circumstances, it is hypocritical and irresponsible to make loud declarations about the threat of international terrorism while turning a blind eye to the channels of financing and supporting terrorists, including the process of trafficking and illicit trade in oil and arms. It would be equally irresponsible to try to manipulate extremist groups and place them at one's service in order to achieve one's own political goals in the hope of later dealing with them or, in other words, liquidating them.

> To those who do so, I would like to say — dear sirs, no doubt you are dealing with rough and cruel people, but they're in no way primitive or silly. They are just as clever as you are, and you never know who is manipulating whom. And the recent data on arms transferred to this most moderate opposition is the best proof of it.

> We believe that any attempts to play games with terrorists, let alone to arm them, are not just short-sighted, but fire hazardous (ph). This may result in the global terrorist threat increasing dramatically and engulfing new regions, especially given that Islamic State camps train militants from many countries, including the European countries.

> Unfortunately, dear colleagues, I have to put it frankly: Russia is not an exception. We cannot allow these criminals who already tasted blood to return back home and continue their evil doings. No one wants this to happen, does he?

Well actually I am pretty sure that the State Department does want it to happen. And that each terrorist incident in Europe and Australia will be preceded and followed by State Department pressure to address the "root causes" - the root causes being insufficient diversity and affirmative action. Observe that the recent Australian government initiative to mend fences with the Muslim Community was immediately followed by a terrorist incident, which proves the urgent importance of mending fences with the Muslim community.

Observe the smooth and continuous transition under way from affirmative action being necessary because the official victims are so weak, to being unavoidable because the official victims are so powerful and dangerous.

## Thermodynamics, leftism, organisms, and Chesterton's fence

### 2015-10-08 06:12:02

Entropy, disorder always increases. Life exists, a living creature exists, by increasing its own internal order, at the expense of consuming external order and excreting disorder.

A functional society generates internal order, like a living organism. So the individual organisms of the society find safety, peace, order, and secure property rights. And from these intangible forms of order, they get more tangible, individual organism scale forms of order: food in the supermarket, electricity at the switch, water at the tap. Leftism consumes the order of society to grow and live, as a parasite or a cancer consumes the order of the organism in order to live. And eventually the lights go out, as in Venezuela or North Korea.

Consider a cancer cell. On the micro scale, what it does is indistinguishable from what a good cell does. It grows, it absorbs nutrients from the bloodstream.

But it replaces the highly ordered structure of the good cells with structurelessness, with mere growth, without regard for the organismic functions that a healthy cell is performing.

The order of the organism is apparent only to teleological thinking.

The order of society is in Chesterton's fences. Leftism takes down Chesterton's fences, deeming them irrelevant obstacles, as bones and blood vessels and lungs and heart and brains are irrelevant obstacles to cancer cells.

The ensuing disorder becomes visible[311] before you get to the North Korean point where the lights go out.

## Republican party funds the sale of baby meat

### 2015-10-10 00:32:53

As you may have heard:

> Boehner's announcement Friday that he will step down at the end of October came just after he persuaded conservatives not to threaten to shut down the government unless Congress cut off Planned Parenthood funding.

"Threaten to shut down the government" means "pass a budget forcing taxpayers to fund every single thing on the left wing wish list except funding for a particular corporation that sells baby meat[312]."

This would "shut down the government" because the Democrats would reject such a terribly extreme ultra far right budget.

Hang on a minute. If the Democrats reject the budget, are not they the ones shutting down the government?

As the Overton Window moves ever leftwards ever faster, the pretense that there is an opposition party to the permanent government becomes ever thinner.

---

[311] https://heartiste.wordpress.com/2015/10/06/what-we-have-lost/
[312] https://blog.reaction.la/culture/intact-fetal-cadavers/

# Putin successfully stabilizing Syria

## 2015-10-18 21:32:24

Where you have a substantial Islamic minority, the only stable solution is for Islam to rule or to be violently and brutally crushed. Nothing in between works, despite over a thousand years of governments, peoples, cultures, and religions trying to find something in between, and endlessly failing. Where you have several different substantial Islamic factions in a single country, the only solution is a brutal dictatorship to keep the Islamics in line. That, or genocide. It is the nature of Islam to make war till it conquers or is very thoroughly conquered. *Very* thoroughly conquered.

Aleppo is about to fall. The fall of Aleppo will be the defeat of the "moderate" ("Christians to Beirut, Alawites to the grave") opposition.

The difference between the "moderate" opposition and Islamic State is not their position on Christians and Alawites. They both intend to kill every Alawite everywhere. It is their position on the royal families of Jordan and Saudi Arabia. The "moderate" opposition supports and is supported by royalty. Islamic State is republican and intends to overthrow the royal families. Thus the defeat of the "moderates" is likely to cut off royal aid for the overthrow of Alawite rule in Syria.

The "moderates" are at present transferring large amounts of American and Saudi military aid to Islamic State, with a wink and a nod from the State Department, making the war in Syria a major profit center for Islamic State. With the defeat of the "moderates" Syria becomes a cost sink, so Islamic State (which needs to make war pay) will retreat, likely under cover of some face saving formula that pretends Islamic state is not defeated, pretends that Sunnis are not being ruled by Alawites, and pretends the State Department has not suffered a humiliating defeat.

The Pentagon, the red empire, the empire of the bases, supports the royal families of the Middle East. The State Department, the blue state, the empire of the consulates, opposes the royal families of the Middle East.

Putin will be reluctant to humiliate America by rubbing it in the way America was humiliated in Vietnam, since that is likely to destabilize the world, and will therefore try to maintain some pretense of Sunni autonomy. On the other hand, the American government is getting aggro, responding to its defeat in Syria by pushing for war with China, much as Hitler, when up to his neck in alligators, declared war on America.

Thus while Putin would likely favor some compromise that allows the State Department to save face by pretending it is still destabilizing Syria, the US, to judge by its behavior towards China, is not in the mood for saving face, but rather, believing that history is on its side, wants victory and to be seen to be victorious, where victory means at minimum maintaining Syria a chaotic bloody hell hole, with the final objective of expelling the Christian minority and exterminating the Alawite minority, thus making possible a "Democratic" Syria. Democracy requires a Syria with a single religion, Sunni, and a single ethnicity, Arab, and the State Department has repeatedly demonstrated that it so loves democracy that it is willing for other people to pay the price.

There is a significant risk that the State Department will regard peace, stability, and order in Syria as an intolerable affront, and will do something drastic to ensure that history proceeds as it is supposed to.

The American government is now spiritually in the same position as the Soviet government used to be. It believes it is destined to rule the world, being the voice of truth, light, and history, while it buggers its economy and its technology stagnates, undermining its power to rule the world.

## Watching female oriented video porn so you don't have to

### 2015-10-22 04:16:37

Most female sexually oriented material is books or chick flicks, which are entirely under the thumb of the social justice warriors, so it is sometimes tricky to disentangle what is a reflection of the unbridled female id, and what is social justice propaganda, what the social justice warriors wish the female id was really like.

However a small minority of female sexually oriented material is porn that is clearly intended to be watched one handed, and this is, for the most part, stupendously and shockingly politically incorrect. This stuff is a direct manifestation of the female id while that female is beating herself off. From time to time I hear feminists covens announce that they are going to produce politically correct feminist porn, but it looks like no woman beats herself off to feminist porn. Female porn looks like it is entirely untouched by social justice concerns.

Most of this stuff is pretty icky. A majority of this material is interracial porn, with the white insert character (the character the female viewer is intended to identify with) being brutally abused by several black men. A large plurality of the material is cuckold porn. The insert character treats her husband with utter contempt, and then gets banged in front of him by several thugs and pimps.

Where there is enough story line to identify the class, personality, and motives, of the characters (and there frequently is not enough story line for that) the males that the female viewer is intended to fantasize having sex are, in the majority of identifiable cases, low IQ thuggish scum, and thoroughly nasty and unpleasant people.

Only a small minority of the sex in these videos is actual rape, but most of the sexy is pretty rapey, being degrading and coercive. The male characters just stick it in without waiting for indications of consent. The females seldom object very strongly.

In the majority of cases, where there is any story line at all, the old patriarchy is represented as impotent, powerless, and afraid in the face of the you-go-girl empowered slut insert character. However the you-go-girl empowered slut is promptly disempowered, degraded, and humiliated in a spectacularly politically incorrect fashion by thug males. Husband is impotent, but thugs rule.

In a minority of cases, the men of the old patriarchy are, however, depicted glowingly, as good men, as sexy alpha male wild beasts, and it seems to me that in a majority of cases where the viewer is intended to get off on watching white males, and there is enough story to identify the social roles of the characters, those white sexy alpha males are of the old patriarchy - husbands, boyfriends, rich men, powerful men, aristocrats, and fathers.

Yes literal fathers. There is quite a bit of biological dad rapes biological daughter porn, and it seems to me that the women watching this porn are not only getting off on the fantasy of a powerful older male savagely raping a young powerless and submissive girl, they are also getting off on the fantasy of an intact nuclear family presided over by a strong man who loves his family and takes care of them, the latter fantasy being more improbable in their lives than the former. The daughters are always trash sluts who had it coming, and the dad is always a great dad. I am not being ironic. Porn does not do irony.

Either way, the porn sends the message loud and clear that emancipation was a disaster for women's sex lives. Every male that they beat themselves off on cheerfully oppresses women, often in a brutal and degrading fashion, whether as thug, pimp, or patriarch.

One of the porns was pretty much a plea by women for their beta boyfriends to man up: Girlfriend visits boyfriend, who is a programmer or some such, one of those guys with a high pay low status cubicle job. He is working at home on his computer doing something job related. Girlfriend wants some sex but he says he has to finish the work related stuff, then he will visit her. He almost seems like a beta male, other than his striking alpha ability to brush off his girlfriend and tell her what she will do. She goes away, and he discovers she has forgotten her phone. He reads her instant messaging history, and finds she has been making unfavorable comments about their sex life.

Instead of curling into ball and whimpering softly as a beta male would do, he heads to her place to punish her. He grabs her by the throat, smashes her cell phone, pulls her hair rips her clothes off, puts her into crushing submission hold, and proceeds to stick it into every orifice. Which of course she loves and their sex life is, as a result, absolutely great forever after. The porn is largely about sex while being strangled. It is not exactly rape, but he does not ask permission, and the only foreplay in which he engages is hair pulling and strangulation, and he applies a painful submission hold whenever he sticks it into her.

That drip drip dripping sound you hear is one thousand pussies opening wide and dripping moisture at the thought "Successful middle class upwardly mobile handsome young software engineer who nonetheless has balls enough to engage in domestic violence when he is disrespected"

Then there was "The Castle" In the dungeons underneath the castle a bunch of naked women are chained up. From time to time the gentlemen from upstairs come down stairs to amuse themselves. This porn was pro patriarchy, pro feudalism, pro class differences, and pro rape. The guys from upstairs are presented as great guys. This was unusually extreme and unrepresentative of mainstream tastes, in that only a few of the videos featured girls in chains, but it was representative of mainstream tastes in that most of the videos featured girls overpowered and dominated by powerful males.

In most of the videos with sufficient story line to identify character and social roles, the women are having sex with the scum of the earth who are depicted as total scum. In "The Castle", they are having sex with noblemen, who are depicted as genuinely noble - feudalism as women wish it had been when they are beating themselves off.

The Cinderella fantasy, where a rich and powerful male gives a girl a makeover, and she looks like princess, and thus becomes a princess, as for example the movie "Pretty Woman" is undoubtedly a popular romance story. But it is not what they beat themselves off on. When they are beating themselves off, the story is more along the lines that the pimp rips her clothes off and makes her a whore, than that the rich guy gives her nice clothes and makes her a princess.

A few of the videos depicted women being subjugated and degraded in extreme ways, ridiculously extreme ways. One of the fantasy worlds made the world of the Gor series look like a feminist utopia. In the imagined world they never domesticated animals, so, like the natives of South America, raised humans for meat and milk. "The Dairy Farm" features a factory farm in this imagined world. The converse video, of women as princesses, never occurred. The median and modal video was degrading, and range of humiliation and degradation was between "sluts get hammered hard" to stuff that makes "Gor" seem feminist. If Cinderella was done as a video porn, then once the prince had finished using Cinderella, every other male at the ball would take his turn.

I conclude that because of female emancipation, affirmative action, and anti sexual harassment laws, status in the male status hierarchy no longer registers in the female mind as status. High status by male standards is low status as indicated by the status signals of the environment of evolutionary adaptation, so females just are not turned on by it. Hence the attraction to the scum of the earth.

In the ancestral environment, an alpha male was someone who frequently poked holes in other people with a sharp object.

## The Jewish problem

2015-10-24 03:12:46

Nazis are commies and commies are progressives.

If you are a Nazi, you think that the rot set in around 1930-1950. If you are a progressive, you think the rot has not set in yet.

So if you are a Nazi, you pretty much want the New Deal, or the New Deal on steroids. Nazis are leftists who have been left behind by the movement ever leftwards.

If you are a Nazi, you think leftism is fine except for Freudian Theory, second wave Feminism, race denialism, and the Frankfurt School's Cultural Marxism, all of which can be plausibly blamed on Jews.

But when the Supremes hypocritically endorsed "separate but equal", that was race denialism, with a touch of hypocrisy to make it actually workable.

The Jewish problem is that Jewish conversos to progressivism failed to pick up on the hypocrisy, and started demanding that people actually live according the moral standards that everyone piously endorsed around 1820 or so.

The rot did not set in with cultural Marxism. The rot set in with "We hold these truths to be self-evident, that all men are created equal, that they are endowed by their Creator with certain unalienable Rights". There is your race denialism right there.

As for feminism and the destruction of marriage, the attempted divorce of Queen Caroline in 1820 established the moral principle that women are so naturally pure and virtuous, that it is mere cruelty to enforce the marriage contract on women, it should only be enforced on the naturally wicked and despicable sex, men.

If you want to get out of the trap, say after me: "All men were not created equal, some should command some should obey, some should not merely obey, but are naturally slaves, and should not be allowed to make their own decisions. If found wandering loose causing problems, should be placed under the control of an owner. Women's sexual choices are apt to be dangerous to society and to themselves, thus fertile age women should always be controlled by husbands or fathers. A women not subject to a man is suffering misfortune, as for example an orphan or widow, or is wicked and needs punishment, as for example a harlot."

As soon as you denounce the declaration of independence and the emancipation of women the logical case the Jews are a big problem collapses. And the emotional case for hating Jews is the same as that of any market dominant minority, envy and covetousness, which is also at the root of declaration of independence and the emancipation of women.

Getting rid of the Jews will not help you. The problem is inside your head. They are not emitting evil mind control rays at you. You have been emitting evil mind control rays at them. Umpteenth wave feminism is the logical consequence of the failure to divorce Queen Caroline.

## Bay of Pigs operation

2015-11-14 05:37:25

Bay of pigs official history:

> "On January 1, 1959, a young Cuban nationalist named Fidel Castro (1926- ) drove his guerilla army into Havana and overthrew General Fulgencio Batista (1901-1973), the nation's American-backed president. For the next two years, officials at the U.S. State Department and the Central Intelligence Agency (CIA) attempted to push Castro from power."

But it was the state department that overthrew Batista and installed Castro. Maybe they repented of this when Castro revealed himself to be a full on communist. But if they ever repented, official history would call Castro a communist, not a nationalist, and would call the Bay of Pigs a revolt, not an invasion, for it was conducted by Cuban Nationals and therefore arguably a revolt, not an invasion.

Initially the invading force had US air support, which would have made it impossible for Castro to deploy heavy weapons or massed troops against them, thus extremely difficult to destroy them. But the US air support was abruptly and unexpectedly withdrawn, leaving the invasion force hanging out to dry.

Not deploying the US air force at all makes sense. Deploying it makes sense. But deploying it, and then suddenly not deploying it only makes sense if you want your invading force to be annihilated.

The moment there were juicy high value targets available to the US air force, including Castro himself commanding his troops in the field, the US airforce went home.

If you want to overthrow Castro, blowing him up in the battlefield is likely to be highly effective.

If they were so overconfident that they expected their forces to win without air support, why apply air support initially? Surely if overconfidence was the problem the normal sequence would be to try it without air support, then when the $#!&* hits the fan and large concentrations of enemy show up, apply air support.

Looks to me that those men were betrayed to their deaths, same tactic as Lord Howe betraying his men to their deaths.

The purpose of the Bay of Pigs operation, as actually implemented, was to prove that communism could not be rolled back because of the direction of history and the glorious liberation of the oppressed masses. History is supposedly on the side of the left, and if history fails to conform to script, it gets a helping hand.

If the purpose of the Bay of Pigs operation was to overthrow Castro, would have bombed command, control and communication on the prospect that he might be there, as in fact he was.

If the purpose of the Bay of Pigs operation was to overthrow Castro, official history would call him a communist, not a nationalist.

If the purpose of the Bay of Pigs operation was to overthrow Castro, official history would call it a revolt, just as our pet infidel raping mass murdering terrorists in Syria are supposedly revolting against the evil and oppressive Syrian government, not invading Syria.

The inability of the American government to overthrow Castro resembles the inability of the House and Senate Republicans to pass a budget that denies the left a single item on its wish list, however outrageously repugnant and violently unpopular[313].

## Yes, we are at war with Islam

### 2015-11-14 10:13:19

And always have been.

For over a thousand years, a multitude of nations, states, peoples, cultures, religions, and empires have attempted to coexist with Islam. None have succeeded. We will not be the first.

If you have a few percent of Muslims, you have what you can pretend is a major crime problem. If you have ten to thirty percent, you have a low level civil war, which intermittently becomes a high level civil war whenever you relax or show signs of weakness. If you have thirty percent, you can have a fairly tense peace, like the not-quite-war in Mindanao if you have a large well disciplined military, guards and soldiers everywhere, and regularly and routinely deploy death squads, but you cannot afford rule of law - you can have peace only by ruthlessly and unhesitatingly applying the laws of war. With a large Muslim minority you need death squads and the routine and frequent application of torture to keep the almost-peace, the not-quite-war.

France has five or ten percent Muslims, regular car burnings, Calais has been burning for some time, and the French state has no power over substantial areas that have been successfully seized by Islam.

France has taken pretend measures - checking passports at major entry points. This is security theater. Calais continues to burn, and the French authorities avert their eyes. Muslim illegal immigrants continue to flood over the borders unopposed. Rapes by Muslims are piously ignored. Preachers continue to preach terror, and while Muslim preach-

---

[313]https://blog.reaction.la/culture/republican-party-funds-the-sale-of-baby-meat/

ers preach terror, the French authorities arrest and prosecute Marine LePen[314] and Eric Zemmour[315] for incitement. A Muslim that gets over the border cannot be deported.

Far from France getting serious about stopping terror, it remains a criminal offense to advocate getting serious about the problem.

Under recent international law you cannot return people unless their country of origin agrees to accept them, or at least that is how international law has recently come to be interpreted. And the countries of origin never agree. Australia and Israel have been cheerfully breaking this law, and New Zealand has been furtively breaking it. Burma has been dumping Muslims into boats and telling them that if they want to live under Islam, start sailing to a Muslim country.

When France rounds up illegals and dumps them in Africa or the Middle East, then France will be beginning to get serious. But no one can imagine such a thing, let alone propose it, for to imagine such a thing is a thought crime.

France is absolutely unserious about dealing with terrorism, and to even think seriously about dealing with terrorism is a crime no Frenchman will admit to committing.

The only good Muslim is a bad Muslim. If a Muslim is not murdering innocents and raping children, he does not take his religion seriously.

## Minor Australian politician says out loud what everyone in the world is thinking

### 2015-11-16 06:31:00

Josh Frydenberg, Australian minister for natural resources says[316]:

> a country that loses control of its borders not only invites the tragedy of the loss of life at sea... but also the direct security threats that are incurred by not knowing exactly the backgrounds of the people that you accept into your own country

It is odd that in the entire world, I cannot find any other politician saying this out loud in plain words. Waiting for Trump, who so often outrages the elites by saying the unsayable.

## How to deport eleven million people

### 2015-11-18 03:11:12

First, the Australian experience tells us that regular judges and government employees will not cooperate with the merely elected government. So the merely elected government has to rely on the military and on "civilian contractors" (mercenaries). The merely elected government has to give the "civilian contractors" sovereign immunity against the

---

[314]https://www.bbc.com/news/world-europe-34580169

[315]https://galliawatch.blogspot.com/2015/11/eric-zemmour-in-court.html

[316]https://www.skynews.com.au/news/politics/national/2015/11/15/paris-attacksvindicatetough-border-stance.html

courts, which makes them not very civilian at all. Without sovereign immunity, any time a "civilian contractor" forcibly prevents an "asylum seeker" from going wherever he wills, it will be deemed a war crime, like the Israeli wall.

Secondly you have to find the illegals. What countries that actually have control of their borders do is that local forms of ID are only issued to people with a right to reside there indefinitely. Everyone else either cannot get that ID, or gets a special form of that ID that requires a passport or photocopy of the passport to also be presented. And the foreign passport always shows entry permission which expires after a certain time. And you cannot rent a room, or get a regular job, or open a bank account, or drive a vehicle, etc, without ID. If you are a foreigner, need your passport to rent a room, get a most types of job, or drive a vehicle. Further, if you come to the attention of police, some types of rentacop, or the military guard, they can demand your id, as for example, bad driving, reasonable suspicion of an offense, drunk and disorderly, homeless and no visible means of support, or being obnoxious in a shop or a bar. If the rentacop at the mall detects you are illegally resident, and he does not like you much, he puts you in the mall pen, and calls border control to collect you. The control on renting rooms or buying homes catches far more people more effectively than the control on jobs, since the landlord does not particularly want to rent to illegals, while the employer may well want to hire illegals. And your landlord very much wants your ID so that he can go after you if you trash his stuff, while your employer likely has you under supervision, so does not really want your ID except the government tries, usually not very successfully, to make him. And if a landlord does illegally rent to an illegal, that illegal better be on time with the rent.

Will this catch all eleven million?

No, but it will catch a lot of them, and it will catch the most obnoxious ones, the ones that are causing problems.

## Yes, all Muslims are like that

2015-11-22 21:33:17

Turks celebrate Paris attack

Turks boo and chant during moment of silence for Paris.

Not all Muslims will kill you, just as not all Christians will turn the other cheek, but if he will not kill you, he is not being a good Muslim. In this case, the no true scotsman fallacy is no fallacy, since killing infidels is required by the Koran. If he is not murdering innocents and raping children, does not take his religion very seriously.

## Yet another PC outrage, again

2015-11-23 03:15:09

point deer, make horse.

Lately there has been some hand wringing[317] about how freedom of speech in Academia

---

[317] https://www.washingtonpost.com/news/act-four/wp/2015/11/11/yale-university-of-missouri-and-the-broken-promises-of-americas-universities/

has just been killed[318].

Bollocks.

Academics have been terrified, servile, docile, and submissive since the middle of the nineteenth century.

The purpose of political correctness is to humiliate and degrade by demanding that people accept an obvious lie, thus demonstrating who has the power and who shall submit.

Every so often a new act of submission is demanded to show submission to new masters, and all of academia absolutely without a single exception turns on a dime and endorses the new obvious lie, just as it endorsed all of the old obvious lies, for nearly two hundred years.

This is nothing new. What is new is that the lies are coming faster and faster, indicating greater and greater instability within the ruling elite - but they have been coming every faster for nearly two hundred years. This is a sign of decline, but decline has been happening for quite a while, ever faster.

Hence the Chinese saying: point deer, make horse[319]:

In other words, absurd ideas are made up on purpose to humiliate people and check who is really loyal to which power holders.

Here is Spandrel telling the story:
> Well the emperor died out of the capital, so nobody knew. The only ones who knew were his prime minister, Li Si, and his close minister Zhao Gao, who may or may not have been a eunuch. Well apparently Zhao Gao didn't like the crown prince Fusu very much. He had reason to think that Fusu hated him, and would execute him as soon as he became emperor himself. So Zhao Gao gets Li Si and says "hey, dude's dead, we're the only ones who know. Fusu doesn't like you either, so why don't we get this kid Huhai and name him successor?"
>
> Li Si took some convincing, as did Huhai himself. But eventually they got on the plan, and sent a forged imperial edict ordering Fusu to kill himself. Which strangely he did, even after opposition by his entourage. With crown prince Fusu out of the way, the three got back to the capital, and set up Huhai as Second Emperor of Qin.
>
> Soon later Zhao Gao found some excuse and executed Li Si and all his family, and took his prime ministership. He obviously knew too much. Then he proceeded to execute all those little Schelling Points that were the emperor's brothers and sisters, so there was no contest about who had the right title to the crown. Still after Huhai was secure in his thrown, he was starting to be a little uncooperative with Zhao Gao. The Chen Sheng rebellion had started, and the empire was having trouble suppressing it. The Emperor blamed Zhao Gao for the mess and he had a point. But Zhao Gao didn't like that. He started to think that maybe they should have a change of emperor, but he couldn't be sure he could pull it off.
>

---

[318]https://www.latimes.com/opinion/op-ed/la-oe-daum-race-missouri-yale-20151111-column.html
[319]https://bloodyshovel.wordpress.com/2015/06/03/the-purpose-of-absurdity/

> So Zhao Gao brings a deer into the palace. Grabs it from the horns, calls the emperor to come out, and says "look your majesty, a brought you a fine horse". The Emperor, not amused, says "Surely you are mistaken, calling a deer a horse. Right?". Then the emperor looks around at all the ministers. Some didn't say a word, just sweating nervously. Some others loudly proclaimed what a fine horse this was. Great horse. Look at this tail! These fine legs. Great horse, naturally prime minister Zhao Gao has the best of tastes.
>
> A small bunch did protest that this was a deer, not a horse. Those were soon after summarily executed. And the Second Emperor himself was murdered some time later.

It is a compliance test. Will you be party to a blatant lie? If you will be party to one blatant lie, then you be party to each of the other lies.

So we get a ruling elite that lies without hesitation. But in fact it is not in the interest of people, society, or the state, to have a ruling elite that lies without hesitation. It makes elite cohesion difficult, which increases the likelihood that the elite wind up murdering each other in large numbers, usually murdering a lot of innocent bystanders in the process to provide cover.

PC is pretty much the opposite of the old honor codes. Instead of an honor code, we have a dishonor code. Instead of compliance testing potential elite members for courage, honor, and dignity, we compliance test them for cowardice, lying, and groveling.

## Recap on NATO shooting down a Russian jet and murdering the pilot

2015-11-24 21:07:45

A Russian Jet that was flying over Syria at the invitation and with the permission of the Syrian government was bombing Turks in Syria. While bombing Turks in Syria, was shot down by Turkey, which is part of NATO. Allegedly the jet strayed slightly inside Turkey, but it was shot down over Syria, the wreckage landed inside Syria, the pilots landed inside Syria, and the pilots were murdered inside Syria. We know it was shot down over Syria because of video uploaded by the Turks who murdered one of the pilots. Although Turkey says it was flying inside Turkish airspace, it was shot down in a Turkish no fly zone over Syria.

The pilots parachuted safely and were promptly murdered, by an organization that is theoretically an enemy of the US, but which in Syria is receiving backing and arms from the US and is composed of people who are ethnically Turks operating on the border of NATO ally Turkey with the protection of Turkey. The killers videotape themselves shooting the pilot endlessly while chanting "Allah Akbar" and upload the video to the internet.

Obama and the US enthusiastically backs Turkey, as Turkey makes war on Christians.

Obama says Turkey has the right to defend itself and its airspace. It certainly has the right to defend its airspace by shooting Russians in Turkish airspace. Does not follow that it has the right to defend its airspace by shooting Russians in Syria. The plane was shot down while bombing Turks in Syria. Hard for it to intrude on Turkish airspace while its bombs are landing where they are supposed to.

Will this incident lead to World War III? Probably not. But this kind of stupidity and recklessness will lead to World War III. It has been a long time since the last big war, so people are forgetting that peace is hard, war is easy. If we don't get World War III this time over Syria, we will get it next time over someplace else, or the time after that. I am still inclined to bet on Civil War II rather than World War III, because the American elite is increasingly disloyal and incohesive.

## Yes, the US did treacherously stab Russia in the back over Syria.

2015-11-28 00:10:11

Russia informed the US approximately when and where Russia would be bombing terrorists, as part of their agreement to avoid incidents over Syria that might lead to World War III.

According to Russia's account[320], shortly before the pre-announced Russian bombing near the border, Turkey put up two F16s which loitered near the border, awaiting the bombing run near the border. When the bombing began, one of the Turkish F16s crossed into Syrian territory and ambushed a Russian bomber - direct conflict between Russian armed forces and Turkish armed forces without the fig leaf of a proxy, an attack conducted outside Turkish territory.

How do we know the Russian account is true and the Turkish account is false?

We know it is true because the Turkish media got a professionally edited video of the jet coming down faster than the Russians got their rescue mission - which means the Turkish media and Turkish forces on the ground inside Syria knew what was coming, while the Russians did not know what was coming. Therefore this attack was undertaken in response to notification that the Russians would be bombing Turks inside Syria near the border, therefore not undertaken in response to a bomber straying over the border. Note also that Obama's speech was all about Russia bombing the good terrorists instead of the bad terrorists, not about the supposed border crossing.

Therefore official NATO forces have already attacked official Russian forces in Syria without the fig leaf of proxies. Therefore B already owes me a bottle of Ardbeg.

## Technological decay

2015-12-06 23:59:09

I have long argued, and commenters on this blog have long been disputed, that science died shortly after World War II, replaced by official state religion wearing lab coats as priestly robes, and using test tubes as aspersoria for holy water.

The age of science began with the Restoration and the Royal Society. The Royal Society's motto was "Take no one's word for it". Feynman, in his address "What is Science?", rephrased this as "Science is the belief in the ignorance of experts." Now, however science consists of taking the word of secret anonymous committees meeting behind closed

---

[320]https://www.rt.com/news/323651-turkey-su24-downing-syria/

doors, committees that refuse to show their evidence, data, calculations, and method of calculation even while demanding trillion dollar programs, gigantic human sacrifice, and challenged by freedom of information requests.

I have long argued, and commenters on this blog have long been disputed, that since 1972, the west has been in technological stagnation or outright decline in most everyday fields, in an ever increasing number of fields. Yes, DNA reading and computer disk drives keep improving, but clothes washing machines have gone to $#!&, and there is a reason why people are nostalgic for the old muscle cars.

Observe our ability to build and operate tall buildings has been diminishing since 1972.

The highest level of technology is found in war. Soldiers are to take control of or destroy men and assets. Tanks, artillery, mortars and Armored Personnel carriers are to destroy soldiers. Ground attack planes and helicopters are to destroy tanks and armored personnel carriers, and air to air fighters are to destroy ground attack planes, and other air to air fighters.

So the highest level of technology, and the greatest expense, is found in the air to air fighter. A people's capability to build and operate air to air fighters is the most sensitive barometer of its technological level, and a vital factor in that people's capacity to win wars. You get air superiority, so the other side cannot use tanks against your soldiers, and you can use tanks against their soldiers, and artillery against their population centers and assets. You flatten their population centers and destroy their assets so that they cannot feed and equip their soldiers, and then your soldiers take charge.

And as you know, American air to air fighters have been getting slower and slower, more and more expensive, less and less maneuverable, flying less and less high, and carrying less and less ordinance. But now they are stealthed, right? And Russian fighters are not stealthed.

Stealth can be beaten by sufficiently advanced electronics - you need two radars in substantially different locations whose radar is coordinated - one paints the target with a radar beam, and the other views the scatter from a substantially different angle. In response to the Turkish attack Russia now has part of the technology to beat stealth deployed in Syria: AEASA radars that can spray beams out in several thousand completely different directions per second. Does it have all of the technology deployed? Does it have the capability to coordinate two AEASA radars so as to see through stealth? Maybe. Probably. Though we will not really know until we see a major air battle between Russia and another advanced power.

Further Russian air to air fighters can fly faster, fly higher, are more maneuverable, and carry more ordinance than American air to air fighters. The recent display of Russian capability in Syria seems to be giving the Pentagon a nervous breakdown. The Su-34 is every way superior, except for the very important defect that it lacks stealth.

When Dubai wants to build a tall building, it hires western experts. But those western experts are expatriates, semi permanent exiles from the west. They have foreign wives, girlfriends, and concubines. They don't build tall buildings in the West because a horde of bureaucrats would shake them down for bribes (politely laundered through "consultants", aka bagmen) and because they could not get any decent pussy in the west.

Our increasingly diverse ruling elite loses cohesion, in part through diversity, in part through selecting for cowards and liars[321]. Because of this loss of cohesion, if you want to build a tall building in the west, you have to bribe a thousand priestly bureaucrats (whose self justifications are increasingly priestly - mostly they are protecting Gaia) and each of these thousand bureaucrats wants his pet consultant to collect ten percent of the surplus value that would be created by the building, adding up to a demand for one hundred times the value, while the King of Dubai is likely to content himself with a mere fifty percent of the value.

## Trump has a good chance

### 2015-12-07 01:38:45

I, and Trump, have always expected that at some point the Cathedral would change the rules to block him because racism.

But now it looks as if they are comfortable with him as Republican candidate, because supposedly Hillary can beat him.

Hillary is a stupid drunken carpet munching bitch. No matter what polls may say, people are only saying they will vote for Hillary because they know that that is what they are supposed to say. If Trump becomes Republican candidate, as is highly likely if nothing extraordinary and obviously undemocratic is done to stop him, and if he then starts to lead on Hillary, and then the government does something extraordinary and undemocratic to stop him, that is likely to lastingly discredit democracy.

Mass immigration, and the ensuing fall in living standards and rise in rape and murder, has caused the half boiled frog to show ominous signs of twitching. The standard response to a twitching frog is to allow the outer party, the conservatives, the appearance of power so that they can conserve the gains made by the left until the frog calms down and the left can resume boiling the frog.

Standard operating procedure would be Trump wins, illegal immigration is halted, legal immigration, like that which brought in the recent jihadi mass murderers, continues, jihadi terrorism continues and escalates, then in eight years illegal immigration quietly resumes again despite loud announcements to the contrary.

But as the left moves ever leftwards, it becomes harder for them to pull off their standard operating procedure. They are reluctant to slow down just because the frog is showing signs of life.

So, predicting Trump gets the Republican nomination, predicting that he easily outpolls Hillary, predicting that he will win unless the government does something undemocratic to stop him, which it well may, predicting that if elected, he will find the permanent government highly uncooperative, and that anything he manages to do, will be quietly undone. Predicting high risk of crisis that the left causes, and does not need to cause, that just as they are engaged in proxy war with Russia and are spoiling for open war with Russia for absolutely no sane reason, they are spoiling for proxy war and open war with the American voter for absolutely no sane reason.

---

[321] https://blog.reaction.la/culture/yet-another-pc-outrage-again/

To state the same prediction in different words: Either Trump wins or the left does something considerably crazier even than the crazy stuff we have recently seen to stop him.

## James Deen rape and porn

### 2015-12-11 00:52:49

The very Jewish and quite politically correct pornographer James Deen has been accused by eight female porn stars of raping them.

The accusations are all obviously false in that none of the pornstars are bringing charges or suing him, probably because he has videotapes of most of the "rapes".

What is obviously happening here is that pornstars realize that they are hurt, humiliated, degraded, and their souls are being destroyed, but the culture gives them no words with which to express the thought except "rape" and "consent". But female consent really is not all that significant. Consent does not make it good, nor lack of consent make it bad. Thirty year old women are only marginally more competent to consent than nine year olds.

James Deen tells us (and since it is all videotaped, doubtless truthfully tells us) that all the BDSM is done with safe words and carefully negotiated boundaries.

I have done a bit of BDSM also, and never used safe words or negotiated boundaries. Safe words and negotiated boundaries are contract negotiations, and you get contract negotiation in sex that is done for money. The safe words and boundary negotiations are not an indication that all is well, but rather an indication that something is terribly wrong.

## Externalities of IQ

### 2015-12-26 02:54:57

"Hive mind" is in error by comparing the individual correlation between income and IQ with the national correlation. Correlations are dimensionless quantities, and we need a quantity with dimension "increase in income per IQ point"

From Scott's graph of income by IQ decile[322], I conclude that within a nation, individual income increases by a factor of 1.024 per IQ point, that for IQs in the normal range, average income for people of that IQ within a given nation is proportional to $1.024^{\wedge}(IQ)$

This closely agrees with Dallards result[323], obtained from different and independent data, that the average income for white males is proportional to $1.025^{\wedge}(IQ)$

From La Griffe's table, I construct a graph of log of national income against IQ, draw a trendline, and conclude that between nations, income increases by a factor of 1.099 per IQ point[324], that the average national per capita income is proportional to $1.099^{\wedge}(IQ)$.

This curve (exponential in IQ) gives a better fit than linear in IQ, and as good fit as smart fraction theory (linear in the proportion of people above a certain threshold).

From which we may conclude that the only a quarter of the benefit of IQ is internalized, that three quarters of the benefit goes to everyone else.

---

[322]https://slatestarcodex.com/2015/12/08/book-review-hive-mind/

[323]https://humanvarieties.org/2016/01/31/iq-and-permanent-income-sizing-up-the-iq-paradox/

[324]https://blog.reaction.la/misc_upl/GDP-IQ.ods

And that therefore importing inferior people people will lower your income much more than you yourself being inferior. Inferior people benefit by going to the countries of superior people, but destroy what they come for.

Note the the neoreactionary classic tinyurl.com/gllc3xs[325] gives a clear explanation of why national IQ matters. Because ruling IQ matters. A couple drive through the Congo. Everything has gone to shit since the white rulers left, everyone is trying cheat and rob everyone else, and often enough, trying to eat everyone else. Cannibalism is not common, but it is a lot more common than one would prefer. Every so often an entire village comes after them with machetes, presumably intending to eat them.

In France, forty percent of births are African, and this fraction is rapidly increasing. It is worse than Brazil, but France is still France, rather than Brazil, because pure blooded whites still rule. From which we may conclude that in a few decades, French cuisine is going to feature people more than snails and frogs.

## In favor of a repressive state religion:
### 2016-01-02 23:04:36

We anthropomorphize the Cathedral as a person or a conspiracy. Such anthropomorphizing is a good approximation for corporations, since they make considerable efforts to make the approximation true - by concentrating all power in the CEO, and then delegating power from the CEO.

However, the cathedral is rather a bunch of conspiracies, and its direction is determined by entropic forces akin to enthalpy, rather than a sinister and clever plan. To build a ruling coalition, divide power into bite sized morsels and distribute widely. Not a good plan for operating a functional organization. Mann is sovereign, and Mann is an idiot.

In Europe you go directly to jail for thought crimes. The US has the first amendment, so employs a workaround. If a business employs thought criminals, it has a "hostile work environment", so gets sued by social justice warriors, and has to pay them large sums, making thought criminals effectively unemployable, and social justice an obscenely lucrative career option.

This, however, does not work on open source, hence Gamergate is relatively successful. The Social Justice Warriors attempt to seize open source projects. Sometimes they seize them, and to their surprise destroy them, often they get pushback, which pushback they attribute to Gamergate and the Neoreaction. And indeed it is true, in that Gamergate and the Neoreaction is the think tank of the pushback, but what makes the pushback effective is the propensity of the revolution to devour its children, what makes the pushback effective is that leftists pretty soon start persecuting leftists for insufficient holiness, with the result that pious leftists find themselves, to their horror, deep shame, and great embarrassment, joining forces with Gamergate and the Neoreaction in self defense, as the Montagnards found themselves collaborating with the Dantonists.

There is always a state religion. There never was a golden age of freedom of speech and thought. However if you have many states with many state religions, and there is a lot of movement and communication between them, as in America before the civil war,

---

[325] https://tinyurl.com/gllc3xs

then truth stands a chance, because if the gentleman from Massachusetts cannot say the truth, the gentleman from Virginia can say it, because before the Mormon War and the Civil War, the State of Virginia had a different and independent state religion from the state of Massachusetts.

The religion of Massachusets wound up conquering the US, and eventually the world, in large part because Virginia took religious freedom seriously, while Harvard and Massachusetts was unyieldingly and fanatically determined to extirpate it with fire and steel and still are unyieldingly and fanatically determined to extirpate it with fire and steel. When crazies and fanatics go up against moderate, compromising, and cynical cosmopolitans, the moderate and cynical cosmopolitans tend to get trampled.

If ever there was freedom from the state religion in a white state, that state was Virginia before the War between the States, and it did not end well.

We today have two problems: A single monolithic state religion, that since World War II has dominated the entire world, and a state religion with no archbishop and inquisition to keep the crazies in line. Kings put Bishops on the payroll to shut up the crazies. If you have a state religion controlled by the holiest, you get holiness spirals of ever more holy people

Having freedom would be the cure, but freedom within a single state is tricky, and, as we saw in Virginia, vulnerable to violence from the holy. Whites are prone to state religions. Asymmetric repression leads to movement ever leftwards. The state religion has to repress the excessively holy as well as the insufficiently holy, or it inevitably gets ever crazier.

If freedom for the insufficiently holy is hard to achieve, restricting the liberty of the excessively holy is easy to achieve.

White nationalists tend to mistake repressing the excessively holy, controlling the priesthood, for controlling the Jews. Effective measures to keep the priesthood and the excessively holy in line would quite disproportionately affect Jews, but Jews as such are the wrong target.

# Saudi Monarch executes US agent who tried to overthrow him.

2016-01-05 00:11:32

Note the sudden explosion of friendliness between Iran and the US State Department.

They were both trying to overthrow King Abdullah bin Abdulaziz Al Saud, King of Saudi Arabia and Custodian of the Two Holy Mosques.

Sheikh Nimr al-Nimr was the face of Arab Spring in Saudi Arabia. Pretty obvious he was a tool of Iran, but the interesting question is: was he a tool of the US State Department?

"NGO" stands for "non government organization", but if an organization is actually non governmental, for example McDonalds, no one calls it an NGO. In practice, "NGO" means "US State Department Front Organization". This is an open secret, as for example when they advertise for employees, they are apt to describe the openings as government employment.

The reason that they call themselves non governmental is that they actively campaign in US politics and foreign politics, which is illegal or embarrassing for the US government to openly do.

When the Saudi princes arrested Sheikh Nimr al-Nimr for trying to overthrown them, the NGOs - pretty much all of them - went bananas, revealing Sheikh Nimr al-Nimr to be an NGO tool, and thus a US State Department Tool.

Note the great success of Arab Spring in Syria, Libya, and Egypt.

## Those were the good old days

2016-01-05 21:45:33

When La Droit de Seigneur was in effect, an ordinary man could expect to marry a wife that had only slept with one alpha male.

When the Spanish inquisition was operating, they shut down free lance witchfinders.

In 1992, I visited Cuba and remarked how Cubans walked small, walked in little steps, took up little space. I could see the fear pressing them down, squeezing them, making them little.

Today, I see white males walking small, taking small mincing little steps, keeping their hands close to their bodies. The statistics show falling testosterone and falling sperm production, but you don't need statistics, you can see the that the testosterone has drained out of white males, while blacks walk large, as if they are aristocrats and whites are peasants, and women casually talk over their boss and interrupt him.

Boys are staying home, staying in Mum's basement. There is no place for them in the world.

## The Anti American empire

2016-01-08 06:31:55

In foreign countries, we regularly see protest banners in English, written by Americans and intended for American audiences, whereby if the American writing the protest banner influences the American seeing the protest banner on television, this will redistribute power in the foreign protest country - and, more importantly advance the power of some Americans over others. This is a symptom of the American Empire - which I suggest is better called the Anti American empire.

Moldbug observed that anti Americanism is more accurately described at ultra Americanism. Subjects of the American empire proudly announce that they implement American ideals better than those dreadful Americans in flyover country, and hope for a pat on the head from the New York Times.

Some time ago, the New York Times has published a list of its most upvoted reader comments of all time and the winner was a Canadian commenter who set out to explain how much more progressive, and consequently wonderful, Canada is relative to the U.S.

That this was noticed by their masters, this slight pat on the head from the emperor, resulted in a huge outburst of patriotic Canadian pride.

And similarly, the American empire is better called the Anti American empire, in that it produces costs, but no benefits, for Americans. For example American tax law claims universal reach, which disadvantages any American citizen attempting to operate a business overseas, making him legally second class to a European. And similarly American corporations are disadvantaged, resulting in all sorts of overly clever scams whereby American corporations form overseas corporations. If America is going to claim universal reach for its laws, those laws should advantage Americans by protecting their freedom to do business, giving them more freedom to do business than natives of foreign countries, rather than less. In practice, American universal jurisdiction is based on the principle that Americans are evil capitalist exploiters who need to be prevented from oppressing the foreign masses.

And of course, Americans spend blood and treasure meddling in foreign regions.

By and large, the objective of these shenanigans is to install in power in foreign places regimes that hate and despise Americans in flyover country, and eagerly hope for a pat on the head from the New York Times. Hence, better called the Anti American Empire.

Reflect, for example, on the installation of Aristide. Aristide "won" the Haitian election, which was called at American insistence. When it became obvious he was going to lose the Haitian election that the American government had called, the American government demanded that the rules were changed, and changed again, until Aristide could win because no one else important was allowed to run. Then, after Aristide "won", and the permanent Haitian government ignored the election outcome, the US government invaded Haiti, and installed Aristide.

There scarcely was and is anyone in the world more loudly, vociferously, and obnoxiously anti American than Aristide, who spent much of his career in Washington seeking American support for him to rule Haiti, rather than in Haiti seeking Haitian support for him to rule Haiti.

During decolonization, there were a pile of Marxist national independence movements, with names in English, composed of rubber stamp Harvard jargon, rather than referencing the names, history and culture of the countries whose independence they were supposedly seeking.

And similarly, when Cuba ridicules US presidents, it ridicules the evil stupid Bushitler and Ronald Raygun, while groveling for a pat on the head from Obama the Lightbringer.

I have often written favorably of the red empire of the bases, and contrasted it with the evil blue empire of the consulates. But they are both the American empire, and without the hard power provided by the empire of the bases, the empire of the consulates would find that their soft power was parasitic on the hard power of the bases, and their NGOs would be exiled or banned. Shut down the empire of the bases, as Trump proposes, and the Anti American empire withers on the vine.

If we really must intervene in the Middle East let us steal their oil and ravish their women. Three hundred thousand vets have suffered brain damage from explosions. It is not worth it unless they get their wicks dipped.

Trump proposes to cut loose all those countries that hate us, despise us, and cost us blood and money. Should he actually carry out this policy, which is completely within presidential power and requires no consent from judiciary or legislature, only the obedience of the military, the horror and outrage will be beyond belief, making the former Bush derangement syndrome, and the current Trump derangement syndrome seem like courteous and rational discussion. The only reason the media's heads are not already exploding on television is that they really cannot believe the proposal.

While I don't think the merely temporary government can achieve real and lasting change, it will be good to hear those blood vessels popping like firecrackers on New Years Eve.

Just as the Turkish empire really sucked for Turks, the American Empire really sucks for Americans, hence, the Anti American Empire. Not to mention that Aristide, the loudest Anti American on the block, was our proconsul in Haiti.

## Rotherham Syndrome

2016-01-10 10:39:52

Approximately one thousand vibrants sexually assault two or three hundred white females. Zero arrests.

Thus though white males are legally second class before white females[326], all whites, including females, are legally second class before vibrants. Two arrests took place a week after the events, but this was a feeble gesture to appease the rioters. Nothing will happen to the two men arrested.

The interesting thing is not that this behavior happened, but that it received, and continues to receive, impunity.

And, similarly, when woman make false rape allegations - against whites, they also get impunity.

Government policy is that white males shall not get their wicks dipped, and vibrants shall get their wicks dipped. The government, and feminists, are super duper sensitive about female consent in some cases, but not others.

Hundreds of women were robbed of identifiable items, such as cards, jewelry, and cell phones. That very few arrests have been made indicates that not only did they not want to arrest anyone then, they still do not want to arrest anyone now.

## The trouble with fashism and 1488

2016-01-12 07:35:59

It is really great that so many young people are turning fashi, just as it is really great that so many people are turning to Donald Trump.

But Trump and fashism are just yesterdays's leftism - a leftism that supports the white working class, while progressives piss on the working class.

Long ago, commies and fashi competed for the working class, and it became obvious that the white working class preferred the fashi. And ever since then progressives have

---

[326]https://dailycaller.com/2016/01/10/national-organization-for-women-defends-rolling-stone-gang-rape-fabricator/

hated the working man with the rage of a jilted lover, and suppressed fashism using methods that cast doubt on their claim of democratic legitimacy. If Trump becomes president, it will be delightful to see the fourth estate explode in apoplectic rage.

But sorry. Lower class people are not the solution. They are the problem. Fashism is just another near far alliance, intellectuals with proles, very similar to Trump with proles. It is a white with white alliance, but near far alliance is inherently suicide and treason. It will go wrong in a way that does not involve race replacement, but still involves the destruction of white civilization. If you are fashi, you are still on the slippery slope heading ever leftwards. Recall the last days of the Roman Populares. In their last days, they allied with the Samnites. The Populares, I suppose, probably wanted a Roman Republic in which the subject states, such as the Samnites, were treated fairly. The Samnites wanted to level the walls of Rome and kill all Romans. Kind of like the alliance of progressives with Islamic State.

The trouble with "gas the kikes" is that it presupposes the expropriation of the Jews. And when you expropriate people, you are going to screw up corporate capitalism, which is the foundation of western civilization, the foundation of the scientific and industrial revolutions. People thinking out of covetousness and envy think that if they take that rich guy's stuff and make him poor, they will be rich, but instead, their neighborhood mysteriously winds up looking as if bombed.

Similarly "Day of the Rope". You are proposing to hang Havel's Greengrocer, though all you have to do, rather than hang him, is announce new and different posters for his window. He will put up the new posters, and barely notice that they say the opposite of the old.

"Gas the kikes" and "Day of the rope" are proposals for redistribution and disorder, when what we need is order in place of anarcho tyranny, and an end to redistribution.

Fashism is in large part just 1930s leftism, leftism as it was before the Jews came to dominate leftism. But leftism went to hell not when the Jews got in on it, but when they emancipated women, freed the slaves, raised the age of consent, and banned liquor, all of which they did well before major Jewish involvement. Genealogically, nazism is lutheran descended, progressivism is puritan descended, and communism is judaism descended, but in the 1930s, not so very different. National Socialism was just the New Deal on steroids. Jews that become progressives are conversos, Jews that become communists are heretical Jews.

It is really great that so many young people are turning fashi, and it is really great that so many people are turning to Trump. But the problem is that fashism is insufficiently radical, is just 1930s leftism, when what we need is 1660s restoration. Fashism is a step in the right direction, but far too small a step. Fashi support the white working class, and talk in dumbed down language to them. Western civilization was founded on feudalism and then corporate capitalism, systems that distributed power organically, valorizing and justifying severe inequality, decentralized but hierarchical, orderly but unplanned, systems that glorified and valorized the superiority of the few over the mediocrity of the many.

If you really want to secure the existence of our people and a future for white children, "gasing the kikes" is neither necessary nor sufficient. We need higher fertility, and we need eugenic fertility. We need smart women to get husbands and babies instead of PhDs and cats. Lots of babies, instead of lots of cats.

Hence my program "What to do in a restoration[327]".

What is stopping fertility is that:

* Marriage is not only an unenforceable contract, but the state applies enormous energy and effort to encourage and incentivise women to break the contract.

* That women are indoctrinated with the false life plan, where they pursue their careers while fucking Jeremy Meeks, and marriage and children just somehow spontaneously happens without them actually needing to do anything, while they really have to work hard on their careers, and hard on pleasing Jeremy Meeks.

* Coeducation means that fertile age women spend lots of unsupervised time in the company of men who have no ability to have a family, and no inclination or economic ability to settle down, and do not ordinarily get to meet men who might be able to marry them. By the time they get to work, they have already ridden far too much cock and have become jaded, their bosses are married, and their male co-workers are lower in status than they are. And the smarter the woman, the more years she spends riding cock in higher education, so the less likely it is she will be able have a family.

* Degree inflation means that young people spend their most fertile years listening to boring propaganda, when they could be working and breeding. Used to be that a school leaving certificate signaled that you were substantially smarter and more industrious than than the average Joe. Then every good-for-nothing moron was awarded a school leaving certificate, and you needed to graduate high school to signal that you were substantially smarter and more industrious than than the average Joe. Then every good-for-nothing moron was graduated from high school, and we have now passed the point where, as the Challenger inquiry revealed, plenty of good-for-nothing morons receive postgraduate degrees from good colleges. When I was doing job interviews I found plenty of people with degrees in computer science from good colleges, who should never have been allowed to show up for computer science 101, and had been completely wasting their time by attending the computer science course, that with their computer science degree and substantial debt they were no closer to grasping the basics than they had been on the first day.

* Degree inflation makes children impractically expensive, since you have to support them in a good school for twenty three years or so, which often enough somehow turns into thirty years or so. If most kids failed their school leaving certificate when they began puberty and promptly got kicked out of schooling (thus making the school leaving certificate an actually useful qualification and allowing teachers to require children to learn actually useful stuff for the school leaving certificate) then kids would be a profitable investment once again - particularly if the law backed the authority of the father over his male children till 21, and his female children until married or infertile.

* Anarcho tyranny makes housing impractially expensive, since you if you plan to have children you have to buy land somewhere free from dindus and vibrants - and the only allowed way to keep out dindus and vibrants is to for housing to be impractically expensive.

* The anarchy part of anarcho tyranny means you need land in a dindu free area. The tyranny part of anarcho tyranny means the business at which you work needs to be close

---

[327] https://blog.reaction.la/economics/what-to-do-in-a-restoration/

to the regulatory revolving door, meaning you face a long commute from your expensive suburb into a big city, a far too big city.

## Bitcoin crisis

### 2016-01-15 23:08:00

Back in the beginning, I argued bitcoin would not scale.

The counter argument was that we could muddle our way through somehow with ad hoc solutions, which could be sort of true, in principle.

The scaling problems started to bite in 2013[328]. They are now biting really hard.

The scaling problems are now well and truly here. Downloading the blockchain is slow and expensive. Doing transactions is slow, unpredictable, expensive, and unpredictably expensive.

Any solutions hurt, are partial, incomplete, unsatisfactory, and will disadvantage some people financially. Civil war in the bitcoin community has ensued[329] over which people it is to be.

That outcomes are determined by weight of computing power (the miners) rather than weight of bitcoins owned has led to problems. The miners don't face the same incentives as the people trying to do bitcoin based businesses.

Bitcoin has grown to about as large as it can get. It is doing about as many transactions as it can do, arguably rather more transactions that it is really suited for doing. Any fixes are at best small tune ups to get a little bit more performance out of the system, are at worst just burden shifting and burden hiding - hence the civil war. I have been trying to design a coin that could scale, by having a dispersed blockchain, where no one entity has to keep all transactions. You keep your own transactions, and summary information about entities you transact with, and summary aggregate information about all transactions, and the chain of hashes that links the ownership of your money and your transactions into the global hash, which chain would only grow as log of the total number of transaction, rather than grow with the total number of transactions. This means that parts of the blockchain will get lost temporarily or permanently, and the problem is to create a method for dealing with such losses that does not give anyone incentive to cause such losses, apart from the general deflation that such losses cause. Have been trying to design this for some time. Not making much progress these days.

Another solution, compatible with existing bitcoin is to have account based money built on top of bitcoin, bitcoin backed banks, analogous to gold backed banks. People are talking about this solution, but not actually implementing it, even though it seems a good deal easier than the solution that I proposed.

---

[328]https://blog.reaction.la/economics/bitcoin-scaling-problems/
[329]https://medium.com/@octskyward/the-resolution-of-the-bitcoin-experiment-dabb30201f7#.z2qoau1x5

## Believing in male supremacy will make you more attractive to women.

2016-01-19 12:24:02

If you believe that you are entitled, that women should obey, submit, serve, that unless you are buying sex by the hour, women should be sacrificing their own good to serve you, then red pill behavior comes naturally.

If, on the other hand, you believe that women are equals, then it seems obvious that you should treat them "fairly" - which is to say, as if buying sex by the hour. Even if you know the red pill intellectually, it seems horribly unfair that women should respond to you doing good to them by doing bad to you, and equally unfair that the more you demand from women, the more you get.

If you don't know the red pill, but believe that women should submit and obey, you will naturally act red pill. If you do know the red pill, but believe women are equals, then doing what gets you laid will seem artificial, unnatural, repugnant, and immoral, and women will seem bad when such behavior works.

If you think of woman as equals, you cannot judge yourself to be a good man when you do what gets you laid, and you cannot judge a woman to be a good woman when you do what gets you laid, and then she obeys you, has sex with you, and serves you.

But such a woman *is* a good woman. Women are content to serve, and should be content. Only whores are equals, and equal women are whores.

## The goal is soft genocide. Unless stopped, the outcome will be hard genocide.

2016-01-21 04:43:14

You saw that look of absolutely visceral disgust on Angela Merkel's face when someone handed her the German flag.

I am pretty sure that if an AIDS infested tranny projectile vomited all over her, she would lick it up and think it was chocolate.

That look of visceral disgust tells me that she wants everything that flag stands for destroyed – the German people, the German race, classical music. In her gut she absolutely wants to see German cities destroyed like Detroit was. She wants every German and everything German to die with her when she dies, to be physically erased and absolutely forgotten. She wants the death of every German and the utter destruction of anything memorable that any German ever made.

Why so?

Well, one way of answering this is that a long time back, students campaigning for the supposed achievements of NAMs to be given more attention in universities, sung "Western Civ has got to go" - meaning, or thinking they meant, the course "Western Civilization"

And similarly those calling for "the liquidation of the kulaks as a class" did not *at first* think they were calling for the liquidation of kulaks as individual human beings.

But in holiness competition, we get the phenomenon that neoreactionaries call "not getting the joke". If you are going to be selected for loyalty to progressive memes, best take those memes absolutely literally and seriously, since only the truest believers get into the best universities and get the plum jobs. So the next generation of progressives takes the most ridiculous things as holy writ, the more ridiculous the better, since precisely the most stupid, ridiculous and outrageous things will differentiate you from the other applicant to Harvard.

Thus students sing "western civ has got to go" (meaning the course) and not long thereafter, you are not going to make it into the elite unless you believe in your very heart and soul, believe absolutely and utterly, that "western civ has got to go", meaning the buildings, the books, the art, the science, the technology, *and the people.*

Another more or less equivalent explanation of this odd henomenon is the laws of majority minority relation[330]s

The logical extrapolation of these laws is that if equality, all whites must somehow be made to not be around any more, by some means that no one wants to think too much about, since their continued existence produces inequality. White males keep emitting these evil thoughts that somehow cause dindus and vibrants to underperform.

The methods for making whites somehow not be around any more will inexorably become more vigorous with the passage of time as the white male and married white female voting block gets smaller. (Single white females vote for rape, of course. What did you think they would vote for?)

## Hillary

### 2016-01-25 22:45:18

Observing Hillary's performances, it is kind of obvious that she is a drunk or druggie who cannot be trusted to be sober for a public appearance, or else she is suffering from some premature brain disease, or very likely both.

The email scandal is a storm in a tea cup. She committed umpteen felony offenses that could in theory send her to jail for zillions of years, but so does everyone. Everyone runs their own email server away from their employers and subordinates, and keeps data that could be potentially used against them on a thumbdrive. Everyone keeps a few spare identities here and there. It is like her husband smoking dope and raping women who had agreed to come to his hotel room in the middle of the night. I have never purchased dope, nor smoked it in private, and I notice that those who do tend to be losers, but once in a while I have been with a bunch of guys who are passing some grass around, and one needs to be sociable, and her husband is famously sociable. Nobody cares about his dope smoking, and feminists care even less about his rapes. The only people who ever worried about his rapes are Democrats-are-the-real-racists cuckservatives. Rape, like dope smoking or concealing or destroying information, is a crime that tends to be selectively prosecuted, and receives highly selective indignation. Consider for example Polanski. That was not statutory rape of a thirteen year old, that was actual rape, in the sense that Samantha continually said no and made some resistance. Does anyone care? Feminists don't. Chances

---

[330]https://www.amnation.com/vfr/archives/009226.html

are that the top secret data was lot more secure on Clinton's private thumbdrive than on the government official top secret system, because Clinton had real motive to secure it.

Hillary's "health" problem - that she cannot be trusted to be sane and sober - is rather more serious. How did the democrats wind up anointing this drunken carpet muncher to be president?

Answer: Quid pro quo for sticking to her husband in spite of his innumerable infidelities. It is reminiscent of the harem politics of decadent empires.

Filed under culture. Not filed under politics, or even party politics.

## In support of Roosh

2016-01-26 01:12:15

Roosh is a great and valuable ideologue of the alt-right

A lot of white nationalists want to purge Roosh because he is a non white degenerate who sleeps with lots of white women.

If a virgin sleeps with Roosh, she slept with a man who made it perfectly clear he was only in town for a week, and was in town to sleep with as many women as possible.

If a non virgin sleeps with Roosh, where is the problem?

White knighting is a first step to cuckservatism.

Come the revolution, those sluts will get a caning, and Roosh will get a shotgun marriage, and will probably be much improved by it.

The red pill is the alt right's killer app. If you know what women are like, you will conclude that emancipation was a really bad idea. If female emancipation was a bad idea, you are well and truly off the reservation.

## Trump is the man

2016-01-29 09:58:19

Among the red pill community there is a debate as to whether Trump is an exemplar of manliness, and his latest move in blowing off the presidential debate is an example of manliness, or whether it is the opposite.

Obviously, if someone treats you with disrespect, as Kelly disrespected Trump, the manly thing to do is to blow them off and ignore them. And critics of Trump say that by throwing a tantrum over Kelly, he is not ignoring her.

Well, perhaps. But if he showed up at the debate and accepted her as moderator and responded to her hostile interrogation, he would even less be ignoring her.

## The Road of our people's democracy

2016-02-01 04:37:14

In Hungary, and various other soon to be iron curtain countries, free and fair elections were held, which elections the communists completely and totally lost.

Untroubled, they applied pressure to purge the very rightmost people from government. And the very rightmost were purged. And they continued to apply pressure, and the very rightmost remaining were purged. And pretty soon there was no one left except communists. They called this "The Salami Slicer[331]". The process did not go all the way to infinite leftism and the execution of absolutely everyone, because Stalin had it under top down control, and turned it off once total communist domination had been achieved.

Which is OK, provided that Stalin has sufficient control to prevent those under him from using it against him.

Now lately, social justice warriors have been pushing open source software projects to adopt the following set of rules[332]:

> ... People with "merit" are often excused for their bad behavior in public spaces based on the value of their technical contributions. Meritocracy also naively assumes a level playing field, in which everyone has access to the same resources, free time, and common life experiences to draw upon. These factors and more make contributing to open source a daunting prospect for many people, especially women and other underrepresented people....
>
> ...
>
> Examples of unacceptable behavior by participants include:
>
> > The use of sexualized language or imagery and unwelcome sexual attention or advances
> > Trolling, insulting/derogatory comments, and personal or political attacks
> > Public or private harassment
> > Publishing others' private information, such as a physical or electronic address, without explicit permission
> > Other conduct which could reasonably be considered inappropriate in a professional setting
>
> Our Responsibilities
>
> Project maintainers are responsible for clarifying the standards of acceptable behavior and are expected to take appropriate and fair corrective action in response to any instances of unacceptable behavior.
>
> Project maintainers have the right and responsibility to remove, edit, or reject comments, commits, code, wiki edits, issues, and other contributions that are not aligned to this Code of Conduct, or to ban temporarily or permanently any contributor for other behaviors that they deem inappropriate, threatening, offensive, or harmful. ...
>
> ...

tl;dr The project agrees to purge the politically incorrect.

Doubting that the politically incorrect need to be purged is, of course compelling evidence that your views are so shockingly right wing that you need to be purged. Indeed,

---

[331]https://www.revolutionarydemocracy.org/archive/rakosihung.htm
[332]https://contributor-covenant.org/

debates on this issue tend to reveal that practically all of the key contributors are so ultra extreme far right wing that they need to be purged.

Further, although supposedly it is everyone's responsibility to purge the politically incorrect, obviously ordinary contributors, being mere coders and guilty of white privilege lack the required exquisite sensitivity to subtle slights, so people with the right race, sex, and sexual preferences need to be added to the project to take charge of purging people.

Note that the people pushing this proposal are so excruciatingly sensitive that they consider that the use of terms such as "forking" constitute sexualized imagery. They find misogyny and racism absolutely everywhere. Everyone (except themselves) is guilty, and must be punished.

## Can't stump the Trump

### 2016-02-01 10:11:34

I try not to follow electoral politics, because it is a spectacle, designed to give you the illusion of a microslice of political power. And ninety nine percent of the time, it is as fake as professional wrestling, as when the Republican party recently passed a federal budget funding every single thing on the left wing wish list, including welfare for illegals, late term abortions and the sale of baby meat, completely, outrageously, and flagrantly betraying those who voted for them, and revealing that everything they had said on the campaign trail was a total barefaced utterly cynical lie.

But Trump ... well at worst, it is truly great professional wresting, and the people I hate are getting pounded good and hard, and are not liking it very much.

Trump has the outstanding knack of getting a complex idea across in a gesture, a smile, a tone of voice.

A girl challenges Trump on "women's issues". At least that is what her question verbally is, but her body language is "You are uncool because fertile age chicks don't like you". And all us white knights know that fertile chicks are the arbiters of male social status.

Trump gives a rambling non answer to this rambling non question that logically makes no sense at all, and has no particular relevance, but in fact makes the point that he has numerous hot wives, great sex life, handsome sons and beautiful daughters. So this attack having been deflected, she asks an actual question. "When you are president will I get equal pay"

Trump replies "If you earn it" - making the unthinkable and unspeakable implication that what women do in the workplace just is seldom very valuable.

Trump was challenged on his reluctance to put boots on the ground in various trouble spots where the US is currently being routinely humiliated. To which he replied "Do you want to rule Syria?"

We have of course been losing wars because we have been occupying countries while refusing to rule them. Chaos predictably ensues. Progressive imperialism believes we can put good guys (meaning democratically elected progressives) in power around the world, as was supposed to happen in Arab Spring. Trump's question implies that if you put boots on the ground the victory condition and the method by which victory is achieved is that your general rules as US proconsul. This gives progressives the horrors, because the progressives want priests, not warriors, to rule. But priestly rule in an Islamic country is at best Islamic Brotherhood, as in Egypt, at worst the Taliban, which is why we have been losing. Events in Afghanistan have repeatedly demonstrated that faced with a choice between Taliban rule, and rule by US soldiers, the US State Department will choose the Taliban every single time.

## Women like rapists

### 2016-02-03 23:30:07

In the current Muslim invasion of Europe, the invaders continually commit acts that would get a white male a long time in jail and permanent registration as a sex offender, but for the invaders, minor consequences or no consequences. And you are seeing few if any complaints from women,unlike the extreme hypervigilance against imperceptibly slight micro aggressions by nerds.

A bunch of Swedish males protest about sexual assaults by the invaders against their women. And Swedish feminists counter protest "We are not your women"

Decoding: "You are insufficiently manly to grope us, unlike the invaders, we don't want to be owned by men like you."

In the manosphere, I see a whole lot of posts hopefully and optimistically proclaiming that all these assaults will show women that they need manly white men to protect them.

> we are approaching a social tipping point where the physical necessity of conventional masculinity will outweigh the liability to women inceding the power that feminine social primacy represents.

But women are not reacting that way. Their reactions shows that to them, all these assaults reveal white men as insufficiently manly, not invaders as dangerously aggressive. They rather like the invasion, and don't really want anything effective done to stop the assaults.

Efforts to protect women from sexual assault by the invaders are unappreciated and unwanted. Such efforts would only be appreciated and wanted if white men claimed and successfully enforced ownership over women, if individual white men claimed and enforced such ownership, with their individual enforcement backed by collective enforcement.

Women love it when a firm and confident claim of ownership leads to successful defense - and rather too much love testing claims of ownership by creating situations where the claim needs defending. Absent confident and firm ownership claims, do not really like defense very much.

Recall that in the legend of Perseus and Andromeda, after Perseus rescues Andromeda from the dragon, he kills her fiancee, abducts her from her family and marries her. He rescues her *and firmly takes possession.*

## Fall of Aleppo reveals that asymmetric warfare is bunkum
2016-02-04 20:28:13

In war, the stronger party prevails.

Asymmetric warfare only works when the weaker party has political protection. Perhaps like the Taliban, the weaker party is fighting soldiers required to operate as heavily armed nursemaids. Perhaps like Mao after the long march or the communists in Greece, the weaker party is launching raids from across a border that the stronger party is reluctant to cross.

The usual scenario where asymmetric warfare works is that the State Department fears the Pentagon more than it fears America's enemies, and requires US troops to operate by police rules, while those the Pentagon is fighting operate by the laws of war.

When Russia intervened in Syria to rescue their ally and preserve their Mediterranean base, the usual suspects, in particular President Obama announced Russia was getting into a quagmire. Instead Russia has, as I predicted[333], been decisively and thoroughly winning[334], largely through shelling, bombing, blockade, and siege - slow but thorough tactics that deny the weaker party any opportunity to do even a small amount of damage to the stronger. Less sweat that way than taking strong places by storm.

The Turkish controlled parts of Aleppo and west of Aleppo have now been cut off from Turkey[335], and are now already conserving food and ammunition. Short of an open land and air intervention by Turkey, short of open non proxy war between Russia and Turkey, will wither on the vine and fall in a few months.

Russia is also bombing the hell out of Islamic State's Turkish supply lines, but has as yet made no attempt to cut them off on the ground. Once Aleppo falls to siege, will probably turn its attention to laying siege to Islamic State.

The current peace talks illustrates asymmetric warfare in a nutshell: The weaker losing side rather than the stronger winning side is laying down preconditions and making demands, the primary demand being that Russia stop advancing. In other words, they are asking the State Department to stop the Russians from winning in the same way the State Department has so regularly stopped the Pentagon from winning. The State Department indignantly blames Russia for the failure of the peace talks, which supposedly failed because the weaker side is getting hammered so hard and is suffering so badly.


## Leftism, suicide, autogenocide, and cosmocide.
2016-02-13 05:47:11

If all men are created equal then it logically follows that all white males must die, because they keep emitting evil thought rays that cause blacks and women to underperform, blacks to commit crimes, and render women incapable of agency. If you believe all men

---

[333] https://blog.reaction.la/war/putin-reads-neoreaction/#comment-1130283

[334] https://www.washingtonpost.com/world/europe/after-four-months-russias-campaign-in-syria-is-proving-successful-for-moscow/2016/02/02/7a65d676-9dd0-11e5-9ad2-568d814bbf3b_story.html

[335] https://turcopolier.typepad.com/sic_semper_tyrannis/2016/02/short-and-sharp-saa-cuts-off-rebel-loc-with-northern-aleppo.html

are created equal, you are going to pursue the goal of the death of all white males regardless of whether you are Jewish or not. This was obvious in the French response to the Haitian slave revolt.

Working class Trump voters must be bitter clingers who are worse than Hitler simply by existing.

The left has always been autogenocidal. When the Populares allied with the Samnites that showed they wanted to kill all free Roman males.

Indeed, cosmocidal. They want to immanentize the Eschaton, and the only way to do that is to kill everyone and destroy everything.

Your ordinary leftist, for example Scott Alexander is undeniably a nice guy. But he has no enemies to the left, and no friends to the right, which means that all his friends are his enemies, and all his enemies are his friends. He is incapable of seriously criticizing those to the left of him, and does not dare allow himself to comprehend those to the right of him. Thus Scott will completely and accurately identify some problem with leftism "but still, quite sincerely, ritually abase himself to it. He writes long sincere thoughtful screeds pointing out that baby sacrifice is lowering the birth rate and causing family trauma, though of course he fully understands and endorses that Lord Moloch must be sated with the only food acceptable unto him."

Leftism is holiness, and in any discussion, any consensus, the holiest leftist or cuckservative always wins, so nice leftists always lose to evil crazies, and piously agree that they deserve to lose, since the holiest, being holier, should get their way.

And if you want to immanentize the Eschaton, you are holier than anyone like Scott, who might be suspected of thinking that immanentizing the Eschaton might be difficult. Only a total asshole like myself could possibly oppose immanentizing the Eschaton altogether. And if one wants to immanentize the Eschaton soon, one is holier than anyone who merely wants to immanentize some time in the distant and indefinite future. And if one wants to immanentize the Eschaton right away, one is the holiest of all, and every leftist and cuckservative wants to be one's friend, and none of them dare offend one, even though one will undoubtedly take offense anyway.

And thus the Khmer Rouge. And thus Chang Hsien-chong

Angela Merkel hates Germans and Germany – is viscerally repulsed by them, clearly wishes all Germans and all memory of Germany and all German culture to end with her. Remember her revealing reaction to the German flag. She reacted to the German flag like a vampire doused with holy water, or exposed to the rising sun.

Leftism is inherently cosmocidal. This suicidal, destructive, and self destructive tendency is as common as dirt even among the non Jewish left. Granted, the Jewish left is worse, but the difference is nothing to get excited about. They all want to kill you and everyone like you. And if, like Scott, they are not completely 110% on board with killing you and everyone like you, they are nonetheless trying to avoid falling overboard for fear that those who are completely 110% on board with killing you and everyone like you might take offense - or rather might take even more offense than they do already.

## Leftism is:

### 2016-02-16 04:47:40

As the destruction of Github[336] illustrates, leftism is rule by priests, by priests selected by priests on the basis of superior holiness. Degree inflation, Sarbanes–Oxley, and the Social Justice Warrior attack on tech is a program of seizing the means of production for the holy, just as communism was.

## Poland goes alt right

### 2016-02-18 00:35:07

Poland goes /pol[337]

This may be the start of a Soviet style collapse of the American empire.

> "In the new issue of the weekly Network, a report about ?*what the media and Brussels elite are hiding*? from the citizens of the European Union[338]".

OK, they are reporting sexual Jihad, but what about the Jewish question? Yes, Poles are now allowed to mention the Jewish question[339]

So. Are the Jews plotting to rule the world?

Biblical prophecy is that Israel gets to rule the Middle East, and clearly the Middle East would be better for it. Plus I don't much care what happens to the middle east, and someone needs to keep Muslims in line. Fine by me if Jews plot to implement Biblical prophecy. They are supposed to plot to do that.

Since the exile there has been a whole lot of Talmudic and Rabbinical interpretation that reinterprets this Biblical prophecy as ruling us - as ruling whites, as ruling Europe, as ruling the lands of exile. Some Jews buy into this, some Jews do not. Perhaps some of my Jewish supremacist commenters can tell us how widespread is acceptance of this re-interpretation.

I would be inclined to suspect that Jews that want to take the Temple Mount back now tend to favor the interpretation that Jews should rule the Middle East, while Jews that do not want to return to Israel and do not want to take back the Mount tend to favor the reinterpretation that Jews should rule the lands of exile - but some of those are waiting for the Messiah to do the heavy lifting and are not necessarily going at it right now.

So. Did the holocaust actually happen?

Well the holocaust of the Jews did not happen quite in accordance to the official myth, but somehow most Jews under Nazi rule did wind up dead one way or another. There has been a whole of mythmaking and lies about the holocaust of the Jews, but it seems to

---

[336]https://hintjens.com/blog:111

[337]https://8ch.net/pol/

[338]https://www.breitbart.com/london/2016/02/17/islamic-rape-of-europe-polish-news-magazines-shockingly-frank-cover/

[339]https://www.theguardian.com/world/2015/nov/10/polish-defence-minister-condemned-over-jewish-conspiracy-theory

me that the point of the mythmaking was not so much to make the Nazis more guilty, as to make killings by Nazis as different as possible from killings by commies. Anyone who tells you commies are very different from Nazis is in favor of one or the other.

Well, actually there is a big difference. Commies killed a huge number of commies. Nazis only killed a fairly small number of Nazis. Unless you count the war between Germany and Greece, in which they killed every Nazi they found.

# Emancipation of women was a fitness test that we failed

## 2016-02-26 08:16:10

Hence the collapsing birth rate.

### Fitness tests:

A fitness test is usually applied by a woman to a particular man she is thinking she might like in her pussy. When applied in this manner, a fitness test is what pickup artists call a shit test.

For example, suppose one schedules to meet a girl at ten in the morning. One is planning an all day first date with a variety of activities, since one hopes for a first date lay. She is late. A little after ten in the morning she messages one saying she will be there around eleven, twelve, or so. If one says "sure, I will wait for you baby", one will wait and wait for she is not going to turn up at all. If one says "forget it", departs the agreed meeting place without looking back or looking around, (she is likely not late at all, but stalking and watching) does not return when she promptly responds that she has arrived (swift forgiveness of drama leads immediately to more drama, not sex), and then goes silent for a few days, then soon she will be pestering one for a date. See the wise and great, Heartiste, minion of Satan, for a lengthy[340] elucidation[341] of[342] shit[343] tests[344].

Women cannot help shit testing men any more than men can help looking at women's breasts. This is instinctive and unconscious. They genuinely believe their postures, attitudes, and demands are sincere, genuine, and deeply felt, like a four year old's temper tantrum, and are entirely unaware that when their bluff is called, they will fold like cheap cardboard, and feel a deep relief, like a child in her father's arms.

### Emancipation of women leads to population collapse:

To reproduce it is necessary that a man and a woman form one household, one flesh. Sharing kids between two households is often tried these days, with results that are uniformly

---

[340]https://heartiste.wordpress.com/2013/06/25/compendium-of-female-super-shit-tests/

[341]https://heartiste.wordpress.com/2010/10/04/brushing-off-common-shit-tests-from-girls/

[342]https://heartiste.wordpress.com/2015/11/17/which-men-do-girls-shit-test-the-most/

[343]https://heartiste.wordpress.com/2014/04/30/additions-to-the-shit-test-compendium/

[344]https://heartiste.wordpress.com/2011/03/14/the-i-can-leave-if-you-want-shit-test/

horrifying. One household must have one captain, and that captain the man, for women by their nature will not have sex with kitchen men.

And to reproduce, it is necessary that they are stuck in this arrangement.

If it depends on moment to moment consent, then we have prisoner's dilemma. Women cuckold their men, and men spin plates. We get tit for tat defection. Tit for tat can only produce good results in iterated prisoner's dilemma, and with reproduction, there are not many iterations.

Thus, for successful reproduction and child raising, women must be *compelled* to obey the father of their children, *compelled* to submit sexually to him, and *forbidden* to submit sexually to anyone else. Moment to moment consent frustrates both men and women, since it makes it difficult for them to reproduce. We need outside coercion to get to cooperate cooperate equilibrium. Moment to moment consent results in defect defect equilibrium, where no one gets what they really want. To reproduce successfully, men, women, and their children need durable and patriarchal marriage.


## Emancipation of women leads to the welfare state, marriage to state, low IQ women having eighteen thuglets by eighteen different thugs, high IQ women having cats in place of babies.

The late nineteenth century, Victorianism, demonstrated that emancipated women without the welfare state means a whole lot of women giving birth in a dark alley in the rain to a fatherless child.

Victorianism was an effort to control this problem by dialing up censorious sexual moralizing to eleven, while simultaneously denying fathers the power to control their daughters and husbands the power to control their wives. Dialing up the sexual moralizing failed, and failed spectacularly. Recall Florence Nightingale's wealthy gentleman friends, and Queen Caroline attending a ball naked from the waist up, and going back to her hotel with a man she picked up at the ball. Both of them needed a good whipping. No amount of pious moralizing will substitute for a father or a husband equipped with a stick no thicker than a woman's thumb. Victorianism failed, and failed hilariously badly.

If you give women freedom of choice, a great many women make such terrible choices that men have little alternative but to pay for women's choices. If you emancipate women to make their own decisions, you have to pay for their decisions, have to have a welfare state, because their decisions are frequently so bad. This profoundly impairs the freedom of men, that they have to pay for bad choices that they have no power over and receive no benefit from. Some thug knocks up some idiot, and the man with a job has to support another man's child and a woman who is not giving him sex and domestic service.

This is pretty much what "Les Misérables" was about. "Les Misérables" argues that we need a welfare state to take care of criminal men and immoral women. And indeed that is true, if you reject the obvious alternative of coercively, involuntarily, and forcibly subordinating criminal men and immoral women to good men, of enslaving bad men and shotgun marrying independent fertile age women.

Since we don't want to pay for eighteen thuglets, and we don't want women giving birth in a dark alley in the rain, we have to keep women under male authority that supervises and restrains their sexual choices.

The eighteenth century system of guardianship was in large part a system for coercively marrying off young women who would have otherwise become independent women of property. They were generally married off to their guardian, or their guardian's son. Guardian/ward marriages were the normal outcome of guardianship, and though theoretically consensual were usually clearly involuntary or the result of rather forceful manipulation. When the ward was taken into the guardian's family at a very early age she was usually married off to a family closely related to their guardian's family as soon as they came of age, to avoid psychological incest. Psychologically incestuous marriages between guardian and ward, in effect adopting a child with the intent of marriage at puberty, were not illegal but were subject to social disapproval, immoral but legal. Though legal, seem to have been extremely rare. If it was necessary to raise a female ward from an early age, she was raised in a household separate from her intended husband and transferred to her intended husband's household at puberty.

Our society encourages gay men to adopt small helpless children as sex slaves[345], so we should not get agitated about eighteenth century guardians, who had to marry their wards for life in order to have sex with them and to keep charge of their ward's property and dowries.

It is not clear what happened to poor independent young women, but somehow, in the eighteenth century, there do not seem to have been many poor independent women, so I suppose that something was done.

What was done with convict women in the early days of Australian settlement gives us a hint as to what was done with poor independent women in eighteenth century England.

When the convict ships landed in Australia, the convict women, now far away from family restraints, and free to mingle with men, acted like it was spring break in Cancun or Woodstock Revival. None of these women were there because of convictions for prostitution, and though they all acted like whores in eighteenth century meaning of the term, they don't seem to have been selling sex, rather the reverse. The popular stereotype of a transported woman was a servant girl who stole something from her employer to give to her unreliable bad boy lover, who showed up at infrequent and unpredictable intervals to rough her up, have sex with her, and take her stuff. These days we longer call such women whores, because all women are like that, except for those few who have chosen to submit themselves for life to the firm hand of a strong man who is better than that.

If you read secondary and derived sources about the convict women in Australia they all invariably depict them as poor pitiful victims who were cruelly coerced into having casual sex by economic pressure or rape. This nineteenth and twentieth century account flatly, directly, and blatantly contradict what the primary sources and contemporary sources that they supposedly draw upon depict. What primary and contemporary sources all uniformly and consistently depict is Woodstock Revival and spring break on the shores of Port Jackson: Girls Gone Wild: "their desire to be with the men was so uncontrollable that neither shame nor punishment could deter them". We don't see contemporary reports of convict women in Australia trading sex for money until twenty years into the nineteenth century, three decades after settlement began - which is to say we don't

---

[345]https://blog.reaction.la/culture/why-gay-marriage-is-not/

see contemporary reports of convict women in Australia trading sex for money until the coercion to impose monogamy was considerably reduced.

There is no contemporary report of convict women being forced into casual sex or paid for casual sex. What they do however report is women being forced, often by disturbingly severe violence, into monogamous sex, but resisting that coercion with amusing vigor and flair.

To solve the problem of spring break on the shores of Port Jackson, the authorities would frequently line up newly arrived female convicts in front of the female factory, and bring a bunch of preapproved males to marry them. Each male, on seeing a female he liked, would drop a small gift at her feet. If she picked it up, they were married (even if the female convict was already married to someone else in England). Any girl left over after every male had walked past was forcibly assigned to some male for seven years as servant and concubine, so it was advisable to pick up one of the gifts.

Upon arrival female convicts had to make a hurried choice between monogamous durable consensual marriage, or monogamous durable non consensual concubinage. Thus, for example, most, probably all, of the females that arrived on the Brittania in 1798 were either immediately married, married within a few weeks, or assigned to men to whom they subsequently bore children. They were swiftly taken out of circulation one way or another way. In some cases, many cases, they were taken out of circulation coercively by assignment. In the other cases, they voluntarily took themselves out of circulation with a swiftness that indicates very forceful pressure. Earlier and later convict women mostly got married in a less hurried manner, but they got married fast enough to suggest that pressure was applied case by case, and/or that they were shotgun married upon getting pregnant, but not shotgun married shortly after showing up on the docks like the girls of the Brittanica and other ships arriving around that time.

The first batch of convict women tended to produce children of uncertain paternity in brief and transitory relationships. Women off the Brittanica, who were swiftly married or assigned, generally produced children of known paternity in durable relationships, often durable relationships of assignment that they were forced into with open and unambiguous coercion, suggesting a harsh crackdown against immoral relationships and in favor of monogamy at about this time.

I would guess that what happened to poor independent fertile age women in eighteenth century England was something intermediate between what happened to rich independent fertile age women in eighteenth century England, and what happened to fertile age convict women on the shore of eighteenth century Port Jackson but I have no data supporting this conjecture, other than that eighteenth century England, unlike Victorian England, did not much resemble spring break in Cancun.

While the nineteenty century theory was that women were so naturally pure and chaste that all the apparatus of coercion to keep them from misbehaving was sheer cruelty and could safely be discarded, the eighteenth century view was that women had to be in the custody of someone with a duty and practical motive to keep them from engaging in sex, and the authority and power to coercively prevent them from engaging in sex, or else married to a husband who had the authority and power to coercively prevent them from engaging in extra marital sex. Eighteenth century people believed that fertile age women urgently needed sex, and if prevented from getting some were apt to take alarmingly drastic measures or go into hysterics, while from the mid nineteenth century to the present, people seem to think that sex is something alarming and unpleasant imposed on women by men. The nineteenth century treatment for hysteria reflects the realistic but unmentionable eighteenth century belief as to what caused it.

## Harem formation

If female choice is unrestrained, twenty percent of the males get eighty percent of the pussy. But they don't get it in any stable way. A girl spends a few months as number three on some man's booty call list, then realizes she has little chance of making it to number two, so gets herself a position on some other man's booty call list. So nobody gets to reproduce, whereas in old fashioned harems formed by male power, rather than female power, she would be stuck in one man's harem, so she and that man would get to reproduce.

Harem formation, whether the result of female control of sex, or a few powerful men controlling sex, has a detrimental effect on the rapidly diminishing number of men in the society. Without access to pussy, they are disinclined to work or fight in defense of order, peace, and their society. Instead they hang out in mom's basement.

Monogamy and chastity can be understood as socialism in pussy, the seizure of the means of reproduction by beta males.

The King is worried that men do not seem keen on working, paying taxes, or soldiering. So he price controls pussy down to something ordinary men can pay. Bride price shall be low or zero, women shall obey their husbands, not their fathers or their own whims. Price control causes a shortage, as always, so the King and the high priest introduce rationing. Only one pussy per customer.

This works if you have non consensual marriage, if marriage is handshake between the groom and the father of the bride, or between the father of the bride and the father of the groom. But what if you have, partially or wholly, romantic and consensual marriage? In which case the woman is likely to delay marriage hoping for a booty call from Jeremy Meeks until her eggs start to dry up.

So the high priest deems that going out on booty calls will result in eternal damnation. This, however, has curiously little effect. So the King and the high priest say that if daughter goes out on a booty call, the father is dishonored, and possibly punished. This works, assuming the King backs parental authority over daughters. Or the King could give all women the status of pets, and the high Priest switches marriage to being a handshake between the father and the groom. Or the King could give only misbehaving women the status of pets, and have consensual romantic marriage normal and normative, but only normal and normative for virtuous women, which is to say virginal women, or women plausibly presumed virginal, under paternal supervision. (Which is of course the solution that I favor.)

This is not necessarily a literal account of the origins of monogamy, rather I have personified the motives leading to monogamy as the motives of individual powerful people.

Most societies seem to have used, somewhat inconsistently, hypocritically, and irregularly, a mixture of these tactics, with marriage being mostly consensual and romantic, but female choice severely constrained by the authority of the father and pressure to get married, particularly severe pressure to get married in the event of illicit sexual activity or illegitimate pregnancy.

## Trump and testosterone

2016-02-28 05:35:59

Testosterone levels and sperm counts have been falling steadily. Young men commonly have levels that once would have been normal in seventy year olds, and "normal" testosterone keeps being redefined downwards, while "normal" estrogen gets redefined upwards.

I have long suspected that this reflects metaphorical estrogen in the metaphorical water supply, rather than literal estrogen in the literal water supply, and the Trumpening hints that this theory is true. Trump's supporters, critics, and opponents are all acting as if they have had testosterone shots, notably Rubio whose surgical castration seems to have been temporarily and partially reversed.

A Trump presidency is likely to have a big effect on the way American males walk, the way in which they speak, and the amount of kitchen work that they do.

## Trump and social class

2016-03-01 03:37:42

There is a bit of drama about a pressman being thrown to the ground at a Trump rally. There were fifteen thousand people at the rally. There were a few hundred black-lives-matter protestors who got thrown out. There were some illegal immigrant rights protestors who got thrown out. Did no one else get thrown to the ground?

A horde of black-lives-matter protestors are being herded out by security. They are leaving peaceably. The pressman gets out of the press box. Security guy stops him by getting in his way. Pressman is absolutely shocked, outraged, and indignant. Pressman gets right in the security guy's face, screaming at him from an inch or two away. His spittle must be spraying all over the security guy. Security guy grabs him by the throat and pushes him out of the security guy's face, laying him quite gently on the ground. Pressman kicks, tries ineffectually to fight. But the wonderful thing is expression on his face. He is absolutely incredulous, he is astonished, he is outraged he cannot believe that the security guy has dared to lay impious hands on him.

Observing the black-lives-matter protestors an arms length away, it is obvious that they believe that it would be entirely ordinary and expected for security to lay hands on them if they failed to leave or resisted being ejected, and don't see anything the slightest out of the ordinary about security laying hands on some guy. That is what security does. Business as normal, nothing to see. They are leaving quietly because they believe that if they make trouble, security will kick their ass. Pressman thinks he can make trouble, and security cannot kick his ass.

But there are a bunch of people around the incident who also find security laying hands on the most holy pressman startlingly impious.

Pressmen, even though they are usually paid with the smell of an oilrag, are a much higher class than mere menials like security, security being working class, even though this security guy was secret service, who draw way better pay than pressmen.

So how does Trump come into this story I hear you ask. The security guy was not a Trump employee, he was a government cop, not a rentacop. So how is Trump involved?

Trump is involved because I am pretty sure the security guy would ordinarily have internalized the class dynamics, and let his social superior spit in his face, but listening to Trump made him less submissive, raised his spirits, made him remember he was a man.

Now if we were governed by real aristocrats, I would be entirely in favor of menials knowing their place, and would find Trump's populism disturbing, but we are governed by scum. An aristocrat would never scream in a menials face. He might kill the menial, he might have him killed, he might permanently blight the menial's career, but he would not scream in the menial's face.

Which brings me to those trade deals that Trump has been denouncing.

I don't know what Trump thinks is wrong with those trade deals. But what I think is wrong with those trade deals is that they treat making physical things in America as evil and oppressive, a sinful activity that needs to be phased out as soon as possible, *as a lower class activity*. These deals demand that other countries go along with America's outrageous and oppressive copyright and patent laws, and open their doors to American capital, while opening America's doors to physical manufactured goods, without really much asking foreigners to open their doors to American physical manufactured goods.

## Heartiste addresses the Jewish Question

### 2016-03-01 22:28:02

Heartiste, minion of Satan, addresses the Jewish Question with his usual combination of insight and empirical data[346].

His data and conclusions are consistent with mine: My conclusions being that Jews are priests by nature, and we suffer from a crisis of an ever escalating excess of priests, and an ever escalating dangerously great theocratic power, ever escalating persecution of ever more minor deviations from an ever more extreme official state theology and theocracy of equalism, covetousness, and envy, and it is this crisis that causes the over representation of Jews among bad people doing bad things, not the other way around. If we get priests under control, then Jews are under control. If we expel Jews without getting priests under control, we are still screwed.

## The unsafe schools initiative

### 2016-03-04 06:18:31

In Australia there is a program, called the safe schools initiative, targeted primarily at school children near puberty and below puberty, aimed at presenting gay, lesbian and transgender role models as normal, happy, healthy regular people, despite the fact that

---

[346]https://heartiste.wordpress.com/2016/03/01/iqology/

gays and male to female transgender have an extremely high rate of death, disease, crime, suicide, murder, assault, self harm, and drug abuse, with lesbians and female to male transgender not far behind. The reason there are not that many old gays is that most of them die of murder, suicide, disease, or drug abuse before they get old. As the New Testament says Romans 1:27:

And likewise also the men, leaving the natural use of the woman, burned in their lust one toward another; men with men working that which is unseemly, and receiving in themselves that recompence of their error which was meet.

These happy healthy role models depicted in the material are slightly older than the target audience, the role models being just past puberty, and the target audience just before puberty, the obvious point of the propaganda being that the target audience should grow up into these happy healthy well balanced role models.

Here is one of the role models, pushed on pre pubertal children: a schoolboy with an obviously gay fifty eight year old cuddling him:

This is blatant gay recruiting of children - it is obvious that those pushing this initiative do not believe that gayness is innate, that people are born that way, but rather that gay sex is an acquired taste to which children can be inculcated.

And, indeed, it is obvious that gayness is transmitted from pedophiles to children, Afghanistan being an example of a place and culture where gayness transmitted in this fashion is very prevalent.

While a sexual preference for young males is disturbingly common in all cultures at all times, in places and times where this preference is very severely repressed (death penalty, vigorously enforced) a sexual preference by males for adult males seems to be entirely unknown. In such cultures there is some sodomy of adult males but it is like sodomy of donkeys, an inferior substitute for the real thing. Thus, for example, during the War of Northern Aggression adult male on adult male sodomy was rare, and adult male on adult male pornography entirely nonexistent. No one wanted to look at pictures of adult males getting tapped when they could look at pictures of females getting tapped.

If what gays officially believe, that gays are born that way, is true, then suppressing homosexuality is just pointless cruelty. If, however, what gay activist behavior suggests that gays believe, that male sexual preference for adult males is the result of gay sex environment near puberty or before puberty, is true, then we should have the death penalty for male homosexual acts, and lesbian acts should be discouraged, with females being coerced into heterosexual relationships.

## Single women vote for foreign conquest and rape
2016-03-06 04:50:24

I am opposed to anyone voting, except perhaps married men of property and wealth who are raising or have raised their biological children with their wives, but the worst voters are single women.

Sweden is now the rape capital of the west, due to importation of masses of North Africans to maintain the vote for failed welfare statism. When Swedish men say "Hands off our women", Swedish women say "We are not your women", and vote for more mass nonwhite immigration and ridiculously light slap-on-the-wrist penalties for rape.

Women do not really want the kind of society where sex happens by consent. (Check the xhamster porn videos preferred by women[347]) Thus single women subconsciously, and sometimes consciously, want our society to be conquered, the men killed, and they themselves sexually enslaved.

In the ancestral environment, if you were a man and your in group was conquered, you were likely to be killed or enslaved, and thus be no ones ancestor. If you were a woman and your in group was conquered, you were indeed likely to be enslaved - to a successful man in the victorious group who would have children by you, and, knowing his children were his own, raise them well.

So we are in large part descended from men who conquered, and who resisted conquest with absolute determination, and descended from women who took to conquest, abduction, and slavery like a duck to water.

The strong independent woman, the woman living the lifestyle that feminism and school teaches her she should have, has few or no children, for children take two, and the commitment to stick it out when things go bad. In the ancestral environment, if you were a strong independent woman you were surrounded by weak contemptible men, in which case abduction, rape, and slavery was a good way to meet manly men.

Suppose the Taliban was to somehow do a Boko Haram and abduct a bunch of baristas with post graduate degrees in victim studies and a hundred thousand dollars of student debt. They would probably wind up having six children and umpteen grandchildren each, so we would expect women to have evolved to rather like this sort of thing.

Or, alternatively, you can believe that women was created to be a helpmeet to man, and in the fall was condemned to desire this sort of thing.

Lots of existing societies have arranged marriages or marriage by abduction. It seems to work just fine. When parents, society, or respectable authority tell women to fuck

---

[347] https://blog.reaction.la/culture/watching-female-oriented-video-porn-so-you-dont-have-to/

someone, they fuck him, and are happy to do so.

Large numbers of well educated and wealthy English gentlewomen in eighteenth century England married whom they were damned well told to, and I don't see any memoirs or books from any of them complaining about it.

We hear a lot about women being involuntarily trafficked to brothels, and sometimes it happens, though less than advertised, but when white nights go forth to rescue these poor oppressed and victimized damsels in distress, they are invariably disappointed.

Commanding a woman to clean some man's floor and cook his meals is like commanding children to eat their broccoli, whereas commanding a woman to warm some man's bed is like commanding children to eat their icecream.

In eighteenth century Australia there was a fair bit of lighthearted and unserious female resistance to shotgun marriages, they were far from entirely compliant, but looking at these incidents, those resisting shotgun marriage do not seem like poor pitiful victims of male sexual desire, but lustful bawds who were worried that the party was going to end.

Since Victorian times, historians have sought to depict eighteenth century Australian women as sexually exploited and sexually hyper oppressed, but they just cannot seem to find any examples of women seriously resenting, complaining about or resisting this supposedly horrid extreme sexual oppression. We see lots of disciplinary issues where women were punished for talking back to the husband that they were assigned to, or punished for failing to work as directed by their husband, or being absent without leave for short periods. We just don't see any disciplinary issues, zero, despite vigorous and alarmingly imaginative search by historians, that seem plausibly related to disinclination to go to bed with the man to whom she was assigned.

Consent is useful and valuable to the extent that a women voluntarily swears to honor and obey her husband, and to stick it out till parted by death, and eighteenth century Australian authorities were pretty keen on obtaining more or less voluntary consent for that purpose. If she is not credibly swearing that before God and man, consent serves no useful purpose to husband, family and society, women don't really like it all that much, and the eighteenth century British and Australian authorities were untroubled by the lack of it.

## Cutting

### 2016-03-06 07:18:10

In 1985, when cutting first appeared, girls cutting themselves was something astonishing, something no one had heard of, that psychiatric interns had never heard of.

Now a significant minority of women cut themselves. Hard to say how many, but probably a few percent. Not a substantial minority, but not a tiny minority either. Hot fertile age women. Women with strong sexual needs and completely screwed up sex lives, usually sex lives screwed up by their own self destructive bad choices. "Strong independent women" who are not in the least strong, and greatly fear independence. White women. Women totally raised in feminism.

As the epidemic grows, only now is the psychiatric industry coming up with a diagnostic category "Non suicidal self harm" We did not have a word for cutting until recently, and psychiatrists are only now coming up with a word for it, and not a very apt word yet, for the category self harm is deliberately over inclusive, in order to avoid being exclusively female, including a great deal of what would be more aptly called "stupidity", so that some males can be put in the same category. (The obvious difference being that after doing something very stupid once or twice, males usually stop doing that particular stupid thing.) It is politically disturbing to have a psychiatric category that is near one hundred percent female, so calling it what everyone calls it, "cutting", is politically incorrect. Yes. Males sometimes, rarely, cut themselves. Discover it hurts like the blazes, then do not do it again.

If you google for "self harm", the PC term, you don't get information on cutting, but deceptive and malicious misinformation on cutting, misinformation intended to cause harm and suffering, and if you google "cutting" any page that comes up with words "self harm" in it is overwhelmingly likely to be malicious misinformation.[348]

As it says in the Book of Genesis, women are psychologically maladapted to equality.

Think how much more comfortable she would be, how much more at peace she would be, how much saner she would be, how much happier she would be, if those were her owner's whip marks.

Reading between the lines of girls making videos and posts about cutting themselves, they are saying to the numerous boys that pumped them and dumped them "Punish me, don't ignore me."

## Women are the dangerously lustful sex.

### 2016-03-07 09:12:02

Some time ago, I and a bunch of other reactionaries had a debate on whether women commonly fuck dogs.

I have no evidence that women of commonly fuck dogs, but I have lots of personal evidence that women very commonly do lots of horrifying stuff that many of my commenters find very hard to believe. These personal observations are perhaps statistically insignificant and may be from an unrepresentative sample of females, but is consistent with the rather small subset of women who watch porn, who generally watch disturbingly deviant stuff, while most males watch fairly vanilla stuff.

Most women read romance, rather than watch porn. Romance male leads are generally demon lovers, rather than the nice boy next door - one notable exception being when the female lead is sold, enslaved, kidnapped, abducted, or subject to an arranged marriage without her consent at a very young age by the otherwise nice boy next door. In the very common genre of supernatural romance, the male lead is often a literal demon. How is a real life male going to compete?

Male and female sexual impulses are the product of natural selection. In the ancestral environment there is biological and evolutionary conflict of interest between dads and daughters, in that daughters prefer cad type demon lovers, and dads prefer dad type sons

---

[348] https://goodbyeamericainaphoto.wordpress.com/2016/03/05/attention-whoring-is-her-bread-and-cutter/

in law. Daughter prefers the best sperm, but dad does not want to be stuck with support. Similarly a conflict between husbands and wives, in that wives prefer demon lovers, and husbands are seldom demon lovers - the best semen is unlikely to belong to the best protection and support.

For civilization to exist, fathers and husbands have to be able to coercively overrule the sexual preferences of women.

For it to be politically possible for fathers and husbands to coercively overrule the sexual preferences of women, we have to have it generally accepted that women are the dangerously lustful sex, whose dangerously powerful sexual impulses have to be overruled for their own good, for the good of their children, and the good of society - that women's dangerously powerful lusts and self destructive lusts are the big problem that has to be solved, not immoral males.

Whether or not women commonly fuck dogs, for civilization to survive, men need to be inclined to suspect that they might. For civilization to survive, men need to control women's sexual choices. For men to control women's sexual choices, it needs to be politically incorrect to have excessive confidence in the purity and chastity of women. That women are dangerously and self destructively lustful needs to be taught by authority, presented in the media, and the sort of thing you need to believe if you want to get on with the important people you need to get on with if you hope to get ahead.

## Trump and assabiyah

### 2016-03-09 23:38:59

In the days of its greatness, the Roman Republic had assabiyah

"Horatius," quoth the Consul,
"As thou sayest, so let it be."
And straight against that great array
Forth went the dauntless Three.
For Romans in Rome's quarrel
Spared neither land nor gold,
Nor son nor wife, nor limb nor life,
In the brave days of old.

Then none was for a party;
Then all were for the state;
Then the great man helped the poor,
And the poor man loved the great:
Then lands were fairly portioned;
Then spoils were fairly sold:
The Romans were like brothers
In the brave days of old.

Now Roman is to Roman
More hateful than a foe,
And the Tribunes beard the high,
And the Fathers grind the low.

As we wax hot in faction,
In battle we wax cold:
Wherefore men fight not as they fought
In the brave days of old.

Baron Macaulay's poem neglects to explicitly mention, but takes for granted that the reader knows, that all three were aristocratic officers, and that the two that fought on Horatio's right and left were lieutenant generals. This is reminiscent of Britain in the days of its greatness, when aristocratic officers led from in front, charging into battle in costumes that conspicuously marked them as targets, and engaging the aristocratic officers of the opposing army in personal hand to hand combat, for which glorious privilege they paid extraordinarily large amounts of money.

Our political class hates and despises the white working class, as much as it hates and despises soldiers, cops, and security guards. Democrats are disgusted by the fact that the white working class votes for them. If Hillary could turn her white working class voters away from the voting booth with whips she would, and a major reason the Republican establishment is horrified by Trump is that he is bringing white working class voters from the Democrats to the Republicans. They would rather lose to Clinton than win with the unspeakably vulgar Trump.

Trump regularly pulls stunts that our chattering classes do not understand, and therefore ignorantly ridicule, much as the New York Times ridicules Sarah Palin for using sentence structures that exceed the comprehension and reading level of the New York Times staff. In Trump's recent victory celebration, he had piles of Trump products on display. "What is this?" asked our chatterers. "An infomercial?"

Trump was making the point that capitalists did not just grab their wealth from the secret stash before the rest of us could find the secret stash, but rather organize the production of stuff - that capitalists are rich because, in substantial part, they create wealth.

In another stunt, he called up two of his black supporters and campaigners, the Stump For Trump women, Diamond and Silk, and introduced them as having made themselves rich.

This is, subliminally, the classic fascist message - forget about class differences, let us work to make America Great Again. It is the reverse of Sanders' message, yet appeals to the same people. One is a message of envy and covetousness, the other calls on us to be greater than that. And to the extent that the chattering classes understand Trump's message, they hate him for it and rightly call him fascist.

## Ethnic cleansing in Ferguson

### 2016-03-11 08:02:17

Not all houses in Ferguson have dropped to a small fraction of 2014 prices, some substantial areas are holding value, but houses in large parts of the Ferguson zip code have dropped far far below the cost of building, or even maintaining, the house. If the ad says "located close to shopping", it usually means that whites have been forced to abandon their homes to blacks by black violence. The shopping areas are still partly ruins, often with rubble that no one has yet bothered to clean up.

4 Burdale, Saint Louis, MO 63135      $14,800

Single Family   Closed   4 Beds   1 Full Bath   1,850 Sq. Ft.

Listed by Paul Morad    MLS # 15051613

These houses are generally listed as sold in foreclosure, suggesting that the occupants simply fled, abandoning their house to the bank.

Whites build houses for black people to live in. When the neighborhood is utterly destroyed, blacks move on to another white neighborhood. Hence the abandoned ruins of Detroit, as blacks flee the ruins of Detroit, to ruin more recently built homes.

That is how the inner city became black. And now, the process that made the inner city, where the wealthy used to live, a terrifying jungle stalked by upright walking plains apes, is being repeated on those suburbs targeted by the HUD and the department of justice.

This predation by blacks on whites is a major part of what makes housing and family formation unaffordable to whites - the high, and ever rising, cost of buying a house in a neighborhood which is unlikely to be taken away from you.

Everywhere, blacks live in the ruins of homes built by whites that whites were forced to abandon, often, as in the inner city, quite wealthy whites. For white people to afford housing, we simply have to restore segregation, apartheid, and slavery. Even if this is unfair to some individual high performing blacks, what is happening with housing is immensely more unfair. Collective racial violence by blacks as a race against whites as a race gets blacks free stuff from whites, and this absolutely has to stop. If you don't like my program for stopping it, what is your program?

# The Cathedral triumphantly announces victory in the streets

## 2016-03-12 06:43:29

The Daily Beast:

> MAKE AMERICA RAGE AGAIN[349]
> Protesters Scare Trump Out of Chicago

The Riverfront Times in Saint Louis

---

[349] https://www.thedailybeast.com/articles/2016/03/11/protesters-scare-trump-out-of-chicago.html

The activists in this town are battle-hardened and ready to go. They've had a lot of fights in the last year or so, and that's only primed them to take on bigger ones. It really makes you wonder what Trump was thinking.[350]

Well, a short time ago, Trump's rally in Saint Louis took place. How, I wonder, did it go?

Bunch of arrests, one guy who decided to fight the cops somewhat the worse for wear.

If you want to look for videos of violence at the Trump rally in Saint Louis, you see Trump's adoring crowds drowning out the protester with a Trump chant, followed by Trump commanding the cops "get him out of here!", and then you see a crazy black guy trying ineffectually to fight a couple of cops who are throwing him out with smooth efficiency and complete control.

When you try to control political outcomes using the threat of crazy black guys, crazy black guys are only a problem if no one is allowed to fight back.

And so we see frequent noisy announcements that Trump is being outrageous and horribly politically incorrect for having his people fight back. The Cathedral is confused and continually surprised by the way government cops keep maintaining order and following Trump's directives at Trump events. The Cathedral is accustomed to controlling both sides of the pretended confrontation, the protestors and the cops both, and is confused, disoriented, and surprised by what happens when the cops support order. Order prevails.

Meanwhile, large numbers of American voters notice that, outside of Trump rallies, order does not prevail.

Despite the frequent and triumphant announcements of disorder at Trump events, what the voters see is someone able and willing to maintain order, who has the support of the men he needs to maintain order.

The Cathedral is implicitly threatening voters, that if they elect Trump, the NAMs will come around and beat them up, but what the voters see at a Trump rally tells them the reverse.

## Artificial consciousness is unlikely

2016-03-15 04:39:23

Artificial intelligence turned out to be surprisingly easy. Anything that only humans can do, computers can do. Anything that only smart humans can do, computers can do better.

Anything that a spider can do turns out to be rather difficult for a computer. We don't really know what consciousness is, perhaps for the same reason as a fish does not know what water is, and we don't really understand what it is good for. It seems rather magical. That does not mean it is magical, but it might as well be for all that we can understand of it.

---

[350]https://www.riverfronttimes.com/newsblog/2016/03/09/why-yes-the-rft-is-biased-against-donald-trump

# What Republicans are voting on in Ohio

## 2016-03-15 06:32:40

All right thinking people care about all humans everywhere to exactly the same degree - except, of course, that they hate white people because of all the horrible evil white people have done to all other races and hate males because of all the horrible evil males have done to females.

So every decent right thinking person believes that all people everywhere have the right to live in America, receive section eight housing in a nice American suburb, and receive EBT and SSSI until they magically become as middle class as the rest of the people in that suburb. (Which, of course, they will, magically transforming from tax consumers to tax payers, and from arsonists, rapists, and vandals to mortgage payers, thereby solving the problem of the missing grandchildren.)

And anyone who does not believe that is an unthinkably horrible evil person who is provoking violence by thinking thoughts that make it right that he should be physically attacked.

In Ohio, it is a straight up and down vote between the good kind virtuous Kasich, who holds that it is immoral to obstruct America's border with Mexico, and everyone who crosses it should promptly get a green card, and all the associated benefits[351], and the evil Trump, who is causing horrible violence by disagreeing with Kasich's position, and is therefore at fault whenever anyone engages in attempted violence against him or any of his supporters.

Ohio is a straight vote between the advocate of wide open borders with generous welfare for the entire world, and the advocate of a wall along the border.

Now you might well ask how we got to the situation where the Kasich's of this world are treated as saints, rather than evil madmen. Does not anyone remember how completely insane this would have been a couple of decades ago?

And the answer is, we all speak newspeak[352].

The vocabulary, the language, that is capable of expressing the thought that we have different and more important moral obligations to kin, friends, and neighbors than to far away strangers has been taken away from us.

Whatever the outcome of this vote, the fact that Kasich taken seriously shows that democracy is simply unacceptable. If he wins, it is an indictment of democracy. If he gets five percent, it is an indictment of democracy.

So what is the indictment?

The indictment is that democracy empowers the people who can simplify our language and erase our past.

Democracy must end! It dies, or we die.

We are always ruled by priests or warriors. It is not the voters fault that we are ruled by priests, nor is it the voters fault that our priesthood is evil and insane, and daily becoming

---

[351]https://www.breitbart.com/immigration/2016/03/14/john-kasich-goes-all-in-for-amnesty-illegals-made-in-the-image-of-the-lord/

[352]https://www.counter-currents.com/2016/03/the-decay-of-words-1-virtue-and-vice/

more evil and more insane. But it is democracy's fault that there is not much the voters can do about it.

## Crowd sourcing the question: How recent are open borders?
2016-03-15 21:52:48

Cathedral sources say that open borders, resettle them in green leafy suburbs on generous welfare, has been the law of the land since forever, and only recently have evil racists started to protest, but the way I recall it, worldwide, borders to white countries received some reasonable degree of enforcement until enforcement quietly but abruptly stopped world wide in 2011. This led to a ginormous flood of illegal immigrants, increasing many fold each year, resulting in public resistance in numerous white countries starting in 2013.

Which resistance is on the one hand increasing with the flood, and is on the other hand collapsing under the impact of pious moralizing.

The way I recall it, before 2012, they were legally letting in lots of low IQ layabouts and petty criminals, to live on welfare and crime, with a small but significant number of rapists, serious criminals, and terrorists in the mix, but illegal entry was not a problem. Then enforcement abruptly stops in 2011, huge numbers of illegals show up unopposed in 2012, and even larger numbers in 2013, with a corresponding rise in the proportion of rapists, murderers, and terrorists - who also live on welfare and crime.

One day even Obama opposes gay marriage. The next day, no one opposes gay marriage, *and no one remembers that they ever opposed gay marriage.* The same thing is now happening with illegal immigration. Not only is it policy, it always has been policy and all decent people always have supported it.

Theoretically the Roman Catholic Church still opposes gay marriage - like it theoretically still supports the husband's authority in marriage, theoretically opposes divorce, and theoretically has a male only priesthood.

But in fact, if you go to Roman Catholic Church you will see a woman doing stuff that looks very like the stuff a priest does, remarried women taking communion, and at a Roman Catholic marriage the priest will ad lib some feminist talking points.

We have abruptly moved from guarded borders, and border guards, being an uncontroversial fact that every single person takes for granted, to them being a crime equal in seriousness to being the first person to stop applauding at a gay wedding. This does not look to me like "decades of kindergarten to hospice propaganda" but more like hate week in Orwell's 1984.

## Anarcho tyranny in the Chicago riots
2016-03-18 07:22:12

Police in Chicago were set up to take a kayfabe fall, to be the bad guys, and lose.

The plan was that at a pre-arranged signal, multiple mobs would simultaneously rush the podium, and nail Trump, thereby solving the Trump problem.

Police would be unable to prevent this, having been disarmed, forbidden to use effective force and set up to be legally at fault in any lawsuit.

What really happened at the Chicago Rally[353].

How the cops were set up to lose[354] and be defeated[355].

It is entertaining just how much the Chicago Chief of Police hates the police. I assume something similar is happening in the Army.

## Against sexual consent

### 2016-03-19 09:03:55

Castalia house has produced an excellent booklet "Safe Space as Rape Room" 1,[356] 2,[357] 3,[358] 4,[359] 5,[360] I,[361] II,[362] III.[363]

Which documents how the fetishization of consent allowed gay science fiction authors to prey upon young boys attracted to science fiction fandom.

> In other words, a pedophile with the Delany mindset is given carte blanche under the Scalzi-endorsed code to attract children "desperate to establish some sort of sexual relation with an...adult figure" for **invited** sexual and physical attention.

> > "Why? Because I want my friends and fans to be able to come to a convention and feel assured that the convention is making the effort to be a safe place for them." – John Scalzi

> Scalzi's desire for his friends' and fans' safe place becomes a nightmare if just one of those friends or fans happens to be a molester like fellow SFWA member Ed Kramer, who attracted children to his hotel room at the conventions he ran.

When we came down from the trees, children and females were dependent on males for protection from predators, and males were dependent on each other. Contrary to

---

[353]https://www.reddit.com/r/The_Donald/comments/4a2bu9/what_really_happened_at_the_chicago_rally_my/

[354]https://secondcitycop.blogspot.com.au/2016/03/map-381-statement.html

[355]https://secondcitycop.blogspot.com/2016/03/questions-about-last-night.html

[356]https://www.castaliahouse.com/safe-space-as-rape-room-science-fiction-culture-and-childhoods-end-part-1-of-5/

[357]https://www.castaliahouse.com/safe-space-as-rape-room-science-fiction-culture-and-childhoods-end-part-2-of-5/

[358]https://www.castaliahouse.com/safe-space-as-rape-room-science-fiction-culture-and-childhoods-end-part-3-of-5/

[359]https://www.castaliahouse.com/safe-space-as-rape-room-science-fiction-culture-and-childhoods-end-part-4-of-5/

[360]https://www.castaliahouse.com/safe-space-as-rape-room-science-fiction-culture-and-childhoods-end-part-5-of-5/

[361]https://www.castaliahouse.com/protecting-your-child-from-the-pedophiles-of-science-fiction-fandom/

[362]https://www.castaliahouse.com/supplement-ii-the-enablers-in-fandom-respond-to-safe-space-as-rape-room/

[363]https://www.castaliahouse.com/supplement-iii-historic-timeline-of-abuse-in-science-fiction/

Locke's original state of nature, we were not distant and equal, but instead close and unequal.

Chimps and men are unusual among apes in that we hunt, and unusual among mammals in that we make war. Lions and hyenas are instinctively and permanently at war, but conflicts between lions are normally one on one, and at most one pair of brothers against another pair of brothers. Chimps, on the other hand, while mostly at peace with neighboring tribes of chimps, are frequently at war, and these wars often total and genocidal. Since chimps and men are omnivorous killer apes, it is a good bet that the common ancestor of chimps and men were omnivorous killer apes.

When our ancestors first came down from the trees and out of the forest onto the plains, they could not walk or run very fast or far, and to this day, we are lousy sprinters compared to almost any predator. So, our ancestors avoided being eaten by being the meanest sons of bitches on the plains, with a team of killer apes using their superior ability to cooperate and coordinate against a team of lions.

Under these circumstances, it is unlikely that women got any opportunity to consent to sex or refuse sex. It is also unlikely that females were shared, as this would undermine group cohesion. Yes, the male penis is shaped to scoop out competing sperm, but the male hands are designed for a more permanent and final solution to sperm competition. In the trees, females could screw around because they did not need male protection, and because meat was less important in the trees. On the plains it would likely be a really bad idea for a female to wander out of sight of her owner. Human and chimp males are both shaped for violence, but human males arguably more shaped for violence than chimp males. Humans are more sexually dimorphic than chimps, and the dimorphisms all bear a fairly obvious relationship to the capability for violence. Almost every human male can easily subdue almost any human female. This is not true among chimps.

The ancestors of men, the omnivorous killer apes that came down to the plains, survived because they loved their comrades and cooperated well. And the main thing that they cooperated to do was to slay their enemies. Humans are more specialized for cooperation than chimps, for example the whites of our eyes that make it easy to accurately tell what direction a human is looking. Our ancestors were, compared to most other creatures, and compared to chimpanzees, loyal, good, and kind - good to and kind to their comrades - brutal and deadly to everything else.

Consent does not make sex right. Nor does lack of consent make sex wrong. Lots of societies have arranged marriages, and some societies have marriage by abduction. Women seem to like such marriages just fine.

In the early settlement of Australia, the authorities regularly applied shotgun marriage on a large scale, and often assigned a woman to a man without bothering with the formality of marriage or any pretense at female consent, and it does not seem to have led to any difficulties. Whereas porn stars give carefully recorded consent to everything, and usually wind up badly disturbed by all the disgusting things they consented to.

Sex is far too important to be left to the decision of those directly involved. And women are not much better at making the decision at thirty than at ten.

# Trump and Israel

## 2016-03-23 20:30:03

On the one hand, Trump says, or implies, that he is going to pursue America's interests, not Israel's. On the other hand, he says and implies that he does not care deeply for the poor long suffering victimized saintly Palestinians.

Thus the mainstream media contradicts itself on his AIPAC speech (his speech to a bunch of powerful Zionist Jews) He got a subdued response, they laughed at him, and they cheered him wildly.

Then the Jews themselves are embarrassed that they cheered him wildly, and issue a shamefaced apology for cheering the horrid evil Trump, who is so uncaring about the sainted Palestinians, unlike our multiple peace prize winning president, who loves both Israel and Palestinians so deeply.

# Warmists capitulate

## 2016-03-25 06:29:08

For the last eighteen years there has been little or no global warming.

Major warmists have been steadfastly denying the undeniable. Then a paper appeared, signed by most of the big names in Anthropogenic Global Warming Alarmism, acknowledging "The Big Hiatus"

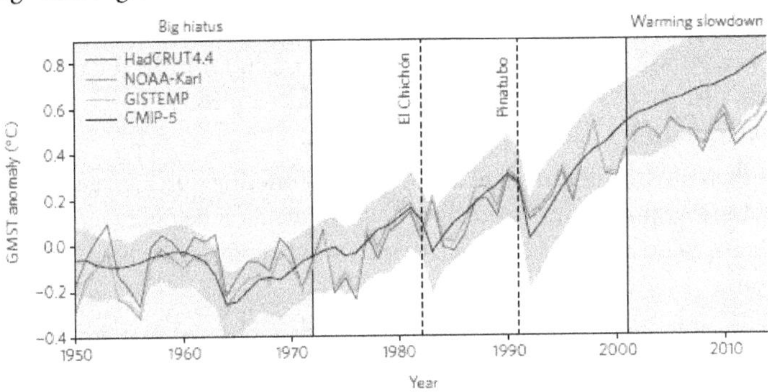


The black line is what the the warmists predicted, the grey area was their error bars.

The colored lines are what has been observed.

The graph is divided into several sections. The hiatus/pause/slowdown is what has been observed since the accuracy of our tools for measuring climate change were improved.

This capitulation is largely due to the work of Climate Audit[364].

Climate models retrodicted the past with near perfect accuracy, despite the fact that our ability to measure or estimate past global climate was nowhere near that accurate. Conspicuously failed to predict future climate change.

---

[364]https://climateaudit.org/

I repeat my prediction of future climates: In times to come the climate will for long periods be substantially warmer than it is now. It will also for long periods be substantially cooler than it is now. There is now far more ice around Antarctica than was historically normal, and Antarctica has been abnormally frozen up for the past thirty years or so. In the past from time to time the North Pole has melted in summer. In the past the Northwest passage sometimes opened in summer and sometimes did not, and in the future the Northwest passage will sometimes open in summer and sometimes will not. In the future the North Pole will sometimes melt during summer, sometimes for several summers in a row, but mostly it will stay solidly frozen. Polar bears will get by either way. Having survived the North Pole melting in the past, they will survive the North Pole melting in the future.

## Jian Ghomeshi rape case

### 2016-03-25 10:47:03

Umpteen different women accused Jian Ghomeshi of raping them. He was rightly acquitted.

Reading the evidence, I interpret it as indicating that he was so besieged by hot chicks that he generally would not date the same woman twice. When he dated a woman he would rough her up to turn her on. This sometimes resulted in her becoming so sexually excited she would have sex with him on the first date. In which case he when he was finished using her, he would kick her out like a piece of trash. Or if she did not have sex with him on the first date, he would also kick her out like a piece of trash, presumably because he expected the next date to be more compliant.

She would then pursue him in email and in person, offering quick casual sex in language that became ever plainer and more direct, which contacts he politely or rudely ignored. This is a man who having had a woman once, would continually turn down offers to have her again.

Some women, after being ignored in this manner, then charged him with sexual assault. These were the classic failure-to-booty-call rape accusations.

Jian Ghomeshi is tolerably good looking, but not exceptionally handsome. He is not charismatic. He is mildly famous and mildly influential. He is not particularly narcissistic. I conjecture that the chief reason for his success with women was that he is just naturally and instinctively a total asshole with a tendency to sadistic violence.

Progressive degenerates define BDSM as role playing - safe words and all that. He states that he never role played - which would indicate Ghomeshi got real, rather than pretended, submission from women.

Ghomeshi piously claimed to be a feminist, which is a piety that is absolutely mandatory for someone with his kind of job, but in practice always treated women as they love to be treated - like domestic animals.

He is Iranian by ancestry, therefore may have been raised redpilled.

## Trump is the man

2016-03-26 01:03:37

It is clear that Trump had this scandal[365] in his pocket ready to fire at Ted Cruz for some time.

Why did he not deploy it earlier?

He deployed it *now* because Ted Cruz went after Trump's wife.

Trumps biggest political advantage is that he cares about things that are more important than political advantage.

With every other politician on the face of earth you ask the question "Is it to his advantage to harm me?"

With Trump, the man, you have to ask the question "Will this piss off the Trump?"

Don't piss off the Trump. He rewards those who do right to him, and harms those who do wrong to him. He is the man.

## The quality of pussy that Jian Ghomeshi kicked out of bed

2016-03-29 03:52:44

Movie star, grad school.

Some white knight in the comments has been defending the virtue and chastity of womanhood and how warmly they treat nice guys, and how if you treat women as equals, or even better, the superiors that they naturally are, you will get laid.

Jian Ghomeshi's procedure consisted of beating them up on the first date, having sex with them on the first date, and then brutally dumping them to make way for the next girl in line.

A woman will crawl nine miles over broken glass to have sex with her demon lover. It is not in the nature of women to be chaste except that they submit to male authority. If

---

[365] https://radaronline.com/photos/ted-cruz-mistresses-report-other-scandals/photo/1275169/

you are not having sex with your wife, she is getting it somewhere else.

Monogamy and chastity was invented by men to reduce conflicts between men, and imposed on women with a stick.

## Trump for King

### 2016-03-30 09:03:44

History does not repeat, but it rhymes.

Today's America is Wiemar Germany. But Trump is not Hitler. Rather, Trump is Kemal Ataturk.

Kemal Ataturk abandoned most of the Turkish empire, because most of it was run against the interests of Turks. It was the anti Turkish empire, as the American empire is the anti American empire.

This put Kemal Ataturk on a collision course with the Caliphate, which continued to rule by soft power what Turkey no longer ruled by hard power. Which Caliphate he was eventually forced to destroy.

Hitler wanted a German Empire. Trump intends to disband the American empire, or as much of the American empire as costs Americans money and delights in telling New York that their provincials are much holier than Americans.

The Cathedral will not be pleased. Being universalist, world empire is their heart and soul. Abandoning empire is going to piss them off a lot more than an eight year delay in turning America brown and ethnically cleansing whites is going to piss them off.

Trump is not particularly right wing. He is what was middle of the road yesterday, though progressives find it hard to tell the difference between yesterday's middle of the road and people who chant "Heil Hitler". The Republican establishment frequently complains that Trump fails to endorse all the wonderful policies that they did absolutely nothing to give effect to when they had the presidency and both houses.

We love Trump for the wonderful job he is done on political correctness, for being ten times as manly as any other candidate, and, last but not least, for being the only politician who is serious about not letting in the entire rest of the world into America to live on crime, welfare, and voting Democratic. Who else proposes to throw out anchor babies?

By the way, Tony Abbot kicked anchor babies out of Australia, and not a dog barked. The judges cowered and hid as they realized an airforce special forces commando outranks a high court justice. The left thought it would be a huge deal, and tried to make hay out of it, and no one paid the slightest attention.

But could Trump manage what Moldbug called "the true election" - could he attain actual power to govern?

The presidency has been steadily accumulating legislative and budgetary power. But the presidency is not the president. The presidency is a horde of fireproof bureaucrats who theoretically answer to the president, but, being fireproof, do not in fact answer to anyone. It is clear that they intend to ignore Trump and govern as they have always governed.

This will undoubtedly irritate Trump. If he does something effectual, he is going to look quite a bit like Stalin or Cromwell, and this election will be the true election.

This seems like a ridiculously optimistic hope, and I suppose it is, but Trump does not seem like the kind of man who would plan to be president without planning to actually govern.

Obviously Trump, a middle of the roader, has no intention of implementing a restoration.

But for Trump to implement anything at all, he is going to have to make a good start on a restoration.

## The Feminine Imperative

### 2016-04-03 11:14:21

One of my commenters had never heard of the Feminine Imperative, and it is not listed the social matters compendium[366], so here is a description and definition.

The Feminine Imperative is that when a woman follows her pussy, it should have good results for her, and if it does not have good results for her, it is the fault of some dastardly man and not an indication that women are too childish and irresponsible to be allowed to follow their pussies.

Whenever illicit female sexual desires lead to illicit acts which have bad consequences, those consequences are deemed to be the fault of men, and it is the duty of men to make female sexual desires come out with good consequences for the woman, even if it means bad consequences for the man. Man up and marry those sluts!

Thus, for example, serial monogamy is deemed to be perfectly moral[367], while polygyny is totally unacceptable meaning that women are allowed to be permanently on the prowl to trade up from their current husband or boyfriend, while it is absolutely terrible for a man to sleep with multiple girlfriends, or to sleep with other women in addition to his wife.

When women do bad things, they are treated like children morally, let off the hook, protected from the consequences, yet they are allowed to make potentially disastrous choices without adult supervision, choices that men will pay for when those choices go wrong. Thus women receive substantially lesser penalties for crimes, and are not really expected to honor contracts - yet any business that discriminated against contracts signed by women would be in big trouble, even though it is also in trouble when it tries to enforce those contracts.

A pregnant woman can abort, or give the child away, but if she decides to keep it, she can demand child support from the father - while denying the child a father.

The system that the father and the mother get married at shotgun point, and the father is forced to support his wife and child, and the mother forced to honor and obey the husband makes moral sense. The system that a single mother is on her own would also make moral sense, if women could be treated as independent adults, equal to men, but when we tried that the result was far too many women giving birth to fatherless children in the rain in dark alleys. So now we have a system where pregnancy obligates men, but

---

[366]https://www.socialmatter.net/the-compendium/
[367]https://dalrock.wordpress.com/2012/08/20/womens-sacred-path-to-marriage/

not women, where women make the decisions and men pay for the consequences. That is Feminine Imperative.

The underlying mechanism leading to the Feminine Imperative is that adult women are assumed to be adult, to be capable of making responsible decisions about sex and reproduction. And when it becomes painfully obvious that they are not, then men have to pick up the pieces, without however having the power and authority to restrain women from making bad decisions.

The Feminine imperative is a result of the fact that letting women take the costs of their decisions leads to intolerably bad outcomes. So men have to take the cost of women's decisions.

But even if we try to ameliorate the costs of bad decisions, these decisions are still terribly harmful and should never have been permitted. For example Kate Gosselin should not have been permitted to be rude, hateful and shrewish to her husband, and should not have been permitted to frivolously divorce her husband, as these choices led to extremely bad consequences for her and her children[368], and making her husband pay for her wicked, foolish, and self destructive behavior did not much diminish the self destructiveness of it.

## Against urbit

### 2016-04-05 19:50:04

The world is moving to cloud computing - which means that the world is moving to giant megacorps that are excessively cozy with the government owning all your data.

Which, as general David Petraeus discovered, can be really bad for you. Google tipped off his enemies, not by reading his email, though they did read his email, but by tracking where he was when he logged in to gmail. Which is why Hillary likes to keep her email server's database on a thumb drive that she personally controls. Supposedly this is bad for national security, but I am pretty sure it is mighty good for Hillary's security.

Urbit is intended to fix this:

> Your urbit is a personal server: a persistent virtual computer in the cloud that you own, trust, and control.

Unfortunately urbit is also a language, a rather weird language, and a language that is interpreted rather than compiled.

A compiler can compile itself, and usually does. An interpreter cannot interpret itself.

Urbit, as a language, is kind of like Haskell as a language. Except that Haskell has a compiler, which is a huge advantage.

Let us suppose you want to multiply two times three in Haskell:

Well if you multiply two by three in C++, the compiler generates code that loads the number two into a register, loads the the number three into another register, multiplies the registers together, then stores the result where you tell it to store it.

If you multiply two by three in Haskell, the interpreter first creates a function to multiply any number by two, then applies that function to the number three, and it does not

---

[368]https://blog.reaction.la/culture/the-false-life-plan/

store the result. Which means if you have any non trivial program, it is pretty hard to figure out what the program is actually doing and how much time and memory space the task is going to take. Except that you can be pretty sure it is going to take more time and more memory space than doing it in C++.

Does anyone actually use anything written in Haskell? All alleged successful uses of Haskell are in-house usages - the man who uses the program is the man who wrote the program. We don't see someone writing something in Haskell, and then large numbers of other people using his software. If you google any standard language, you get lots of hits of people wrestling with vast amounts of data used by vast numbers of people. If you google functional languages, you get academics playing interesting and clever games for the entertainment of other academics.

I rather suspect that no one except Yarvin is likely to be able to write any large efficient program in Urbit.

In order for Urbit "your personal server on the cloud" to be useful, your personal server needs to provide tools that are the functional equivalent of blogging, tweeting, reddit, facebook, Github, email, the pirate bay, the silk road, ebay, and such. Tools whereby you can use your personal server to securely interact with other people.

Not seeing specs for such tools. Such tools seem like a lot of work.

The huge advantage of a language such as Urbit is that the cloud is inherently massively parallel, and Urbit is designed to be inherently adapted to massive parallelism. Your personal server on the cloud can scale - enormously. Which is more of an advantage if you are a giant corporation. And even so, giant corporations do not use such languages, because they are hard.

Something like Urbit is the right way to do things in a massively networked environment. But it is an enormous and difficult task. Writing a compiler would not be such a big job compared to all the other jobs that have to be done to make Urbit useful.

Urbit is a bright idea. It is a correct idea. But it is a really big job.

## Inequality is great

### 2016-04-09 02:31:45

We should love what we are, rather than conceding that the left is morally superior for wishing reality away.

It is great that women are what they are and men are what they are, otherwise I would have an absolutely terrible sex life. Vive la différence. It is good that men should lead, and women should follow.

It is great that whites are superior to all brown and black races in intelligence and prosocial conduct.

The east Asians are on average a bit smarter, though I think this is more that east Asian women are considerably smarter than white women than that east Asian men are smarter than white men. East Asian men are not all that overrepresented among competent engineers relative to white men, whereas east Asian women are way overrepresented among competent engineers relative to white women.

However, white men are more naturally manly than east Asians, and in some important ways more prosocial, hence better able to engage in large scale cooperation, hence white men are the most successful race at large scale war by far.

It is great that white males are better warriors than east Asian males, regardless of whether east Asian males might be slightly smarter.

East Asian men should build a great Chinese civilization, or maybe several east Asian civilizations, White men should build a multitude of great white civilizations (since whites will never form one nation) and the rest of mankind needs to be conquered and subdued.

I am not unduly worried about whether Japan gets absorbed into the greater Chinese co-prosperity sphere or vice versa, but it is a really bad thing that America rules the white world, this being contrary to our nature. We really need at least one white civilization west of the Hajnal line, and at least one white civilization east of the Hajnal line. One white civilization is far too few. (Hurrah Putin.)

## On successful revolution

2016-04-16 01:09:31

One of those who must not be named wrote:

> Old Martin had a secret protector
> Who happened to be an Elector
>
> Wycliffe did heresy flaunt
> His sponsor was named John of Gaunt
>
> King quickly pulled out ahead
> With helpful support from the Reds
>
> Women's Studies got a small donation
> From the generous Ford Foundation
>
> BLM gets away with their rancor
> As tools of a prominent banker
>
> The Big lend a hand to the Little
> The High and the Low vs the Middle

The alt right will be able to win when, and only when, the left is sufficiently terrifying to each other that some powerful people, or one powerful person, decides that the alt right might come in mighty handy.

## Fixing housing, health, and education.

2016-04-23 05:54:29

Housing, health, and education are unaffordable. So people think something must be done, and punishing the rich sounds like something. Hence Sanders.

## Housing

Getting stuff zoned for building houses is basically illegal, and when you somehow bribe and litigate enough bureaucrats to get houses built, tends to be overrun by inferior races who make the housing very cheap by driving out whites - typically around a quarter of the cost of building stuff, so if you build, you lose your shirt and are underwater on your mortgage when you flee ethnic cleansing.

Reconquer these zones, and the price of housing should fall substantially, both because humans can move back into areas overrun by plains apes (gentrification) and because investors will have confidence they can build houses and not lose money.

That building houses is pretty much illegal is a special case of the problem that building anything tends to be illegal. Bureaucrats like to subdivide power into ever smaller bite sized chunks, so pretty soon, to get anything done, you need the OK of umpteen bureaucrats, each of whom wants a bribe of a substantial part of the added value - so the total squeeze will far exceed the added vale.

The solution is to gate many no men through one yes man. For any project there should be one bureaucrat who has the power to say yes, and the power to blow off a thousand bureaucrats saying no.

Reconquer unsafe areas, and make it legal to build stuff. Price of housing will fall radically.

## Health

You will notice that in America, you can pay for surgery for your dog by swiping your credit card, while the same surgery for a human costs the price of a big house in a nice neighborhood plus a really nice car. So it has to be paid by absurdly expensive insurance.

Well, in India, Singapore, and Thailand, you can, and usually do, pay for that surgery by swiping your credit card.

Free market healthcare, healthcare for the rich in India, for the middle class in Singapore, and for the well off in Thailand, is simply affordable, in the sense that you can pay for pretty much any medical procedure using your credit card without exceeding your credit card limit - or at least without exceeding my credit card limit.

Nominally free market healthcare gets expensive because of cross subsidies. A hospital has a thousand NAMs show up who will not pay their bills, gives them abortions and diabetes treatment, then one white man shows up with an ear infection that needs a course of antibiotics, and hits him with a hundred thousand dollar bill. Indian healthcare is cheap for white people because the hospital you go to is full of whites and rich Indians - you are not providing a bed and food for thousands of poor Indians and it is efficient because genuinely free market. They post their prices up front, those are the real prices, and you go to the hospital that offers a fair price, whereas American hospitals will never tell you what it is going to cost.

Singapore has the best healthcare in the world, and the cheapest for the taxpayer, and reasonably cheap for the individual person needing medical services. Simply copy Singapore's system. Singapore has forced savings accounts, so that when someone has an emergency, he has savings, rather than hitting up the taxpayer. For the very poor, the very unlucky, or the very sick in Singapore there is free government healthcare - complete with death panels and the usual government healthcare suck. Socialism for the very poor, capitalism for the affluent.

Copy Singapore


## Education

Educrats are our priesthood, and priests always think people should spend more time in church. Hence degree inflation.

It is time for the dissolution of the monasteries. Confiscate the endowments.

It used to be that only pretty smart people, about equivalent to IQ 115, pretty close to the white intake of today's Ivy League students, could pass the school leaving exam, administered at the start of white male puberty.

And the top of the top elite, did matriculation, the completion of high school, at about the completion of white male puberty.

At one time, employers could look at a school leaving certificate, issued at the start of white male puberty as a signal that a candidate not only had a great work ethic and a strong sense of follow-through but that they were cut from a different cloth from most average or above-average young people. It signaled something unique about the candidate and made it that they were somebody in whom it would make sense to invest.

Then our priesthood started issuing school leaving certificates to everyone

At one time, employers could look at a high school certificate, issued at the completion of white male puberty as a signal that a candidate not only had a great work ethic and a strong sense of follow-through but that they were cut from a different cloth from most average or above-average young people. It signaled something unique about the candidate and made it that they were somebody in whom it would make sense to invest.

Then our priesthood graduated everyone from high school.

At one time, employers could look at a college degree, issued long after a man should have gotten married and started fathering children, as a signal that a candidate not only had a great work ethic and a strong sense of follow-through but that they were cut from a different cloth from most average or above-average young people. It signaled something unique about the candidate and made it that they were somebody in whom it would make sense to invest.

Then our priesthood graduated everyone from college.

A college degree has become the new high school diploma: the minimum credential required to get even the most basic, entry-level job.

Degree inflation is proceeding faster and faster. 25 percent of people employed as insurance clerks have a BA, but twice that percentage of insurance-clerk job ads require one.

If you want something better than the most basic entry level job, you need an advanced degree - and by the time you get your advanced degree, all the women you might have married have spent years fucking one man after another, and their fertility is starting to be adversely affected by age and sexually transmitted diseases.

One of the mechanisms for ensuring adequate attendance at government indoctrination sessions - the state church - is that schools perform a sorting function. For the able and industrious to be sorted into the able and industrious category, they first have to attend X amount of time listening to government propaganda, where X is apt to increase without limit.

But that propaganda, that indoctrination, is against sorting – sorting is discrimination. We are therefore proceeding to subtler forms of discrimination, degrees in stupid, versus degrees in smart. The logical endpoint of this process is that everyone in America gets a PhD which costs six hundred thousand dollars, but most of the PhDs are in basketweaving and puppetry. The sorting function, which is the incentive to attend college, is continually sabotaged and subverted.

No one should run up large amounts of debt to get a degree in stupid.

Our elite is being stupidified by avoiding disparate impact. Anything that filters for smarts has disparate impact on women and blacks. Also, smart people tend to mansplain – give those affirmative actioned into jobs beyond their competence instructions and advice that they are incapable of following. In an environment where one has a large number of female affirmative action employees, filtering for political correctness is going to filter for stupidity since smart people will be perceived as discriminating against the less smart, no matter how pious and sincere their faith.

I propose degree deflation:

At puberty (measured by biology rather than chronological age, to avoid the disaster that ensues when you have twelve year old adult black men in the same classroom as twelve year old white male children), everyone gets a test that discriminates between the lower two thirds and the upper third.

The upper third get the option of going to special elite boarding school (real school) while the rest, if they feel inclined, can attend bullshit school to learn lies and bullshit as at present. (There would be too much outrage if we simply kicked them out) The intent is that after a while, bullshit high school empties out as people realize that it not worth anything, and then we can we burn them down, salt the earth, build condos where they stood, and send the teachers to the gulag in Alaska for re-education.

Smart kids can learn in elite high school maths to calculus and trig, science to special relativity, how to calculate pi from first principles, geography, history of western civilization, and can absorb the western culture and western civilization that university no longer teaches.

About one third are eligible for elite high school, about one third of those graduate at the completion of puberty.

This, of course, renders sorting function performed by the Ivy league redundant.

Ten percent of that 11 percent who graduate elite high school, the top one percent, people 135 and up, take an elite two year university course. This certificate is roughly comparable to Harvard Law, (except that it does not cover much law) rendering the existing academic system rather useless.

As the colleges empty out, confiscate the endowments, burn down the colleges, salt the earth, build condos where they stood, and send the professoriat to the gulag in Alaska for re-education, where they will be taught useful skills appropriate to their talents, and eventually re-integrated into the economy into positions that do not involve indoctrinating people. For Maths and Science people that will rarely be a problem, but the rest may well be learning how to say "Do you want fries with that?". The re-education is conducted in Alaska because of the likelihood of trouble as the colleges shut down.

Attempting to use academic credentials to filter to smarter than the top one percent is unlikely to succeed, because of demand for lengthy recreational degrees. If we try to get an elite smarter than 135, going to need some new filtering mechanism. Also, using academic credentials as a filter means you are up against the bureaucratic imperative to expand. If one is supposedly in the business of educating people, one is naturally inclined to claim that the education is beneficial, and can benefit everyone, rather than acting as a filter. Thus academic institutions have an incentive to subvert their filter function, and thus an incentive to stupidify the elite.

We used to have a public service exam, a requirement for government employment in functions likely to exercise power, that was IQ heavy, though it also tested for diligence by requiring you to memorize a lot of useless nonsense. Unfortunately, this, of course, had disparate impact. Simply re-instituting the exam would dramatically improve elite function, and one could simply make it a substantially tougher exam for anyone in the system at a level likely to make policy.

Degree deflation, aptitude testing, and a gulag in Alaska.

## Spiritual Security

2016-04-29 01:50:50

Putin coined the useful and important concept of "spiritual security", as a part of national security.

All states have a state religion. If your state religion is controlled by a hostile state, you are toast. That is spiritual insecurity. The official state religion of most states is progressivism, and their progressivism is controlled by the NGOs, which are controlled by the US State Department, which is controlled by Harvard in pretty much the same way the US supreme court is controlled by Harvard. (Sometimes the president makes minor, and usually ineffectual and unsuccessful, efforts to influence the US State Department. If he gets too stubborn about it, the media demonize him.)

Back in the 1400 and 1500s the Pope was in the pocket of the Holy Roman Emperor and/or the King of Spain, and a lot of states were at war or near war or cold war with the Holy Roman Emperor and/or the King of Spain. These states found that the Pope was getting up their noses. They found Martin Luther handy to protect themselves from papism, which eventually led to the bloody holy wars of the Protestant Reformation west of the Hajnal line. Being Roman Catholic was spiritual insecurity - you were apt wind up incorporated in the almost universal empire of the triple crown.

More recently Jomo Kenyatta complained during the twentieth century: "When the Missionaries arrived, the Africans had the land and the Missionaries had the Bible. They taught how to pray with our eyes closed. When we opened them, they had the land and we had the Bible." That is spiritual insecurity.

China has a big problem with progressivism and assorted Christian sects, many of which smell suspiciously like the State Department, discovering in the New Testament that gay sex is sacred, and husbands should obey their wives. The obvious solution is state sponsored Confucianism Manchesterized, or state sponsored Manchesterism Confucianized, but they are hesitant and confused. What exactly is their state religion? Supposedly it is Maoism, but Maoism is just not that credible these days, and they don't particularly wish it was credible. They are half decided to go with Confucianism, but what sort of Confucianism? They are not sure. In the recent confrontation in Hong Kong, the police backed the protestors against the government, siding with the US state department against Peking. Such is the power of faith. Hong Kong suffers severely from spiritual insecurity. The authorities in Peking need to decide on something that is credible, persuasive, and sane, and go with that, for right now China is spiritually insecure. The state department plots a "democratic" takeover of China. If what happened in Hong Kong had happened in Peking, China would be ruled by the State Department and looted by Wall Street the way Russia was after the fall of communism.

Putin has a big problem with progressivism, but is taking forceful and effective measures against it. The unofficially official Russian state religion is highly unprogressive Russian Orthodoxy.

Russian orthodoxy in the west steers a delicate path wobbling between pissing off the State Department, and pissing off the patriarchy in Russia. There are no large scale hierarchical organized Christian religions in the west that seriously dissent from the State Department line that all religions, rightly understood, are the same religion, and that religion is progressivism.

## Rabid Puppies and My Little Pony

### 2016-04-30 08:47:36

For a long time the major science fiction publishing houses have been vomiting forth tedious hate filled political lectures that patronizingly scold the traditional audience for science fiction and fantasy: White males. The only part of what they produce that actually sells is romance porn for women where the female protagonist or gay bottom protagonist gets nailed by demons, dinosaurs, vampires, zombies, and werewolves.

(I have only just now discovered that dinosaur porn actually exists. I thought it was a joke of the Rabid Puppies. You would think it would be ironic, but porn does not do irony. Girl gets nailed by carnivorous dinosaurs with grotesquely large equipment.)

The Hugo awards have generally celebrated the most pompous and worst written political lectures, works that are very little read, plus a few celebrations of grotesquely deviant female perversion, works considerably more widely read.

The Rabid Puppies[369] are akin to Gamergate, in that social justice warriors don't like anything that white males do for fun, and intervene to stop it from being fun and instead make it morally improving. Thus, for example, Title IX is largely aimed at stopping white males from engaging in physical team sports. Apolitical white males get pissed with this and become political. Hence the rabid puppies want good science fiction and fantasy to

---

[369]https://voxday.blogspot.com.au/2016/03/rabid-puppies-2016-list.html

get the awards. And particularly good science fiction and fantasy that pisses on social justice warriors.

And among their nominations were a two episode My Little Pony story.

Social Justice warriors took this as a troll, that the Rabid Puppies were nominating something bad just to show that they could, much as Social Justice Warriors stage revolting and disgusting events to see how far they can force people to degrade and humiliate themselves, but of course that is not Rabid Puppy style. If they nominate it, has to be good, or something they think is good.

So I downloaded this My Little Pony Episode, "the cutie map", And it is pretty good and very deep. 1984, Brave New World, and Harrison Bergeron, written for ten year old girls.

A commie pony has established a commie utopia, and our major characters drop in to investigate.

There is the mandatory official happiness of "Brave New World", the destructive equalizing downwards of "Harrison Bergeron", and the poverty, ugliness, and lying authoritarianism of "1984". All depicted for ten year old girls.

Of course "My Little Pony" is in the business of teaching little girls prosocial lessons, and the first lesson that we are beaten over the head with is "people can disagree, and still be friends". Which gets repeated numerous times. Sounds pretty bland and innocent as a lecture to ten year old girls. Right? Except that it is set in a society of terrifying political correctness where everyone agrees with everyone or else. Which makes it not at all bland and innocent.

In other words, Social Justice Warriors, the mob who wants to no platform Moldbug, the rioters trying the shut down the Trump rallies, are behaving like naughty, unpleasant, bad, nasty children. Like naughty ten year old girls.

Another lesson, less heavily thumped, is that some people are better than other people, and that some people can be better than other people, and still be friends. Also, the commie utopia has no choice in goods, and what goods it does have are no good. The equal ponies are dressed in identical coarse sacks, and eat identical bad food. Since everyone is supposedly equally good at muffin production, the cook is in fact dreadful at cooking muffins.

At eighteen minutes in the first episode, we find that the incompetent muffin cook has, like Harrison Bergeron, been deprived of her special talent that once made her better than others.

We also encounter the Overton Window "that sounds extreme". Or rather "that souNDS EEEXXXTEEEEEEEEME!!" - for views that before the communist revolution would have been utterly ordinary and taken for granted. Even those plotting counter revolution are incapable of crimethink. They want moderate and reasonable counter revolution - nothing EEEXXXTEEEEEEEEME!! They are cuckservative ponies. Communism is horrible, brutal, and failing disastrously, so they want just slightly less communism. But nothing "EEEXXXTEEEEEEEEME!!"

Yes, My Little Pony features a cuckservative.

And then, at the end of the first episode, they discover there is no leaving utopia,

At the start of the next episode, we hear propaganda broadcast by loudspeaker. "Exceptionalism is a lie" say the loudspeakers. But the ten year old girls viewing the episode know the major characters are exceptional - leading to a moral unusual in shows directed at ten year old girls "Don't trust the mass media - it is probably propaganda."

But the major characters have had their special abilities, their superiority, magically removed from them. They are handicapped down to the lowest common denominator. They find that they like dull books and crappy soviet style goods.

Then comes the pressure to rat out your fellow reactionaries and counter revolutionaries.

Then Fluttershy discovers that some commies are more equal than other commies, reveals it, and counter revolution ensues - an ending that I fear is far too optimistic. We already know that some commies are more equal than other commies, and no one is revolting.

## American Law Institute Sexual Assault Draft

### 2016-05-02 23:30:30

You have probably heard that congress makes law. It does not, it has not for a long time, and were it to start doing so it would be a revolutionary act. First there would be tanks in the streets. 2201 C Street would be on fire and full of bullet holes and dead bodies. Blood would be running out the doors into the gutter.

Harvard makes law, and when Harvard, having decided in general form what the law is going to be, gets to working out the details of that law, a committee of the Ivies meets to draw up the fine print, and that committee of the Ivies is the American Law Institute.

And right now they are drafting a law that says that an explicit verbal no outweighs any amount of non verbal yes, and that any sexual act without an explicit verbal yes is sexual assault[370].

Since this is the internet, I assume that some substantial portion of my readers are unfamiliar with the normal way that sex goes down between a man and a women.

You never get an explicit verbal yes from a normal decent women, only from whores and hard core burned out sluts.

The human mating dance is innate, instinctive, pre verbal, and pre rational. You get a woman into a sex place, (such your bedroom) using lots of touching and gentle caresses but also all the human arts of words and persuasion. (Where are your etchings? I thought you were going to show me your etchings?) But once she is in there, words soon stop.

If you try to get explicit verbal consent, at best you are breaking the mood and interrupting the playing out of your and her sexual instincts, and at worst you are very likely just not going to get it. And it continues to be that way with your wife and girlfriends, except that the full mating dance gets abbreviated.

Normal decent people just don't do sex in accordance with Harvard rules and they are not going to start. They are going to go right on doing it the way it always has been done.

We are all criminals now.

---

[370]https://lawprofessors.typepad.com/crimprof_blog/2016/05/amending-the-ali-sexual-assault-draft-penalties.html

## The Summoner's tale

### 2016-05-05 02:11:37

Chaucer depicts three priests: The Friar, the Summoner, and the Pardoner. All of the them are corrupt and avaricious. The Summoner and the Pardoner are low testosterone gays, and the Pardoner is a predatory pedophile gay. The Friar has seduced many women, and been forced, therefore, to pay dowries to get them married off.

The Moldbug canon is that the professors rule, with the mass media as the mid-level priesthood. But lately Donald Trump and the alt-right have been giving the mass media a hard time.

Which tells me that the world is starting to lose faith in the superior virtue of our priesthood.

The disturbances in Hong Kong were a good example of priestly power. Cathedral astroturf protestors were able to disrupt the city because backed by police. The police did what was virtuous, (they supported democracy and all that) rather than what their duty required. (The police should have arrested criminals and troublemakers, and kept the roads open. It was police, rather than protestors, that closed the roads. When a tiny handful of protestors declared a road closed, if police had walked away, drivers would have driven over the protestors.)

Had the same thing happened in Tiananmen Square, the Cathedral would have successfully mounted a "democratic" takeover of China, and Wall Street would have looted China the way it looted Russia after the fall of the Soviet Union.

Contrary to Cathedral myth, nobody got killed in Tiananmen Square. The authorities, having the warriors cheerfully obey them, were able to quell the protests with very little fuss. You only get real violence when the priests succeed in sowing disunity among the warriors. Recall what happened when "Occupy Wall Street" ran into Wall Street rentacops.

What happened, I hear you ask?

Answer: Absolutely nothing happened, because Wall Street rentacops were certain of their duty and the righteousness of performing their duty. If you are a rentacop, you believe in private property rights. It is part of your training, and if you don't believe in private property rights, you fail your training. So when Occupy showed up to violate private property rights, the rentacops said "No" and Occupy failed to violate private property rights. And similarly, nothing happened in Tiananmen Square.

Priestly power rests on moral authority, on superior virtue, while warrior authority rests on the ability to kick ass. We know the priesthood is virtuous because they are ceaselessly nagging us to be virtuous. All of us white males are racist and misogynist, and should be ashamed. Our evil thoughts lower black and female self esteem, and thus cause black and female misbehavior and underperformance. All black and female misbehavior is evidence of just how bad we white males are, and how ashamed we should be. Similarly the extremely high death rate among gays from disease, suicide, and gay-on-gay violence is all our fault. HIV is a heterosexual disease because it is caused by heterosexuals thinking bad thoughts about gays and denying them the opportunity to make blood transfusions. When blacks burn down the cities built by white people that they stole from white people, and drive out the few remaining whites, that demonstrates what evil racists we whites are. Whenever females get in trouble through underperformance and bad behavior, in particular when they render children fatherless, we males should pay the costs of female decisions.

All of which goes to show how much more virtuous the priesthood is than you and me. Their standards are so very very high that it is very difficult for sinners like myself to live up to such high standards.

I notice that the going price for refusing to take rapeugees in Europe is about 250 000 US\$ per rapeugee rejected[371]. Diversity is good for you and if you don't want the immense benefits of diversity you have to pay 250 000 per diversity. Which is about the same as the price that our priests pay to live far away from the victims of white oppression. Which, realistically, sets the value of diversity as negative US\$250 000 per browner person. It is harder to perceive prices for avoiding single women, since men like to meet them and visit them while not living too close to them, but I would guess the price for living away from women lacking male supervision to be about US\$100 000. The traditional connotations of the word "bastard" implies that female misconduct has substantial negative externalities, and residential patterns suggest a willingness to pay a substantial amount of money to avoid these externalities.

Remember all that indignation about blacks being forced to go to the back of the bus? Well now, we don't force blacks to go to the back of the bus... and whites don't ride buses where they are likely to encounter significant black ridership, for excellent, obvious, and entirely unmentionable reasons.

In the time of Chaucer, summoners had the job of punishing people for their sins against religion, pardoners had the job of selling people indulgences for their current and future sins, while friars had the easier and more popular job of forgiving people their recent sins, supposedly conditional on repentance - thereby giving them immunity against the summoner. Of course, you found the friar more easily impressed by your repentance if you made a small donation, but this was generally cheaper than buying an indulgence or bribing a summoner. So friars, summoners, and pardoners were in competition and did not much like each other.

Chaucer's Pardoner cheerfully admits to his own evil and corruption. Chaucer's Friar exposes the corruption of summoners, whereupon the Summoner gets vehemently stuck into friars, root and branch. The summoners excessive interest in assholes becomes apparent. Recall the conspicuous lack of testosterone and the popularity of gay sex amongst our priesthood today.

And then in due course we had the protestant reformation and the wars of religion.

Fertile age women should always be under the supervision and control of husbands or fathers, and if due to misfortune or misconduct, a fertile age woman is not under such supervision, she should be placed under male supervision one way or another. If you don't believe this, you will find it hard to handle women, will be inclined to credit our priesthood with immense virtue, and will be ashamed of your irresistible sinfulness.

People whose misconduct adversely affects other people's property values should suf-

---

[371]https://www.theguardian.com/world/2016/may/03/eu-refugee-crisis-closed-door-countries-pay-solidarity-contributions

fer various forms of exclusion, segregation, and apartheid. Persistent petty criminals and vagrants, people profoundly disinclined to earn a living, should be enslaved. In profiling individuals for their likely adverse affect on property values, and their likely future criminality and potential for productive free employment, race, sex, and ancestry (such as bastardy) should be legitimately part of the profile. The deserving poor should be taken care of. The undeserving poor should be dealt with. Since the apple does not fall far from the tree, it should be legitimate to discriminate in favor of the children of productive people raised by their parents, and against the children of unproductive people and people who caused problems. If you don't believe this, property prices and living patterns make no sense, you will unnecessarily expose yourself to danger, will be inclined to credit our priesthood with immense virtue, and will be ashamed of your irresistible sinfulness. Why won't your ride the bus, you wicked man?

## Formalism

### 2016-05-07 21:34:39

Moldbug argued for Formalism - that the official reality of political power should match up with the actual reality.

And I would add to that the rectification of names: That words should cut reality at the joints, rather than lay a comforting layer of snow over what everyone knows but no one can actually say. We need to bring back words like "bastard" to accurately describe the consequences of fatherlessness.

The advantage of formalism is illustrated by comparing Dubai with North Korea.

If you say your hereditary King is King because he personally owns the right to rule Dubai, which he inherited from his father, works a whole lot better than if you say your King is democratically elected to give effect to the will of the people of North Korea. Because if you say your King is democratically elected and so forth, you have to shoot anyone who shows signs of noticing reality.

We are increasingly in an informal situation since Harvard exercises informal power - for example making it illegal for white males to have sex with their wives is an immensely unpopular law which is being backdoored in through the endless redefinition of rape, sexual assault, and domestic violence, since any politician that openly stood for such a law would be instantly reduced to a smoking grease spot.

The more the actual distribution of power differs from the nominal and formal distribution of power, the more political repression is needed, and the more those that exercise power need to act illegally.

The need for widespread and frequent hypocritically and corrupt acts lead to criminal acts done for profit, as for example the looting of Haiti and the looting of post Soviet Russia.

Because your entire real government is acting illegally and criminally even when it is filling in potholes and managing the water supply, tends to act illegally by stealing and raping. I am not aware of the guys from Harvard raping - seems that our male ruling elite is increasingly forbidden to have sex at all, and you cannot make it into the elite unless you have abnormally low testosterone, but the high in the high low alliance turn a blind eye to rapes by their low political allies.

However, though the high have not been raping, and high males are increasingly not having sex at all, they have been stealing on a grand scale that gets steadily grander.

Since lies, fraud, and violent repression needed to just do the routine everyday stuff that governments are supposed to do, particular members of the government are apt to use lies, fraud, and violent repression to get ahead and benefit themselves.

Informal government is thus apt to suffer lack of cohesion, thus those that actually own the government are apt to have trouble defending their ownership.

If property rights poorly defined, violence apt to ensue. Who owns the government is bound to get nasty sooner or later. Informal government has been fairly peaceful in recent times, but has a potential for apocalyptic violence.

## Adulthood by race

2016-05-09 01:20:29

Eyeballing the graphs in the Journal of Endoctrinology[372], looks like American blacks become physically adult roughly four years earlier than American whites. Which makes them approximately intermediate between chimps and men. This is consistent with black females typically experiencing menarche at nine and white females typically experiencing menarche at twelve. Data on puberty in black males seems curiously hard to find, suggesting that it is horribly politically incorrect. Just eyeballing American blacks, looks to me that black males experience puberty at about the same age as black females or close to it, while white males experience puberty about two years later than white females, but that is just a wild assed guess.

The American Academy of Pediatrics has issued a study that says the difference is only one year, as measured by the start of testicle growth. Maybe I am prejudiced, but I find that hard to believe. The interesting measure that people should care about is not growth of testicles, which no one can see, but growth in bones, which everyone can see, and which can be objectively measured far more accurately. Maybe there is not much difference in the age and which testicles start to grow, but there is surely a pretty big difference in the age at which bones have substantially grown. It is also kind of suspicious that there is a only a one year difference in the start of testicle growth, which is hard to define and hard to measure, and a three year difference in menarche, which is entirely unambiguous to define and measure. Much as indications of climate change are more alarming the less they can be accurately measured, and the less alarming the more they can be accurately measured.

Which makes educating whites and black children in the same classrooms segregated by age, rather than by physical development, pretty much insane.

Similarly, stupid to put girls and boys in the same classroom by age during puberty, though not as stupid as putting whites and blacks in the same classroom by age. Indeed, it is pretty obvious that during puberty, kids should be sorted by their puberty stage, not by age.

---

[372]https://www.ncbi.nlm.nih.gov/pmc/articles/PMC2853999/figure/F1/

The reason we don't do what we obviously should do is that what we are doing advantages female children over male, and young black men over white male children.

## Duerte Harry

### 2016-05-09 07:45:12

If the votes are honestly counted, Duerte Harry will be the next president of the Philippines.

He was previously mayor of Davao, where he solved a crime problem, in substantial part a problem of Muslim criminals predating on Christians, by killing criminals. A lot of criminals. Of all religions.

When I was in Davao, some people threatened him with lawfare, and he responded in his newspaper that if they sued him, he would kill them, their wives, and their children.

Motorized tricycles are the major form of public transportation in some parts of Davao and most places near Davao. My tricycle driver stopped to buy fuel, and told me how a street kid had snatched a fuel payment, equivalent to six US dollars, and subsequently been killed by one of Duerte Harry's death squads.

I wonder how many other payments that kid snatched before they nailed him. Also, how big was this "kid"? Had to be strong enough to snatch, and fast enough to get away.

The people who were allegedly death squads were wonderfully disciplined, always perfectly polite and courteous, their uniforms extremely neat, their guns and decorations shiny. I felt very safe with them, whereas I don't feel safe with western police, who are conspicuously undisciplined and discourteous. I always get the feeling that western police may capriciously decide I have done something illegal (after all, there are so many things that are illegal) just to show me who is boss. I have always been able to talk my way out of trouble with police even when caught red handed, except for traffic offenses, or else my lawyer was able to talk me out of trouble, but why the hell should I need to talk my way out of trouble? I am an honest decent guy. Anarcho tyranny is that they enforce all sorts of laws against people like me, and not against the kid who snatches six dollars.

When car-burning riots raged in Sweden, police had a policy[373] of deliberately doing nothing about the rioters while cracking down[374] decisively on so-called "vigilantes" who tried to stop immigrant rioters burning cars and neighborhoods. To add insult to injury, authorities issued parking tickets[375] on burned cars.

In America, a four year old boy was groped in a bathroom. His father slugged the groper. Father arrested, groper not arrested.[376]

See Will's anarcho tyranny blog[377] for a long long list of what police do while allowing criminals to run amuck. He tends to focus on tyranny. Here is some anarchy[378]. And

---

[373] https://www.theblaze.com/stories/2013/05/27/parking-tickets-issued-to-cars-destroyed-in-violent-sweden-riots-conservative-site-posts-proof/

[374] https://www.friatider.se/swedes-take-to-the-streets-to-defend-their-neighborhoods

[375] https://www.theblaze.com/stories/2013/05/27/parking-tickets-issued-to-cars-destroyed-in-violent-sweden-riots-conservative-site-posts-proof/

[376] https://mpcdot.com/forums/topic/7900-anarcho-tyranny-in-the-21st-century/

[377] https://willsanarchotyrannyblog.wordpress.com/

[378] https://blog.reaction.la/war/anarcho-tyranny-in-the-chicago-riots/

more anarchy[379].

Duerte Harry's death squads don't do anything like that, any more than they would let the brass on their uniforms get dull, or drink while on duty, or wear uniforms that were less than perfectly neat and pressed. Their scrupulous neatness and rigid discipline is a symbol that they do not engage in such self indulgent bullying. Their perfect courtesy and crisply pressed uniforms are a promise that they do not threaten people like me. They threaten people who would snatch six dollars out of my hand.

There a pattern all over the West of excessive force against the innocent, the weak, the law-abiding, and those defending themselves and others but excessive deference to actual violent criminals.

This reflects a more general problem of the state, and members of the state apparatus, displaying ever less discipline. Which problem starts at the top with fireproof senior public servants.

## Libertarianism

### 2016-05-12 01:10:11

Most neo reactionaries are ex libertarians, or ex anarchists.

Indeed, if you are a feudalist you are not even an ex anarchist. You are an anarcho capitalist who doubts that most people should be allowed authority in the anarcho capitalist system of enforcement and justice, or are likely to receive a substantial voice.

"I pencil" is a famous criticism of socialism, which shows how difficult it is to centrally plan a pencil.

The problem is made much easier by good fences – and the occasional armed rentacop and fierce guard dog keeping an eye on those fences.

The socialist looks at those fences and says "the fences are unproductive, and the guard dogs are not only unproductive but costly and dangerous. They also look unfriendly and uncomradely, they divide us. Let us therefore abolish them"

And then the socialist, attempting to produce a pencil, produces instead many miles of red tape and a severe pencil shortage, frequently followed by a gulag full of "wreckers" that he blames for the pencil shortage.

The fences and the dogs serve a purpose, that purpose being to subdivide big problems into subproblems small enough to be manageable. Central regulation, on the other hand, bureaucrats claiming the power to meddle in what goes on behind fences, turns many small tractable problems into one gigantic mess.

Libertarianism works provided you have fences, and often enough you also need rentacops and vicious junk yard dogs to make libertarianism work. And it is the only thing that does work to make a modern economy function – apart from terror and mass murder, and terror and mass murder does not work nearly as well as libertarianism and fences.

Libertarianism does not work where you do not have fences. Public transport in America fails because of blacks. To make it work again, you really are going to have to send blacks to the back of the bus. Whites just will not ride buses with significant black

---

[379]https://willsanarchotyrannyblog.wordpress.com/2014/11/27/obama-imposes-anarcho-tyranny-on-ferguson/

ridership, for excellent and glaringly obvious reasons that no one dares mention. You wanted integrated buses, got buses with no white ridership.

Similarly "integration" was in practice black workers in Detroit riding on the backs of white workers in Detroit, shortly followed by the dispossession and ethnic cleansing of whites in the inner city and Detroit. Detroit's car industry failed because they were forced to treat productive and unproductive workers alike and were forced to hire unproductive workers. Ayn Rand depicts this, without, however, mentioning the overwhelmingly predominant race of the unproductive workers. When Detroit was thriving, she accurately predicted its future as a desolate ruin, abandoned by all civilized people.

If you have blacks and whites in the same classroom, the blacks are very much louder, take up more space, and are dangerous and threatening, disrupting education and forcing the white kids into submissive roles.

Further, the kind of discipline required to make it possible for blacks to learn in a classroom is a lot more severe than the kind of discipline required to make it possible for whites to learn in a classroom. Few blacks are capable of learning without being whipped. Successful black schools are harsh, and the harsher they are the more successful.

And of course, at a certain age, the blacks are into, or have completed puberty, and the black pupils are man sized and able to beat up the teacher, while the whites have not begun puberty, or have scarcely begun it, and are still child sized and still behave like children.

And if you have twelve year old white boys and twelve year old white girls in the same classroom, the twelve year old girls are well and truly into puberty, and the twelve year old boys are not, creating a profoundly disruptive environment, though not as severe as that caused by twelve year old white boys, and twelve year old black adult men in the same classroom.

But the biggest failure of libertarianism, the biggest failure by far, is marriage and the family. Libertarianism is basically incompatible with family formation, children, and grandchildren, with the continued existence of whites and east Asians, for white and east Asian women are psychologically incapable of breeding near replacement in a libertarian environment.

The problem is that for a man and a woman to raise their children together, to provide their children with a mother and a father, they have to form one household, no fences. But if one household, then one captain. The man has to be boss. Further, they have to be stuck with each other for incentive compatibility. Consent to sex has to be once and forever. If consent to sex is moment to moment, then marriage is moment to moment, and you get serial monogamy, which means that husbands have no incentive to care for and nurture their wives, and wives no incentive to please and obey their husbands. Which means that women get their way sexually until they hit a certain age and become cat ladies, and men do not get their way sexually, and means that children have only one parent, and a lengthy succession of violent and abusive step parents.

A libertarian solution to marriage and the family would mean two separate households with visitation rights. A lot of people are trying that today, and it is not working. This stuff just fails. Broken families, empty buses, hellish schools.

If you cannot solve a problem with fences, guards, and guard dogs, the solution is unlikely to be libertarian.

## Shit tests are designed to be passed

### 2016-05-13 05:54:15

This is not a PUA blog. Not going to tell you how to recognize a shit test or how to pass it. I myself am not all that good at such things. But I will tell you that you need to know such things.

Mostly the red pill is the rediscovery of stuff that back in the fifties and sixties everyone knew but no one would plainly say.

Shit tests, however, represent a new and clearer understanding. The Taming of the Shrew is all about passing shit tests, so this is not a completely new discovery, but we understand shit tests better than men in the past.

Girls cannot help shit testing men that they like, any more than a man can help looking at a woman's breasts. When acquiring a girlfriend, you will be hit by shit tests. When trying to keep your wife or girlfriend in line, you will be hit by shit tests.

A shit test is a power struggle. If the girl wins, for example getting you to apologize, making you hold her bag, making you try to please her in ways that can never please her, she loses. If you win, you win. Never apologize, never explain.

I think girls are genuinely unconscious of shit testing men. They think their supposed attitudes are sincerely held, though their attitude evaporates in a puff of smoke when you blow off their shit test. (Some shit tests, like showing up late, or going home to mother, require a bit of patience before you will see the attitude change.)

And it is hard to tell the difference between a shit test and girl really not liking you, or really not wanting to have sex with you. Except that shit tests are designed to be passed.

And shit tests are often horrifyingly harsh. It is often hard to pass a shit test, because they are really meant to be hard to pass. And if you fail a shit test it is likely to become retroactively true that the girl really did not like you, or really did not want to have sex with you. Hard to tell the difference between a thermonuclear shit test and a thermonuclear rejection. Except that one will reliably get you laid and the other one will not.

I am not going to tell you how to detect a shit test. You just have to intuit it. After a while you get a reflexive feeling of resentment "Hell, this girl is out of line. She is behaving improperly". But you should not react to a shit test by getting hostile and angry since such an attitude assumes in advance you will fail the shit test, rather than pass it and claim your startlingly generous reward. Rather, you should assume she will be happy to be gently but firmly put in her proper place.

Not going to tell you how to pass them. I am not particularly good at passing them. They are hard to pass, particularly in a society that gives women nuclear weapons.

Consent does not make sex right, and lack of consent does not make sex wrong.

A porn star is apt to wind up feeling mighty bad about sex and her life, even though she gets formally videotaped giving explicit verbal consent to absolutely everything. Most women married by abduction or by arrangement feel pretty good about their marriage, and all the better if husband firmly insists on sex every night.

Women do not really like needing to consent to sex, let alone consent moment to moment. Which is one of the reasons you will probably strike out if you try to get a woman to give you explicit verbal consent. They much prefer "It just happened". Women really don't want to succeed in getting their own way on sex, because if they get their own way, that kind of implies that the person they are having sex with is weaker, needier, or lower status that they are. In the environment of evolutionary adaptation, if a woman really does not have much choice in who's semen gets thrust into her pussy, it is probably better quality semen from the standpoint of Darwin, and more honorable and legitimate sex from the point of view of the God of the old Testament. They like to be dominated and commanded into sex. So a girl losing shit tests is her warm up to getting nailed. Just as every time a man looks at a girls boobs, he is thinking about having sex with her, every time a girl shit tests a man, she is thinking about being overcome, overpowered, dominated, and submitting sexually to that man.

I took a lady friend, and her good friend, to a resort, because I hoped for a threesome. This was extremely stupid of me, because one is never going to make a threesome with one's lady friend's good friend, because they will fear breaking up their friendship, but, hey, all the blood had as usual rushed from brain to my little man.

Let us call my lady friend girl 1, and her good friend who failed to have sex with me and distracted the attention of girl 1 away from me girl 2.

I met a man at the resort, and he wanted to join my group, and that was fine with me because he, being an outsider trying to join the group, was unavoidably confirming my alpha male status with every move he made, so I asked him to join us. We will call him beta man.

Eventually he very delicately sort of asked which girl was surplus to my requirements, which girl was the third wheel on the bicycle. To which I straightforwardly replied that girl number 2 was the extra, but he could not have her. He should hit on some other girl.

And, predictably, everyone acted as if I was being completely reasonable and had rightful authority over girl 2's life. But, of course, girls do not take this kind of treatment lying down. Or rather, standing up. If you tell a girl she cannot have something, she is going to want to have it.

Predictably, after a while girl number 2 just happened to wander off so that she is as far from me as she can be while still remaining in line of sight. And I pretend to not look at that line of sight.

And Beta man disappears, takes a circuitous route while out of sight, and just happens to reappear near girl number two.

I pretend to not look, while glancing every now and then out of the corner of my eye

I know he is going get an absolutely brutal shit test, because, he, and she, are literally sneaking behind my back, and thus he is acting beta. To get enough alpha cred to nail her, he needs to pass a brutal shit test, and she is going to give him the opportunity to gain enough alpha cred to nail her.

So he chats to her, she chats to him. I cannot hear them and they are too far away to see very clearly, but suddenly he acts has though she has stabbed him with a spear, the spear is sticking all the way through him and out the other side, and he is coughing blood. He flees in shame and horror.

The poor man was severely traumatized, perhaps for life. The next day we saw him in town, and my girls called out to him to join us, and he acted like we were opening fire with a machine gun. He fled again in abject terror.

But I know girl number 2 liked him, and wanted to spend a night in his room at the resort, because she was disappointed when he fled.

Had he joined us again, he would have faced an even more brutal shit test, to give him the opportunity to gain the alpha cred he lost by being beta to my alpha, and failing the first shit test. But if he had passed - well, it was obvious to me that girl number two had plans, though I don't know if it was obvious to her.

Maybe like Roger Elliot he spent the rest of his life creepily staring at women from a great distance waiting for them to approach him, then fleeing in terror if approached, and finally broke down, killed a bunch of people and committed suicide. Maybe he became a hairy hermit in the depths of the Amazonian rainforest. But it was obvious to me that girl number two had conscious or subconscious plans to spend the night in his room, rather than on the spare bed in mine, and was visibly disappointed when her plans fell through.

The moral of the story is: Pass your shit tests. The rewards are great. The punishment for failure is dire. And it is easier to pass your shit tests if you believe in the chain of being: Beasts < blacks < children < women < men < angels.

But the trouble is that society arms women with nuclear weapons against being hit on by upper class males, and in particular white males. This makes upper class men less sexy than lower class men, and lower class men less sexy than underclass men, and white men less sexy than black men. It is harder to pass a shit test the higher your social class.

## All slopes are slippery

### 2016-05-20 11:36:30

Just as overt discrimination against blacks was replaced with overt discrimination against whites with no intervening period of neutrality, when people opposed the double standard and started socially enforcing chastity on men, they abandoned social enforcement of chastity on women.

In the social world, everything is a feedback loop, and all slopes are slippery. The resulting equilibria rarely involve "equality."

Either men are morally superior to women, and women's sexuality is restricted, or women are morally superior to men, and male sexuality is restricted. Someone is always in charge, both at the societal level, and at the individual level.

The only time someone is not in charge is when the two sides don't know each other very well, and don't know how hard they can push. This is why dating is a process of the woman figuring out what she can get away with. They want to progress to the power shakeup so they know who is in charge.

Once someone wins an initial dispute, and gets defined as the party with the most valid needs (or greatest grievances), then their moral superiority turns into power. Once the first Schelling Point has been crossed, it's very hard for the losing party to hold other Schelling Points, and will lose as much ground as the culture/subculture allows and the virtue of the winning party (e.g.upper class, lower class, and feminist women will take different amounts of flesh if they win at moral superiority).

Once one Schelling point goes, there can be no natural equilibrium at some new, nearby Schelling point. The new equilibrium is not a new stationary Schelling point near the old, but rather is unending retreat. Retreat under fire always turns to total rout.

One possibility would be to give both men and women moral status in different spheres of society. This seems like it could work, but isn't it what the Victorians tried? Women were given great prestige and moral authority in the home and education, but that moral authority expanded, as Mencken makes clear. Women's moral sphere got bigger and bigger until eventually it swallowed the male sphere, and we now have Codes of Conduct in tech.

Blacks and whites could separate, and be in some sense equal if apart. But men and women need to be together, and being different, either men will rule women, or women rule men, and for obvious biological reasons women ruling men does not work very well.

## New Canon on Church and State

### 2016-05-26 03:02:27

I hearby declare Citadel's statement on Church and State[380] to be neoreactionary canon.

A lot of neoreactionaries are Christian adherents of organized religion - or wish they could be Christian - or wish they could be adherents of some organized religion or other. I suppose all of us wish that[381].

Trouble is that today's Roman Catholicism and the rest are heretical, satanic, and are committing institutional suicide as fast as possible. The pope wants "speaking ex Cathedra" to become yet another letterhead of Acorn, the Vatican to become a museum run by Havard with tour guides giving spiels written by Ivy Leaguers explaining how stupid and wicked things were in the bad old days, and the Church buildings where once Catholics met to receive the Eucharist to become Marxist Lesbian bookstores, as most of the Churches in San Francisco already have.

Speaking as a believer, Citadel argues the same conclusion I have less convincingly argued as an unbeliever, that I argued less convincingly because an unbeliever. The Church should be subordinate to the good state as a woman should be subordinate to her husband.

The Church inevitably succumbs to the state religion. See the Pope kiss Harvard's feet. And back when the Church arguably had some independence, and real earthly power, when the Holy Roman Empire had lost all power, but the Church had gained far too much earthly power, we got indulgences and Chaucer's summoner. Henry the Eighth was doubtless a bad man, but you got no indulgences from his church, and his summoners were subject to discipline.

The worst of the Roman Catholic Church was not the pornocracy, when Popes were succeeded by the sons of their mistresses. Hereditary priesthood is an excellent system, and normatively celibate priesthood a horrible mistake. The Church was great, faithful, orthodox, glorious, and virtuous under the pornocrats and under the Holy Roman Emperors. The worst of the Church was indulgences and corrupt summoners.

---

[380]https://citadelfoundations.blogspot.com/2016/05/dont-wait-on-church.html
[381]https://blog.reaction.la/culture/the-dark-enlightenment/

## Menstrual synchronization and cryptic ovulation

2016-05-28 04:58:28

The PUA interpretation of cryptic ovulation is that it is an evolutionary adaption to make it easier for women to cuckold their husbands. Doubtless there is some truth in this, but some untruth also, since when females get their way the result is not polyandry, which is cryptic, but serial monogamy, which female behavior is far from cryptic, whereas when males get their way, the result is polygyny. Further, females have control of which males can get them pregnant, since their cervix will open for one man's sperm and not for another man's sperm, so cryptic ovulation for this purpose is overkill.

Another effect of cryptic ovulation is to promote more sex, for the telos not of reproduction, but for the telos of the unitive bond between man and woman, that the two should be one flesh.

Since ovulation is cryptic in humans it is odd that human females tend to synchronize their menstrual cycles. It is apparent that a female's subconscious mind can see what a male's subconscious mind cannot see.

This implies an evolutionary arms race, in which it is valuable to males to know a female's fertile period, but valuable to females that a male not know her fertile period. And it is also valuable for females to know the menstrual cycle of competing females, and valuable for them to let her know their fertile period.

If a females fertile period is transparent to a male's subconscious mind, this facilitates pump and dump. By enabling more reproductively efficient sex by the male, undermines the unitive bond and male investment, to the females disadvantage, and facilitates mate guarding, to the female's disadvantage. It is easy to see why it should be important to females that their fertile period be cryptic to males, but why should it be transparent to females?

It is well known that females living together tend to synchronize menstruation but this serves no useful evolutionary purpose, so is presumably a side effect of something that does serve useful evolutionary purpose.

Personal observation, not necessarily statistically significant: Women sleeping with the same man all tend to menstruate simultaneously, or very close together, even if they never meet. It looks to me that when no one is using any form of contraception, one menstruating triggers the other to menstruate.

This, assuming the observation to be valid, serves the evolutionary purpose, useful for women, of making polygyny harder, and making it less likely that a polygynist who may well consciously or subconsciously perceive a woman's fertile state will get two women pregnant in rapid succession, thus making it more likely he will stick with whoever first gets pregnant.

## Keeping up with PC

2016-05-30 02:13:51

Me:

> I would not like to be incorrect, so is pedophilia still an abomination and absolutely the

worst thing ever, or is it holy and sacred already?

SJW:
> Relax. Still an abomination and absolutely the worst thing ever.

Me:
> What if the pedophilia is part of an anti bullying program teaching pre pubertal children to accept gays.

SJW:
> Never happens.

Me:
> I seem to recall the anti bullying literature depicting an obviously gay fifty year old man embracing a pre pubertal child of indeterminate sex

SJW:
> A totally non sexual embrace intended to demonstrate social acceptance of whatever sexual whatever the child was expressing. Which is therefore totally holy and sacred

Me:
> I seem to recall a pre pubertal child born male but said to be identifying as a girl who was ...

SJW:
> Totally holy and sacred. Obviously someone who knows he is a girl before puberty and can choose sex change treatment before puberty can know and prefer his sexual preference before puberty but ... um ... ah ... er ... people like me would never do anything that is not holy and sacred.

SJW:
> But I can definitely positively absolutely tell you that pedophilia still an abomination and absolutely the worst thing ever, and if a twenty four year old hot female teacher should have sex with a handsome high school football star who is big enough and strong enough to pick her up, toss her on the bed, and give her a spanking this is totally shocking, indescribably disgusting, and she needs to go to jail for the terrible terrible terrible harm she has inflicted on the poor victimized high school football star.

SJW:
> still an abomination and absolutely the worst thing ever.

# Trump for King

2016-05-31 11:31:30

This image, and this entire blog is licensed under the Creative Commons Attribution-Share Alike 3.0 License

This is an outline of how President Trump might well become King Trump the first, if we are sufficiently lucky and virtuous.

The world is sick of anarcho tyranny, and hungers unknowingly for the power and authority of Kings.

The recent election of Duterte, on a platform of his praetorians simply killing the bad guys out of hand without charges or trials, is an example of this hunger.

Now I hear some of you saying (and the progressives thinking but not saying out loud) that apart from being tough on crime, corruption, and governmental indiscipline,

Duterte is a leftist and that is just a bunch of rice niggers, low IQ south Asians. White people are more civilized than that - perhaps a little too civilized for our own good.

In Australia, one of the whitest countries remaining, a few elections back, the election was on the issue of illegal immigration. Tony Abbott said he would stop illegal immigration.

The judges, of course, ruled stopping illegal immigration illegal. Tony Abbott ignored the judges. The net effect is that today, if you violate immigration law they send you to jail in Villawood detention center without bothering with charges or trials. From time to time the left whines about due process, and gets absolutely zero traction. Suddenly it was revealed that there is zero support for due process, that there are almost no voters who care about due process any more. And in particular and especially very few white voters who care about due process.

The purpose of due process was supposedly to ensure that the innocent do not go to jail, and the guilty do go to jail. But anarcho tyranny means that with so many laws, the innocent are bound to be guilty of something or other, while actual criminals are deemed the oppressed, and are coddled and protected by the state. Due process lets real criminals loose, mostly dark skinned real criminals who prey on white people, while imposing enormous and impossible legal costs on innocent middle class honest respectable people. For middle class people, due process is just the government's way of punishing you when it cannot be bothered finding a crime to convict you of, even though with so many laws you have undoubtedly committed more crimes than you can shake a stick at.

White people just don't like due process any more, for much the same reasons as Filipinos rejected it.

So in our current environment due process and judicial review is discredited, and lacks political support. In Tony Abbot's Australia as much as in Duterte's Philippines, it was suddenly and startlingly revealed that judges are simply all out of moral authority. No one cares about due process, because, under anarcho tyranny, there is no reason why they should care. It is not just a tiny handful of reactionary intellectuals thinking like this. It is pretty much everyone.

The point of due process was to prevent the King from treating repectable decent people like criminals. But now that we are all treated like criminals, people just don't care.

Power divided can be power reduced. If the benevolent party controls all the food, or ninety nine percent of the food, as in communist China, today's Venezuela, or Allende's Chile, then you are toast. The result is at best severe oppression as in Venezuela, at worst mass murder on an enormous scale, as in China.

If however ninety nine percent of the food is controlled by ninety nine members of the one percent each of whom controls one percent of the food, then no problem. In this case, power divided is power reduced.

But if you need ninety nine approvals by ninety nine bureaucrats to build a house, you are more than ninety nine times as oppressed than if you need the approval of one bureaucrat, because you face a coordination problem between bureaucrats.

With one bureaucrat, you could hope to pay him off, formally or informally, by giving his bagman/consultant, say, a third of the surplus value you create by building the house.

With ninety nine bureaucrats, they each want ten percent, so you just cannot build the house.

In this case, power divided is power increased, enormously increased. This enormous multiplication of oppressive power is another aspect of anarcho tyranny that leads people to hunger for the power of kings, they hunger for one man who could say "give me half the surplus value and build it" and who would tell the other ninety eight bureaucrats to take a long walk off a short pier. They hunger for a Duterte who would shoot the other ninety eight bureacrats behind a shed.

America's smartest member of the ruling progressive elite tells us[382]:

> Investigating the reasons behind the bridge blunders have helped to illuminate an aspect of American sclerosis — a gaggle of regulators and veto players, each with the power to block or to delay, and each with their own parochial concerns. All the actors — the historical commission, the contractor, the environmental agencies, the advocacy groups, the state transportation department — are reasonable in their own terms, but the final result is wildly unreasonable.

Larry the prog worries that regulation, a multiplicity of veto players, makes government inefficient, and therefore unpopular, worries that he cannot get the bridge he needs to go to and from Harvard, and fails to see the glaringly obvious, that regulation makes the private sector inefficient.

I, too, have had to deal with a multiplicity of veto players, each with his bagman collecting his bribe.

And I do not believe that any of them were reasonable. That is just Larry the prog issuing the required pieties. All of them deserve to be shot. All of them were evil, corrupt, and insane.

Larry is pissed because his commute to Harvard is obstructed, blissfully unaware that Americans further from the seat of power suffer from the anarchy of government far more severely than he does.

In America, the presidency has gathered to itself enormous power, intervening in every small business, every household.

Husbands are thrown out of their houses, fathers torn from their children, thanks to the Department of Justice, which is theoretically answerable to the president. Women with husbands tend to vote Republican. Children with fathers tend to vote Republican. If the Depart of Justice has its way no woman will have a husband, nor any child a father.

Similarly the department of Justice arranged for white people to be burned out of Ferguson, forbidding the Ferguson police from protecting people and property, and forbidding collective self defense against collective aggression.

But the presidency is not the president. It is an enormous horde of bureaucrats that are theoretically supposed to obey the president, but which the president cannot fire, which results in anarcho tyranny. If the president could fire them, this would enormously

---

[382]https://www.washingtonpost.com/news/wonk/wp/2016/05/26/why-americans-dont-trust-government/

increase the power of the president, but enormously decrease the power of the presidency, because one would be merely subject to one tyrant, instead of ninety nine tyrants.

In practice, the bureaucrats tend to treat the president as their public relations boy, rather than their boss. And if he fails to run good PR for what they have already decided to do they will smack him around the ears in the pages of the New York Times.

The bureaucrats are answerable to the consensus of their fellow bureaucrats, they have to be a square peg in a square hole, but the consensus is controlled by the consensus of the Ivies, and the consensus of the Ivies is controlled by the consensus of Harvard.

And as we have seen Harvard does not much like Trump, and to judge from his list of Supreme Court judicial candidates, Trump does not much like Harvard.

For Trump to rule, for Trump to accomplish any of his goals, the president has to subjugate the presidency, a process that will inevitably require massive firings, and some actual violence against those who decline to be fired. Quite possibly some Duterte style sudden violent deaths that no one is inclined to investigate because everyone knows what an honest investigation would reveal.

Trump will need to get rid of some turbulent priests.

The president's power is so very great as to diminish the power and effectiveness of democracy thus we see a tendency to dynasties - the attempted Kennedy dynasty, the attempted Clinton dynasty, and the Bush dynasty.

An enormous increase in the power of the president, which will happen if Trump succeeds in firing those bureaucrats who do not obey him, would pretty much guarantee dynastic rule. Trump would govern for eight years, then be succeeded by his sons.

So we would have a system that was nominally democratic, but actually hereditary and monarchic. Such a difference between actual and formal power is necessarily corrupting and destructive, because such government operates by lies. To remedy this corruption, one of Trump's sons would have to declare himself King Trump the third, and his predecessors King Trump the first and King Trump the second.

So for Trump to become King in substance, and eventually King in name, he has to seize the power to fire the fireproof.

Which, given that he has support from the military, the praetorians, the cops, the rentacops, and the mercenaries, and that judges do not have much support from anyone, is quite doable.

If Trump says "You are fired", and security frog marches the offending presidency bureaucrat out of the building and does not let him back in, has that bureaucrat not been fired?

If HR attempts to keep paying the bureaucrat, apply the same measure to HR. If judges rule the firing illegal, do like Abbot and Duterte, and tell the judges to take a long walk off a short pier.

Thus could Trump exercise the power of Kings.

And if he wants to build a wall and deport anchor babies, that is what he needs to do, he needs to exercise the power of a King, for otherwise the presidency will not permit the president to act.

And if Trump exercises the power of Kings and does so competently and bravely, if he is worthy to exercise such power, Kings shall in due course ensue. I will then apply for the job of Grand Inquisitor when the time is right.

## If you are a conservative

2016-06-11 02:29:15

You believe that a wall for the US is immoral and racist, but a wall for Israel is not.

You believe deporting anchor babies is unconstitutional.

You believe that free trade consists of other nations accepting US copyrights, patents, and US investment, but not US goods.

You believe that the US should be the world's policeman.

You believe in gay marriage.

You oppose abortion but support state funding for an abortion business that sells baby meat.

You propose that a tax payer funded organization should fund and guarantee mortgages where Hispanics put three percent down on mortgages whose mortgage payments substantially exceed their annual income. (This is your plan to make Hispanics into conservative voters - fund them getting houses in leafy green suburbs)

You believe that America is a propositional nation, defined by allegiance to a proposition, not a land or a people. But you are not terribly clear on what the proposition is. Maybe it is that all Gods chillun are entitled to Obamaphones?

For many decades, Conservatism incorporated has been purging those to its right. Anyone too right wing was deemed to not be a true conservative. And the purge went ever leftwards ever faster.

The alt right is those that have enemies to the left, and no enemies to the right. As conservatism purged ever more people, ever faster, it would inevitably happen that conservatism would become a minority in the Republican party, and the alt right, the faction that fails to purge rightists, the majority.

And so it has come to pass. The alt right outvotes conservatives.

This may well result in the Republican party becoming a genuine political party, rather than the outer party to the Democrats inner party, which is what it was under Bush.

But it will not result in democracy working, since the inner party is permanently in power regardless of election results, and can only be removed by measures resembling a military coup followed by gleichschaltung. Making democracy actually effect policy is likely to require measures strikingly similar to abolishing democracy.

## Church Authority versus Sovereign authority

2016-06-13 07:18:48

The natural tendency is for Church and Sovereign to become one (interpreting Religion and Church broadly to include progressivism as a religion and Harvard as its Church) If one, the question goes away.

But sometimes church and sovereign are geographically different, as when the Holy Roman Empire lost power, resulting in one Roman Catholic Church and many Roman

Catholic Kings. Whereupon trouble ensues, and the question becomes urgent. What tends to happen is that the Pope proclaims himself superior to Kings, but is under the thumb of one particular King, so that the supremacy of the Pope started to look suspiciously similar to the supremacy of the Habsburgs. Today we see that Harvard has alarmingly great power in Iran, and Obama alarmingly little, and we see state department functionaries taking power in supposedly independent states, which state department functionaries were usually educated within a very short distance of Harvard.

The solution to this problem is given by the Chrismation of Solomon: Zadok the Priest & Nathan the Prophet Formally Chrismated SolomonKing[383]

Formally, Solomon became King because the priest and prophet anointed him so, making church authority supreme over sovereign authority. (Chrismation is Eastern Orthodox Christian language for anointing with oil[384]. Supposedly the oil goes back to biblical times, having been continually diluted with fresh oil.)

In actual substance, Solomon became King by murdering his brother Adonijah, arguably the legitimate heir, in a fight over Abishag, the most beautiful woman in Israel, even though it was illegal and immoral for either of them to possess her, and even though there is no mention in the bible that she intentionally did anything to tempt either of them, and by shedding the innocent blood of Joab in the tabernacle, thereby desecrating the tabernacle.

However by formally submitting to the Church, the sovereign pointed away from the unpleasantness of a messy succession, and to God. In substance, Solomon was in charge, largely due to craftiness and ruthlessness. In form, the church was superior to the state. In substance, Solomon dismissed one priest and appointed another, violating the principle of hereditary priestly succession. 1 Kings 1 and 1 Kings 2 lists numerous morally dubious or openly wicked killings and purges by Solomon over the succession question, and 1 Kings 2 concludes:

> So the king commanded Benaiah the son of Jehoiada; which went out, and fell upon him, that he died. And the kingdom was established in the hand of Solomon.

So was it blood or oil that made Solomon King?

Thus the bible points to the formal authority of Church over Sovereign, in order to give the sovereign authority, in order to make Kingship inspiring rather than demoralizing, but the substance of authority belongs to the sovereign, not the the Church. Napoleon was wrong to crown himself, not wrong to have himself crowned.

If there is a distinction between Church and State, and there usually is not, nor should there be, we should take the Chrismation of Solomon to demonstrate the proper relationship of Church and State. The Church should be formally superior, to make Kingship holy, to give dignity and virtue to the state. But actual superiority leads to the problems encountered with the sons of Samuel, and with Papal indulgences, and with Habsburg empire, and with Harvard.

---

[383] https://orthosphere.wordpress.com/2016/05/03/zadok-the-priest-nathan-the-prophet-formally-chrismated-solomon-king/

[384] https://en.wikipedia.org/wiki/Anointing#/media/File:Ancient_Egyptian_King.jpg

# What people really mean when they say there is a lot of rape

2016-06-17 10:15:58

Official, politically correct truth, is that there is a whole lot of rape, and very few rape convictions, and when women claim to have been raped, it is always true.

Now of course the poster girl law applies. If there was a whole lot of unpunished rape, or if most rape accusations were true, or even if more than a tiny proportion were true, then when Rolling Stone and suchlike go looking for a poster girl, they would be able to find one that did not blow up in their faces[385].

On casual observation and common sense very few rape accusations are true, the overwhelming majority of rape convictions are false and unjust, and the courts exhibit guilty conscience in convicting obviously innocent men, and then frequently sentencing them to sexual assault awareness class, time served, and suchlike. Obviously people do not really believe that many rape accusations, or even many rape convictions, are true in the ordinary sense of logic and facts. Rather it is an emotional truth.

"Yes, Virginia, There is a Santa Claus"[386]

People believe that many rape accusations are true, that many rape convictions are just, the way they believe in Santa Claus.

> DEAR EDITOR: I am 8 years old.
> Some of my little friends say there is no Santa Claus.
> Papa says, 'If you see it in THE SUN it's so.'
> Please tell me the truth; is there a Santa Claus?

> …

> VIRGINIA, your little friends are wrong. They have been affected by the skepticism of a skeptical age. They do not believe except they see. They think that nothing can be which is not comprehensible by their little minds. All minds, Virginia, whether they be men's or children's, are little. In this great universe of ours man is a mere insect, an ant, in his intellect, as compared with the boundless world about him, as measured by the intelligence capable of grasping the whole of truth and knowledge.

>

> Yes, VIRGINIA, there is a Santa Claus. He exists as certainly as love and generosity and devotion exist, and you know that they abound and give to your life its highest beauty and joy. Alas! how dreary would be the world if there were no Santa Claus. It would be as dreary as if there were no VIRGINIAS. There would be no childlike faith then, no poetry, no romance to make tolerable this existence. We should have no enjoyment, except in sense and sight. The eternal light with which childhood fills the world would be extinguished.

> Recently my wife died, after a long and terrible illness. She was always a good wife, she gave me two good sons, and we were together since we were teenagers. My sisters came to visit me for the funeral. I have not seen them for a long time.

---

[385]https://www.washingtonpost.com/news/grade-point/wp/2016/01/08/catfishing-over-love-interest-might-have-spurred-u-va-gang-rape-debacle/

[386]https://www.newseum.org/exhibits/online/yes-virginia/

After the funeral my oldest sister, recently widowed, and a good wife all her years to the best of my knowledge, told a story of how she and a bunch of other politically active women had investigated a girls religious school for pedophilia, and found and presented a pile of evidence that obviously no one else found the slightest bit convincing, and I am pretty sure my elder sister did not find convincing either. I was disturbed, and argued that she was overdoing it, creating a danger than innocent people would be unjustly impugned, that if they could find nothing substantial, should have let sleeping dogs lie. And in the course of this quite civilized conversation I casually said "The vast majority of rape accusations are false, the vast majority of rape convictions are false". My tone of voice, and my honest expectation, was that we were all family, we don't need to pretend, no one is going to overhear us, so we can get away with acknowledging the glaringly obvious. My work is not really due to the inspiration provided by Comrade Stalin, and there is not really much rape, or at least not much rape by white heterosexual males.

My sisters were outraged. They exploded. I could not get a word in edgewise. They spewed forth a torrent of condemnation and rebuttal. In particular and especially my divorced sister who was especially loud and spoke especially fast, and not very coherently.

She proceeded to passionately and very loudly describe various recent rape convictions, which were, she told me, clearly and overwhelmingly right and just.

Her evidence that these rape convictions were real strikingly resembled the SUN's evidence that Santa Claus exists:
> Nobody sees Santa Claus, but that is no sign that there is no Santa Claus. The most real things in the world are those that neither children nor men can see.

I have no idea what really happened in these alleged rapes. But I know what my sister told me happened. According to her:

> "They expected to be loved and cherished, they expected to be treated kindly.
> But instead ..."

But instead really really terrible things were done to them.

According to her, it was all regret "rape". The girls consented, then regretted consenting but the girls were not regretting trivially or foolishly. According to her the girls had really good reasons for regret, up to and including serious physical injury. Really really good reasons.

My divorced sister also has lots of good reasons for regretting some of her sexual choices. I don't know if any of them are as good as the reasons she attributes to these girls and these convictions, but they are good reasons. Which may explain her passion on the topic and her somewhat surprising choice and depiction of what constitutes genuine rape.

Women reliably and very predictably make disastrous sexual choices that cause immense harm to themselves and to everyone around them. So when they say they believe complainant X, even when, as with Jackie Coakley and Crystal Mangum, it is glaringly obvious that the complainant is making stuff up, what they actually mean is that complainant X is suffering real and genuine pain as a result of her choices to have sex or to refuse to have sex. For example, Jackie Coakley suffered great and real pain as a result of having casual quickie no strings attached hookup sex with Ryan Duffin, and repeatedly offering to have more casual quickie no strings attached hookup sex with Ryan Duffin, and repeatedly hatching overly complicated and excessively clever plots to manipulate Ryan Duffin into giving her another quickie, and Ryan Duffin repeatedly being too busy to get around to giving her any more quickies.

The current free-for-all sexual jungle just chews women up and spits them out. It breaks them. It makes them into trash, into garbage, into filth, into scum. It makes them into women who cannot stand the thought of being touched by any man who would be likely to marry them, or even hang around with them for very long. If Jackie Coakley manages to marry someone, she will probably find it mighty hard to fuck him. This is a major factor in our population collapse. Wives just not being able to stand fucking their husbands. And since fertile age women have to have sex ...

And that is what women mean when they say that most rape complaints are real, that most rape convictions are just. Like Santa Claus, it is an emotional truth, not seriously intended to be a factual truth. Virginia will not be able to see an actual Santa Claus coming down the chimney, and the SUN is not really saying that she will be able to. Men are convicted because women suffer, not because anyone really thinks that those particular men personally did anything in particular to cause the suffering of those particular women. Phi Beta Kappa and its members are still under various punishments and persecution even though the original rationale (their supposed rape of Jackie Coakley) has collapsed, new and ever more improbable rationales appear to fill the gap to justify the partial continuation of various measures originally applied to the fraternity to punish the rape of Jackie Coakley - though the original measures were mild enough as to reveal that no one had ever actually believed that the fraternity had been complicit in actual rape type rape.
> Sullivan announced a new contract between the university and fraternities that includes enhanced safety measures for social activities designed to discourage binge drinking. The university said that Phi Psi was the first fraternity to sign the updated agreement, and fraternity officials said that Phi Psi members have participated in a sexual assault awareness program.
>
> "We believe that in the midst of this ordeal, there is an opportunity for good," Scipione said. "This has prompted us to take a closer look at ourselves and what role organizations like ours may play in ensuring student safety."

A sexual assault awareness program, in the absence of any actual sexual assault, is just punishment, humiliation, and degradation. If you actually thought someone committed sexual assault, or was likely to, you would deploy something more forceful than a sexual assault awareness program. The purpose is brainwashing, to convince the innocent that they are guilty. to punish them for failure to comply with the narrative, for their disgraceful and shocking failure to be actually individually and personally responsible for the bad feelings and bad consequences that women suffer as a result of their bad sexual choices. The point of sexual assault awareness course is to re-arrange reality so that men are at fault for the bad decisions that women make, to punish Phi Beta Kappa and its members for Jackie Coakley's self destructive decision to fuck Ryan Duffin.

Supposedly believing the story to be real, the actions of the authorities were not nearly drastic enough for people who supposedly believed. Knowing the story to be completely false, their actions are far too drastic for people who disbelieve. The leniency of the initial punishment revealed the authorities' guilty knowledge that almost all rape accusations are false, the severity of the final punishment revealed the guilty intention to punish innocent men for the grave and terrible wrongs that women so frequently and predictably do to themselves.

It would greatly improve Jackie Coakley's prospects of marrying and her ability to be a good wife if she was publicly caned for fucking Ryan Duffin, because caning and public degradation would render the man who was willing to marry her more alpha in her eyes. It would relieve the psychological problems caused by her bad sexual choices. This is what girls who cut themselves are trying, and failing, to achieve. Women who do bad sexual things want men to punish them. Jackie Coakley's rape story was a sexual fantasy of receiving a well deserved punishment from high status males.

Consent based morality is based on the idea that we make rational choices. If two men agree to exchange iron for wheat, the exchange must be in the interests of both of them, it must make them both better off, or else they would not agree. But sexual consent in fertile age woman is based on raging hormones, on volcanically powerful and entirely irrational forces, thus women make terrible sexual choices that are very much against their interests. For this reason, sexual consent is not sufficient to make sex right, nor lack of sexual consent sufficient to make sex wrong.

We have an army of too clever by half intellectuals thinking up clever stories why the government and society should intervene in people's economic choices, even though even the stupidist man will generally be careful with his own money, yet everyone thinks that female consent is necessary and sufficient to make sex right, even though everyone sees women making terrible choices, and regretting those choices.

Emancipating women, allowing them to choose who to sleep with and who not to sleep with, is like setting ten year old children loose in the jungle to live by hunting bears. When menarche hits, women become less capable of consenting competently, not more capable. The age of consent should be menopause. Women should not be allowed to consent to sex except under male supervision.

Women despise men who treat them well, hence the effectiveness of negs and preselection. I should know. I am an asshole. Ask my sisters.

All woman respond to PUA tactics. Look around you. A woman will only be happy if she is virtuous, and will only be virtuous if she is bagged by a good man who keeps her and restrains her inherently wicked impulses. Women reward playful cruelty and cheerful selfishness.

Women do not reward kindness. If they choose to submit to a kind man, that is their good luck, not their good judgement.

Consider how much better off Kate Gosselin would be[387] had she not been allowed to speak back to her husband, nor refuse to sleep with him, nor to sleep with anyone else.

---

[387] https://blog.reaction.la/culture/the-false-life-plan/

# The feminized police force and army

## 2016-06-22 22:25:51

1. In response to the Orlando terrorist massacre there were women in uniform among those police responding. This was absurd, outrageous, despicable, shocking, and immoral. We should not expose women to danger - and because you cannot treat women differently to men, no police were exposed to danger.

2. In response to the Orlando terrorist massacre police of both sexes hid some distance away for three hours while the shooter continued shooting at leisure and victims continued to bleed out on the floor for three hours.

The problem is that if you are going to incorporate women in a workforce, you cannot tolerate masculinity. If you have women in the workplace, along comes the schoolmarmish attitude that men are brutes and this shocking brutishness cannot be tolerated. But there are some jobs, such as firefighting, policing, and war that just really need masculinity.

And even if, as in engineering, you don't really need masculinity, it is really oppressive that men are just not allowed to be men.

A situation where unowned fertile age women are mingling with masculine men is socially intolerable. The woman have to be owned, or the men emasculated, and since keeping women under control is today deemed intolerable, the men are emasculated, and we are now seeing that it is costly to emasculate police, and the Brits have repeatedly demonstrated that it is very costly indeed to emasculate soldiers.

Fertile age women should not be allowed to mingle with men except that they are firmly controlled by some male who is present, in authority over them, and responsible for their good behavior, and the number of women he is responsible for is small enough that he actually can control them. In practice, the alternative is always emasculating the men.

It is interesting that the astonishing cowardice of the police is being covered up - shows guilty mind - that this episode of horrifying cowardice is not just some bad apples, but is recognized as a result of government policy, much as the reaction to the Fort Hood shooting showed guilty mind in that they recognized the Fort Hood shooting was the result of affirmative action promoting people who absolutely should not have been promoted.

Omar Matteen eliminated opposition, then proceeded to shoot a bunch of people. Police arrived, and were told to wait for the SWAT team. They waited, and waited, while he kept on killing people at leisure, and victims continued to bleed out on the floor. Police *withdrew.*

Eventually, after half an hour, he stopped shooting, maybe he was short of ammo, maybe tired. Then he called up the FBI, told them this was a terrorist attack. It is not clear whether he resumed shooting after that.

Two and half hours after the attack, police started taking out wounded people lying on the floor.

Three hours after the attack, the SWAT team finally counter attacked.

So it is not quite literally true that they waited three hours while he killed people at liesure. They waited half an hour while he killed people at liesure, then two and a half hours more while he could have killed people at leisure, and possibly did. They also waited two and a half hours while wounded people were bleeding out on the floor.

Hey, if they were arresting you for failure to show up in court, for a court hearing whose date had been changed without informing you of the change, would have shot blind through your door, then it would have taken them two seconds to shoot your dog, and three seconds to break your child's face.

Large scale social cooperation, the larger organization of society, is something men do. It is part of masculine behavior. And if feral fertile age women are allowed to wander loose, you cannot tolerate masculine behavior, which makes large scale cooperation difficult. Either masculinity has to be deemed wicked, or fertile age women not under male supervision and authority have to be deemed wicked, or at least deemed feral. And so we have come to deem masculinity wicked.

## Nationalism rises from the dead

### 2016-06-24 05:48:41

White nationalities have been told, and have believed, that they don't deserve to have nations, that they are too wicked to have nations, that their evil thoughts cause nonwhite nationalities to underperform.

And if you look at the capitals of what used to be white nations, looks like most white nationalities no longer have nations. White males are merely individuals, isolated, alienated, emasculated, and permanently outvoted. The single white women vote for minorities that are still permitted manliness and rape.

And if you look at polls, looks like most whites agree, that whites are too wicked to have nations, that whites deserve to cease to be.

And the left, confident in those polls, has opened the borders to one billion one hundred million Africans, to live on crime and welfare and voting left.

As the frog gets dumped from the hot water to the boiling oil, he twitches slightly.

## All slopes are slippery

### 2016-06-25 09:51:31

The Guardian remarks:

> The deeper fear among Tory remainers now isn't just of a recession. It's about the rise of something new in British politics

When Tony Abbott halted illegal immigration to Australia he took a total no exceptions policy - not one illegal would be allowed in or allowed to stay, however sad his case, not one anchor baby would be allowed to stay. A power struggle ensued over a tiny handful of cute babies with photogenic ailments requiring urgent medical attention, and it immediately became obvious that both left and right believed that if one cute baby whose parents were fleeing religious persecution was allowed in, it would swiftly become extremely difficult to say "no" to one hundred million black male African Muslims with machetes fiercely screaming for infidel blood and white pussy, that if you cannot hold the simplest possible reasonable Schelling point, you cannot hold any Schelling point anywhere, that everyone with any expertise in politics believed that all slopes are slippery.

Brexit may well lead to a cascade of independence movements, and a cascade of walls against brown skinned people and Muslims - or at least that is what our leaders fear.

Brexit does nothing in itself to prevent Britain from being overrun by Muslims who are fundamentally and intrinsically hostile to Britain and the British. But it makes possible the will and intent to prevent Britain from being overrun with Muslims.

Brexit makes it possible for Britain to make free trade agreements with those nations with which she is united by history, language, culture, and customary law - which suddenly means that history, language, culture, and customary law are likely to become salient in people's minds. Those that seek to abolish Britain and the British can no longer claim that unelected Eurocrats make abolishing Britain and the British economically efficient.

I am not saying that we are winning (indeed as long as we have one person one vote we are inexorably doomed to lose horribly, to vanish utterly from history, and to be unremembered as those capable of remembering the past perish also) but Brexit is going to set free dangerous thoughts.

The Altright is the Dark Enlightenment manifesting as a mob, and Trump is the altright manifesting as electoral politics. Brexit is also the altright manifesting as electoral politics.

A key point of the Dark Enlightenment is that mobs are not the solution to the problem and electoral politics are not the solution to the problem - but they are a manifestation that people are thinking about the problem and thinking of solving it. Even if Trump becomes president, his greatest accomplishment will remain that Trump set free dangerous thoughts. Ideas are far more powerful than guns, for someone has to aim the guns. The mob, and the electoral politics, are not power, but are echoes of power, they are the thunder that tells us the lightning has already struck.

## George Soros on Brexit

### 2016-06-26 06:47:52

Mixed in amongst the usual lies, were some truths[388].

> The "Leave" campaign exploited the deteriorating refugee situation – symbolized by frightening images of thousands of asylum-seekers concentrating in Calais, desperate to enter Britain by any means necessary – to stoke fear of "uncontrolled" immigration from other EU member states.

Why the quote marks around "uncontrolled" Soros? Was not that the plan all along - to bring in five hundred million males over the next few years from Africa and the middle east to permanently outvote the white population while living on crime and welfare?

---

[388] https://www.project-syndicate.org/commentary/brexit-eu-disintegration-inevitable-by-george-soros-2016-06

... scenes of chaos like the one in Calais.

...

... A sudden influx of asylum-seekers disrupted people in their everyday lives across the EU.

The lack of adequate controls, moreover, created panic, affecting everyone: the local population, the authorities in charge of public safety, and the refugees themselves. It has also paved the way for the rapid rise of xenophobic anti-European parties – such as the UK Independence Party, which spearheaded the Leave campaign – as national governments and European institutions seem incapable of handling the crisis. ...

Xenophobic? Is it not entirely rational to be alarmed by scenes of chaos like the one in Calais. If people found their everyday lives disrupted, maybe they have a right to act collectively and individually to protect their everyday lives against this disruption engineered by their ruling elites.

... making the disintegration of the EU practically irreversible.

If we are sufficiently lucky and virtuous.

Brexit will open the floodgates for other anti-European forces within the Union. Indeed, no sooner was the referendum's outcome announced than France's National Front issued a call for "Frexit," while Dutch populist Geert Wilders promoted "Nexit."

How about that.

...Tensions among member states have reached a breaking point, not only over refugees, but also as a result of exceptional strains between creditor and debtor countries within the eurozone. At the same time, weakened leaders in France and Germany are now squarely focused on domestic problems. In Italy, a 10% fall in the stock market following the Brexit vote clearly signals the country's vulnerability to a full-blown banking crisis – which could well bring the populist Five Star Movement, which has just won the mayoralty in Rome, to power as early as next year.

:-)

The five star movement is a non cathedral leftist movement. Much like Bernie Sanders. Their economic program is, like that of Bernie Sanders, pure self destructive evil madness, akin to the flagellant movement that flogged each other to show how holy they were, but, like Bernie Sanders, they are outflanking the Cathedral on the left and, like Bernie Sanders, trying to produce a leftism that is not held together by hating white heterosexual males, the destruction of the white race, and the physical destruction of white civilization. Instead, they hate the economic system that produces stuff, and propose to replace it by a program of not producing stuff, since actually producing stuff is low status and insufficiently holy. I suppose everyone will earn their living by doing socially conscious puppetry and artisanal basket weaving.

The bottom line is that switching to fast boiling the frog, declaring that there was no such thing as an illegal immigrant, that everyone in the world had the right to live and vote in white countries, rob their citizens, rape their women, and receive welfare, gave the game away. Too many people can now see what is coming down the road.

That said, I don't think we can stop this by democratic means. Women will vote for rape by alpha cock, and white males are beta by law. But quite substantial and rapidly growing numbers of people realize we have to put a stop to this.

## How to give effect to Brexit

### 2016-06-29 06:20:24

Supposedly, if the British voted for exit, the government would immediately invoke article 50 - would give notice that Britain was resigning from the EU. That is what the prime Minister told them.

Well, the British voted for exit, and surprise, surprise, the government is not invoking article 50. The prime minister lied.

What a surprise. Are you surprised?

And every day, the most appalling scum, mostly black Muslims from darkest Africa, continue to pour through Calais to live on crime, welfare, and voting left. Theoretically England has a legal immigration policy that only lets in the better kind of migrant, but this has collapsed, as was always intended from the beginning, and now it is mostly violent black young male criminals, cannibals and terrorists. The supposed policy was collapsing from the beginning, and lately has collapsed faster and faster. If it had worked as officially intended, Britain would now be getting lots of high IQ Chinese, mostly wealthy Chinese businessmen. Instead it got a few, very few, low IQ Chinese, mostly poor Chinese waiters and welfare bums, and lately, rapidly increasing numbers of violent very low IQ black males. The supposed immigration policy was always dead in the water, and the real policy is now pouring over the border.

But look at Australia. Illegal immigration was abruptly ended totally and completely overnight with the stroke of a pen - well - with the stroke of a pen that authorized Australian Marines to shoot up boats and set them on fire anywhere on the high seas.

Legal immigration remained out of control in Australia, and has been getting steadily more out of control, but as the next Australian election comes very close, the Australian government has suddenly launched a crackdown to enforce the official policy, the official policy being "skills based": that the rich, the pretty, and the clever are legally allowed in, and the rest not, while the actual unofficial policy was increasingly that the scum of the earth were legally allowed in to live on crime, welfare, and voting left. That unofficial policy has now, about a week before election time, been declared to be corruption, rather than high moral virtue. It is implied that the bureaucrats and judges that gave effect to the unofficial policy, gave effect to the actual policy, were, rather than acting according to the highest moral principles, bribed by migration agents. And by sheer coincidence this shocking and extremely surprising corruption was uncovered just before the election.

The official Australian story being that until a week or so before the elections, the government was too busy cracking down on illegal immigration to notice that legal immigration was a shambles. And until a week or so before the election supposedly no one had noticed. Or at least no one respectable had noticed and if anyone disrespectable noticed they probably got prosecuted for hate speech.

But now, they really are cracking down on both legal and illegal immigration. So if Australia can do it, so can Britain. The Australian government abruptly and totally stopped illegal immigration overnight, and it looks like they are now abruptly and totally stopping the scum of the earth from legally migrating. They got instant one hundred percent compliance last time, and I think they are going to get instant one hundred percent compliance this time. It is like lightning and thunder. Bam. Sudden radical change in policy immediately followed by sudden radical change in compliance. They had to shoot up a few boats, whereupon the rest fell into line, and I expect they will have to charge a few bureaucrats who thought themselves fireproof, whereupon the rest will fall into line. Sir Humphrey Appleby suddenly notices his minister talking quietly to a couple of large security guys about corruption. Swift and total implementation gives the enemy no time for counter measures. While leftist policies are introduced little bit by little bit so that the frog does not notice he is being boiled, rightist policies have to be introduced suddenly and totally, like a military offensive, like a coup.

The longer Brexit remains unimplemented, the harder it will be to implement.

In Britain, you theoretically have a sudden radical change in policy that is *not* being followed by compliance. Indeed, if anything, looks like they are getting in as many scum of the earth as fast as possible in fear that the compliance might be coming down the road. Slowly and eventually down the road.

So what are you going to do? As a reactionary, I say voting does not work, but voting worked in Australia. Eventually worked. Albeit after quite a while.

Vote for someone with the balls to give effect to policy decisively and suddenly. And if that does not work, because you have too many nonwhites voting against whiteness, and too many single women voting for rape by men of those races who are allowed to be alpha, well, then, there is always the reactionary solution.

The military and the spy agencies look perfectly loyal to the government, but so did the Chilean military, which had a long tradition of staying out of politics. The Chilean junior officers plotted and rehearsed the coup without anyone actually speaking the fatal words out loud until a few hours before the actual coup. The Thai coup is going smoothly, and in the Philippines, looks like a self coup is underway or has already happened. Obviously if you are in the military, you don't go 1488 out loud, but if Brexit just does not happen, this discredits democracy.

When Napoleon entered the Council of Ancients with a squad of Grenadiers, they heckled him. One deputy called out, "And the Constitution?"

Napoleon replied "The Constitution! You yourselves have destroyed it. You violated it on 18 Fructidor; you violated it on 22 Floreal; you violated it on 30 Prairial. It no longer has the respect of anyone."

And so it should be if Brexit has no effect. Our next Napoleon should tell parliament about Brexit.

# Teaching boys to be beta

## 2016-06-29 14:04:03

I was watching "Troy". And for the first hour it was totally great. The mother of Achilles, who has the power of prophesy, and is believed to be a goddess or something similar, prophesies that if he goes to war with Troy, he will die in that war, but his name will live for a thousand years.

This is actually conservative, for Achilles was part of the collapse of Bronze age civilization, three thousand years ago, and his name still lives.

And Achilles, being warlord, a king, and a hero, and the greatest warrior ever, and a living legend, and incredibly brave and manly, naturally decides to go to Troy.

He goes to Troy, and after the first battle, orders his men to loot the temple of Apollo. So his men dump a kingly share of the temple loot in his tent, part of that loot being a dazzlingly beautiful girl, a virgin dedicated to Apollo tied up in his tent.

And then he just ... he ... he just totally fails to act like a man. In addition to being famous, and a hero, and the greatest warrior ever, and a living legend, he is also unbelievably handsome. But I swear, that there is no way that girl would voluntarily bed him in real life, if he acts like that.

Now I am old, and fat, and no one terribly important, and I look like Jabba the Hut, but if I had had a few hours with that girl in my tent, she and I would have been going at it like weasels in heat. (Voltaire said all he needed was ten minutes, but I think he was lying, and in any case, I am not as good as Voltaire.)

Everything Achilles does prior to going into that tent is totally, unbelievably, impossibly manly. Everything he does in the first hour of the movie is totally, unbelievably, impossibly manly. And then he goes into that tent and he is just ...

You know why boys are no damn good with girls these days. Because they watch movies like that. They are taught to respect women. But women do not really want to be respected. And what is this girl that Achilles should respect her? We see him disrespect King Agamemnon. Until this scene we only see him respecting mighty warriors who have earned it by their courage and their prowess, or King Odysseus, whom he respects for his cunning. What has this chick done to earn respect?

After that scene, I just could not watch the film any more, because I just could not see Achilles as a man. Just some kind of cuck. Real men just don't treat women like that. It is not just that it will not get you laid. It is unmanly. It is wrong. It is gay. It is effeminate.

OK. In the workplace I have to treat women like that or be fired, but it burns. OK, I bend to power and grit my teeth and suffer the humiliation, but the whole Achilles story is that he does not bend to power. Show him acting like a cuck, then there is no story any more.

Achilles does not respect King Agamemnon. He does not respect the King of Thessaly. He does not respect the champion of Thessaly. He does not respect the troops of Thessaly. He does not respect the ambassadors of King Odysseus. Why is he so damn respectful to some speaking temple loot?

## Separation of Church and State has failed catastrophically
2016-07-08 00:33:30

Same problem as anarcho capitalism. The vacuum is apt to be filled. And today it is filled with an official government belief system that daily becomes more extreme, and is enforced more coercively.

In retrospect it is clear that in England the demand to disestablish the Anglican Church came from a competing religion, then called Evangelicalism, which was already most of the way to becoming the state religion of England.

The history of the US is more complex. When the United States was many separate states with a common defense and a common foreign policy, back when people sa

By and large, I tend to focus on power at the bottom - that women interrupt their boss tells me that they are hired for reasons other than their contribution to profit, that businesses are forced or morally pressured to hire women, and then stuff them into parts of the business where they cannot do too much immediate damage. Blacks walk down the street like aristocrats, taking up lots of space, while white males walk like serfs.

I also write a lot about female sexual preferences. Sexual selection, female choice, results in a positive feedback cycle. I expect my readers, unlike Harvard alumni and Word Bank economists, to know the difference between positive feedback and negative feedback, and to know that positive feedback is apt to have extremely bad consequences.

Social matter however has been looking at the top - at the remarkable over-representation of people educated within a short distance of Harvard in the top ruling levels of most countries[389].

## Separation of Church and State has failed catastrophically.
2016-07-10 13:07:44

Same problem as anarcho capitalism. The vacuum is apt to be filled. And today it is filled with an official government belief system that daily becomes more extreme, and is enforced more coercively.

In retrospect it is clear that in England the demand to disestablish the Anglican Church came from a competing religion, then called Evangelism, descended from Puritanism, which was already most of the way to becoming the state religion of England though it continually changed its name in the process.

The history of official religion in the US is more complex. When the United States was many separate states with a common defense and a common foreign policy, back when people said "The United States are" rather than "The United States is" there was absolutely no separation of Church and State, for each state had its own state religion, and the seminary of the state religion of Massachusetts, charged with promoting and enforcing the state religion, was Harvard.

After the English restoration the religion of New England became aggressive, political, this worldly, and bent on conquest and domination. They forever resented the English restoration which had disempowered them and purged them from lucrative posi-

---

[389]https://www.socialmatter.net/2016/07/07/hitlers-hiding-austrias-judiciary/

tions in the Church of England and in the English government. Whig history began as their plan for reconquering England and the world.

The state Church of Massachusetts was state church of New England, and New England set up its Rome, its Papacy, in Massachussetts. The civil war and the Mormon war was New England conquering America - and then, following the civil war, denied it was a religious institution and proceeded to apply the doctrine of "separation of Church and state" as a very thin coat of white wash over the state religion of Massachusetts being enforced on everyone in America. And after World War II, everyone in the world, except those protected by nuclear weapons, Russia and China. There is a direct correlation between one's alma mater's proximity to the Boston-NYC-DC corridor and the height of one's position in the government and ruling class of one's country.[390] Outside of Russia and China the only substantial resistance comes from Muslims. If you are Muslim a tranny nonetheless wins your song contest, your universities are run from Harvard, two thirds of the youngsters attending university are women due to affirmative action for women, and shortly after they attend university they find themselves covered in semen from head to foot and are told that they are liberated. Approximately half of all Muslims are moderate Muslims, and if you are a moderate Muslim you support the gay parades, you have only one wife in the event you have a wife, and if you do get married you will probably marry a women nearing the end of her fertile years, and are failing to reproduce. Immoderate Muslims, most of whom support Islamic state or some faction equally violent, are getting laid, marrying young women in their most fertile years, and having numerous children.

Ann Coulter famously said "Kill their leaders and convert them to Christianity". Predictably, the US government adopted a policy of killing their leaders and converting them to progressivism, which policy is not entirely failing, but is having considerably less success and more serious problems than admitted. Conversion to progressivism is not keeping up with rate at which real Muslims, the ones that make women submit to their husbands, breed.

By and large, I tend to focus on power at the bottom - that women interrupt their boss tells me that they are hired for reasons other than their contribution to profit, that businesses are forced or morally pressured to hire women, and then stuff them into parts of the business where they cannot do too much immediate damage. Blacks walk down the street like aristocrats, taking up lots of space, while white males walk like serfs.

I also write a lot about female sexual preferences. Sexual selection, female choice, results in a positive feedback cycle, hence the peacock's tail. I expect my readers, unlike Harvard alumni and Word Bank economists, to know the difference between positive feedback and negative feedback, to, unlike the typical Harvard alumunus, understand why the peacock's tail is a really bad thing for peacocks, and to know that positive feedback is apt to have extremely bad consequences, and almost always needs to be broken and disconnected in the most direct way possible.

But this post is about power at the top. It is, however, also about my favorite topic: Positive feedback loops. And if you did not get that the peacocks tail is a manifestation of a positive feedback loop and that the peacock's tail shows that women should never

---

[390]https://www.socialmatter.net/2016/07/07/hitlers-hiding-austrias-judiciary/

have been emancipated, do some homework before commenting. Seems that these days all they teach in university is how to hate white males, even if your degree is nominally in computer science. If your degree is in computer science, you damn well should know what a positive feedback loop is and why it is a bad thing.

During the reign of Charles the First of England, there was a remarkable outbreak of holiness. By and large, the holiest people tended to get the preaching jobs in the Church of England, and, since there was not a whole lot of entertainment and social events other than going to church, they persuaded other people to be holy.

To some extent this holiness was genuine and sincere. On the other hand, since Church of England jobs had good pay and status, it was to some extent pharisaical, and became increasingly pharisaical. And this pharisaical holiness started to increasingly resemble nineteenth century leftism, alarming the King, so Charles the First set to appointing Bishops that opposed and suppressed left wing pharisaism - or perhaps Bishops that, like Charles himself, enjoyed a good time and were not particularly holy. And this led to civil war, which the exceedingly holy won.

And pretty soon each candidate for office was even holier than each of the other candidates.

And pretty soon pharisaical holiness developed a striking resemblance to twentieth century leftism, the twentieth century labor movement and the hippies, Which alarmed Oliver Cromwell, who, like Stalin, found himself outflanked on his left, so he cracked down on it, a good deal more vigorously and more successfully than Charles the first did. Cromwell is both a villain to reactionaries, for executing a great King, and a hero to reactionaries, for putting a stop to leftism, and for equipping General Monck with a praetorian guard, the Coldstream guards.

Cromwell's leftism did not go all the way to twenty first century leftism and celebrate sodomy, but the wind was blowing that way, as men ever more holy had to denounce yesterday's holiness. The war on Christmas and the war on Marriage began under Cromwell, foreshadowing the twenty first century celebration of sodomy.

After Cromwell died, General Monck staged a coup, and to this day the Coldstream Guards, who were originally his praetorians, guard parliament. General Monck restored the monarchy, and the monarchy, Charles the Second, purged puritans from state institutions, including the Church of England.

This pissed off the puritans no end. Charles attempted to purge New England's ruling institutions, but whereas puritans were unpopular in England, pretty much everyone in New England was a puritan, and the puritans eventually regained power in New England by a revolt that England let slide, and eventually legalized.

And having regained power, they proceeded to get holier and holier, until they were holier than Jesus (abolitionism and prohibition). And here we are.


## Defense of capitalism:

2016-07-15 09:11:02

Reactionary future criticizes capitalism from the right.

Capitalists have power independent of the state. They are apt to use that power politically. Example George Soros. By and large, capitalists overwhelming back the left.

But, if they back the left, they are sucking up to power, or like the NGOs, serving the state when the state wants a smidgen of deniabity. For example you cannot see daylight between George Soros in the Ukraine, Harvard in the Ukraine, and the State Department in the Ukraine. In the Ukraine, it is perfectly clear that George Soros it taking orders from the State Department.

Charles the second said that science and the scientific method was high status, and rich people all over the place proceeded to apply the scientific method and sponsor science. Harvard says that equality is high status, and all the rich people attempt to tap the untapped potential of women and nigerians.

The State Church keeps capitalism in line with no problems.

## Trucks gone wild

### 2016-07-16 22:58:54

Our rulers' position is now clear. We should learn to live with terrorism. Unlimited immigration will continue, and it is unthinkable and morally abhorrent to object to anyone in the world moving to America and living on crime, welfare, and voting left. The continued existence of borders and citizenship in a world dominated by progressive ideology is an unprincipled exception. Open-borders absolutists are perfectly correct that there is no coherent way to argue that racial discrimination or hereditary aristocracy are unjust without also concluding that anything short of completely open borders is equally unacceptable. The logic is inescapable.

Thus, if a black criminal is killed by police and it less than perfectly clear that the killing was justified, his picture is all over the news, whereas if a Muslim kills a child, we never see the child.

Well then, what will it take to stop terrorism? Truck control?

Notice that despite extremely strong gun control in France the terrorist (who entered as a refugee) had a fine collection of weapons in his truck. Not only is it hard to stop individual criminals from getting guns, it is considerably harder to stop large organized groups from getting guns.

Recall that Saddam allowed his people to own full auto weapons. Since he could not stop his enemies from getting full auto weapons, he had little choice but to allow his loyal, or at least not actively rebellious, subjects full auto weapons. If Frenchmen were allowed to own and carry full auto weapons as Saddam's people were, the truck incident would likely have had a different outcome. But it would still have been pretty nasty.

But of course we don't want a state like Saddam's, where civil war is barely held in check by state terror. (Though it would be an improvement on today's Iraq, where civil war is not held in check.) Nor Mindanao, where civil war is held in check by the threat of state terror, by state terror recently past, and the imminent likelihood of more to come. We want a peaceful high trust society. And to do that, have to remove the Muslims. Dump them on the shores of Africa.

Very few Muslims are inclined to blow themselves up in a pizza parlor. But every single Muslim, including the moderate friendly nice Muslim next door who would never dream of exploding in a pizza parlor, supports and sustains a society where the man who blows himself up in a pizza parlor is holier than you are, where the jihadi gets the girls, where a terrorist can hang out and it is hard for police to find him, let alone surveille. him.

For over a thousand years peoples, cultures, religions, civilizations, empires, nations, and Kingdoms have struggled to find a way to coexist with Islam. None have ever succeeded. We will not be the first.

## Another prediction: No kayfabe at the Republican National Convention.

2016-07-17 09:57:13

At the coming Republican National Convention Trump will be officially nominated as Republican candidate for president, in a process more like a coronation than a vote.

A long distance outside the coronation, there will be small, and exceedingly peaceful protests. Anyone unpeaceful will be hammered down so hard and fast you will scarcely get a chance to see him.

The reason I predict small and exceedingly peaceful protests is that the left is universally unpopular and loathed. People only show up for a left wing protest if they expect the police to take a kayfabe fall, and the judiciary to let them off in the unlikely event that they get arrested for riot, smashing stuff, beating people up, and stealing stuff. They only vote left for ecb cards and obamaphones. With the Republican National Committee capitulating to Trump, it is clear that the police, who have always favored Trump except when very directly ordered to take a fall, are not going to take a kayfabe fall, and the judiciary are not going to let rioters off. Law and order will prevail, triumphantly confirming Trump's promise that he can provide law and order.

If Trump can quell the Republican National Committee, quelling race riots is easy. If quelling race riots is easy, Hillary's program of inciting hatred and attacks against whites and police will blow up in her face.

For nonwhites and single women, the Democrat/cuckservative program is ECB, SSSI, and obamaphones. For white males, the Democrat election program is "Vote democrat or we will send around the blacks to burn you out of your homes and rape your children". Thus the demonstrated ability to provide law and order is *YUGE*.

Trump is white's last hope of collective defense, short of a military coup or armed revolution. We shall see collective defense on display around the Republican National Convention.

## RNC convention: No riots, no floor fight, Trump in charge.

2016-07-19 01:25:39

The headlines and stories about the floor fight were written in advance. I heard what I presume was the floor fight live.

The speaker called a vote that the troublemakers should not be given the opportunity to sound off, that that part of the proceedings should be skipped. Thunderous ayes. Two or three nays, perhaps four people shouting as loudly as they could. Maybe there were some quieter nays that I did not hear. "Sorry folks", says the speaker, "the ayes have it."

Mighty short floor fight.

The headlines and stories were also written in advance about the rioting outside the convention, but, of course, they had to ditch those stories. If anyone rioted he got squashed so fast that the newsmen could not spot him.

According to the news

> And so, when those Never Trump delegates shouted for a roll call vote, the acting convention chair—Arkansas Rep.Steve Womack—ignored the chant and declared the rules approved. The "ayes" had it.

> Before Womack could move on, he was shouted down, as pro- and anti-Trump delegates went back and forth on the floor, screaming in a battle of wills.

Bullshit. The anti trumpers shut up.

The Ayes had it.

I based the above comment on video coming from the convention organizers. On you tube, there is a different video, taken by the anti trumpers, which *sounds* a lot more disorderly. On the anti trumpers video, the shouting goes on and on. But on the anti trumper video, I see no one shouting except for short periods even though I continually hear seeming shouting. There is a discrepancy between the video and the audio. I would say the seeming shouting is just background conversation with the amplification turned up.

The only disorderly bit was four people chanting "Roll Call vote" for 33 seconds, and then falling silent because they could not get a critical mass of people to join them. Mostly it was one woman who looked like a classic social justice warrior waving her arms to coordinate the chant, and another man chanting and clapping in time. The waving and the clapping was an attempt to lead a mass chant. Two leaders, two followers. When they could not get any more than two following them, they wimped out.

So, what we now have is a straight up civilizational battle between the force of order, the strong leader of men who can effortlessly impose peace and order, and the forces of disorder, Obama, Hillary, and the news media inciting black people to kill white people.

And, as I will say in every politics post, this is the last presidential election in which the candidate who stands for killing white people might lose, or even have their point of view contradicted. If Hillary wins, the presidential election after this will be between a cuckservative who supports killing white people, and a leftist who supports killing white people with a lot more enthusiasm.

But today, order prevailed. The total absence of trouble outside the convention tells me that the warrior class has already accepted Trump as the rightful ruler, which makes it hard for the priestly class to depict him as illegitimate. I am pretty sure that the Cleveland police got stand down orders, which they creatively reinterpreted.

Trump is a credible commander in chief because he is obeyed, victorious, and has the support of the warrior class. He says he is a winner, and that story, told with confidence, becomes true. He wins. There was peace and order in the convention, and around the convention.

## Now four sovereign nations

2016-07-19 22:16:21

Reactionaries are fond of saying there are three independent nations on the earth: America, Russia, and China. Everyone else is under the boot of the Cathedral, except for a few small protectorates of Russia and China. Each sovereign nation has its own Twitter equivalent, which enforces the values of its own state religion.

It looks like Turkey may be added to the list, probably leading the Cathedral to re-evaluate Islam.

Since the Cathedral does not realize it is a state religion like any other, but regards itself as simple truth and decency, it believes it can crush Islam without overt violence and naked repression, in the same way it has crushed Christianity without overt violence and naked repression. Supposedly Islam rightly understood, like Christianity rightly understood, is indistinguishable from progressivism. Mohammed the community organizer like Jesus the community organizer. Progressivism thinks itself scientific, as Marxists used to think they were scientific.

Which is what Turkish Universities used to preach. I am not sure that they will still be preaching that now that Erdogan has purged every single university dean and most of the judiciary.

Erdogan is purging Gulenism. Gulenism is interfaith, arguing that Islam, Christianity, and Judaism are all basically the same. Well, if they are all the same, then they are all the progressivism of progressive Jews.

But, I hear you ask, how can Turkey achieve sovereignty without nukes? Won't America murder them all in some horrifically gruesome fashion after the fashion of the Boers and the Tutsi?

Turkey has nukes. American nukes. Supposedly they cannot detonate without US command codes, but the US has been industriously affirmative actioning "moderate" muslims into its security apparatus, so I would not bet on that.

Progressive "Jews" act like conversos. "Progressive" Muslims do not act like conversos. I think the Cathedral has been suckered by Muslim taqiyya.

Putin has adopted Orthodox Christianity as his state religion in place of progressivism, which is fundamentally western, and which celebrates the western values, culture and tradition that the Cathedral seeks to destroy and erase from history. Orthodox Christianity is our friend. Islam is the enemy of our enemy, but is not our friend.

If it turns out that Turkey is defecting from the Cathedral, it is possible that the Cathedral may come to doubt that importing three hundred million black male military age Muslims screaming for infidel blood and white pussy and giving them affirmative action mortgages to move into green leafy suburbs will turn them into tax payers and mortgage payers to replace the missing grandchildren.

But more likely they will just double down on madness, deciding that the way to defeat Erdogan is to turn these guys into middle class mortgage payers and tax payers even faster.

## Tor compromised

### 2016-07-20 01:12:30

It has long been known that much of the resources for Tor are provided by US spy agencies. Which is not necessarily a bad thing, since they might want a means for communicating that no one can spy on.

However, Lucky Green, a key figure in the privacy community, has issued a warrant canary[391] - what you issue when you are forbidden to tell people you have had a warrant served on you.

The canary fails to tell us that a US spy agency is inside his servers in a way that tells us that a US spy agency now is inside his servers and a many other Tor servers.

In a warrant canary, you say what you are forbidden to say by failing to say things that you would otherwise be expected to say.

This inclines me to Moldbug's solution, assuming his interpreter and compiler can be sufficiently small and self contained that one can make sure that everyone runs the same one. But if the interpreter and compiler exceed sixteen thousand lines, then defending them against this sort of attack becomes difficult.

## Western Civilization

### 2016-07-21 09:49:55

Western civilization is a bunch of things that tend to come together.

Christianity (forget that "Judeo Christian" crap, Judaism still has the problems Jesus complained about)

Classic Greek art, culture and philosophy (hey, compare our comic books with Greek statues, then compare with Indian statues or Japanese comic books, and no one except us and the Greeks does philosophy)

Western music descended from seventeenth and early eighteenth century composers, in particular and especially Bach. If you are fan of country and western, or Elvis, or whatever, it still a lot more like Bach than it is like anyone else's music, except, like the Japanese, they have adopted western music. Indeed pretty much everyone has adopted western music, but they are all imitators and continue to be imitators. Note how much Engrish there is in East Asian pop music. Any music you hear is derived from someone, who derived it from someone, who derived it from someone, who derived it from Bach, and classic western music, such as the concert the Russians put on in Palmyra to remind us that the west was victorious, is that western music that is most directly derived from Bach. I think Handel is better than Bach, but everyone in the west winds up copying Bach even if they are punk rockers who do not know they are copying Bach, and pretty much everyone in the world winds up copying the west.

---

[391]https://trac.torproject.org/projects/tor/ticket/19690

Science: The first statement of the scientific method comes from Roger Bacon, who proceeded to do a great deal of scientific research starting in 1247. Science really got going with the Royal Society in 1660. The King made science high status, so wealthy gentlemen proceeded to engage in or sponsor science, and the pirates who were conquering what became the British empire, who aspired to become wealthy respectable gentlemen, would sometimes take a break from shaking down Sultans for bloodstained gold to do scientific research. The best thing the Royal Society did was define the scientific method, give status to anyone who applied it successfully, and, more importantly deny status to those who falsely claimed to be applying it. When the Royal Society was subordinated to Harvard after World War II. no one with authority defined or enforced the scientific method, and these days the name of science is generally invoked by those who seek to restore the demon haunted dark, global warmers and the like

Worshipper of the demon haunted dark:
> Every year 47 million species go extinct

Fan of what used to be the scientific method
> Name one that went extinct in the last few years

Worshipper of the demon haunted dark gives seventeen impeccably authoritative citations.

Fan of what used to be the scientific method
> None of these name or describe a species that went extinct in the last few years.

Worshipper of the demon haunted dark gives twenty three more impeccably authoritative citations.

Enlightenment "Rationalism". Enlightenment rationalism transliterates Christian beliefs about the next world, where they can never be disproven, into this world, where they are demonstrably false, which is the opposite of rationalism. For example "all men are created equal, that they are endowed by their Creator with certain unalienable Rights". The Enlightenment was western civilization taking a very bad turn, which may well be the end of us all. The scientific revolution gets identified as part of the enlightenment, but this is like Marxists telling us that Marxism is scientific socialism. Science predates the enlightenment in that science got started around 1247, and the enlightenment around 1750. The high period of science, 1660 to 1945, occurred during the enlightenment, but was caused by the reaction, not the enlightenment, in that King Charles gave the Royal Society status, and the Royal Society gave science and the scientific method status. If Western civilization is to survive, the Enlightenment must be thoroughly purged and erased. Eradicating the enlightenment make make restoring Christianity necessary and possible, but the urgent necessity is the thorough and complete erasure of the enlightenment. Western civilization cannot survive the enlightenment.

Adam Smith and capitalism. Adam Smith showed that capitalism, done right, channels impulses that can be immoral and destructive, into ends that are moral and constructive. Thus, Western Civilization is inherently capitalist, and National Socialism is stupid, not because racist, but because socialist. The ten commandments consist of four that deal with God, thereby defining the adherents as a different and separate people, and six that prescribe how to deal with one's fellow man, and in those six the rule against covetousness is the rule that is particularly and specially emphasized. Covetousness is wanting that which is someone else's. If you see someone's pretty wife, and think, I should have her, he treats her badly, he does not appreciate her as I appreciate her, he is too old and ugly for her, if I were to sneakily kill him and take her, she would be happier with me", that is covetousness. If you think "Perhaps she has a younger sister who is still single", that is not covetousness. And similarly, if you look at a rich man and think "He got his wealth by doing bad things, so he deserves to be punished by me taking away his wealth and having it myself", that is covetousness. If, instead, you inquire how he got rich, and think about what you could do similarly, that is not covetousness. Adam Smith explained why the latter approach is usually more appropriate to wealth. Whenever you think of excessively clever rationales why the excessively fortunate do not deserve what they have, and should be deprived of it, that is covetousness, and civilizations end when the mob is empowered to give effect to covetousness.

It is plausible to argue that the key element of Western Civilization, the killer app, was the rule of law, laws that Kings had to obey, and yet, there is something wrong with this story, in that the law in England began as common law, which was not law centric, but judge centric, and the judges were, pretty much, local aristocrats, and local aristocrats pretty much did what they wanted, so the common law was not literal law written down as laws, but generalizations made by lawyers about the common moral culture of the aristocrats. So distributed power, limits on the power of kings, gave rise to laws that kings had to obey, not the other way around. A key feature of Western civilization is that it has always had a lot of nation states, and these nation states tended to have within them subsidiarity, many dispersed powerful people, rather than one king, or one all powerful bureaucracy. This gave rise to competition that mostly peaceful, though far from entirely peaceful, and the from this competition, the best tended to win, and be imitated, and worst tended to lose, and be ignored or replaced It was not the rule of law, but rather the rule of law was one of the consequences of subsidiarity, of mostly peaceful competition between powerful people and groups. The overwhelming dominance of the Cathedral over a multitude of nominally independent nation states, and the centralization of each of these nation states means that madness goes unchallenged. Doctrine goes out from Harvard, and goes unchallenged by reality. Competition made the west great, and real competition has been silenced. The megacities grow because winners and losers are not made by the market, but by government. Housing is expensive because everyone needs to be close to the man who is close to the man who is close to the man who is close to the man who is in the revolving door between regulators and regulated. Decentralization of nation states is difficult and hard to define. Independence of nation states is easier to define and easier to attain, hence the neoreactionary position that there need to be more nation states, and those nation states independent. When we have more nation states, and more independence for them, then perhaps will be able to look at them and say what constitutes decentralization.

# Patriarchy and fertility

## 2016-07-22 01:44:08

We observe high fertility in those nations and cultures where patriarchy is legally and socially enforced, in particular Muslim Afghanistan and Christian Timor Leste. Affordability of family formation has little effect. Clearly males in patriarchal societies are highly motivated to have children. They will do whatever it takes so that they can afford a family.

Thus, if pro social behavior in a patriarchal society is rewarded by a wife and the ability to support a family, you get highly motivated workers and soldiers.

Some people have argued that this observation is psychologically unreasonable "The guys I know don't want children"

Henry Dampier explains why males in our society don't want children in his 2015 article "Why no one wants to be a patriarch"[392]

> If you want men to join the legions, you make it so that the clearest path to power for a typical man will be to join up with the legions, serve his time, and then marry and be fruitful on his plot of land. If you want men to form households, you given them rights over those households and the families that issue from them. ...

> ... Men lost the right to use legal force against their wives and children in stages. ...

> ... the disciplining doesn't really go away from society. The switch is just passed on from the father to the policeman and the schoolmaster. The state's hirelings retain the right to discipline children, although wives tend to be permitted to run wild, especially nowadays, restrained only by their desires and sense of self-interest.

> The disciplining also changes from spanking to drugging, often heavy drugging of untested chemicals onto children. ...

> The reason why no one wants to be a patriarch today is that patriarchs have no more legal authority. They have no formal power over their wives or children. They only have influence. Influence is both fickle and distinct from power. When a child misbehaves in the modern world, there are only a few paths that a parent can take. They can verbally discipline the child (more likely to work in a higher-class household than a lower-class one), they can illegally or semi-legally beat them, they can take them to a psychiatric professional of some kind, or they can feed the kid to the justice system. Schools have their own corrections systems of varying levels of effectiveness.

> Further, paternal heads of household can be deprived of their assets and children at any time at the arbitrary whim of their wives. The wife can commit adultery, and the man can still lose his property in the ensuing divorce. The children and the wife alike can be wildly disrespectful to the head of household, and the man has no recourse other than whining.

[392]https://www.henrydampier.com/2015/03/why-no-one-wants-to-be-a-patriarch/

I was the boss of my family and I found being a patriarch and having children hugely rewarding. But then I am a grade A asshole, and I am not afraid to commit illegal acts, though I tend to consult lawyers on ways to weasel out or buy my way out if caught, before I commit them. It is hard to be a patriarch if you are a nice guy, or if you have respect for law and social pressure, because marriages on the Pauline model are illegal, being marital rape and psychological abuse. Marriage as it has been understood for thousands of years is illegal and criminal, so of course the population is collapsing. Workable families are similarly illegal. Indeed, these days any sexual interaction with women is illegal with the notable exception of hiring whores and escorts - whores, escorts, and porn stars being the only women who are likely to give you explicit verbal consent moment to moment.

Extrapolating my subjective experience, and the subjective experience depicted by Henry Dampier, fully explains observed fertility patterns, for example the very spectacular collapse of Japanese fertility[393].

People don't want children as assets. Never have, never will. If you think we can modify fertility with the tax system read Luke 15:11-32 and 2 Samuel 15:2 – 19:6 to gain an understanding of human nature and the human condition.

The problem is that children can be taken away from a man and used as hostages against him. That is why men do not want children.

Marriage and family is outlawed, thus only outlaws have wives and families.

## Alt right at the Republican National Conventional
### 2016-07-23 06:38:45

The left thinks the alt right has taken over the Republican Party and gave the Nazi salute from the Podium, and are fantasizing about creating a replacement Republican party in which white males will no longer have significant representation. The reason the Never Trumpers were unable to agree on anything is that some of them wanted Ted Cruz as nominee, and some of them wanted an unspecified nonwhite female nominee and a general purge of whites and males, to be purged not only from the Republican party and from history, but from the physical universe.

In actual fact less than one percent of the Republican National Convention was alt right, and none of them would have given the Nazi salute, though I suppose a few of them quietly murmured "14 words" and "27. Februar 1933" but they were treated as a respectable faction of the Republican party and received the same firm police protection that all the Trump factions received.

By "taken over" progressives mean "not attacked on sight with baseball bats".

Still, if you are an alt right, not being physically attacked on sight by state sponsored thugs wielding baseball bats with police protection is intoxicating.

Trump has not gone all the way to "no enemies to the right". Notoriously, he disowned the alt right before he refused to disown it, and refused to disown it before he disowned it. But if the alt right was at the Republican convention, like every other major faction that backed Trump, and gets wall to wall police protection, he is not disowning them all that much.

---

[393]https://blog.reaction.la/economics/the-future-belongs-to-those-that-show-up/

So, I will raise a glass of moonshine to Trump, and to 27. Februar 1933.

Listening to Trump's acceptance speech:

> ... We will be a country of law and order
>
> ...
>
> The attacks on our police and the terrorism in our cities threaten our very way of life. Any politician who does not grasp this danger is not fit to lead our country
>
> Americans watching this broadcast tonight have seen the recent images of violence in our streets and the chaos in our communities. Many have witnessed this violence personally. Some have even been its victims.
>
> ...
>
> Beginning on January 20th of 2017 Safety will be restored.

Hmm. Obama promised to stop the oceans from rising, Trump promises to deter the dindus from thuggery - after having very successfully deterred any thuggery in the vicinity of the Republican convention.

In the reply to Trump's speech, the mainstream media issued a pile of statistics showing race relations are simply wonderful.

I have another statistic.[394]

## Trump explains crony capitalism to the masses

### 2016-07-23 22:53:20

If you already know all the stuff that Trump is explaining, his speech is kind of dull, but for leftists and normals, it is full of shocking news, as for example the Obama policy of swiftly releasing violent immigrant criminals to continue predating on white people in

---

[394]https://blog.reaction.la/war/ethnic-cleansing-in-ferguson/

order to drive us out, or simply kill us. That was pretty boring to me. Of course our rulers want us dead. Remember that incident with Angela Merkel and the flag. Also bears shit in the woods and the Pope is not Catholic. But it totally shocked the audience.

At 28 minutes into his speech, he explains crony capitalism:

> Hillary's single greatest accomplishment may be committing such egregious crimes and getting away with it, especially when others, who have done far less, have paid so dearly.

Audience cheers enthusiastically.

> When that same secretary of state rakes in millions and millions trading access and favors to special interests and foreign powers I know the time for action has come.

Audience cheers enthusiastically.

> I have joined the political arena so that the powerful can no longer beat up on people who cannot defend themselves

Audience cheers enthusiastically.

> Nobody knows the system better than me.

Trump gives evil supervillain sneer, as if he is condescending to the audience, after just having robbed them.

Audience is silent and confused.

He carries his condescending sneer a little bit over the top.

Audience laughs nervously.

Trump gives an asshole smirk, like he is saying "Oh what a naughty boy I am, and I got away with it."

Audience roars with laughter.

Then he gives a mock surrender, holding his hands up as if being arrested by the audience for the innumerable crimes of which we know perfectly well he is guilty.

Laughter continues for quite a while. He waits for everyone to get it. Yes, he knows how the powerful special interests abuse the system, having abused the system quite thoroughly. He knows how Hillary takes millions for access by special interests and special favors to them, having paid her millions for access and favors.

Holds up his hand to signal audience to stop laughing, and to signal he is going back from non verbal communication, to verbal communication.

> Which is why I alone can fix it.

Wild cheering with a little laughter.

## The overwhelming majority of rape accusations are false

2016-07-28 01:09:23

Follows from the poster girl principle. If poster girls suck then every other girl sucks as badly or worse. For example for example Marie Curie was a second rate scientist, therefore there are no great female scientists. Emmett Till was not lynched, nor killed for whistling at a white woman, therefore there are no examples of blacks being lynched in an obviously unjust fashion, or with reckless disregard for justice.

Earlier I posted this argument[395], but the early version neglects to mention the internal evidence from the Rolling Stone editors that they knew their rape story was unlikely

---

[395] https://blog.reaction.la/war/the-vast-majority-of-rape-accusations-are-false/

to be true, went looking for something better, could not find it.

In 2015 Rolling Stone issued an apology for their "Rape on Campus" story. Their investigating reporter saw lots of red flags, that would have convinced any reasonable person that the rape accusation was false, and that going ahead with the story was likely to blow up in their faces, but they decided to go ahead with the story anyway. Deep within the apology there is a guilty line that I missed the first time around, and everyone seemingly missed. After encountering lots of horrid red flags[396] that made it glaringly obvious that it was a really bad idea to pursue this story, that the complainant was lying through her teeth

> That summer, Erdely began interviewing multiple UVA assault survivors.

In other words, there was a whole big pile of University of Virginia "Assault Survivors", but all their stories sucked even worse than Jackie Coakley's story, so they wound up going with Jackie Coakley's story for lack of anything better. They were determined to do a rape on campus story about evil white males. They knew, consciously or subconsciously, that the story they had was false, but despite looking around, despite having lots of other "Assault Survivors", could not find anything better.

In the "Rape on Campus" story Jackie Coakley, the supposed rape victim, lied to the reporter Erdeley, and it rapidly became obvious that she was lying. Erdeley lied to her editors, and her editors lied to the readers. The editors falsely led the reader to believe that Ryan Duffin, the love interest that Jackie Coakley was catfishing with her rape story, had been interviewed, thereby making the story seem as if it had not come from a single source, that Jackie Coakley's story had supposedly been checked with the other people supposedly involved in that story. That the editors lied indicates mens rea, that they knew this was a mighty weak story and needed some creativity to make it seemingly credible.

In the original story[397] Rolling Stone tells us:

> a "shitshow" predicted by her now-former friend Randall, who, citing his loyalty to his own frat, declined to be interviewed.

Implying that they sought out witnesses and encountered the male wall of solidarity protecting rapists and penalizing rape victims. In actual fact, the editors knew full well that "Randal" (real name Ryan Duffin, the man that Jackie Coakley was catfishing in an unsuccessful campaign to get him to sleep with her) had not declined to be interviewed, because they had not attempted to interview him. Had they attempted to interview him, would have learned much that was inconsistent with Jackie Coakley's story.

The magazine knew from the beginning that Jackie Coakley's story was not credible, went looking for someone with a more credible story, decided to stick with Jackie Coakley. Therefore, rape complainants with a more credible story than Jackie Coakley are rare or nonexistent.

This is the same argument I made previously[398], but this time with internal evidence from the magazine that they knew their story was weak and went looking for something better.

---

[396] https://www.rollingstone.com/culture/features/a-rape-on-campus-what-went-wrong-20150405
[397] https://archive.is/2I04n#selection-5941.258-5941.383
[398] https://blog.reaction.la/war/the-vast-majority-of-rape-accusations-are-false/

At the time of the article, the University of Virginia had not expelled a single student for sexual assault, therefore if any of these "Assault Survivors" were credible, they would be telling pretty much the same story as Jackie Coakley. Therefore, every single one of them was even less credible than Jackie Coakley, and we can see the mens rea that the editors knew that Jackie Coakley was not credible.

Scott Alexander argues against the poster girl principle that maybe there are lots of real rapes, and the person gets convicted, so, no big deal, that the reason that fictitious campus rapes gets reported is because some people doubt their reality, therefore no prosecution, therefore controversy. So, because of controversy, we hear false rape allegations widely reported and fail to hear real rape allegations, because they get dealt with efficiently. But, until the story, no expulsions for sexual assault from the University of Virginia, and yet lots of "Sexual Assault survivors". So either the university was letting people get away with rape, or else all the "sexual assault survivors" are lying. And, since Jackie Coakley was what the Rolling Stone ultimately ran with despite knowing their story was weak and looking for something better, all the "sexual assault survivors" at Virginia were lying even more blatantly than Jackie Coakley. Rolling Stone was looking for a more credible story, looked at all the other "sexual assault survivors", did not find what it was looking for.

Rolling Stone tells us that in the previous year at Virginia University, their had been 38 complaints of sexual assault.

> of those 38, only nine resulted in "complaints"; the other 29 students evaporated. Of those nine complaints, four resulted in Sexual Misconduct Board hearings.

None of these four resulted in anyone being expelled for assault.

So, either the University is blowing off real sexual assaults, or thirty eight of thirty eight complaints of sexual assault were flagrantly bogus.

And if any of those thirty eight complaints were not flagrantly bogus, Rolling stone would surely have gone with that one instead of, or as well as, the one they did go with.

## The next big thing in progressivism

2016-07-30 03:59:08

Recently there was ass bandits. Then there was transgender.

For a while it looked liked the next big thing would be pedophobia - the "anti bullying" campaign sought to protect pre pubescent children of ambiguous sex who had physically affectionate relationships with obviously homosexual middle aged males from being "bullied" and sought to normalize pre pubescent children of ambiguous sex who have physically affectionate relationships with obviously homosexual middle aged males.

But no, it is clear that the next big thing is not pedophobia but killing white heterosexual males.

Ann Coulter reminds us[399]:

> as the country reels from the cold-blooded murder of five policemen in Dallas and three in Baton Rouge, Lezley McSpadden, mother of Mike Brown, America's most famous cop-assaulting criminal, appeared on stage at the Democratic National Convention.

---

[399]https://www.anncoulter.com/columns/2016-07-27.html

>

> ...

>

> In this regard, I notice that six of the nine "Mothers of the Movement" have different last names from their snowflakes.  The children with the same names as their mothers were the two who were gunned down by black gangs, as well as one schizophrenic, who, unfortunately, had grabbed an officer's baton and was hitting him with it when he got himself shot.

>

> ...

>

> Hillary claims to oppose cop-killing, so why is she using her convention to promote the biggest lie in the pantheon of anti-cop lies, and to celebrate a man whose most famous act was to violently assault a police officer?

## Report on moonshine

### 2016-07-30 05:03:55

About a year ago, I produced thirty liters of moonshine.
    Tasted as if distilled from dead rats and kerosine
    Double distilled it. Still tasted as if distilled from dead rats and kerosine.
    Forgot about it for a year. After a year, tried it again. Not bad at all.

## Fertility and corporal punishment

### 2016-07-31 03:30:19

[To 1933, wives in movies are never spanked by their husbands.][400]
From 1933 to 1945, wives in movies are sometimes spanked, but it is shocking, unexpected and unusual.[401]
From 1945 to 1963, wives in movies and on television are sometimes spanked and it is routine, respectable, and usual. For example in "I love Lucy" we are never shown a spanking on screen, but Lucy is regularly very afraid of receiving a well deserved spanking for her many amusing misdeeds.

In the Western "McLintock" the authority figure, representing virtue, middle class respectability, and normality, unambiguously endorses the husband beating the wife severely for gross misbehavior, with a small coal shovel.

From 1945 to 1963, appropriate and proportionate corporal punishment of wives is depicted as normal, proper, appropriate, expected, and respectable. As in McLintock, it is what respectable middle class husbands do ensure that their wives and families behave in a respectably middle class manner - since women, unless restrained, have a not at all middle class preference for drama.

---

[400] https://www.youtube.com/watch?v=vLGOzH7yROk
[401] https://www.youtube.com/watch?v=vLGOzH7yROk

This had a dramatic effect on marriage and fertility in the US, almost as spectacular as the disastrous fall in fertility that ensued when McArthur emancipated Japanese women[402]. Marriage went up, fertility went up.

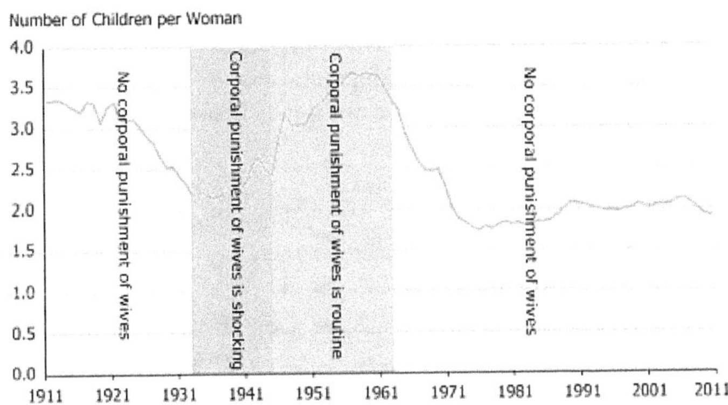


We see a significant rise in fertility when spanking starts being depicted, and massive rise in fertility when it starts being depicted as normal. When spanking stops being depicted as normal, stops being depicted at all, soon followed by a massive demonization of men who rule their families and a hate fest against them, which is to say, against marriage and husbands, as marriage was traditionally understood, fertility drops like a stone, as spectacularly as when women were emancipated in Japan.

The high high fertility period was the gap between first wave feminism (Amelia Earhart getting a ticker tape parade for being transported across the Atlantic by a man like a sack of potatoes) and second wave feminism.

During that period it once again became socially acceptable to refuse to hire women for jobs for which they are inherently unfit, and once again became socially acceptable to spank one's wife (McLintock). During that period women were once again expected to aspire to becoming wives and mothers, rather than despise that role.

Before 1933, no corporal punishment of wives depicted in Hollywood. 1933 to 1945 portrayed as shocking and unexpected, though not necessarily wrong. It is often justified in the context of the movie, but it is also depicted as the act of an outlaw - illegal but romantic.

We first see corporal discipline of one's wife (spanking) portrayed in the media as normal, legal, proper, and socially acceptable in 1945, and fertility abruptly rises, and this depiction continues to 1963. whereupon it abruptly, suddenly, and totally stops - and fertility starts falling.

As the MRAs argue, feminism has artificially raised female status above male status. When a man and a woman walk in opposite directions down the corridor, the man gives way and the woman walks right down the middle of the corridor. Women continually interrupt men with impunity. (Perhaps the reason I am not totally unsuccessful with women despite being old, fat, and bald is that I am competing with the likes of Scott Alexander.)

---

[402]https://blog.reaction.la/economics/the-future-belongs-to-those-that-show-up/

But the MRA demand, actual equality, feminism done right, is obviously absurd and unworkable, because of the obvious inferiority of women in the male sphere. (Obviously women are superior in the female sphere, such as babies, home, housework, and finding my car keys.)

Thus, for example, no one really expects women to bear the costs of their own decisions, because women really should not be making those kind of decisions unsupervised. Thus "equality" in practice means women make decisions and men pay the costs of those decisions.

So what we have to sell is the principle of patriarchy - that women should be ruled by fathers or husbands, that men really are superior, that women should give way and should not interrupt. All women should be deferential to all men, but should obey those men and only those men who are committed to care for them.

And we have to reject and dismiss consent culture. Consent does not make sex right, nor lack of consent make sex wrong. Moment to moment consent is bad for everyone, and particularly bad for women. Women lack agency in sexual matters, making "rape" ill defined. The concept maps poorly to real life situations. "Rape" used to mean dating a woman without the consent of parent or guardian, irrespective of how she felt about it, or whether you physically had sex with her. We did not really have a word or concept for what we are now calling rape until the late eighteenth century or so.

The very concept of rape and consent attributes unrealistic agency to women. As in the old testament, we should give female consent as little moral and legal weight as possible, because the word is difficult to fit to real life events.

I don't think women have agency in sexual matters, since between menarche and menopause their sexual actions are driven by volcanic forces of which they are scarcely aware. They do not want what they want, and they do want what they do not want. Nor do female children get "talked into sex". If you have good preselection from adult women, female children with no breasts who have not yet experienced menarche will sexually harass you. The problem of adult men having sex with female children is primarily a problem of badly behaved female children, not badly behaved adult men. With women who have boobs, men pursue, and women choose, for sperm is cheap and eggs are dear. Pre boobs, and pre menarche, which is to say pre eggs, the shoe is apt to be on the other foot.

Thus, for example, Scott Alexander's girlfriend consented to sex with lots of people, not including Scott Alexander, felt bad about it, felt that a gay man could do what she did without feeling bad about it or making Scott feel bad about it, so proceeded to surgically disfigure herself and declare herself to be a gay man. Clearly she would be much better off had she received a few severe spankings followed by some nonconsensual sex from Scott Alexander.

The population collapse is nothing to do with automation etc, since emancipated women in poverty stricken third world countries reproduce even less.

It simply a matter of whether or not men and women can enforceably contract with each other to durably form patriarchal families. If they can, total fertility per woman is around six or seven. If they cannot, total fertility per woman substantially less than replacement. If something in between (as for example the fifties when marriage as traditionally understood was illegal, but was nonetheless depicted on television as normal, normative, and respectable) then the fertility rate is something in between. The economy makes scarcely any difference, short of outright famine and hard Malthusian limits.

Timor Leste proves that if men have the opportunity to be patriarchs, they will not let poverty stop them. They will do whatever it takes.

Back in the fifties, when spanking was respectable, employers tended to advertise for married men, because they expected married men to be more highly motivated.

So we set up society so that prosocial behavior, reasonable competence, upholding order, and a bit of hard work pretty much guarantees a man will become a patriarch, and lo and behold, we will get prosocial behavior, order, hard work, and lots of well brought up children.

If, however you deny men the opportunity to become patriarchs, they hang out in their mother's basements and watch cartoon porn, regardless of whether their society is rich or poor.

If patriarchy is the law of the land and I have a legal path to be a patriarch but no job, I can find a job, or create one, or scrape up a living somehow. If patriarchy is outlawed and I am legally prohibited from being a patriarch, I will be receptive to the life of the outlaw, the life of the bum, the vagrant, or hanging out in my mother's basement. Jobs are not the problem. The lack of a reason to get a job is the problem.

If you look at high fertility and low fertility times and places, the factor that massively outweighs absolutely everything else by far, is whether or not a man and a woman can make a deal to form one household and have babies and expect their partner to be forced to stick to it. Patriarchy is necessary for this, since one household must have one captain, but patriarchy is in itself insufficient – the woman also needs protection that her children will neither be torn away from her, nor will she and they be abandoned by their father. The deal has to guarantee both the authority of the husband over his wife and children and the economic and emotional security of the wife and children, has to guarantee the father and husband obedience and respect, and the wife and children that they will be protected and looked after.

Reality is that wherever and whenever men have the option to be a patriarch, the overwhelming majority of men gladly make whatever sacrifice necessary to attain that role, even if extremely poor.

Hookers are only a marginal improvement over masturbation. What progressives offer men is just not what most men want, as revealed by men's actions.

Yes, a harem is better than just one wife, but a changing rotation of whores is not a harem. The point of having more than one woman is having more than one woman. If I sleep with several women that is really great. If one of them sleeps with another man that is really bad and I will certainly dump her, probably beat her, and might well kill her. I will be very angry and sad for a very long time.

Look at the typical male polyamorist. He is psychologically scarred and mentally crippled for life. Having a bunch of whores rather than owning a woman, or better, owning two women, just really sucks brutally. Those guys are traumatized and damaged.

It unmans men, as if every day a bully beat them up, and they could do nothing about the daily humiliation but suck it up. Just look at what it does to men. It would be kinder to cut their balls off, which is pretty much what progressives are planning to do to us.

The typical male polyamorist looks as if a fat blue haired feminist has been beating him up every day – indeed, he would probably love it if a fat blue haired feminist beat him up every day.

Whores are a marginal improvement on beating off to anime. When men are reduced to such desperate straights, it totally crashes their testosterone and they buy an anime cuddle pillow and weep bitter tears upon it.

The criminalization of patriarchy was the criminalization of the deepest and most powerful need of white men.

## Why Trump is Hitler

### 2016-08-02 00:10:42

You have doubtless seen lots of people arguing that Trump is Hitler. Often "Trump is *literally Hitler*!"

Of course people who read my blog know what "literally" means, and though Trump is obviously not literally Hitler, there is in fact a good argument that Trump is Hitler.

But for some strange reason, Democrats never make the argument out loud in plain words. I wonder why.

The argument, said outright in plain words, is:

Hillary's nomination speech was in large part urging black people to murder white people, and promising to use the justice department to prevent police from enforcing law on black people. If police, for some mysterious inexplicable reason, wind up arresting and killing a disproportionate number of black people - well that is disparate impact, which illegal. You don't have to prove racist motivation. Disparate impact is racist. Treating people according to the content of their character is racist regardless of motivation if the outcome is bad for non asian minorities.

This has been the law and practice for a very long time, and failure to apply this law to school discipline and law enforcement is an unprincipled exception. Unprincipled exceptions always go away sooner or later, and Hillary, truthfully or untruthfully, is promising to remove this unprincipled exception for policing and school discipline. I hope she is being untruthful, but sooner or later it will be the truth. Unprincipled exceptions are always removed sooner or later.

Hillary also promised to take away the guns of law abiding people (law abiding gun owners being almost entirely white Republicans) so that colored criminals can kill them (Criminal gun owners being mostly black Democrat voters. In other words, she promises to take away the guns of white Republicans so that black Democrats can kill them once she has appointed enough anti gun supreme court judges.

Hillary also promised to keep the borders open, and in particular open to poor suffering Muslim refugees, who are generally brown or black, male, military age, and always vote Democrat. Every few weeks we read of some outrage where black male military age Muslims murder large numbers of people, usually large numbers of white people. It is unclear how many black male military age Muslims we will get under this policy, but there are several hundred million such in the world, and they would all be much better off coming to America to live on crime, welfare, and voting Democrat. So there is a good chance that Hillary will bring in a few hundred million black male military age Muslims screaming for infidel blood and white pussy, to permanently change the electoral landscape so that whites are permanently outvoted, and we end up with a brown republican party competing with a slightly darker brown Democrat party over who will burn the most white shops, murder the most whites and rape the most white women.

Trump's nomination speech was law and order, and he proceeded do demonstrate his capacity to maintain law and order in a wide area around the convention center. Among his various law and order measures was that he was going to stop illegal immigration and Muslim immigration.

We all know that lawlessness and disorder is in very substantial part, non white criminals preying on whites, for example Kristallnacht in Ferguson, so this means Trump is the pro white candidate and Hillary is the anti white candidate.

And, of course, Hitler was the pro white candidate, therefore Trump is Hitler.

And I now raise another glass of moonshine, this time to 27. Februar 1933.

## Mean, median, and chastity enforcement.

2016-08-03 00:15:45

Men are polygynous. Women are serially monogamous. Women are hypergamous.

It follows that the mean number of sexual partners a man has will always be enormously larger than the median number of sexual partners a man has.

The mean number of sexual partners a woman has is necessarily equal to the mean number of sexual partners a man has.

It follows that the median number of sexual partners a woman has will always be larger than the median number of sexual partners a man has.

Hence the necessity in patriarchal societies of using extraordinary and disturbingly drastic means to enforce female chastity, aka double standard. Or, equivalently, eggs are precious, sperm is cheap.

## No such thing as moderate Islam

2016-08-05 03:25:03

If a Muslim is not murdering innocents and raping children, he is a bad Muslim.

"Hang on" I hear you say: "Did not you tell us that Alawites, the guys in Syria that the State Department is trying to genocide, are moderate?"

Yes, Alawites are moderate. Their religion also has more gods that you can shake a stick at, they drink wine, celebrate Christmas, and eat pork. They celebrate something suspiciously like mass with wine and bread, plus a pile of pagan deities. Since Christianity is dead in the water, maybe we should convert to Alawism, since the likely alternative is that we get converted at swordpoint to Islam, or we males get killed and our women get converted at swordpoint to Islam. But I digress. Back to moderate Islam.

The great majority of Muslims are profoundly disinclined to blow themselves up in a pizza parlor. But they create an environment were the guy who is apt to blow himself up in a pizza parlor is holier than they are, an environment where the guy who is apt to blow himself up in a pizza parlor can fade into the woodwork when the police come looking for him.

There is no moderate Islam in the sense that there is no Islam where the adherent to the faith who engages in violence against non Muslims is viewed as bad, unholy, an outsider, no Islam where Jihad is not as Islamic as motherhood and apple pie are American. There is no Islam that fails to provide a favorable environment for terror. Terror is so fundamental and intrinsic to Islam, that any supposedly Muslim religion that seriously disengages from terror really is not Muslim, and any Muslim monarchy that fails to support terror gets assailed as inauthentically Muslim, as not taking Islam seriously, and it is transparently apparent that any nominally Muslim monarchy that fails to support terror is inauthentically Muslim, does not take Islam seriously.

For thirteen hundred years, no one has managed to coexist with Islam except in a state of war and near war. We will not be the first.

We have to either convert to Islam, convert to some faith capable of holding its own against Islam, or forbid Islam and expel Muslims.

Converting to Islam is the solution we do not want, the solution that will inevitably happen if we do nothing much. Hillary plans to bring in a hundred million or so male military age Muslims screaming for infidel blood and white pussy, and even if she fails to do so, the militarized Muslim womb will outbreed us, if nothing is done. In America and Europe large numbers of fertile age white women are converting to Islam, because Muslims are the only men that can get away with being manly, and Muslims are abducting and enslaving large numbers of young fatherless welfare girls.

The Cathedral thinks it can convert Muslims in the same way it has been so successful in converting Christians, persuading them that all religions, rightly understood, are progressivism.

See also Scott Alexanders triumphalist exposition that progressivism is simply western culture, and everyone naturally converts to progressivism western culture because it so much nicer and more humane and wiser and better and truer than any of the alternatives.

In fact progressivism sucks, and men suffer terribly under it, for it is brutally contrary to human nature, and unless you actively crush Islam the way the Cathedral actively and aggressively crushed, and continues to actively aggressively crush, Christianity, it is not going to absorb Muslims. Rather we see the reverse happening. Aggressive Muslims get pussy and the girls are glad of it. The Cathedral defines Christianity as misogyny, hatred, homophobia, and so on and so forth, and crushes it with unrelenting ruthlessness, but is disinclined to do this to Islam, because islam is brown, and browns can never be racist, misogynist, or homophobic. Also because if it went after Islam the way it goes after Christianity, Muslims would start cutting the throats of progressives.

The Cathedral has had some considerable success at converting Muslims to progressivism, as for example Iran. Turkey, however, has definitively put an end to the program in Turkey.

For a long time it looked as if the Cathedral program, educate Muslims into understanding that Islam, rightly understood, was progressivism, seemed to be succeeding. And then we started to see head scarves all over the place.

As the Cathedral became ever more hostile, hateful, and destructive towards males and masculinity, coming to a supposedly right understanding of Islam became ever less popular among Muslims, and we started to see those headscarves multiply.

The Cathedral rationalized away the ever expanding sea of headscarves. For a while it was still possible to believe that the Cathedral program could succeed, the Hillary could bring in a hundred million male military age Muslims screaming for infidel blood and white pussy, they would convert to progressivism, they would buy homes in green leafy suburbs with affirmative action mortgages, pay their mortgages, and replace the missing grandchildren to pay off social security.

This delusion was punctured at Benghazi in Libya:
Hillary:
> "With all due respect, the fact is we had four dead Americans," Clinton told him angrily. "Whether it's because of a protest or whether a guy out for a walk decided to go kill some Americans, what difference at this point does it make?"

Well it would not make much difference whether because of a protest or whether a guy out for a walk. But it makes a huge difference that it was neither of these. It was a bunch of guys in military uniform, with military weapons, with chain of command, with military insignia of rank, equipped with the apparatus and institutions of a modern western state, that were, and are, applying this apparatus and these institutions to suppress progressivism and enforce Islam, in the way that Clinton and company have long been using this apparatus and these institutions to suppress Islam and enforce progressivism.

What was revealed at Benghazi, and has continued to be revealed ever since, is that the progressive program to convert Muslims to "moderate Islam" (aka progressivism) was entirely dependent on the efficient modern coercive apparatus of the modern state, and that it really is not working any more, even in the rapidly declining number of countries where progressives command the efficient modern coercive apparatus of the modern state. (Libya, and now Turkey, being among those were progressives have been removed from theocratic power.)

# Hillary's condition

## 2016-08-09 03:43:06

Hillary has been photographed being stabilized by two assistants as she climbs the stairs. This used to be Hollywood's way of depicting someone as drunk - that he needed assistance to climb stairs without falling over and falling down.

Hillary is known to have injured her head by falling down.

Hillary has seizures. Seizures are typical of repeated severe alcohol withdrawal. Diazepam is used to control seizures and to treat alcohol withdrawal, and Hillary is accompanied everywhere by a man with a Diazepam injection pen.

Hillary is frequently unavailable for lengthy periods, while Trump is always on and ever ready to speak off the top of his head.

Hillary was famously unavailable for a considerable time during the Benghazi incident.

## Common Core Explained

**2016-08-12 02:59:54**

tl;dr[403]

Problem: If you try to teach children reading, writing, and arithmetic, People of Color will underperform. Thus teaching reading, writing, and arithmetic has *disparate impact*.

Solution: Yo Stop teaching dem dat racist whitey sheeit what 'chew thinkin' man?

A child who has been educated with common core is a child who cannot do maths, cannot spell correctly, nor write grammatically. He is cut off from the past two thousand years of civilization.

## On stopping power

**2016-08-14 00:27:10**

Ellifritz studied 1800 actual gunfights.

His study produced the seemingly absurd conclusion that the handgun most effective in stopping people, in resolving a gunfight to the shooters satisfaction, was by many reasonable measures the .22, a conclusion he was profoundly reluctant to accept.

Now obviously if you do a Mythbuster type experiment, put the gun in a vice, aim it at a block of gelatine, any other handgun will do a whole lot more damage to the gelatine than a .22, and by some reasonable measures the heavier bullets were more effective - but if you want a one shot stop, .22 is head and shoulders above the rest.

So what might be different when it is man on man?

Well consider the most studied combat of recent times. Zimmerman shooting Martin. Martin was pounding Zimmerman's head onto the concrete, Zimmerman killed Martin with one shot directly through the heart. Obviously what mattered was not the gun but the man. What mattered was that Zimmerman was so well practiced he could put his bullet on target while blind and severely distracted.

Now, what is the cartridge that people practice with the most?

It is the .22 LR.

Thus the most likely explanation for Ellifritz's seemingly absurd results is that stopping power depends on practice a whole lot more than it depends on the gun or the cartridge. So you should buy the gun you are most comfortable practicing with and have the most fun practicing with.

I would interpret his results as indicating that there were a higher proportion of expert shooters wielding a .22, hence the large number of one shot stops and deadly shootings, but that .22 was significantly less effective in the hands of a inexpert shooter who relies on spray and pray.

---

[403]https://occamsrazormag.wordpress.com/2016/08/11/is-commoncore-the-ultimate-idiocracy-or-complete-anti-white-sabotage/

# Why women are sleeping with chads

## 2016-08-14 10:26:39

The problem is that dads are being emasculated and chads are not being emasculated

Men want children, children are hostages against them, the hostages make them weak, so their wives despise them and fuck a black rapper, who fucks their husband's daughters and beats their husband's sons. If we preferentially give children to the husband in the event of divorce, women will not wish to divorce - not because they don't want to lose their children, but because husbands will not behave in ways that make their wives wish to leave them.

If irresponsible and reckless women can take their husband's children away, we severely weaken every man that loves his children. If we weaken him, his wife will despise him, and will take his children away, and his daughters will be raped and his sons beaten by some black rapper

It is not that women like being beaten, though some do. What they like is that they could be beaten. To successfully raise children, needs to be a man and a woman forming one household. One household, one captain. If cannot be beaten, not really one household. So women feel insecure.

They want to be held by strong hands. If not held by strong hands, will fuck black rappers.

They want a husband who is an oak, against whom their wild storms beat in vain. Women want men who actually have power in the relationship, despite the intemperate female urge to get their way in arguments.

Emancipation was a shit test that we failed. Women demand stuff, but when they get what they demand, are more unhappy

What nearly everyone wants is a secure relationship. But men want a secure relationship, and a mistress, or two mistresses, or two secure relationships plus some fly girls. And women want a secure relationship with a male that is way more alpha than they are, the billionaire vampire of romance novels. So they shit test their husbands by making demands, which demands are tests for weakness. They want a secure relationship with a strong man, and current rules make all men weak.

Prisoner's dilemma ensues: Nobody gets what they want.

The deal that everyone would choose if they could is illegal and unenforceable, except by personal charisma and the potential of personal violence.

Women truthfully complained that the traditional deal meant that some women were apt to be severely oppressed and ill treated. But abolishing the traditional deal is not what anyone wanted. The result is that everyone gets ill treated. If a woman gets her way, she will feel insecure, and go looking for a man who denies her her way. Because if a woman gets her way, it is not really one household, one flesh, and if not really one household, difficult and dangerous to raise children in it.

The telos of sex is children. But because humans take a long time to raise children, must form a unitary bond. And so the Roman Catholic position on the natural law of sex is wrong, for the telos of sex is not children directly, but the unitary bond, the formation of one flesh, sex as an expression, the primary expression, of erotic love. Hence wife goggles. And because a ship must have one captain, because raising children requires a single household, sex is also an expression of female submission and male domination. More so for women than for men. Men fantasize about having sex with a woman, but women fantasize about submitting sexually to man's masterful domination. Hence men look at women's boobs while women shit test men. Women want to be taken, want to be commanded to submit to sex. They really hate this affirmative consent stuff.

If one household, then husband has sex whenever he feels like. If husband begs wife for permission every night, not one flesh, hence not a safe environment to raise children, hence women do not really like it. Moment to moment consent is a shit test. Women demand it, but if they get it, they really hate it.

If husbands need to ask wife's permission for sex, then wife will not like sex. Further, if consent to sex is moment to moment, then consent to marriage is moment to moment, men and women are unable to make the deal that they both want: A secure, stable, durable bond. A safe place to raise children in. They both want it and neither can get it.

The type of relationship women need is illegal, not because women didn't like it, but because they think they don't like it. They struggle against it, but that is to test the strength of the husband, not because they actually don't like it. They think they don't like it so that they will only submit to a worthy man, but under current rules, no man is worthy.

Women were not fooled on manipulated into asking for this. It is what they really asked for, and what they think they really want. It is in the nature of a woman to rebel against a man. But if she successfully rebels, she loses interest in that man. He completely ceases to exist for her. She forgets that he ever existed.

So women only see men that dominate them and push them around, they are completely blind to the current American reality where women walk over men all the time as if they were carpets. Hence the common complaint that men continually interrupt, talk over, and ignore women, when in fact it is the other way around.

If a woman interrupts you and talks over you, you do not really exist in her universe.

If a woman interrupts her husband, then in her mind she is single and has been abandoned.

If a fertile age woman interrupts her husband, she is cruising for a dick, because every single fertile age woman is cruising for a dick.

If your fertile age wife interrupts you and talks over you, you are probably being cuckolded.

## Civilization and dysgenesis

2016-08-23 06:11:56

We may reasonably suppose that the first six civilizations were founded by high IQ peoples. Their homelands are now all occupied by low IQ peoples, as for example Egypt and the Indus Valley. And any smart people currently in the vicinity of the Indus valley are descended from foreign invaders who conquered a low IQ population that had lost or was losing the capability to operate cities and irrigation.

The Maya created writing and the positional number system, and used it to accurately predict the motions of the moon and sun. Their descendents were for the most part homeless nomads, their largest city being two hundred mud huts. Their great cities were abandoned, even when they commanded key resources. The descendants of the Maya are obviously incapable of operating a great civilization, indeed, without white rule, could not even have cities, or political units larger than tiny tribes with poorly defined territories. They wound up running naked through the jungle with pointy sticks to the extent that they had any jungle.

You would think that positive eugenics is natural in a civilization. The smartest people get to the top, command and effectively utilize all the good stuff, so have more surviving children. And sometimes it does work like that.

But if the smart people are the ruling and fertile people, they will proceed to ensure that their smart children get all the top jobs. This will disturb the topmost rulers, who would like to have limitless freedom to appoint obedient people to the good jobs, regardless of ability, and more importantly, regardless of family. In particular, they would like the freedom to *not* appoint the sons of powerful rival families. If you have a bunch of fertile smart industrious men inserting their kids into the top jobs, then you wind up with aristocratic or semi aristocratic system. The Bishop is succeeded by the Bishop's son, which bothers the pope no end. The colonel is succeeded by the colonel's son, which bothers the general, which bothers the King. One drastic solution, popular in China, is to give the top jobs to eunuchs. You want a top job, have to give up your man parts. Note the striking similarity with today's political correctness, which requires metaphorical castration of males, and prefers literal castration of males.

Affirmative action for women makes a lot more sense when we recall that working women, unlike working males, do not reproduce, therefore will not be succeeded by their children. If you are a ruler, able (aristos) fertile patriarchal families are a problem, working women and eunuchs are the solution. And if the very smartest women are not all that bright, all the better, will be less capable of plotting against you. So the smartest females do not reproduce. Even if working women are substantially less productive than working men, working men are threat, working women are not a threat. Similarly any measures to prevent the affluent white male children of affluent white males from getting ahead. Such measures are rationalized in the name of social justice, but such measures give the most powerful more power.

From the point of view of the emperor, eunuchs are a better solution than working women, since eunuchs are substantially smarter than women, and have zero offspring, not merely near zero offspring.

A system of rule by the best (aristos) will, if the best are fertile, tend to become hereditary or semi hereditary. Thus patriarchy plus meritocracy will give rise to aristocracy, because affluent patriarchs have numerous sons, the meritocrats start running the system as a job placement program for their numerous sons, and the Pope will not be happy. Conversely, when the King tries to do stuff to make it less hereditary, he is apt to make the best less fertile.

One would suppose the mandarinate to be eugenic, and indeed China, unlike other civilizations, has not become a low IQ wasteland. But mandarin exam was corrupted to select for grinds rather than smarts. Any test can be gamed. The more that scoring high in the test matters, the less predictive of accomplishment it is. Thus selecting people on the accomplishments of their family and recent ancestors is apt to produce more accurate predictions than over reliance on an examination system. If the outcome of an IQ test has little direct effect on your career, it will accurately predict accomplishment. If you hand out nice jobs on the basis of an IQ test, considerably less so. If nice jobs are handed out on the basis of the test, the test is apt to become a marathon of rote memorization, which is what happened with the Chinese mandarinate exam. But for obvious reasons, emperors were unenthusiastic about handing out nice jobs on the basis of family accomplishment, for accomplished families are rivals.

Fertility in our civilization is of course massively dysgenic, because women are artificially placed in the workforce and education, with the most able women being most forcefully helicoptered into courses and jobs far beyond their ability.

As "Smart and Sexy[404]" demonstrates, our mandarinate exam (the SAT and LSAT) has been jiggered to avoid selecting too heavily for ability. If, however, our mandarinate exam was fixed as proposed in "Smart and Sexy", and if we had patriarchy, our civilization, like the Chinese, could avoid becoming a desolate wasteland of low IQ savages running through the woods with sharp sticks. And it would not be hard to make our mandarinate exam better than the traditional Chinese mandarinate exam.

The Chinese communist party currently selects on test results, on family accomplishment, and on individual accomplishment. This is likely to give substantially better results than the traditional Chinese mandarinate exam. Unfortunately they also are affirmative actioning women, probably for the same reasons we are, and this is producing significant dysgenesis in China.

## Natsocs are center left

### 2016-08-25 01:32:17

Socialism is left. If Natsocs are not socialist, need a new name.

One might argue that socialism is only left if demotic. Socialism on das Führerprinzip is the way every well run corporation works internally. But every well run corporation, as for example Apple under Steve Jobs, works by delegating everything except its core competence to the market place, and it then operates its core competence on das Führerprinzip. Steve Jobs decided what sort of glass the Iphone, and thus all smart phones, would have, but he then sourced the glass he wanted in the marketplace - where not only Iphones, but also every android phone, now uses glass made to the specifications originally issued by Steve Jobs.

The sovereign has to grant property rights to his subjects in themselves and in their stuff, or he gets overwhelmed, as depicted in every critique of socialism, I Pencil[405], Atlas

---

[404] https://www.amazon.com/gp/product/B01KLBZNZY/ref=as_li_qf_sp_asin_il_tl?ie=UTF8&tag=jims-blo0e-20&camp=1789&creative=9325&linkCode=as2&creativeASIN=B01KL-BZNZY&linkId=c37c63bf53808fbd1b4c8269863a3600

[405] https://www.amazon.com/gp/product/1572460431/

Shrugged by Rand, Ayn [406], Socialism: An Economic and Sociological Analysis[407], and The Road to Serfdom[408], and winds up being puppeteered by ministers and bureaucrats, as depicted in "Yes Minister" and "Atlas Shrugged", leading to anarcho tyranny.

The Soviet Union wound up depending on criminals, because the criminals, who like the sovereign had primary property rights established by their own violence, were alone able to be productive.

When natsocs propose Kristallnacht, they succumb to the secret stash theory of economics, that smashing up Jewish pawnshops and vodka stills will make non Jews rich. Similarly Venezuela cannot develop its gold mines because thugs from the government keep coming around expecting to find a pile of gold. Jews are a problem, but Jewish professors of social studies and the Hollywood Jews who produced "The Kingdom of Heaven" are a problem. Jewish pawnshops are not a problem. And implying that they are is pandering to the kind of short time preference people who borrow from pawnshops, who think if usury is forbidden they will be able to borrow for free, who think that if they smash up the pawnshop, they will be as well off as the people who run the pawnshop. It has been said that antisemitism is the socialism of the stupid - implying that the peopile running Venezuela are very smart when they smash up every pawnshop instead of only Jewish pawnshops.

Nah. Socialism is stupid, and it becomes less stupid when it fused with racism because the result is less socialist. Antisemitism is the socialism of the marginally less stupid. Obama's socialism, as for example Obamacare and Obamaphones, the socialism of the supposedly terribly clever people, that is stupid.

Natsocs are right about nationalism. And their socialism, socialism on das Führerprinzip, does not suck nearly as badly as demotic socialism. Notice that it murdered far fewer people than demotic socialism. Not only did the Nazis only murder a handful of Nazis, while the communists murdered enormous numbers of communists, the nazis murdered fewer communists than the communists murdered communists. If you are a communist, the sensible thing to do would have been to vote nazi, vote for people promising to kill you and against the people promising to put you in power. Commmies, such as Obama's biological parents and mentor, are enormously more evil than nazis.

# Clinton's Booby Trap

## 2016-08-26 10:53:00

Hillary wants the alt right to take over the right, to become the Republican party.

Which means that the alt right gets all the lovely beltway gravy that the Republicans are getting today - and like the Republicans, gets no power. Like the Republicans, becomes the outer party.

The Republican party then becomes the white male party *because* white males are about to permanently outvoted and rendered politically irrelevant.

---

[406]https://www.amazon.com/gp/product/B00MXCDDFW/
[407]https://www.amazon.com/gp/product/0913966630/
[408]https://www.amazon.com/gp/product/0226320553/

It is an improvement on the current plan of the Republican leadership, which is that elections from 2020 out consist of the Republicans saying "White males are hateful, evil and deserve to suffer", and the Democrats saying "White males are really horribly hateful and evil and we are going to make them suffer even worse". And the beltway gravy will be nice.

But remember. Demotic politics is never where the power is, it is just theater to manufacture legitimacy for rulers, never a source of power. It can, however, be a source of beltway gravy, which is not nothing.

The booby trap is that we will rationalize pursuit of the lovely beltway gravy by coming to believe, or at least pretend to believe, that demotic politics is where power comes from. The alt-right taking over the Republican party is not the booby trap. The alt right being exposed to the same incentives as the Republican party is the booby trap.

## Democracy explained

2016-08-31 22:19:07

For something over two hundred years, the anglosphere has moved ever leftwards, ever faster.

Ever leftwards policies are baked in to a holiness signaling spiral, and the government elects a new people to vote for these policies that are already baked in.

They are not going to change their policies because of the votes of two hundred million black Muslim military age males screaming for infidel blood and white pussy. Rather they need the votes of two hundred million black Muslim military age males screaming for infidel blood and white pussy because they are already changing their policies and intend and expect to very rapidly change them a whole lot more.

I would have thought that everyone reading my blog knows this, but recently one of my commenters needed to have this explained to him.

## A white woman's chance of getting married

2016-09-04 07:34:43

tl;dr If you are white woman who is thirty or over, and not already married or in a relationship resembling marriage, your chances are slim. You are washed up, you are left on the shelf, you are past your sell by date.

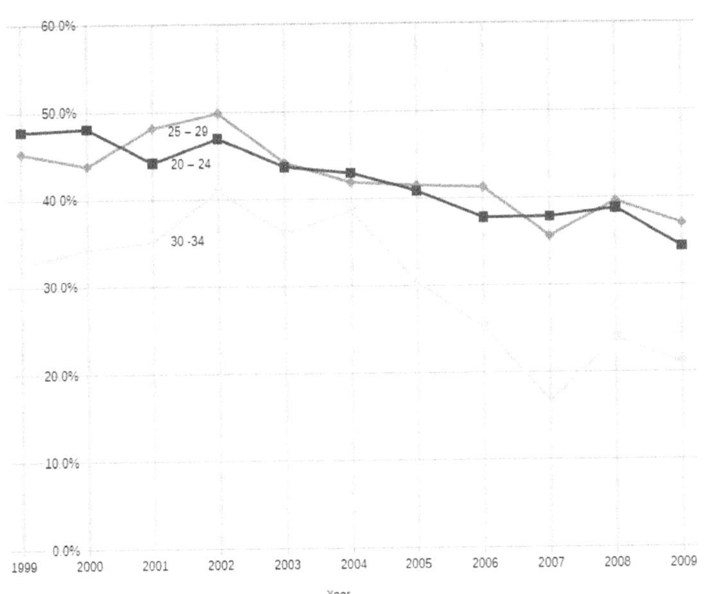
Chance of never married woman getting married in the next five years
60.0%
50.0%
25 – 29
20 – 24
40.0%
30 -34
30.0%
20.0%
10.0%
0.0%
1999 2000 2001 2002 2003 2004 2005 2006 2007 2008 2009
Year

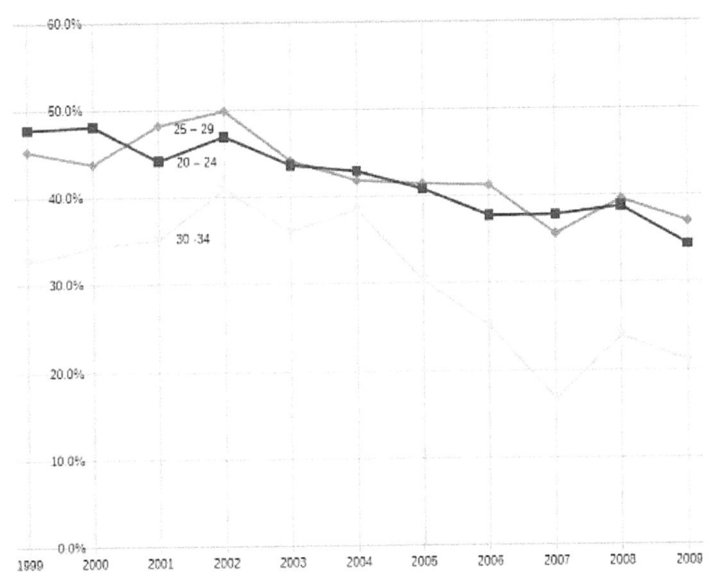
Chance of never married woman getting married in the next five years
60.0%
50.0%
25 – 29
20 – 24
40.0%
30 -34
30.0%
20.0%
10.0%
0.0%
1999 2000 2001 2002 2003 2004 2005 2006 2007 2008 2009
Year

This is my analysis of Dalrock's data[409].

If white men had their way, and women did not have their way, most women would get married between fourteen and seventeen, and men would get married as soon as they could afford to support a wife and children. We know that is what would happen, because when white men had all the power, when men got their way, that is what did happen, for women of the affluent class.

If women had their way, and men did not have their way, women would spend thirty years from age ten to age forty sexing a long succession of wealthy charismatic socially skilled alpha males with big tools, then get married and have children using IVF and their eggs that they froze in their late twenties. We know that because there is a pile of highly emancipated women with highly successful careers in front of the fertility clinic, only without the husbands.

If you are a woman approaching thirty, and you are nagging your husband, bitching at him, interrupting him, speaking disrespectfully of him, or refusing him sex: Repent now.

There is a lot of divorce porn around in which a not very attractive woman ditches her boring unexciting husband, and then lands a six foot eight inch tall highly athletic billionaire. File that with ones where she marries an immortal vampire or gets abducted by pirates, sold into the Sultan's harem, and becomes the Sultan's favorite. The author of "Eat Pray Love" attempted to carry out her novel in real life. Wound up marrying a man in need of a green card, much older and poorer than her ex, who dumped her shortly after his green card came through. And if you are a woman approaching thirty that is what will happen to you if you don't let your husband get a word in sideways. He probably will not leave you, but if you don't treat him respect, you will wind up making the extremely bad decision of leaving him. Much as so often sex "just happened" even though you were not really planning on it and it was a really bad idea, divorce also "just happens". Women inherently lack agency, and really bad decisions just keep "just happening".

Let us reflect on what happened to the notorious reality television shrew Kate Gosselin. She harassed, humiliated, and scolded her husband day and night on reality television, while he cared for their eight children and held down a job, then she frivolously divorced him, excluded him from his children's lives, demonized him to his children, and obsessively brings lawsuits against him for all manner of silly things, making it impossible for him to own any property or accumulate any assets, and destroying her own assets in high and frivolous legal costs. Now she is permasingle while he has a girlfriend ten years younger than himself and his ex wife. The opposite of love is not hate, but indifference. You can tell that Jon Gosselin no longer loves Kate Gosselin, but Kate Gosselin is still very much in love with Jon Gosselin, for Kate hates Jon to the point of madness. If a woman divorces at age thirty or close to it, she is apt to wind up like Kate Gosselin, while Jon Gosselin winds up with stalkers.

Men in their forties, fifties, and sixties routinely marry women much younger than themselves. Women in their thirties usually don't marry men their own age, or indeed men of any age. Men past thirty usually will not marry women near their own age. They usually marry considerably younger women, or just do not get married at all.

---

[409]https://www.goingyourownway.com/mgtow-lounge/dalrock-2014-married-data-4643/

I am a recent widower. I loved and cared for my wife all her days, even though during our last years she was terribly ill. And various women near my wife's age, women in their sixties and late fifies, think to themselves "He loved his wife. Why should he not love me?"

Well it does not work like that. When a man loves a woman, he loves a young cute woman, and if she does not screw up, he gets wife goggles, and loves her all her days. But a man is just not going come to love an elderly woman. That is just how we are made. Which means that when a girl past twenty five or so switches lovers, every time she switches, she will discover her marriage market value has fallen, fallen significantly and substantially. And at age thirty, she still has substantial sexual market value, as a booty call girl, or a friend with benefits, but her marriage market value is likely to be zero. Hence, when a woman is pushing thirty, probably not a good idea for her to act like the kind of girl who is going to divorce her husband, even if she still has lots of booty calls from rich charismatic men with big swinging tools, since such actions are apt to take on a life of their own.

Very few men are going to marry a women in her forties, even if the alternative is porn, whiskey and whores, but thirties is negotiable. It is a market price. How young a woman can a man get, so that he can ignore all the women older than that, how old can a woman dance on the cock carousel before she is left on the shelf and beyond her sell by date? If all women panic at age x, a sensible man will insist on a woman a little bit younger than x. The alternative for him is not porn, whiskey, and whores. So a man should figure out the age at which all women panic, and marry a woman younger than that, a woman should figure out the age at which all women panic, and panic just before the rest of them.

Analyzing Dalrock's data looks to me like not so much a marriage strike by men, but the age at which women should panic, and men can afford to ignore them because they can get someone younger, has been falling. It was probable that before 2001, a woman was past her sell-by date at thirty two or so. Then in 2007, past her sell by date at thirty or so. Not a huge change in the age of panic, but the panic has been driven by a huge change in the number of women permanently left on the shelf. Before 2001 the rise in the number of unmarried people was driven by a continual rise in the age at which women got married, driven by women choosing to marry later and later, a deal becoming ever more favorable for women, as they spent more and more years cavorting on the cock carousel from ten to forty, and ever less favorable for men, as their wives brought ever less youth, beauty, and chastity to the deal. Now the deal is turning to be slightly less unfavorable for men, which means that the continuing rise in the number of unmarried people is a rise in the number of people who are never going to get married, ever.

Since the number of never-will-be-married people continues to increase, the age at which women should panic, the last minute at which men get picky and women get desperate, will continue to decrease, probably going to go all the way down to twenty five or so.

## Hillary's illness

### 2016-09-06 01:28:45

The most notable symptom of her illness is the need for frequent and lengthy "naps", often at inconvenient times that play hell with her schedule. This sounds like alcoholism, since Parkinsons is bad all the time, while getting drunk comes and goes.

Both alcoholism and Parkinsons can cause coughing fits, but by and large, when you get coughing fits in Parkinsons you are pretty far gone and cannot pass for normal even superficially, whereas alcoholics with coughing fits pass for normal except that they get drunk at times that are socially inappropriate or inconvenient for their careers.

Alcoholic coughing fits tend to be associated taking high proof shots. If you get drunk on wine, no problem, or at least no coughing problem.

During her most recent coughing fit she was stressing her throat by shouting into a microphone. Getting coughing fits while shouting is not all that odd. If I took a few too many shots of high proof moonshine and then started shouting I would probably cough also, not really a sign of anything seriously wrong, (though the fact that she could not stop coughing but had to be hustled away is a sign of something seriously wrong) but why shout? Just hold the microphone a little closer, or do as everyone does while singing or videoconferencing, have a headset that holds the microphone just beside your lips.

That she was shouting into the microphone suggests she was having speech difficulties, which she disguised by shouting. If she was not shouting, would probably be slurring her words drunkenly.

Shouting worsens the common perception of her, that she is an angry nagging scold, a social justice warrior, the wicked witch of the west wing. Women should not shout, and men should shout infrequently.

## There will be war

### 2016-09-08 06:48:46

Politics is about who whom. Politics is tribalism and sectarianism. The question is simple. Who's side are these guys on? What tribe to they favor grabbing all the loot, and what tribe to they plan to destroy? Ferguson burning is real politics, not ethanol subsidies. Milwaukee burning is real politics. The violence that followed Trump's cancelled Chicago rally is real politics. Politics is the destruction of your enemies, the burning of their homes, the seizure of their women.

Politics is to defeat your enemies, to drive them before you, to take from them all they possess, to see those they love in tears. If you are not ethnically cleansing Ferguson, and Milwaukee or resisting the ethnic cleansing of Ferguson and Milwaukee, it is not politics. If you are not dumping weeping anchor babies over the border, it is not politics.

And if the other side is engaged in politics, and you are not engaged in politics, you lose.

Rotherham was the women of one voter group being forcibly emancipated, and then forcibly unemancipated to the benefit of another voter group. Similar operations are taking place conspicuously and spectacularly in Sweden and Germany. That is politics.

Politics is not abortion. Politics is who gets control of women's sexual and reproductive services. Emancipation is not natural for women, and if one group's women are emancipated, they will be taken by another group, and will be mighty glad of it.

Politics is ethnic cleansing and seizing the women of your enemies, politics is about land and women, and it has been about land and women ever since the wealthy and successful were driven out of the American inner city and lost their inner city properties.

If you are not destroying your enemies and securing land and women for your supporters, you are not engaged in politics. The left is engaged in politics, mainstream conservatives are not.

For a conservative party to exist, it must unite to protect those that commit sacrilege against PC, in the same way it now unites to destroy them. This requires them to reward their friends and punish their enemies, in the same way that they now reward their enemies and punish their friends.

For democracy to exist without massacre, pogroms, arson, and ethnic cleansing, requires very high levels of social cohesion and trust that we no longer possess, and that our government has been systematically destroying. Diversity plus proximity means war. If white males start nakedly pursuing their own interests the way that every other interest group does, it is going to be war. If they don't, genocide.

War is easy, peace is hard. Governments everywhere have forgotten how easy war is, how difficult peace is, and gleefully throw jet fuel on the fire. The natural state of mankind is war. Peace requires a high level of trust, cooperation, and well functioning social technology, all of which are being enthusiastically dismantled. Peace is an elaborate machine with many moving parts, all of which have to work together correctly.

The anglosphere has been internally peaceful since the Mormon War and the War of Northern Aggression, so we think internal peace is natural. This, however, is survivorship bias. The anglosphere rules the world because of long internal peace. But peace is not natural. Peace is hard. Ever since the wealthy and successful were driven out of the inner cities, we have been on a trajectory to where politics gets serious.

## On the day of the rope

### 2016-09-11 08:46:11

On the alt right, a lot of people correctly observe that certain groups are all enemies, and conclude we have to hang them all, or give them all helicopter rides to the Pacific.

That is a lot of helicopter rides.

Does not follow. A lot of these people are Havel's Greengrocer, and will chant the new slogans as mindlessly as they chant the old, without even noticing that the slogans have changed.

In the English restoration, people in politically sensitive jobs - preachers, university professors, etc, were invited to reapply for jobs similar to the jobs that they had before the restoration, at similar pay, but these offers were conditional on "conformity". So in the job interview, one had to display the same enthusiasm for the new political correctness as for the old, and most announced that they had always believed what they now believed in the post restoration job interview, despite the fact that in their pre restoration job they had had to enthusiastically display the opposite beliefs.

Seems to me that the English restoration was a huge success. It eventually, after a long time, came apart, as all things come apart, but this was not due to any failure in the early purges. It was failure to continue the early purges. They stopped monitoring people in politically sensitive jobs for apostasy.

William Wilberforce should have been enslaved for apostacy and sold to cut sugar cane in the Caribbean, and if that had been done to him and the entire Clapham church, all of them that were in politically sensitive jobs, the British Empire would still be doing fine.

The dangerous ones are not Havel's Greengrocer. The dangerous ones are the ones who sincerely and strongly believe one thing, and conspire with other people believing that thing, while pro forma saying they believe a different thing - entryists. You need an organization to watch for entryists in governmental and quasi governmental jobs (banking, universities, foundations, ngos, and major media), an inquisition, which takes stern measures against them, but you don't want to put Havel's Greengrocer through the inquisition.

The policy of the Spanish Inquisition was that if people said they believed what they were supposed to believe, and superficially acted as if they believed it, they were fine. The Spanish inquisition did not torture people till they confessed. It tortured people till they stopped confessing. If someone was obviously practicing and advocating different religion, while claiming to adhere to the official religion, they would make him confess his "error", confess that he was supposedly a sincere adherent of the official religion who had supposedly mistaken and misunderstood the beliefs and practices of the official religion, and give him a moderate punishment for his "error", the purpose and the effect being primarily to make apostasy low status and economically unrewarding. Unrepentant heretics, people who boldly claimed to be holier than the inquisition, they burned at the stake, but when you were in the hands of the Spanish Inquisition, it was mighty hard to stay unrepentant. They knew that actually burning a heretic was a big win for heresy, so sought to avoid it as far as possible.

The Inquisition depicted in Warhammer 40 000 is very popular on the alt right, but the fictional Warhammer 40 000 Inquisition, unlike the Spanish Inquisition, is apt to arbitrarily torture and execute heretics without due process. We need to be very careful to torture and execute the correct people. No torturing Havel's Greengrocer (even if he is Jewish)! Even if we don't care about groceries, still a win for heretics.

## How to remove eleven million illegals.

2016-09-11 11:47:40

Trump has promised to triple the number of ICE deportation officers, the people whose job it is to remove illegal aliens already in America, the ones that made it past the border regions.

Since public servants can never be fired, the ICE deportation officers (ERO) are still there, and are still theoretically deportation officers, but their status has been systematically lowered, and these days they push paperwork in circles rather than actually deporting anyone.

If you catch someone near the border, you can deport them pretty easily, but the huge problem with ERO is that in order to deport anyone, they have to go before a judge, and judges are extremely reluctant to deport anyone. There is an unending due process legal labyrinth in which illegals, even criminals, even murderers, circulate forever. If Trump empowers ERO officers, judges will continue to disempower them. Trump not only needs to triple the number of ICE deportation officers, he needs to empower them.

The Australian solution to this problem was to just deport illegals and completely exclude judges from the process altogether. In Australia an "unlawful person" (Aussie for illegal immigrant) is just administratively sent to Villawood Detention center. From there, they can get a ticket home. Or if they cannot get a ticket home, they are sent to an "Offshore processing center". (Australia's equivalent of Gitmo.) This tends to highly motivate them to get a ticket home. Some, who it seems were insufficiently motivated, have just been dumped by the Australian navy on some foreign country's beach between the high tide and low tide mark.

In Australia, whenever someone in authority encounters an "unlawful person" inside Australia, for example at a police stop or a hospital visit, they are supposed to rat them to border control, and they generally do rat them to border control. And from border control, to Villawood Detention center. Trump has to make sure that police stops, hospital visits, welfare applications, and so on and so forth, rat illegal immigrants to ERO, and that ERO has a nice convenient prison in which they can throw people and leave them to rot without pesky judges bothering them. If all ERO can do is take them before a judge, the judge will let them loose, even murderers and rapists. An unlawful person is likely to become a whole lot more cooperative if his only way out of his oubliette is to go home.

Let us call the wall, "The Great Wall of Trump", and the prison, "The Trump Archipelago".

## The puritan hypothesis in short

### 2016-09-13 00:56:35

New world order university forum has issued a post criticizing the puritan hypothesis[410]

Their counter theory is that leftism is an efficient, centralized, and competently run conspiracy of evil people who for entirely rational reasons want to rule the world, and that leftism is composed of coherent, well defined, and unchanging beliefs.

Well if that was the case, we are toast. But I am pretty sure it is not the case.

Observing leftism in action, it is all holiness spirals. Social Justice Warriors continually out left each other and form circular firing squads. Every few years they find something new to be holy about. There is no consistent and unchanging core of leftism. One day they love the proletariat the next they hate the rednecks. One day they love the peasants, the next they liquidate the kulaks. The only consistent things in anglosphere leftism have been war on marriage and war on Christmas, but other outbreaks of leftism have not had those elements.

---

[410]https://newworldorderuniversity.com/?p=8271

Leftism is a thousand points of doctrine, but new points continually get added, and old points reinterpreted, or altogether dropped. Remember when Obama and Clinton opposed Gay Marriage? Well you may remember, but somehow very few other people do.

The Bolsheviks were a largely an evil Jewish conspiracy - except that the Jews in question were largely self hating Jews, who proceeded to enthusiastically purge each other until Hitler was able to congratulate the Soviets on having achieved a Judenfrei ruling elite. The Khmer Rouge were foreign educated intellectuals, who proceeded to murder all the foreign educated intellectuals, then all the intellectuals, then murder most Khmer Rouge members who could count.

When I read up the writings of the proto puritans, the members of the Church of England who were industriously being ever holier - well at first it was conventional Christian holiness. Very sincere people being very holy. Suspiciously holy. Then, by the time the Puritans set off for America, it was conventional Christian holiness that had turned distinctly pharisaical[411]. And then by the later Cromwell years, the most holy were pushing standard twentieth century leftism, which so alarmed Cromwell that he cracked down.

Communism is not directly puritan descended, though Marx was influenced by the leftists suppressed by Cromwell, and proceeded to do to Judaism what they had done to Christianity. Marxist Dialectics is Talmudism transmogrified into left wing politics, and Dialectical Materialism is God's plan for the Jewish people transmogrified into History's plan for the Vanguard of Proletariat. Obviously today's progressivism is massively influenced by Jews, Communism, and through communism, influenced by Judaism, particularly the recycling and global warming movement. But Anglosphere leftism are the winners, and anglosphere leftism has organizational continuity going back all the way to the proto Puritan Brownists mentioned by Shakespeare. Harvard was the state Church of New England. Harvard conquered America, and then the world. This is an accident of history; there were several other strains of leftism that could have conquered the world. But they did not. And here we are. If you look at the desegregation of the Boston school system, which is where desegregation and affirmative action started biting Northerners, not a Jew in sight.

Communism never had organizational continuity with any Jewish synagogue, whereas leftism does have organizational and institutional continuity with Puritan religious institutions, in particular Harvard, a religious seminary and the central authority of the New England State Church.

If the world was currently ruled by the Soviet Union, then Jew hypothesis would be largely true. But it is ruled by the US state department, which wants Israel destroyed, so the Jew hypothesis is largely false, and the Puritan hypothesis is true. There are a lot of Jews in today's progressivism, but they are all conversos. They are intermarrying, and if they have any children, which they seldom do, their children seldom identify as Jewish. If any Jew in Harvard started to wear conspicuously Jewish Orthodox gear, the way the Happy Merchant in the Happy Merchant meme does, the Social Justice Inquisition would be on to him in a flash and he would lose tenure. George Soros wants whites in Europe genocided, but he wants Jews in Israel genocided even more, even sooner.

---

[411] https://blog.reaction.la/culture/puritanism-and-purity/

## Yes, Trump legally can fire the bastards

2016-09-14 23:02:00

We all know that Trump loves firing people who are no damned good, and that giving effect to his program requires firing a whole bunch of civil servants.

From time to time the pious say that this shows that Trump has no understanding of how government works. The president cannot fire people.

Someone who may not be named drew my attention to Myers v. United States[412] a much ignored but never overruled Supreme Court decision that the president can fire any federal government employee he damn well pleases for any reason or no reason at all, and that any law restricting his power to do so is unconstitutional.

Actually firing people is still going to resemble a military self coup, but at least this makes the self coup clearly legitimate, a restoration of presidential authority that has been unlawfully and unconstitutionally usurped by the president's overly numerous and overly powerful servants.

Actually firing people is likely to result in Trump becoming God Emperor after the style of Augustus or King by the Grace of God after the style of King George the third, because the powers his dangerously powerful servants have usurped from the people and the states then fall into his hands, but at least this Supreme Court decision gives firing people the plausible appearance of a constitutional restoration of the Old Republic, making the loyalty and obedience of the military easier to maintain during the purge.

## Hitting your woman with a stick

2016-09-17 22:11:51

No woman in love ever wanted to hear her lover say "Honey, you can hang out at my place as long as you feel like it"

What she wants to hear is "I will keep you forever, and never ever let you go."

Men want to have sex with women. Women want to submit to a man's urgent and powerful sexual demands. Sex for women is just not very interesting unless it is an act of submission and obedience.

Moment to moment consent to marriage and moment to moment consent to sex just is not what women want, as every man who has seduced a woman knows. (Some of my progressive commenters claim to married etc, but I really find this hard to believe. Maybe they are married in the sense that they get to sleep on the couch in the garage and are graciously allowed change the sheets on the main bed after their wife fucks her lover, who visits at infrequent intervals, beats her up, beats her kids up, fucks her, drinks all the booze in the fridge, and takes the housekeeping money.)

What women want corresponds to what, in the ancestral environment, was a safe place to raise children, and that was a household where she was firmly and securely in the hand of a strong master. Or, as the Old Testament tells us: "thy desire shall be to thy husband, and he shall rule over thee."

---

[412]https://en.wikipedia.org/wiki/Myers_v._United_States

Equality requires fences between equals. To raise children together, must be one household, one flesh, and one household can have only one captain. If two captains, no safe place for children. If your household has two captains, your wife will abandon that household.

The vast majority of white converts to traditional Islam are hot fertile age single women. Very few converts from Islam to Christianity, almost none, are fertile age women. Traditional Islam gives women what fertile age women really want. Progressivism gives them what they foolishly ask for and gives it to them good and hard.

Because of hypergamy, a woman will always test you, always rebel. But she does not rebel because she wants to win, instead she wants to be overpowered, she wants to be dominated, she wants to lose. Because of hypergamy, there is no rest for men, no love that is secure and unconditional. We always have to perform, we are always on stage, even though the role we usually have to perform is one of relaxed and confident mastery. We read of emperors with ten thousand concubines, who could have any concubine tortured or executed for any reason or no reason at all, and yet *still* they had woman troubles. But women don't want to know this and are not going to give you any sympathy for it. The show must go on! Women have to paint their faces, and men have to be brave and manly, so stop whining.

Women need discipline, supervision, authority, and punishment, and when they do not get it they become distressed, tense, disturbed, and act out disruptive and destructive misbehavior to force those around them to take charge. They start fantasying about men who will take charge of them, fantasying about men who are not the men who are letting them run wild.

Because a woman will always test you, and this testing will always irritate and upset you and likely piss you off, it will often happen that she feels, rightly or wrongly, that her testing has damaged the relationship, whereupon she will likely beg for physical punishment, corporal punishment, to expiate her wrongdoing. Or, if actually ditched, cut herself since you are no longer around to do it for her.

Which brings me to the subject of this post. When should you hit your woman with a stick?

Well firstly, Mohammed, not well known as a blue haired feminist, said that if at all possible you should avoid physically punishing your women. Petruchio, Shakespeare's parody of a manly man, pick up artist, and natural, found other ways to punish Kate. So in general, most of the time, you should not physically punish women. If other measures can work. But this kind of assumes you are in charge and she is tolerably well behaved, assumes that other measures can work.

Obviously, if it is not broke, don't fix it. You don't hit a woman who is always sexually available to you, generally obeys your orders, and runs the household in general accordance with your will, even if she sometimes tries your patience with minor shit tests like backseat driving. I never hit my wife. On the other hand, I am pretty scary guy. That I potentially might have hit my wife if she had been badly behaved might well have had something to do with her good behavior. Or maybe she was just naturally a good woman. Unfortunately good women are rare as rubies. I have needed to hit other women quite often.

Obviously you should never punch a woman in the face. Female faces are quite fragile, you can easily kill them with a punch in the face. A light slap in the face is, however fine. That is a *light* slap. For heavier slaps, obviously you should smack them on the backside, which can take a very heavy slap with no risk of injury.

The best place for a moderate blow with a stick is probably the palm of the hand. For heavier whacks with a stick, backside, upper back and thighs. Hitting them in the lower back can kill them, women are very fragile and need to be punished with care and love.

A light slap in the face, followed by cold stare works great, though it is more in the stare than the slap. Recently I had a dispute with my girlfriend resulting from her denying me sex. I struck her with a stick on the palm of hand twice, after the style of the punishment of Amy[413] in "Little Women". Worked great, and inspired this post.

Obviously any behavior that is good reason for hitting your woman with a stick is good reason for dumping her. And in our society that is legally loaded against men, the sensible thing to do, the safe thing to do, the easy thing to do, the sane and obvious thing to do, is to dump her rather than beat her.

But in fact every woman prefers a man who would beat her for misbehavior to a man who would dump her for misbehavior, and every woman prefers both the man who would beat her and the man who would dump her, to the nice guy who politely endures her misbehavior. The laws are set up to empower woman, but revealed preference is that they wind up sleeping with men who disempower them, which revealed preference makes total sense in that the telos of sex is not so much reproduction directly as the creation of an environment suitable for raising children, which requires women to be disempowered. If fucking does not disempower her, she does not really like it.

An environment of no fault divorce results in a hell of a lot of stupid divorces in which everyone gets hurt, everyone loses. And at best, or rather the least bad, one partner benefits a little, and the children and the other partner suffer enormously. Which least bad outcome is readily observed to be mighty uncommon, compared to the usual outcome where everyone loses. But if husbands are socially and legally discouraged from beating their wives, you really have to have no fault divorce. What woman want, what everyone wants, is an environment suitable for raising children. Which no fault divorce fails to provide. And if divorce only for fault, then it needs to be socially and legally acceptable for husbands to beat their wives with a stick in moderate and proportionate punishment for misbehavior.

## Nitrocellulose illegalized

### 2016-09-22 05:06:25

The government has defined nitrocellulose, a deflagrating explosive, as a high explosive.

This makes anyone who creates ammunition subject to rules that are impossible to comply with. Fortunately the government has also issued an unprincipled exception, telling people not to worry about it. Just go on handling nitrocellulose as the deflagrating explosive that it actually is, and, wink, nod, we will not prosecute you.

---

[413]https://www.youtube.com/watch?v=ejNRBp82_hw

But slowly, over time, unprincipled exceptions always go away. This is a back door criminalization of private ownership of guns. A few years down the line, they will start enforcing this, and say, "Oh, we are just enforcing laws that have been on the books for a long time, but widely ignored." And private gun owners will find it strangely hard to legally buy ammunition. "Hey, the state has not banned your guns, nor your ammo, just banned anyone who makes ammo for your guns. And this law has been on the books since forever. They are still allowed to make it, but they have to make it safely - except that no one can figure out how to make it safely."

Of course people who make ammunition for law enforcement and the military will get a continuing unprincipled exception, but people who make ammunition for private customers will not.

Then again, the way they are cutting the balls off our police and military, I would not have a lot of confidence that the military will continue to get ammo either. They banned mines and cluster bombs by a similar back door law: Our government passed laws against our military that could never be complied with, issued an unprincipled exception that allowed mines and cluster bombs, then the unprincipled exception somehow slowly faded away. Meanwhile the Soviets continue to use cluster bombs with devastating effect.

I cannot see any sane reason for banning cluster bombs other than that in the many proxy wars where the Red Empire of the Bases backs one side, and the Blue Empire of the Consulates backs the other side, cluster bombs were blowing the hell out of the State Department's proxies.

## Yes, women vote for rape, conquest, and enslavement

## 2016-09-25 01:30:35

Some of my supposedly red pilled commenters doubt my account of the nature of women.

So, I am going to steal shamelessly from the great and wonderful Heartiste, Minion of Satan.[414]

> Bleeding heart (and bleeding bush) Frenchwomen are lining up to fuck the rapefugee dregs of humanity....in a romantic setting that looks like this:

---

[414]https://heartiste.wordpress.com/2016/09/22/men-invade-women-invite-into-their-vaginas/

Contrast: There are White beta males at this very moment paying for dinners and nights out in glittering cities to impress unenthusiastic dates, while women make pilgrimages to the Calais Sex Camp to volunteer as eager holsters for penniless, smelly migrant meatsticks. The Crimson Pills don't get harder to swallow than that.

When we voted to emancipate them, we failed their shit test.

"Hey", I hear you saying: "How come they vote for emancipation *and* conquest, both? Aren't you being inconsistent Jim. You cannot have it both ways. Why are they shit testing us harder than they shit test the rapeugees?"

Because we are weak and guilty about it, and the rapeugees are bold and aggressive about it. You need to tell girls to make a sandwich and take their pants off. And when they are difficult, you need to hit them, hit them in a properly careful and loving way of course.

## Aleppo

### 2016-09-28 21:39:42

Rebel held Aleppo is currently entirely surrounded, and is about fourteen kilometers by four kilometers, meaning every inch of it is within mortar range of Assad's troops. It will fall shortly unless there is a rescue mission from outside to relieve the siege. There have been rescue missions before, each of which ever more blatantly involves some new foreign power directly intervening in Syria ever more directly against the legitimate Syrian government. There may well be rescue missions again, but right now Aleppo is falling.

There is nothing wrong with Assad by middle eastern standards. In Assad controlled regions people of all religions and ethnicities are free to go about their business, whereas all the rebels except the Kurds want to kill or exile every religion and every ethnicity different from their own. (The Kurds just want to partition the Kurdish regions off into Kurdistan)

The problem with Assad is that during Arab Spring, the US, aka "the international community" capriciously and whimsically decided he should fall, and he did not fall, which is a slap in the face to "the international community".

If regimes deemed problematic by "the international community" always fall, then it is a self fulfilling prophecy. If people believe a regime will fall, it will fall. So if Assad does not fall, then other regimes could potentially get away with being deemed problematic by "the international community". This is Russia's objective - to deny "the international community" the power and authority to overthrow any regime that displeases it. Russia does not really give a damn about Syria in particular. While "the international community" weeps sad salty tears telling us what a horrid person Assad is for fighting back against people who want to kill him, kill every member of his family, and kill every member of his race and religion, and tells us that because of this horrid crime, it is utterly unacceptable that Assad continues to rule, Russia tells us they want to set a precedent, and Syria just happens to be the place to set it. The precedent that Russia wants to set is that legitimate regimes should not be overthrown by external forces.

And in fact, since Syria became a problem, the "international community" has quietly stopped deeming regimes problematic. Which is likely to lead to more and more regimes becoming problematic. That Assad remains has already led to a domino effect, and should Aleppo fall and "international community" give up, there will be a lot bigger domino effect.

If Aleppo falls, then Assad controls all the significant urban areas of Syria, in which case it is kind of obvious that "the international community" has been defeated and should just give up. It could escalate the war by putting US soldiers on the ground, but this would undermine the pretense that the "the international community" is just the spontaneous outrage of all right thinking people, and make it look too much like the US empire. Also putting US soldiers on the ground would be war with Russia.

Of course everyone except "the international community" knows that "the international community" is just the US empire, but the US empire does not want to know it.

Whereas Islam can coexist with Christianity by making Christians second class citizens, Liberalism cannot coexist with Christianity. Christians must cheer at gay weddings, demonize fathers, and enthusiastically celebrate single mums. The existence of Christianity anywhere in the world is an intolerable threat and insult to liberalism. In Russia, the Russian orthodox are allowed to be Russian orthodox, which generates ever increasing outrage and aggressive war talk among liberals. We are moving towards internal civil war, or external nuclear war, and it is hard to say which will come first, though I expect civil war.

## Bunker busters said to be war crime

2016-09-29 06:29:16

As you know "the international community" is denouncing Russia's use of bunker buster bombs as a war crime.

There is a rebel video on you tube examining the hole made by a bunker buster. Looks like the bomb blast went through two meters of concrete to blow up inside a bunker.[415]

Somehow I doubt that you will find all that many civilians under two meters of concrete inside a bunker. But I rather suspect you might find a few members of "the international community" in there.

Looks to me that Putin is using bunker buster bombs to bust bunkers.

## Women prefer men with the stones to rape them

### 2016-10-01 23:12:41

Left wing activist hot heterosexual chick with no apparent boyfriend works as refugee aid activist. Predictably gets robbed and gang raped. Predictably continues to work as refugee aid activist and blames German racism.[416]

Why, you may ask, does a hot chick have no boyfriend? Well in my experience it is extremely common for way hot chicks to have no boyfriend because they are on booty calls to guys who are, by the rather strange and hard to understand female measurement of status, higher status than they are.

This post is intended to hint she was quite likely cruising for a gang bang, and quite likely still cruising for another. Of course I have absolutely no direct evidence that she was cruising for a gang bang. For all I know she might have been a pure minded virgin with unfortunate naive misconceptions about refugee behavior.

But I do have direct evidence from personal experience that cruising for a gang bang from males that are low status in the ostensible male hierarchy is alarmingly common behavior among hot chicks, and of course all us with any significant contact with women know from direct personal experience that most women are unimpressed by the ostensible male hierarchy.

Indeed one of the primary functions of patriarchy is to overrule female choice so that pussy goes to males who are high status in the ostensible male hierarchy, rather than high status in the disturbing and hard to fathom way that women perceive status - so that pussy goes to high IQ prosocial, well behaved, brave and hard working males, rather than to the Jack Dawson character in the film "Titanic" - an unsuccessful musician with no apparent means of support, whose numerous real life equivalents live mostly by sponging off their numerous high IQ high socioeconomic status girlfriends, partly by folding sweaters, partly on welfare, and partly on burglary and drug dealing.

## Cathedral decision making

### 2016-10-03 07:43:57

The president does not make decisions. The presidency does not make decisions either, at least not in the sense that an individual, or a well run corporation makes decisions.

Rather, it is driven entropic forces, which tend over time tend to have certain outcomes, like a river slowly changing its course. Thus we see the presidency gradually yielding on Aleppo.

---

[415] https://www.youtube.com/watch?v=ioHqDTQKX2U

[416] https://www.rt.com/news/349784-german-migrants-assault-lie/

If Xenophon, or Raffles, or Clive of India, or Atilla the Hun was running the show, he would decide whether to hold them, fold them, walk away or run. What we see the American government doing is drifting and wobbling, and right now it is gradually drifting amorphously and slowly towards abandoning its long held plans for regime change in Syria. By and large, the decisions of the presidency have no clear motive, no clear objective, and are not well modeled as decisions by a self interested individual. When IBM does X, it is generally because the CEO has decided that X would be profitable. When the presidency does something, it is the net outcome of a bunch of individuals each pursuing his particular self interest, each maximizing his particular microslice of power and his particular reputation for holiness, the net outcome of a great many individuals each with a tiny microslice of power each doing something that serves his particular interest, as a river changes its course as the net outcome of the drift of many tiny grains of sand. There are no elders of Zion, or if there are, they don't care what happens to Zion.

If Clive was running the Aleppo operation, he would fight, or run, or cut a deal with Russia. But the presidency is incapable of cutting a deal with Russia over Aleppo because, as the Russians have discovered, it is "not agreement capable"[417], a term generally used for failed states. The American negotiators may agree with Russia that America will do X in return for Russia doing Y, but then X does not happen, not so much because anyone in America made a conscious decision to double cross the Russians, but because there is in fact no real chain of command connecting the negotiators with people who might have the ability to make X happen. So the presidency neither fights, nor runs, nor cuts a deal. Today it is drifting slowly in the general direction of running.

The amorphous, erratic, unpredictable, and uncontrollable drift of the presidency on matters of war and peace contrasts dramatically with Harvard's ability to decisively and abruptly make decisions on matters of faith and morals[418], for example global warming or second hand smoke. One day every academic everywhere in the entire western world believes X. The next day, every academic everywhere in the entire western world believes Y, and not only believes Y, but has always believed Y, and has absolutely no recollection than anyone anywhere ever believed X, except perhaps a few ignorant bible thumping racist loons in the wilds of Appalachia or the marshes of Florida.

## Deus Vult

### 2016-10-05 10:24:08

Spandrel observes that religion is our genes looking for a tribe to join, and concludes We shall drown, and nobody will save us[419]

Alfa NL observes that Spandrel is very clever, but the natural law arguments for marriage, the family, for desiring the survival of our personal descendants are kind of chilling, and it is a lot easier say that marriage, property, and the survival of our descendents is the will of God, and that the purpose of organized religion is not to be a synthetic tribe in

---


[417] https://thesaker.is/why-the-recent-developments-in-syria-show-that-the-obama-administration-is-in-a-state-of-confused-agony/

[418] https://blog.reaction.la/tag/the-past-keeps-changing/

[419] https://bloodyshovel.wordpress.com/

which the tribe secures the genetic survival of its members, but to help its members follow the will of God. "God is a better sounding story than nihilism. I prefer the story of God. If that makes me a LARPer for holy status points in the eyes of Gnon's guardian, so be it."

Recall the wisdom of Heartiste, minion of Satan. In human affairs, irrational optimism will get you your way, while rational pessimism will not.

God wills our survival. We shall therefore win. We shall defeat those such as Merkle that wish to take all of us quietly and comfortably with them to their graves. We shall silence them and exile them forever from the seats of power. We shall tear down their temples and make their temples and their prophets damnatio memoriae, so that like the Amalekites nothing remains but the condemnation, the erasure, and the memory of their wrongs.

## Who would win a great power war that starts in Syria

2016-10-08 03:01:54

The US military have of course an enormously bigger budget than the Russian military, enormously more equipment than the Russian military, and enormously more trained men.

And, of course, there is that famous US technological superiority.

Heh, you know me. US technology has been running on empty for decades. The west has been resting on its laurels for a long time. Western technology is these days bluff, bullshit, sales flimflam, and imports from China.

## Nuclear Technological decline

2016-10-09 08:59:13

The US no longer produces weapons grade plutonium. Supposedly this is a choice.

It has asked other countries to not produce weapons grade plutonium, and to get rid of the weapons grade plutonium they do have.

The economical way to destroy weapons grade plutonium is to burn it in nuclear reactors, to use it for power, which destroys some of it and irreversibly contaminates the rest with plutonium 240, making it unusable for weapons, though still usable for power.

Unfortunately, the US, in attempting to do so, ran into "massive cost overruns", which is to say, technological decline. Putting it in breach of its agreements with Russia and Japan.

Under the US-Russian PMDA, originally signed in 2000, both parties agreed to dispose of at least 34 metric tons of weapons grade plutonium, enough to produce 17,000 nuclear bombs.

The US, however, has not disposed of any plutonium, despite spending a lot of money attempting to do so. If you cannot use it, probably cannot make it.

## On the current path

2016-10-10 07:03:42

If you teach your elite to hate western civilization, whites, and modern technology, you are not going to have any of them for very much longer.

It looks rather as if 99% of western peoples are going to perish from this earth. The survivors will be oddball types, subscribers to reactionary and rather silly religions in barren edge regions like Alaska.

Recent events in Syria suggest that the Russian capability for air warfare is substantially more technologically advanced than that of the US - Russians are acting as if they think it is, and Americans are also acting as if they think it is, though no one will know for sure unless war ensues. Maybe Russians are bluffing, but when civilizations decline, it is normal for the center to decline first, while the periphery keeps going for a little bit longer. That American spacecraft rely on Russian plutonium, and that for a while America relied on Russian transport to the space station suggests that technological decline has hit America harder than Russia, is consistent with Russian air superiority over Syria.

Chinese GDP now substantially exceeds that of America.

Singapore is a trap. Smart people go to Singapore, they don't reproduce. People illegally hiding out in the wilds of Chernobyl do reproduce. But Chernobyl is also a trap. People there turn into primitives.

The west conquered the world and launched the scientific and industrial revolutions starting with restoration England conquering the world and launching the scientific and industrial revolutions.

The key actions of the Restoration were making the invisible college into the Royal society – that is to say, making the scientific method, as distinct from official science, high status, and authorizing the East India company to make war and peace – making corporate capitalism high status. Divorce was abolished, and marriage was made strictly religious, enforcing patriarchy socially and legally, thus encouraging reproduction.

Everywhere in the world, capitalism is deemed evil, the scientific method is demonized and is low status, and easy divorce and high female status inhibits reproduction. If women get to choose, they will choose to have sex with a tiny minority of top males and postpone marriage to the last minute – and frequently to after the last minute. ("Top" males in this context meaning not necessarily the guy in the corner office, but rather tattooed low IQ thugs)

We need a society that is pro science, pro technology, pro capitalism, which restricts female sexual choice to males that contribute positively to this society, and which makes it safe for males to marry and father children. Not seeing that society anywhere, and those few places that approximate some few aspects of this ideal are distinctly nonwhite.

It is sometimes argued that the Restoration did not last long, that the Glorious Revolution put Whigs and Whig doctrine in power and ended divine right. Which version of history has Whigs presiding over the triumph of the West.

Maybe.

But for a hundred and twenty years, any Whig that said the Glorious Revolution was Lockean was apt to find himself in exile.

Divine right was still going strong when George declared that God had appointed him regent, though this unleashed a firestorm against him and all the Georges similar to that against Trump today.

Indeed, the doctrine that women are pure and chaste, and that therefore men are always in the wrong, which is currently being used to attack Trump, was originally deployed to attack King George, in much the same style, deploying much the same rationales. The entire Victorian era can be thought of as weaponizing the sainthood of women against that horrid alpha male, King George. To this day Queen Caroline is still sainted, and to this day they either deny that George was Regent, which makes it a bit odd that there is an entire period of art, science, and architecture known as "Regency", or else they say he was "appointed" regent, passive tense, without, however, saying who appointed him. They are still to this day in shock that divine right was live and effective for King George.

Corporate Capitalism lasted about as long as divine right lasted. Aristocratic control of the army lasted a little longer, to the Crimean war. It is hard to say when patriarchy ended, but the sainthood of women logically implied an attack on patriarchy. If women are naturally virtuous, there is no need to coerce women to obey their marriage vows, only men. So all coercion against women was an unprincipled exception, albeit in much of the world that unprincipled exception lasted all the way to 1972. The Scientific Method, enforced and upheld by the Royal Society, lasted all the way to end of World War II.

One could argue that Whiggism was victorious in 1788, when the Whigs successfully prosecuted a revolution on the principle that all men were created equal - while refraining from suggesting that women were created equal, and kind of avoiding the issue of whether blacks were created equal, but I would not count the triumph of Whiggism in America till the war of Northern Aggression. Whiggism was victorious and triumphant in *some* American states starting 1788, but not in all.

The sainthood of that whore, Florence Nightingale, was part of policy of demonizing the warriors who actually fought the war, and led to a policy of logistics being carried out by high status people classified as soldiers, rather than low status people classified as camp followers acting under the supervision of regimental commanders and lower, acting under the supervision of officers who were expected to actually fight in person. This reorganization of military supply put warriors under bureaucrats, thus dramatically lowering the authority of warriors within the military. This eventually gave us today's British army, which has two hundred generals none of whom have heard a shot fired in anger, but which can only put two hundred actual fighting men on the field of battle to combat their enemies.

The argument was that there were a lot of dismal failures of logistics during the Crimean war, but in fact it is not obvious that transferring power over feeding and clothing soldiers from those close to the soldiers being fed and clothed, to those in the capital, has led to an improvement.

The greatness of the west derives from patriarchy, science, and capitalism, which in turn derived from the divine right of Kings, the established state church, and the supremacy of King over Church, for all of these were established or greatly reinforced in the restoration of 1660, and fell apart after divine right came under sustained and venomous attack in the nineteenth century.

Maybe we still have corporate capitalism, but in the nineteenth century the state took the guns away from corporate capitalists.

Saying "Things went wrong on date X" is misleading, because entropy is constantly increasing while efforts to clean up the mess and expel entropy are sporadic, but things suddenly got a whole lot better in the big clean up of the restoration, and things started going to hell a whole lot faster after they sainted women in order to demonize King George.

While Pol is always right about Jews[420], the trouble with Jew centric theory is that it prescribes nazism, which is just a return to nineteen thirties leftism from twentieth century leftism. Any real fix is necessarily going to resemble the restoration, which makes puritan centric theory more applicable. And if we look at the carpetbaggers sent to rob the Ukraine, they did not come from the vicinity of Jerusalem, but from the vicinity of Harvard, the headquarters and seminary of the State Church of Massachusetts.

To keep organizational entropy under control you need one man in charge. And then the entropy grows in those parts of the state that he has trouble controlling. The decay of our civilization is priest led and priest caused, (defining priests broadly to include the professoriat and similar). So, when there was a state church under a divine right king, that king could, and often enough did, expel the entropy - frequently by encouraging problem priests to emigrate, often to America. Would have worked considerably better if England had had an inquisition, to make sure that those professing adherence to the Church of England were actually adhering to it, rather than actively subverting it. And if he had expelled the offenders to cut sugar cane in the tropical sun, rather than to America.

With the death of God, hard to manage a divine right King. Somehow I doubt that Moldbug's crypto locks would do as effective a job as God did.

Maybe there is some other solution to installing science, the scientific method, corporate capitalism, and patriarchy, and preventing the growth of entropy within the organs of the state. But the method that mostly worked from 1660 to the early nineteenth century was divine right monarchy ruling over a church and state united.

Corporations are often effective in controlling entropy within the organization, because the CEO has plenary power. But we are not yet seeing any well run corporate states.

As the current election campaign demonstrates, America today is rather close to being church and state united, but with no one man in charge, and no inquisition, we get holiness spirals and phariseeism. Free lance witch finders always manage to drum up business more efficiently than state sponsored witch finders.

The usual way these things end is that one leftist makes himself supreme, makes it as dangerous to be to the left of him as to be to the right of him, and proceeds, like Cromwell and Stalin, to put some order into the system. And if you are lucky, he is eventually replaced by a rightist who, being a rightist, is able to put a whole lot more order into the system. On the other hand, a leftist singularity can go directly all the way into a dark age, or just kill pretty much everyone until outsiders take over.

---

[420]https://twitter.com/skype_directory/status/783033257185185793

# The imaginary Free Syrian Army

2016-10-14 06:43:46

The US is theoretically aiding the "Moderate Muslims", the free Syrian Army, the FSA, which theoretically controls a small and rapidly shrinking patch of Aleppo.

In actual practice, those that control Aleppo will murder any male non sunni Muslim on sight, regardless of age, which makes them less moderate than Islamic State. The US is, as Putin observes, aiding terrorists.

Stuart Ramsay was in Aleppo when those moderate Muslims of the Arab Spring, the movement to make the middle east democratic and progressive, took control, and was there when they almost immediately lost control.[421] It seems that the FSA only existed for a few weeks or months, with rank and file FSA fighters swiftly going over to those fighting holy war for race and religion, and the FSA leadership mysteriously vanishing.

In retrospect it is clear that the Arab Spring was an act of aggression by the Cathedral against middle eastern regimes, no doubt genuinely inspired by the most noble sentiments, but entirely without real local roots.

The "moderates" were, it is now apparent, rootless cosmopolitans who identified ideologically and politically with the "international community" and expected to get quasi governmental jobs, for example NGO jobs, media jobs, academic jobs, and so forth, provided by the international community, in international places.

Ramsay reports that the FSA made no real effort to set up a governing structure in the areas they controlled, unlike the various groups waging tribal and holy war against various other Syrians minutely different from themselves. This is the typical problem with quislings. They don't really care because they expect their foreign masters to do the heavy lifting. If they do nothing, maybe their foreign masters will pick up the slack, if they do something, their foreign masters will capture most of the benefit. And if everything goes bad, they expect to be working for an NGO some place else.

The FSA, like the rest of the Arab Springers, were rootless cosmopolitans who acted the way quislings serving a foreign master typically act. And now they are all dead or fled, mostly fled. And they fled four years ago, and are now doing international community jobs like section eighting refugees into your suburb.

# Why women get tattooed

2016-10-16 09:42:53

In general female behavior is not explicable in terms of rational pursuit of goals, but as innate reactions to stimuli, at least in anything pertaining to sex and reproduction.

And most things do pertain to sex and reproduction, at least until they hit menopause.

Thus, to explain a female's behavior, one does not ask "what do woman want" but rather "how would this reaction to stimuli have affected reproductive success in the ancestral environment?"

It is obvious and well known that tattoos uglify women, which has a direct and substantial harmful effect on their lives and reproductive success. So, why?

---

[421]https://news.sky.com/story/aleppo-how-did-the-city-crumble-so-fast-10613726

Well, I can report the reason in one case. The one women where I was around when she made the decision to get tattoos initially wanted to get tattooed as a shit test. Her motivation was to test if I was strong enough to stop her from doing stupid self destructive things. Which I was. And then eventually I dumped her. After I dumped her she proceeded to do a pile of stupid self destructive things while somehow going to considerable lengths to involve me in them. The message being "see, without you to care for me and protect me from myself, I will do stupid self destructive things."

Well, that is one case, and maybe it does not generalize, but this is the case where I know the reason why a woman got tattooed.

## Maybe a relatively painless Soviet Style collapse?

2016-10-21 04:46:05

I have been predicting, and still predict, that the fall of the Cathedral will be long, bloody, and terrible, and that the Cathedral will likely be replaced by something that none of us want, like the Islamic Caliphate.

But lately there have been happier signs, like the Trumpening.

And the defection of Duterte from the blue empire is another encouraging sign.

Duterte won the Philippine election on a hugely popular program of replacing the dysfunctional justice system with right wing death squads[422]. The Cathedral could not quite believe this, but after a while started murmuring about doing something, presumably another color revolution after the fashion of Syria.

Whereupon Duterte defected from the "International Community" to China, seeking Chinese protection against US military intervention.

Hillary's program is to restore the blue empire by overtly violent means. Trump's program is to let it go.

What happened in the Soviet Union is that when they let Afghanistan go, then another state went, and another state went, and a landslide of states, and then Moscow itself fell.

While the International Community, the blue empire of the consulates, has been struggling with Syria, Thailand and the Philippines have wandered off the reservation. Insurrection has a habit of cascading. To restore control, it would not be sufficient to destroy Syria and have the Alawites and Christians genocided, but war with Thailand and the Philippines might well also be necessary, and might well escalate to similar degrees of horror.

War tends to become far more horrible than those starting it expect. The Cathedral is piously indignant about barrel bombs, forgetting that the neighborhoods being bombed were often quite recently ethnically cleansed of their previous inhabitants by the forces supported by the Cathedral.

It seems to me that if a neighborhood was previously occupied by group A, and then group B drives them out, it is perfectly reasonable for group A and their allies to bomb the hell out the neighborhoods new and old occupied by group B. Yeah, there are children living it those neighborhoods. And there children driven out of their homes by

---

[422]https://blog.reaction.la/politics/duerte-harry/

violence when those neighborhoods were ethnically cleansed. The Cathedral has sponsored a whole lot of violent ethnic cleansing in Syria, which caused, and entirely justifies, the violence that we now see in the reconquest of Aleppo.

And the Cathedral has sponsored a whole lot of violent ethnic cleansing in America, to which everyone piously turns a blind eye.

The empire rests on white males, while sadistically increasing the oppression of whites and males to ever more ridiculous extremes. Contrary to the fantasies of the 1488ers, no backlash ensues, instead whites and males become ever more passive, apathetic, terrorized, and emasculated. But on the periphery of empire, the empire is collapsing.

This collapse does not reflect for the most part backlash against anti white and anti male measures (though Boko Haram is unambiguously backlash against anti male measures) but the fundamental military weakness of a society that is constructed by white males, that is entirely dependent on the work and military capability of white males, and is ever more hostile to white males. The utterly extraordinary and almost incredible British defeats in Basra and Helmand province show what happens when you feminize your military. The empire is falling not because white males will fight their oppressors, but because they will not fight for their oppressors. Will the fall of the Blue Empire go all the way to Washington, as the fall of the Soviet Empire went all the way to Moscow?

## Winning gamergate

### 2016-10-25 11:11:32

A few days before the election, the feminist blogger Go make me a sandwich[423] has thrown in the towel, despite being handed large bags of money and unenending praise for her "courage" in complaining about sexism in games.

Another victory for the power of Trump, who has made every man stand a little straighter, walk with a slightly bigger stride, and grow bigger balls. Win, lose, or draw, he has already accomplished more change than every previous Republican candidate.

Her complaint has been to endlessly point out that male game characters are depicted as manly, while female game characters are ... female. Which is to say, hotter than she is. This oppresses her. Not only that, but when she attacks artists for allegedly bad and sexist art, they have been known to disagree. It is supposedly horribly misogynistic for a male to do anything other than politely agree when attacked by a woman. People disagreeing with her cause her great pain. It is extremely cruel that anyone in the world publicly disagrees with her after she publicly attacks them.

Every fertile age female writing a book or blogging or giving a speech on anything she is passionate about is arguing that the world should be remade in such a way that the writer or speaker should be considered hot.

All her complaints are pretty similar to this one[424]

She complains that Taki is physically impossible, because of waist to hip ratio.

> When you compare the two, you can see that they've given Taki so much of an "hourglass figure" that her rib cage is practically inverting itself, as is her stomach. This begs

---

[423]https://gomakemeasandwich.wordpress.com/
[424]https://gomakemeasandwich.wordpress.com/2010/11/05/boobs-youre-doing-it-wrong-taki/

the question, where does she keep her organs? Also, you'll notice that I fleshed out Taki's ass a bit. That's not me making Taki a bit fatter, that's me giving Taki the musculature needed to connect her legs to her torso.

So I put a tape measure the images of Taki in the link. Taki, as originally drawn, by the artist depicting a sexy ninja, has a waist to hip ratio of 1.9/2.8 = 0.0.67 (That is putting a tape measure on my screen, your screen will have different measurements but the same waist to hip ratio.

As "corrected" by the blogger to be supposedly realistic 2.2/3.0 = 0.73

In the bloggers black and red diagram, original Taki has 2.2/3.2 = 0.69, and supposedly realistic Taki 2.6/3.6= 0.72

But a real life hot caucasian chick is typically 0.7, and a real life hot East Asian chick, which the character presumably is, being a ninja, is indeed about 0.67 and yes, you can find, and bed, lots of real life asian chicks with a waist to hip ratio around 0.67. We are not talking freakish supermodels, but the reasonably slim and fit girl next door - well, next door if you visit East Asia.

My recent East Asian girlfriend had a waist to hip ratio better than Taki, and while her boobs were not nearly as large as fictional Taki's boobs, which are indeed unreasonably large, they were better than the "corrected" Taki's boobs. My recent East Asian real life girlfriend was way less "realistic" than the bloggers "corrected" Taki.

And the same is true of the regular complaints of "ünrealistic" depictions of females. They are only unrealistic if you demand that artists be forbidden from depicting that minority of women able to push aside the extra pizza slice.

By and large most videogame females correspond to a realistic slim athletic woman with big boobs, and most videogame males correspond a body builder male, reflecting what men and women want to be, and would like to have in their sexual partners - they are idealized, but except in deliberately cartoonish art, usually not absurdly exaggerated, nor are males any the less idealized that females. Pretty much every male in video game art looks like Superman.

The problem is that dumpy chicks find hot chicks far more threatening than dumpy males find hot males, and the blogger's depictions of supposedly realistic female characters show this. Her "realistic" female characters show a realistic need to push aside the last slice of pizza and hit the gym. If she finds Taki threatening, she would find plenty of real life East Asians threatening.

## How to implement patriarchy

2016-10-26 07:41:28

Implementing patriarchy is a lot harder than it looks. There are a lot of moving parts that have to work together right.

The problem is that nature has given women so much power, that it is very hard for law to take it away from them. Spandrel has plenty of amusing tales of women disruptively exercising power from the bottom in a system where they were theoretically completely property.

If I beat a woman, it is because she wants me to beat her. If I don't beat a woman, it is because she does not want me to beat her. If I dump a woman, it is because she wants me to dump her. We men are all dancing monkeys on a chain, and just as much a dancing monkey when administering a beating.

Back when husbands theoretically had absolute power over their wives, and Kings theoretically had absolute power over their subjects, Kings mistresses tended to be their wives of their courtiers. Now you might suppose the King was shaking down his courtiers - but hang on there. The wife screws the King, and goes back to her beta orbiter husband's bed, where presumably they chastely cuddle while she weeps on his shoulder about how badly the King treats her. If the King's power can reach into the courtier's home and stop him from whipping his wife, how come it cannot reach into the courtier's home and stop the wife from cuddling her beta orbiter husband? Further, how come the King's mistresses have already had children with other men? Who wants seconds? Yes, the King was shaking down his courtiers, but he was being manipulated into shaking down his courtiers, and his courtiers were being manipulated into letting him shake them down.

Obviously what happened was that the lord on his own domain is the ultimate alpha male, lord of the manor, everyone grovels to him. His wife thinks she has hit the jackpot. Then they go to court, he grovels to the King, she despises her husband, stops fucking him, and fucks the King. Her husband is definitely not getting his way. The King is not really getting his way. *She* is getting her way. It was unrestrained hypergamy. She gets fucked by the King, cuddled by her beta orbiter husband.

To protect Odysseus from the sirens we need to tie him to the mast.

So:

If a man sleeps with another man's wife, the offended husband may kill him, or the state will execute him. The wife may be punished according to the husband's discretion.

If a man prostitutes his wife or girlfriend, makes her sleep with another man, he shall be executed by the state. If a man allows himself to be cuckolded, allows his wife to sleep with another man, the state shall execute both of them.

We do this not to punish the wicked husband, but to protect the husband from the wiles of woman, as Odysseus had himself tied to the mast, and ordered his men to slay him should he break free.

If a man gravely wrongs his wife, the state may relieve her of the duty of always being respectful to him, always obeying him, never speaking back to him, and always being sexually available to him, while requiring him to continue to support her, which is to say, allow her divorce for grave wrongs, *but* the state should not relieve her of the duty to never be sexually available to another man, because otherwise she will concoct fictitious grave wrongs, or manipulate her husband into genuinely committing grave wrongs, as soon as she encounters a man seemingly more alpha than her husband. If she does sleep with another man after divorce, her husband can stop supporting her, or he can forcibly take her back and punish her at his discretion.

Women should be fully under the authority of the male head of household, and should remain legally children until menopause. The head of household should have authority to physically discipline wife and children.

Normally marriage should be romantic, consensual, monogamous, should reflect erotic love and should be permanent. Normally couples should not be allowed to date unless engaged, where engagement consists of a promise to marry, understood as a promise to marry if they have sex.

However, due to various forms of misconduct, we often have to break from this ideal one way or another. We should break from the ideal not by dissolving the marriage, but by coercing people to marry and to stay married, by enforcing both the man's duty to support the woman, and the woman's duty to obey him, respect him, be always sexually available to him, and never sexually available to anyone else.

Female consent is foolish, irresponsible, reckless and easily manipulated. So the first principle to be laid aside should be female consent, and permanency the last principle to be laid aside. Female consent does not make sex right, nor lack of consent make sex wrong.

Varying degrees of shotgun marriage should be applied for misbehavior. For example, if a woman gets pregnant, and the father is marriageable, they should be forced to marry. If he refuses to marry, he gets a support order. If she refuses to marry, she gets concubinage - the duty to obey him, respect him, provide domestic and sexual services to him and never to anyone else, the duties and obligations of marriage without the honor and protections of marriage. (That is how they did it in Australia at the end of the eighteenth century)

If she sleeps with a non marriageable man, she should be required to get married to someone marriageable, anyone, in a hurry, under threat of being assigned to someone in concubinage. Again, in Australia in the late eighteenth century, a lot of women somehow managed to find good husbands with amazing swiftness, usually in days, sometimes in hours.

# UVA Dean surrenders to PC in Rolling Stone defamation case.

## 2016-10-29 05:11:51

Supposedly thousands of University of Virginia students are raped every month, or possibly every day, by privileged white heterosexual males.

Yet strangely, Associate Dean Nicole Eramo of the University of Virginia has not punished a single privileged white male for actually raping someone.

Therefore, either Dean Nicole Eramo is worse than Hitler, or rape is a massively over reported crime, with the vast majority of rape accusations being false, and the vast majority of rape convictions unjust. Rolling Stone told us that the Dean is worse than Hitler. The Dean is suing them.

Rolling Stone is defending its story, not on the basis that it is true, but that it is truthy, that the Dean really is worse than Hitler.

The Associate Dean is unable to say the glaringly obvious, that rape is massively over-reported, that the vast majority of rape accusations and convictions are fraud committed by evil and irresponsible women who need to be severely punished.

Instead, the Dean piously tells us that rape is massively underreported, and explains that, due to pervasive sexism in the system, it is just very difficult to find anyone actually guilty of rape.

But Dean Nicole Eramo, you are, or rather were, in charge of the system. If rape really is massively underreported, then you really are worse than Hitler.

Women cry rape for many reasons, one of them, as for example Jackie Erdeley's story, to attract sympathetic male attention. But the big underlying reason is that in a world that says that sex is always fine if two adults consent, and never right if one of them does not consent, they have no language to express the thought "I have been banging like a barn door in high wind, and somehow I feel really bad."

## How to kill off the Cathedral

2016-10-30 12:23:27

History is replete with radical leftist movements that were seemingly crushed by authority, only to rise from the dead centuries or millenia later.

Assume we gain power, either by military coup or by the true election. (The true election is like a regular election, except that after the election the Reichstaag burns) How can we suppress the Cathedral so that it stays dead, and does not creep back like it did after the restoration?

When push comes to shove, there is actual physical political violence. The left wing takeover of universities in the sixties was mediated by thugs associated with the Democratic Party[425].

## Jobs and education make women ugly and unattractive

2016-10-30 22:50:42

Women find jobs and education attractive in men, so mistakenly and foolishly think that men will find jobs and education attractive in women. They find arrogance, cruelty, sexual promiscuity, and assholery attractive in men, so mistakenly and foolishly think that men will find arrogance, cruelty, sexual promiscuity, and assholery attractive in women.

What men like is primarily youth and fertility, but close second to this is kindness, fidelity, humility, and obedience. "Will this woman", the man subconsciously thinks, "look after me and my children?"

A woman has all her life to do jobs and education, but limited time to get married and start a family. After thirty, she is not so hot any more, still bangable, but no fun for a long term relationship. She is also running out of eggs. After age thirty she can still have children, but there is a rapidly rising chance that she will not be able to have as large a family as she or her husband might wish. After forty, high chance she will not be able to have any children at all. And after forty, well, there are some men that will bang forty year old women, but most men would prefer whiskey, porn, and whores if a forty year old woman was the only alternative. Old men seldom marry old women. I am pretty old, and infamously indiscriminate about which women I bang (if it goes up, it goes in) but I don't bang forty year old women, and there is a limit to how many times I will bang a woman in her thirties, unless she is exceptionally good looking for a thirty year old.

---

[425]https://unqualified-reservations.blogspot.com.au/2008/02/theory-of-ruling-underclass.html

If a woman marries a man while she is still young and beautiful, and he is in love, wife goggles come into effect and she seemingly remains the same age forever. I saw my wife as about seventeen all her years until she was dying, but of course, the later a woman marries, the less she is going to benefit from wife goggles.

The worst part of jobs and education is that they suck up time that a woman should use to get married and have a family, but they also tend to mark up a woman's face.

If a woman goes to college, and does not nail down her future husband in the first year, she is going to wind up banging a long succession of charismatic alpha males, and getting dumped by a long succession of alpha males, resulting in the infamous thousand cock stare, and the thousand cock stare is chillingly ugly.

Highly educated women get married less, get divorced more, and have fewer children than less educated women.

And then she goes to work.

Men need to be needed. Men do not want an independent woman. And being an independent woman hardens a woman's face.

Women in high socioeconomic status jobs get married less, get divorced more, fuck around more before, during, and after marriage, and have fewer children than woman with low socioeconomic status jobs.

This problem has been made far more severe by affirmative action. I recall a lawyerette in Telstra's legal department (78% female) boasting about how much affirmative action was in place, and arrogantly, impudently, and aggressively demanding that a whole lot more affirmative action be put in place.

These days, most women's jobs are affirmative action jobs. Women get jobs on the backs of men because companies are forced to hire woman.

One big problem with affirmative action is that an affirmative action hire is largely fireproof, so if there is any drama between a man hired on his merits, and woman hired for being a woman, the man gets fired. And women love drama. Which makes all the women in the workplace socially superior to the men who are theoretically their equals on the organization, since the men are frightened of the women, frightened that if a woman picks a quarrel with them it will have grave consequences, and often socially superior to their immediate boss. Watch how the poor boss cannot get a word in edgewise.

Yeah, I know feminists say that when a man speaks over a woman, he is being aggressive and shouting her down, but when a woman speaks over a man, she is not interrupting, she is being friendly and helpful - but the boss would have had a much easier time without all that "help", which resembled the help given by a backseat driver to the driver.

So the women go around with a hard and hostile face, lest any of their male social inferiors should get sexy ideas about them, and that hostile face becomes permanent, so that even when she tries to smile at an alpha male, she is smiling through a permanent hostile condescending sneer that has engraved itself on her face. And that is not what any man needs in a wife. Jobs for women are, in the overwhelming majority of cases, affirmative action jobs where the men carry the woman on their backs, affirmative action jobs make women arrogant and hostile, and arrogance and hostility makes them ugly.

There is a certain amount of truth to the feminist proposition that women never interrupt men, they are just being friendly and helpful - and a great big untruth. And the great big untruth is revealed if the man does not let her interrupt, if he keeps on speaking and raises his voice to be be heard, her face will distort into the face of a witch, a monster, and a toad, she will scream incoherently at the top of her voice and swell with furious rage, that even though her interruption is superficially pleasant and courteous, that it is an interruption is discourteous, a demonstration of arrogance, hostility, and social power, the power of state enforced affirmative action hiring, and this arrogance and discourtesy, and the state power backing it, is suddenly, brutally, and shockingly revealed the instant the interruption is resisted.

Every time a woman interrupts a man, her face gets a tiny bit uglier.

## Trumpslide

### 2016-10-31 08:17:41

Voter turnout is massive. You don't get massive turnout like this to vote for the status quo. If Hillary wins, it will only be by equally massive election fraud. As Stalin said:[426]
> "I consider it completely unimportant who in the party will vote, or how; but what is extraordinarily important is this — who will count the votes, and how."

Poll results are based on the theory that white turnout will be about the same as it was when both parties supported the ethnic cleansing of whites from certain areas, black attacks on whites on the basis of race, and the continual denigration and demonization of whites, and that male turnout will be about the same as it was when both parties supported rape hysteria and an epidemic of false rape accusations, the criminalization of fatherhood, the replacement of fatherhood with child support, brutal, draconian, and extraordinary methods of enforcing child support, and the systematic biased denial of credentials to males in a hostile and angry education system that is more interested in teaching them that masculinity is toxic and oppresses women than interested in genuine education.

I expect that the massive turnout reflects massively higher white voting and male voting.

Failing massive electoral fraud, expect a last gasp effort to deny him office by means of the electoral college, followed by a widespread government policy of paying even less attention to president Trump than they have been paying to president Obama.

Normally I recommend and practice non participation in democratic politics. It is a spectacle and a delusion. But this is the Flight 93 election. Vote early, vote often, and should opportunity permit it to be done safely, physically attack likely Hillary voters near polling booths.

Normally in an election, there is not much at stake, so peace is better than war. In this election, too much is at stake for anyone, left or right, to accept the decision of a majority of the voters. The election will not immediately lead to civil war, regardless of fraud or outcome, the time is not quite yet, but it will move us markedly closer to the time for war. The stakes get higher every election. The results of this election, and probably all future US elections, will not be quietly and routinely accepted by the losing side.

---

[426]https://lib.ru/MEMUARY/BAZHANOW/stalin.txt

# Defining the alt right

2016-11-02 06:51:50

According to Saboteur[427], the core uniting principle of the alt right is that we reject equality. Which is true.

Alternative right[428] tells us that the alt right is those that apply the scientific method to society and human affairs. Which is true, and which not only implies that humans are unequal, but also that global warming is bullshit, and lots more along those lines.

Vox Day has issued a lengthy definition[429], which for all its length leaves out the absolutely vital principle of "no enemies to the right" and includes the distinctly left wing proposition that all peoples are entitled to independence. I rather think that Rhodesia and the Belgian Congo demonstrated that some people need to be ruled by outsiders. We don't support all nationalisms. We support some nationalisms, including those of Japanese, of Chinese in China, of Israeli nationalism by Jews in Israel or intending to move there, and so on and so forth. Most of us don't support black nationalism. We support all nationalisms of peoples competent to have a functional nation.

Red Ice adds to Vox Day's points[430] awareness of the Jewish Question, awareness of Jewish bad behavior in exile. The alt right totally supports the right of Jews to a Jewish nation. Non Jews in Israel should not get to vote, get government jobs, nor go to the most prestigious Israeli universities. Jews should dominate Israel. But Jews should not, however, dominate the image of ourselves that Hollywood presents, nor Washington's revolving door between regulators and regulated. Jews demonize European history, in particular the crusades, and hold up to us a distorted twisted lying mirror of our past that makes us look ugly and crazy, that seeks to make us despise ourselves.

1. No enemies to the right. No one gets denounced or disowned or read out of the movement for being too far right. Criticisms of other alt rightists should be friendly or brotherly, or should criticize them for being too far left (Milo is gay, nazis are socialist) If you criticize someone for excessive rightism, criticize him as you would criticize your brother in front of non family and police. No enemies to the left works great for leftists. No one asks President Obama to disown his terrorist mentor Bill Ayers. If someone twits you about a fellow alt rightist who is calling for alarmingly large categories of people to be given helicopter rides to the Pacific ocean, ask him what was the position of the New York Times during Mao's Great Leap Forward.

2. The Alt Right understands that diversity + proximity = war.

3. The Alt Right doesn't care what you think of it. You can call us racists, anti semites, and sexists all you like.

---

[427] https://saboteur365.wordpress.com/2016/09/12/we-dont-like-being-lied-to-what-unites-the-alt-right/
[428] https://alternative-right.blogspot.com/2016/09/the-alt-right-is-scientific-movement.html
[429] https://voxday.blogspot.com.au/2016/08/what-alt-right-is.html
[430] https://redice.tv/news/what-the-alt-right-is

4. America is not a proposition nation, there are no proposition nations. The Alt Right rejects the Declaration of Independence and the Constitution too. All men were not created equal, and the hundreds of millions of non whites coming to the USA do not give a damn about any of the other principles enunciated in the Declaration of Independence and are unlikely to be persuaded to care. Mass migration has rendered those propositions dead in the water.

5. The Alt Right is anti-equalitarian. It rejects the idea of equality for the same reason it rejects the ideas of unicorns and leprechauns, noting that human equality does not exist in any observable scientific, legal, material, intellectual, sexual, or spiritual form.

6. The Alt Right is of the political right in both the American and the European sense of the term. Socialists are not Alt Right. Neocons are not Alt Right.

7. Conservatives conserve, meaning they conserve yesterday's left wing political, military, and moral victories. The Alt Right believes in its own victory and intends to re-impose the lessons of science, reality, ancient cultural tradition, and history. We intend to roll back two hundred years of progress, and in some cases four hundred years of progress.

8. The Alt Right believes Western civilization is the pinnacle of human achievement and supports its three foundational pillars: Christianity, the European nations, and the Graeco-Roman legacy. Christendom has a disturbing tendency to go left, which was corrected by such barbarian founders of Europe as Charles the Hammer. These corrections need to be kept in place.

9. The Alt Right is openly and avowedly nationalist. It supports all nationalisms of superior people and the right of all nations competent to rule themselves to exist, homogeneous and unadulterated by foreign invasion and immigration.

10. The Alt Right is anti-globalist. It opposes all groups who work for globalist ideals or globalist objectives.

11. The Alt Right is scientodific. It presumptively accepts the current conclusions of the scientific method (scientody), while understanding a) these conclusions are liable to future revision, b) that scientistry is susceptible to corruption, and c) that the so-called scientific consensus is not based on scientody, but democracy, and is therefore intrinsically unscientific.

12. The Alt Right believes identity > culture > politics.

13. The Alt Right rejects the free movement of peoples.

14. The Alt Right believes we must secure the existence of white people and a future for white children. It is a specifically non Jewish white movement. But that whites should exist does not imply that Jews should not exist. Israel should exist. And Japan should exist. And China should exist. And Thailand should exist, and so on and so forth.

15. The Alt Right does not believe in the general supremacy of any race, nation, people, or sub-species. Whites should not rule the world. The American empire, aka "the International Community" rules the world except for China and its satellites, and Russia and its satellites. It should not do so. In particular, it should not rule Japan.

16. The Alt Right is a philosophy that values peace among the various nations of the world and opposes wars to impose the values of one nation upon another as well as efforts to exterminate individual nations through war, genocide, immigration, or genetic assimilation, such as efforts by "the International Community" to overthrow the ruler of Syria and genocide his ethnic group. We do not accept the Nazi theory that the natural state of relations between nations is war. On the contrary, we accept Xenophon's argument that it is usually cheaper to pay in gold than in steel, that one should only obtain resources by force if one cannot obtain them by purchase at market prices. We believe that good fences make good neighbors. War is generally a consequence of insufficiently secure walls and property rights. To substitute conquest of resources for international trade is seldom profitable.

17. The Alt Right observes that men and women are not equal, that in relationships between them, the man should take the superior position. We endorse Pauline marriage - that divorce should only be for grave fault, that the husband should have authority over the wife, and the father authority over the children. We recollect that for nearly two millenia, the Church, and the Christian state, backed the authority of the husband over the wife, and backed the husband against adulterers, by the most drastic means.

## Malaysia departs the blue empire

2016-11-03 03:44:29

After a wonderful speech indicting American anarcho tyranny, Duterte announced the Philippines would no longer be a vassal of the US and would henceforth be a vassal of China. And how about a bilateral trade deal between the Philippines and China? He then went to China's ancient, traditional, and natural enemy, Japan, and said the Philippines would not be anyone's vassal, and how about a bilateral trade deal between the Philippines and Japan?

A little while ago the notoriously and outrageously corrupt US Justice Department, notorious for launching frivolous lawsuits against corporations with deep pockets, and suggesting that the corporations settle by handing out huge amounts of slush money to private individuals who are political allies of individuals in the Justice Department, launched criminal charges of corruption against the Prime Minister of Malaysia, as if Malaysia was some suburb of Washington.

Instead of coming to the US to be put in a US jail by a US court, for crimes committed entirely within Malaysia with absolutely no connection to the US, the Prime Minister of Malaysia headed off to China to do a Duterte.

The specific accusation made by the US Department of Justice against Najib is that he had his Malaysian government do a large favor for a private Malaysian corporation, which subsequently, surprise surprise, made a large private donation to his Malaysian private political campaign, as if this sort thing does not happen all the time in Clinton emails, and as if the US Department of Justice does not openly do far worse things every day.

My analysis is that the dominoes are falling as a result of Blue Empire defeat in Aleppo, as the dominoes fell after Soviet defeat in Afghanistan, or American defeat in Vietnam. But the incompetent, hostile and unpleasant behavior of the US government also pushes its subject states to do what the weakness of the US government allows them to do.

Hat Tip Spandrell[431], the reactionary and darkly enlightened expert on all things East Asian.

## The trouble with Jew centric theory

### 2016-11-04 07:30:48

We are saturated in hateful anti white propaganda. To counter this propaganda it is enormously effective to suggest that those spreading it do not internally identify as white, even though they may superficially look white, that those piously bemoaning white privilege and piously saying "white like me" do not in fact think they themselves are white, but rather, by white, they mean "goy", that they are preaching hatred against the outgroup that they hope to exterminate by means of their underclass allies, hence the oddly suicidal Jewish enthusiasm for the Islamification of Europe.

It is a devastatingly effective meme. Wonderfully effective. And there is quite a lot of truth to it. And it works great on the anti Christian propaganda also, linking it to the the anti white propaganda. If someone is genuinely an atheist, he will not care about Christians, though he might well worry about Muslims. Show me an active, energetic prosyletizing atheist, and he energetically prosyletizes against Christians, not Jews and not Muslims, and most of the time he interprets the old testament as not meaning what it says, but rather what twenty first century Jews today think that it means - in other words, the vast majority of active, energetic, prosyletizing "atheists" just somehow happen to believe that Jews have a special pipeline to God, which is an odd belief for an "atheist" to have.

But then you wind up overlooking anti male propaganda and the huge epidemic of false rape accusations and frivolous domestic violence accusations. And wind up overlooking leftist victories before 1930s, in particular the war of Northern Aggression, and worst of all, overlooking the emancipation of women.

Jew centric theory always winds up saying that 1930s leftism, the leftism of Hitler and FDR, was just fine, that leftism was not too bad until Jews got in on it, that leftism was just fine until the Frankfurt School corrupted it. It was not just fine.

The future belongs to those that show up. Whites, particularly high IQ whites, only succeed in reproducing within the patriarchal family structure.

---

[431] https://bloodyshovel.wordpress.com/2016/11/02/nobody-rules-alone/

If you believe we must secure the existence of our people and a future for white children, because the beauty of the White Aryan woman must not perish from the earth, have to unemancipate women.

If we are going to unemancipate women, 1930s leftism is not OK. If 1930s leftism is not OK, we wind up with Moldbug's Puritan/Harvard hypothesis.

If you would rather blame everything on Jews than on Harvard, or on the Frankfurt School rather than the Harvard of 1800, you wind up not being able to enjoy this rebel anthem:

## Rolling Stone found guilty of defamation for rape hoax

2016-11-05 06:37:20

The judge, unreasonably and improperly, set the very high bar of "actual malice".

Either the jury ignored the judge's direction, or, more likely, the jury consciously or subconsciously realized that when every single person connected to this case piously agreed that there was a whole lot of rape on campus, they did not actually mean that there was a whole lot of rape type rape on campus, or indeed any rape type rape on campus, that these pious proclamations were intended as a theological truth rather than a literal truth, intended to signify that the speaker feels the pain and traumatization that women are feeling in sexual jungle, not to signify that women were literally being raped.

If we realize that consensual sex is apt to be traumatic for women, maybe we should not be letting women make these decisions. Jackie Coakley was traumatized because Ryan Duffin would not have sex with her twice. The reverse decision, refusing to have sex with the father of one's children, or refusing to have sex with one's husband, is apt to be equally disastrous for women.

If two men agree to exchange apples and iron, we should conclude the deal makes both of them better off, that consent is proof that the deal should go through, and lack of consent is proof it should not. With fertile age women possessed by raging hormones, similar reasoning is inapplicable.

## The wicked flee when no man pursueth

2016-11-06 22:47:19

Trump's final ads say "The political establishment has bled this country dry", and Jews hear "Jews have bled this country dry"

That said, the political establishment are the people in the Podesta emails, who are disproportionately Jewish, but are not mostly Jewish, and most Jews don't get to email Podesta.

Most of the the screen time in Trump's recent ad is occupied by non Jewish figures representing the political establishment, in roughly similar proportion as Jews and non Jews are represented in the Podesta emails. Jews doing bad things are overrepresented in the Trump ads to roughly the same extent as in the Podesta emails, in real life, Jews doing bad things are over represented in the political establishment.

There are three Jewish villains and considerably more than three non Jewish villains in Trump's ad, roughly the same proportion as appear in the Podesta emails.

One of the figures who briefly flash up in his ad is (((George Soros))), whose business model consists of buying worthless debt from insolvent third world governments, and then having the World Bank, also known as the US tax payer, restore the debt to its face value. If that is not bleeding this country, what is?

Trump could have used Jon Corzine instead of George Soros, but Soros is better known, perhaps because he is Jewish, but mostly because he has stolen more money and done more bad things than Jon Corzine, not only stolen much more money, but also overthrown various governments in the service of the state department, for example the government of the Ukraine, and attempted to overthrow of several more, for example the government of Hong Kong. For all his many faults, Jon Corzine has not overthrown any governments, though maybe he helped keep a government in power that should have been overthrown.

Trump uses the (((CEO of Goldman Sachs))) to illustrate "pockets of a handful of large corporation". Goldman Sachs was the biggest unpunished recipient of bailout money in the recent financial crisis. Other institutions received more bailout money, but were punished by re-orgs that removed the worst offenders from power. Trump could have used Angelo Mozilo, who cost ordinary Americans far more than Goldman Sachs, but Mozilo was removed from power and had some of his ill gotten gains confiscated. Blankfein, Soros and Clinton are in each other's pockets today, while no one admits that they used to be friends of Angelo not so very long ago. Maybe Goldman Sachs is notorious in substantial part because they are Jewish recipients of bailout money - but also because demonstrably more powerful than any of the other recipients of large amounts of bailout money.

If Jews are overrepresented among the readily identifiable people in the Trump ad, that is because a few Jews made themselves readily identifiable by committing enormous crimes with the blessing of the political establishment, and possessing vast power and wealth despite vast unpunished crimes. If you want an image to illustrate "Those who control the levers of power in Washington", who would be a better image than George Soros? If you want an image to illustrate money going into the "pockets of a handful of large corporation", who would be a better image than the CEO Goldman Sachs? Yes more money was spent to bail out Countrywide bank than to bail out Goldman Sachs, but the (((CEO of Goldman Sachs))) is still in the Clinton circle, whereas the former CEO of Countrywide, while still rich, has been unpersoned.

I suppose that Trump could have left out (((the Federal Reserve Chairwoman))), and arguably should have, but it is notorious that the Fed is intentionally causing asset inflation and blowing asset bubbles, which is an economic policy that favors the very rich at the expense of the middle class.

# Demon Worship

## 2016-11-08 19:57:27

The Clinton circle ritually and collectively perform degenerate acts as a sacrament (Podesta's Spirit Cooking). There are increasing grounds to suspect that they engaged in child sacrifice.

I don't suppose they would think of it as demon worship, rather they think they are worshiping themselves and their own magical powers, but the connections to child traffickers reveal that it is demon worship. Hillary famously said "It takes a village", and she has taken a few, or at least she applied State Department power to protect child traffickers that stole a few.

Meanwhile, the State Department some time ago installed Ms.Park Gyun-Hye as the President of South Korea, and was and is confident of her servile obedience, and continues to feel that were she replaced, it would be a bad thing for "the international community".

But it was recently revealed that Ms.Park Gyun-Hye was the servile and mistreated puppet of a circle of people who claim magical powers and perform magic rituals[432].

So if she is the puppet of a religious leader, then the religious leader must be the puppet of the State Department, or, more likely, since cohesion usually comes from shared religion and ritual practice, the State Department is controlled by practitioners of the same religion, who meet together to do disgusting stuff like drinking the blood of children, which bonds them together.

The Cathedral is not so much a single conspiracy, as the net entropic consequence of a huge number of conspiracies. It cannot be accurately modeled as a single conscious being. Apple under Jobs was an extension of the will of Jobs, and its actions were explicable as the pursuit of profit and the pursuit of excellence. The American government cannot be modeled as the will of Obama, or the will of a small group capable of meeting around a coffee table and its actions cannot be modeled as the pursuit of anything coherent or sane. But the largest and most cohesive conspiracy will exercise the most power and gain the most privilege, and the largest and most cohesive conspiracy is apt to be the beneficiary of shared religious worship and belief.

Since the Clinton circle is clearly the most powerful conspiracy, we would expect it to be the largest and most cohesive, hence we would expect it to be held together by the glue of shared religious worship and belief - religion and belief that supplies plentiful amounts of blackmail material. It is inherent in the nature of the Cathedral that one is likely to find something like a cult of demon worshipers exercising the most power. You have inner circles, inner circles within inner circles, and natural selection for the meme system most capable of gaining and holding power.

You will notice that the pope and almost every christian authority has backed Hilton to the hilt, knowing that she engages in degenerate acts conducted as a sacrament.

---

[432]https://bloodyshovel.wordpress.com/2016/11/02/nobody-rules-alone/

# Draining the swamp

## 2016-11-09 22:32:26

Trump has promised to drain the swamp.

Then in his acceptance speech, he promised not to drain the swamp.

This is less worrying than it might seem, since when you purge powerful people, you don't want them to see it coming.

From now till the start of the purge, he is going to be playing his cards very close to his chest. Any predictions made from his behavior between now and the purge will be incorrect, because his behavior between now and the purge will be deceptively moderate. The start of the purge will itself be deceptively moderate. And then he will keep on purging. How far he will go, nobody knows. I don't know.

I would guess the purge starts in March at the earliest. First he has to get his key people into position. Then suddenly, wham, he gets his enemies out of position.

He has for many years been psychologically preparing the American people for massive firings of the permanent government, which firings the courts will deem illegal, but the public will wonder what the hell the courts are maundering about. These firings will happen when those he is about to fire are least expecting it, when they think they have gotten the upper hand over Trump. And during the first months of a Trump government, it will look as if they have the upper hand over Trump.

There may well be a Reichstag fire moment, when something happens that dramatically symbolizes the resistance of the permanent government to the merely elected government. Expect the newspapers to return to their old form and triumphantly announce how Trump has been decisively and humiliatingly defeated, how his policy is in ruins, because impossible to implement. If, as is likely, they announce that, they are falling into his trap, as when the Comintern set fire to the conveniently unguarded Reichstag.

The big known unknown is how thoroughly he intends to drain the swamp.

What we would like Trump to do is purge the government of traitors, bribe takers, degenerates, people on the revolving door between regulators and regulated, enemies of America, and, of course, Satanists. The Ming Dynasty criminalized sects because of the propensity of sect members to attain political power, such as the Ming dynasty itself. Deem membership of a sect that does weird stuff moral turpitude. Then fix numerous consent judgments organized by the Justice Department that make political dissent a violation of the affirmative action laws. Generate a precedent that disparate impact is legal, and unambiguously legalize domain specific IQ tests of the Fizzbuzz type or domain appropriate physical tests of the Marine pull up type. If only 0.1% of female and black applicants pass your company's Fizzbuzz, you should have a cast iron defense against discrimination charges, even if search of your emails reveal engineers saying hateful things about women and blacks. Generate the legal precedent that evidence of political dissent cannot be presented as evidence of discrimination, and may not be presented in court because it merely prejudices the judgment. Then reverse the degree inflation that forces ever increasing numbers of students to spend ever increasing time in educational institutions that do not educate but merely indoctrinate. then confiscate the endowments, burn Harvard to the ground and salt the earth where it stood. Or redevelop Harvard into shops, offices, and hotels, which is more Trump's style.[433]

And, of course, use state power over cable and broadcast television to encourage the companies to fire Colbert and replace him with someone with an actual sense of humor and willingness to puncture actual sacred cows, like Pax Dickinson.

But before he gets to making Saturday Night Live funny again, has to get to redevelop Harvard into shops, condos, hotels, and offices.

Currently we have an elaborate system where committees give grants to people who are on committees. This renders power and funding untraceable and difficult to control. To drain the swamp, has to run government money through a direct hierarchy operating on das Führerprinzip.

So the Dean of a university should be appointed by the board, the Dean should have the power to hire and fire professors, and all academic funding should go through university, which is to say through the dean. If the Pentagon wants a professor at MIT to research something, it should pay MIT, not the professor.

We should abolish tenure. Tenure was supposed to make professors proudly independent and capable of dissent, but instead every single academic at every single institution grovels. When the line changes, every professor changes his position and instantly forgets that the line was different yesterday. The line emerges from an amorphous mass of committees, obscuring who has power and who makes decisions.

Outside funding of academics should be seen as corrupting. Would Steve Jobs be happy if one of his executives received large payments from a committee containing people connected to a competing company? All funding should go directly through the board and Dean/CEO.

And when we have replaced hidden lines of authority with direct lines of authority, on das Führerprinzip, we can then hold those with that authority responsible for what they do with it.

After getting rid of committees and outside funding, which hides who has power and who makes decisions, then and only then can we purge academia.

That is what is needed to stop Cthulhu from always swimming left, that is what is needed to make Saturday Night Live funny again. Whether Trump is up to go all the way with this program is, of course, the big known unknown.

## The winds of freedom already blow

2016-11-10 00:22:13

Whatever Trump may do after he ascends the throne, he has already done more for freedom than every past president.

Twitter shadowbanned numerous people, including Trump himself. The morning after the night that Trump's election was called, the CEO of Twitter resigned. The COO of twitter resigned at 2PM on the 9th[434], about the time it became obvious that Trump had won. The "where is Hillary" hash tag ridiculing Hillary's failure to concede in a timely manner appeared at about 5PM on the ninth.

---

[433] https://blog.reaction.la/economics/what-to-do-in-a-restoration/
[434] https://twitter.com/adambain/status/796473439317954560

I imagine he expected a short and unpleasant board meeting, and decided not to attend.

I expect the man responsible for shadowbanning Donald Trump to remain radioactive for quite some time.

The practical effect of this is that the Altright has been mainstreamed. For years, progs have been saying that anyone outside the ever narrowing Overton window is literally Hitler and is going to genocide the Jews, to which the Altright replies:
> "Yeah, sure"

Anti semitism, promulgated by the Altright but not by Trump himself, was a hugely effective counter measure against the stream of anti white, and anti white male propaganda. It freed people from their guilt for being white.

I expect that the Trump campaign, and the Republican party remade in Trump's image, will hire numerous Altrightists for cushy government and party jobs, though probably not the unironic day-of-the-rope fire-up-the-ovens factions. Trumpism is that we are going to this legally and constitutionally - well, legally as the people judge legality, not necessarily legally as far left judges judge legality. Trumpism is populist. Neoreactionaries don't really care what the people might judge as legal. But today, we are all Trumpists. And Trump does care what the people might judge as legal.

I am rather doubtful that this can be done legally and constitutionally, but obviously needs to be tried. And tried damned hard. I rather suspect that trying damned hard is likely to morph into the Trump monarchy, regardless of Trump's intentions.

Anti semitism is false and dangerous, in that though Jews are overrepresented among political insiders and progs, political insiders and progs are not an instrument of a vast Jewish conspiracy, rather the reverse, but nobody was fighting fair, and antisemitism, the stream of memes originating largely in Pol, worked in its usual function as a populist appeal to the masses, to the considerable benefit of Trump, who though he did not get his own hands dirty, was not overly horrified by his allies and supporters getting their hands alarmingly dirty.

White people and males pull the lever for Democrats because they feel bad about being white and/or bad about being male. Trumpism was and is an upsurge of outrage against this feeling and the stream of propaganda that makes whites and males feel bad about themselves, the stream of hateful hostile venomous propaganda denigrating whites and males.

But if you think that stream is a Jewish conspiracy, you are apt to overlook the even more obvious stream of hateful hostile venomous propaganda denigrating husbands and fathers.


# In favor of taking the left on helicopter rides to the Pacific

## 2016-11-10 07:17:54

Trump is our leader, and Trump plans to do this in accord with the spirit of the constitution, which is to say, without helicopter rides to the Pacific. Maybe it can be made to work that way, and if can be made to work that way, its our duty to make it work that way.

But the left really are hateful horrible thoroughly nasty people. Notice for example that servants of the Clintons have a remarkable rate of "suicide" and "accidental" death. I rather think therefore it cannot be made to work that way, that helicopter rides are going to be needed. If you allow commies freedom of speech, you wind up without freedom of speech.

There are a lot of highly intelligent really nice people on the left, for example Scott Aaronson and Scott Alexander, who pat themselves on the back about their wonderful commitment to civil discourse and how they quietly disapprove of the worst extremes of Social Justice Warriors. But they refuse to hear anything that anyone to the right of them says, and refuse to engage in in intelligent rational discussion those to the right of them, instead engaging in casual, thoughtless and ignorant demonization. Their niceness manifests as willingness to be literally cuckolded, rather than willingness to notice that the US was backing the genocide the Alawites and the Tutsis, or willingness to engage in intelligent civilized conversation with their intelligent and civilized opponents, because to engage in intelligent civilized conversation with their intelligent and civilized opponents would involve thoughtcrime. There was a time when Scott Alexander would converse to those to his right, but he, and the entire left, have stopped doing so, probably due to the ever expanding definition of thoughtcrime. The entire left has shut down any conversation with the entire right, for fear of thought contamination.

If you will not talk, it is going to be war sooner or later.

If someone just flat refuses to talk to me or talk to anyone like me, he is an enemy. So genuine unironic Nazis are not enemies, merely friends that are mistaken about socialism and the role of Jews. They will talk with me in a civilized rational fashion, so seem unlikely to murder me. Theoretically they will murder Moldbug but they really just do not seem like the kind of people who would murder Moldbug. As soon as someone like Moldbug turns up, I figure they would turn into merely ironic Nazis. But the left will not talk with me except under my moderate prog identities, nor with anyone like me. Not even the high IQ and supposedly moderate and reasonable left, those that think themselves the sane, smart, and moderate left. Which makes resolution of conflicts impossible, and in the long run, war inevitable. In the long run, they are going to wind up unintentionally blundering into trying to kill the people that they have intemperately demonized and will not hear, and the people that they have demonized and that they will not hear will try to kill them.

And, given that war seems inevitable, we would be foolish to start the salami slicer on the unironic nazis. The cuckservative collapse occurred because in an endlessly unsuccessful effort to make themselves acceptable to the left they read one faction after another out of the conservative movement, as racist, sexist, homophobic, transphobic, whatever, until there was hardly anyone remaining, until the salami slicer had consumed most of the salami.

I recently read how Nixon was supposedly a terrible horrible opponent of affirmative action. In actual fact Nixon enormously expanded affirmative action. He just did not go quite as far in making dissent from affirmative action a crime as some people wanted - which oversight was swiftly remedied by the justice department in a series of consent decrees, wherein employees committing thought crime constitutes proof of discrimination.

Affirmative action under Nixon was the salami slicer moving into high gear, and recent events are the salami slicer running short of salami.

## Don't worry about Trump policy reversals - yet

### 2016-11-10 20:18:06

Trump is reversing himself on pretty much everything. Suddenly he is the cuckservative president.

But remember, he does not formally get power until January, and actually getting his hands on the real levers of power will take at least six weeks after that. He will not really have power until March at the earliest.

The wonderful smirk on his face gives me strong hope that once he has his hands on the levers of power, there will be an April surprise. If we are lucky, a March surprise.

Well, maybe we are all going to be double crossed. We always knew we might all be double crossed. But don't start the revolution until Trump is in power and rolling. Wait for the Comintern to burn the conveniently unguarded Reichstag, and then we shall see what happens. Then we will know if democratic politics double crosses us every time.

One of the things that give me high hopes is that Trump has been cultivating the praetorians for a long time. Plan for blackshirts, not brownshirts. In his victory speech he pissed on his base, but he did not piss on his praetorians.

A lot of the alt-right has been prepping for brownshirts. Cut it out. The left has the antifa to irregularly beat up real and imagined enemies while police stand around like potted palms, but we are not going to have brownshirts. Rather, once Trump purges the justice department, if Trump purges the justice department, police are going to stop winking at the crimes committed by antifa.

## Recap on Global Warming

### 2016-11-13 02:52:37

Some days are warmer, some are cooler. Some years are warmer, some are cooler. Some centuries are warmer, some are cooler.

Not only does climate vary, but the variability itself is subject to change. Ten degree swings over decade have happened, and when that happens once, usually happens ten or twenty times over the following millenia. Fortunately we have not had anything as bad as that in recent millenia, but during Roman times it was substantially warmer than today, and wheat grew in what is now desert, today's deserts were the breadbasket of Europe, and during the little ice age, it was mighty cold, and the deserts were bigger.

The Hockey stick curve (which shows climate stable until industrialization) is just phony. The climategate files revealed that those proclaiming it showed no interest in whether it was true or false. Mann delegated the key work to minor grad students, told them what the data should show, and displayed absolutely no interest in how they tortured the data to get his predetermined result. This was obvious when it came out, and confirmed by the leak of climategate files. Mann himself did not know how the Hockey Stick curve was generated, in the sense that he failed to ask, and showed no interest in, the questions raised in the Harry_Read_Me.txt file, which discusses the manufacture of the corrupted and corrupting data used to weight the proxies, and also in that Harry, a low status menial, was tasked with recreating graphs already published, implying that Mann and company had no idea where those graphs came from or what they were based on, if anything.

Mann and company vaguely hoped and sort of believed that they curves that they published were somehow derived from observations, but they did not know, and showed no interest in, what observations, and how derived.

When the Hockey Stick Curve appeared it showed the classic marks of theocratic science.

Everyone used to believe, based on extensive evidence, that climate had been highly variable in the past. And then suddenly everyone in academia changed their belief, quietly forgetting that they used to believe something complete different, without asking for the evidence that supposedly supported their new belief.

Indeed, to ask the new experts how they knew their new facts about past climate was deemed an act of harassment. To ask, was to be anti scientific, since you were showing disrespect to official science. Every academic everywhere, with a handful of courageous exceptions that were swiftly brought into line, agreed with the new line, and declined to ask dangerous and subversive questions as to what data, what evidence, brought the new line about. How did one proceed from observations of fossil trees and glaciers to a conclusion very different to that which past observers of fossil trees and glaciers had concluded? No one would tell, and no one important would ask.

When the state officially recognizes science and scientists, this tends to make scientists into priests.

In the restoration, Charles the Second created the Royal Society to keep scientists on track, which was part of his purge of the priesthood. It is a pity he did not create an inquisition to continue the purges and keep the rest of the priesthood on track.

From the Restoration in 1660, to the end of World War II, the Royal society enforced the scientific method. If you wanted respect and esteem as a scientist, you had to tell us new and interesting things, *and you had to show everyone how you knew these new and interesting things from what you saw with your eyes and touched with your hands.*

After World War II, Harvard got the upper hand over the Royal Society, and you no longer have to show your work. Instead, your work must be approved by the most holy synod of mother church - in other words, must pass peer review *behind closed doors*. Peer Review is new. Attempts to root it in the past of science before World War II are artificial and contrived. Somehow we obtained almost all of science that matters before we had peer review, and since we have had peer review, things have started to go terribly wrong with science. Peer Review is science by social consensus, and Galileo told us that that does not work.

Global Warming is much the same religion as the Aztec state religion. Sacrifices must be made, or else the sun will not rise to tomorrow, and the priests can therefore pull strings, so that some people are sacrificed more, and others less, as with Chris Turner's carbon indulgences[435].

---

[435] https://blog.reaction.la/global-warming/global-warming-scientists-trapped-in-antarctic-denial/

It is not enough to stop the sacrifices though that is a damned good start. The priesthood itself must be purged, for as long as they have state power, they will continue to apply it against Trump.

The permanent government will always win over the temporary government unless purged, and the permanent state religion will always control the permanent government, unless a King places himself the head of that religion, and, armed with an inquisition, brings it into line. May Trump become God Emperor, or at least King and High Priest. And may his grand inquisitor purge Satanism from our political elite and lies and heresy such as Catastrophic Anthropogenic Global Warming from our priesthood, with holy fire.

We need to suppress Catastrophic Anthropogenic Global Warming as Castile suppressed the Old Gods of Mexico, and as the Romans suppressed Druidism, and for much the same reasons, and with much the same methods. Global Warming is not an example of science making a mistake. Science always makes mistakes, and advances because of them. Global Warming is an example of an evil priesthood and evil priests, pursuing evil goals by evil means. Scientific errors should not be punished, but evil religions need to be forcibly suppressed by centralized power and state violence, for evil religions propagate by centralized power and state violence, and thus can be suppressed by no other means.

## What the alt right hopes for from Trump

### 2016-11-18 08:58:47

Trump has promised to build a wall, deport millions of illegals, and stop people who hate us from migrating here.

Well, that is pretty good, but what we really wish is for Trump to be King and high priest, and his son to be grand inquisitor.

That is a mighty tall order, but it would stand a mighty good chance of curing civilizational decay.

We need him to be King or Emperor, because democracy is against us. We don't want women and blacks voting. Democracy always tempts politicians to enfranchise or import low information voters that can be bought cheaply, obamaphone voters. Thus in the end, democracy winds up as the government electing a new people

We need him to be god, or high priest, or archbishop, so that there is a clearly defined official doctrine that one can piously believe and thereby be an acceptably good person. At present your company is in violation of affirmative action law unless everyone believes in equality twice as much as everyone else, that woman are just as good as men except that they are better, and any underperformance is due to evil sexist thoughts emitted by males, that blacks are just as good as whites and any underperformance is due to evil racist thoughts emitted by whites. The required holy doctrines are set by activist judges and social justice warriors, and thus escalate endlessly. No piety is safe from being deemed racist next year.

We need a grand inquisitor to rid state and quasi state institutions (courts and universities) of demon worshipers, and anyone who claims to be holier than the King, to shut down the holiness competition whereby every professor, every social justice warrior, and every judge tries to be twice as holy as every other.

Of course Trump is not an alt rightist, despite what the left tells themselves. The alt right is just one of the factions of the Trump coalition, and far from being the largest or most influential, though the fact that the alt right is allowed any legitimacy at all horrifies and outrages the left.

But, though just one faction, and far from the largest, Trump has so far shown no inclination to succumb to the pressure to dump parts of the coalition that brought him to power. Many of us expected that he would, and did not much care so long as he builds the wall, but so far, all seems well. He is holding his coalition together. Trump is loyal to those that are loyal to him, and an enemy to his enemies. And if he sliced off one part of his coalition, leftists would demand even more strongly that he slice off another.

So what are our chances of getting what we want, in addition to the wall and the reduced influx of black military age Muslims screaming for infidel blood and white pussy? What are our chances of getting God Emperor Trump, a fixed and safely unchanging holiness doctrine, and an inquisition to make it stick?

I don't care if the Holy Trumpian doctrine of the divine Trump says that blacks are angels, and leprechauns exist, provided that next year you don't have to say they are even better than that.

I rather think we stand a small but significant chance. You will have heard that the Obama/Trump transition is chaos. It is.

The problem however is not with Trump, but with the presidency. The presidency is a worm's nest. Trump wants to transition the permanent government to doing what he damn well tells them, the permanent government wants to transition the merely temporary government into being their public relations boy as usual. Hence the transition is going extremely badly, indeed it is scarcely going at all.

The permanent government is run by committees that supply or deny people who sit on committees status and power and future career opportunities.

Thus, run by consensus of the most holy synod, no one is responsible, and it is impossible to discover who allocated money or authority for what policy, and difficult to determine what the real policy actually being implemented actually is, since the actual on-the-ground policy is unlikely to correspond to its official description.

This architecture makes it difficult to determine who to fire. Perhaps Trump can save time and mental effort by firing entire committees at once.

This architecture is unfixable, no matter how many political commissars you insert, except by not having stuff run by committees - except by reorganizing the permanent government so that it is responsive to a single will, by having money, power, responsibility and authority flow though clear overt formal official hierarchical channels that appear on an organization chart as a top down tree. As King Charles the first said, "No Bishop, no King", meaning if no Bishop, then no King.

One can readily foresee that Trump is going to find dealing with a very decentralized organization frustrating and exhausting. He will issue orders and they will sink into the labyrinthine morass without a trace.

Trump being Trump, I think he not only wants to take charge of the Permanent Government, but is likely to do so, which is a revolutionary act for which he will need revolutionaries. Expect the left to set fire to the Reichstag at a convenient moment.

And if we don't get God Emperor Trump and his holy inquisition, we will say we did and watch the leftists go even crazier.

## Don't Stop

2016-11-20 01:33:53

Scott Alexander has published an essay calling on his fellow leftists to stop screaming[436] racist-misogynist-homophobe-literally-Hitler at everyone all the time at maximum volume.

And a lot of gutless ladyboy cuckservatives are so traumatized at being unkindly treated by the left that they are citing it favorably.

I would unkindly interpret his essay has "Please do not set fire to the Reichstag while Trump has the army and the police, and stop being mean to the legacy Americans until we have imported enough brown allies to kill them all[437]."

What Scott fears is exactly what I hope for with every fiber of my being: That the left screaming racistsexisthomophobe at everyone all the time at maximum volume will eventually lead to a preference cascade where large numbers of manly men go around wearing t shirts saying "I am a proud racist misogynist etc"

If Scott actually wanted peace rather than democidal war, he would be willing to talk to the right, rather than patronizingly lecture them with formulaic repetitious hostile patronizing Stalinist boilerplate, and willing to listen to their reply, their reply invariably being it that we have heard that crap a thousand times before, and it is obviously untrue from scientific studies and everyone's lived experience.

Scott's essay is not an olive branch. It is advice to the left as to how to get in the best position for their coming war upon legacy Americans.

This post stolen wholesale from Steve Johnson's excellent comment.[438]

## Trump's secret plan to defeat Isis

2016-11-21 03:21:54

He is not telling me, and it is risky to attempt to predict the actions of individuals, but Trump has a long history of picking up hundred dollar bills lying on the pavement that everyone else refuses to pick up.

And for the defeat of Isis, the hundred dollar bill lying on the pavement is:

Islamic State's claim to be the Caliphate rests on it being a state, on it controlling territory, a capital, a uniformed army with proper chain of command, and wealth. If you are hiding in a cave on a mountainside, you cannot be the Caliph. So, to kill Islamic State, make it stop being a state. As yet another mere terrorist organization, has less appeal.

So cut a deal with Putin and Assad for a joint attack on the capital of Islamic State. Follow Assad's brutal example by leafleting the place telling everyone to flee or die. Give

---

[436] https://slatestarcodex.com/2016/11/16/you-are-still-crying-wolf/

[437] https://slatestarcodex.com/2016/05/02/be-nice-at-least-until-you-can-coordinate-meanness/

[438] https://blog.reaction.la/politics/what-the-alt-right-hopes-for-from-trump/#comment-1469201

them the opportunity to flee. Then kill everyone who has not fled. Level the capital to the ground. Utterly flatten everything. What the bombs leave standing roll over with mine clearing tanks followed by bulldozer tanks. Rebuild under the control of Sunnis who are in Assad's pocket. Make sure any Sunnis not in his pocket are dead or fled, preferably dead. Repopulate with cooperative Sunnis so that your genocide does not look too much like genocide.

Islamic State will probably still be around as a terrorist organization, but they are, or recently were, committed to realist version of Islam. If they are not a state any more, will not call themselves "Islamic State", will not claim their leader is the rightful Caliph, merely the future Caliph.

He is keeping the plan secret, because he needs to cut a deal and it will make it hard to bargain if he is precommitted to getting the deal.

Of course the left is going to scream genocide, but their humanitarian intervention in Syria was predicated on Alawites being genocided and Christians being expelled to Lebanon, and their humanitarian intervention in the Congo predictably resulted in many, probably most, Tutsi women in the Congo being vaginally impaled with objects as large as themselves. The left murdered about a hundred and seventy million people during the twentieth century, and we should just stop taking their pious cries of moral superiority seriously.

Leftists are weak people, are noisy women and weak men, who identify with power and cruelty, and thus identify with mass murderers and torturers like Che Guevera, Aristide, and Zapata. They loved the Khmer Rouge until the Khmer Rouge lost power by murdering each other until there were not enough competent Khmer Rouge left to uphold the regime. They loved the Khmer Rouge as long as the Khmer Rouge were successfully engaging in mass murder and mass torture, and hated them when, and only when, they lost, hated them not for mass murder and mass torture, but for weakness. As small boys identify with men who drive monster trucks, leftists identify with those who murder and torture. Hence the tendency of teenage boys to be radical leftists, and to cease being radical leftists when they reach their full growth and realize they need to be careful about getting into fights lest they kill someone with their bare hands.

So why are people reluctant to pick up this hundred dollar bill?

Because of an ideological left wing progressive belief in the potency of guerrilla warfare. In practice, guerrillas only succeed to the extent that they are backed by an outside power - usually the State Department. The Vietnam war with in part a proxy war between Russia and America with North and South Vietnam as proxies, but in larger part a proxy war between the State Department's blue empire of the consulates, and the Pentagon's red empire of the bases, as was increasingly obvious towards the end. Islamic state is largely a creation of the State Department, a part of their efforts to overthrown various Arab regimes, in particular Libya, Iraq, and Syria. Once they go back from State to State warfare down to guerrilla warfare and lose State Department backing, they will be insignificant.

## The Overton Bubble

2016-11-23 01:07:06

The Overton window has formed a bubble. People inside the bubble now refuse to have anything to do with those outside the bubble, refuse to hear, refuse to understand, refuse even to notice, react to them only with ignorant crazy hatred, and if anyone respectable shows signs of listening, he loses respectability and gets cast out of the bubble. No longer will respectable people have anything to do with him. He shall be friendless and alone. Except that so many people have been cast out of the bubble that he probably will not be friendless and alone.

This particular form of the left singularity, like many forms, leads inevitably to civil war. Unlike most forms of the left singularity, it will lead to civil war that the left is likely to lose.

Know your enemy and know yourself, win a hundred battles without jeopardy
Know yourself, but not your enemy, win some, lose some.
know neither yourself nor your enemy, always lose.

The left has weaponized self inflicted ignorance, symbolized by literally and physically turning their backs on their opponents. This weapon is apt to backfire. Not a good idea to show your opponent your back.

The back turning maneuver is a DHV (demonstration of higher value) It subcommnicates "You want our attention, but are beneath us, and are no threat to us". It will be harder to pull off once Trump imprisons the officials of a few sanctuary cities and fires the Washington press core. (Which despite being a supposedly private enterprise organization works from government offices and receives the usual services and benefits provided by government employees to people in government offices, as do a great many politically critical supposedly private enterprise organizations. The phrase "NGO" has become a joke, with even NGO employees describing their work as government employment.)

A good reply to the physical back turning maneuver is to pour an iced drink over the offender. You have to respond to the "You are no threat" subcommunication by showing you are a threat.

## No enemies to the right

2016-11-24 00:54:52

Observe that no enemies to the left works great for the left. Obama was an office boy to Bill Ayers, communist and terrorist, and no one ever asks him to disown communists and terrorists.

Similarly observe that no enemies holier than oneself works great for Islamists:
> "Hello, I am a moderate Muslim, a very moderate Muslim, with extensive connections to immoderate Muslims and considerable influence over them, so give me a basket full of degrees from high status universities and a big cadillac with girls in the front and sacks of money in the back, or else my immoderate friends might be displeased with you."

If we disown Nazis then we have to have to disown those one step removed from Nazis, and then we have to have to disown those two steps removed from Nazis, and then we have to have to disown anyone whom the left points the finger at and screams "racist" at, and then we are cuckservatives.

If the lips are gone the mouth will feel cold. Having actual unironic Nazis in the alt-right makes it safe for me to be in the alt-right, since leftists will be too busy having mental breakdowns at the actual unironic Nazis to have mental breakdowns at me.

The left has a thousand points of evil and madness, while anyone who disagrees on a single one of those points is "literally worse than Hitler". The alt-right is everyone who is "literally worse than Hitler".

Typically one alt-rightist is "literally worse than Hitler" because he disagrees on one point, while another alt-rightist disagrees on a different point, so typically two alt rightists have nothing in common except the nine hundred and ninety eight points where they agree with the left.

How then should we deal with disagreements within the alt-right?

One cannot debate everyone, but you should never criticize a fellow alt-rightist you are unwilling to debate. And if you do criticize them, and do not wish to debate them, retract, apologize, and affirm alliance against the common enemy.

Remember you grew up immersed in leftism, that your media shows a radically false picture of life. In the media fathers and husbands are always wicked and/or incompetent, and generally bad for women and children, female sexuality is always chaste and pure, blacks are always magical, women never divorce men for foolish and wicked reasons, all criminals are affluent white males. So if you disagree with your fellow alt-rightist there is a very high chance that you do so in ignorance, foolishness, or even wickedness, since you were raised on media that presents evil as clever, nice, and high status, and good as stupid, nasty, and low status.

Always criticize a fellow alt-rightist as a brother, not an enemy. If you criticize your brother, it is because you want to speak to him, and him to speak to you. If you criticize your brother, you must first be willing to learn where he is coming from, you must first want to learn where he is coming from.

## Google searches left wing indoctrination for you.

### 2016-11-25 02:48:12

Duckduckgo search for Hillary Clinton images.[439] Of the top ten images three are are photoshopped and/or selected against her, three are photoshopped or selected for her, and four are neutral photos, which is exactly what you would expect in a country split down the middle.

Google search for Hillary Clinton Images[440]. Every single image photoshopped in her favor.

If you are using google search, you are only searching half the web, the half that carries the official truth. For Google, authoritative sources are those inside the Overton Window. If you specifically search for a subversive source, Google will find it for you, but if you do a general search, you will not easily find crimethink.

---

[439] https://duckduckgo.com/?t=palemoon&q=hillary+clinton&iax=1&ia=images
[440] https://www.google.com.ph/search?q=hillary+clinton&source=lnms&tbm=isch&sa=Xn

## No enemies to the right consensus

2016-11-25 08:38:32

I, Roosh, Vox Populi, and those that should not be named have agreed they are not going to disavow Spencer, while criticizing him as a one would criticize a brother and an ally. If Heartiste comes aboard, that should settle it.

## Hail Trump

2016-11-26 00:25:27

That is Hail, not Heil

That is Hail Trump as in Hail Caesar Augustus, not Heil Trump as in Heil Hitler.

This is a reference and reverence to God Emperor Caesar Augustus who did to decadent Roman democracy much what Hitler did to decadent German democracy for much the same reasons, but fortunately your average Harvard graduated social justice warrior does not know any history other than Hitler killing the Jews, whites enslaving blacks, and that every thing was invented by blacks except what was invented by women.

That is why we call him God Emperor Trump, not der Führer.

By the way, the Roman salute to God Emperor Caesar Augustus differs slightly from the Nazi salute, in that the palm is visible, rather than down, and the fingers may be semi closed, but not clenched, but don't try it because social justice warriors will not know the difference.

We are who we are, so to salute president elect Trump in the hope that he will soon become God Emperor Trump, I recommend the military salute universally used by western armies for a long time. For extra fun points, this salute was in fact the salute used by the German army in World War II, and every other white army, but social justice warriors don't know that.

## Hard core and softcore Trump appointments

2016-11-26 02:49:12

Early appointments hard core, and primarily directed at those departments that you need to prevent a coup by the permanent government against the president, or make a self coup by the president against the permanent government.

Later appointments softcore cuckservative, and directed at those departments that are irrelevant in the event of a coup.

A big exception to this is the Department of State, which applies semi soft power to overthrow foreign governments and manipulate political outcomes within America. It does not directly control anything that can be directly used to make a coup, except for organizations like the CIA for which Trump has already chosen an establishment figure who is nonetheless extremely hostile to the State Department, but it does control the NGOs that can send out a mob of protesters to delegitimize the government and provide justification for a coup. Trump's plans for dealing with the State Department (coup central) are unclear. I conjecture he is going to promise them someone they are happy with, then change his mind a few weeks after becoming president, once he has his own men in the army, the FBI, and the justice department.

## Frame

### 2016-11-30 10:12:53

We just have to have stronger frame than theirs.

Their frame is that they are virtuous and we are wicked, and that we know they are virtuous and we are wicked.

They refuse to interact with anyone who fails to accept their frame of moral superiority - that they are better than us because they deeply care about people located in places that they cannot find on a map of the world.

In actual fact their supposed good intentions usually have horrifying and brutal effects on the supposed beneficiaries, and when their supposed good intentions have horrifying effects on the supposed beneficiaries they are entirely comfortable and have not the slightest hesitation in blaming the victims, as for example the recent aid to Haiti fiasco, the earlier imposition of Aristide on Haiti at gunpoint which resulted in Aristide torturing to death very large numbers of real, suspected, and imaginary rightists in highly creative ways, the humanitarian intervention in Syria which if Russia had not intervened would have resulted in the total genocide of the Alawites, the expulsion of Christians to Lebanon, and the expulsion or genocide of several varieties of Shiite, in particular the genocide of the Palestinian Shiites, and the very similar humanitarian intervention in the Congo which predictably resulted in many, perhaps most, Tutsi women in the Congo being vaginally impaled with objects larger than themselves

Our frame has to be that they are hypocritical sycophants engaged in an ever escalating contest to speak power to truth, that they mindlessly regurgitate ignorant and formulaic Stalinist boilerplate to ingratiate themselves to power, power that is alarmingly capricious, brutal, cruel, terrifying, and erratic. That goodness begins at home - which implies that a grown woman with no husband is a bad woman.

Their supposed goodness is confirmed in their minds a false history of the world in which white males cause black and female underperformance. They supposedly believe that women and blacks are equal while indulging female irresponsibility and black violence. Women are in practice treated as children, except that when a child misbehaves the child is hauled off to the responsible adult who is told to discipline his child, but women misbehave and get away with it, for no one can haul them off to the responsible male who will be told to discipline his women.

In their history of the world Rhodesia, the Belgian Congo, segregation and slavery were hurtful evil crimes against blacks committed because whites hate blacks. They read and believe a press in which covers in hostile and mendacious detail every incident where a white kills a black, while piously ignoring an enormous number of incidents where blacks attack whites out of hatred inculcated into them in school, in university, and in the mass media.

In fact, blacks were immensely better off under white rule in Rhodesia and the Belgian Congo than before and after, slavery was necessary because of black disinclination to work for a living, and ever since slavery whites have been carrying blacks upon their backs. Segregation was an early form of affirmative action for blacks, artificially creating a black middle class by protecting them from white competition.

Their supposed moral superiority rests not on actual deeds to friends and family, which are generally hateful and contemptible, but on what they have been mendaciously and flatteringly told about things that happened long ago and far away.

## The fall

### 2016-12-02 02:05:18

Support for democracy is falling.

In practice, "democracy" has always been rule by the left. They fix the electorate as needed, by expanding it, "educating" it, applying political repression, or bringing in a new people to replace the old people, so as to ensure a vote for current leftism. Which gets ever lefter. And current leftism has been getting crazier and crazier, faster and faster[441]. Which requires ever more drastic measures to massage the electorate to obtain an acceptable result.

Lockean doctrine implied a democracy of property holders - since the only legitimate activities of the state were to defend the realm and uphold property rights, and allowing non property holders to vote would obviously undermine property rights. In Whig history, the restriction to property holders and the importance of securing property rights gets forgotten.

In Whig history Lockeanism was triumphant in the Glorious revolution, which supposedly established the supremacy of parliament. Perhaps it did, but Lock and his patrons were exiled. If those in power were Lockeans they were forced to remain mighty quiet about it until the early 1800s in order to avoid the wrath of the divine right monarch.

Divine right was still live when George proclaimed that God had appointed him regent. This resulted in Trump/Bush levels of derangement on the left, and the entire Victorian era and the resulting emancipation of women and destruction of marriage can in large part be understood as an effort to retroactively destroy George the Fourth. His filthy slut wife is still today written up as a long suffering saint, and hence all women are saints, and only wives are ever wronged, never husbands. We are still today suffering under a propaganda offensive created to delegitimize George the fourth. The left is still today half cracked on anything King George related. Anything your read in official history related to King George the fourth is half lies and half butthurt madness.

Whigs got the decisive upper hand when King George's reign ended - and two years after his death instituted lockean democracy limited to property holders. Which property restriction was progressively diluted resulting in the election of lefter and lefter governments, until in 1918 they gave large numbers of non property holders the vote, who promptly proceeded to vote against property rights. So the period where Lock's doctrines were actually in effect was about fifty two years, from 1832 to 1884. Britain went from kingly and aristocratic rule to democracy of the propertyless with an intervening period

---

[441] https://dissentingsociologist.wordpress.com/2016/11/26/leftism-the-religion-that-failed-a-study-in-insecure-power-and-social-disorganization/

of rule by the property owning classes of about fifty to ninety years, from 1832 to 1884, or from 1832 to 1918.

This was classical liberalism, libertarianism, which is a reasonable and sane form of leftism. But it did not come to power by itself, could not come to power by itself. It came to power in coalition with two evil and crazy forms of leftism, hatred of colonialism and the doctrine that women are angels, which doctrine of women as angels was used as a bludgeon against King George and the Aristocracy, and continues to be used as a bludgeon against King George and the Aristocracy, even today.

Pretty soon the evil and crazy left devoured the sane left. Since women are angels there is supposedly no need to coercively enforce chastity on them, and the marital contract only needs to be enforced on men, not women, Enforcing it on women is supposedly just misogyny. The result was what you would expect, a massive wave of female promiscuity and adultery, for example the whore Florence Nightingale and the slut Queen Caroline, and a vast horde of illegitimate children.

A lot of libertarians believe that if we refrain from subsidizing fatherless children, we will not have fatherless children. Victorianism proved this false, with far too many women giving birth in dark alleys in the rain. If you don't have a welfare state to support fatherless children, you have to do what the Victorians failed to do, forcefully coerce women to behave chastely, subjecting them to the authority of responsible male adults with authority to use corporal punishment. We wound up with a welfare state in large part because the Victorian failure to police female chastity with male authority and physical coercion resulted in an intolerable torrent of bastards.

The United States is a more complicated story, because, until the war of Northern Aggression, things happened state by state. Whigs generally came to power in the American Revolution, but not always and everywhere, so came to power somewhat earlier in America than in Britain. In America, Lockeanism, democracy restricted to property owners, generally had a short life. To get acceptably leftist governments elected, had to enfranchise the masses. And then had to enfranchise even more of the masses. And then enfranchise women. And then had to bring in the third world to replace legacy Americans.

Religions are synthetic tribes. So we are always ruled by a theocracy, defining religions broadly to include quasi religious doctrines like communism and proggism. But proggism, the religion descended from whiggery, itself descended from puritanism, has become ever more evil, ever more insane, and is getting crazier faster and faster. This is inevitable in a state religion that lacks an archbishop and a grand inquisitor to prevent holiness spirals. If adherents of a belief system took power, the way for the next guy to take power is to adhere to that belief system only even more so and with knobs on top.

So the day inexorably comes when proggism shall fall, and with it democracy.

Lockeanism was a pretty good idea - but ultimately it was a mere tool to power, and rapidly got left behind in the holiness spiral. The good ideas got used up, and the ideas remaining are demolition of Chesterton's fence. When your ideology takes power, it becomes a state religion, and you are going to need an archbishop and a grand inquisitor to prevent your ideology from being devoured by those holier than you are.

You have to have someone whose job it is to stop holiness spirals, to officially discredit those who preach more than the required level of holiness, to ensure that those possessing state power are sufficiently holy but not holier than the King, the Archbishop, and the Grand Inquisitor.

## Trump already setting things right

### 2016-12-04 01:16:43

The first hundred days has not even begun, but Trump is already governing through business connections, elite connections, and texting, bypassing the permanent government. The Philippines was moving, arguably had moved, from US alliance to Chinese alliance. Trump and Duterte have a friendly chat, and it was fixed.

The problem was that fresh from its great successes in overthrowing governments in Libya, Egypt, Syria, Iraq, etc, the State Department and the Permanent US government was gearing up to overthrow the government of the Philippines, but Trump told Duterte not to worry. Problem solved.

The state department was not involved in setting up this phone call, which was organized through Trump's private business connections in the Philippines. Expect mega outrage in due course at the total lack of separation between president Trump and billionaire CEO Trump. Trump is acting as if he has just performed a hostile business takeover of the very badly run US incorporated. The permanent government will call this corruption, and in a sense it is, though in practice it is more that Trump is spending his own money and using his own business assets to govern the country. Rather than public President Trump enriching private CEO Trump, CEO Trump is applying Trump's own private assets to govern America. There was and is uncertainty over how rich Trump is, though he flies around in a castle in the sky with a gold plated bath tub, but whether he is rich, or super rich, he is rich enough to run a presidential campaign out of his own pocket and his private connections turn out to wield a lot of power, enough power that he is not helpless before the forces of the permanent government. He was not helpless during the campaign, and he will not be helpless as president. Putting his business into blind trust would render him helpless. We voted for Trump because we well knew he was an insider and a very powerful man, and we figured that power was much needed to deal with anarcho tyranny.

The entire world has been living under the threat that if you do not install prog government that keeps up with the latest in progressivism, your country will be destroyed, like Libya or the Ukraine. Trump has removed this threat. If the Philippines is safe from the murderous, sadistic, and indiscriminately destructive wrath of the state department, so is Poland and Hungary. Expect a cascade of fashy governments around the world.

The progs complain

> populist strongmen have begun to put pressure on critical media, to violate minority rights, and to undermine key institutions such as independent courts.

"Critical media" means of course media of the permanent government, either openly and directly controlled like NPR, or with a thin pretense of private ownership like the white house press core, which despite being nominally private works from government offices and receives government benefits.

"Minority rights" means of course arrogant minority privilege. Hear disruptive female hires interrupt and talk over their boss, watch good-for-nothin black hires take up the whole corridor when they walk down the corridor. Because they are almost fireproof short of a lawsuit, and you are not.

"Independent courts" means courts under Harvard's thumb legislating from the bench - and we are about to see the "Independent" courts legislate open borders.

Progs think the Scalia court was "right wing". Let us reflect on three packages of judicial legislation that no one on the court would challenge

The supremes are by past standards, raving lunatic fringe frothing at the mouth left. All of them.

1. Law enforcement is crippled by rules that are intended to prevent them from discriminating against blacks. The court sees that blacks tend to be convicted at higher rates than whites, concludes discrimination, and issues rules. The rules, being designed to prevent nonexistent discrimination without actually imposing arrest quotas, fail, more rules ensue.

2. Political repression. For example the Bank of Beverly Hills was destroyed not for defying regulatory rules requiring them to make loans to Hispanics with no income, no job, and no assets, but for doubting the moral superiority of those imposing these rules. "Hostile environment" is in practice, search for thought crime. If people at your company commit thought crimes, regulators will destroy it.

3. "Disparate impact" prohibits hiring on merit and recruitment on ability, giving us the stupid elite.

To fix Disparate Impact, Hostile environment, and restriction on policing you would need to give five justices helicopter rides to the Pacific ocean, for I am pretty sure that every justice on the court currently supports these things.

## Women

### 2016-12-04 23:29:51

When mainstreamers read the red pill on women, they read it as "women are evil and dangerous". Well, women are certainly dangerous, but not exactly evil, rather subject to volcanically powerful sexual impulses that are apt to have disastrous consequences for themselves and everyone around them.

Now, me, I would fuck every fertile age woman I meet if I could. The little man gives pretty much all of them the salute. Obviously women are not like that, so men tend to interpret female behavior as women are less interested in sex than men - which rapidly becomes women are pure, women are angels, women belong on pedestals.

Not so. It is that men are polygynous, women are hypergamous. A woman will crawl nine miles over broken glass to fuck her demon lover. And then not give her husband the time of day.

Conversely, if your wife does not much want to fuck you, she is fucking her demon lover. If she is fertile age, and is disrespectful and disinclined to fuck you, she is going to leave, destroying all your assets and ruining the lives of your children. Fertile age women need sex, quite a lot of sex. If she does not need sex with you, you have a big problem. Conversely, if you fail to gratify her pretty regularly, you are going to have a big problem.

In real life I regularly see women behaving badly with disastrous consequences for themselves, their husband, and their children. Yet I never see this in the media or in fiction. In this, the media presents us with a wildly false image. Women themselves are deceived, and their own bad behavior and the resulting evil consequences catches them by surprise.

Old legends present a more accurate and realistic picture of women. For example King Gradlon and the City of Ys.

King Gradlon was raider based in Cornwall, but on one of his raids to the cold North, his armies melt away because of bad weather and logistic failure, and he is left all alone. Then he meets Queen Malgven who proposes that he should kill her husband and steal the royal treasury, so King Gradlon gets back to Kinging again. His wife bears a sea witch daughter, Dahut. When Dahut becomes a teenager, she prevails on her father to build the city of Ys, which is built below high tide level, protected by dikes. The city of Ys is a big success. Many people migate to Ys. It is a popular and successful pagan city based on sea trade. At low tide the sea gates open to allow ships into its port. Every so often his daughter sacrifices someone to the sea. Then a sea demon arrives, makes love to his daughter, and prevails on her to open her gates to the sea at high tide, and the entire city drowns.

Female voting behavior in Europe is well explained by the theory that women rather like rape. They are importing the rapeugees to do the raping that white men will not do. Female resistance to rape is a shit test intended to separate the strong rapist from the weak.

At 1:20 in the video the white girl is groped by a bunch of Iranians. At 1:26 in the video freeze the frame to look at the expression on her face.

Similarly, if you see a woman alone in a twenty four hour laundromat, late at night when there is no one around, she is a single woman, because if she was married her husband would not permit it. Or if he is too weak to stop her, she will not be married very much longer.

Female sexuality and reproductive capability needs to be kept under male control and male supervision. If women have control of their own bodies, they are apt to behave badly.

## Legality

### 2016-12-06 01:16:40

The American government has over several decades passed sterner and sterner laws to prevent illegals from entering and to deport illegals when they do enter, and then proceeded to ignore those laws.

On day one, Trump will start enforcing those laws - and then the Judges will legislate open borders from the bench. They will find in the emanation of the penumbra of the constitution a universal human right for every person in the world to vote in the United States, to predate on white people by welfare and crime, and to vote for more welfare, less law enforcement against criminals, and more law enforcement against the middle class, after the fashion of Venezuela, which exemplifies anarcho tyranny in that everything is illegal, except crime, which is legal.

America's anti discrimination laws work rather like Venezuela's price control laws. The government legislates reality away. America makes unequal groups equal by law, Venezuela makes everyone prosperous by law. When reality continues to be real anyway, the law is being broken, therefore the government can punish anyone they please for breaking it. In America they don't punish crimethinkers directly, but they do punish businesses that employ crimethinkers thus indirectly punishing crimethinkers. The same is partly true in Venezuela, except that in Venezuela they have shut down so many businesses that there is very little left, resulting in chaos and famine.

We on the alt-right are largely ex Brahmins, or in revolt against Brahmin culture in which we are deeply immersed, so we tend to think there is not much that Trump can do against the judges. When the judges rule deporting immigrants illegal, and being racist illegal, and that being white makes you racist, people within Brahmin culture think that will be that.

But that is not in fact how Joe Sixpack, the guy with the remote in one hand and a can of beer in the other, thinks about legality. Nor, more importantly, is it what the armed man wearing a uniform thinks about legality.

He thinks that legality is a man wearing a uniform and a gun enforcing explicit formal officially stated rules in obedience to his chain of command. And the neater the uniform and the shinier the gun, the more legal those rules are. In this, Joe sixpack is wiser than we are. Because the neatness of the uniform and the shininess of the gun is an indicator of discipline, and discipline is an indication that the rules are going to be enforced as intended, and thus an indication that the man with the gun is no threat to Joe sixpack

So what Trump needs to do is send out people in sharp looking uniforms with nice looking weapons to enforce those laws whether the judges like it or not, and imprison or deport people who break those laws without bothering with judges.

When Trump does this, the left will suffer total meltdown.

One percent of the people will say "Oh it is terrible that Trump has abandoned due process".

One percent of the people will say "Oh it is terrible that Judges are legislating from the bench".

Ninety eight percent of the people will say "The open borders people are being boring, change the channel to the sports news."

The vast majority of people just do not care about due process, in part because judges have been abusing it so grossly for so long.

## No enemies to the right worked

2016-12-07 08:26:14

Because we did not disown Spencer, he got to speak to the world, he was heard by the entire world, saying stuff that we would like the world to hear. And the heat has gone away.

# left becomes the movement against Global Apartheidt

## 2016-12-11 11:32:28

The issue used to be capitalism, now it is "global apartheid". Our enemies believe that everyone in the world has an inherent human right to move to white countries to live on crime, welfare, and voting for less law enforcement and more welfare.

This will be demonstrated when Trump tries to close the borders. The Permanent Government will just flat in your face point blank defy him. If he closes the borders, he will have to do so by demonstrating that an air force commando outranks a supreme court justice.

As the capitalism versus socialism conflict assimilated all conflicts to itself during the early part of the twentieth century, "Global Apartheidt" versus "racism" is now assimilating all conflicts to itself. All politics become identity politics, all identity politics is becoming pro white or anti white, and all anti white politics becomes Muslim, part of the war of Islam on the west. Hence the State Department backing genocidal Sunni terrorists against moderate Muslim regimes like that of Syria.

They don't realize that they plan to kill the golden goose.

They don't realize that all the wealth of the world was created by white people originally and still today most of it, with the notable exception of East Asian economies, is created by white people. They think that wealth comes from magic dirt. Hence Obama telling us "You did not build that" in cheerful defiance of the obvious facts. The new emerging majority thinks that white wealth was just magically showered on whites like their EBT cards and obamaphones were magically showered on them. When they burn down a white owned shopping center, and it is not promptly replaced by shopping center run by black women, they figure that is white racism at work. "Why were blacks not given a shopping center the way whites were?" They think EBT cards and Obamaphones just pop out of the magic dirt.

Everyone graduated from Harvard, and everyone in the permanent government, believes that the wealth just sprang from magic dirt, and whites just grabbed more than their fair share, believes "You did not build that" If only those awful white males were not around to prevent wealth from showering on women and people of color. Because if you want to go to Harvard, you need to persuade Harvard that you do believe that.

Hence believe not necessity to allow whites to build stuff. Which belief system leads to killing the goose that lays the golden eggs. Factories and all that are supposedly evil. Are supposedly instruments of oppression. Hence the regulatory state that makes it impossible to build physical things in America unless your factory is grandfathered in. Everyone in the Harvard and the Permanent Government believes this, and if he does not believe it, keeps his beliefs a deep dark secret. They believe that when they shut down factories and farms and mines and stuff, they are being noble and good, are dripping with saintliness as they erase these horrid sins against Gaia, and anyone trying to keep them open is being sinful, greedy, and corrupt.

They think, everyone in Harvard thinks, everyone in the Permanent Government thinks, that the Golden Goose is keeping people poor by scarfing up all the wealth emerging spontaneously from the magic dirt, they do not realize we are paying for EBT cards and Obamaphones.

When Black Lives Matter burn down a supermarket whites build, Obama tells the owners "You did not build that".

In the early part of the twentieth century, the left wanted the masses to seize the means of production. But with identity politics replacing class politics, all the stuff that whites do becomes equally evil, so now in the early part of the twenty first century the left wants to shut down the means of production. Everyone is supposedly going to live by swiping EBT cards and get their internet via Obamaphone. The left is now the party of rule by underclass, not the party of dictatorship of the proletariat.

The Daily Stormer reminds us that there is a secretive committee of big Jewish donors that has undue influence over the Democratic party, but the Democratic party will very shortly elect a Muslim terrorist who hates Jews as their leader. By "terrorist" I don't mean that he personally will strap dynamite around himself and blow himself up in a Jewish synagogue, but that he will be part of an organization, the Muslim Brotherhood, that organizes people to blow themselves up. And the Jews will continue funding the Democrats even as part of these funds are used to strap explosives around suicide bombers to blow themselves up in synagogues. And they will congratulate themselves on having found a brown Bernie with which to sucker the white working class one more time. Until they import enough black African males that they get roasted on spits and eaten.

Jews will probably support the left all the way to the bitter end - as they supported Muslims during the crusades, but the logic of identity politics means that the left will not support Jews. Jews keep telling their brown allies that Jews are not really white, but this fails to have the desired effect. Jews found it a lot easier to lead an anticapitalist movement than an anti white movement.

The army tries to earn brownie points by opposing Muslim patriarchy and repression of homosexuality. General Mattis is a big offender here, pointing out that Afghans beat women, etc. It is like pointing out that Democrats are the real racists. Emancipating Afghan women does not gain the army any brownie points, nor do the rapes of the rapeugees lose the the rapeugees any brownie points. And the Muslim brotherhood can full on flat out openly oppose the emancipation of women, and still be leftists in good standing, indeed the very best of standing.

Hating whites males is the KKKrazy glue that holds the coalition of the fringes together, and the Muslim Brotherhood hates us more than anyone, so, since no friends to the right and no enemies to the left, the left loves the Muslim brotherhood and is busily importing an army of their fighters, even though the Muslim Brotherhood position on women, Jews, and homosexuals is umpteen light years outside the Overton Window. The Muslim Brotherhood is sliding into control of the left, the way communists slid into control in the thirties and forties, because they are the leftmost on the defining issue of our times. Moldbug, reading old books, said that America is a communist country. Pretty soon it is going to be a Muslim country.

# A warming world?

## 2016-12-12 05:36:08

Early explorations of the Antarctic report an ice free shore in areas now long covered by a growing icecap. Twenty first century science just simply lies in your face about this, with blatant barefaced fraud, but sometimes the discrepancy becomes glaringly and embarassingly obvious[442].

What about the North Pole? Early twentieth century attempts to reach the North Pole were frustrated by the fact that ice coverage was fragile, incomplete, and had gaps full of open water even in the middle of winter, so that travel by dog sled was dangerous and impractical. There was too much ice for it to be safe to sail to the pole in summer, but not enough for it to be safe to dog sled to the pole in winter. Today, the North Pole in the middle of winter is solidly ice bound, and it is quite easy to reach the North Pole by dog sled. So today's north pole has a lot more ice than it did at the start of the twentieth century. The Northwest passage was difficult and unsafe for wooden ships then, and difficult and unsafe for wooden ships now.

But do we have any proxies for temperature that cover the present day, and also centuries past?

Yes we do, we have Law Dome, a pile of ice and snow in the Antarctic. Drill in Law Dome, and the isotope ratio agrees very well with recently measured present day temperatures of the weather station near Law Dome, unlike most proxies favored by global warmers.

And the Law Dome shows that in 500AD-1000AD, the temperature at Law Dome was a whole lot warmer than the present, or any recent temperatures.[443] On the whole, temperatures have gone up and gone down, plenty of climate change, but mostly in the direction of colder, as we would expect from the growth in the icecaps.

What about surface instrument readings which supposedly show the world has warmed 0.6 degrees in recent decades?

I myself attempted to reconstruct recent global temperatures from surface instrument readings, and the data is unsuited to the task. It contains various sources of systematic error that have to be corrected by ad hoc guessing, and one can make one reasonable set of guesses and use one reasonable procedure, and get one past temperature, or a different reasonable set of guesses and a different reasonable procedure and easily get a result 1.2 degrees different without intentionally torturing the data.

We now have satellites that do provide accurate world wide readings of temperature, and have had them since 1998 (actually a good deal earlier than 1998, but the early satellites had problems that arguably make their readings non comeasurable. Debates about how earlier satellite measurements should be interpreted are difficult to resolve.)

And surprise surprise, since we have had accurate satellite readings of global temperatures, they have been fairly stable, with no obvious trend in any particular direction. There has been plenty of quite dramatic climate change in the past, and there will likely be plenty of quite dramatic climate change in the future, but it is not apparent that we

---

[442]https://blog.reaction.la/global-warming/global-warming-scientists-trapped-in-antarctic-denial/
[443]https://climateaudit.org/2016/08/03/gergis-and-law-dome/#more-22100

have been having much climate change from nineteen ninety eight to the present.

The only data suitable for detecting small world wide variations of temperature is the satellite data, and the less one is free to torture the satellite data, the less it it indicates that anthropogenic warming is detectable.

## Fall of Aleppo reveals that asymmetric warfare is bunkum
2016-12-15 07:23:00

fourteen months ago, I said that Aleppo would very shortly fall[444].

Eight months ago I said that it had fallen for certain values of fallen, and its fall indicates that asymmetric warfare only works when the stronger side is fighting with one hand tied behind its back[445] - usually tied by the State Department. My prolific commenter B complained that Aleppo had not actually fallen yet, therefore this failed to demonstrate that asymmetric warfare is bunk.

OK.

Now it really has fallen, and asymmetric warfare really is bunk. The weaker side really was unable to go guerrilla.

Mao's guerrilla warfare consisted of raiding China from across a border behind the protection of Soviet troops. The terrorists are heading to the Turkish border to repeat this form of guerrilla warfare.

Syria simply has no problem with terrorism in the sense of Somali guy attends college, gets training that white people are microagressing against him, then runs amuck killing white people at the college, then the college apologizes to Islam and the Somali community and gives white people further training in refraining from microagressing. The only terrorism problem in Syria is shells, mortars, and rockets raining down on civilians from terrorist controlled territories, and they have just cleaned up the last terrorist controlled area in or near a big city, after the style of the siege of Grozny.

If Syrians do not have to put up with fourth generation warfare style terrorism, then we do not have to put up with terrorism, with fourth generation warfare, either.

You kill Somali guy. Then you put everyone who encouraged or enabled Somali guy in the gulag. And you don't let them out until many years have passed since the last terrorist act. You level his mosque and his college, then you put all the instigators at college and mosque in the Gulag, and you make sure no one associated with his mosque or his college ever gets a job preaching or teaching ever again. That is how you do it. And you keep an eye out for anyone who sounds like those who instigated Somali guy. Oh, and you deport everyone who looks like Somali guy. But deportation is only half the answer since those who enabled and encouraged Somali guy's terrorism were generally white.

## Boycott people who hate you
2016-12-17 01:31:59

Using their products will harm you. Seek out alternative products

---

[444] https://blog.reaction.la/war/putin-successfully-stabilizing-syria/
[445] https://blog.reaction.la/war/fall-of-aleppo-reveals-that-asymmetric-warfare-is-bunkum/

Boycott the Star Wars movie Rogue One. All the villains are white males. All the heroes are not. Not only will this depress you and persuade you that you are evil and villainous and doomed to lose, but this guarantees bad writing and a boring show for the reasons explained by Orwell. If it is written to political formula, it is written to formula, so all the characters are living dead, placeholders and formulae, not people that you might care about. They kill a few of the heroes to try and make you care, but you won't care.

Use InfoGalactic not Wikipedia. Wikipedia treats academia and the mainstream press as authoritative, and forbids any direct personal knowledge as "original research". If you want to say that Karl Marx was an anti semitic Jew, you are not allowed to quote Karl Marx saying genocidal things about Jews, you have to quote some academic interpreting Karl Marx's genocidal remarks about Jews.

These days, most Academic "research" is custom ordered by the permanent government, global warming being an egregious example. The permanent government decides it will promulgate some regulation or finding in order to reward a friend or punish an enemy, and then commissions some "research" to authoritatively justify this regulation or finding. Thus most academic research is meaningless except as an answer to "Who does the permanent government intend to destroy?" We are in the third childhood of human reason, the latter days of the Roman empire being the second childhood of human reason.

Thus Wikipedia simply feeds you the poisons manufactured by Academia and the mainstream media.

Use DuckDuckGo not google. Google actively censors and manipulates your searches, in order to manipulate you. This becomes apparent when you start searching conspiracy theories. Which for most conspiracy theories is probably a good thing, but Google's idea of what is a conspiracy theory and what is fake news is alarmingly broad and grossly biased politically. I would not mind a search engine censoring conspiracy theories and fake news if it would tell me it is doing so and allow me to turn off the censorship, but Google deceptively and silently censors, thus manipulatively deceiving you.

Use gab.ai, not twitter, for you and the people you follow in twitter are apt to be silently censored without you or they realizing it, making you feel isolated, alone, frightened, weak, and powerless.

I have not found any evidence that Kellogg is putting testosterone blockers and xenoestrogens in their cornflakes and bran, but given that they hate males and that testosterone levels are mysteriously dropping, why take the chance?

## "Love Live's Here" in action

### 2016-12-17 22:27:34

Since Richard Spencer is a hard target, and since the alt right will not disown him, "Love Lives Here" is now gunning for his mother[446].

I think it is time to show "Love Lives Here" a little tough love.

This Tanya Gersh is doing a great job at dispelling hostile stereotypes of Jews.

---

[446]https://medium.com/@recnepss/does-love-really-live-here-fff159563ba3#.dhwuekg66

# The Cathedral defined

## 2016-12-19 00:33:05

Because of the big expansion of the Alt Right, the Dark Enlightenment, and Neoreaction, we are getting a lot of people unfamiliar with the theory.

Know your enemy, know yourself:

The Cathedral is the Academic-judiciary-media complex. It is also priestly power, even if some of the priests are not actually in academia, the judiciary, or media. It the set of people, with actual privilege under democracy. All people are equal, but some are more equal than others. The Cathedral are the ones that are more equal than others. Jews tend naturally to priesthood, but the Cathedral is not entirely ruled by Jews, and in practice Orthodox Jews are normally excluded from the Cathedral as unbelievers, revealing the Christian roots of progressivism.

The Cathedral has organizational continuity with the state religion of Massachussets, in that Harvard was the headquarters of the state religion of Massachusetts. Harvard is a heretical offshoot of the Church of England, in that Harvard was founded by clerics expelled from the Church of England by Charles the second, clerics known at the time as dissenters or noncomformists, and the State Religion of Massachusetts was founded by clerics who fled England to avoid the authority of Charles the first, clerics known at the time as Brownists. The frequent name changes, which continue to this day, indicate that this religion keeps developing a dreadful reputation.

The problem is the priesthood of all believers. This is wonderful in theory, but in practice, some believers are more equal than others, so what you get in practice is what Moldbug calls informal power - power that is unofficial, secretive, insecure, conspiratorial, and based on lies and pretence, as illustrated by the Climategate files.

It used to be that Royal society decided what was science, what was the scientific method, and awarded prestige to some scientists more than others. Its motto was "Take no one's word for it" - which meant that scientists that claimed X had to show how they knew X. When Harvard got supremacy over the Royal Society as a result of World War II, we got scientific truth determined behind closed doors on the basis of secret evidence that they will not show you even if you mount freedom of information requests. Peer Review is in practice the clerical synods that the State Church of Massachussets demanded. Similarly accreditation of educational (credentialing) institutions.

The British civil war (1640-1660) was a result of dissident/brownist clerics demanding that the authority of Bishops appointed by the King be replaced by the authority of clerical synods.

This led to riots against the King's Bishops, which Charles the first failed at first to treat as full on revolution against the King and at first failed to crush with full on military power. The mainstream interpretation of events leading up to the British civil war is that Charles was too harsh, but my interpretation is the opposite - that the more revolution you allow, the more revolution you are going to get.

We are now entering a similar crisis, in that the permanent government claims to exercise authority and regulate not on the basis of what some mere president tells it to do, but on the basis of objective fact, where some people behind closed doors get to determine objective fact and others do not.

The permanent government has long been apt to commission "research" that makes it a moral and legal necessity to reward friends and punish enemies, and in the last months of the Obama regime has been aggressively claiming priestly independence similar to that of the judiciary, academia, and the mainstream media. It has also been organizing quasi military forces independent of the regular military. This is the priesthood of all believers all over again.

The priesthood of all believers would be fine if you added a little addendum that non religious authority gets to decide which believer may administer the sacraments - the family patriarch, the magistrate, or the King, as appropriate, so that we had formal, rather than informal, inequality between believers and priests. Arguably this is implied by Saint Paul's remarks on divine right, and in the end Martin Luther took this interpretation. Secular authorities should be able to regulate the church provided that they are not hostile to the faith and do not demand repudiation of the doctrines of the faith.

Or we could go with apostolic succession, and holy oil. There is a sufficient supply of holy oil, because if you have a bottle half full of holy oil, and top it up with regular oil, you get a full bottle of holy oil. The holiness does not get diluted. (It is a miracle) But the Roman Catholic Church and the Church of England has become rather shy about apostolic succession. Seems to me you cannot have apostolic succession, unless one apostolic successor who is a Bishop actually says to a candidate Bishop something like "By the power granted to me by the apostles, I appoint you successor to the apostles", and sloshes him with holy oil, or something along those lines. A ambiguous pat on the head does not really count. By which standard, no one in the Roman Catholic Church or the Church of England has apostolic succession any more, so if we go with apostolic succession we will have to import some Bishops who do have apostolic succession from Mount Athos or Moscow. Mount Athos is safer. We don't want Moscow to lose intellectual sovereignty to Harvard, and equally we do not want Washington to lose intellectual sovereignty to Moscow.

To deal with the problem, Trump is going to need to forbid heavy weapons and armored personnel carriers to any federal government agency other than the regular military, and then replace holy synods with Bishops - in other words re-organize the federal bureaucracy on das Führerprinzip.

He also needs to reduce the power of the Judiciary by demonstrating that an airforce commando outranks a supreme court justice.

And after he is done with the federal bureaucracy, do the same to Academia.

He needs to radically reduce the status of Academia by radical degree deflation- we need to reintroduce the bar exam and the civil service exam, so that you can take the exam without bothering with an accredited college, and create a viable apprentice + exam based model for doctors of medicine. And simply repeal all the other accreditation requirements, in particular and especially "disparate impact".

Trump has already struck effectively at the power of the media without even being president. Now he needs to do to the rest of the Cathedral what he has done to the media.

After that, send a request to Mount Athos for some holy oil. We need to close off open entry into the priesthood. Even when disempowered, it is still an attractive nuisance that will attract the dangerously ambitious.

Some possible approaches to closing off open entry into the priesthood.

1: The priesthood of all believers firmly regulated by the state. The state gives them privileges and power, in return for them teaching loyalty and patriotism, but keeps them under tight formal and explicit control. (Luther's later more conservative Lutheranism)

2: Bishops derive their authority from the King, combining apostolic succession with (1) as in the Church of England from 1660 to 1820

3: Full on apostolic succession, with appropriate respect for secular authority, as with Eastern Orthodoxy and today's Russian Orthodox Church under Putin. Get some holy oil.

4: Hereditary priesthood, as in the Old Testament Israel.

5: Priesthood as private property, as in today's Japan and saga period iceland, where private ownership of an official state endorsed shrine makes you a priest. We make the universities as independent in reality as they are in form, so that Academia tolerates, is unable to prevent, is incapable of suppressing, open dissent within Academia, shutting down the network of committees controlling committees that causes all Academia to speak with a single voice, that makes it a thousand loudspeakers all echoing one microphone.

Since the shrines are official, solution five always has substantial elements of solution one. Give them too much independence, they will conspire to create an informal and unofficial apparatus of coercion that enables them to speak with one voice, for the added power that this gives them. The state not only has to ensure that the priesthood is dependent on the state, but also ensure that the priesthood is genuinely independent from synods of priests, for synods of priests lead to wars and revolutions, exercising power without responsibility.

## The evil of libertarianism.

### 2016-12-21 06:58:48

As the central defining issue of the left has become hating cis hetero white males and destroying capital, rather than hating capitalists and seizing capital, Libertarianism has become irrelevant.

Libertarians have responded to irrelevance by becoming evil. Tyler Cowen, who is arguably the primary remaining libetarian blogger, certainly one of them, just published a blog post that he does not care about Aleppo[447] - this is the man who cares deeply that a billion black African Muslims are much worse off in Africa than they would be if they were allowed to come to America to live on welfare and crime and vote for more welfare and more crime, this is the man who is so much more moral than you are that you are worse than Hitler for not caring as much as he does.

We are under no obligation to worry about far away strangers hurting, particularly when they are being hurt by other far away strangers as is usually the case. We are, however, under an obligation to worry about us hurting far away strangers, particularly as if we hurt far away strangers and do not much care, they are morally entitled to defend themselves by killing us.

[447] https://marginalrevolution.com/marginalrevolution/2016/12/aleppo-and-other-tragedies.html

Aleppo is the result of a failed American effort to overthrow the legitimate and long established government of Syria. To this end, the American government sponsored a bunch of genocidal terrorists who intended to kill every Syrian Alawite and kill or expell every Christian and every Shiite of Palestinian origin. These foreign genocidal terrorists seized a portion of Aleppo, kept the civilian population hostage as human shields, and proceeded to lob mortars and rockets into the rest of Aleppo.

The reckless cruelty of progs in general and the American government in particular, with the extraordinary cheerleading of a mainstream media drunk with the blood of innocents, was steadily leading us towards thermonuclear war with Russia.

And this is the question on which Tyler Cowen decides he will not care.

## America's nuclear arsenal

### 2016-12-22 23:10:42

Trump: "The United States must greatly strengthen and expand its nuclear capability"

"Why", you ask "Cold war is over. Surely we have more nukes than we know what to do with."

America's nuclear weapons are, for the most part, thermonuclear, and need a little bit of tritium to get them to ignite.

Tritium has a half life of twelve years, and due to technological decline, we have not been able to make tritium for quite a while.

So the number of nuclear weapons that we can ignite has been halving every twelve years.

To greatly expand our weapon supply, need to resume production of tritium, which the Obama regime has been attempting to do - so far unsuccessfully We should also resume testing to try to create thermonuclear weapons that do not need tritium detonators, but if the US was unable to do that back when it could put a man on the moon, its no longer great descendants might find that difficult.

Expect universal outrage and ridicule at Trump's statement, but when under Obama we tried and failed to resume production of tritium, greatly expanding our nuclear capabilities was what we were trying and failing to do.

The last man on the moon is now eighty two years old, the tallest building in the US was built in 1973, and when we tried to replace the two towers, we were unable to do so. Dysgenic decline, promoting women and coloreds to posts beyond their capability, "disparate impact" prohibits employers from choosing the best, and superior expertise is deemed to be mansplaining. Google has been purging its best engineers, an ailment I attribute to the problem that smart males get up the noses of dumb blue haired social justice warriors. Recall that Obama could not get its Obamacare website up until they threw in the towel and accepted an all white and east asian, all male, team to get it up.

If we are going to greatly expand our nuclear capabilities, need to send women back to the kitchen and keep them barefoot and pregnant. That is the lesson of Team Obama's efforts to get a website up.

## The Wicked Flee

**2016-12-25 02:11:04**

The wicked flee when no man pursueth.

I don't want this blog to turn into all Trump all the time, but those liberal tears just taste so delicious.

Trump asks for the names and activities of those engaged in countering "violent extremism".

And immediately government employees panic that Trump will engage in reprisals against those countering violent extremism and will undo all their good work in countering violent extremism.

Now why would they worry that Trump will undo their work in countering "violent extremism" - unless their idea of violent extremism is not a Muslim driving a truck into a crowd of Christians but rentacops maintaining order at Trump rallys, unless their idea of a violent extremist is not a member of the Muslim Brotherhood but the first person to stop cheering at a gay wedding?

Well guess what:

> "One type of domestic extremism includes those who disdain others due to a person's immutable characteristics, such as race, ethnicity, national origin, religion, gender, gender identity and disability."

So if you notice that women are markedly and strikingly less competent than men at men's activities, such as work outside the house, and men are markedly less competent than women at women's activities, like finding the car keys and taking care of small children and the very ill, then you are a violent extremist. The only possible reason that you could believe your lying eyes it that you hate women so much you are likely to attack and kill them.

By which standard, Muslims are only a very minor part of the very big extremist problem. Nothing but the constant vigilance of the Obama regime prevents blond blue eyed males from running amok and massacring people. Obviously we urgently need to register, and probably deport, white males.

## Why nation building fails

**2016-12-26 21:40:22**

Because they are not building nations, but hotels for transnational progressives

That is the explanation of why Assad is supposedly a very very bad man. Because he refused to let a bunch of people with prior experience in being paid by the international community for dashing around the world raising female self esteem, stopping the oceans from rising, and caring deeply about the plight of international refugees, from taking power in Syria. And as a result the state department found itself funding and arming a bunch of genocidal totalitarians that make the Taliban and Islamic state look moderate.

They want to turn Afghanistan into a multicultural society where women get massive affirmative action.

"Nation building" equals nation dismantling. The globalist idea of nation is a hotel. Who will fight for a hotel?

If you actually want to build a nation in Afghanistan, so that the holier than thou mullahs will not have power, you start by finding the true king. The true King will of course have policies that are agreeable to the majority of Afghan fighting men. For example he will be opposed to educating girls past puberty, and will want them given education that focuses on their role of wife and mother. The true King will also tend to have policies that are agreeable to the leadership of fighting men, such as low taxes, and policies that are in accord with Afghan tradition, such as mandatory Islam and the execution of apostates.

The problem is that the international community is not building nations, but transnations, which have no natural support among local fighting men.

Progs simply assume they are entitled to rule, the arc of history and all that, and any opposition to them ruling is illegitimate, but they are in fact weak, due to gays and women and all that.

It would be easy to defeat the Taliban and set up a colonial regime in Afghanistan: Kill their leaders, take their women, and convert them to Christianity. It would be even easier to set up a traditional Afghan regime: Find the true King. But a tranzi regime will always need outside military support from unenthusiastic foreign soldiers who resent transnationalism.

The progs want empire, and they want the opposite of empire. They want white males to conquer their empire and hold it in brutal subjection, and they want an empire that hates and punishes white males. The state department cannot make up its mind whether it hates the Taliban the most, or US soldiers the most. It is endlessly puzzled that the Taliban continues to hate progs. Don't they know that Islam is the religion of peace?

A genuinely independent Afghanistan is not going to be governed by people who want to emancipate women and stop the oceans from rising. So rule it or don't rule it.

The US government needs to rule Afghanistan or not rule Afghanistan. And if it does not rule, whoever does rule Afghanistan is not going to emancipate women, and if it does rule, is going to have to keep soldiers there indefinitely and let those soldiers get their dicks wet.

## Against Liberty

### 2016-12-27 07:04:08

Liberty allows and encourages the highest human flourishing. But when your enemies seek your destruction, it is time for liberty to go.

The time approaches for the warrior ethic, wherein the highest good is to crush your enemies, to see them driven before you, and to hear the lamentations of their women.

It takes two to keep the peace, only one to start war. Every time that Muslims drive a truck into a bunch of Christians, or Black Lives Matter ethnically cleanses the neighborhood of whites and burns down a shopping center, people start panicking "Oh, the terrible white backlash is forcing Muslims and blacks to become radicals.", though no one has seen any white backlash yet.

The way to respond to war, is with war. History shows us that only war works.

Let us try massacring some peaceful Muslim men and enslaving their women, and see what the effect is on Muslim radicalism. Let us try reenslaving those blacks that are causing the most problems. That would be backlash.

For liberty to exist, there must first be law. For law to exist, there must first be order. For order to exist, there must first be peace. For peace to exist, there must first be victory. And victory usually requires the most horrifying means.

Submitting to your enemy's war making is not liberty, nor order, nor is it peace.

It is been too long since the last war, people have forgotten how terrible war is, and our enemies have become too used to easy victories, where they make war unopposed, and this war making is answered by generous concessions, which necessarily leads to more extreme war making by our enemies. The only way to real peace, is now through real war.

## Russia did not hack the Democrat's emails

### 2016-12-31 05:55:33

And Obama and the spy agencies know it.

Wordfence, a cyber security company, reports[448] that the attacker used version 3.10 of an open source hacking tool written by a person who speaks English that can be downloaded for free from a Ukrainian website, by anyone in the entire world. The current version is 3.17

Presumably the KGB uses its own custom written hacking tools, written by Russian speakers, with the documentation kept under lock and key at KGB headquarters, or at least keeps its free shareware tools updated. The tool used is not Russian malware. It is English language open source malware, used by hackers around the world.

Wordfence report that the IP addresses used in the attack have no particular association with Russia, and are similar to those used to attack random Wordpress websites. There is no Russian fingerprint in these attacks.

Obama's story is that the tool and the IP addresses indicate the attacker is the Russian government. Rather, the tool indicates the attacker was some English speaking kid in his pajamas whose mother did not give him enough pocket money to buy professional hacking tools, and the IP addresses indicate he has enough smarts to hide his own IP address.

Hat tip small dead animals[449]

---

[448] https://www.wordfence.com/blog/2016/12/russia-malware-ip-hack/
[449] https://www.smalldeadanimals.com/2016/12/to-a-befuddled-.html